WAHHĀBISM

Wahhābism

THE HISTORY OF A MILITANT ISLAMIC MOVEMENT

COLE M. BUNZEL

PRINCETON UNIVERSITY PRESS
PRINCETON & OXFORD

Published by Princeton University Press
41 William Street, Princeton, New Jersey 08540
99 Banbury Road, Oxford OX2 6JX

press.princeton.edu

First paperback printing, 2025
Paperback ISBN 9780691241616
Cloth ISBN 9780691241593
ISBN (e-book) 9780691241609

LCCN: 2022056529

British Library Cataloging-in-Publication Data is available

Editorial: Fred Appel & James Collier
Production Editorial: Jaden Young
Jacket/Cover Design: Katie Osborne
Production: Erin Suydam
Publicity: Kate Hensley & Charlotte Coyne
Copyeditor: Elisabeth A. Graves

Jacket/Cover Image: *Kitāb radʿ al-ḍalāla wa-qamʿ al-jahāla*, Islamic Manuscripts, Garrett no. 3788Y, Special Collections, Princeton University Library

This book has been composed in Arno (Classic)

CONTENTS

Illustrations vii

Maps and Figures viii

Preface xiii

Note on Conventions xvii

Introduction 1

1 Muḥammad ibn ʿAbd al-Wahhāb and His Discontents 29

2 The Doctrine of Ibn ʿAbd al-Wahhāb I: The Taymiyyan Background 92

3 The Doctrine of Ibn ʿAbd al-Wahhāb II: The Key Components 127

4 The Warpath of Early Wahhābism: The First Saudi State (1741–1818) 191

5 The Reassertion of Enmity: The Second Saudi State (1823–1887) 228

6 The Persistence of Enmity: The Rashīdī Interregnum (1887–1902) 261

7 The Decline of Enmity: The Rise of the Third Saudi State (1902–1932) 294

Conclusion: The Fall and Rise of Militant Wahhābism 329

Appendix 343

Glossary 347

Bibliography 351

Index 377

ILLUSTRATIONS

Maps

1. The Arabian Peninsula in the eighteenth century viii
2. Najd in the eighteenth century ix

Figures

1. The Āl al-Shaykh x
2. The Āl Suʿūd xi

Tables

1.1. Wahhābī epistles quoted in early refutations 91
A.1. Dated or roughly datable early refutations of Wahhābism 343
A.2. Undated early refutations of Wahhābism 345

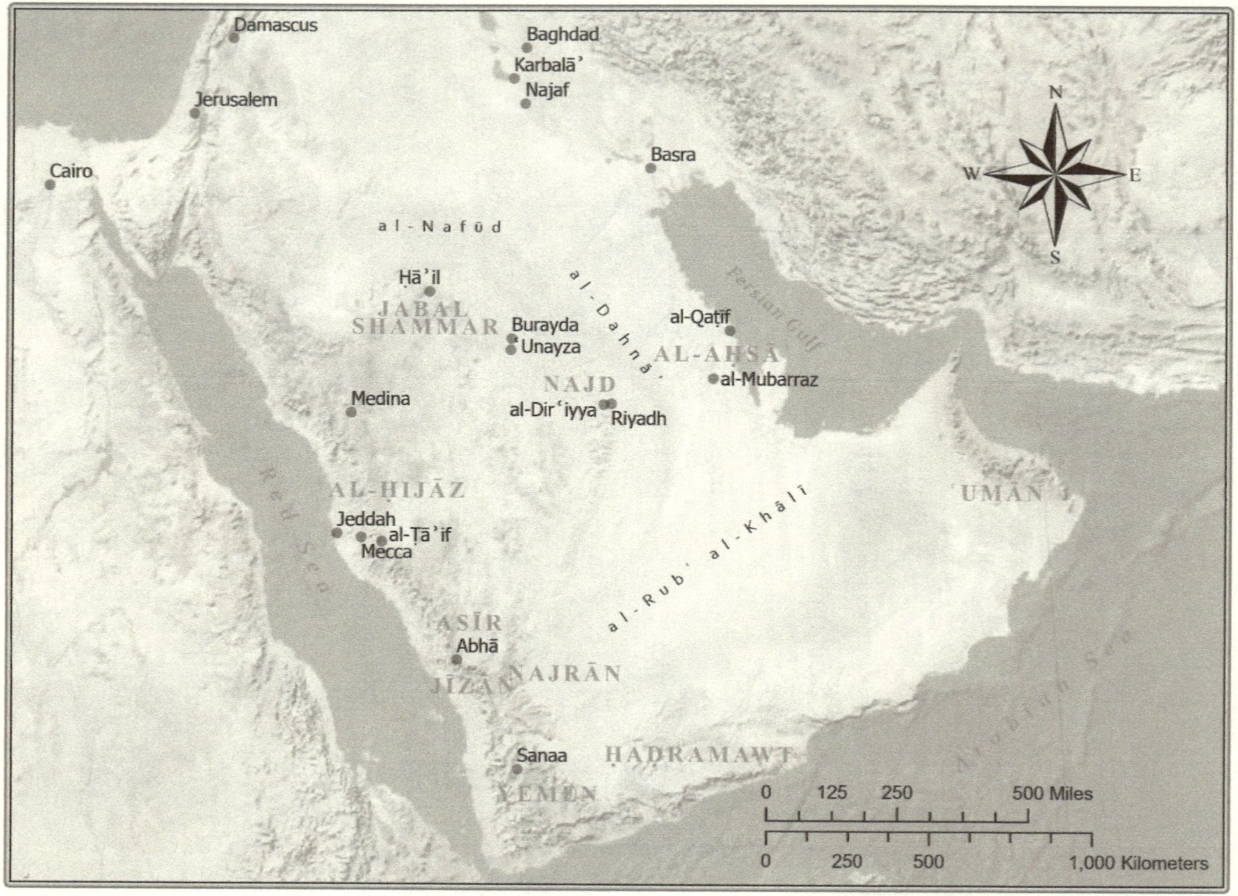

MAP 1. The Arabian Peninsula in the eighteenth century

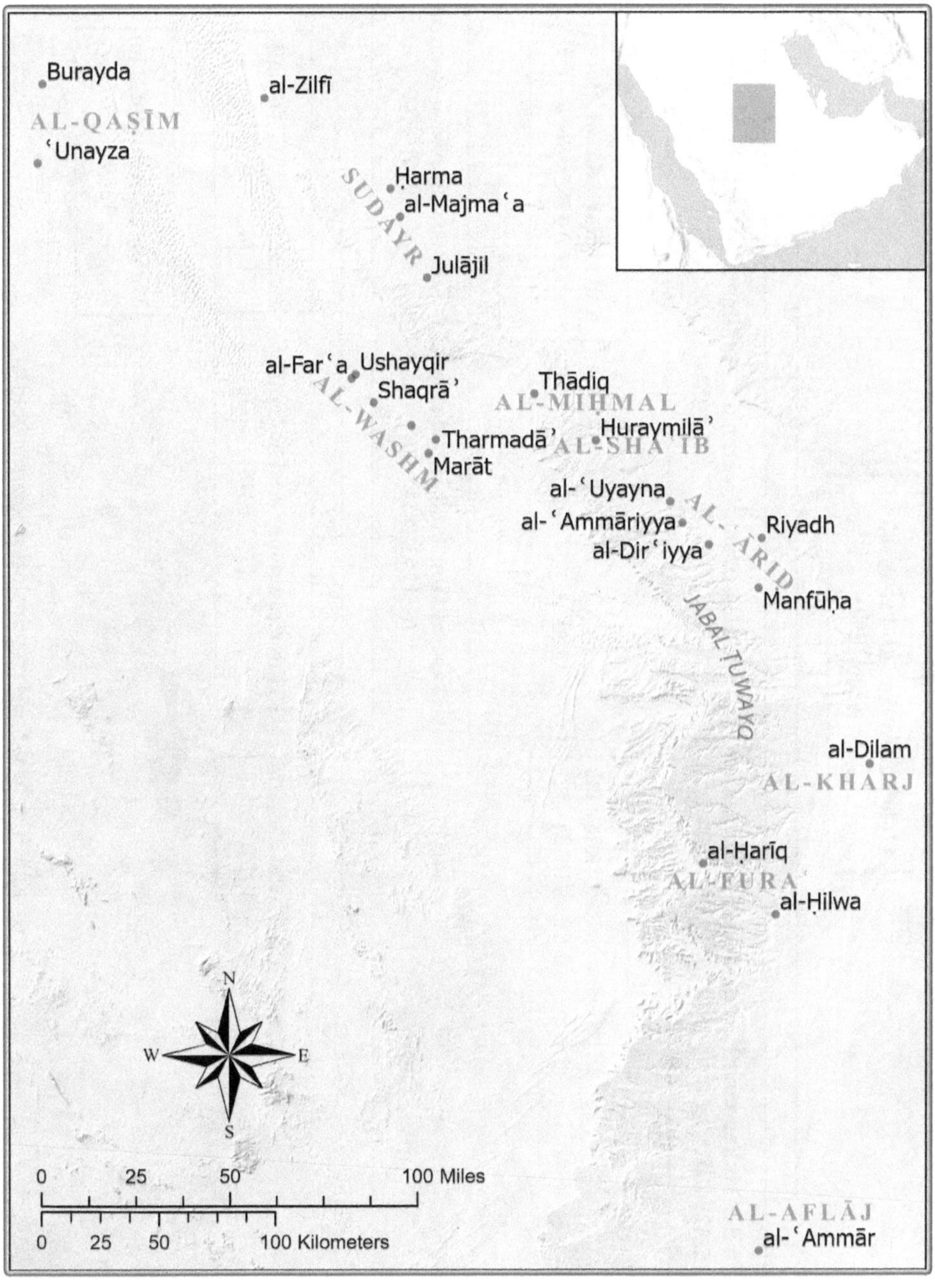

MAP 2. Najd in the eighteenth century

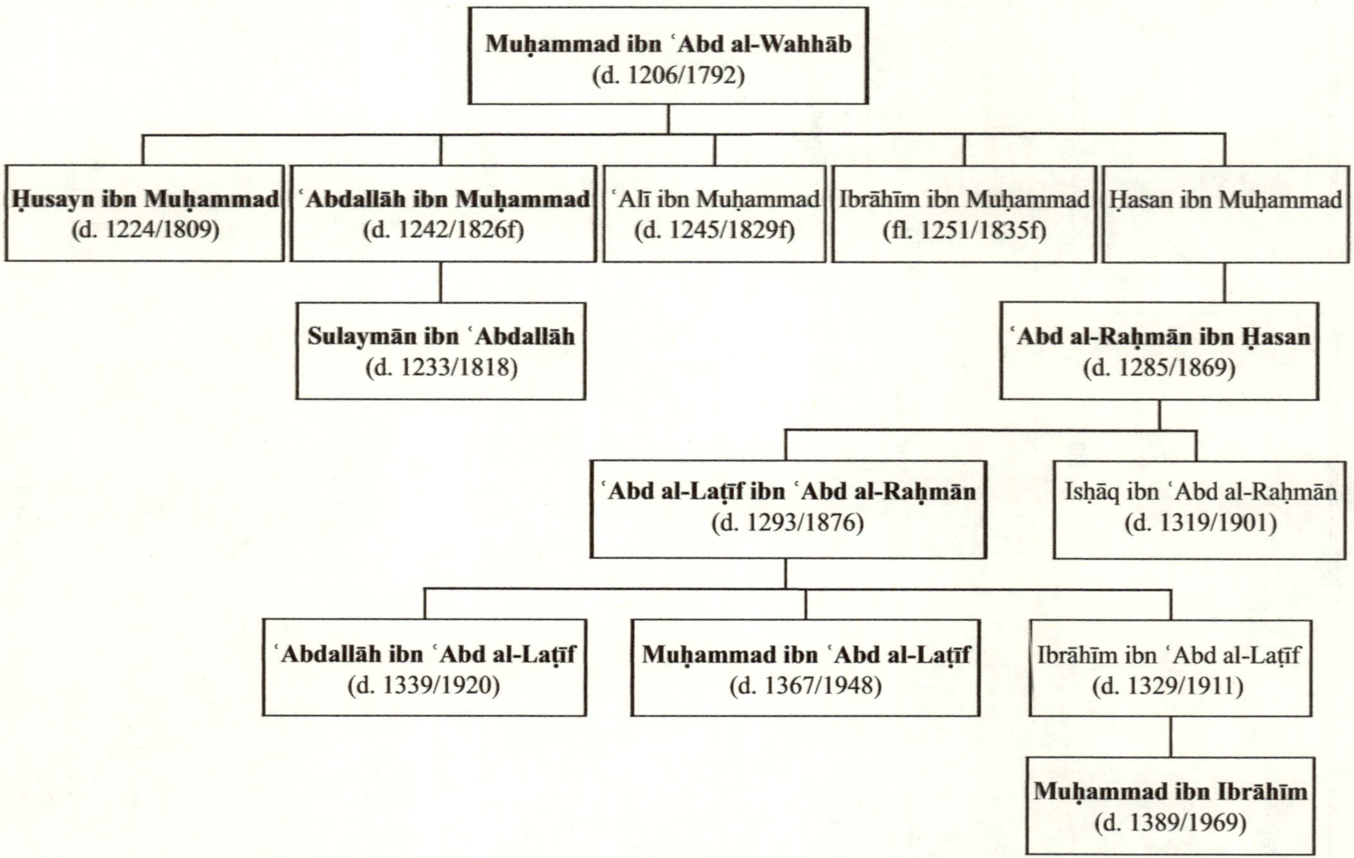

FIGURE 1. The Āl al-Shaykh (principal scholars in bold)

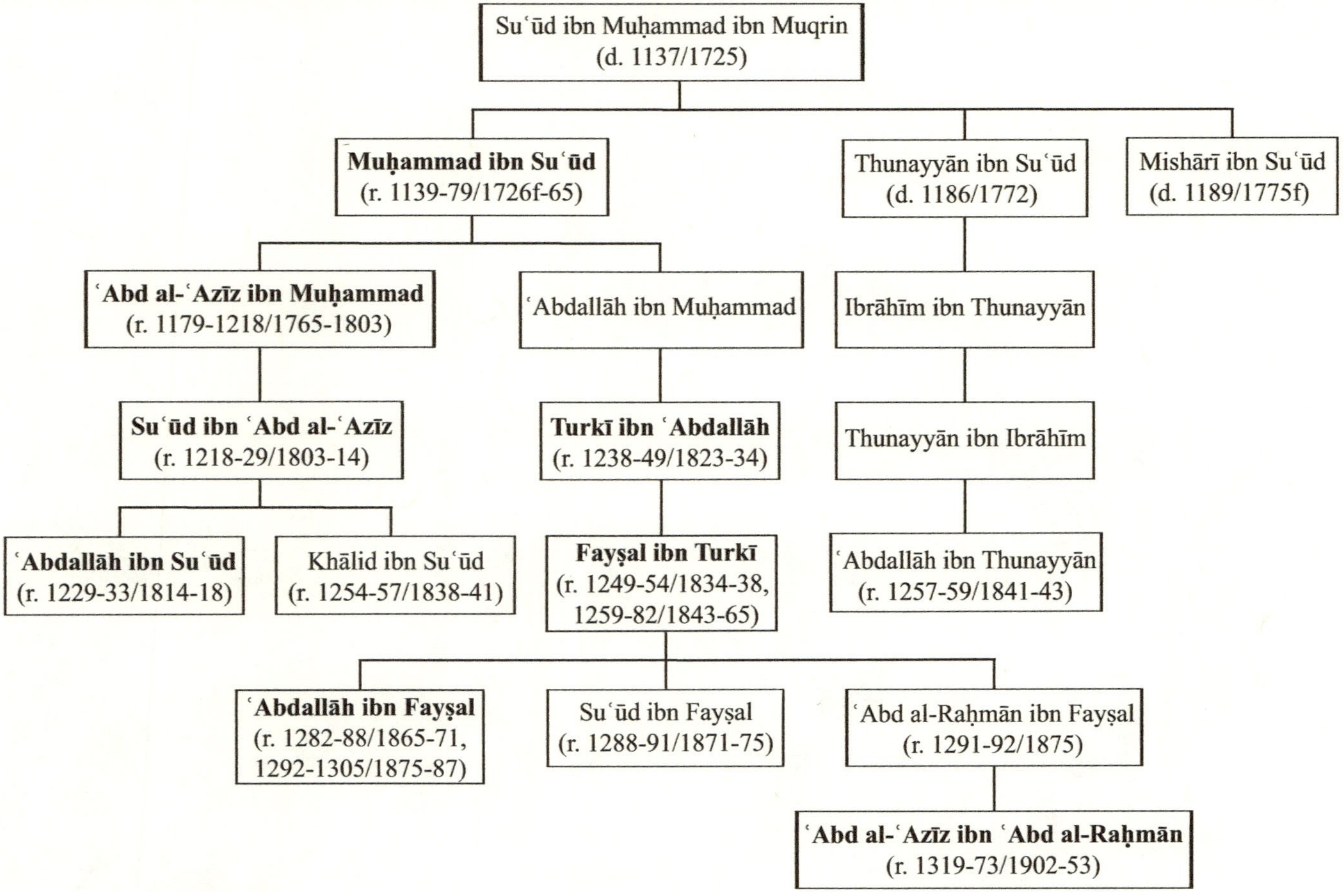

FIGURE 2. The Āl Suʿūd (principal rulers in bold)

PREFACE

THIS BOOK has its origins in a much more modest plan to study the life and career of a single Wahhābī religious scholar, Sulaymān ibn Siḥmān. Born in the western Arabian region of ʿAsīr in the mid–nineteenth century, Ibn Siḥmān migrated at an early age to central Arabia, where he rose to become one of the leading Wahhābī scholars of his generation. At the time of his death, in 1349/1930, he was the most prolific author in the Wahhābī movement's history, having written numerous refutations, in prose and in verse, of the movement's many enemies. His prodigious literary output shed extraordinary light on the travails of the Wahhābī community during a tumultuous half-century that witnessed both the decline of Saudi political power in the late nineteenth century and its later resurgence in the form of the modern Saudi state in the early twentieth century. His writings also helped to clarify what the Wahhābīs stood for and believed at this time. Ibn Siḥmān, along with his colleagues, was adamantly opposed to what he saw as the mainstream religious currents in the Islamic world, in particular the popular customs of grave visitation, which he considered to be polytheism. Those who participated in such customs, or merely tolerated them, were in his view not Muslims at all but, rather, polytheists and were to be condemned as such. Ibn Siḥmān pronounced *takfīr* on the Ottoman Empire on the grounds that it espoused polytheism, he opposed the travel of Wahhābī Muslims to any area outside Wahhābī control, and he repeatedly stressed that true Muslims were duty-bound to show hatred and enmity to those deemed polytheists. Wahhābism was, at this point, still a radical Islamic movement: intolerant, adversarial, and uncompromising. Ibn Siḥmān was that movement's chief spokesman and defender. He was perhaps the most important Wahhābī scholar alive during the turn of the twentieth century, yet almost nothing had been written about him in English.

The problem with writing a biography of Ibn Siḥmān, however, was that in the context of Wahhābism his religious views were not exactly novel. His fiery tone and passion for refutations were to some extent unique, as was his penchant for writing in verse, but the ideas that he articulated were anything but original. Nor should they have been, as this was not a religious community that prized originality in the first place. Ibn Siḥmān's role, as he understood it, was to continue the mission (*daʿwa*) of Muḥammad ibn ʿAbd al-Wahhāb, the eponymous founder of Wahhābism, by reiterating his ideas and those of his successors among the Wahhābī scholars. Appropriately, his writings were shot through with lengthy quotations of earlier Wahhābī authorities, including, in addition to Ibn ʿAbd al-Wahhāb, Ḥusayn ibn Ghannām, ʿAbd al-Raḥmān ibn Ḥasan Āl al-Shaykh, ʿAbd al-Laṭīf ibn ʿAbd al-Raḥmān Āl al-Shaykh, and Ḥamad ibn ʿAtīq. These were the leading lights of the Wahhābī tradition from its inception up to the late nineteenth century, and to a very large extent they bore a consistent religious message. That message consisted of an emphasis on purifying the religion of all perceived elements of polytheism, as well as a requirement that true Muslims dissociate from, and show hatred and enmity to, the so-called polytheists. What these scholars represented, together with Ibn Siḥmān, was what might be called traditional or unreconstructed Wahhābism—a radically exclusivist and fiercely provocative Islamic movement. This militant Wahhābism was the version championed by the movement's religious authorities for nearly two centuries, from the 1150s/1740s to the 1340s/1920s, when the modern Saudi state sought to tame the Wahhābī religious establishment and come to an accommodation with the broader Islamic world. In this context, Ibn Siḥmān's writings can be seen as the last major articulation and defense of the militant Wahhābī heritage.

In the course of my research on Ibn Siḥmān, I gradually came to the realization that I could not tell his story without first coming to grips with the Wahhābī tradition that he so passionately sought to defend. Accordingly, the scope of my inquiry broadened to include the entire Wahhābī period from the movement's origins in the 1150s/1740s up until the establishment of the Kingdom of Saudi Arabia in 1351/1932. Here I found that much work remained to be done. With few exceptions, Western scholars of Islam had not taken a serious interest in Wahhābism. A great deal of source material had yet to be scrutinized, and some had yet to be uncovered. Much of the secondary literature fundamentally misunderstood key aspects of Wahhābī history and doctrine, and while several important and pathbreaking studies of the Wahhābī movement were available, none of these adequately captured what I found to be one of the key Wahhābī doctrinal tenets—namely, the duty to show hatred and enmity to those accused of polytheism. There was also a gap in the literature as regards the nature of the Wahhābī doctrine and its relationship to the ideas of Ibn Taymiyya and Ibn Qayyim al-Jawziyya. All of this would need to be addressed in a proper study of Wahhābism from its origins to the period up to and including the founding of the modern Saudi state. The result of my expanded research is a book of considerably wider scope than a biography of Ibn Siḥmān. It probes the nature of the Wahhābī doctrine, examines the early history of the Wahhābī movement, and covers the efforts of subsequent Wahhābī scholars to refine, preserve, and defend the Wahhābī heritage into the early twentieth century.

While the book was written primarily with a view to understanding Wahhābism on its own terms and in its own context, it should be noted that it is also informed in some degree by my parallel interest in the modern Sunnī *jihādī* movement. In recent decades, *jihādī* groups and actors have embraced the premodern Wahhābī tradition as their own, seeing it as the embodiment of sound Islamic creed with its emphasis on doctrinal exclusivism and militant activism. Wahhābism has become the *jihādī* movement's ideological backbone. Wahhābī texts abound on *jihādī* websites and are frequently quoted by *jihādī* scholars and leaders, who see themselves as the proper heirs of the Wahhābī tradition. There is of course more to *jihādī* ideology than the premodern Wahhābī tradition; the influence of certain Muslim Brotherhood ideas remains key. However, to the extent that Wahhābism forms a crucial part of *jihādī* ideology, this book may be read for background on the ideology of modern Sunnī *jihādism*.

In the course of researching and writing this book, I have incurred numerous debts of gratitude. Above all I should like to thank Bernard Haykel, who supervised an earlier version of this work in the form of a Ph.D. dissertation at Princeton. So much of what went into this book, from research in Saudi Arabia to rare manuscripts from India, Iraq, and elsewhere, was made possible by him. Michael Cook, also at Princeton, was likewise an invaluable resource and source of support, and I was most fortunate to have him as a teacher and adviser. Muhammad Qasim Zaman and Khalid El-Rouayheb provided valuable comments on an earlier version and informed my thinking in numerous ways. Jon Hoover read and commented on the chapters on Ibn Taymiyya, and I am grateful to him for saving me from errors and pointing me in the right direction in a number of matters. My thanks go as well to the two anonymous reviewers, who read the manuscript carefully and whose comments certainly improved the final product. The introduction was made better by the input of my Hoover colleagues Valentin Bolotny, Amber Boydstun, and Jackie Schneider. Over the years I have had many fruitful discussions with scholars on subjects pertaining to Wahhābism, especially Daniel Lav, Saud Al-Sarhan, and Michael Crawford. The book would have looked a lot different were it not for their unique insights and knowledge. I alone, of course, am responsible for the views presented herein.

The Abdallah S. Kamel Center at Yale Law School and the Hoover Institution at Stanford provided the space where I was able to complete the manuscript. At Yale I am grateful to Tony Kronman and Owen Fiss for welcoming me to the center and for hosting a workshop on one of my chapters. At Hoover I owe a special debt to Russell Berman, chairman of Hoover's Middle East and Islamic World Working Group, for his encouragement and support, in this project as in others. In Saudi Arabia I was fortunate to be hosted twice by the King Faisal Center for Research and Islamic Studies, on both occasions with the financial support of the Princeton Institute for International and Regional Studies. I am grateful to the staff at the center for welcoming and assisting me and for organizing an early talk I gave on Ibn Siḥmān. I am also grateful to those who assisted me at other institutions in Saudi Arabia, including the King Abdulaziz Foundation for Research and Archives, the King Salman Library at King Saud University, and the King Fahd National Library. My research in the kingdom was greatly enhanced by the friendship and support of Abdulrahman Alshuqir, Abdulaziz Alrasheed, and Ahmad Shanbary, who took it upon themselves to open doors I did not know existed. Abdulrahman and Abdulaziz facilitated my travel to Ḥā'il, where I had the good fortune of gaining access to the Ṣāliḥ ibn Sālim Āl Bunayyān family library, with its trove of little-known manuscripts. My thanks go as well to the Āl Bunayyān family for their hospitality.

My editor at Princeton University Press, Fred Appel, believed in this project from the beginning, and I am grateful to him and his colleagues for seeing it through to completion. My superb copyeditor, Elisabeth A. Graves, did a masterful job reviewing the manuscript, and I am grateful to her as well. Kelly Seeger has been with me through all the stages of this book. Her love and support were vital to getting me across the finish line.

NOTE ON CONVENTIONS

THE SYSTEM I have used for transliterating Arabic is essentially that of *The Encyclopedia of Islam Three*, with two minor differences: (1) I prefer to indicate the elision of alifs with a half ring (e.g., *fī ʾl-masjid*, not *fī l-masjid*, and *wa ʾl-kitāb*, not *wa-l-kitāb*), and (2) I prefer to spell out the words *ibn* and *bint* as opposed to shortening them to "b." and "bt."

Most dates are given according to both the *hijrī* and Gregorian calendars, in the format AH/CE. The letter *f* appended to a year indicates that and the following year (e.g., 850/1446f = 850/1446–47).

The abbreviations EI^1, EI^2, and EI^3 refer to the first, second, and third editions of the *Encyclopaedia of Islam*, respectively. Translations from the Qurʾān are borrowed or adapted from A. J. Arberry, *The Koran Interpreted*. All other translations, unless otherwise noted, are my own.

Introduction

SOMETIME IN THE middle of 1155/1742, an epistle by Muḥammad ibn ʿAbd al-Wahhāb arrived in the city of Basra in southern Iraq. Ibn ʿAbd al-Wahhāb, a preacher from the central Arabian region of Najd, had recently launched an Islamic reformist movement in his home region predicated on a doctrine of strict monotheism (*tawḥīd*). Rumblings about his controversial movement had already reached Basra, some four hundred miles away from Ibn ʿAbd al-Wahhāb's location in Najd, but this was the first piece of writing by him to arrive in the city. In the epistle, cast as an explication of the confession that "there is no god but God" and of *tawḥīd*, Ibn ʿAbd al-Wahhāb warns that polytheism (*shirk*) has spread far and wide in the Islamic world, primarily in the form of the supplication (*duʿāʾ*) of saints and prophets during the visitation of graves, meaning appealing to them for earthly gain or heavenly reward. For Ibn ʿAbd al-Wahhāb, such practices, while at the time a widespread feature of Islamic ritual in the Arab Middle East as elsewhere, were unambiguously *shirk*, and those participating in them were to be regarded as polytheists (*mushrikūn*). It was incumbent on those seeking to profess Islam, he wrote, to abandon these practices and to direct all forms of worship to God alone. Only then would they satisfy the conditions of the confession that "there is no god but God" and of *tawḥīd*. This, however, was not the only thing required of them. It was also necessary, Ibn ʿAbd al-Wahhāb continued in the epistle, that they show hatred and enmity to the polytheists and the false gods that they worship. After setting out the requirement of directing all worship to God, he goes on to explain the second requirement:

> Do not think if you say, "This is the truth. I follow it and I abjure all that is against it, but I will not confront them [i.e., the saints being worshipped] and I will say nothing concerning them," do not think that that will profit

> you. Rather, it is necessary to hate them, to hate those who love them, to revile them, and to show them enmity.[1]

Here, then, was the true test of faith. The complete Muslim was one who not only worshipped God exclusively but exhibited hatred and enmity to perceived idols and polytheists, the polytheists in this case being professed Muslims seen as engaged in tomb-centered rituals.

The epistle that arrived in Basra in 1155/1742, known as the *Kalimāt fī bayān shahādat an lā ilāha illā ʾllāh* (Words in Explication of the Confession that There Is No God but God), is one of Ibn ʿAbd al-Wahhāb's earliest known writings.[2] It was circulating several years before the historic alliance he would strike with the Āl Suʿūd (i.e., the family of Suʿūd), in approximately 1157/1744f, and the subsequent rise of the Saudi state, which would spread Wahhābism across the Arabian Peninsula by force of arms. Despite its early date, however, the message that the epistle contained was illustrative of the doctrinal thrust of the Wahhābī movement for generations to come. This was a message of theological exclusivism combined with militant activism, of directing all worship to God alone and showing hatred and enmity to polytheism and polytheists. In many other letters and epistles, Ibn ʿAbd al-Wahhāb would elaborate this same message with similar wording, and as before it was the second part of his formulation, the requirement of confrontation, that he presented as the true test of faith. Adherence to *tawḥīd* had to be accompanied by a profession of hatred and enmity, by a demonstration of unfriendliness and hostility, before one could be considered a true Muslim. In another epistle, for instance, he writes: "Islam is not sound without showing enmity to the polytheists; if one does not show them enmity, then he is one of them, even if he has not committed it [i.e., *shirk*]."[3] And in another epistle he makes the point again, writing that "a person's religion and Islam are not sound, even if he professes *tawḥīd* and eschews *shirk*, unless he shows enmity to the polytheists and openly professes enmity and hatred of them."[4]

In Ibn ʿAbd al-Wahhāb's writings, the required confrontation with alleged polytheists was most commonly expressed in the language of hatred (*bughḍ*) and enmity (*ʿadāwa*), together with the related notion of dissociation (*barāʾa*). The phraseology of these three elements derives from the Qurʾān, and specifi-

1. al-Qabbānī, *Faṣl al-khiṭāb*, f. 65a.
2. For more on this source and the embedded epistle, see chapter 1.
3. *al-Durar al-saniyya*, 10:107.
4. Ibid., 8:113.

cally Q. 60:4, in which the Prophet Abraham declares his separation from the polytheists around him. In the verse, Abraham and his followers are seen declaring to their polytheist community: "We dissociate [*innā buraʾāʾ*] from you and that which you worship apart from God. We reject you, and between us and you enmity and hatred [*al-ʿadāwa waʾl-baghḍāʾ*] have shown themselves forever, until you believe in God alone." In the Wahhābī doctrine, unsurprisingly, Abraham is considered the exemplar par excellence of the duty of confronting polytheists, but so is the Prophet Muḥammad. The latter, in Ibn ʿAbd al-Wahhāb's telling, was uncompromising in exhibiting hatred and enmity to the polytheist Quraysh, even during the period of his preaching in Mecca, often seen as the peaceful phase of his career.

In addition to *bughḍ*, *ʿadāwa*, and *barāʾa*, Ibn ʿAbd al-Wahhāb invoked *takfīr*, or publicly charging with unbelief, in the context of the duty of confrontation. He thus deemed it obligatory for Muslims to pronounce *takfīr* on those he considered polytheists—that is, to condemn them as unbelievers or excommunicate them. *Jihād*, in the sense of warfare against unbelievers, was another element in this mix. As Wahhābism grew in tandem with the rise of the first Saudi state, the obligatory confrontation with polytheists expanded to include not just verbal but armed confrontation as well. Ibn ʿAbd al-Wahhāb thus wrote in one of his later epistles: "If a person wishes to be a follower of the Messenger [i.e., Muḥammad], then it is incumbent on him to dissociate from this [i.e., *shirk*], to direct worship exclusively to God, to reject it and those who commit it, to condemn those who practice it, to show them hatred and enmity, and to wage *jihād* against them until the religion becomes God's entirely."[5]

Ibn ʿAbd al-Wahhāb died in 1206/1792, but his teachings would be preserved by generations of Wahhābī scholars after him. Some of the most important of these scholars were his direct descendants, known by the patronymic "Āl al-Shaykh," or "family of the shaykh." While occasionally these men refined and reformulated certain Wahhābī doctrinal principles, their main task, as they saw it, was to safeguard and perpetuate the doctrine of Ibn ʿAbd al-Wahhāb, who in their view had rediscovered the true and original message of Islam.

Like Ibn ʿAbd al-Wahhāb, these scholars perceived *shirk*, in the form of the supplication of saints and prophets, as having spread far and wide in the Islamic world, and they called on people to worship God as one and to confront polytheists with hatred and enmity. Sulaymān ibn ʿAbdallāh Āl al-Shaykh (d. 1233/1818), for example, a grandson of Ibn ʿAbd al-Wahhāb's, underscored

5. Ibid., 1:146.

"the command to show enmity to the polytheists, to hate them, to wage *jihād* against them, and to separate from them."[6] ʿAbd al-Raḥmān ibn Ḥasan Āl al-Shaykh (d. 1285/1869), another grandson, wrote that "God has made it obligatory to dissociate from polytheism and polytheists, to reject them, to show them enmity and hatred, and to wage *jihād* against them."[7] His son ʿAbd al-Laṭīf ibn ʿAbd al-Raḥmān Āl al-Shaykh (d. 1293/1876), a great-grandson of Ibn ʿAbd al-Wahhāb's, proclaimed that "it is inconceivable that a person could know and practice *tawḥīd* yet not show enmity to the polytheists. It cannot be said of one who fails to show enmity to the polytheists that he knows and practices *tawḥīd*."[8] Another important Wahhābī scholar, Ḥamad ibn ʿAtīq (d. 1301/1884), argued that hatred of polytheists borne in the heart is insufficient and that believers must *manifest* their hatred of polytheists. Hatred, he wrote, "is of no benefit until its signs are manifested and its effects are made clear.... [A person] has not met his obligation until enmity and hatred are demonstrated by him, and the enmity and hatred must be evident, manifest, and clear."[9] Likewise, Isḥāq ibn ʿAbd al-Raḥmān Āl al-Shaykh (d. 1319/1901), a great-grandson of Ibn ʿAbd al-Wahhāb's, maintained that "hating them in the heart is not enough; it is necessary to manifest enmity and hatred.... This is manifesting the religion. It is necessary to express enmity openly and to pronounce *takfīr* on them publicly."[10] The Wahhābī scholar Sulaymān ibn Siḥmān (d. 1349/1930) put this idea into verse:

> Manifesting this religion is clearly pronouncing to them
> that they are unbelievers, for indeed they are an unbelieving people,
> And evident enmity and manifest hatred,
> this is manifesting [the religion] and [proper] condemnation.
> By God, such is not what is apparent among you.
> O those with understanding, have you no notice?
> This, and not enough is bearing hatred in the heart
> and love in it—this is not the measure.
> Rather the measure is to bear it
> openly and clearly, for they have gone astray.[11]

6. Āl al-Shaykh, *Majmūʿ al-rasāʾil*, 56.

7. *al-Durar al-saniyya*, 8:190.

8. Ibid., 8:359.

9. Ibn ʿAtīq, *Sabīl al-najāt wa ʾl-fikāk*, 44–45.

10. *al-Durar al-saniyya*, 8:305.

11. Ibn Siḥmān, *ʿUqūd al-jawāhir* (al-Rushd ed.), 1:321 (meter = *rajaz*).

Many of these Wahhābī scholars were writing at a time when the Wahhābī movement was weak and insecure. By emphasizing the duty of hatred and enmity, they sought to ensure that Wahhābism would remain distinct and separate from the larger Islamic world, a world they perceived to be dominated by the forces of *shirk*. Of crucial importance to them was maintaining the antagonistic posture toward the polytheist other that Ibn ʿAbd al-Wahhāb had made central to his doctrinal program. Whether opposing polytheists by means of verbal denunciation or armed confrontation, or merely dissociating from them and keeping them at a distance, the Wahhābī scholars from the mid–eighteenth to the early twentieth century were committed to upholding the original Wahhābī message of theological exclusivism and militant activism, a message already on display in the epistle that reached Basra in 1155/1742.

Wahhābism and the Three Saudi States

The term *Wahhābism* (*al-Wahhābiyya*) refers to the predicatory movement (*daʿwa*) launched by Muḥammad ibn ʿAbd al-Wahhāb in the mid–eighteenth century. It may also refer to the distinctive doctrinal content of that movement. The subject of this book is Wahhābism as it was from the mid–eighteenth to the early twentieth century, a period when, far from being the quietest version of Islam that it would later become, Wahhābism was a provocative and activist faith, one that encouraged and even demanded confrontation with those Muslims seen as polytheists. Given its militant character, this form of Wahhābism will occasionally be referred to here as *militant* Wahhābism to distinguish it from the less aggressive, though still highly intolerant, form that would become the standard in Saudi Arabia beginning in the early twentieth century.

In doctrinal terms, Wahhābism is a Sunnī Islamic movement, meaning that it situates itself within the legal and theological tradition of Sunnī Islam. More specifically, it appeals to the tradition of the Ḥanbalī *madhhab*, or school of law, the smallest of the four law schools in Sunnī Islam; and even more specifically, it appeals to the authority of a small number of mostly Ḥanbalī scholars from the fourteenth century, in particular Ibn Taymiyya (d. 728/1328) and his student Ibn Qayyim al-Jawziyya (d. 751/1350), who lived most of their lives in Damascus under the Mamlūk Sultanate. Like the Wahhābīs, these fourteenth-century Ḥanbalī scholars were extremely hostile to what Western academic literature has called the "cult of saints," a term denoting the ritual practices associated with visiting the burial sites of saints and prophets, including asking them for worldly favors and pleading with them for divine intercession.[12] In Arabic these practices are captured by the term *ziyāra* (visitation), or *ziyārat al-qubūr* (visitation of graves).[13] When Ibn ʿAbd al-Wahhāb began his movement in central Arabia in the mid–eighteenth century, it was the practitioners of the cult of saints, or *ziyāra*—that is, Muslims who worshipped at graves and appealed to the dead—who were the principal targets of his wrath. By engaging in such practices, he believed, they were associating others in God's oneness and so committing *shirk*. In justifying this belief, he appealed specifically to the ideas of Ibn Taymiyya and Ibn al-Qayyim, quoting both their words and the scriptural evidence that they cited. This is not to say, however, that the Wahhābī and Taymiyyan versions of Islam were identical; much of this book is in fact concerned with examining the differences between Wahhābī and Taymiyyan thought, in addition to their similarities.

The term *Wahhābī* is in origin a pejorative coined by the enemies of Ibn ʿAbd al-Wahhāb to stigmatize his movement as deviant and heretical. For most of Wahhābism's history, its adherents have rejected the label as offensive, preferring to call themselves Muslims (*Muslimūn*) or monotheists (*muwaḥḥidūn*), their view being that the Wahhābī form of Islam is nothing but a revival of the pure and uncorrupted version.[14] Even so, the Wahhābīs have long recognized that theirs is a distinct movement in Islam, one captured by the term "the Najdī mission" (*al-daʿwa al-Najdiyya*). The latter term, which goes back to at least the mid–nineteenth century,[15] may be understood as synonymous with the Wahhābī movement. The argument sometimes made by Saudi royals and officials that Wahhābism does not exist—an argument based on the idea that Wahhābī teachings reflect nothing but true Islam—is thus misleading.[16] The term *Wahhābism* is used here not in any derogatory sense but only as a neutral descriptor, in keeping with Western academic convention.[17]

12. See, e.g., Goldziher, "Cult of Saints in Islam."

13. *EI*³, s.v. "Grave Visitation/Worship" (Richard McGregor).

14. For a period of some fifty years, however, beginning in the 1300s/1880s, some of the leading Wahhābī scholars embraced the "Wahhābī" epithet as a point of pride, as will be seen below.

15. See, e.g., *al-Durar al-saniyya*, 9:258, 10:466, 14:409.

16. For this argument, see, for instance, Mahdi, "There Is No Such Thing as Wahhabism."

17. In the 1940s, the scholar George Rentz sought to introduce the term *Unitarianism* as a more neutral alternative to *Wahhābism*, but this did not catch on. See Rentz, *Birth of the Islamic Reform Movement in Saudi Arabia*.

In more recent decades, the Wahhābīs have seized on another term as an appropriate label for their distinctive version of Islam: Salafism (*al-Salafiyya*). The Salafī label, to be sure, is not inappropriate for Wahhābism. The term *Salafism* comes from the name for the first three generations of Muslims, *al-salaf al-ṣāliḥ* (the pious ancestors), whom Salafīs purport to emulate in belief and practice. The Wahhābīs certainly fit the popular conception of Salafism today as a purist religious orientation in Sunnī Islam, one that combines a fundamentalist hermeneutics (that is, direct engagement with the source texts of revelation) with a commitment to the doctrinal tenets of Ibn Taymiyya and Ibn al-Qayyim.[18] However, while Wahhābī scholars did occasionally use the "Salafī" epithet before the modern era,[19] Salafism was not a popular name for Wahhābism before the mid–twentieth century, when the Wahhābīs embraced it as part of an attempt to improve their image.[20] Wahhābism is better understood as a subset of the broader Salafī movement rather than as the embodiment of Salafism itself, particularly since, as will be seen, Ibn ʿAbd al-Wahhāb departed from Ibn Taymiyya and Ibn al-Qayyim in significant ways.

As noted above, Ibn ʿAbd al-Wahhāb and his followers believed that *shirk* was pervasive in the Islamic world on account of the prevalence of the cult of saints. The proper response, in their view, was a renewed commitment to the principle of *tawḥīd*, understood as worshipping God as one and directing all forms of worship to Him alone, combined with an insistence on manifesting hatred and enmity to *shirk* and those seen as practicing it. What manifesting hatred and enmity to polytheists meant in practice is not usually spelled out by the Wahhābī scholars, but the general idea was clear enough: Muslims must actively oppose and antagonize those perceived as committing *shirk*. In Wahhābī Islam as originally conceived, true Muslims are expected to be spirited antagonists, not passive believers. They are impelled by their monotheistic doctrine to show hostility to those who violate their strict understanding of *tawḥīd*. The obligatory confrontation with polytheists also included the ideas of dissociation (*barāʾa*) and excommunication (*takfīr*), and when the Wahhābī movement became enveloped in the

18. For this understanding of Salafism, see Haykel, "On the Nature of Salafi Thought and Action." On contending views of Salafism in the modern period, see Lauzière, *Making of Salafism*.

19. See, for instance, *al-Durar al-saniyya*, 12:367, 504.

20. Commins, "From Wahhabi to Salafi."

expansionary warfare of the first Saudi state, the idea of *jihād* against polytheists was included as well.

The success of Wahhābism owed to a large extent to its association with the Āl Suʿūd dynasty, or what is sometimes referred to as the House of Saud. After launching his mission in the Najdī town of Ḥuraymilāʾ in 1153/1741, Ibn ʿAbd al-Wahhāb moved shortly thereafter to al-ʿUyayna, another town in Najd, where his movement continued to spread. In approximately 1157/1744f, he made the fateful decision to relocate to the nearby town of al-Dirʿiyya, whose ruler was a certain Muḥammad ibn Suʿūd (r. 1139–79/1726f–65). The latter pledged his support for Ibn ʿAbd al-Wahhāb, who in turn pledged his support for the Saudi ruler. The small emirate of al-Dirʿiyya, which embraced Wahhābism as its official religious ideology, grew over a period of decades into what would be known as the first Saudi state (ca. 1157–1233/1744f–1818), which at its height encompassed most of the Arabian Peninsula and threatened to conquer Iraq and Syria. The state's conquests were undertaken in the name of extending the ambit of true Islam (i.e., Wahhābism), and Ibn ʿAbd al-Wahhāb justified the state's expansion as legitimate *jihād* for the sake of eradicating *shirk*. The first Saudi state would be destroyed in 1233/1818 by an invading army sent from Muḥammad ʿAlī's Egypt, but the alliance between the Saudi dynasty and the Wahhābī scholars survived, having become an alliance between the Āl Suʿūd (the descendants of Ibn Suʿūd) and the Āl al-Shaykh (the descendants of Ibn ʿAbd al-Wahhāb).

Within five years of the first Saudi state's destruction, the Saudi-Wahhābī partnership reemerged in a second Saudi state, which had its capital in Riyadh. The second Saudi state (1238–1305/1823–87) extended its sway across central and eastern Arabia but never managed to reconstitute the full territorial expanse of the first. It came to an end in 1305/1887 following a long civil war. The third and final Saudi state, also with its capital in Riyadh, was launched in 1319/1902 by a young member of the Saudi family named ʿAbd al-ʿAzīz ibn ʿAbd al-Raḥmān Āl Suʿūd (r. 1319–73/1902–53). Over the next twenty-five years, ʿAbd al-ʿAzīz succeeded in recovering most of the territory of the original Saudi state and in 1351/1932 gave his expanded realm the title of the Kingdom of Saudi Arabia, which it retains to this day. Like the first Saudi state, the second and the third Saudi states also justified their expansionary warfare as *jihād* for the sake of eradicating *shirk*, and in this they enjoyed the support of the Wahhābī scholarly establishment, led by Ibn ʿAbd al-Wahhāb's descendants.

Throughout this period, the Wahhābī scholars continued to promote Ibn ʿAbd al-Wahhāb's original religious message centering on the proper worship of God in accordance with *tawḥīd* and the necessary display of hatred and enmity. Even when the Wahhābī movement was on the defensive, as it was during the latter part of the second Saudi state and prior to the founding of the third, the scholars refused to adopt a more accommodationist stance, devoting their energies to opposing any kind of harmonious coexistence with non-Wahhābī Muslims. Any attempt to dilute Wahhābism, to tamp down its exclusivism and militancy, was vigorously opposed. Yet, during the third Saudi state, and especially after 1351/1932, the militancy at the heart of the Wahhābī movement began to ebb. ʿAbd al-ʿAzīz Āl Suʿūd, the Saudi ruler, prevailed upon the Wahhābī scholars to tone down Wahhābism's more extremist tendencies that had kept it a sect apart for almost two hundred years. At the beginning of his reign, Wahhābism was still seen as a dreadful heresy by the majority of the Islamic world. ʿAbd al-ʿAzīz sought to change this perception as he made his country into a modern state, and to a large extent he would succeed. At his direction, the scholars gradually relaxed their adversarial posture toward the larger Islamic world. The general principles of Wahhābism were in theory left unchanged, but in practice they were not adhered to with the same intensity as before. Neighboring Muslim countries such as Egypt and Iraq were no longer viewed as lands of *shirk* to be either conquered or avoided. Over time, Wahhābism was domesticated, developing into a quietest form of Islam that taught proper worship, policed Saudi society, and emphasized obedience to the ruler.

This book is not about this later Wahhābism but, rather, about Wahhābism as it was before its taming and co-optation by the modern Saudi state. It aims to show that Wahhābism, from its emergence in 1153/1741 to approximately 1351/1932, was a distinctly militant form of Islam, one founded in a radical spirit of exclusion and confrontation that would persist for nearly two hundred years. The leading Wahhābī scholars during this period never ceased to emphasize the duty of showing hatred and enmity to those Muslims they deemed polytheists. Their insistence on this duty was of central concern, and so it will be of central concern to this book.

This is not the first study to posit such a distinction between an earlier era of militant Wahhābism and a later one defined by a less militant form. David Commins, for instance, has written of the "taming of Wahhabi zeal" under ʿAbd al-ʿAzīz and his "calculat[ing] that survival in the international arena required that he curb Wahhabism's xenophobic impulses."[21] Similarly, Guido Steinberg has described how "the puritanical character of the Wahhabi community... gradually had to give way to external influences" as ʿAbd al-ʿAzīz pursued the modernization of his kingdom.[22] "Wahhabism as a religious movement," he writes, "underwent a process of change between 1925 and 1953 that makes plausible the distinction made by Werner Ende between old Wahhabism and Wahhabism."[23] Abdulaziz Al-Fahad has written of the "slow and painful process that transformed Wahhabism from a puritanical, exclusivist, and uncompromising movement into a more docile and accommodationist ideology that is more concerned with practical politics than ideological rigor."[24] Similarly, Nabil Mouline has described early Wahhābism in terms of a "counterreligion." A counterreligion is an exclusivist and militant form of monotheism, one that approaches the outside world with an "antagonistic character" and "rejects and repudiates everything that went before and what is outside itself as 'paganism.'"[25] In Mouline's view, Ibn ʿAbd al-Wahhāb was the founder of just such a counterreligion, one that "refus[es] all compromise" and in which "exclusion is the golden rule and interaction with other groups is possible only in the framework of conversion or confrontation."[26] The history of later Wahhābism, by contrast, is that of Wahhābism's "transformation from a counterreligion into a religion that interacts more openly with the Other."[27]

Yet while the idea that Wahhābism began as something aggressive and uncompromising and later developed (or degenerated) into something more complaisant and docile is generally well recognized, the more precise nature of the Wahhābī doctrine in the militant era remains to be examined and explored. The idea of Wahhābism as a counterreligion fits well with the idea of

21. Commins, *Wahhabi Mission*, 71–72.

22. Steinberg, *Religion und Staat in Saudi-Arabien*, 609.

23. Ibid., 610. The year 1925 marked the consolidation of Saudi rule over the Ḥijāz, while 1953 was the year of ʿAbd al-ʿAzīz's death. As alluded to here, in a series of articles the German scholar Werner Ende discussed the relationship between modernist Islam and what he called the "old Wahhabism" (*Alt-Wahhabiya*) of conservative Wahhābī scholars. See Ende, "Religion, Politik und Literatur in Saudi-Arabien."

24. Al-Fahad, "From Exclusivism to Accommodation," 516–17.

25. Assmann, *Moses the Egyptian*, 63, 3.

26. Mouline, *Clerics of Islam*, 58, 14.

27. Ibid., 264.

militant Wahhābism developed in this book, though here the Wahhābī counterreligion is defined by its specific doctrinal tenets, including a particular conception of *tawḥīd* and the requirement to show hatred and enmity to polytheists. This book explores the origins and content of the Wahhābī doctrine in exhaustive detail, and it examines the persistence of that doctrine in the century and a half after Ibn ʿAbd al-Wahhāb's death in 1206/1792.

About a half century after his death, in the mid–nineteenth century, the Wahhābī scholars introduced a distinction between hatred (*bughḍ*), on the one hand, and enmity (*ʿadāwa*), on the other. The pioneer of this development was Ḥamad ibn ʿAtīq (d. 1301/1884), who theorized that hatred was to be understood as something internal, a feeling, while enmity was something external, hatred made manifest. It was not enough, Ibn ʿAtīq wrote, for Muslims to hate polytheists; they had to show them enmity as well, in the sense of openly condemning and confronting them. The display of enmity was more important than the hatred harbored in one's heart. In his words, "Hatred that is not accompanied by manifest enmity is profitless."[28] The spirit of Wahhābism, to borrow his phrase, from the mid–eighteenth to the early twentieth century, was one of "manifest enmity" (*al-ʿadāwa al-ẓāhira*), a visible and unremitting hostility toward the vast majority of the Islamic world seen as having fallen into *shirk*.

Yet while the idea of manifest enmity pervades this book, this is not its sole focus. The book aims to provide a comprehensive treatment of the religious thought of Muḥammad ibn ʿAbd al-Wahhāb and his successors, as well as a full account of the history of the movement that he began, from its origins to the early twentieth century. Drawing on an array of original primary sources in Arabic, including rare manuscripts that have yet to be examined before, it reconstructs the polemics between Ibn ʿAbd al-Wahhāb and his scholarly enemies; examines the content of his religious thought, including its origins in the ideas of Ibn Taymiyya and Ibn Qayyim al-Jawziyya; charts the rise of the first Saudi state from a minor political entity to an expansive empire; and traces the persistence of militant Wahhābism through several generations of Wahhābī scholars who, after the collapse of the first Saudi state, sought to preserve the spirit of manifest enmity at all costs. While the book draws on a growing secondary literature on Wahhābism, and on an even more promising literature on the theological and legal thought of Ibn Taymiyya and Ibn

28. Ibn ʿAtīq, *al-Difāʿ ʿan ahl al-sunna*, 30–31.

Qayyim al-Jawziyya, it is primarily the product of my own reading and interpretation of primary sources in Arabic. If "[a]rchaeology is the methodology of history," as R. G. Collingwood has observed, then this is a work of both excavation and reconstruction, of the discovery and synthesis of a wide range of materials with a view to reconstituting something of the history and doctrine of this historical movement.[29]

Before turning to an overview of the chapters that follow, it will be necessary to lay some of the groundwork for what is to come. A working knowledge of three subjects in particular is essential for following this book's discussion of the history and doctrine of Wahhābism. These subjects are the geography and demography of central Arabia, the field of Wahhābī studies, and the sources available for the study of Wahhābism.

Geography and Demography of Central Arabia

The Arabian Peninsula, also known as Arabia, is the landmass in the southern Middle East bounded by the Red Sea to the west, the Persian Gulf to the east, the Arabian Sea to the south, and the lands of the Fertile Crescent to the north.[30] Known in Arabic as "the island of the Arabs" (*jazīrat al-ʿarab*), it is characterized by meager rainfall and desert conditions, the main exceptions being the historical Yemen and Ḥaḍramawt in the southwest and the fertile coastlands along the Persian Gulf, including Oman in the southeast and the cluster of oases known as al-Aḥsāʾ in the northeast. Al-Aḥsāʾ, often pronounced al-Ḥasā, corresponds to what is now the Eastern Province of modern Saudi Arabia. In the far west of the Arabian Peninsula is the region of the Ḥijāz, home to the holy cities of Mecca and Medina, and south of there lie the regions of ʿAsīr and Jīzān. All three belong to a long coastal plain known as the Tihāma. The center of the Arabian Peninsula is defined by a great plateau stretching hundreds of miles north to south and east to west and set off on three sides by vast, sandy deserts—the Great Nafūd to the north, the Dahnāʾ to the east, and the Empty Quarter (*al-Rubʿ al-Khālī*) to the south. In Arabic this plateau area is known as Najd, meaning "upland," and it is here where Wahhābism arose.

Historically, Najd was isolated and desolate, seen by the surrounding areas as being of little importance either politically, culturally, or economically. Given

29. Collingwood, *Idea of History*, 491.

30. See *EI*[3], s.v. "Arabian Peninsula" (Robert Hoyland).

its relative remoteness and harsh living conditions, the great Islamic empires, including the Ottomans, paid it little heed and did not attempt to rule it directly. Najd was not so remote as to be entirely ignored by those in its vicinity, lying as it did along the trade and pilgrimage routes connecting the holy cities of the Ḥijāz to Iraq and eastern Arabia, but no one would have expected that a religious or political movement of any significance was poised to arise there.

At the time of Wahhābism's emergence, the people of Najd were predominantly Sunnī Muslims belonging to the Ḥanbalī *madhhab*. For reasons that remain unclear, Ḥanbalism had become the dominant *madhhab* in Najd sometime around the fourteenth century.[31] While there was also a Ḥanbalī presence in the predominantly Shīʿī region of al-Aḥsāʾ in eastern Arabia, as well as in parts of Syria, including Damascus, Ḥanbalism was otherwise marginal in the world of Sunnī Islam at this time. The dominance of Ḥanbalism in Najd goes some way in explaining the rise of Wahhābism in the eighteenth century, given that the Ḥanbalī tradition preserved the ideas and writings of Ibn Taymiyya and Ibn al-Qayyim. However, many of Ibn ʿAbd al-Wahhāb's early opponents, as will be seen, were themselves devout Ḥanbalīs, and they contested his use of these fourteenth-century Ḥanbalī authorities.

In terms of social classifications, Najdīs generally fell into the categories of settled peoples (*ḥaḍar*) and nomads (*badw*, i.e., bedouin).[32] The *ḥaḍar* resided in towns and made their livelihood in agriculture, crafts, and trade, while the *badw* moved from place to place practicing animal husbandry and engaging in raiding and extortion. The *badw* were defined by strong tribal affiliations, the dominant tribes in the early Wahhābī period being the ʿAnaza, the Ẓafīr, the Muṭayr, the Qaḥṭān, and the ʿUtayba. The *ḥaḍar*, for their part, were essentially detribalized, meaning that they no longer organized according to tribal identity—though most maintained an ancestral tribal affiliation. While it is often said that Wahhābism emerged in the desert, in reality it was the product of townspeople, the *ḥaḍar*, who maintained the culture of religious learning. As will be seen, Ibn ʿAbd al-Wahhāb had no love for the *badw*, condemning them as polytheists.

The region of Najd was divided into a number of districts or subregions, most of which lay along Jabal Ṭuwayq, a long mountain range extending some five hundred miles north to south and rising to about eight hundred feet at its

31. al-Shuqayr, "al-Madhhab al-Ḥanbalī fī Najd," esp. 92–93.

32. For a good introduction to *ḥaḍar-badw* dynamics, see Al-Fahad, "Raiders and Traders," 237–41.

highest point.[33] In the eighteenth century, these districts were, from north to south, al-Qaṣīm, Sudayr, al-Washm, Thādiq, al-Miḥmal, al-Shaʿīb, al-ʿĀriḍ, al-Kharj, al-Furaʿ, and al-Aflāj. Each was host to a number of towns or settlements (*qurā*; sing. *qarya*) where settled life was made possible by the presence of oases and *wādī*s (i.e., dry river valleys beneath which groundwater is sometimes accessible). Wahhābism took root in the district of al-ʿĀriḍ, sometimes known as Wādī Ḥanīfa, after the *wādī* on which it is situated. Al-ʿĀriḍ was home to the towns of al-ʿUyayna, al-Dirʿiyya, al-Riyāḍ (i.e., Riyadh), Manfūḥa, and al-ʿAmmāriyya. Al-ʿUyayna, the birthplace of Ibn ʿAbd al-Wahhāb, had the distinction of being the dominant town in al-ʿĀriḍ, as well as the most populous and most politically powerful town in all of Najd. Each of the other districts likewise had a dominant town. These were ʿUnayza in al-Qaṣīm, Julājil in Sudayr, Tharmadāʾ in al-Washm, Thādiq in al-Miḥmal, Ḥuraymilāʾ in al-Shaʿīb, and al-Dilam in al-Kharj. Farther to the north lay the elevated region of Jabal Shammar, with its principal town of Ḥāʾil. Jabal Shammar is sometimes regarded as separate from Najd, sometimes as an extension of it.

The political scene in Najd at this time was fractious and undeveloped. The region had not seen significant state formation in centuries, the most recent case being that of the Banū ʾl-Ukhayḍir, an ʿAlid dynasty that ruled from southern Najd in the ninth to eleventh centuries.[34] Indeed, the basic patterns of social, political, and economic life had not undergone significant change in centuries, at least none that can be reliably detected,[35] a fact that makes the rise of Wahhābism and the first Saudi state all the more intriguing.

Wahhābī Studies

Unlike some other movements in Islamic history, Wahhābism has not received a great deal of attention from Western scholars of Islam. From the eighteenth century to the early twentieth century, there were hardly any studies of the movement by Western academics and none that could be considered well informed. In one sense this lack of attention was understandable, as the Wahhābīs were throughout this period a minority sect in Islam, viewed by the great majority of the Islamic world as dreadful heretics. They were located in

33. On the geography of Najd, see Al Juhany, *Najd Before the Salafi Reform Movement*, 23–37, 149–52.

34. Ibid., 45–47.

35. For more on this point, which is contested, see chapter 4.

a remote area of Arabia to which few had access, and apart from the short-lived occupation of the holy cities in the early 1200s/early 1800s, they were not a particularly significant force in political or military terms. The lack of scholarly attention to Wahhābism may also have been related to what George Makdisi identified as the relative neglect of Ḥanbalism among Islamicists. As Makdisi wrote, "[T]he nineteenth century [was] the great enemy of Hanbalite studies," and "[h]ad it not been for the interest shown by the Salafī movement in Egypt and the Wahhābīs of Saudi Arabia in the Hanbalites, Hanbalism might well have remained even longer, perhaps forever, among the 'insignificant' schools in the mind of Islamists [i.e., Islamicists]."[36]

The pioneers of Wahhābī studies in the West were European travelers to Arabia who wrote accounts of their journeys, beginning with the German Carsten Niebuhr's *Beschreibung von Arabien,* published in 1772.[37] Though few of these men (and in a few cases women) penetrated the Wahhābī heartland of Najd, they nonetheless sought to learn all they could about the controversial movement capturing the attention of so many inhabitants of the Arabian Peninsula. Influenced by their anti-Wahhābī informants, as well as by their own prejudices, such early travelers helped to spread many false and misleading reports about what the Wahhābīs believed. These included the idea that the Wahhābīs rejected the authority of the Qurʾān and the *ḥadīth* and the related idea that Wahhābism was analogous to Deism in Europe. Such misapprehensions found their way into early Orientalist scholarship. What appears to be the earliest Western scholarly treatment of Wahhābism, a short article published in 1805 by the French Orientalist Antoine-Isaac Silvestre de Sacy (d. 1838), took its cues from Niebuhr and an anonymous traveler. Building on their misunderstandings, Sacy speculated that the Wahhābīs derived from the tenth-century Ismāʿīlī movement known as the Qarmaṭians, who seized the Black Stone from the Kaʿba in Mecca in 317/930.[38]

Over time, the information conveyed by travelers improved. Considerable progress was made with the publication in 1829–30 of two posthumous works by the Swiss traveler Johann Ludwig Burckhardt, *Travels in Arabia* and *Notes on the Bedouins and Wahábys.* Burckhardt, who traveled through western Arabia in 1814–15, rejected the prevailing view in Europe that Wahhābism was a kind of Deist movement, seeing it as very much within the parameters of

36. Makdisi, "Hanbalite Islam," 219.

37. On the travelers and their views, see Bonacina, *Wahhabis Seen Through European Eyes.*

38. Sacy, "Observations sur les Wahhabites."

orthodox Sunnī Islam. Relying on the accounts of well-informed sources in the Ḥijāz, which had recently been occupied by the Wahhābīs, as well as some former adherents of the movement, he portrayed Wahhābism as reformist and puritan. "I think myself authorised to state," he wrote, "from the result of my inquiries among the Arabs, and the Wahabys themselves, that the religion of the Wahabys may be called the Protestantism or even Puritanism of the Mohammedans."[39] In saying this, he rightly emphasized the Wahhābīs' hostility to saint veneration, comparing the cult of saints in Islam with hagiolatry in Catholicism ("Mohammedan saints are venerated as highly as those in the Catholic church, and are said to perform as many miracles as the latter").[40] The analogy with Protestantism may have been flawed, but it was certainly an improvement on the analogy with Deism. Burckhardt, however, though better informed than his predecessors, still wrongly claimed that the Wahhābīs rejected the authority of the *ḥadīth*,[41] and he never ventured into Najd.

The first to make the journey was an Irish captain in the army of the East India Company, George Forster Sadleir, who attempted to intercept the retreating Egyptian army in 1819. His account, however, says little about Wahhābism.[42] After Burckhardt's, the most thoroughgoing treatment of the movement by a nineteenth-century European traveler was written by the Englishman William Palgrave, who also made it to Najd during his journeys in Arabia in 1862–63.[43] Having read a number of Wahhābī doctrinal texts, and having conversed with Wahhābī scholars in Riyadh, Palgrave came to the conclusion that Wahhābism was an authentic expression of original Islam—pure and unadulterated. Ibn ʿAbd al-Wahhāb was to be praised for having "learned to distinguish clearly between the essential elements of Islam and its accidental or recent admixtures." He had "discovered amid the ruins of the Islamitic pile its neglected keystone"—namely, monotheism—and having done so "dared to form the project to replace it, and with it and by it reconstruct the broken fabric." "The Wahhabee reformer," Palgrave wrote, "formed the design of putting back the hour-hand of Islam to its starting-point; and so far he did well, for that hand was from the first meant to be fixed." Ibn ʿAbd al-Wahhāb

39. Burckhardt, *Notes on the Bedouins and Wahábys*, 1:102. Also quoted in Bonacina, *Wahhabis Seen Through European Eyes*, 6n7.

40. Burckhardt, *Notes on the Bedouins and Wahábys*, 2:108.

41. Ibid., 1:102.

42. Sadleir, *Diary of a Journey Across Arabia*.

43. Palgrave, *Narrative of a Year's Journey*, esp. 1:363–79.

had looked upon the "corruptions and overlaying of later times," including the supplication of "intercessors and mediators, living or dead," and the "honouring [of] saints or tombs," as "innovations, corruptions, and distortions," and he had "resolved to consecrate the remainder of his life to the restoration of this primaeval image of Islam . . . the authentic religion of Mahomet." Yet while Palgrave saw much in Ibn ʿAbd al-Wahhāb to admire, believing the reformer's conclusions to have been just and logical, he was nonetheless no admirer of Islam. For this reason he objected to Burckhardt's view that Wahhābism was analogous to Protestantism. The analogy was flawed, he wrote, because Islam, unlike Christianity—"a religion of vitality, of progress, of advancement"—was "stationary," "[s]terile," and "lifeless" and thus "justly repudiates all change, all advance, all development." Ibn ʿAbd al-Wahhāb was to be commended for having sought to return Islam to "its primal simplicity," but the Islamic religion was simply unworthy of comparison to its Christian counterpart.[44] Palgrave's portrayal of Wahhābism was thus not an entirely flattering one; nonetheless, he did well to highlight the atavism at the heart of the Wahhābī project and its hostility to perceived innovations such as the cult of saints.

In the twentieth century, the European travelers who touched on Wahhābism would be even more accurate in their depictions and in some cases, though not all, even more sympathetic. The most prolific and influential of the European travelers in the twentieth century was Harry St. John Philby, a British civil servant and explorer who later settled in Arabia, where he converted to Islam and became a close adviser to the Saudi leader. Philby was also a scholar who was the first to make extensive use of Wahhābī primary sources in narrating the history of Saudi Arabia. His many books, none of them specifically devoted to Wahhābism, were for decades an indispensable source for anyone working on the Arabian Peninsula.[45]

In the early twentieth century, European Orientalists were finally beginning to show interest in Wahhābism. Perhaps the earliest was the great Hungarian Orientalist Ignaz Goldziher, who devoted several pages of his 1910 *Vorlesungen über den Islam* (Lectures on Islam) to a description of the Wahhābī movement. The description, while not very detailed, holds up quite well. Goldziher emphasized the Wahhābīs' fierce opposition to the cult of saints and the unmistakable influence of Ibn Taymiyya.[46] In 1927, the Dutch scholar Roelof Willem

44. Ibid., 1:364–65, 370–73.

45. See, among other titles, Philby, *Arabia*; Philby, *Saʿudi Arabia*.

46. Goldziher, *Introduction to Islamic Theology and Law*, 241–45.

van Diffelen published a doctoral thesis on the Wahhābī doctrine, presenting a more detailed analysis of Ibn Taymiyya's influence that also holds up quite well.[47] Diffelen's study would be cited by David Margoliouth, the Laudian Professor of Arabic at the University of Oxford, in his 1934 entry on Wahhābism in the first *Encyclopedia of Islam*.[48] The state of knowledge of Wahhābism in Europe had thus improved dramatically since Sacy's 1805 article. Yet Margoliouth's entry also showed how little scholarly work had been done on the subject to this point. His main sources were European travelogues and several manuscripts in the British Library, including one that presents an unreliable account of Ibn ʿAbd al-Wahhāb's life.[49] The French Orientalist Henri Laoust provided a more extensive treatment of Wahhābism in his 1939 study of Ibn Taymiyya, in which he devoted a chapter to Wahhābism.[50] This was to remain the authoritative account of the Wahhābī doctrine for decades to come, though its focus was the reception of Ibn Taymiyya more than Wahhābism itself. In the later twentieth century, the historian Michael Cook was one of few scholars to give the movement significant attention, examining its origins and the rise of the first Saudi state in two seminal articles.[51] However, the field still awaited a fuller and more comprehensive account of Wahhābism's origins and history.

Much greater attention would be paid to Wahhābism following the terrorist attacks of September 11, 2001, which brought newfound scrutiny on Saudi Arabia and its associated religious doctrine. The head of al-Qāʿida, Osama bin Ladin, was a Saudi national, as were fifteen of the nineteen hijackers who murdered nearly three thousand people in New York, Washington, D.C., and Pennsylvania. Rightly or wrongly, Wahhābism was seen as providing part of the

47. Diffelen, *De leer der Wahhabieten*. I am grateful to Daniel Lav for bringing this book to my attention.

48. *EI*[1], s.v. "Wahhābīya" (David Margoliouth).

49. On this source, which was likely written at the request of a British official in the Gulf in 1233/1817, see Cook, "Provenance of the *Lamʿ al-shihāb*."

50. Laoust, *Essai sur les doctrines sociales et politiques de Taḳī-d-Dīn Aḥmad b. Taimīya*, 506–40.

51. Cook, "Expansion of the First Saudi State"; Cook, "On the Origins of Wahhābism." See further his *Commanding Right and Forbidding Wrong in Islamic Thought*, 165–92. Other significant contributions to the field of Wahhābī studies in the twentieth century were made by Richard Hartmann, Werner Ende, George Rentz, Esther Peskes, ʿAbdallāh al-ʿUthaymīn, and Alexei Vassiliev, whose works are cited where appropriate. Vassiliev's *The History of Saudi Arabia* (2000), translated from the Russian, is the best available general history of Saudi Arabia in English.

ideological motivation for the attacks. The body of Wahhābism-focused scholarship thus grew rapidly. Key contributions included David Commins's general history of the movement, Michael Crawford's biography of Ibn ʿAbd al-Wahhāb, Abdulaziz Al-Fahad's articles on the evolution of the Wahhābī doctrine and Najdī society, and Guido Steinberg's and Nabil Mouline's respective studies of the Wahhābī scholarly class.[52] Unfortunately, the post-9/11 period brought forth a number of polemical and apologetic studies as well. Some scholars would seek to vilify Wahhābism as the source of all Islam's modern ills, while others would go in the opposite direction, presenting so rosy a picture of Wahhābism as for it to be unrecognizable.[53] Yet despite these kinds of contributions, in general the new scholarship on Wahhābism over the past two decades has vastly improved the state of the field, even if there remains much more to be done.

Sources for the Study of Wahhābism

For most of the period covered in this book, Arabia was a manuscript culture, meaning that the printed word was a rare sight. The Wahhābīs would begin printing their works in India and Egypt in the late nineteenth century, though the printing press did not arrive in Arabia until the early twentieth century. When the Wahhābīs started to make use of these presses, some of the first works they printed were compendia of Wahhābī texts. The most comprehensive of these was *al-Durar al-saniyya fī ʾl-ajwiba al-Najdiyya* (The Splendid Pearls of Najdī Responsa), which was arranged and edited by the Wahhābī scholar ʿAbd al-Raḥmān ibn Qāsim (d. 1392/1972) and published for the first time in Mecca between 1352/1933f and 1356/1937f.[54] This remains, in updated form, the most

52. See Commins, *The Wahhabi Mission* (2006); Crawford, *Ibn 'Abd al-Wahhab* (2014); Al-Fahad, "From Exclusivism to Accommodation" (2004); Al-Fahad, "The 'Imama vs. the 'Iqal" (2004); Steinberg, *Religion und Staat in Saudi-Arabien* (2002) (researched before 9/11); and Mouline, *The Clerics of Islam* (2014).

53. See, for example, the anti-Wahhābī polemic by Hamid Algar (*Wahhabism: A Critical Essay*) and the philo-Wahhābī book by Natana DeLong-Bas (*Wahhabi Islam: From Revival and Reform to Global Jihad*). The latter, which has drawn fierce criticism from scholars of Islam, portrays Ibn ʿAbd al-Wahhāb as a protofeminist averse to *jihād*. For some of this criticism, see Kearney, "Real Wahhab"; and see the review by Laurent Bonnefoy in *The Journal of Islamic Studies* 17 (2006): 371–72.

54. A more complete edition was published in Riyadh between 1385/1965 and 1388/1968f, followed by a new and updated edition published between 1402/1981f and 1417/1996. All

complete collection of Wahhābī texts and is frequently cited in this book. A much smaller collection is the one-volume *Majmūʿat al-tawḥīd* (The Compendium of *Tawḥīd*), which was printed in Mecca in 1343/1925 following the publication of several Indian lithograph editions.[55] Another collection, similar in scope to *al-Durar al-saniyya*, is *Majmūʿat al-rasāʾil wa ʾl-masāʾil al-Najdiyya* (The Compendium of Najdī Epistles and Responsa), which was published in Cairo between 1344/1925f and 1349/1930f.[56] This book was the product of a collaboration between the Wahhābī scholars in Najd and the Islamic modernist scholar Rashīd Riḍā in Egypt. A much shorter compendium of Wahhābī texts, titled *al-Hadiyya al-saniyya wa ʾl-tuḥfa al-Wahhābiyya al-Najdiyya* (The Splendid Gift and the Wahhābī Najdī Present), was published in Egypt before this, in 1342/1923f, also with the assistance of Riḍā.[57] Much later, in 1398/1977f, a multivolume book consisting of all the works of Ibn ʿAbd al-Wahhāb was published in Riyadh, though most of these texts had appeared earlier in one form or another.[58] Many more works by Wahhābī scholars have been published as stand-alone texts, some of them in critical editions. Others still remain in manuscript form in various libraries in Saudi Arabia.

Another important source for the study of Wahhābism is the Najdī historiographical tradition. Before the rise of Wahhābism, it is fair to say, Najdī historiography was generally undeveloped and unsophisticated. Such histories as there were were threadbare in character, merely recording important events in annalistic fashion with little or no detail.[59] Wahhābism wrought massive change in this regard, as its adherents produced historical works of far greater depth and detail, probably because they saw themselves as writing the story of a great and important Islamic movement.[60] By far the two most important

---

subsequent versions are reprints of this third edition, including the one used here: Ibn Qāsim, ed., *al-Durar al-saniyya fī ʾl-ajwiba al-Najdiyya*, new ed., 16 vols. (Riyadh: Warathat al-Shaykh ʿAbd al-Raḥmān ibn Qāsim, 1433/2012). While the third edition appeared following the editor's death, all the changes and additions were made by the editor himself. Some of the content of the original was rearranged, but none was removed. See al-Qāsim, *al-Shaykh ʿAbd al-Raḥmān ibn Qāsim*, 85.

55. Yāsīn, ed., *al-Kitāb al-mufīd fī maʿrifat ḥaqq Allāh ʿalā ʾl-ʿabīd al-musammā Majmūʿat al-tawḥīd*.

56. Riḍā, ed., *Majmūʿat al-rasāʾil wa ʾl-masāʾil al-Najdiyya*.

57. Ibn Siḥmān, ed., *al-Hadiyya al-saniyya*.

58. Ibn ʿAbd al-Wahhāb, *Muʾallafāt al-shaykh*.

59. Cook, "Historians of Pre-Wahhābī Najd."

60. al-Jāsir, "Muʾarrikhū Najd min ahlihā (1)"; al-Jāsir, "Muʾarrikhū Najd min ahlihā (2)."

histories for the early period of Wahhābism are those by Ḥusayn ibn Ghannām (d. 1225/1810f) and ʿUthmān ibn Bishr (d. 1290/1873), and since these books will be cited frequently in this study, it is worth saying more about them and their respective authors here.

Born in eastern Arabia, in al-Aḥsāʾ, in 1152/1739f, Ibn Ghannām was a scholar known for his specialization in the sciences of the Arabic language, a fact that goes some way in explaining his predilection for flowery rhymed prose and obscure vocabulary.[61] When Ibn Ghannām embraced Wahhābism is unclear, but we know that he moved to al-Dirʿiyya from al-Aḥsāʾ in the years preceding the Wahhābī conquest of his home region in 1210/1796. He appears to have belonged to the Mālikī *madhhab*, which had some adherents in al-Aḥsāʾ. (Wahhābism, as shall be seen, was primarily creedal in emphasis, and thus one's legal affiliation was not necessarily an impediment to conversion.) In al-Dirʿiyya Ibn Ghannām worked as a language teacher instructing a generation of Wahhābī students in Arabic, including the sons and grandsons of Ibn ʿAbd al-Wahhāb, and he also served as something of a court scholar. He is known to have composed at least two works at the behest of the Saudi ruler ʿAbd al-ʿAzīz ibn Muḥammad Āl Suʿūd (r. 1179–1218/1765–1803), the successor to the first Saudi ruler, one of which was his history. Titled *Rawḍat al-afkār wa ʾl-afhām li-murtād ḥāl al-imām wa-taʿdād ghazawāt dhawī ʾl-Islām* (The Garden of Thoughts and Reflections for the Inquirer into the Condition of the *Imām* and the Enumeration of the Raids of the Muslims), where the *imām* refers to Ibn ʿAbd al-Wahhāb, the book is divided into two volumes. The first consists of a biography of Ibn ʿAbd al-Wahhāb and an account of the rise of his movement, complete with many of his letters, epistles, *fatwās* (legal responsa), and writings of Qurʾānic exegesis. The second volume, which bears the secondary title *Kitāb al-ghazawāt al-bayāniyya wa ʾl-futūḥāt al-rabbāniyya* (The Book of the Exemplary Raids and Lordly Conquests), is a chronicle of the period 1157–1212/1747–97f, with some discussion of the years immediately prior.[62] While neither volume is dated, one can be sure that the project was

61. For his biography, see Ibn Bishr, *ʿUnwān al-majd*, 1:299; Āl al-Shaykh, *Mashāhīr*, 185–201; Āl Bassām, *ʿUlamāʾ Najd*, 2:56–58; al-Qāḍī, *Rawḍat al-nāẓirīn*, 1:104–5. For his birth year, see Jaḥḥāf, *Durar nuḥūr al-ḥūr al-ʿīn*, 1045–46.

62. The edition of *Rawḍat al-afkār wa ʾl-afhām* used here is *Tārīkh Ibn Ghannām al-musammā Rawḍat al-afkār wa ʾl-afhām*, 2 vols., ed. Sulaymān al-Kharāshī (Riyadh: Dār al-Thulūthiyya, 1431/2010). The only other serviceable editions are that published by Maṭbaʿat Muṣṭafā ʾl-Bābī al-Ḥalabī in Riyadh in 1368/1949 and that published by al-Maṭbaʿa al-Muṣṭafawiyya in Bombay in 1337/1918. The latter, however, is missing the larger part of Ibn ʿAbd al-Wahhāb's *fatwās* and

completed no later than 1216/1801, as in this year Ibn Ghannām finished a second book that refers to *Rawḍat al-afkār wa ʾl-afhām*.[63] An important feature of Ibn Ghannām's history, in addition to its elaborate prose, is its stark portrayal of non-Wahhābī Muslims as polytheists and unbelievers. The Wahhābīs are made out to be the revivers of true Islam who are waging *jihād* against their heathen enemies, and their conquests are presented in terms of the early Islamic conquests.

Ibn Bishr's history was written much later than Ibn Ghannām's, in the 1250s–70s/1830s–50s. Born in Sudayr in 1210/1795f, Ibn Bishr, unlike Ibn Ghannām, had little experience of the first Saudi state, though he had studied in al-Dirʿiyya in the years just before its destruction in 1233/1818.[64] The author of several other books on various subjects, Ibn Bishr is said to have been close to the rulers of the second Saudi state, though we know little in detail about his life and career. His history, *ʿUnwān al-majd fī tārīkh Najd* (The Sign of Glory in the History of Najd), consists of two volumes, the first completed in 1251/1835 and the second in 1270/1854.[65] The first volume includes a biography

---

the beginning of his Qurʾānic exegesis (the elision occurs in vol. 1, p. 232, l. 4, between the words *ʿAbd al-Dīnār* and *wa-qāla*; the missing text is supplied in al-Kharāshī's edition at 1:452–535). In all three of these editions, the second volume ends abruptly, mid-poem, in the section devoted to the year 1212/1797f. This has led to speculation that the remainder of the book is missing. At least three manuscript copies I have examined, however, show the complete section for 1212/1797f, after which the book ends. One of these states that this was the final year that Ibn Ghannām chronicled (*wa-hādhā ākhir mā arrakhahu ʾl-shaykh Ḥusayn ibn Ghannām*). See Ibn Ghannām, *Rawḍat al-afkār wa ʾl-afhām*, ms. Lucknow, f. 232a. For the other two complete manuscripts, held at the British Library, see Cureton and Rieu, *Catalogus codicum manuscriptorum orientalium*, 436 (nos. 953–54), 576 (nos. 1260–61). The edition by Nāṣir al-Dīn al-Asad, published by Maṭbaʿat al-Madanī in Cairo in 1381/1961, was an attempt to render Ibn Ghannām's rhyming prose in a modern idiom; in the process the content was supplemented, rearranged, and bowdlerized. While some scholars continue to cite it, it should be avoided.

63. Ibn Ghannām, *al-ʿIqd al-thamīn*, 28. For the completion date (Ṣafar 1216/June 1801), see 251. *Al-ʿIqd al-thamīn* is a *ḥadīth*-based creedal work that includes a synopsis of Wahhābī history.

64. On him, see Āl Bassām, *ʿUlamāʾ Najd*, 5:115–26; al-Qāḍī, *Rawḍat al-nāẓirīn*, 2:120–22.

65. Ibn Bishr, *ʿUnwān al-majd*, 1:417, 2:236. There have been many editions, but the one used here (edited by Muḥammad al-Shathrī, 1433/2012) is the most reliable, as it is based on a rare manuscript of Ibn Bishr's final and updated version of the book. In addition to numerous small changes, in this version the *sawābiq* (the entries for years prior to the rise of Wahhābism) are not peppered throughout the book but, rather, arranged chronologically. The complete manuscript of this version has been printed in full as Ibn Bishr, *ʿUnwān al-majd fī tārīkh Najd* (Riyadh: Maktabat al-Malik ʿAbd al-ʿAzīz al-ʿĀmma, 1423/2002).

of Ibn ʿAbd al-Wahhāb and treats the years 850–1237/1446f–1821f; the second covers the period 1238–67/1822–50f. As will be noticed, Ibn Bishr begins his history much earlier than Ibn Ghannām, in 850/1446f as opposed to 1157/1744f. The reason for this is that he situated his work within the larger Najdī historiographical tradition, which often starts with the events of that early year. Perhaps related to this is the fact that Ibn Bishr's work tends to be less extreme in its portrayal of non-Wahhābī Muslims, even though Ibn Bishr was still by all accounts a committed Wahhābī. His work is highly valuable for the later years of the first Saudi state and for the years of the second Saudi state through 1267/1850f. Ibn Ghannām's is more reliable for the earliest years of the Wahhābī movement.[66]

While the histories of Ibn Ghannām and Ibn Bishr are the most important sources for Wahhābī history between the 1150s/1740s and 1260s/1850s, they are not the only Wahhābī chronicles produced during that period. Three contemporaries of Ibn Bishr authored important chronicles as well: Ḥamad ibn Laʿbūn (d. ca. 1277/1860), Muḥammad al-Fākhirī (d. 1277/1860), and ʿAbd al-Wahhāb ibn Turkī (fl. 1257/1841f). Ibn Laʿbūn's history, which covers the years 800–1257/1397f–1841f, is the fullest account of the three, and Ibn Bishr actually borrows from it frequently.[67] Also of some value are two Wahhābī chronicles that survive only in French translation. The first of these is an abridgment of the work of a certain "Suléiman il Nedjedi," which relates Wahhābī history through the year 1224/1809f.[68] The other was written by a

66. A helpful introduction to these texts is George Rentz's 1947 dissertation for the University of California, Berkeley, titled *Muḥammad b. ʿAbd al-Wahhāb (1703/4–1792) and the Beginnings of Unitarian Empire in Arabia*. Rentz's study consists of a straightforward narrative of early Wahhābī history based on the two chronicles, pointing out where they sometimes disagree. It was finally published as *The Birth of the Islamic Reform Movement in Saudi Arabia* in 2004.

67. See Ibn Laʿbūn, *Tārīkh*; on his use of Ibn Bishr, see ʿAbd al-ʿAzīz ibn Laʿbūn, *Nuqūlāt ʿUnwān al-majd min tārīkh Ibn Laʿbūn*. Al-Fākhirī's book, which spans the years 850/1446f to 1277/1860f (brought through to 1288/1871f by his son), is quite meager by comparison. See al-Fākhirī, *Tārīkh*. Ibn Turkī's book, like Ibn Laʿbūn's, covers the years 850/1446f to 1257/1841f but is much spottier in its coverage. Noteworthy is that its author was a fierce opponent of Wahhābism living in Iraq. See Ibn Turkī, *Tārīkh Najd*. One may also mention here the chronicles of Ibn Yūsuf (fl. 1207/1792f) and Ibn ʿAbbād (d. 1175/1761f), which treat Najdī history through the beginning of the Wahhābī period (1173/1759f and 1175/1761f, respectively). See Ibn Yūsuf, *Tārīkh*; Ibn ʿAbbād, *Tārīkh*. The chronicle of a slightly earlier scholar, Ibn Rabīʿa (d. 1158/1745f), misses the Wahhābī period by just ten years. See Ibn Rabīʿa, *Tārīkh*.

68. The text was translated and abridged in 1818 by Jean Baptiste Louis Rousseau; see Rousseau, *Mémoire sur les trois plus fameuses sectes du Musulmanisme*, 27–35.

certain "cheykh Abderrahman el-Oguyeh," whom we can likely identify as ʿAbd al-Raḥmān ibn Ḥasan Āl al-Shaykh (d. 1285/1869), a grandson of Ibn ʿAbd al-Wahhāb's who was taken to Egypt in 1233/1818. His chronicle covers the history of Wahhābism through the year 1225/1810f.[69]

As for the period that followed, the most valuable histories were written by the scholars Ibrāhīm ibn ʿĪsā (d. 1343/1925), from Ushayqir in al-Washm, and ʿAbdallāh al-Bassām (d. 1346/1927), from ʿUnayza in al-Qaṣīm. Ibn ʿĪsā's chronicle is presented as an extension (*dhayl*) of Ibn Bishr's *ʿUnwān al-majd*, bringing the chronology forward to 1340/1921f.[70] Al-Bassām's work starts in the ninth/fifteenth century and ends in 1344/1925f.[71] The chronicles of Ibn ʿĪsā and al-Bassām were some of the last contributions to traditional Najdī-Wahhābī historiography, as the mid–twentieth century saw the emergence of a new Saudi historiography centered on Saudi nationalism.[72] An important exception to this pattern was the extensive chronicle of Ibrāhīm ibn ʿUbayd Āl ʿAbd al-Muḥsin (d. 1425/2004), from Burayda in al-Qaṣīm. His multivolume chronicle, titled *Tadhkirat ulī ʾl-nuhā wa ʾl-ʿirfān bi-ayyām Allāh al-wāḥid al-dayyān* (Reminding the Wise and Perceptive of the Days of God, the One, the Requiter), was written over a period of decades and was published in full only in 1428/2007. Its eight volumes cover the years 1268–1421/1851f–2000f in traditional annalistic fashion.[73] Āl ʿAbd al-Muḥsin's work is rich in historical detail for the period before and during the rise of the third Saudi state.

Another kind of source is the Wahhābī biographical dictionaries, though these, it must be acknowledged, are a rather late source. The Wahhābīs only took to the genre of the biographical dictionary in the mid–twentieth century, before which time it was the histories that were the principal source for biographical information on scholars and other notables. Nonetheless, while these more modern works should be treated with caution, many of them preserve unique documents and collate otherwise disparate information. The standard Wahhābī biographical dictionaries today are three: *Mashāhīr ʿulamāʾ Najd wa-ghayrihim* (The Famous Scholars of Najd and Others) by

69. See Mengin, *Histoire de l'Égypte*, 2:449–544. For the author's identification as the "petit-fils du célèbre ebn-Abdul-Wahab," see 1:vi.

70. Ibn ʿĪsā, *ʿIqd al-durar*. He also wrote a more comprehensive, though less detailed, chronicle covering the period from the eighth/fourteenth century to 1339/1920f. See Ibn ʿĪsā, *Tārīkh baʿḍ al-ḥawādith*.

71. al-Bassām, *Tuḥfat al-mushtāq*.

72. Determann, *Historiography in Saudi Arabia*, 50ff.

73. See Āl ʿAbd al-Muḥsin, *Tadhkirat ulī ʾl-nuhā*.

ʿAbd al-Raḥmān ibn ʿAbd al-Laṭīf Āl al-Shaykh (d. 1406/1986), from Riyadh;[74] *ʿUlamāʾ Najd khilāl thamāniyat qurūn* (The Scholars of Najd Through Eight Centuries) by ʿAbdallāh ibn ʿAbd al-Raḥmān Āl Bassām (d. 1423/2003), from ʿUnayza;[75] and *Rawḍat al-nāẓirīn ʿan maʾāthir ʿulamāʾ Najd wa-ḥawādith al-sinīn* (The Spectators' Garden of the Achievements of the Najdī Scholars and the Yearly Events), by Muḥammad ibn ʿUthmān al-Qāḍī, also from ʿUnayza.[76] Āl al-Shaykh's book is devoted exclusively to Wahhābī scholars, while Āl Bassām's and al-Qāḍī's works cover Najdī scholars in both the Wahhābī and pre-Wahhābī eras. Several more Wahhābī biographical dictionaries treat the scholars of particular subregions or cities in central Arabia.[77]

Beyond the Wahhābī tradition, there are numerous other sources of value for the study of Wahhābism that tend to be underexploited. One kind of source is the early refutations of the movement, which will be examined in detail in chapter 1. Another is the historical works of non-Wahhābī scholars who paid attention to Najd, such as the Egyptian ʿAbd al-Raḥmān al-Jabartī (d. 1240/1825), the Najdī Iraqi ʿUthmān ibn Sanad (d. 1242/1827), the Yemeni Luṭf Allāh ibn Aḥmad Jaḥḥāf (d. 1243/1827f), the Iraqi Kurd Rasūl Ḥāwī al-Karkūklī (d. 1243/1827f), and the Ḥijāzī Aḥmad ibn Zaynī Daḥlān (d. 1304/1886).[78] While these men were generally hostile to Wahhābism, some of them, including al-Jabartī and Jaḥḥāf, were fairly nuanced in their views. The non-Wahhābī biographical tradition is also of value, especially the Ḥanbalī biographical dictionary *al-Suḥub al-wābila* by the anti-Wahhābī Muḥammad ibn Ḥumayd (d. 1295/1878), the ʿUnayza-born Ḥanbalī *muftī* of Mecca.[79]

74. Āl al-Shaykh, *Mashāhīr*. The first edition appeared in 1392/1972f; it built on the author's earlier *ʿUlamāʾ al-daʿwa*, published in 1386/1966.

75. Āl Bassām, *ʿUlamāʾ Najd*. The first version of the book, *ʿUlamāʾ Najd khilāl sittat qurūn*, appeared in 1397/1976f in three volumes. The updated version was published in 1419/1998f in six volumes.

76. al-Qāḍī, *Rawḍat al-nāẓirīn*. The first edition appeared in two volumes in 1400/1980. For a short collection of later Wahhābī biographies, see Ibn Ḥamdān, *Tarājim li-mutaʾakhkhirī ʾl-Ḥanābila*.

77. These include Ṣāliḥ al-ʿUmarī's work on the scholars of al-Qaṣīm and ʿAlī al-Hindī's (d. 1419/1998) on the scholars of Ḥāʾil. See al-ʿUmarī, *ʿUlamāʾ Āl Salīm*; al-Hindī, *Zahr al-khamāʾil*. A newer and more comprehensive dictionary of the scholars of Ḥāʾil is al-Ruday ʿān, *Manbaʿ al-karam*.

78. al-Jabartī, *ʿAjāʾib al-āthār*; Ibn Sanad, *Maṭāliʿ al-suʿūd*; Ibn Sanad, *Sabāʾik al-ʿasjad*; Jaḥḥāf, *Durar nuḥūr al-ḥūr al-ʿīn*; al-Karkūklī, *Dawḥat al-wuzarāʾ*; Daḥlān, *Khulāṣat al-kalām*.

79. Ibn Ḥumayd, *al-Suḥub al-wābila*. The book largely omits the Wahhābīs but is valuable for the information it provides on their Ḥanbalī opponents in Najd and elsewhere. For more

This Book

The book consists of seven chapters. Chapter 1 sets the scene by examining the life and early career of Ibn ʿAbd al-Wahhāb and the numerous refutations of him by his scholarly opponents. The refutations are drawn from all over the globe, many of them surviving only in unique manuscripts. As will be seen, they are an extraordinary untapped source for the study of early Wahhābism, helping us to reconstruct the polemics between Ibn ʿAbd al-Wahhāb and his enemies and to follow the trajectory of his movement. The refutations are helpful in giving both a sense of what the debate over Wahhābism was all about and a sense of the tenor of that debate. Wahhābism's opponents did not confront it politely; many people wanted Ibn ʿAbd al-Wahhāb dead, even before his movement had adopted violence. Further, the refutations are helpful in allowing us to date some of Ibn ʿAbd al-Wahhāb's letters and epistles, given that many of the refutations are dated and quote Ibn ʿAbd al-Wahhāb's writings.

The next two chapters are concerned with Ibn ʿAbd al-Wahhāb's doctrine and its relation to the religious thought of Ibn Taymiyya and his disciple Ibn Qayyim al-Jawziyya. Ibn ʿAbd al-Wahhāb's teachings, it is argued here, cannot be understood without reference to their Taymiyyan underpinnings. While Ibn ʿAbd al-Wahhāb's reliance on these scholars has been widely acknowledged, the relationship between Taymiyyan and Wahhābī thought has yet to be rigorously studied. Chapter 2 focuses on the Taymiyyan background of Ibn ʿAbd al-Wahhāb's doctrine, examining some of the distinctive features of the religious thought of Ibn Taymiyya and his pupils that would come to play a role in Wahhābism. Chapter 3 examines the key components of Ibn ʿAbd al-Wahhāb's doctrine, which I identify as fourfold: (1) the division of *tawḥīd* into two kinds, (2) *takfīr*, (3) *al-walāʾ waʾl-barāʾ* (association and dissociation, particularly its negative aspect), and (4) *jihād*. The chapter shows how Ibn ʿAbd al-Wahhāb, for each of these components, borrowed from the ideas of Ibn Taymiyya and Ibn al-Qayyim while also modifying them substantially, generally taking their ideas in a more radical direction.

Chapter 4 concerns the development of Ibn ʿAbd al-Wahhāb's movement from its precarious beginnings as a mere predicatory movement to its lofty heights as the religious engine of the first Saudi state (ca. 1157–1233/1744f–1818). While it has been argued that Wahhābism was in essence apolitical in

---

on this book and its author, see Commins, "Traditional Anti-Wahhabi Hanbalism in Nineteenth-Century Arabia."

character, this chapter shows that Ibn ʿAbd al-Wahhāb was by no means indifferent to politics and indeed played an active role in the political realm. His movement's development followed a pattern analogous to the development of early Islam, which began without any discernible political objective but gradually transformed into a movement combining both religion and politics. At the height of the first Saudi state, Ibn ʿAbd al-Wahhāb's heirs invoked another legacy of the early Islamic polity, quoting the Prophet Muḥammad's menacing letter to the king of Byzantium while they threatened to invade Iraq and Syria. The chapter seeks to establish that the state's ambitions went beyond Arabia and that if not for external intervention, the first Saudi state may well have expanded further northward.

The next three chapters are about the reassertion, persistence, and decline of militant Wahhābism following the demise of the first Saudi state in 1233/1818. Throughout this period, the Wahhābī scholars, from ʿAbd al-Raḥmān ibn Ḥasan Āl al-Shaykh to Sulaymān ibn Siḥmān, worked to safeguard their doctrine from internal corruption and external attack. They were often on the defensive, given the political environment in which they were operating, and their principal concern was staving off normalization with non-Wahhābī Muslims. They repeatedly forbade travel to non-Wahhābī lands by emphasizing the duty of showing hatred and enmity to polytheists. The chapters examine these scholars' lives, their environments, and their literary exploits. Chapter 5 takes up the scholars' efforts to revive the spirit of militant Wahhābism during the second Saudi state (1238–1305/1823–87), focusing in particular on the period known as the second Egyptian occupation (1253–59/1837–43) and the period of the Saudi civil war (1282–1305/1865–87). Chapter 6 looks at the scholars' travails during the political ascendancy of the Āl Rashīd (1305–19/1887–1902), a dynasty that ruled from Ḥāʾil in northern Arabia. This was a period when a revisionist form of Wahhābism, one that played down the idea of *takfīr* and of showing hatred and enmity, was on the rise in the al-Qaṣīm region of Najd. Chapter 7 tracks the activities of the scholars during the rise of the third Saudi state (1319/1902–present), focusing on their approach to the zealous Wahhābī fighters known as the Ikhwān and their acrimonious relationship with Rashīd Riḍā, a modernist Muslim scholar in Egypt who advocated an "enlightened" form of Wahhābism. At the beginning of this period, these scholars envisioned the new Saudi polity as one that would never fly foreign flags or host foreign embassies, let alone form alliances with Christian powers. That was not to be the nature of the state that came to be known, in 1351/1932, as the Kingdom of Saudi Arabia.

The book's conclusion considers the further decline of militant Wahhābism in Saudi Arabia over the succeeding decades and its subsequent revival, in modified form, by the ideologues of Jihādī Salafism, the radical Sunnī Islamic movement that considers itself the true and rightful heir of the Wahhābī tradition. The *jihādīs* regard militant Wahhābism as an inspiring example of a fiercely puritanical and uncompromising movement that approached its polytheist enemies with hostility and *jihād*, and they regard later Wahhābism as a perversion and betrayal of the original.

1

Muḥammad ibn ʿAbd al-Wahhāb and His Discontents

[A]s in the case of Eckhart and Marie des Vallées, the most significant texts have been preserved for us thanks to a mine of hostile commentaries.

—LOUIS MASSIGNON, *THE PASSION OF AL-HALLAJ*

THIS CHAPTER SURVEYS the life and career of Muḥammad ibn ʿAbd al-Wahhāb, from his birth in 1115/1703f through to the flourishing of his movement in the 1170s/1750s amid the rise of the first Saudi state. In doing so, it also examines the anti-Wahhābī refutations of his many scholarly opponents in Najd and beyond, who viewed the Wahhābī movement with alarm and sought to discredit Ibn ʿAbd al-Wahhāb from the very beginning.

The most important sources for the life of Ibn ʿAbd al-Wahhāb are naturally the Wahhābī ones, in particular the histories of Ibn Ghannām and Ibn Bishr, discussed in this book's introduction. An even earlier Wahhābī source, Muḥammad ibn Gharīb's *al-Tawḍīh ʿan tawḥīd al-khallāq* (The Clarification of the Oneness of the Creator), provides another account of his life,[1] while yet another is furnished by his grandson ʿAbd al-Raḥmān ibn Ḥasan Āl al-Shaykh

1. Ibn Gharīb, *al-Tawḍīḥ*, 1:165–98. To my knowledge this is the earliest surviving biography of Ibn ʿAbd al-Wahhāb by someone from within his movement; it was written sometime between 1194/1780 and 1203/1789. Ibn Ghannām's and Ibn Bishr's accounts, by contrast, were written no later than 1216/1801 and 1251/1835, respectively. For more on *al-Tawḍīḥ* and Ibn Gharīb, see further below in this chapter.

in a work known as *al-Maqāmāt* (The Assemblies).[2] Another indispensable source is the writings of Ibn ʿAbd al-Wahhāb himself. While not a prolific author by the standards of Islamic scholarship, Ibn ʿAbd al-Wahhāb left behind a reasonably large corpus that sheds much light on his preaching and other activities. This corpus includes numerous epistles and letters; a collection of *fatwā*s and sermons; a number of bare-bones theological tracts consisting of proof texts with minimal commentary, the most noteworthy being *Kitāb al-tawḥīd* (The Book of God's Oneness); similarly unadorned works of Qurʾānic exegesis and *ḥadīth* commentary in the form of lists of takeaways or important points; several abridgments of Islamic texts including two Ḥanbalī law books and Ibn Qayyim al-Jawziyya's *Zād al-maʿād* (Provisions for the Hereafter), a book of prophetic guidance;[3] and a short biography of the Prophet based mainly but not solely on Ibn Isḥāq's famous *sīra*.[4] While much attention has been paid in the existing literature to *Kitāb al-tawḥīd*, often seen as the main repository of classical Wahhābī doctrine, far more important to understanding Wahhābism as a historical movement are Ibn ʿAbd al-Wahhāb's letters and epistles (*rasāʾil*; sing. *risāla*).[5] The significance of these *rasāʾil* lies in the fact that they show him preaching to and interacting with the society around him. They were the main instrument by which he spread his message, and in them we see him explaining to his intended audience what it is they ought to believe and how they ought to act on those beliefs. The *rasāʾil* are thus the real repository of classical Wahhābī doctrine, and they are a key source for reconstructing Ibn ʿAbd al-Wahhāb's life and career. Yet another key source that will be drawn on here, and one that has thus far been neglected in the study of Wahhābism, is the corpus of anti-Wahhābī refutations. Many of these refutations were written in response to Ibn ʿAbd al-Wahhāb's *rasāʾil*, and together with the *rasāʾil* they help to illuminate the nature of his doctrine and the course of his career as a preacher.

2. This was completed in 1283/1866; see Āl al-Shaykh, *al-Maqāmāt*, 140.

3. These abridgments are ʿAlāʾ al-Dīn al-Mardāwī's (d. 885/1480) *al-Inṣāf fī maʿrifat al-rājiḥ min al-khilāf* and Abū ʾl-Faraj Ibn Qudāma al-Maqdisī's (d. 682/1283) *al-Sharḥ al-kabīr ʿalā ʾl-Muqniʿ*; see Ibn ʿAbd al-Wahhāb, *Muʾallafāt al-shaykh*, 2:2 (*Mukhtaṣar al-Inṣāf wa ʾl-Sharḥ al-kabīr*).

4. See Ibn ʿAbd al-Wahhāb, *Mukhtaṣar sīrat al-rasūl*. And on this text, see Riexinger, "Rendering Muḥammad Human Again"; Riexinger, "Der Islam begann als Fremder."

5. In this book *letter* is generally used to mean a letter to a particular person or persons, while *epistle* is generally used to mean an open letter or one to a particular area or areas; the Arabic *risāla* contains both meanings.

The Arabic word *radd*, translated here as "refutation," denotes an Arabic literary genre going back to the earliest centuries of Islam.[6] Traditionally, the refutation was a theological polemic directed against specific persons, religions, or sects (e.g., Muʿtazilism, Khārijism, Shīʿism). In the mid–eighteenth century, the emergence of the Wahhābī movement in central Arabia gave rise to a new subgenre of the refutation, that of Wahhābism and its founder. In the early 1150s/early 1740s, a number of heated anti-Wahhābī tracts appeared almost simultaneously in and around the Arabian Peninsula. In the Ḥijāz, al-Aḥsāʾ, and southern Iraq, Sunnī Muslim scholars took aim at what they considered a new heresy gaining strength in Najd and were merciless in their denunciations. They condemned the leader of the perceived heresy in the strongest possible terms, asserting, among other things, that he was mentally ill, that Satan had whispered into his ear and misled him, and that he was claiming prophecy. The doctrine emanating from Najd was evidently scandalous to these men of religion, a direct challenge to their authority and a grave affront, as they saw it, to certain centuries-old standards of Islamic belief and practice. Some of the refutations came directly in response to Ibn ʿAbd al-Wahhāb's epistles; others were written at the request of Najdī opponents of the new creed. In the face of this flurry of refutations, Ibn ʿAbd al-Wahhāb and his followers held their ground. In a number of counterrefutations, they reaffirmed their views and sought to demonstrate the errors and false claims of their enemies.

The anti-Wahhābī refuters were by no means neutral witnesses to the rise of the Wahhābī movement. Many of their charges were false and misleading. Nevertheless, the refutations are a uniquely valuable source. Not only do they highlight the intensity of the odium theologicum between the Wahhābīs and their opponents, drawing our attention to the main issues in dispute, but they also allow us to see how Ibn ʿAbd al-Wahhāb's movement developed over time. This is because the refutations are often dated, or otherwise roughly datable, and because they often refer to Ibn ʿAbd al-Wahhāb's activities and writings. Some of them even quote his epistles or reproduce them in their entirety, thus allowing one to ascertain the *terminus ante quem* (latest possible date) of the quoted or embedded epistle. Very few of Ibn ʿAbd al-Wahhāb's works are otherwise datable. Sometimes Ibn Ghannām tells us when or where a text was written, and other times internal evidence, such as a correspondent's name, can be brought to bear to help with dating. The refutations, however,

6. See *EI*[2], s.v. "Radd" (Daniel Gimaret).

allow one to assign dates to Ibn ʿAbd al-Wahhāb's writings as never before as we reconstruct the war of words between the early Wahhābīs and their enemies.

Much as historians of early Islam have used contemporary non-Muslim accounts of the rise of Islam to supplement and enrich their understanding of Islamic origins,[7] so, too, can historians of Wahhābism draw on contemporary anti-Wahhābī sources to improve and enhance their understanding of the early Wahhābī movement. Only recently have historians begun to probe the anti-Wahhābī refutations for their value as historical sources.[8] This chapter builds on their work by drawing on a greater wealth of source material, much of which has only recently come to light. Most of the refutations that will be examined here have not been discussed in previous scholarship.[9] While some of them have been published, the majority remain in manuscript form, preserved in different libraries around the world, including in the United States, the United Kingdom, Germany, India, Iraq, and Saudi Arabia. Several more are partially preserved in two later refutations, Ibn Dāwūd al-Zubayrī's *al-Ṣawāʿiq wa ʾl-ruʿūd*, completed in 1210/1795, and ʿAlawī al-Ḥaddād's *Miṣbāḥ al-anām*, completed in 1215/1801, which will be discussed in due course.[10]

This chapter has three parts. The first provides a brief account of Ibn ʿAbd al-Wahhāb's background and early preaching as described in the Wahhābī sources, ending just before his arrival in al-ʿUyayna in approximately 1155/1742. This was a time when his movement was growing and he was beginning to send out epistles as part of his predicatory campaign. The next two parts examine some of these epistles and the refutations that engage with them. Thanks to the refutations, we are able to see which of his epistles were circulating and when, and we are able to witness Wahhābism's transition from a nonviolent into a violent movement following Ibn ʿAbd al-Wahhāb's move to al-Dirʿiyya in approximately 1157/1744f. The second part of the chapter exam-

7. See, for instance, Hoyland, *Seeing Islam as Others Saw It*.

8. See Traboulsi, "Early Refutation"; Cook, "Written and Oral Aspects."

9. For two earlier surveys of anti-Wahhābī refutations, see Redissi, "Refutation of Wahhabism in Arabic Sources"; Āl ʿAbd al-Laṭīf, *Daʿāwā ʾl-munāwiʾīn*. Redissi's article does not cover the early period in depth, while Āl ʿAbd al-Laṭīf's more extensive study is mainly concerned with refuting the refutations. A survey of some of the more obscure refutations may be found in al-Bassām, "Min asbāb al-muʿāraḍa." Some of the earliest refutations are discussed in Crawford, "*Daʿwa* of Ibn ʿAbd al-Wahhāb Before the Āl Saʿūd."

10. Ibn Dāwūd, *al-Ṣawāʿiq wa ʾl-ruʿūd*; al-Ḥaddād, *Miṣbāḥ al-anām*. For a list of the refutations that I have managed to find, dated and undated, see the appendix.

ines the epistles and refutations of the al-ʿUyayna period of his preaching; the third part, those of the al-Dirʿiyya period.

This chapter does not purport to examine Ibn ʿAbd al-Wahhāb's religious thought in detail, though many aspects of his doctrine will be introduced here. The chapter's purpose, rather, is to lay the groundwork for the more rigorous discussion of his doctrine that follows by constructing as accurate an account as possible of Ibn ʿAbd al-Wahhāb's life and early career, examining how his preaching was received by his opponents, and introducing some of his most important *rasāʾil.*

The Early Life and Career of Ibn ʿAbd al-Wahhāb

Muḥammad ibn ʿAbd al-Wahhāb was born in 1115/1703f in the settlement of al-ʿUyayna,[11] by all accounts the leading town in Najd in the earlier eighteenth century in terms of wealth, population, and political heft.[12] The ruler of al-ʿUyayna at the time of his birth was ʿAbdallāh ibn Muḥammad ibn Muʿammar (d. 1138/1725f), a member of the Āl Muʿammar family that had reigned in the town since the fifteenth century.[13] As was noted above, each of Najd's subregions was dominated by a particular town. Al-ʿUyayna was the dominant town in the subregion of al-ʿĀriḍ, but it was also the largest and strongest of all the towns of Najd and was engaged in long-standing conflicts in al-Shaʿīb (with Ḥuraymilāʾ) and in al-Kharj. The next largest town in al-ʿĀriḍ, and the closest competitor with al-ʿUyayna for subregional dominance, was al-Dirʿiyya. In the early eighteenth century, al-Dirʿiyya's leadership was contested by the Āl Waṭbān and Āl Muqrin families (both of the Murada clan),[14] but in 1139/1726f Muḥammad ibn Suʿūd of the Āl Muqrin assumed control, and henceforth rule

11. See Ibn Ghannām, *Tārīkh,* 1:208; Ibn Bishr, *ʿUnwān al-majd,* 1:61; Ibn Laʿbūn, *Tārīkh,* 329; al-Fākhirī, *Tārīkh,* 114. Ibn Gharīb gives 1115/1703f without birthplace (*al-Tawḍīḥ,* 1:165); Sulaymān al-Najdī gives Ḥuraymilāʾ without birth year (Rousseau, *Mémoire sur les trois plus fameuses sectes du Musulmanisme,* 27); and ʿAbd al-Raḥmān "el-Oguyeh" gives 1116/1704f and al-ʿUyayna (Mengin, *Histoire de l'Égypt,* 2:449).

12. Al Juhany, *Najd Before the Salafi Reform Movement,* 106–7, 150.

13. Ibid., 105.

14. Ibid., 104. The tribal origins of the Murada, and hence of the Āl Suʿūd, are contested. In the modern period, Saudi rulers have located the family's origins in the sedentary Banū Ḥanīfa, but previously the dominant view had their origins in the nomadic ʿAnaza; see Samin, *Of Sand or Soil,* 195–97.

in the town would remain in his family line, the Āl Su'ūd.[15] By the time Ibn 'Abd al-Wahhāb reached the age of twenty-four, the two largest towns in al-'Āriḍ, al-'Uyayna and al-Dir'iyya, each of which would play host to him and his religious project, were ruled by the Āl Mu'ammar and Āl Su'ūd dynasties, respectively.

The family into which Ibn 'Abd al-Wahhāb was born, the Āl Musharraf, was one of the leading scholarly families in Najd.[16] The religious tradition in Najd, to reiterate, was dominated by Ḥanbalism, and so the family was versed in the Ḥanbalī *madhhab*. The family's origins can be traced to a town in al-Washm called Ushayqir, the traditional center of Najdī religious learning. Ushayqir was Najd's educational hub, known for producing scholars who would go on to assume teaching positions and judgeships in the various towns. Among these scholars were members of the Āl Musharraf. In the mid–seventeenth century, family members held the judgeships in Riyadh and al-'Uyayna.[17] Later in the century, Sulaymān ibn 'Alī (d. 1079/1669), Ibn 'Abd al-Wahhāb's paternal grandfather, served as the judge (*qāḍī*) of al-'Uyayna, where he was remembered as a teacher and unrivaled legal authority.[18] 'Abd al-Wahhāb ibn Sulaymān (d. 1153/1741), his son and the father of Ibn 'Abd al-Wahhāb, was a scholar of lesser renown who also held the judgeship of al-'Uyayna.[19] He served in this position until 1139/1726f, when a new ruler came to power and dismissed him. Thereafter he settled in Ḥuraymilā', a town in the district of al-Sha'īb, where he held the position of *qāḍī* till his death in 1153/1741.[20]

15. Al Juhany, *Najd Before the Salafi Reform Movement*, 104. See further, for the date of Muḥammad ibn Su'ūd's assumption of power, Ibn 'Abbād, *Tārīkh*, 82; Ibn La'būn, *Tārīkh*, 381; Ibn Bishr, *'Unwān al-majd*, 1:73.

16. Al Juhany, *Najd Before the Salafi Reform Movement*, 117, 134–35.

17. al-'Uthaymīn, *Muḥammad ibn 'Abd al-Wahhāb*, 28. The *qāḍī* (judge) of Riyadh was Aḥmad ibn Nāṣir (d. 1049/1639f or 1048/1638f); the *qāḍī* of al-'Uyayna was 'Abdallāh ibn 'Abd al-Wahhāb (d. 1056/1646f).

18. Al Juhany, *Najd Before the Salafi Reform Movement*, 132. For his biography, see Ibn Bishr, *'Unwān al-majd*, 1:40–41; Ibn Ḥumayd, *al-Suḥub al-wābila*, 2:413–15; Āl Bassām, *'Ulamā' Najd*, 2:366–72. Ibn Ḥumayd gives al-'Uyayna as his birthplace, while Āl Bassām gives Ushayqir.

19. On him, see Ibn Ḥumayd, *al-Suḥub al-wābila*, 2:675–81; Āl Bassām, *'Ulamā' Najd*, 5:40–43.

20. See Ibn Rabī'a, *Tārīkh*, 87; Ibn La'būn, *Tārīkh*, 385; al-Fākhirī, *Tārīkh*, 125; Ibn Bishr, *'Unwān al-majd*, 1:73; Ibn 'Īsā, *Tārīkh ba'ḍ al-ḥawādith*, 78; al-Bassām, *Tuḥfat al-mushtāq*, 185. The new ruler was Muḥammad ibn Ḥamad ibn 'Abdallāh ibn Mu'ammar (d. 1142/1729f), a grandson of the previous ruler. Ibn Ghannām does not mention the dismissal, merely recording that 'Abd al-Wahhāb chose to move to Ḥuraymilā' and not specifying a date (*Tārīkh*, 1:212).

Muḥammad ibn ʿAbd al-Wahhāb was trained to be a religious scholar from a young age, as was his brother, Sulaymān.[21] According to Ibn Ghannām, he received his early education at the feet of his father in al-ʿUyayna.[22] At the age of twelve, in approximately 1127/1715f, he married (or perhaps contracted a marriage) and performed the *ḥajj*, the pilgrimage to Mecca; afterward he returned to al-ʿUyayna to resume his studies with his father. Sometime later he would leave Najd for a course of study abroad.[23]

It was not unusual for aspiring Najdī scholars to embark on such journeys, the most common destinations at the time being al-Aḥsāʾ, the Ḥijāz, and Damascus.[24] With his privileged background, Ibn ʿAbd al-Wahhāb would have been well positioned for such a trip. Ibn Ghannām relates that he traveled first to Medina, then to Basra, and finally to al-Aḥsāʾ, the bulk of his time studying (*akthar lubthihi li-akhdh al-ʿilm*) being spent in Basra.[25] After an unknown period, which seems to have included multiple trips back and forth from Najd to Basra, Ibn ʿAbd al-Wahhāb returned to Najd for good, settling in Ḥuraymilāʾ, where his father was now the *qāḍī*. Unfortunately, the sources do not afford us a much more specific time line than this. We can be fairly certain that he began studying in Basra no later than 1137/1724f, when he was about twenty-one years old, as one of the anti-Wahhābī sources locates him there at that time.[26] We can also be certain that he did not settle in Ḥuraymilāʾ before 1153/1741, the year his father died. Most likely he returned and established himself in Ḥuraymilāʾ in the late 1140s/late 1730s.[27]

According to Ibn Ghannām, it was during his time in Basra that Ibn ʿAbd al-Wahhāb began spreading his religious views, preaching among certain

21. It is unclear from the sources whether Sulaymān was older or younger than Muḥammad.

22. Ibn Ghannām, *Tārīkh*, 1:208.

23. Ibid., 1:209–10.

24. Al Juhany, *Najd Before the Salafi Reform Movement*, 133.

25. Ibn Ghannām, *Tārīkh*, 1:210, 212. For the variant itineraries recorded in the Wahhābī and non-Wahhābī sources, see Cook, "On the Origins of Wahhābism," 191–98. Nearly all the Wahhābī sources agree that Ibn ʿAbd al-Wahhāb visited only the Ḥijāz, Iraq, and al-Aḥsāʾ, usually in that order. The story of his travel to and residence in Iran is almost certainly a fabrication.

26. Ibn Dāwūd, *al-Ṣawāʿiq wa ʾl-ruʿūd*, f. 32b, where the author states that he heard this from his teacher Muḥammad ibn Fayrūz, who heard it from his father, ʿAbdallāh ibn Fayrūz.

27. This is because Ibn ʿAbd al-Wahhāb left Ḥuraymilāʾ for al-ʿUyayna in about 1155/1742, as we shall see shortly, and both Ibn Ghannām and Ibn Bishr note that he lived in Ḥuraymilāʾ for a number of years (*sinīn, muddat sinīn*). See Ibn Ghannām, *Tārīkh*, 1:215; Ibn Bishr, *ʿUnwān al-majd*, 1:85.

people (*ba ʿḍ al-nās*) in his personal gathering space (*majlis*).[28] The people in Basra would engage him in debate over the matter of visiting graves and supplicating the dead. Ibn Ghannām quotes him as saying: "Some of the polytheists of Basra would come to me and relate their specious arguments [*shubuhāt*] to me. As they were seated before me, I would say, 'Worship in its entirety is not valid but to God alone [*lā taṣluḥu ʾl-ʿibāda kulluhā illā lillāh*].' All of them would be astonished, and not a mouth would make a sound."[29] In this telling, Ibn ʿAbd al-Wahhāb was beginning to articulate his views on *tawḥīd*, but only in a limited fashion; he was not yet seeking to lead a movement or cause serious trouble.

A more dramatic episode in Basra is related by Ibn Bishr, who suggests that Ibn ʿAbd al-Wahhāb was preaching there in a more outspoken fashion. According to Ibn Bishr, when Ibn ʿAbd al-Wahhāb condemned certain forms of unbelief and religious innovation (*ashyāʾ min al-shirkiyyāt wa ʾl-bidaʿ*) in Basra, he was persecuted and driven out of the city, nearly dying from thirst on his way to the nearby town of al-Zubayr. He was saved by a traveler who gave him drink and carried him the rest of the way on his donkey. From al-Zubayr he sought to go to Damascus but fell short of funds, and so he returned to Najd via al-Aḥsāʾ.[30] While this story of Ibn ʿAbd al-Wahhāb being violently driven out of Basra is possibly true, it is more likely that he preached discreetly and without fanfare in the city, as indicated by Ibn Ghannām. Ibn Bishr was writing considerably later than Ibn Ghannām, and the Basran scholars who later refuted Ibn ʿAbd al-Wahhāb do not mention his presence in the city, which would seem to confirm that he kept a low profile there.

Both Ibn Ghannām and Ibn Bishr, among other of Ibn ʿAbd al-Wahhāb's biographers, relate that during his travels he studied with a number of different teachers. None of them, however, seems to have been the inspiration behind his distinctive doctrinal views. Ibn Ghannām states that Ibn ʿAbd al-Wahhāb studied with a group (*jamāʿa*) of teachers in the Ḥijāz, Basra, and al-Aḥsāʾ, naming just one: ʿAbdallāh ibn Ibrāhīm ibn Sayf (d. 1140/1727f), a Ḥanbalī from the Najdī district of Sudayr who was living in Medina.[31] Ibn Ghannām notes that Ibn Sayf provided Ibn ʿAbd al-Wahhāb with two *ijāzas* (*wa-ajāzahu*

28. Ibn Ghannām, *Tārīkh*, 1:212.

29. Ibid.

30. Ibn Bishr, *ʿUnwān al-majd*, 1:83–84.

31. Ibn Ghannām, *Tārīkh*, 1:210. On Ibn Sayf, see Ibn Ḥumayd, *al-Suḥub al-wābila*, 1:44; Āl Bassām, *ʿUlamāʾ Najd*, 4:6–10; al-Qāḍī, *Rawḍat al-nāẓirīn*, 1:425.

min ṭarīqayn), or licenses of authorization to transmit a text.[32] Ibn Bishr likewise identifies Ibn Sayf as one of Ibn ʿAbd al-Wahhāb's teachers, also mentioning two others: the Ḥanafī Muḥammad Ḥayāt al-Sindī (d. 1163/1750) in Medina and a certain Muḥammad al-Majmūʿī in Basra.[33] Al-Sindī may well have been a teacher of Ibn ʿAbd al-Wahhāb's, as one of the anti-Wahhābī sources similarly relates that Ibn ʿAbd al-Wahhāb frequented al-Sindī's study circle in Medina (*yataraddadu ʿalā ʾl-shaykh Muḥammad Ḥayāt*).[34] It should be noted, however, that according to another anti-Wahhābī source, al-Sindī was among Ibn ʿAbd al-Wahhāb's early refuters.[35] As for al-Majmūʿī, there is no reference to him in any other source; he may well be fictitious, though Majmūʿa was at least a real area within Basra.[36] Muḥammad ibn Gharīb, in his biography of the Wahhābī founder, names four teachers with whom Ibn ʿAbd al-Wahhāb allegedly studied: in Medina, the Ḥanbalī Ibn Sayf and the Ḥanafī ʿAlī Afandī ibn Ṣādiq al-Dāghistānī (d. 1199/1785) and, in al-Aḥsāʾ, the Ḥanbalī Muḥammad ibn ʿAfāliq (d. 1163/1750) and a certain ʿAbd al-Laṭīf al-Aḥsāʾī.[37] Apart from Ibn Sayf, all of this is questionable. There is no record of Ibn ʿAbd al-Wahhāb studying with either al-Dāghistānī or Ibn ʿAfāliq, and Ibn ʿAfāliq, like al-Sindī, was one of Ibn ʿAbd al-Wahhāb's early refuters. Notably, he would accuse Ibn ʿAbd al-Wahhāb of having had no teachers (*lā sanada lahu wa-lā mashyakha*).[38] ʿAbd al-Raḥmān ibn Ḥasan Āl al-Shaykh, for his part, names Ibn ʿAbd al-Wahhāb's teachers as three: Muḥammad Ḥayāt al-Sindī in Medina and the Ḥanbalī ʿAbdallāh ibn Fayrūz (d. 1175/1762) and the Shāfiʿī ʿAbdallāh ibn ʿAbd al-Laṭīf (d. 1181/1767f) in al-Aḥsāʾ.[39] That these men were his teachers is certainly plausible. It is clear from one of Ibn ʿAbd al-Wahhāb's letters that he

32. Ibn Ghannām, *Tārīkh*, 1:210–12. The *ijāzas* appear to have been for two *ḥadīths*; Ibn Ghannām reproduces the chains of transmission for these going back to the Prophet. Cf. Ibn Gharīb, *al-Tawḍīḥ*, 1:166–72, where two similar chains are outlined.

33. Ibn Bishr, *ʿUnwān al-majd*, 1:82–83, 70. On al-Sindī, see Nafi, "Teacher of Ibn ʿAbd al-Wahhāb."

34. al-Ḥaddād, *Miṣbāḥ al-anām*, 10.

35. Ibn Dāwūd, *al-Ṣawāʿiq wa ʾl-ruʿūd*, f. 82b. The source is a refutation (partly quoted here) by Muḥammad ibn al-Ṭayyib al-Maghribī, who writes at the end of his refutation: *wa ʾl-shaykh Muḥammad Ḥayāt kataba lakum mā ẓahara lahu saddadahu ʾllāh.*

36. Cook, "On the Origins of Wahhābism," 193.

37. Ibn Gharīb, *al-Tawḍīḥ*, 1:166–67. On al-Dāghistānī, see al-Murādī, *Silk al-durar*, 3:215. On Ibn ʿAfāliq, see the section on his refutation below.

38. Ibn ʿAfāliq, *Tahakkum al-muqallidīn*, f. 42b.

39. Āl al-Shaykh, *al-Maqāmāt*, 67–68.

at least met ʿAbdallāh ibn Fayrūz,[40] and it is clear from the same letter that he met Ibn ʿAbd al-Laṭīf, though the description of their encounter suggests mutual learning, not a student-teacher relationship.[41] What is undeniable, however, is that both of these men later opposed Ibn ʿAbd al-Wahhāb and wrote refutations of him.[42]

Why, one may well ask, were Ibn ʿAbd al-Wahhāb's biographers so eager to mention these anti-Wahhābī scholars as being among his teachers? The answer seems to be that the biographers were concerned with rebutting the accusation that Ibn ʿAbd al-Wahhāb had no scholarly pedigree, a common charge leveled against him by his opponents, and thus they sought to construct one for him to bolster his résumé. Ibn Gharīb wrote his account of Ibn ʿAbd al-Wahhāb's life directly in response to the accusation that Ibn ʿAbd al-Wahhāb had failed to study with teachers who could lead him to the right path (*wa-lā qaraʾa ʿalā man yahdīhi ilā ʾl-nahj al-qawīm*).[43] What appears to have happened is that the biographers went out of their way to look for teachers to identify, ignoring the fact that some of them were staunch opponents of Wahhābism. Over time the list of teachers grew longer, and the influence imputed to them was exaggerated. Ibn Bishr even makes three of these teachers out to be Ibn ʿAbd al-Wahhāb's doctrinal allies. First, he relates a story in which Ibn Sayf, in Medina, shows Ibn ʿAbd al-Wahhāb a collection of books being prepared as weapons (*silāḥan*) to be used against his hometown of al-Majmaʿa in Sudayr.[44] The implication is that Ibn Sayf, like Ibn ʿAbd al-Wahhāb, considered the religious practices in Najd to be polytheistic and thus desired to impose a proper understanding of Islam on its people. In a second story, Muḥammad Ḥayāt al-Sindī is seen, in the company of his pupil, condemning certain visitors to the Prophet's tomb who supplicate the Prophet and seek his help (*yadʿūna wa-yastaghīthūna*).[45] The suggestion is that al-Sindī's view of such visitors is the same as Ibn ʿAbd al-Wahhāb's, namely, that they are committing *shirk*. In a third story, Ibn Bishr relates that the mysterious Muḥammad al-Majmūʿī approved

40. Ibn Ghannām, *Tārīkh*, 1:251 (letter to Ibn ʿAbd al-Laṭīf).

41. Ibid., 1:246.

42. Ibn Fayrūz's refutation is quoted in Ibn Dāwūd, *al-Ṣawāʿiq wa ʾl-ruʿūd*, ff. 196b–97b. Ibn ʿAbd al-Laṭīf's, which is lost, is discussed by Ibn ʿAbd al-Wahhāb in a letter to its author; see Ibn Ghannām, *Tārīkh*, 1:246–62.

43. Ibn Gharīb, *al-Tawḍīḥ*, 1:163.

44. Ibn Bishr, *ʿUnwān al-majd*, 1:83; noted in Cook, "On the Origins of Wahhābism," 192.

45. Ibn Bishr, *ʿUnwān al-majd*, 1:83. The condemnation is made in the words of the Qurʾānic Moses (Q. 7:139); noted in Cook, "On the Origins of Wahhābism," 192.

of (*istaḥsana*) Ibn ʿAbd al-Wahhāb's condemnation of *shirk* in Basra and paid a price for it (*laḥiqa . . . baʿḍ al-adhā*) at the hands of the Basrans.[46] All of these stories are suspect, as none of these teachers—at least not Ibn Sayf or al-Sindī—is known to have had any sympathy for Ibn ʿAbd al-Wahhāb's subsequent preaching. ʿAbd al-Raḥmān ibn Ḥasan takes a different approach, suggesting that his grandfather was intellectually superior to the men under whom he studied. Countering the enduring charge that Ibn ʿAbd al-Wahhāb had not studied with teachers (*lam yatakharraj ʿalā ashyākh fī ʾl-ʿilm*), he asserts that his grandfather belonged to a prominent scholarly family in Najd and studied with some of the leading scholars of the day, both in Najd and beyond.[47] But he also highlights his grandfather's willingness to challenge some of these men, noting that Ibn ʿAbd al-Wahhāb debated some of the scholars in al-Aḥsāʾ on certain issues (*baḥatha maʿahum fī masāʾil wa-nāẓara*).[48]

Both Ibn Ghannām and Ibn Bishr agree that it was in Ḥuraymilāʾ, following his studies, that Ibn ʿAbd al-Wahhāb launched a full-fledged predicatory campaign. According to Ibn Ghannām, in Ḥuraymilāʾ Ibn ʿAbd al-Wahhāb began publicly to condemn polytheism and to call on people to direct worship to God alone.[49] Ibn Bishr adds that he came out openly with his mission in Ḥuraymilāʾ (*aʿlana bi ʾl-daʿwa*) only after his father died, in Dhū ʾl-ḥijja 1153/February–March 1741.[50] While Ibn Ghannām fails to mention this detail, it is very likely true. As Ibn Bishr has it, Ibn ʿAbd al-Wahhāb and his father had a tense relationship in Ḥuraymilāʾ. When Ibn ʿAbd al-Wahhāb criticized the religious innovations and polytheism (*al-bidaʿ wa ʾl-shirk*) in the area, there followed an exchange of words between the two men (*waqaʿa baynahu wa-bayna abīhi kalām*), meaning a serious confrontation.[51] The story finds corroboration in the anti-Wahhābī refutation of Ibn Dāwūd al-Zubayrī, who states that Ibn ʿAbd al-Wahhāb's father and brother were the first to censure him for his doctrinal views (*awwal man ankara ʿalayhi*). Ibn Dāwūd further notes that Ibn ʿAbd al-Wahhāb did not speak openly about *takfīr* before his father's death (*qabl mawt wālidihi*).[52] In an endorsement of Ibn Dāwūd's refutation, the

46. Ibn Bishr, *ʿUnwān al-majd*, 1:83–84.

47. Āl al-Shaykh, *al-Maqāmāt*, 62.

48. Ibid., 68.

49. Ibn Ghannām, *Tārīkh*, 1:213.

50. Ibn Bishr, *ʿUnwān al-majd*, 1:85. For his death date with month, see Ibn Laʿbūn, *Tārīkh*, 406; al-Fākhirī, *Tārīkh*, 129.

51. Ibn Bishr, *ʿUnwān al-majd*, 1:85.

52. Ibn Dāwūd, *al-Ṣawāʿiq wa ʾl-ruʿūd*, ff. 40b, 122a.

anti-Wahhābī scholar Muḥammad ibn Fayrūz (d. 1216/1801) describes the relationship between Ibn ʿAbd al-Wahhāb and his father as an acrimonious one. He notes that his own father, ʿAbdallāh ibn Fayrūz, once wrote to Ibn ʿAbd al-Wahhāb's father to urge him to set his son straight (*an yanṣaḥahu*), only for Ibn ʿAbd al-Wahhāb's father to lament that his son was disobedient and beyond his control (*iʿtadhara bi-khurūjihi min ṭāʿatihi*).[53] While none of this is mentioned by Ibn Ghannām, the story of an alleged conflict between Ibn ʿAbd al-Wahhāb and his father would find its way into the later Wahhābī tradition as accepted fact, as would the story of him beginning his mission only after his father died. There is indeed every reason to believe that ʿAbd al-Wahhāb ibn Sulaymān, an establishment figure, would have opposed his son's radical views. It is possible that Ibn ʿAbd al-Wahhāb felt restrained by his father's presence and thus hesitated to promulgate his doctrine until the latter was gone.

In Ḥuraymilāʾ, according to Ibn Ghannām, when Ibn ʿAbd al-Wahhāb began preaching about *tawḥīd* and urging people to cease committing *shirk*, he attracted a group of loyal followers, men who would preach alongside him and emulate him in word and deed. There were others from beyond Ḥuraymilāʾ who journeyed to the town to meet with Ibn ʿAbd al-Wahhāb and learn from him directly. His name became well known in the towns of al-ʿĀriḍ—al-ʿUyayna, al-Dirʿiyya, Riyadh, and Manfūḥa—but his reception there was for the most part not positive. Nonetheless, his movement continued to grow.[54]

It was also in Ḥuraymilāʾ, according to Ibn Ghannām, that Ibn ʿAbd al-Wahhāb authored what is perhaps his best-known work, *Kitāb al-tawḥīd*.[55] The book, which would come to be seen as the foundational text of Wahhābism, attracting commentaries by later Wahhābī scholars, is mostly a collection of Qurʾānic verses and *ḥadīth*s divided into chapters with short commentary in the form of lists of points. Though it offers almost no overt criticism of the contemporary religious environment,[56] the chapter titles provide something of a rundown of all the alleged polytheistic practices in Najd and elsewhere, including supplicating (*duʿāʾ*) and seeking the help of (*istighātha*) saints and prophets, seeking blessings from trees and stones, wearing rings and strings to

53. Ibid., ff. 1b–2a.

54. Ibn Ghannām, *Tārīkh*, 1:212–15; cf. Ibn Bishr, *ʿUnwān al-majd*, 1:85.

55. Ibn Ghannām, *Tārīkh*, 1:215. ʿAbd al-Raḥmān ibn Ḥasan Āl al-Shaykh puts the place of authorship in Basra (*al-Maqāmāt*, 66).

56. I have identified only two overt references to the contemporary scene; see Ibn ʿAbd al-Wahhāb, *Kitāb al-tawḥīd*, 172, 261.

ward off evil, and sorcery and astrology. As David Commins has suggested, *Kitāb al-tawḥīd* likely served as a kind of textbook for classroom instruction.[57] It does not seem to have played a major role in Ibn ʿAbd al-Wahhāb's preaching. Indeed, it would be impossible to know from its contents alone what its author was trying to accomplish, as it lacks the polemical quality of his letters and epistles.

While the biographies seek to identify the names of Ibn ʿAbd al-Wahhāb's teachers, at most these are portrayed as his allies; none is presented as a key source of inspiration. The general portrayal of Ibn ʿAbd al-Wahhāb in the biographies is as a humble servant of God who rediscovered the original message of Islam, the true meaning of *tawḥīd,* through divine inspiration. As will be seen, the claim of divine inspiration was one that Ibn ʿAbd al-Wahhāb would even make himself. Ibn Ghannām's portrait is instructive. In his creedal work *al-ʿIqd al-thamīn,* he gives a short account of the rise of Wahhābism prefaced by an account of the rise of Islam.[58] He describes the Prophet's career, including his call to *tawḥīd* in an environment afflicted by *shirk,* the hostility that this engendered, and the warfare and political success that followed. Next, he explains how things went wrong with the introduction of change (*taghyīr*) and innovations (*bidaʿ*) in the religion, especially after the twelfth century. The situation continued to deteriorate until, in the mid–eighteenth century, God "expanded the breast of one whom He won over to Islam and whom He guided, lay bare to him the ways of His instruction and His guidance, and made clear to him the path of guidance."[59] In the Qurʾān, the Prophet is the one whose breast was expanded by God (Q. 94:1), so Ibn Ghannām here is describing Ibn ʿAbd al-Wahhāb in pseudo-prophetic terms, in a sense as the Prophet's successor. It was by means of him that "God erased the darkness of polytheism and skepticism and doubt" that had overtaken the world, and thus he was following in the Prophet's footsteps.[60] Similarly, ʿAbd al-Raḥmān ibn Ḥasan claims that Ibn ʿAbd al-Wahhāb received his unique understanding of the foundations of the religion not from any of his teachers but, rather, from God Himself (*aẓhara ʾllah lahu min uṣūl al-dīn mā khafiya ʿalā ghayrihi*).[61] There is, however, one further influence on his grandfather's thinking of which

57. Commins, *Wahhabi Mission,* 13.

58. Ibn Ghannām, *al-ʿIqd al-thamīn,* 17–28.

59. Ibid., 24.

60. Ibid.

61. Āl al-Shaykh, *al-Maqāmāt,* 65–66.

ʿAbd al-Raḥmān ibn Ḥasan takes note: the works of Ibn Taymiyya and Ibn Qayyim al-Jawziyya. In al-Aḥsāʾ, according to ʿAbd al-Raḥmān, Ibn ʿAbd al-Wahhāb encountered some of their works with ʿAbdallāh ibn Fayrūz and was enamored of them.[62] Remarkably, this is the first reference in any of the biographies to the role of the two fourteenth-century scholars—remarkable, as their influence on Ibn ʿAbd al-Wahhāb was no secret to anyone involved in the early Wahhābī controversy and was in fact frequently discussed and widely debated.

Refutations and Epistles: The al-ʿUyayna Period

Within a year or so of his father's death in 1153/1741, Ibn ʿAbd al-Wahhāb relocated from Ḥuraymilāʾ to his hometown of al-ʿUyayna. According to Ibn Bishr, Ḥuraymilāʾ was a difficult place in which to preach his controversial doctrine. The town was politically divided between two tribes, neither of which was capable of imposing order and providing security. After an assassination attempt by certain townspeople upset with his preaching, Ibn ʿAbd al-Wahhāb decided to leave for a more secure location.[63] Al-ʿUyayna, as the largest and most powerful town in all of Najd, would have been an attractive destination as a new base of operations. Upon Ibn ʿAbd al-Wahhāb's relocation, the ruler of al-ʿUyayna, ʿUthmān ibn Muʿammar (r. 1142–63/1742f–50), quickly became an enthusiastic supporter of his. In Ibn Ghannām's telling, Ibn Muʿammar gave his full backing to Ibn ʿAbd al-Wahhāb and his missionary efforts, commanding his people to obey the newly arrived preacher (*wa-amara ʾl-nās lahu bi ʾl-ittibāʿ*).[64] Ibn Bishr adds that Ibn ʿAbd al-Wahhāb married the ruler's paternal aunt, al-Jawhara bint ʿAbdallāh, thus cementing his ties to Ibn Muʿammar through marriage.[65]

In al-ʿUyayna, according to both accounts, Ibn ʿAbd al-Wahhāb continued gaining new followers, both in the town and across al-ʿĀriḍ. In a sign of his growing support, Ibn ʿAbd al-Wahhāb began to take action in his campaign against *shirk* by destroying certain objects of veneration. On one occasion, he set out with Ibn Muʿammar and a group of men to destroy the domes and mosques built above the graves of certain of the Prophet's Companions in

62. Ibid., 68.

63. Ibn Bishr, *ʿUnwān al-majd*, 1:85–86; cf. Mengin, *Histoire de l'Égypte*, 2:449.

64. Ibn Ghannām, *Tārīkh*, 1:215.

65. Ibn Bishr, *ʿUnwān al-majd*, 1:85–86.

al-Jubayla, an area near Riyadh. One of these was the tomb of Zayd ibn al-Khaṭṭāb, the brother of the second caliph, ʿUmar ibn al-Khaṭṭāb. Ibn ʿAbd al-Wahhāb and his followers also cut down certain trees in al-ʿĀriḍ that were being venerated by the people of Najd. Ibn ʿAbd al-Wahhāb is said to have taken an axe to one of these trees himself.[66]

It was also in al-ʿUyayna that Ibn ʿAbd al-Wahhāb began writing epistles setting out the main lines of his doctrine and sending them to nearby towns and areas.[67] The beginning of this epistolary activity inspired some of the first anti-Wahhābī refutations.

The earliest extant refutation of Wahhābism that is dated was written by a Shāfiʿī scholar in Basra named Aḥmad ibn ʿAlī al-Qabbānī (fl. 1159/1746).[68] Al-Qabbānī was the most prolific anti-Wahhābī scholar during the al-ʿUyayna years of Ibn ʿAbd al-Wahhāb's preaching, authoring three refutations. The first of these, titled *Faṣl al-khiṭāb fī radd ḍalālāt Ibn ʿAbd al-Wahhāb* (The Decisive Statement in Refutation of the Errors of Ibn ʿAbd al-Wahhāb), was completed in mid-Shawwāl 1155/mid-December 1742, according to the lone surviving manuscript in Baghdad.[69] As al-Qabbānī relates at the beginning of his work, in mid-1155/mid-1742, an epistle by Ibn ʿAbd al-Wahhāb, described as the judge of al-ʿUyayna (*qāḍī ʾl-ʿUyayna*), reached Basra (*waradat ʿalaynā*). Sometime thereafter an unidentified person (*baʿḍ al-nās*) asked him to compose a commentary on it in order to expose its errors and defend the practices related to the cult of saints.[70] This he would do at length, never failing in the

66. Ibid., 1:86; Ibn Ghannām, *Tārīkh*, 1:215–16.

67. Ibn Bishr states that this began in al-Dirʿiyya (*ʿUnwān al-majd*, 1:92), but the evidence from the early refutations proves otherwise.

68. Little is known about al-Qabbānī apart from the names of some of his books (Traboulsi, "Early Refutation," 377–79, 382), his Shāfiʿī allegiance (Cook, "Written and Oral Aspects," 162), and the year of his birth, 1108/1696f (al-Ḥusaynī, "Makhṭūṭ nādir").

69. al-Qabbānī, *Faṣl al-khiṭāb*. This and the two other refutations by al-Qabbānī are part of a study and edition being prepared by Bernard Haykel and Samer Traboulsi. I am grateful to them for sharing the first and second of these texts with me. The third was discovered by Michael Cook in the Princeton University library and is discussed in his "Written and Oral Aspects."

70. al-Qabbānī, *Faṣl al-khiṭāb*, f. 4b. The Iraqi historian ʿAbbās al-ʿAzzāwī (d. 1391/1971) likewise notes the arrival of Ibn ʿAbd al-Wahhāb's epistle in the middle of this year, relying on

course of his commentary to heap abuse on the Wahhābī founder, described as, among other things, "Satan's deputy" (*khalīfat Iblīs*).[71]

In the course of his lengthy refutation, al-Qabbānī preserves the full text of the epistle by Ibn ʿAbd al-Wahhāb, which also survives in slightly different form in the Wahhābī tradition.[72] Following the opening invocation, the epistle begins with the statement "These are words in explication of the confession that there is no god but God" (*hādhihi kalimāt fī bayān shahādat an lā ilāha illā ʾllāh*),[73] and so we will refer to it here as the *Kalimāt fī bayān shahādat an lā ilāha illā ʾllāh*, or the *Kalimāt* for short. It is thanks to al-Qabbānī's *Faṣl al-khiṭāb* that we can be sure that the *Kalimāt* was written no later than mid-1155/mid-1742 and that we know it was circulating as far away as Basra at this time. Whether it was sent there by the Wahhābīs for the purpose of preaching or whether it was being spread by Ibn ʿAbd al-Wahhāb's opponents for the purpose of exposing him as a heretic is unclear. Whatever the case, the *Kalimāt* epistle allows us to see exactly what Ibn ʿAbd al-Wahhāb was preaching at this early point in his career.

The main theme of the *Kalimāt fī bayān shahādat an lā ilāha illā ʾllāh* is the pervasiveness of *shirk* in the contemporary Islamic world and the proper understanding of *tawḥīd*. In the epistle Ibn ʿAbd al-Wahhāb begins by condemning the association of other beings in worship with God (*al-shirk bi ʾllāh*) and warning that the destination for those who commit *shirk* is hellfire, regardless of one's piety and good works on earth. He goes on to explain that the supplication of saints and prophets is undoubtedly a form of *shirk* and gives a few examples of such illicit veneration:

> So reflect, may God have mercy on you, on the supplication of other than God [*duʿāʾ ghayr Allāh*] in times of hardship and in times of comfort that has afflicted mankind. Such and such a person intends to travel, so he goes to the grave of a prophet or someone else and comes to it with his wealth in order to avert robbery [*bi-mālihi ʿan nahbihi*]; and such and such a person is afflicted by hardship on land or on sea, so he seeks the help of

---

the same copy of *Faṣl al-khiṭāb* available to me; see al-ʿAzzāwī, *Tārīkh al-ʿIrāq bayna ʾḥtilālayn*, 5:310, 6:336.

71. al-Qabbānī, *Faṣl al-khiṭāb*, f. 68a.

72. *al-Durar al-saniyya*, 2:100–112; *Majmūʿat al-rasāʾil wa ʾl-masāʾil al-Najdiyya*, 4:15–23. The differences between al-Qabbānī's version and the first of these are minimal.

73. al-Qabbānī, *Faṣl al-khiṭāb*, f. 25b.

[*fa-yastaghīthu*] ʿAbd al-Qādir or Shamsān, or a prophet or a saint, that he may relieve him of this hardship.[74]

ʿAbd al-Qādir al-Jīlānī (d. 561/1166) was a Ḥanbalī scholar and the namesake of the Qādirī Ṣūfī order.[75] Shamsān is the name of one of several Najdī saints who are mentioned frequently in Ibn ʿAbd al-Wahhāb's writings. He was buried in the southern Najdī district of al-Kharj, which appears to have been the epicenter of the cult of saints in Najd. According to al-Qabbānī, Shamsān was a *sayyid*, a descendant of the Prophet, who had only recently died (*tuwuffiya min zaman qarīb*).[76] Most of these Najdī saints appear to have been *sayyids*, and presumably this prophetic pedigree conferred on them a status as being close to God. Elsewhere in the epistle, Ibn ʿAbd al-Wahhāb refers to two other Najdī saints, Ḥusayn and a certain "guardian of the place of seclusion" (*rāʿī ʾl-khalwa*), whom al-Qabbānī identifies as Idrīs, the son of this Ḥusayn.[77] Other Najdī saints mentioned by Ibn ʿAbd al-Wahhāb in his writings include Yūsuf and Tāj, the latter being the son of Shamsān. According to Ibn Ghannām, Tāj led an active cult in al-Kharj at the time of the rise of Wahhābism.[78] In another epistle, Ibn ʿAbd al-Wahhāb refers to these saints in terms of family units, as in "Shamsān and his sons and Idrīs and his sons" (*Shamsān wa-awlādahu wa-Idrīs wa-awlādahu*), indicating that the cult of saints in al-Kharj was oriented around these men and their offspring and descendants.[79] In the *Kalimāt* as elsewhere, Ibn ʿAbd al-Wahhāb denounces these holy men as *ṭawāghīt* (sing. *ṭāghūt*), a Qurʾānic term with the general meaning of "idol," though in this context having the more specific meaning of "a person who is worshipped and who allows himself to be worshipped."[80] He further complains that the people of Najd are making vows to these *ṭawāghīt* and giving them votive offerings, accusing these idols of having "devoured people's property" (*akalū amwāl al-nās*).[81]

74. Ibid., ff. 33b–34a (= *al-Durar al-saniyya*, 2:104, with several minor differences).

75. On him, see *EI*³, s.v. "ʿAbd al-Qādir al-Jīlānī" (Jacqueline Chabbi).

76. al-Qabbānī, *Faṣl al-khiṭāb*, f. 33b (= *al-Durar al-saniyya*, 2:104).

77. al-Qabbānī, *Faṣl al-khiṭāb*, ff. 72b, 81b (= *al-Durar al-saniyya*, 2:110, where the names of these saints are not given).

78. Ibn Ghannām, *Tārīkh*, 1:175–76, 2:676.

79. al-Qabbānī, *Naqḍ qawāʿid al-ḍalāl*, ff. 41a–63a, at f. 57a.

80. al-Qabbānī, *Faṣl al-khiṭāb*, f. 68b (= *al-Durar al-saniyya*, 2:110). For more on Ibn ʿAbd al-Wahhāb's understanding of *ṭāghūt*, see chapter 3.

81. al-Qabbānī, *Faṣl al-khiṭāb*, f. 68b (= *al-Durar al-saniyya*, 2:110).

In the *Kalimāt* epistle, Ibn ʿAbd al-Wahhāb urges his readers to desist from appealing to the *ṭawāghīt* and calls on them to worship God alone. It does not matter, he argues, whether one believes in one all-powerful God while making appeals and vows to these holy men; what matters is that God is unified in practice. Believers must direct all forms of worship, including supplication, to God alone, otherwise they are committing *shirk*. This is the true meaning of "there is no god but God" and of *tawḥīd*. However, for Ibn ʿAbd al-Wahhāb, believing as much is insufficient to meet the test of Islam. From here he goes on to say that those who agree with him to this point must take the further step of showing hatred and enmity both to the *ṭawāghīt* and to those who worship them. "Do not think if you say," he writes,

> "This is the truth. I follow it and I abjure all that is against it, but I will not confront them [*lā ataʿarraḍuhum*] and I will say nothing concerning them," do not think that that will profit you. Rather, it is necessary to hate them, to hate those who love them, to revile them, and to show them enmity [*lā budda min bughḍihim wa-bughḍ man yuḥibbuhum wa-masabbatihim wa-muʿādātihim*].[82]

Thus, as the *Kalimāt* epistle shows, at this early date in 1155/1742, Ibn ʿAbd al-Wahhāb was preaching a consciously provocative doctrine aimed at disrupting the popular religious environment in Najd as elsewhere in the Islamic world. Ibn ʿAbd al-Wahhāb wanted his followers not only to believe that the cult of saints constituted *shirk* but also to act on this belief by openly condemning these objects of illicit veneration as well as those seen as worshipping them.

The *Kalimāt*, it should be made clear, was by no means an isolated instance of such preaching, as the theme of condemnation and confrontation features prominently in Ibn ʿAbd al-Wahhāb's early epistles. For example, in another epistle, similar to the *Kalimāt* in content and in structure, Ibn ʿAbd al-Wahhāb rails against the saints in al-Kharj, including Shamsān, Idrīs, and Yūsuf, denouncing them as *ṭawāghīt* and urging his readers to understand that appealing to them constitutes *shirk*. He then urges his readers to pronounce *takfīr* on the *ṭawāghīt* and to show them hatred and enmity and to do the same to those who love them, defend them, or fail to pronounce *takfīr* on them (*man aḥabbahum aw-jādala ʿanhum aw lam yukaffirhum*). This was to be done even to immediate family members, one's siblings and one's children (*wa-law kānū ikhwānahu*

82. al-Qabbānī, *Faṣl al-khiṭāb*, f. 65a (= *al-Durar al-saniyya*, 2:109, with minor differences).

wa-awlādahu).[83] Ibn ʿAbd al-Wahhāb's message was thus intended to be divisive and disruptive. The idea was to emphasize the distinction between the community of belief (i.e., the Wahhābīs), on the one hand, and the community of unbelief or *shirk* (i.e., those seen as participating in the cult of saints or even just tolerating it), on the other, and then to enforce the distinction by means of condemning and confronting the latter group.

Toward the end of the *Kalimāt*, we encounter the text of what was likely, in origin, a separate epistle. In this much shorter second epistle, Ibn ʿAbd al-Wahhāb again makes the case that belief in righteous persons (*al-iʿtiqād fī ʾl-ṣāliḥīn*) is *shirk*, drawing on the examples of both Muḥammad and the Prophet Moses.[84] Here, however, his target is more specific, namely, certain early writers (*baʿḍ al-awwalīn al-muṣannifīn*) who committed *shirk* while being ignorant of their doing so. The example given is the Egyptian Ṣūfī Muḥammad ibn Saʿīd al-Būṣīrī (d. thirteenth century),[85] whose popular odes to the Prophet, according to Ibn ʿAbd al-Wahhāb, contain elements of greater polytheism (*al-shirk al-akbar*). As evidence he cites a line in al-Būṣīrī's poem *al-Burda* (The Cloak), in which the Ṣūfī writes: "O most noble of creation [i.e., the Prophet], none have I to seek refuge in / but you . . ." (*yā akram al-khalq mā lī man alūdhu bihi / siwāka . . .*). This kind of supplication (*duʿāʾ*) of the Prophet, Ibn ʿAbd al-Wahhāb writes, is a form of worship that must be directed to God alone.[86] The attack on al-Buṣīrī, while only a minor aspect of the *Kalimāt* epistle, was commonly invoked by Ibn ʿAbd al-Wahhāb's enemies as evidence of his heresy.[87]

Al-Qabbānī read and understood the *Kalimāt* epistle well. In his words, Ibn ʿAbd al-Wahhāb's principal targets were *istighātha* (calling on the dead for help) and *tawassul* (using the dead as a means to God). He summarizes the epistle as follows:

> What is in it is that *istighātha* and *tawassul* of the Prophet or a saint is major polytheism [*shirk akbar*]; that the polytheism of the unbelievers [at the time

83. *al-Durar al-saniyya*, 2:116–20.

84. al-Qabbānī, *Faṣl al-khiṭāb*, ff. 82a–b, 112b, 116b, 117a, 119a, 121a–b, 122a (= *al-Durar al-saniyya*, 2:111–12, with minor differences).

85. On him, see *EI*[3], s.v. "al-Būṣīrī" (Thomas Homerin).

86. al-Qabbānī, *Faṣl al-khiṭāb*, f. 82b (= *al-Durar al-saniyya*, 2:111).

87. See, e.g., al-Qabbānī, *Faṣl al-khiṭāb*, ff. 82a–112b; Traboulsi, "Early Refutation," 400–401 (quoting ʿAbd al-Wahhāb al-Ṭandatāwī); al-Ḥaddād, *Miṣbāḥ al-anām*, 63 (quoting ʿIsā ibn Muṭlaq); Ibn Gharīb, *al-Tawḍīḥ*, 2:742, 771–73 (quoting ʿAbdallāh al-Rāwī).

> of the Prophet] was less severe than it [i.e., the polytheism of today's unbelievers]; and that the believer who does not approve of *istighātha* yet fails to curse those who practice *istighātha*, and does not show them enmity, hate them, hate those who love them, and dissociate from them and from those prophets and saints they worship apart from God is not a believer.[88]

For al-Qabbānī, as for the other Shāfiʿī refuters, the practices of *istighātha* and *tawassul* were perfectly legitimate, being supported both by the *ḥadīth* and by reason.[89] Ibn ʿAbd al-Wahhāb, by targeting those who engage in *istighātha* and *tawassul*, was effectively pronouncing *takfīr* on the global Muslim community (*umma*). "The purpose of this epistle," al-Qabbānī writes, "is to demonstrate that this Muslim *umma* has associated [other beings] with God in manifest polytheism."[90] To be fair, in the *Kalimāt*, as in many of his epistles, Ibn ʿAbd al-Wahhāb does not plainly condemn the majority of professed Muslims as unbelievers. Rather, he speaks in general terms of polytheists (*mushrikūn*) and unbelievers (*kuffār*), not specifying exactly who is intended. But for al-Qabbānī, as for most of the refuters, Ibn ʿAbd al-Wahhāb's meaning was perfectly clear: he was dismissing the vast majority of Muslims as polytheists.

In some passages of *Faṣl al-khiṭāb*, al-Qabbānī ascribes Ibn ʿAbd al-Wahhāb's proclivity for *takfīr* to Satanic influence, as when he claims that "Satan the damned seduced him and whispered to him, 'You have been filled with knowledge and wisdom and are more knowledgeable of God than anyone in this age, and this Muḥammadan *umma* has disbelieved and strayed from the path of guidance, worshipping idols."[91] He also suggests that Ibn ʿAbd al-Wahhāb is reviving the teachings of Musaylima, the so-called false prophet of Najd who led a revolt against the first caliph of Islam during the "wars of apostasy" in the seventh century. At one point in his refutation, al-Qabbānī asks Ibn ʿAbd al-Wahhāb if he took his evidence for *takfīr* "from the remnants of the pages revealed to the lying Musaylima with you in the areas of al-Yamāma," al-Yamāma being a geographic designation roughly equivalent to Najd.[92]

88. al-Qabbānī, *Faṣl al-khiṭāb*, f. 4b.

89. On the reason-based argument used by al-Qabbānī and his Ashʿarī forebears, see Lav, "Ashʿarism, Causality, and the Cult of Saints." As Lav explains it, "[T]his Ashʿarī argument states that when a Muslim appeals to a deceased prophet or saint for aid (*istighātha*), the request is implicitly, and in truth, directed to Allāh, as He is the true agent (*fāʿil*) in the cosmos" (256).

90. al-Qabbānī, *Faṣl al-khiṭāb*, f. 25b.

91. Ibid., f. 54a.

92. Ibid., f. 55a–b.

These accusations, however, seem to have been leveled mainly for polemical effect. More often al-Qabbānī identified the source of Ibn ʿAbd al-Wahhāb's heretical views as twofold: (1) his willingness to engage in *ijtihād* and (2) his imitation of Ibn Taymiyya.

The term *ijtihād* refers to the use of independent reasoning to examine the foundational Islamic texts, the Qurʾān and the *ḥadīth*, for the purpose of issuing legal judgments. A practitioner of *ijtihād* is known as a *mujtahid*. By Ibn ʿAbd al-Wahhāb's time in the eighteenth century, the number of living *mujtahid*s in the Sunnī Islamic world was widely considered to be low. With the development of the four law schools in Sunnī Islam, the exercise of *ijtihād* by Muslim jurists had become increasingly restricted. Those who issued legal opinions, or *muftī*s, were typically required to adhere to the teachings of their *madhhab*, that is, to engage in *taqlīd*, a term sometimes translated as "imitation." The so-called gate of *ijtihād*, according to many jurists, had been closed, as modern-day scholars no longer possessed the level of religious knowledge of their forebears; only those scholars with supreme command of the texts of revelation and the juristic tradition were deemed qualified to exercise *ijtihād*, the rest being expected to practice *taqlīd* to one degree or another. Later jurists developed typologies of *muftī*s that distinguished different levels of *ijtihād*, the highest being unrestricted or absolute *ijtihād* (*al-ijtihād al-muṭlaq*), a status generally deemed no longer possible to attain.[93] As another anti-Wahhābī refuter, the Palestinian Ḥanbalī Muḥammad ibn Aḥmad al-Saffārīnī (d. 1188/1774), later put it, "[W]hosoever seeks to exercise *ijtihād* in these times . . . has sought the impossible" (*man rāma ʾl-ijtihād fī hādhihi ʾl-azmina . . . fa-qad rāma ʾl-muḥāl*).[94] He compared Ibn ʿAbd al-Wahhāb's purported claim of *ijtihād* to Musaylima's claim of prophecy.[95]

93. On these issues of *ijtihād*, see Vikør, *Between God and the Sultan*, 53–72, 151–61; Hallaq, "Iftaʾ and Ijtihad in Sunni Legal Theory"; Calder, "Al-Nawawī's Typology of *Muftīs*." For a typology of *muftī*s written by a Ḥanbalī contemporary of Ibn ʿAbd al-Wahhāb's in Syria, see al-Saffārīnī, *al-Ajwiba al-najdiyya*, 122–27.

94. al-Saffārīnī, *Jawāb*, 30. On al-Saffārīnī, see further below. Cf. the view of Muḥammad ibn Sulaymān al-Kurdī (d. 1194/1780), who in his refutation remarks similarly that any claim of *ijtihād* today veers toward the impossible (*daʿwā ʾl-ijtihād al-yawm fī ghāya min al-buʿd*) (al-Ḥaddād, *Miṣbāḥ al-anām*, 83). On al-Saffārīnī, who was born in Nablus, see al-Zabīdī, *al-Muʿjam al-mukhtaṣṣ*, 642–47; al-Ghazzī, *al-Naʿt al-akmal*, 301–6; al-Murādī, *Silk al-durar*, 4:31–34; Ibn Ḥumayd, *al-Suḥub al-wābila*, 2:839–46; al-Shaṭṭī, *Mukhtaṣar*, 127–30.

95. al-Saffārīnī, *Jawāb*, 27–28.

Al-Qabbānī, like many of the refuters, accused Ibn ʿAbd al-Wahhāb of purporting to exercise *ijtihād*, an accusation that the latter vehemently denied. In *Faṣl al-khiṭāb*, after summarizing the contents of Ibn ʿAbd al-Wahhāb's *Kalimāt* epistle, al-Qabbānī concludes by saying that "he determined this decisively and stated it absolutely, not confining himself to one of the *madhhabs* of the *imāms* [i.e., Abū Ḥanīfa, Mālik, al-Shāfiʿī, and Ibn Ḥanbal] and calling people therewith to worship God alone."[96] Later he remarks, addressing Ibn ʿAbd al-Wahhāb, "Your *ijtihād* led you to expel the entirety of this Muḥammadan *umma* from Islam."[97] In reality, Ibn ʿAbd al-Wahhāb did not claim the ability to exercise *ijtihād*. As he saw it, his project was about returning Islam to its theological core of *tawḥīd*, and thus the issue of *ijtihād* was irrelevant. His was a primarily theological project, not one about devising legal judgments. The accusation of *ijtihād* was nonetheless a common one leveled by his refuters, one that seems to have been based in the perception of Ibn ʿAbd al-Wahhāb as someone defying the established structures of religious authority of his day. Like a *mujtahid*, Ibn ʿAbd al-Wahhāb appealed directly to the foundational Islamic texts, but he did so as a revolutionary reformer concerned with reestablishing the foundations of the religion, not as a *mujtahid* devising legal judgments and operating within a system that he respected.

The second alleged source of Ibn ʿAbd al-Wahhāb's heretical views, according to al-Qabbānī, was Ibn Taymiyya. Indeed, a major theme of al-Qabbānī's refutation is that the Najdī preacher had taken his ideas regarding *istighātha* and *tawassul* from Ibn Taymiyya, in so doing engaging in "reprehensible emulation" (*al-taqlīd al-radīʾ*) of the earlier scholar.[98] Addressing Ibn ʿAbd al-Wahhāb, he writes: "It is absolutely clear that you have emulated Ibn Taymiyya in what the most distinguished scholars have counted among his faults and his fictions [*hafawātihi wa-khurāfātihi*]. You have followed him in this abominable doctrine of his [*maqālatihi ʾl-shanīʿa*] that the scholars of Islam declared to be unspeakable."[99] By his "abominable doctrine," al-Qabbānī meant Ibn Taymiyya's position on the cult of saints. The *Kalimāt* epistle even appeared to al-Qabbānī to be something of a Taymiyyan plagiarism. "Know that this epistle," he writes in the introduction of *Faṣl al-khiṭāb*,

96. al-Qabbānī, *Faṣl al-khiṭāb*, f. 4b.

97. Ibid., f. 56a.

98. Ibid., f. 52b.

99. Ibid.

> is taken [*ma ʾkhūdha*] from the words of the scholar Taqī al-Dīn Ibn Taymiyya al-Ḥarrānī. When I was starting this commentary, I came across a work of his on this [i.e., *istighātha* and *tawassul*] that was a response to a question about seeking the help of one buried in a grave and about one who makes votive offerings to mosques, shrines, and scholars . . . and I saw that this epistle was taken from its words and its proofs [*ma ʾkhūdha min kalāmihā wa-min adillatihā*].[100]

Contrary to al-Qabbānī's claim, the *Kalimāt* was not lifted from any one work of Ibn Taymiyya's. As will be seen, however, it was derivative of Ibn Taymiyya's ideas. What is important to grasp here is that one of Ibn ʿAbd al-Wahhāb's earliest refuters took notice of Ibn ʿAbd al-Wahhāb's reliance on Ibn Taymiyya and found it to be utterly reprehensible. For al-Qabbānī, as for many other early refuters, Ibn Taymiyya's views regarding the cult of saints were anathema, and Ibn ʿAbd al-Wahhāb was clearly reviving them.

While al-Qabbānī's *Faṣl al-khiṭāb* is the earliest extant refutation that is dated, it is not the first refutation of Ibn ʿAbd al-Wahhāb to have been written. This fact is revealed by al-Qabbānī himself, who in *Faṣl al-khiṭāb* refers to an earlier refutation by an unidentified scholar in al-Aḥsāʾ that he has been unable to obtain. He writes that Ibn ʿAbd al-Wahhāb had begun sending epistles to distant lands (*arsala ilā ʾl-buldān al-baʿīda*) calling on people to worship God alone and that a man from al-Aḥsāʾ had responded with a refutation: "He sent an epistle to al-Aḥsāʾ, an epistle to Basra, and an epistle to al-Shām. A number of trustworthy persons informed me that one of the distinguished scholars of al-Aḥsāʾ [*baʿḍ fuḍalāʾ al-Aḥsāʾ*] undertook to refute his epistle. However, I have not come across that epistle or that refutation."[101] While there were several scholars in al-Aḥsāʾ who refuted Ibn ʿAbd al-Wahhāb around this time, including the Ḥanbalī ʿAbdallāh ibn Fayrūz,[102] the Shāfiʿī ʿAbdallāh ibn ʿAbd al-Laṭīf,[103] and the

100. Ibid., f. 23a–b.

101. Ibid., f. 54a–b.

102. See the fragment in Ibn Dāwūd, *al-Ṣawāʿiq wa ʾl-ruʿūd*, ff. 196b–98a. On ʿAbdallāh ibn Fayrūz, see Ibn Ḥumayd, *al-Suḥub al-wābila*, 3:652–53; Āl Bassām, *ʿUlamāʾ Najd*, 4:487–89.

103. See the response to his refutation by Ibn ʿAbd al-Wahhāb in Ibn Ghannām, *Tārīkh*, 1:246–62. According to al-Ḥaddād (*Miṣbāḥ al-anām*, 70), the refutation was known as *Tajrīd sayf al-jihād li-muddaʿī ʾl-ijtihād* (Unsheathing the Sword of *Jihād* Against the Claimant of

Mālikī ʿĪsā ibn Muṭlaq (d. 1198/1783f),[104] the most well known of these refuters in al-Aḥsāʾ was the Ḥanbalī Muḥammad ibn ʿAfāliq (d. 1163/1750). It is likely that al-Qabbānī was referring to a refutation by Ibn ʿAfāliq known as *Tahakkum al-muqallidīn fī muddaʿī tajdīd al-dīn* (The Emulators' Ridicule of the One Claiming to Renew the Religion), which circulated widely and would be quoted in many of the subsequent refutations.

Ibn ʿAfāliq, who was mentioned above as one of Ibn ʿAbd al-Wahhāb's alleged teachers, is depicted in the biographical sources as the preeminent Ḥanbalī scholar of eastern Arabia, a man whose knowledge spanned a number of fields, including jurisprudence, grammar, poetry, rhetoric, logic, mathematics, and astronomy.[105] As his refutation shows, he had nothing but contempt for the Najdī reformer, whom he saw as a rabble-rouser and an imposter of a scholar. Ibn ʿAfāliq's *Tahakkum al-muqallidīn*, a version of which survives in a manuscript in Germany, takes the form of a letter to Ibn ʿAbd al-Wahhāb, though one clearly intended for a wider readership.[106] Like al-Qabbānī's *Faṣl al-khiṭāb*, it was written in response to a Wahhābī epistle. Ibn ʿAfāliq states at the beginning that "your filthy principles" (*qawāʿiduka ʾl-khabītha*) arrived "in two leaves" (*fī waraqatayn*) written "in your own handwriting" (*bi-khaṭṭ yadika*).[107] This was a reference to an epistle by Ibn ʿAbd al-Wahhāb that is a statement of four principles (*qawāʿid*; sing. *qāʿida*) for arriving at legal judgments (*aḥkām*; sing. *ḥukm*), an epistle that can be identified as Ibn ʿAfāliq quotes from it.[108] The Wahhābī tradition preserves this epistle under the title

Ijtihād). On Ibn ʿAbd al-Laṭīf, see Ibn Sanad, *Sabāʾik al-ʿasjad*, 291–92; al-Nuwayṣir, *al-Muʿāraḍa*, 208–23; al-ʿUṣfūr, *Fatāwā ʿulamāʾ al-Aḥsāʾ*, 2:499n2.

104. See the fragment and summary of his refutation in al-Ḥaddād, *Miṣbāḥ al-anām*, 62–63. On Ibn Muṭlaq, see Āl ʿAbd al-Qādir, *Tuḥfat al-mustafīd*, 2:629–31; al-ʿUṣfūr, *Fatāwā ʿulamāʾ al-Aḥsāʾ*, 2:520n1.

105. On him, see Ibn Fayrūz, *Tarājim mā kāna fī jihat al-Aḥsāʾ min ʿulamāʾ al-Ḥanābila*, ff. 77a–78a; Ibn Sanad, *Sabāʾik al-ʿasjad*, 292; Ibn Ḥumayd, *al-Suḥub al-wābila*, 3:927–28; Āl Bassām, *ʿUlamāʾ Najd*, 6:38–43; al-Nuwayṣir, *al-Muʿāraḍa*, 189–207. I have used the death date given by Ibn Fayrūz, as he was a student of Ibn ʿAfāliq's and his biography is the earliest.

106. Ibn ʿAfāliq, *Tahakkum al-muqallidīn*; on this manuscript, see Weisweiler, *Verzeichnis der arabischen Handschriften*, 104. I am grateful to Michael Crawford for sharing his photocopy with me. Parts of *Tahakkum al-muqallidīn* are quoted in later refutations, indicating that it enjoyed a wide circulation; see Ibn Dāwūd, *al-Ṣawāʿiq wa ʾl-ruʿūd*, ff. 119b–21a; al-Ḥaddād, *Miṣbāḥ al-anām*, 3, 85.

107. Ibn ʿAfāliq, *Tahakkum al-muqallidīn*, ff. 50b, 49b.

108. Compare Ibn ʿAbd al-Wahhāb, *Muʾallafāt al-shaykh*, 2:2:4, 5–6, and Ibn ʿAfāliq, *Tahakkum al-muqallidīn*, ff. 47b, 43a, respectively. A slightly different version of the epistle is found, broken up into two pieces, in *al-Durar al-saniyya*, 4:5–7, 135–39.

Arbaʿ qawāʿid tadūru ʾl-aḥkām ʿalayhā (Four Principles on Which Legal Judgments Are Based), a title derived from its opening lines: "These are four principles of the religion on which legal judgments are based" (*hādhihi arbaʿ qawāʿid min qawāʿid al-dīn allatī tadūru ʾl-aḥkām ʿalayhā*).[109]

Unlike the *Kalimāt* epistle, the *Arbaʿ qawāʿid tadūru ʾl-aḥkām ʿalayhā* is not concerned with issues of *tawḥīd* and *shirk* but, rather, with the field of Islamic jurisprudence, or *fiqh*. Presumably, its intended audience was not the masses but jurists and other scholars operating within the *fiqh* tradition, a tradition that Ibn ʿAbd al-Wahhāb regarded as corrupt. The four principles that he enumerates, each of which is derived from the Qurʾān, are as follows: (1) the prohibition against speaking concerning God without knowledge; (2) the presumption that things are permissible when God is silent about them; (3) the inadmissibility of ambiguous proof texts; and (4) the reality that, as the Prophet said, there are certain ambiguous matters (*umūr mushtabihāt*) between the permitted and the forbidden.[110] What Ibn ʿAbd al-Wahhāb means to say with these principles is that the scholars of *fiqh* have developed an elaborate system for arriving at religious judgments that has no basis in the foundational Islamic texts and that if one were to follow his principles, one would discover that much of what is in the books of *fiqh* is unfounded. He gives the example of the legal maxim that water, in the context of ablution, is of three types, "purifying, pure, and impure" (*ṭahūr wa-ṭāhir wa-najis*), a typology commonly found at the beginning of legal manuals.[111] According to Ibn ʿAbd al-Wahhāb, this typology is derived from ambiguous proofs and thus should be rejected. To those scholars who accept it as valid, he says: "You have fallen upon the path of the people of perversion [*ṭarīq ahl al-zaygh*] in eschewing the unambiguous and following the ambiguous [*tark al-muḥkam wa ʾttibāʿ al-mutashābih*]."[112] In a strikingly bold statement, he asserts that his four principles should be applied to legal manuals between the chapters of purification (*ṭahāra*) and acknowledgment (*iqrār*), these being the first and last chapters of the most popular Ḥanbalī legal manual in Arabia in the mid–eighteenth century, Mūsā al-Ḥajjāwī's (d. 968/1560) *al-Iqnāʿ li-ṭālib al-intifāʿ*.[113] The implicit accusation is that legal manuals like *al-Iqnāʿ* are shot through with unfounded formulations and judgments. In the *Arbaʿ qawāʿid tadūru ʾl-aḥkām*

109. Ibn ʿAbd al-Wahhāb, *Muʾallafāt al-shaykh*, 2:2:3–10.

110. Ibid., 2:2:3–4.

111. Ibid., 2:2:5.

112. Ibid., 2:2:6.

113. Ibid., 2:2:10; al-Ḥajjāwī, *al-Iqnāʿ*.

ʿalayhā, then, Ibn ʿAbd al-Wahhāb is calling for a comprehensive reassessment, and possibly even abandonment, of the books of *fiqh*—an extraordinary proposal for a scholar of his time.

This was the brazenness to which Ibn ʿAfāliq was responding in his *Tahakkum al-muqallidīn*. Naturally, as a senior scholar and representative of the juristic tradition, he did not take kindly to Ibn ʿAbd al-Wahhāb's principles. The aim of this epistle, as he saw it, was to discredit the scholars (*al-ṭaʿn fī ʾl-ʿulamāʾ*) and the institutions of learning that they had developed over centuries.[114] Ibn ʿAbd al-Wahhāb, he says, is speaking before the masses in the voice of *ijtihād* and deigning to draw conclusions directly from the foundational Islamic texts (*istinbāṭ*), when he is completely and utterly unqualified for such a task.[115] "Are you not ashamed," he asks Ibn ʿAbd al-Wahhāb, "to be claiming to renew the religion"?[116] Not only does he not meet the qualifications of *ijtihād*, asserts Ibn ʿAfāliq, but he has shunned the entire system of Islamic religious education: "This man does not say, 'so-and-so related *ḥadīth*s to me' . . . or 'I studied [texts] by audition and I studied *fiqh* with so-and-so,' and 'I studied [texts] by reading with so-and-so.' He has no chain of transmission and no teachers [*lā sanada lahu wa-lā mashyakha*]."[117] Ibn ʿAbd al-Wahhāb, according to Ibn ʿAfāliq, has located all religious knowledge in himself, requiring every intended student of religion, or seeker of truth (*ṭālib al-ḥaqq*), to emigrate to his land (*al-hijra ilayka*).[118] Hoping to expose him as a fraud, Ibn ʿAfāliq proceeds to ask Ibn ʿAbd al-Wahhāb a series of advanced questions about the different branches of religious knowledge, demanding that the Najdī respond in ten volumes (*fī ʿasharat mujalladāt*), as anyone capable of *ijtihād* could surely do, and calling on his supporters to force him to respond within one year.[119] No such response, of course, was forthcoming.

In the developing confrontation between Ibn ʿAbd al-Wahhāb and his opponents, the *Arbaʿ qawāʿid tadūru ʾl-aḥkām ʿalayhā* would attract only minimal attention, though the accusation that Ibn ʿAbd al-Wahhāb condemned the books of *fiqh* and the threefold typology of water would occasionally

114. Ibn ʿAfāliq, *Tahakkum al-muqallidīn*, f. 43a.

115. Ibid., f. 42a.

116. Ibid., f. 45a.

117. Ibid., ff. 49b, 42b.

118. Ibid., f. 49b.

119. Ibid., ff. 43b–49b, 51a–b.

recur.[120] The epistle appears to reflect an early preoccupation of Ibn ʿAbd al-Wahhāb's with the way scholars approached *fiqh*. The critique of *fiqh*, however, was not a prominent feature of Ibn ʿAbd al-Wahhāb's missionary efforts, and indeed he does not appear very hostile to it in some of his other works. It may well be that he assailed the *fiqh* tradition only at the beginning of his movement, later confining his message to matters of creed. Unlike matters of *fiqh*, the issues of *tawḥīd* and *shirk* concern the fundamentals of belief, falling under the rubric of creed or theology (*ʿaqīda, iʿtiqād, uṣūl al-dīn*). Remarkably, in the *Arbaʿ qawāʿid tadūru ʾl-aḥkām ʿalayhā*, these creedal issues are not even discussed.

Ibn ʿAfāliq, however, shows some familiarity in *Tahakkum al-muqallidīn* with Ibn ʿAbd al-Wahhāb's creedal focus. In a brief comment toward the end of his refutation, he criticizes Ibn ʿAbd al-Wahhāb for using a line of Ibn Taymiyya's to the effect that those who supplicate the dead have disbelieved. The line attributed to Ibn Taymiyya is found in al-Ḥajjāwī's *al-Iqnāʿ*, the Ḥanbalī legal manual. Al-Ḥajjāwī has it as follows, in a section devoted to the acts and beliefs that cause one to apostatize (*bāb ḥukm al-murtadd*): "[Whosoever] sets up intermediaries between himself and God, relying on them, calling on them, and asking [things] of them [has disbelieved] as a matter of consensus."[121] Ibn ʿAfāliq does not explicitly say to what end Ibn ʿAbd al-Wahhāb is using this line, but one can infer that it is to pronounce *takfīr* on those who set up intermediaries (*wasāʾiṭ*) between themselves and God in the way described. It is wrong to follow this opinion, says Ibn ʿAfāliq, as it was a minority one that got Ibn Taymiyya into a great deal of trouble in his day. He describes it as "an opinion unique to Ibn Taymiyya [*min al-masāʾil allatī infarada bihā*] and [one] for which he was tried and imprisoned and subject to the fierce opposition of the scholars of his time and those who came after."[122]

Like the Shāfiʿī al-Qabbānī, the Ḥanbalī Ibn ʿAfāliq was accusing Ibn ʿAbd al-Wahhāb both of *ijtihād* and of unwarranted reliance on Ibn Taymiyya. As will be seen, it was very unusual for a Ḥanbalī refuter to criticize Ibn Taymiyya in this way. It was more common for Ḥanbalīs to downplay the severity of Ibn Taymiyya's views, seeking to rescue him from association with

120. See Ibn Dāwūd, *al-Ṣawāʿiq wa ʾl-ruʿūd*, f. 82a (quoting Ibn al-Ṭayyib al-Maghribī); al-Saffārīnī, *Jawāb*, 23.

121. al-Ḥajjāwī, *al-Iqnāʿ*, 4:285.

122. Ibn ʿAfāliq, *Tahakkum al-muqallidīn*, f. 52a.

Wahhābism. This was the approach that Ibn ʿAfāliq, in his later refutations, would follow.

Ibn ʿAbd al-Wahhāb was concerned with winning converts both among the lay townspeople in Najd and in the local scholarly community, but he was much more successful with the former. The local scholars in Najd were known as *maṭāwiʿa* (sing. *muṭawwaʿ*), a term related to the verb *ṭawwaʿa*, "to compel obedience." As Michael Cook has observed, "The *muṭawwaʿ* of a town was, it seems, the *imām* of its mosque, and at the same time the local scholar and religious leader."[123] Some of the *maṭāwiʿ* in Najd were receptive to Ibn ʿAbd al-Wahhāb's preaching early on, but these appear to have backpedaled.[124] Most of them were quite hostile to his movement, seeing it as a profound threat to their authority as scholars, and as the movement spread they began to look for outside help. Writing to the scholarly communities outside Najd, they sought their support in discrediting the controversial preacher.

An early response to these efforts was a refutation by an Egyptian named ʿAbd al-Wahhāb ibn Aḥmad al-Ṭandatāwī (d. 1156/1743), a scholar living in Mecca whose roots lay in the town of Ṭanṭā in the Nile Delta. Al-Ṭandatāwī, a Shāfiʿī, studied at al-Azhar and was a Ṣūfī of the Aḥmadī order.[125] The only known copy of his refutation is held at Princeton University and was made by none other than al-Qabbānī.[126] Titled *Kitāb radʿ al-ḍalāla wa-qamʿ al-jahāla* (The Book of the Prevention of Error and the Suppression of Ignorance), it is a short work followed by the encomia (*taqrīẓāt*) of ten other scholars in Mecca. Al-Ṭandatāwī completed it on 6 Muḥarram 1156/March 2, 1743,[127] just two and a half months after al-Qabbānī finished his *Faṣl al-khiṭāb*. The schol-

123. Cook, "Expansion of the First Saudi State," 672. The word appears to be a vernacular corruption of *muṭawwiʿ*, meaning "one who compels obedience," or *mutaṭawwiʿ*, meaning "one who does good in obedience."

124. Āl Bassām, *ʿUlamāʾ Najd*, 5:339–40.

125. See Traboulsi, "Early Refutation," 380. And for further biographical information, including his death date, see Abū ʾl-Khayr, *al-Mukhtaṣar min Kitāb nashr al-nawr waʾl-zahr*, 333–34; al-Qaṭṭān, *Tanzīl al-raḥamāt ʿalā man māt*, 268. On this manuscript, see Muṭīʿ al-Raḥmān and ʿĪd, *al-Fihris al-mukhtaṣar*, 3:1103 (no. 3973).

126. See the edition in Traboulsi, "Early Refutation."

127. Ibid., 405.

arly opposition to Ibn ʿAbd al-Wahhāb was thus beginning to take form nearly simultaneously in al-Aḥsāʾ, southern Iraq, and the Ḥijāz.

Unlike al-Qabbānī and Ibn ʿAfāliq, al-Ṭandatāwī avoids mentioning Ibn ʿAbd al-Wahhāb by name. Also unlike them, his refutation was not in response to one of Ibn ʿAbd al-Wahhāb's epistles. Rather, as he writes at the beginning of *Kitāb radʿ al-ḍalāla,* he learned of the unnamed man's many heresies from written reports (*khuṭūṭ*) by the scholars of Najd that reached him in Mecca. In these reports, he explains, he learned of a person who pronounces *takfīr* on holy men, including ʿAbd al-Qādir al-Jīlānī, as well as their devotees; prohibits people from practicing *tawassul* of the Prophet, his Companions, and his family members; reprimands people for visiting the Companions of the Prophet buried in al-Jubayla; and opposes the *taqlīd* of the great scholars of previous generations, instructing everyone to draw directly from the Qurʾān and the *ḥadīth.*[128] Al-Ṭandatāwī devotes much of his short refutation to defending *taqlīd* and *ziyāra* and to reproaching Ibn ʿAbd al-Wahhāb for pronouncing *takfīr* on the *umma.* He appears to be the first anti-Wahhābī scholar to argue that the Muslim community cannot have fallen into unbelief, on account of the *ḥadīth* that says: "My community will not agree on an error" (*inna ummatī lā tajtajmiʿu ʿalā ḍalāla*).[129] Later on, al-Ṭandatāwī calls for action to be taken against Ibn ʿAbd al-Wahhāb to stop him from spreading his heresies further. "It is incumbent on those Muslim rulers [*wulāt al-Islām*] who are capable of doing so," he writes, "to restrain him and hinder him till he repents of his horrific acts."[130] Some of the authors of the encomia would go even further in their calls for action.

One of them, the Ḥanafī Amīn ibn Ḥasan al-Mīrghanī (d. 1161/1748), writes that if Ibn ʿAbd al-Wahhāb is insane (*in kāna majnūnan*), then he should be detained and isolated, but "if he is of sound mind, then he is an unbelieving heretic [*kāfir zindīq*] whose killing is a duty for all who are capable of getting hold of him."[131] The author of another encomium, a Ḥanafī named Asʿad ibn ʿAbdallāh al-ʿAtāqī (d. 1169/1755f), states that if Ibn ʿAbd al-Wahhāb is insane (*in kāna bihi junūn*), then "he should be imprisoned, beaten, and treated with

128. Ibid., 391–92.

129. Ibid., 393, 402. For the *ḥadīth,* see Ibn Mājah, *Sunan,* 2:1303 (*Kitāb al-fitan, bāb al-sawād al-aʿẓam,* no. 3950). Cf. Ibn Ḥanbal, *Musnad,* 45:200 (*ḥadīth Abī Baṣra al-Ghifārī,* no. 27224); al-Tirmidhī, *Sunan,* 4:466 (*Kitāb al-fitan, bāb mā jāʾa fī luzūm al-jamāʿa,* no. 2167); Abū Dāwūd al-Sijistānī, *Sunan,* 4:98 (*Kitāb al-fitan, dhikr al-fitan wa-dalāʾilihā,* no. 4253).

130. Traboulsi, "Early Refutation," 401.

131. Ibid., 409. On al-Mīrghanī, see Abū ʾl-Khayr, *al-Mukhtaṣar,* 134–35.

medication for insanity"; but if he is not insane, and if he refuses to repent, then "it has become clear that he is a misled misleader [*ḍāll muḍill*] who should be killed after being publicly denounced so as to deter the likes of him. . . . If my hands could reach him I would kill him myself."[132] Such was the reaction among the scholars in Mecca to the reports being sent by the scholars in Najd. A few years later, in late Muḥarram 1158/late February 1745, the Moroccan-born Muḥammad ibn al-Ṭayyib al-Maghribī (d. 1170/1756f), a Mālikī scholar in Medina, would react similarly to a report that came his way, declaring that "*jihād* against this sinner, and taking action to kill him and relieve all people of his error, are a duty incumbent on all who are able without delay."[133]

The author of some of these reports being sent to the Ḥijāz and elsewhere was a man named Sulaymān ibn Suḥaym (d. 1181/1767f), the *muṭawwaʿ* of Riyadh and one of Ibn ʿAbd al-Wahhāb's most vocal opponents in Najd.[134] In surviving correspondence between the two men, Ibn ʿAbd al-Wahhāb accuses Ibn Suḥaym of complaining to the Ḥijāz about his activities (*wa-tashkūnā ʿind ahl al-Ḥaramayn*), which indicates that Ibn Suḥaym may have been behind the anti-Wahhābī reports that reached al-Ṭandatāwī in Mecca or Ibn al-Ṭayyib in Medina.[135] We can be sure that Ibn Suḥaym was the author of some such reports, if not these exact ones, as Ibn Ghannām preserves a short epistle by him that was sent to Basra and al-Aḥsāʾ.[136]

Ibn Suḥaym's epistle is addressed to all Muslim scholars who come across it (*ilā man yaṣilu ilayhi min ʿulamāʾ al-Muslimīn*), and its stated purpose is to apprise them of the worsening situation in Najd and to elicit written responses. The bulk of the epistle consists of a list of fifteen of Ibn ʿAbd al-Wahhāb's alleged innovations and errors (*min bidaʿihi wa-ḍalālātihi*), which may be summarized as follows:

1. He has destroyed the tombs in al-Jubayla, including that of Zayd ibn al-Khaṭṭāb, as well as a mosque there.

132. Traboulsi, "Early Refutation," 411–12. On al-ʿAtāqī, see Abū ʾl-Khayr, *al-Mukhtaṣar*, 309.

133. Ibn Dāwūd, *al-Ṣawāʿiq wa ʾl-ruʿūd*, f. 82a. On Ibn al-Ṭayyib, see al-Murādī, *Silk al-durar*, 4:91–94.

134. On him, see Āl Bassām, *ʿUlamāʾ Najd*, 2:381–82; al-ʿUthaymīn, *Buḥūth wa-taʿlīqāt fī tārīkh al-Mamlaka al-ʿArabiyya al-Suʿūdiyya*, 91–113 ("Mawqif Sulaymān ibn Suḥaym").

135. Ibn Ghannām, *Tārīkh*, 1:391.

136. Ibid., 1:344–47. For an analysis and partial translation of this epistle in English, see al-ʿUthaymīn, *Muḥammad ibn ʿAbd al-Wahhāb*, 45–46; for an analysis and partial translation in German, see Peskes, *Muḥammad b. ʿAbdalwahhāb*, 70–75.

2. He has burned the Ṣūfī books *Dalāʾil al-khayrāt* and *Rawḍ al-rayāḥīn*.[137]
3. He has said that he would destroy the Prophet's chamber in Medina (*ḥujrat al-rasūl*), where the Prophet, Abū Bakr, and ʿUmar are said to be buried, and replace the gilt waterspout (*mīzāb*) of the Kaʿba with a wooden one.
4. He has said that Muslims have ceased to be Muslims for six hundred years (*al-nās min sitt miʾat sana laysū ʿalā shayʾ*).
5. He has pronounced *takfīr* on those who do not agree with everything that he says (*man lam yuwāfiqhu fī kull mā qāla*).
6. He has written an epistle to us saying that none of his teachers possessed his understanding of the religion.
7. He has pronounced *takfīr* on Ibn al-Fāriḍ and Ibn ʿArabī, two well-known Ṣūfī scholars of the thirteenth century.
8. He has pronounced *takfīr* on the descendants of the Prophet among us (*al-sāda ʿindanā min āl al-rasūl*) on account of their accepting vows (*li-ajl annahum yaʾkhūdhūna ʾl-nadhr*).
9. He has said, against the view that "difference among the *imāms* is a mercy" (*ikhtilāf al-aʾimma raḥma*), that "difference among them is an abomination" (*ikhtilāfuhum naqma*).
10. He has deemed pious endowments to be corrupt (*yaqṭaʿu bi-fasād al-waqf*).
11. He has declared it wrong to pay someone to perform the *ḥajj* on another's behalf (*ibṭāl al-juʿāla ʿalā ʾl-ḥajj*).
12. He has ceased praising the caliph (*taraka tamjīd al-sulṭān*) during the prayer and has called him a sinner (*fāsiq*).
13. He has said that saying prayers for the Prophet (*al-ṣalāt ʿalā rasūl Allāh*) on Fridays at day and at night is an innovation and an error.
14. He has said that the payment taken by judges (*quḍāt*) to resolve disputes is bribery (*rishwa*).
15. He has pronounced *takfīr* on those who say things to ward off the evil of the *jinn* (*dafʿ sharr al-jinn*) in the course of ritual slaughter.

137. *Dalāʾil al-khayrāt* (The Proofs of Good Deeds) is a collection of prayers for the Prophet by the North African Ṣūfī Muḥammad al-Jazūlī (d. ca. 869/1465); *Rawḍ al-rayāḥīn* (The Garden of Sweet Fragrances) is a collection of traditions about Muslim saints by the Yemeni mystic ʿAbdallāh al-Yāfiʿī (d. 768/1367).

Ibn Suḥaym laments that "many of the people of our land have been seduced by him" (*iftatana bihi nās kathīr min ahl quṭrinā*) and ends by calling on those who have received the epistle to respond by expressing their outrage at the heretical preacher, noting that a response is binding on them (*al-jawāb muta ʿayyin*).[138]

Ibn Suḥaym's epistle appears to have achieved a wide circulation, as Ibn ʿAbd al-Wahhāb is found complaining about it in his correspondence. In a letter to the people of al-Qaṣīm, for instance, he notes that some of the scholars there have read it and accepted its claims as true (*qabalahā wa-ṣaddaqahā ba ʿḍ al-muntamīn lil- ʿilm*), and he proceeds to refute some of the accusations. Here he denies having said that Muslims have not really been so for six hundred years, that he said difference among the scholars is an abomination, and that he would destroy the Prophet's chamber and replace the Kaʿba's waterspout; and he denies having burned the books *Dalā ʾil al-khayrāt* and *Rawḍ al-rayāḥīn* or having excommunicated Ibn ʿArabī and Ibn al-Fāriḍ. He even disputes certain points not made by Ibn Suḥaym in the epistle, such as that he claims *ijtihād* and opposes *taqlīd* and considers the books of the four law schools to be worthless.[139] Ibn ʿAbd al-Wahhāb then turns to the charges that he does not dispute. "As for the other matters," he says,

> which are that I say a person's Islam is not complete until he knows the meaning of "there is no god but God"; that I provide instruction in its meaning to those who come to me; that I pronounce *takfīr* on those who make vows [to holy men] if by the vow they seek nearness to something other than God and make the vow for that purpose; [and that I say] that making ritual sacrifice to something other than God is an act of unbelief and that meat so slaughtered is unlawful—these matters are true.[140]

138. Ibn Ghannām, *Tārīkh*, 1:347.

139. *al-Durar al-saniyya*, 1:33–35. Despite what he says here, Ibn ʿAbd al-Wahhāb declares in one of his *fatwās* that those who follow the path (*madhhab*) of Ibn ʿArabī and Ibn al-Fāriḍ are unbelievers, which would suggest that he considered them to be unbelievers as well (Ibn Ghannām, *Tārīkh*, 1:468). In an epistle dedicated to the endowments issue, he explains that he prohibits not endowments in general but what he calls endowments of wrong and iniquity (*waqf al-janaf wa ʾl-ithm*), meaning those set up for the purpose of bypassing inheritance law, i.e., an endowment used to bequeath certain amounts to one's offspring (Ibn Ghannām, *Tārīkh*, 1:364–73).

140. *al-Durar al-saniyya*, 1:34–35. For a similarly worded response to Ibn Suḥaym's accusations, see Ibn Ghannām, *Tārīkh*, 1:348–49 (letter to ʿAbdallāh ibn Suḥaym).

With these words, Ibn ʿAbd al-Wahhāb seems to be trying to downplay the severity of his doctrine, making his use of *takfīr* appear more measured than his opponents claim. He does acknowledge, however, that he is propagating a doctrine of strict *tawḥīd* that requires *takfīr* of certain persons whose acts contravene God's oneness.

Further evidence that Ibn Suḥaym's epistle achieved a wide circulation is furnished by a contemporary source in Basra, al-Qabbānī, who discusses the epistle in a second refutation of Wahhābism. This second refutation, titled *Kashf al-ḥijāb ʿan wajh ḍalālāt Ibn ʿAbd al-Wahhāb* (Lifting the Veil from the Face of the Errors of Ibn ʿAbd al-Wahhāb), was completed in late Rajab 1157/ early September 1744.[141] While mainly an abridgment of his earlier refutation, *Kashf al-ḥijāb* concludes with an additional section devoted to Ibn Suḥaym's epistle. Al-Qabbānī explains at the beginning of his work that he composed the abridgment in response to an appeal by a scholar from Najd (*suʾāl min baʿḍ ʿulamāʾ Najd*), who complained that Ibn ʿAbd al-Wahhāb was distorting the religion and leading the local Muslim community astray.[142] Then, after completing the first draft of *Kashf al-ḥijāb*, al-Qabbānī received another written request from a scholar in Najd. This second appeal was Ibn Suḥaym's epistle, which al-Qabbānī says arrived sometime in 1157/1744f.[143] In the final section of *Kashf al-ḥijāb* he reproduces the epistle in full, together with his own commentary thereon.[144] Given the date of al-Qabbānī's second refutation, we can be sure that Ibn Suḥaym's epistle was written no later than Rajab 1157/ September 1744.

We can also be sure that one of Ibn ʿAbd al-Wahhāb's epistles was written no later than this date, as there is a clear and obvious reference to it in Ibn Suḥaym's epistle. In two places in his epistle, Ibn Suḥaym refers to an epistle

141. al-Qabbānī, *Kashf al-ḥijāb*, f. 298b. On this manuscript, see *Fihrist-i kutubi-i ʿArabī*, 3:538–39; Brockelmann, *Geschichte der arabischen Litteratur*, SII, 532. Al-Qabbānī does not internally title the refutation, but he notes the title in his third refutation (*Naqḍ qawāʿid al-ḍalāl*, f. 42a). Another copy of *Kashf al-ḥijāb*, which I have not consulted, is available in Cairo; see *Fihris al-Khizāna al-Taymūriyya*, 4:112. The fact that *Kashf al-ḥijāb* is not internally titled has led to some confusion. Both catalogs (*Fihrist-i kutubi-i ʿArabī* and Brockelmann) mistake their copy of *Kashf al-ḥijāb* for *Faṣl al-khiṭāb*; Āl ʿAbd al-Laṭīf likewise mistakes his photocopy of *Kashf al-ḥijāb* for *Faṣl al-khiṭāb* (*Daʿāwā ʾl-munāwiʾīn*, 44).

142. al-Qabbānī, *Kashf al-ḥijāb*, f. 4a.

143. Ibid.

144. Ibid., ff. 188b–297b. The differences between Ibn Ghannām's version of the epistle and al-Qabbānī's version are minimal.

by Ibn ʿAbd al-Wahhāb in which the Najdī reformer claimed that none of his teachers possessed his understanding of the religion. In one of these Ibn Suḥaym writes:

> He sent to our lands an epistle by his own hand, with one of his missionaries, in which he swore that this knowledge of his was not known to any of his teachers [*anna ʿilmahu hādhā lam yaʿrifhu mashāyikhuhu*], by whom he claims to affiliate with learning—so he has no teachers!—and that his father did not know it, nor the people of al-ʿĀriḍ. How strange then! If he did not learn it from teachers, and neither his father nor the people of his country knew it, then where does his knowledge come from? Where did he get it? Was it divinely revealed to him, did he see it in a dream, or did Satan teach it to him? All the people of al-ʿĀriḍ saw what he swore.[145]

This forms the sixth of Ibn Suḥaym's fifteen charges against Ibn ʿAbd al-Wahhāb. The same epistle is also mentioned briefly in his fourth charge, which is that Ibn ʿAbd al-Wahhāb said that Muslims had ceased to be Muslims for six hundred years. "The confirmation of this," Ibn Suḥaym writes, "is that he sent me an epistle in which he says, 'Affirm that before me you (pl.) were ignorant and wayward.'"[146] The six hundred years charge notwithstanding, Ibn Suḥaym's description of Ibn ʿAbd al-Wahhāb's epistle is largely accurate.

The missive in question is preserved in Ibn Ghannām's history, where it is described as an epistle to the people of Riyadh and Manfūḥa.[147] As the *muṭawwaʿ* of Riyadh, Ibn Suḥaym would have been one of the first to receive it. The epistle is similar in content to the *Kalimāt fī bayān shahādat an lā ilāha illā ʾllāh*. In it Ibn ʿAbd al-Wahhāb condemns the saints in al-Kharj as *ṭawāghīt*, describing them as "unbelievers and apostates from Islam" (*kuffār murtaddūn ʿan al-Islām*), and he asserts that one's Islam is not sound unless one dissociates from them and pronounces *takfīr* on them (*illā bi ʾl-barāʾa min hāʾulāʾi wa-takfīrihim*).[148] The story behind the epistle appears to have been that the local scholars in Riyadh and Manfūḥa, described by Ibn ʿAbd al-Wahhāb as devils (*shayāṭīn*), were disputing his core message concerning *tawḥīd* and

145. Ibn Ghannām, *Tārīkh*, 1:345–46.

146. Ibid., 1:345.

147. Ibid., 1:401–9.

148. Ibid., 1:403–4.

shirk. Ibn ʿAbd al-Wahhāb countered by arguing that these scholars were ignorant of Islam (*juhhāl*; sing. *jāhil*), and to emphasize the point he explained that he himself had once been ignorant:

> I will tell you about myself. By God, apart from whom there is no god, I sought learning, and those who knew me believed that I had some; yet at that time I did not know the meaning of "there is no god but God," nor did I know the religion of Islam, before this blessing that God vouchsafed [to me] [*qabl hādhā ʾl-khayr alladhī manna ʾllāh bihi*]. Likewise not one among my teachers knew it; if any of the scholars of al-ʿĀriḍ claims that he knew the meaning of "there is no god but God," or knew the meaning of Islam before this time, or maintains that any of his teachers knew it, he lies, fabricates, leads people astray, and falsely praises himself.[149]

Ibn ʿAbd al-Wahhāb's comment here is doubly provocative. Not only does he claim that none of his teachers understood the meaning of "there is no god but God," but he suggests that his knowledge of *tawḥīd* was given to him by God in the form of a blessing (*khayr*). This was nearly to suggest a divine origin of his religious knowledge. That was of course not the point of the epistle. The point, rather, was that the *maṭāwiʿa* of Najd, including Ibn Suḥaym, were not learned in matters of *tawḥīd* and that laypeople should study and understand these matters themselves. It was incumbent on all Muslims, Ibn ʿAbd al-Wahhāb wrote, male and female and learned and unlearned alike, to study and learn them. Nothing that these scholars say should prevent one from doing this.[150] To Ibn ʿAbd al-Wahhāb's enemies, however, what mattered is that he claimed to have been blessed by God with his religious knowledge. In their view, he was brashly dismissing previous generations of Muslims as ignorant unbelievers and behaving as pseudo-prophet, believing himself to be the bearer of divine revelation. Thus in *Kashf al-ḥijāb*, al-Qabbānī describes Ibn ʿAbd al-Wahhāb as "the pretender-prophet of al-ʿUyayna" (*mutanabbī ʾl-ʿUyayna*) and "the pretender-prophet of the lands of al-Yamāma" (*mutanabbī nawāḥī ʾl-Yamāma*).[151] According to Ibn ʿAbd al-Wahhāb, he writes, mankind was in a state of disbelief for six

149. Ibid., 1:402; translation borrowed from Cook, "On the Origins of Wahhābism," 202, with minor changes.

150. Ibn Ghannām, *Tārīkh*, 1:404.

151. al-Qabbānī, *Kashf al-ḥijāb*, ff. 234a, 73a.

hundred years, "until the pretender-prophet of al-ʿUyayna was sent [by God] calling to the religion of Islam."[152]

In Jumādā I 1158/June 1745, approximately ten months after finishing *Kashf al-ḥijāb*, al-Qabbānī put the finishing touches on his third refutation of Ibn ʿAbd al-Wahhāb, which he titled *Naqḍ qawāʿid al-ḍalāl wa-rafḍ ʿaqāʾid al-ḍullāl* (Criticizing the Principles of Error and Rejecting the Doctrines of the Misleaders).[153] The occasion for this third and final effort was the arrival in Basra, in earlier 1158/earlier 1745, of another epistle by the now notorious preacher from Najd. As before, al-Qabbānī would write a disparaging commentary on the epistle, quoting it in its entirety.[154]

This new Wahhābī epistle was a statement of four principles (*qawāʿid*), though unlike the one refuted by Ibn ʿAfāliq, this one was devoted to the issues of *tawḥīd* and *shirk*. The epistle in question was an early version of what would come to be known in the Wahhābī tradition as *Arbaʿ qawāʿid fī ʾl-dīn* (Four Principles Concerning Religion), which in various forms became one of Ibn ʿAbd al-Wahhāb's most influential of catechisms.[155] The *Arbaʿ qawāʿid fī ʾl-dīn* is cast as an epistle for distinguishing between Muslims and polytheists,[156] and in it Ibn ʿAbd al-Wahhāb seeks to show that the *shirk* of the modern-day cult of saints is the same as—and in some ways worse than—the *shirk* of the pagan Arabs at the time of the Prophet Muḥammad. As in the *Kalimāt* epistle and the epistle to Riyadh and Manfūḥa, here Ibn ʿAbd al-Wahhāb condemns the saints of Najd, including Tāj, Shamsān, Ḥusayn, and Idrīs, as *ṭawāghīt*, and he describes as unbelievers those who venerate these holy men by making vows to them and asking

152. Ibid., f. 236a. The six hundred years charge is common in the refutations; see, e.g., Āl Maḥmūd, *Taḥdhīr ahl al-īmān*, 34 (quoting Muḥammad ibn Fayrūz); Ibn ʿAfāliq, *Risāla* I, f. 48b; Ibn Dāwūd, *al-Ṣawāʿiq wa ʾl-ruʿūd*, ff. 81b–82b (quoting Ibn al-Ṭayyib).

153. al-Qabbānī, *Naqḍ qawāʿid al-ḍalāl*, f. 63a. On this manuscript, which is the original version in al-Qabbānī's own hand, see Mach, *Catalogue of Arabic Manuscripts*, 225 (no. 2636); Traboulsi, "Early Refutation," 379; Cook, "Written and Oral Aspects," 162ff.

154. al-Qabbānī, *Naqḍ qawāʿid al-ḍalāl*, f. 41b.

155. See, for the most similar version to this in the Wahhābī tradition, *al-Durar al-saniyya*, 2:27–30.

156. al-Qabbānī, *Naqḍ qawāʿid al-ḍalāl*, f. 42a.

them to relieve harms and supply needs (*tafrīj al-kurubāt wa-qaḍāʾ al-ḥājāt*).[157]

What is unique about this early version of the *Arbaʿ qawāʿid fī ʾl-dīn* is that it actually comprises two sets of four points. The first is more abstract, while the second concerns the current state of affairs in Najd, providing some insight into what was going on there at this time. In the third point of the second set, Ibn ʿAbd al-Wahhāb describes how the struggle in Najd, which he depicts as one between monotheists and polytheists (i.e., between the Wahhābīs and their opponents), has developed into a state of mutual enmity and mutual *takfīr*:

> The third [principle] is that we and they—both sides—pronounce *takfīr* on the other. Among them are those who say, "The people of al-ʿĀriḍ have apostatized and become unbelievers," and have denounced us to Mecca and to the rulers. And we maintain that they are unbelievers, that is, the worshipper and the worshipped [*al-ʿābid wa ʾl-maʿbūd*]. This third [principle], namely, the cutting off of relations and the enmity that is between us [*al-muqāṭaʿa wa ʾl-ʿadāwa baynanā*], has become well known among the monotheists and the polytheists, and is not denied by any of them.[158]

As Ibn ʿAbd al-Wahhāb makes perfectly clear here, he and his followers were pronouncing *takfīr* on both the Najdī saints (i.e., "the worshipped") and those who venerate them (i.e., "the worshipper"). The opponents of Wahhābism, in turn, were pronouncing *takfīr* on the Wahhābīs. Both sides were also dissociating from and manifesting enmity toward the other, though as yet there is no indication that violence had broken out.

Al-Qabbānī's *Naqḍ qawāʿid al-ḍalāl*, though much shorter than his first two refutations, is otherwise much like his previous efforts. Al-Qabbānī describes Ibn ʿAbd al-Wahhāb as "an ignorant and misled man . . . who has claimed unrestricted *ijtihād* [*al-ijtihād al-muṭlaq*] despite being tied down by ignorance, has introduced corruption into the religion, has misled the weak-minded among the inhabitants of those lands, has declared wayward the Muḥammadan community in its entirety, and has pronounced *takfīr* on all those who do not declare its waywardness and unbelief."[159] Al-Qabbānī refers to the continuing

157. Ibid., f. 47a.

158. Ibid., f. 58b; translation borrowed from Cook, "Written and Oral Aspects," 167–68, with minor changes.

159. al-Qabbānī, *Naqḍ qawāʿid al-ḍalāl*, f. 41b.

spread of the nascent Wahhābī movement, noting that Ibn ʿAbd al-Wahhāb continues to lead astray the laypeople (*ʿāmma*) of al-ʿĀriḍ, who, he states, will believe whatever they are told.[160] His contempt for the people of al-ʿĀriḍ, and for the people of al-ʿUyayna in particular, described as cattle (*anʿām*) for their stupidity and gullibility, is evident.[161] It behooves them, he writes, to listen to the scholars who have written against the wayward preacher and to repent of their terrible error.[162] Yet he does not appear very confident that they will heed the scholars' advice.

The Wahhābī movement was evidently still growing at this time, in mid-1158/mid-1745. In this version of the *Arbaʿ qawāʿid fī ʾl-dīn*, Ibn ʿAbd al-Wahhāb suggests that the people of al-ʿĀriḍ were now broadly seen as associated with Wahhābism, indicating that the movement had become dominant in the Najdī subregion. It is clear from al-Qabbānī's refutation that he believed Ibn ʿAbd al-Wahhāb was still residing in al-ʿUyayna.[163] It is perhaps more likely, however, that he had already moved to al-Dirʿiyya.

Refutations and Epistles: The al-Dirʿiyya Period

According to the Wahhābī histories, the reason for Ibn ʿAbd al-Wahhāb's departure from al-ʿUyayna is that Sulaymān ibn Muḥammad Āl Ḥumayd, the leader of the ruling Banū Khālid tribe in al-Aḥsāʾ, prevailed upon al-ʿUyayna's ruler, Ibn Muʿammar, to expel him.[164] As Ibn Ghannām and Ibn Bishr have it, when Sulaymān learned of Ibn ʿAbd al-Wahhāb's activities in al-ʿUyayna, he wrote to Ibn Muʿammar demanding that he either kill or expel the preacher and threatening to withhold the land tax (*kharāj*) that Ibn Muʿammar collected from his landholdings in al-Aḥsāʾ. Particularly upsetting to Sulaymān, we are told, was the recent stoning to death of a confessed adulteress in al-ʿUyayna. In the version of this story related by Ibn Ghannām, a woman had recently come to Ibn ʿAbd al-Wahhāb confessing to her crime of adultery. After confirming the woman's sanity and giving her four days to retract her confession, and after she repeatedly confessed to the crime, Ibn ʿAbd al-Wahhāb ordered that she be stoned in line with the traditional penalty in

160. Ibid., f. 55a.

161. Ibid., f. 42b.

162. Ibid., f. 62a–b.

163. Ibid., f. 57a.

164. Ibn Ghannām, *Tārīkh*, 2:669–71; Ibn Bishr, *ʿUnwān al-majd*, 1:87.

Islamic law. Ibn Muʿammar threw the first stone. News of the punishment—apparently a rarity in Najd at this time—spread quickly and brought further attention to Ibn ʿAbd al-Wahhāb and his movement. Ibn Ghannām claims that this event was particularly upsetting to Sulaymān given his famous appetite for fornication. The ruler in al-Aḥsāʾ was also told, according to Ibn Ghannām, that Ibn ʿAbd al-Wahhāb sought to change the way he conducted his affairs, including preventing him from levying noncanonical taxes (*mukūs*), and even that Ibn ʿAbd al-Wahhāb hoped to unseat him from his rule. Whatever his motive, Sulaymān ordered Ibn Muʿammar either to kill or to expel the troublesome preacher in his town, and Ibn Muʿammar chose the latter course.

Ibn ʿAbd al-Wahhāb's chosen destination was the nearby town of al-Dirʿiyya, ruled by Muḥammad ibn Suʿūd (r. 1139–79/1726f–65). The exact year in which the move took place is not specified precisely or consistently in the Wahhābī sources. Ibn Ghannām states that it happened in approximately (*fī ḥudūd*) 1157/1744f;[165] Ibn Bishr records that Ibn ʿAbd al-Wahhāb arrived in al-Dirʿiyya (*qadima ... balad al-Dirʿiyya*) in 1157/1744f and became settled there (*istaqarra fīhā*) a year later, in 1158/1745f.[166] Piecing this together, one might infer that the move happened sometime in late 1157 of the Islamic calendar, the equivalent of late 1744 or early 1745 of the Gregorian calendar.

One of the attractions of al-Dirʿiyya for Ibn ʿAbd al-Wahhāb would have been that he had already gained a substantial following there, including two brothers of the town's ruler, Thunayyān ibn Suʿūd and Mishārī ibn Suʿūd. Ibn Ghannām relates that the ruler of al-Dirʿiyya immediately embraced the refugee, pledging to protect and support him so long as he promised not to leave al-Dirʿiyya for another town. Ibn ʿAbd al-Wahhāb agreed and, with the support of al-Dirʿiyya's ruler behind him, proceeded with his preaching. Many of his followers from al-ʿUyayna and elsewhere relocated with him to al-Dirʿiyya, which quickly became the new headquarters of the Wahhābī movement in Najd.[167] Unlike in al-ʿUyayna, however, in al-Dirʿiyya the Wahhābī movement

165. Ibn Ghannām, *Tārīkh*, 2:671.

166. Ibn Bishr, *ʿUnwān al-majd*, 1:79, 93. Ibn Laʿbūn states that the move took place in 1158/1745f or early 1157/1744 (*Tārīkh*, 421); al-Fākhirī places it in 1158/1745f or early 1159/1746 (*Tārīkh*, 131).

167. Ibn Ghannām, *Tārīkh*, 2:670–72; cf. Mengin, *Histoire de l'Égypte*, 2:451. Ibn Bishr's account (*ʿUnwān al-majd*, 1:88–89), which I regard as less reliable than Ibn Ghannām's for this period, describes a more elaborate encounter between Ibn ʿAbd al-Wahhāb and Ibn Suʿūd. In this version, Ibn ʿAbd al-Wahhāb tells Ibn Suʿūd that he will acquire great wealth and power, that his realm will expand, and that rule will continue in his family line; Ibn Suʿūd, for his part,

became entwined with the host town's political fortunes. Not long after Ibn ʿAbd al-Wahhāb's arrival in al-Dirʿiyya, Ibn Suʿūd sought to impose his authority over neighboring towns, in tandem with enforcing adherence to the Wahhābī creed. Al-Dirʿiyya grew into an expansionary state, the first Saudi state, and the basis of its expansion was the promotion and spread of Wahhābism. According to ʿAbd al-Raḥmān ibn Ḥasan Āl al-Shaykh, in 1159/1746f al-Dirʿiyya formally brought the nearby towns of al-ʿUyayna, Ḥuraymilāʾ, al-ʿAmmāriyya, and Manfūḥa under its authority. Yet the ruler of Riyadh, Dahām ibn Dawwās (fl. 1187/1773), resisted the call to impose Wahhābism and submit to Ibn Suʿūd and soon after attacked his neighbor Manfūḥa.[168] This narrative finds support in the account of Ibn Ghannām, which states that in approximately (*fī ḥudūd*) 1159/1746f Riyadh attacked Manfūḥa, whose people had converted to Wahhābism and acknowledged Ibn Suʿūd as their overlord.[169] There followed a long war between al-Dirʿiyya and Riyadh. From this point forward, the Wahhābīs were regularly fighting their opponents in warfare, which Ibn ʿAbd al-Wahhāb contended was legitimate *jihād* against polytheist unbelievers.

The newfound belligerency of the Wahhābī movement is reflected in the refutations of the al-Dirʿiyya period, which never miss an opportunity to condemn Ibn ʿAbd al-Wahhāb and his followers for waging war and perpetrating violence on Muslims. A good example is the refutation of a Shāfiʿī scholar in Medina named Muḥammad ibn Sulaymān al-Kurdī (d. 1194/1780), which takes the form of a response to a series of questions put to him about Ibn ʿAbd al-Wahhāb.[170] The questioner, presumably a Najdī, writes that Ibn ʿAbd al-Wahhāb "has appointed himself a leader and requires the Muslim community to follow his words and adhere to his doctrine [*madhhabihi*], compelling them to do so by force of the sword. He holds those who oppose him to be unbelievers, and deems licit their blood and property [*wa-yastaḥillu damahu wa-mālahu*], even if they fulfill the pillars of faith."[171] Al-Kurdī's response is that

---

is seen asking Ibn ʿAbd al-Wahhāb not to interfere with the collection of noncanonical taxes on the people of al-Dirʿiyya, to which Ibn ʿAbd al-Wahhāb responds that the war booty (*ghanīma*) of the ruler's conquests will surpass what he is currently collecting. While this story may well be true, it has the look of back-projection.

168. Mengin, *Histoire de l'Égypte*, 2:451–53.

169. Ibn Ghannām, *Tārīkh*, 2:675–78.

170. al-Ḥaddād, *Miṣbāḥ al-anām*, 82–86; cf. the shorter version in al-Kurdī, *Fatāwā*, 256–61. On al-Kurdī, see al-Murādī, *Silk al-durar*, 4:111–12.

171. al-Ḥaddād, *Miṣbāḥ al-anām*, 82.

all of this is entirely inconsistent with Islamic teachings, as Islam prohibits Muslims from excommunicating and fighting fellow Muslims.

A similar statement is found in a refutation by Muḥammad ibn Fayrūz (d. 1216/1801), the Ḥanbalī scholar in al-Aḥsāʾ who emerged as one of Ibn ʿAbd al-Wahhāb's most outspoken critics in the al-Dirʿiyya period.[172] In an undated refutation written in the context of the war between al-Dirʿiyya and Riyadh, Ibn Fayrūz accuses the Wahhābīs of fighting the people of Riyadh and others on the grounds that they are polytheists. "Ibn ʿAbd al-Wahhāb," he writes,

> has pronounced *takfīr* on a great many Muslims, including the people of Riyadh and others. He has deemed their blood and property licit [*wa-abāḥa dimāʾahum wa-amwālahum*], and he has gone about the lands making pacts with their people to fight the people of Riyadh and others. He has deemed their blood and property licit, and made them out to be as the polytheists whom God commanded His Prophet to fight.[173]

Ibn Fayrūz condemns Ibn ʿAbd al-Wahhāb for comparing his opponents to the unbelievers of the Prophet's time, for the people of Najd, Ibn Fayrūz argues, unlike the pagan Arabs, confess that "there is no god but God"; they pray, pay the alms tax (*zakāt*), and believe in the afterlife, the Qurʾān, and the Prophet; and they do not deny the hour (*al-sāʿa*) or the resurrection (*al-baʿth*) or assign partners to God.[174] In their behavior, Ibn Fayrūz observes, Ibn ʿAbd al-Wahhāb and his followers are mimicking the Prophet and his Companions: "He has placed himself and the people of his country who have followed him and accepted his words in the position of the Messenger of God and his Companions [*maqām rasūl Allāh ṣ wa-aṣḥābihi*], whom God commanded to fight the unbelievers."[175]

172. On him, see al-ʿAtīqī, *Tarjamat Muḥammad ibn Fayrūz*; Ibn Sanad, *Sabāʾik al-ʿasjad*, 290–98; Ibn Ḥumayd, *al-Suḥub al-wābila*, 3:969–80; Āl Bassām, *ʿUlamāʾ Najd*, 3:882–86; al-Qāḍī, *Rawḍat al-nāẓirīn*, 2:226–28; al-Nuwayṣir, *al-Muʿāraḍa*, 224–33; al-ʿAssāfī, *Tarājim al-fuḍalāʾ*, ff. 43a–59a. Al-ʿAtīqī, a student of his, depicts Ibn Fayrūz as "an unsheathed sword against the people of innovation" (*sayf maslūl ʿalā ahl al-bidaʿ*), claiming that he was so active in taking on "the innovation of the people of al-ʿĀriḍ" (*bidʿat ahl al-ʿĀriḍ*) that Ibn ʿAbd al-Wahhāb placed a bounty on his head (*Tarjamat Muḥammad ibn Fayrūz*, ff. 75a–76b).

173. Ibn Fayrūz, *al-Radd ʿalā man kaffara ahl al-Riyāḍ*, 25–26. The title is the invention of the pseudonymous editor, whose edition is made from a unique manuscript in Bahrain.

174. Ibid., 27–34.

175. Ibid., 26.

Similarly, a certain Ṣāliḥ ibn ʿAbdallāh al-Najdī, in Medina, would accuse Ibn ʿAbd al-Wahhāb of assuming the prophetic office (*maqām al-nubuwwa*), of casting his followers as emigrants and supporters (*al-muhājirīn wa ʾl-anṣār*), and of likening their warfare to the *jihād* of the Prophet and his Companions (*jihād al-ṣaḥāba maʿa rasūl Allāh*).[176] While earlier refuters had accused Ibn ʿAbd al-Wahhāb of behaving like a prophet, in the al-Dirʿiyya period they accuse him of imitating the Prophet Muḥammad in the conduct of warfare. A somewhat different approach was taken by the Ḥanbalī al-Saffārīnī in Palestine. Al-Saffārīnī condemns Ibn ʿAbd al-Wahhāb for demanding that people either follow his religious opinions or be fought, saying, "He has deemed licit the blood of those who do not follow him in his error [*wa-abāḥa dimāʾ man lam yattabiʿhu ʿalā ḍalālatihi*]."[177] In saying this, he compares Ibn ʿAbd al-Wahhāb (*hādhā ʾl-aḥmaq*) not to the Prophet but to Ibn Tūmart (d. 524/1130), the founder of the Almohad dynasty in North Africa who famously proclaimed himself the *mahdī* and who, according to al-Saffārīnī, also proscribed *taqlīd* of the four Sunnī law schools. An even more fitting comparison, he goes on to say, is the early Khārijite leader Nāfiʿ ibn al-Azraq (d. 65/685). As he explains, the Azāriqa Khārijite sect, like the Wahhābīs, was known for killing Muslims and deeming their blood, property, women, and children licit.[178] None of the refutations just quoted, it should be mentioned, can be precisely dated; but since they all refer to Wahhābī violence, we can be sure that they all belong to the al-Dirʿiyya period.

If Ibn Suḥaym was Ibn ʿAbd al-Wahhāb's chief scholarly opponent in Najd during the al-ʿUyayna period, in the al-Dirʿiyya period that role would be played by ʿAbdallāh al-Muways (d. 1175/1761f), the *qāḍī* of Ḥarma in Sudayr.[179] Al-Muways had studied in Syria with al-Saffārīnī and others, and he seems to have invoked his academic credentials in denouncing Ibn ʿAbd al-Wahhāb. In one of his letters, Ibn ʿAbd al-Wahhāb taunts him as "your Shāmī" (*Shāmiyyukum*),[180] and in another he claims that al-Muways is flaunting his elite Syrian education—

176. Ibn Dāwūd, *al-Ṣawāʿiq wa ʾl-ruʿūd*, ff. 82b–83a. I have found no biographical information on Ṣāliḥ ibn ʿAbdallāh, though in a letter Ibn ʿAbd al-Wahhāb mentions him as one of his leading opponents; in a play on words, he also refers to Ṣāliḥ as *fāsid*; see Ibn Ghannām, *Tārīkh*, 1:424, 428 (letter to Aḥmad ibn Ibrāhīm).

177. al-Saffārīnī, *al-Ajwiba al-najdiyya*, 129.

178. Ibid., 128.

179. On him, see Āl Bassām, *ʿUlamāʾ Najd*, 4:364–69; al-Qāḍī, *Rawḍat al-nāẓirīn*, 1:415–16; al-Bassām, "Min asbāb al-muʿāraḍa," 43–45.

180. Ibn Ghannām, *Tārīkh*, 1:360 (letter to ʿAbdallāh ibn Suḥaym).

"you see me coming from al-Shām!" (*tarāy jāy min al-Shām*)—as a reason to accept his denunciations of the Wahhābī reformer.[181] While his name is mentioned frequently in Ibn ʿAbd al-Wahhāb's letters and epistles, the only bit of al-Muways's output that appears to have survived is a letter to Ibn ʿAbd al-Wahhāb preserved in a manuscript in Mecca.[182] Here al-Muways rejects the contention that he hates *tawḥīd*, affirming that "we only hate what you, at your whim, have called *tawḥīd*, which entails excommunicating Muslims and deeming their blood and property licit, with no support from God or His Messenger except the way of the Khārijites."[183] As can be seen here, it was in the al-Dirʿiyya period that the refuters seized on the Khārijite theme. Al-Muways, like his teacher al-Saffārīnī, saw the Wahhābīs as akin to the Khārijites, given the exclusivist and violent tendencies of both groups.

Ibn ʿAbd al-Wahhāb was well aware of the arguments being made by his enemies, including the charge of violence. In his words, these arguments were to be understood as *shubuhāt* (sing. *shubha*), a term meaning "specious arguments" or "misconceptions." In the early years of his residence in al-Dirʿiyya, he wrote an epistle known as *Kashf al-shubuhāt* (Exposing the Specious Arguments) responding to some of these arguments. Ibn Ghannām, who preserves the epistle in his history, describes it as "a general epistle to the Muslims" (*risāla ʿāmma lil-Muslimīn*).[184] In Ibn ʿAbd al-Wahhāb's words, its purpose was to equip them with the necessary weapons (*silāḥ*) with which to rebut the *shubuhāt* being spread by "the scholars of the polytheists" (*ʿulamāʾ al-mushrikīn*).[185]

Throughout *Kashf al-shubuhāt*, Ibn ʿAbd al-Wahhāb emphasizes many of the same ideas developed earlier in the *Kalimāt* and the *Arbaʿ qawāʿid fī ʾl-dīn*. Most people (*ghālib al-nās*), he notes at the beginning, are ignorant of the meaning of "there is no god but God." The correct understanding of these

181. Ibid., 1:326 (letter to ʿAbdallāh ibn Suḥaym). The Arabic phrase is in the vernacular.

182. al-Bassām, "Min asbāb al-muʿāraḍa," 44n6; and see the photos at 68.

183. Ibid., 44.

184. Ibn Ghannām, *Tārīkh*, 1:263–81, at 263. An earlier Wahhābī source (Ibn Gharīb, *al-Tawḍīḥ*, 1:178–79) refers to it as *Kashf shubah al-murtāb fīmā ʾltabasa ʿalayhi min al-khaṭaʾ wa ʾl-ṣawāb*.

185. Ibn Ghannām, *Tārīkh*, 1:266.

words is directing all forms of worship to God alone, rejecting what is worshipped apart from God, and dissociating from it.[186] Toward the end, he reminds his readers that saying these words without acting on them is of no help. *Tawḥīd* requires action, and one who understands its meaning but fails to act on it (i.e., by condemning and dissociating from *shirk* and polytheists) has not met the test of Islam; in fact, such a person is a recalcitrant unbeliever (*kāfir mu ʿānid*).[187] Much of *Kashf al-shubuhāt* takes the form of a hypothetical debate between a polytheist (*mushrik*) and a monotheist (*muwaḥḥid*), an approach similar to the one adopted in the *Arba ʿ qawā ʿid fī ʾl-dīn*.[188] Ibn ʿAbd al-Wahhāb instructs his reader in what to say in response to the various *shubuhāt*. Among the arguments that he counters in the epistle are that today's so-called Muslims should not be compared with the unbelievers of the Prophet's time, that it is permissible to ask the Prophet and righteous persons for intercession, that it is permissible to seek the help of the dead, that he is declaring Muslims to be unbelievers, and that whosoever confesses that "there is no god but God" must be treated as a Muslim.[189]

There is another *shubha*, however, that stands out given that it pertains to violence. This is the argument that it is impermissible to fight those who confess that "there is no god but God."[190] Ibn ʿAbd al-Wahhāb notes that his opponents are citing *ḥadīths* in which the Prophet appears to prohibit this. In one of these, the Prophet states: "I was commanded to fight people until they testify that 'there is no god but God and Muḥammad is the Messenger of God,' and perform the prayer and pay the *zakāt*. If they do so, they have secured their blood and their property from me, except as required by Islam, and their accounting will be with God."[191] In another of these *ḥadīths*, the Prophet chides his former slave, Usāma ibn Zayd, for striking a man dead who had uttered the confession of faith. When Usāma protests that the man had said it only out of fear, the Prophet responds: "Did you tear out his heart to see whether he said it [sincerely] or not?"[192] To his opponents' use of these proof texts, Ibn ʿAbd

186. Ibid., 1:265–66.

187. Ibid., 1:280.

188. See Cook, "Written and Oral Aspects," 174–75.

189. Ibn Ghannām, *Tārīkh*, 1:266–79.

190. Ibid., 1:277–78.

191. al-Bukhārī, *Ṣaḥīḥ*, 28 (*Kitāb al-īmān, bāb fa-in tābū wa-aqāmū ʾl-ṣalāt*, no. 25); cf. 273 (*Kitāb al-zakāt, bāb wujūb al-zakāt*, nos. 1399–1400).

192. Muslim, *Ṣaḥīḥ*, 1:96–97 (*Kitāb al-īmān, bāb taḥrīm qatl al-kāfir ba ʿd an qāla lā ilāha illā ʾllāh*, no. 96); cf. al-Bukhārī, *Ṣaḥīḥ*, 807 (*Kitāb al-maghāzī, bāb ba ʿth al-nabī Usāma ibn Zayd*, 4269).

al-Wahhāb retorts that there were always exceptions to the Prophet's instruction not to fight those who say "there is no god but God," noting that the Prophet fought the Jews despite their saying "there is no god but God" and that the Companions fought the apostate Banū Ḥanīfa (i.e., the followers of Musaylima) and the Khārijites despite their saying the same. The Prophet said concerning the Khārijites: "If I could reach them I would kill them as the people of ʿĀd were killed," meaning he would kill all of them.[193] It is thus not an ironclad rule, he says, that Muslims may not fight and kill those who confess that "there is no god but God." With regard to the Prophet's condemnation of Usama ibn Zayd, the proper lesson to be learned from this, in Ibn ʿAbd al-Wahhāb's view, is that one should refrain from fighting a person who outwardly displays Islam (*aẓhara ʾl-Islām*) until it has become clear that the person's behavior contradicts Islam (*ḥattā yatabayyana minhu mā yukhālifu ʾl-Islām*). The unstated upshot of this remark is that the Wahhābīs have already determined that the people they are fighting are unbelievers, despite their outward profession of the faith.

The fact that Ibn ʿAbd al-Wahhāb is seen responding here to an argument concerning violence is significant, as it shows that *Kashf al-shubuhāt* cannot have been written during the al-ʿUyayna period. In other words, it cannot have been written before Ibn ʿAbd al-Wahhāb's move to al-Dirʿiyya in approximately 1157/1744f. While the epistle cannot be dated precisely, we can be sure that it was written sometime between 1157/1744f and 1163/1750, as it is quoted in a series of letters between Ibn Muʿammar and the Ḥanbalī scholar Ibn ʿAfāliq in al-Aḥsāʾ, both of whom died in 1163/1750.[194] Ibn Muʿammar, despite having expelled Ibn ʿAbd al-Wahhāb from al-ʿUyayna, appears to have remained a committed Wahhābī for some time; Ibn ʿAfāliq was trying to convince him to recant his Wahhābī views. In Rajab 1163/June 1750, Ibn Muʿammar was assassinated by Wahhābī loyalists in al-ʿUyayna as he left the mosque after Friday prayer. The story told in the Wahhābī sources is that he

193. al-Bukhārī, *Ṣaḥīḥ*, 639 (*Kitāb aḥādīth al-anbiyāʾ, bāb qawl Allāh taʿālā wa-ilā ʿĀd akhāhum*, no. 3344); Muslim, *Ṣaḥīḥ*, 2:741 (*Kitāb al-zakāt, bāb dhikr al-khawārij wa-ṣifātihim*, no. 1064). According to the Islamic tradition, the people of ʿĀd were an Arabian tribe who opposed the teachings of the Prophet Hūd; they are described in the Qurʾān as having been destroyed by a furious wind (Q. 69:6–8).

194. More precisely, it cannot have been written later than 25 Ṣafar 1163/February ~3, 1750, which is Ibn ʿAfāliq's death date; see Ibn Fayrūz, *Tarājim*, f. 78a. Ibn Muʿammar died a few months later.

had since forsaken Wahhābism and was plotting a rebellion.[195] In his correspondence with Ibn ʿAfāliq, however, Ibn Muʿammar was still a staunch Wahhābī. What remains of the two men's correspondence is an abridged version of two letters by Ibn ʿAfāliq to Ibn Muʿammar, which survive in a unique manuscript in Germany.[196]

In disputing the Wahhābīs' views, and in seeking to convince Ibn Muʿammar to withdraw his support from Ibn ʿAbd al-Wahhāb, Ibn ʿAfāliq quotes from two Wahhābī epistles, the *Kalimāt* and *Kashf al-shubuhāt,* though much more so the latter.[197] To a large extent Ibn ʿAfāliq's letters can be read as a refutation of *Kashf al-shubuhāt,* which Ibn ʿAfāliq repeatedly cites as evidence of Ibn ʿAbd al-Wahhāb's ignorance. As before in *Tahakkum al-muqallidīn,* Ibn ʿAfāliq mocks Ibn ʿAbd al-Wahhāb's scholarly pretentions, claiming that he has no scholarly training or knowledge (*laysa lahu sābiqat ʿilm wa-lā maʿrifa biʾl-ʿilm wa-ahl al-ʿilm*) and claiming that he is "more misled than his family's donkey" (*aḍall min ḥimār ahlihi*).[198] Unlike before, however, Ibn ʿAfāliq describes the Wahhābī movement as belligerent. "Why," he asks Ibn Muʿammar, "are you accepting his [i.e., Ibn ʿAbd al-Wahhāb's] statements, fighting and spilling blood, and dismissing those more knowledgeable of God than he?"[199] Ibn ʿAfāliq complains further that Ibn ʿAbd al-Wahhāb is presenting the military endeavors of the Wahhābīs as *jihād* against unbelievers: "[He] has required you to undertake *jihād,* saying, 'Fight the unbelievers who are near to

195. On the assassination, see Ibn Ghannām, *Tārīkh,* 2:686–88; Ibn Bishr, *ʿUnwān al-majd,* 1:103–4.

196. Ibn ʿAfāliq, *Risāla* I, ff. 36b–55b; Ibn ʿAfāliq, *Risāla* II, ff. 56a–73b. On these manuscripts, see Ahlwardt, *Verzeichnis der arabischen Handschriften,* 2:477 (nos. 2157 and 2158). Ahlwardt casts doubt on the ascription of *Risāla* I to Ibn ʿAfāliq, a view endorsed by Peskes (*Muḥammad b. ʿAbdalwahhāb,* 58–66). This is mistaken in my opinion, as both letters are attributed to Ibn ʿAfāliq by the copyist and are similar in style and substance. For instance, both quote only the same two Wahhābī epistles, the *Kalimāt* and *Kashf al-shubuhāt. Risāla* II has been discussed by Cook ("On the Origins of Wahhābism," 200), while both letters are treated in Āl ʿAbd al-Laṭīf, "Mawqif ʿUthmān ibn Muʿammar." For a not entirely reliable edition of the letters, see al-Radīsī, *al-Radd ʿalā ʾl-Wahhābiyya,* 85–133.

197. For the *Kalimāt,* compare Ibn ʿAfāliq, *Risāla* I, f. 51b, and *al-Durar al-saniyya,* 2:111; and compare Ibn ʿAfāliq, *Risāla* II, f. 65b, and *al-Durar al-saniyya,* 2:109. For *Kashf al-shubuhāt,* compare Ibn ʿAfāliq, *Risāla* I, f. 39a, and Ibn Ghannām, *Tārīkh,* 1:264; and compare Ibn ʿAfāliq, *Risāla* II, ff. 64b, 65a, 66a, 68b–69a, 69b, 70a, 70a–b, 71a, and Ibn Ghannām, *Tārīkh,* 1:263, 264, 264–66, 264, 274, 274–75, 275, 275–76, respectively.

198. Ibn ʿAfāliq, *Risāla* I, f. 53b; Ibn ʿAfāliq, *Risāla* II, f. 62a.

199. Ibn ʿAfāliq, *Risāla* I, f. 40a.

you' (Q. 9:123), such that you have claimed that *jihād* has become obligatory for you."[200] The Wahhābīs, according to Ibn ʿAfāliq, are the clear aggressors (*muʿtadūn*) in the war with Riyadh, and this is indefensible since the Prophet prohibited warfare against those who say "there is no god but God."[201]

Three additional themes that stand out in Ibn ʿAfāliq's letters are (1) the accusation that Ibn ʿAbd al-Wahhāb is imitating the Prophet; (2) the claim that he requires all Wahhābīs to perform *hijra*, or emigration, to lands under Wahhābī control; and (3) the portrayal of Najd as a place with a history of heresy and where bad things are foretold to happen. Ibn ʿAfāliq accuses Ibn ʿAbd al-Wahhāb of having "put himself on the level of a messenger [*anzala nafsahu manzilat rasūl*],"[202] and he further accuses the preacher's followers of treating him as though he were infallible (*maʿṣūm*) like a prophet.[203] Addressing the Wahhābīs generally, he writes, "You have pronounced *takfīr* on the community of His Prophet, deemed their blood and property licit without proof or evidence, and made the land of Musaylima the abode of *hijra*, such that one who does not emigrate there has no Islam and no faith."[204] He alludes to certain people who are picking up and relocating to Najd with their property and families and who are "claiming that it is *hijra* to God and His Prophet."[205] This requirement is especially perverse, in Ibn ʿAfāliq's view, as Najd is the land most detested by the Prophet Muḥammad (*abghaḍ al-bilād ilā rasūl Allāh*) and yet the Wahhābīs have made it out to be the stronghold and establishment of the faith (*maʿqil al-īmān wa-maqarrahu*). He cites a *ḥadīth* in which the Prophet refuses to bless Najd and foretells that it will be the site of "earthquakes and tribulations, and in it will arise the horn of the devil."[206]

A significant difference between Ibn ʿAfāliq's *Tahakkum al-muqallidīn* and these two letters is the approach taken to Ibn Taymiyya. Instead of arguing, as before, that Ibn Taymiyya's position on the cult of saints is wrong and should not be followed, here he defends Ibn Taymiyya, along with his student Ibn

200. Ibn ʿAfāliq, *Risāla* II, f. 58b.

201. Ibn ʿAfāliq, *Risāla* I, f. 49a.

202. Ibid.

203. Ibn ʿAfāliq, *Risāla* II, f. 64a.

204. Ibid., f. 69b.

205. Ibn ʿAfāliq, *Risāla* I, f. 46b.

206. Ibn ʿAfāliq, *Risāla* II, f. 63a. For the *ḥadīth*, see al-Bukhārī, *Ṣaḥīḥ*, 205 (*Kitāb al-istisqāʾ*, *bāb mā qīla fī ʾl-zalāzil waʾl-āyāt*, no. 1037); cf. Muslim, *Ṣaḥīḥ*, 4:2228–29 (*Kitāb al-fitan wa-ashrāṭ al-sāʿa, bāb al-fitan min al-mashriq min ḥayth yaṭluʿu qarn al-shayṭān*, no. 2905).

al-Qayyim, accusing Ibn ʿAbd al-Wahhāb of misconstruing their words.[207] Indeed, one of the main purposes of these letters is to convince Ibn Muʿammar that these earlier scholars cannot be legitimately used to support Wahhābism. To this end Ibn ʿAfāliq emphasizes the distinction between *al-shirk al-akbar* (major polytheism) and *al-shirk al-aṣghar* (minor polytheism), arguing that Ibn ʿAbd al-Wahhāb has failed to distinguish between them as Ibn Taymiyya and Ibn al-Qayyim had. While he acknowledges that committing *al-shirk al-akbar* ejects one from the community of Islam, he claims that excessive acts of reverence for saints and prophets—the kinds of things Ibn ʿAbd al-Wahhāb is complaining about—amount only to *al-shirk al-aṣghar*. These are, as he puts it, merely acts of association in worship (*al-shirk fī ʾl-ʿibāda*).[208] By contrast, *al-shirk al-akbar* is association with God (*al-shirk fī ʾllāh*) or association in God's oneness (*al-shirk fī tawḥīd Allāh*).[209] While these distinctions are not spelled out further, one gathers that for Ibn ʿAfāliq, to commit *al-shirk al-akbar* requires more or less explicit repudiation of God's status as the sole God. These points about *al-shirk al-akbar* and *al-shirk al-aṣghar*, and the issue of Ibn Taymiyya and Ibn al-Qayyim more generally, would be addressed by Ibn ʿAbd al-Wahhāb in his next major counterrefutation, *Mufīd al-mustafīd*.

According to Ibn Ghannām, *Mufīd al-mustafīd* was written in the year 1167/1753f in the midst of a confrontation between al-Dirʿiyya and Ḥuraymilāʾ.[210] More specifically, it was written in response to the anti-Wahhābī activism of Ibn ʿAbd al-Wahhāb's brother, Sulaymān ibn ʿAbd al-Wahhāb (d. 1208/1794), who was the *qāḍī* of Ḥuraymilāʾ. In 1165/1751f, as Ibn Ghannām relates, the people of Ḥuraymilāʾ apostatized, meaning that the town's leaders withdrew their allegiance from al-Dirʿiyya and renounced Wahhābism.[211] There ensued not only physical war between al-Dirʿiyya and Ḥuraymilāʾ but also scholarly war between the two brothers. Ibn ʿAbd al-Wahhāb is said to have scolded Sulaymān for giving his support to the apostasy

207. See especially Ibn ʿAfāliq, *Risāla* I, ff. 44a–49b.

208. Ibid., f. 52a.

209. Ibn ʿAfāliq, *Risāla* II, ff. 66a, 67b–68a.

210. Ibn Ghannām, *Tārīkh*, 2:696.

211. On Sulaymān, see Ibn Ḥumayd, *al-Suḥub al-wābila*, 2:677–81; Āl Bassām, *ʿUlamāʾ Najd*, 2:350–57. And see further, for a valuable study of his refutation, al-Sarḥān, "Ḥaqīqat al-khilāf."

in Ḥuraymilāʾ and for spreading numerous falsehoods about Wahhābism among the town's rulers. Sulaymān emerged at this time as one of Ibn ʿAbd al-Wahhāb's foremost refuters in Najd. According to Ibn Ghannām, for a period of time he composed anti-Wahhābī epistles and sent them to al-ʿUyayna. In 1167/1753f, the courier bearing one of these epistles was apprehended by the Wahhābīs, and on the order of Ibn ʿAbd al-Wahhāb he was executed.[212] In 1168/1755, the Wahhābīs succeeded in reimposing their authority over Ḥuraymilāʾ, whereupon Sulaymān fled.[213]

The only extant refutation by Sulaymān takes the form of a long letter to Ḥasan ibn ʿĪdān (d. 1202/1787f), a man from Ushayqir in al-Washm who appears to have been living in al-Dirʿiyya at this time.[214] The letter that we have is therefore probably not one of those sent to al-ʿUyayna, unless it was written for Ibn ʿĪdān and subsequently repurposed for a broader campaign of anti-Wahhābī propaganda.[215] In 1306/1889, Sulaymān's letter was printed in Bombay as *al-Ṣawāʿiq al-ilāhiyya fī ʾl-radd ʿalā ʾl-Wahhābiyya* (The Divine Thunderbolts in Refutation of Wahhābism), a title that was likely invented by the publisher.[216] We can infer that the letter was written in about 1165/1752f, since Sulaymān refers twice in it to al-Dirʿiyya's adoption of Wahhābism "nearly eight years ago" (*min qarīb thamān sinīn*), this likely being a reference to Ibn ʿAbd al-Wahhāb's move to al-Dirʿiyya in approximately 1157/1744f.[217] Sulaymān's letter is one of the longest refutations to appear thus far. Unlike some of the others, it does not quote Ibn ʿAbd al-Wahhāb's words directly, though it engages with several of his arguments. Like Ibn ʿAfāliq in his letters to Ibn Muʿammar, Sulaymān devotes a good deal of space to proving that Ibn Taymiyya and Ibn al-Qayyim are

212. Ibn Ghannām, *Tārīkh*, 2:691–96.

213. Ibid., 2:736–37. Sulaymān managed to evade capture until 1190/1776f, when the rulers of Sudayr handed him over to al-Dirʿiyya. He quietly lived out his remaining years in the Saudi capital, allegedly repenting of his past opposition to Wahhābism (2:812–13).

214. On him, see Āl Bassām, *ʿUlamāʾ Najd*, 2:51–52; al-Qāḍī, *Rawḍat al-nāẓirīn*, 3:37.

215. As suggested in al-Sarḥān, "Ḥaqīqat al-khilāf," 8.

216. Ibn ʿAbd al-Wahhāb, *al-Ṣawāʿiq al-ilāhiyya*. Some sources refer to it as *Faṣl al-khiṭāb fī ʾl-radd ʿalā Muḥammad ibn ʿAbd al-Wahhāb*; see Ibn Ḥumayd, *al-Suḥub al-wābila*, 2:679; al-Bābānī, *Īḍāḥ al-maknūn*, 4:190.

217. Ibn ʿAbd al-Wahhāb, *al-Ṣawāʿiq al-ilāhiyya*, 50 (*ẓahara qawlukum hādhā min qarīb thamān sinīn*), 51 (*muddatukum qarība min thamān sinīn*); noted in al-Sarḥān, "Ḥaqīqat al-khilāf," 8. If Sulaymān is referring to the beginning of the Wahhābī *daʿwa* more generally, this would put the date of composition around 1163/1749. The first date, 1165/1752f, should be favored, however, as it fits better with the time frame given by Ibn Ghannām and because Sulaymān is referring to his correspondent's lands (*bilād*), likely meaning al-Dirʿiyya.

being misused by the Wahhābīs. Also like Ibn ʿAfāliq, he accuses the Wahhābīs of treating Muslim lands beyond those controlled by al-Dirʿiyya as lands of war (*bilād ḥarb*)[218]—meaning that they must be fought and conquered—and accuses them of deeming licit the blood and property of Muslims.[219] Related to this are the several references to the requirement of *hijra*. "Your doctrine," he says, "is that it is required for the masses to adhere to your doctrine, and that those who adhere to it and cannot manifest it in their land, nor pronounce *takfīr* on the people of their land, are required to emigrate to you."[220] Other themes underlined here include Ibn ʿAbd al-Wahhāb's purported claim of *ijtihād*, the resemblance between the Wahhābīs and the Khārijites, and the portrayal of Najd as a dreadful land.[221]

Another similarity between Ibn ʿAfāliq's letters to Ibn Muʿammar and Sulaymān's letter to Ibn ʿĪdān is the distinction made between *al-shirk al-akbar* and *al-shirk al-aṣghar*. According to Sulaymān, the practices condemned as *shirk* by Ibn Taymiyya and Ibn al-Qayyim belong to the category of *al-shirk al-aṣghar*, not *al-shirk al-akbar*, and thus they do not expel one from the community of believers. For this reason, even though Ibn Taymiyya and Ibn al-Qayyim condemned the presence of *shirk* in certain Muslim lands, they did not consider those lands to be lands of war. In those instances where the *shirk* in question did amount to *al-shirk al-akbar*, Sulaymān says, they did not pronounce *takfīr* on a person until proof had been presented to him (*ḥattā taqūma ʿalayhi ʾl-ḥujja*); meanwhile the accused was to be excused on the basis of ignorance (*yuʿdharu bi ʾl-jahl*).[222]

According to Ibn Ghannām, in 1167/1753f—that is, within a year of Sulaymān's letter to Ibn ʿĪdān—Ibn ʿAbd al-Wahhāb composed a long epistle to the people of al-ʿUyayna refuting his brother's arguments.[223] This counter-refutation, which Ibn Ghannām includes in his history, is known as *Mufīd al-mustafīd fī kufr tārik al-tawḥīd* (The Helper of the Inquirer into the Unbelief of the Abandoner of God's Oneness).[224] In the epistle, Ibn ʿAbd al-Wahhāb refers explicitly to the apostasy of Ḥuraymilāʾ, saying that "the people of

218. Ibn ʿAbd al-Wahhāb, *al-Ṣawāʿiq al-ilāhiyya*, 5, 7.

219. Ibid., 15.

220. Ibid., 44.

221. Ibid., 3–4, 11, 43.

222. Ibid., 6–7, 10–11.

223. Ibn Ghannām, *Tārīkh*, 2:696.

224. Ibid., 2:696–735. For a critical edition based on multiple manuscript sources, see Ibn ʿAbd al-Wahhāb, *Mufīd al-mustafīd*.

Ḥuraymilāʾ and beyond openly revile the religion . . . and they do and say things that are the greatest and most abominable apostasy."[225] He appears to refer to an epistle by his brother, mentioning at one point "the epistle that has reached you" (*al-risāla allatī atatkum*) and describing its author as the leader of the unbelievers.[226] In *Mufīd al-mustafīd*, as in some of his other letters and epistles, Ibn ʿAbd al-Wahhāb underlines the importance of showing enmity to the polytheists and pronouncing *takfīr* on them. Yet, unlike before, he throws violence into the mix as well, arguing that it is a duty to fight the polytheists in addition to showing them hatred and enmity. "May God have mercy," he writes, "on him who considers and reflects upon the command received by Muḥammad from God to show enmity to those who commit *shirk*, near or far, to pronounce *takfīr* on them, and to fight them 'till the religion is God's entirely' (Q. 8:39)."[227] This was an enthusiastic endorsement of fighting the so-called polytheists, which as a practical matter meant supporting the expansionary warfare of the first Saudi state.

Ibn ʿAbd al-Wahhāb's main preoccupation in *Mufīd al-mustafīd* is with what he calls "the issue of *takfīr* and fighting" (*masʾalat al-takfīr wa ʾl-qitāl*).[228] In justifying his approach to these, he quotes liberally from Ibn Taymiyya and Ibn al-Qayyim, seeking to show that these scholars' words, contrary to the claims of his opponents, do in fact lend support to his views.[229] He quotes Ibn Taymiyya, for instance, condemning certain groups of professed Muslims as unbelievers, thus showing that the Ḥanbalī scholar was not opposed to pronouncing *takfīr* on those whose beliefs and behaviors contravened *tawḥīd*. With regard to the distinction between *al-shirk al-akbar* and *al-shirk al-aṣghar*, he asserts that his enemies have misread a passage by Ibn al-Qayyim discussing the two kinds of *shirk*. Despite their claims, he says, practices such as *istighātha* do in fact meet the threshold of *al-shirk al-akbar*, whereas *al-shirk al-aṣghar* pertains only to such minor things as flaunting (*al-riyāʾ*) and swearing by other than God (*al-ḥilf bi-ghayr Allāh*).[230] As in *Kashf al-shubuhāt*, Ibn ʿAbd al-Wahhāb again justifies the use of violence against the opponents of his movement, though here he does so at much greater length, probably because

225. Ibn Ghannām, *Tārīkh*, 2:712.

226. Ibid., 2:710.

227. Ibid., 2:711.

228. Ibid., 2:713.

229. Ibid., 2:700–718.

230. Ibid., 2:707–10. Ibn ʿAbd al-Wahhāb, as will be seen, was generally correct about this.

he was seeking to justify the Wahhābīs' violent campaign to subjugate Ḥuraymilāʾ. Citing more examples of early Muslims who fought people who professed Islam, he highlights the case of Abū Bakr al-Ṣiddīq, the first caliph in Sunnī Islam. During the wars of apostasy following the death of the Prophet Muḥammad, when a number of the Prophet's erstwhile followers refused to pay the *zakāt* to the caliph, Abū Bakr advocated fighting them, despite the fact that they were outwardly Muslim.[231]

Only a few years after it was written, *Mufīd al-mustafīd* would be the focal point of another major refutation of Wahhābism, this one by a prominent scholar in Sanaa named Muḥammad ibn Ismāʿīl al-Amīr al-Ṣanʿānī, better known as Ibn al-Amīr al-Ṣanʿānī (d. 1182/1768).[232] Born into a community associated with the Zaydī version of Shīʿism, Ibn al-Amīr al-Ṣanʿānī was a leading member of a Sunnī reformist trend in Yemen that was similar in some ways to Wahhābism, if not nearly as radical. This reformist trend, which also included Muḥammad ibn ʿAlī al-Shawkānī (d. 1250/1839), championed the authority of the Sunnī *ḥadīth* and advocated *ijtihād* as against *taqlīd*. The members of this trend were also, like Ibn ʿAbd al-Wahhāb, highly critical of the cult of saints. Upon first learning of Wahhābism, in 1162/1748f, Ibn al-Amīr naturally wrote a poem in praise of Ibn ʿAbd al-Wahhāb, describing the Najdī reformer as a man after his own heart, as someone who, like himself, was seeking to revive the religion and defeat ignorance and innovation. Toward the beginning of this poem, he writes:

And the reports about him came, telling that he
is reviving for us the noble religion [*al-sharʿ al-sharīf*] by what he is manifesting,
And exposing publicly what has been concealed of it by every ignorant person
and innovator, thus being in agreement with me.
And he is erecting the pillars of the Sharīʿa while destroying
shrines in which people have strayed from right guidance . . .
Indeed I was pleased by what came to me of his way
having thought that this path was mine alone.[233]

231. Ibid., 2:719–20.

232. On him, see *EI*³, s.v. "al-Amīr, Muḥammad b. Ismāʿīl" (Bernard Haykel); al-Shawkānī, *al-Badr al-ṭāliʿ*, 2:133–39.

233. al-Amīr, *Dīwān al-Amīr al-Ṣanʿānī*, 128–32, at 129–30 (meter = *ṭawīl*).

The Wahhābīs quickly seized on Ibn al-Amīr's poem as a major endorsement. For the opponents of Wahhābism, however, the poem was a scandal. At a time when the Sunnī Islamic world seemed to be united in condemning Wahhābism, here was a major scholar praising it as a just and good reformist movement. Ibn al-Amīr's poem would spread far and wide during this early period, earning him a reputation as a Wahhābī zealot. A number of scholars responded with verse refutations, including one by a colleague of al-Qabbānī's in Basra, the Shāfiʿī Yāsīn ibn Ibrāhīm al-Ṭabāṭabāʾī (fl. 1190/1776f).[234] His poem, copies of which are extant in Germany and the United Kingdom, was completed in Rajab 1168/April 1755.[235] After describing Ibn al-Amīr as a Khārijite aligned with "the Musaylima of Najd," he goes on to refute about a quarter of the offending poem line by line.

In 1170/1756f, after facing a raft of criticism by scholars far and wide, Ibn al-Amīr changed his mind about Ibn ʿAbd al-Wahhāb, recanting his earlier praise poem by authoring a new poem together with a commentary thereon.[236] This poem-cum-commentary is known by several titles, one of which is *Irshād dhawī ʾl-albāb ilā ḥaqīqat aqwāl Ibn ʿAbd al-Wahhāb* (Guiding Those Possessed of Understanding to the Truth Concerning the Statements of Ibn ʿAbd al-Wahhāb). What caused Ibn al-Amīr to revise his views was not the criticism being leveled against him but, rather, the arrival in Sanaa of a new epistle by Ibn ʿAbd al-Wahhāb. This was *Mufīd al-mustafīd,* and it was reading this that convinced Ibn al-Amīr that Ibn ʿAbd al-Wahhāb was no mere reformer like himself. In the prose introduction to *Irshād dhawī ʾl-albāb,* Ibn al-Amīr explains the circumstances that led to his writing the original poem.[237] What he had learned at the time was that Ibn ʿAbd al-Wahhāb prohibited

234. On him, see al-Ḥusaynī, "Makhṭūṭ nādir."

235. Ibn Ibrāhīm, *Radd ʿalā Ibn al-Amīr al-Ṣanʿānī.* For the completion date, see f. 5b; and on this manuscript, see Weisweiler, *Verzeichnis der arabischen Handschriften,* 115. The copy at the British Library is mentioned in Cook, "On the Origins of Wahhābism," 201n95.

236. al-Amīr, *Irshād dhawī ʾl-albāb.* For the poem sans commentary, see al-Amīr, *Dīwān,* 134–40. The attribution of these to Ibn al-Amīr was long denied by the Wahhābīs, who dismissed them as fabrications. The issue is discussed at length in Ibn ʿAqīl al-Ẓāhirī, *Rujūʿ al-Amīr al-Ṣanʿānī,* which concludes that the poem is genuine and the commentary is likely genuine. The senior Wahhābī scholar ʿAbd al-ʿAzīz ibn Bāz (d. 1420/1999) prevailed upon Ibn ʿAqīl al-Ẓāhirī not to publish it; see Ibn ʿAqīl al-Ẓāhirī, *Maʿārik ṣuḥufiyya,* 1:112–13. The Yemeni editor of *Irshād dhawī ʾl-albāb* confirms the attribution of both the poem and the commentary with manuscript evidence.

237. al-Amīr, *Irshād dhawī ʾl-albāb,* 100–110.

religious innovations like those related to the cult of saints and that he had destroyed tombs. Since then, however, new information had come his way, conveyed by two Najdī visitors to Sanaa. One of these, Mirbad ibn Aḥmad al-Tamīmī (d. 1171/1757f),[238] brought with him an epistle by Ibn ʿAbd al-Wahhāb that allowed Ibn al-Amīr to see for the first time that Ibn ʿAbd al-Wahhāb was pronouncing *takfīr* on the entire *umma* and fighting his enemies as unbelievers. This Ibn al-Amīr did not condone. He begins the second poem thus:

> I renounce the poem that I wrote about the Najdī,
> for it has been proved true to me that he is not in agreement with me . . .
> Shaykh Mirbad came to us from his land
> and verified all the things that he is manifesting;
> And he brought epistles written by him
> in which he pronounces *takfīr* on the people of the earth knowingly . . .
> He has vied in spilling the blood of every Muslim
> who prays and pays the *zakāt* and withdraws not from the covenant.[239]

While Ibn al-Amīr seems to mention multiple Wahhābī epistles (*rasāʾil*) here, in the commentary he refers only to *Mufīd al-mustafīd*, which he quotes several times.[240] It is worth noting that there was something about *Mufīd al-mustafīd* that Ibn al-Amīr must have found particularly alarming. This was the fact that Ibn ʿAbd al-Wahhāb had quoted Ibn al-Amīr in the epistle, highlighting a line in the Yemeni's praise poem. Ibn ʿAbd al-Wahhāb had quoted only one line of

238. On him, see Āl Bassām, *ʿUlamāʾ Najd*, 6:416–20. Ibn al-Amīr states that Mirbad arrived in Ṣafar 1170/October–November 1756 and departed eight months later, on 20 Shawwāl 1170/July ~8, 1757; while he does not specify exactly when he composed the new poem and the commentary thereon, Ibn al-Amīr implies that he wrote at least the poem during Mirbad's stay (*Irshād dhawī ʾl-albāb*, 109–11).

239. al-Amīr, *Irshād dhawī ʾl-albāb*, 111 (meter = *ṭawīl*).

240. Ibid., 119–20, 124, 127–28; cf. Ibn Ghannām, *Tārīkh*, 2:720, 712–13. The fact that *Mufīd al-mustafīd* is quoted in *Irshād dhawī ʾl-albāb* means that it cannot have been written earlier than Ṣafar 1170/October–November 1756, the date when Mirbad brought the epistle to Sanaa (see n. 238). While this provides us with a *terminus post quem*, there is no reason to doubt Ibn Ghannām's date of composition of 1167/1753f.

Ibn al-Amīr's poem, and this was related to the authenticity of *ḥadīth,* not *takfīr* and *qitāl.*[241] Nonetheless, it must have been deeply unsettling to the Yemeni scholar to see his own words being used in a Wahhābī epistle advocating views that he regarded as extreme. Perhaps this, more than anything else, was what compelled him to recant.

In refuting Ibn ʿAbd al-Wahhāb on the points of *takfīr* and *qitāl,* Ibn al-Amīr makes many of the same arguments as the refuters before him, including noting that the Prophet forbade killing those who confess that "there is no god but God."[242] He rejects the examples used in *Mufīd al-mustafīd* in support of violence, such as Abū Bakr's willingness to fight those who withheld the *zakāt.* Abū Bakr, he says, only fought them after they persisted in withholding it.[243] Like some of the Ḥanbalī refuters, Ibn al-Amīr draws attention to the distinction between *al-shirk al-akbar* and *al-shirk al-aṣghar,* which he relates to two types of unbelief (*kufr*): unbelief in creed (*kufr iʿtiqād*) and unbelief in action (*kufr ʿamal*). Those who call on saints and make vows to them, among other such practices, have only committed *kufr ʿamal,* not *kufr iʿtiqād.* The proper response is therefore not *takfīr* but, rather, admonishment and instruction to dispel their ignorance (*waʿẓuhum wa-taʿrīfuhum jahlahum*).[244] Also like the Ḥanbalīs, Ibn al-Amīr is concerned with distancing Ibn Taymiyya and Ibn al-Qayyim from Wahhābism. He states at the beginning of his commentary that Ibn ʿAbd al-Wahhāb has misread and misunderstood these two great scholars:

> We saw him to be the kind of man who knows a portion of the Sharīʿa but has not examined it carefully, and who did not study with those who could guide him to the path of guidance, direct him to the beneficial religious sciences, and instruct him in them. Instead, he read some of the works of the Shaykh Abū ʾl-ʿAbbās Ibn Taymiyya and the works of his student Ibn Qayyim al-Jawziyya, and emulated them poorly [*wa-qalladahumā min ghayr itqān*], despite the fact that both prohibit *taqlīd.*[245]

241. *aḥādīthu lā tuʿzā ilā ʿālimin fa-lā / tusāwiya falsan in rajaʿta ilā ʾl-naqdī* ("*Ḥadīth*s that are not ascribed to one with knowledge and do not / equal a penny if you subject [them] to scrutiny"); Ibn Ghannām, *Tārīkh,* 2:720; al-Amīr, *Dīwān,* 129. The quotation is noted in Cook, "On the Origins of Wahhābism," 201n96.

242. al-Amīr, *Irshād dhawī ʾl-albāb,* 113–16.

243. Ibid., 131.

244. Ibid., 134–54.

245. Ibid., 108.

Yet while Ibn al-Amīr recanted his earlier praise and joined the anti-Wahhābī crowd, it must be acknowledged that he never waxed vitriolic in his opposition to Ibn ʿAbd al-Wahhāb, as did all of the other refuters. The Najdī was not a hate figure for him but, rather, a fellow scholar, even if a greatly misled one. Instead of being treated to insulting epithets, he is described throughout the commentary as *al-shaykh Muḥammad.*[246] The tone of Ibn al-Amīr's refutation is measured, and he does not accuse Ibn ʿAbd al-Wahhāb of such things as claiming *ijtihād* and prophecy. Presumably, Ibn al-Amīr still saw something to admire in Ibn ʿAbd al-Wahhāb, even if the latter's approach to *takfīr* and *qitāl* was for him a bridge too far.

At least a quarter century would pass between the recantation of Ibn al-Amīr al-Ṣanʿānī, in 1170/1757, and the next extant refutation that can be fit into the time line. This was a refutation by ʿAbdallāh Afandī al-Rāwī al-Baghdādī (d. 1215/1800f), a preacher in Baghdad who wrote his work at the behest of the city's governor, Sulaymān Bāshā (r. 1194–1217/1780–1802).[247] The Wahhābīs had sent to Baghdad some of Ibn ʿAbd al-Wahhāb's writings, and al-Rāwī was tasked with authoring the response. Part of the response survives in a Wahhābī counterrefutation known by the title *al-Tawḍīḥ ʿan tawḥīd al-Khallāq,* which was likely authored by the Najdī scholar Muḥammad ibn Gharīb (d. 1208/1793).[248] The time lag between Ibn al-Amīr's refutation and al-Rāwī's

246. See, for example, ibid., 132.

247. On him, see al-Baghdādī, *Tārīkh al-usar al-ʿilmiyya fī Baghdād*, 58–60. Curiously, much of al-Rāwī's refutation is borrowed, without attribution, from Ibn al-Amīr's prose commentary. Compare al-Amīr, *Irshād dhawī ʾl-albāb*, 110, and Ibn Gharīb, *al-Tawḍīḥ*, 1:163, 230; and compare al-Amīr, *Irshād dhawī ʾl-albāb*, 135–53, and Ibn Gharīb, *al-Tawḍīḥ*, 1:338, 345–47, 382–83, 405, 409–10, 422–23, 427–28, 440, 446, 450, 453, 461–62, 464–65, 2:495, 498–99.

248. Ibn Gharīb, *al-Tawḍīḥ*. On Ibn Gharīb, see Ibn Ḥumayd, *al-Suḥub al-wābila*, 2:690–91 (misidentified as ʿAbdallāh ibn Gharīb); Āl Bassām, *ʿUlamāʾ Najd*, 6:312–16. The date of al-Rāwī's refutation can be narrowed to between 1194/1780, the year of Sulaymān Bāshā's assumption of power in Baghdad, and 1203/1789, the date of the earliest known manuscript of *al-Tawḍīḥ* ([Ibn Gharīb,] *al-Radd ʿalā ʾl-Wahhābiyya*, f. 227b, on which manuscript, see Browne, *Supplementary Hand-List*, 106). The first edition of *al-Tawḍīḥ* (printed in Cairo by al-Maṭbaʿa al-ʿĀmira al-Sharafiyya in 1319/1901f) was mistakenly attributed to Sulaymān ibn ʿAbdallāh Āl al-Shaykh. The editor of the new edition shows this to be impossible and favors the attribution to Muḥammad ibn ʿAlī ibn Gharīb (d. 1208/1793), following the opinion of several Wahhābī scholars of the nineteenth and early twentieth centuries.

is significant, as it seems to indicate the decline of anti-Wahhābī literature beginning in the 1170s/1750s.

The launching of the Wahhābī movement in 1153/1741 had inspired an outburst of anti-Wahhābī writing. There had been a sense of urgency among the movement's scholarly opponents. Wahhābism, as they saw it, was a dangerous heresy that needed to be confronted and stamped out. Over time, however, the refuters realized that their efforts were not bearing fruit. The refutations did have some impact, of course. Ibn ʿAbd al-Wahhāb did not look upon them with indifference, and in fact he refers to their pernicious influence throughout his *rasāʾil*.[249] The efforts of Ibn Suḥaym, al-Muways, and Sulaymān ibn ʿAbd al-Wahhāb, in particular, likely stalled the progress of the Wahhābī movement in its earliest years. Yet, ultimately, the refuters failed to stop Wahhābism from spreading. Already in the 1140s/1740s, Ibn ʿAfāliq sensed that refuting the Wahhābīs was something of a futile enterprise. As he wrote in one of his letters to Ibn Muʿammar, "You react to every writing that comes your way by rejecting it and cursing and ridiculing its author, even before it is opened and looked at."[250] A few decades later, the sense of futility seems to have settled in, as henceforward the refutation of Wahhābism became more of a niche activity, undertaken only by those with a special interest in the movement.

One such scholar who harbored a special interest in Wahhābism was the Ḥanbalī ʿAbdallāh ibn Dāwūd al-Zubayrī (d. 1212/1797f).[251] Ibn Dāwūd belonged to a group of Ḥanbalī scholars in Iraq who had previously studied in al-Aḥsāʾ with Muḥammad ibn Fayrūz, the leader of the Ḥanbalī community there after Ibn ʿAfāliq. Many of these were Najdī émigrés, including Ibn Dāwūd himself, whose ancestral homeland was in Sudayr. Three other Najdī students of Ibn Fayrūz's had roots in Sudayr as well: Ṣāliḥ ibn Sayf al-ʿAtīqī (d. 1223/1808),[252] Ibrāhīm ibn Nāṣir ibn Jadīd (d. 1232/1817),[253] and Muḥammad ibn ʿAlī ibn Sallūm (d. 1246/1831).[254] In 1208/1793, as the Wahhābī conquest

249. See, for example, Ibn Ghannām, *Tārīkh*, 1:424–26 (letter to Aḥmad ibn Ibrāhīm).

250. Ibn ʿAfāliq, *Risāla* I, f. 55a.

251. On him, see Ibn Sanad, *Sabāʾik al-ʿasjad*, 257–59; Ibn Ḥumayd, *al-Suḥub al-wābila*, 2:619–20; Āl Bassām, *ʿUlamāʾ Najd*, 4:114–15.

252. On him, see Ibn Fayrūz, *Tarājim*, f. 78b; Ibn Sanad, *Sabāʾik al-ʿasjad*, 268–70; Ibn Ḥumayd, *al-Suḥub al-wābila*, 2:429–30; Āl Bassām, *ʿUlamāʾ Najd*, 2:474–77.

253. On him, see Ibn Sanad, *Sabāʾik al-ʿasjad*, 288–89; Ibn Ḥumayd, *al-Suḥub al-wābila*, 1:71–76; Āl Bassām, *ʿUlamāʾ Najd*, 1:423–27.

254. On him, see Ibn Sanad, *Sabāʾik al-ʿasjad*, 277–80; Ibn Ḥumayd, *al-Suḥub al-wābila*, 3:1007–12; Āl Bassām, *ʿUlamāʾ Najd*, 6:292–303.

of al-Aḥsāʾ loomed, Ibn Fayrūz left the area for Basra, which, along with the nearby town of al-Zubayr, became the new home of this anti-Wahhābī community of Ḥanbalīs.[255] In his Iraqi exile, Ibn Fayrūz composed several anti-Wahhābī works urging his Iraqi hosts to wage *jihād* against the Wahhābīs in al-Aḥsāʾ.[256] None of these efforts would bear fruit, however, as the Wahhābīs remained in control of the area for more than a decade after the last anti-Wahhābī campaign was launched from Iraq.

In 1210/1795, Ibn Dāwūd al-Zubayrī completed a long refutation of Wahhābism titled *al-Ṣawāʿiq wa ʾl-ruʿūd raddan ʿalā ʾl-shaqī ʿAbd al-ʿAzīz Suʿūd* (Lightning and Thunder in Refutation of the Damned ʿAbd al-ʿAzīz Suʿūd), a lone copy of which survives in a library in Patna, India.[257] Preceding the main text is an encomium (*taqrīẓ*) by Ibn Fayrūz, in which he tells something of the story of Ibn ʿAbd al-Wahhāb's rise (*shayʾan min nashʾat al-ṭāghiya al-murtāb*).[258] Among other things, he recalls the epistle to Riyadh and Manfūḥa in which Ibn ʿAbd al-Wahhāb had claimed that his understanding of the religion came to him as a blessing (*khayr*) from on high; Ibn Fayrūz retorts that this was in fact a revelation from Satan (*waḥy awḥāhu Iblīs ilayhi*). While he goes on in the *taqrīẓ* to praise Ibn Dāwūd and his work, it seems that Ibn Fayrūz had concluded by this point that writing such refutations was of little benefit. In his refutation, Ibn Dāwūd notes that his teachers advised him against writing it, as doing so would be a waste of

255. For the date of his departure, see Ibn Ghannām, *Tārīkh*, 2:922; on his move to Basra, see Ibn Ḥumayd, *al-Suḥub al-wābila*, 3:974.

256. The first is a poem written in 1211/1796f in support of a tribal chief's campaign in al-Aḥsāʾ ordered by Sulaymān Bāshā (al-ʿAssāfī, *Tarājim al-fuḍalāʾ*, ff. 47a–49a); Ibn Ghannām would write a verse counterrefutation of it (*Tārīkh*, 9:952–56). The second is a poem eulogizing the same tribal leader, Thuwaynī ibn ʿAbdallāh, who was assassinated in 1212/1797, and encouraging his successor, Ḥamūd ibn Thāmir (d. 1242/1826f), to finish the job (al-ʿAssāfī, *Tarājim al-fuḍalāʾ*, ff. 52a–54b). The third is a letter to Sulaymān Bāshā's deputy or steward (*ketkhüdā* in Turkish; *katkhudā* or *kahyā* in Arabic) setting out the arguments in favor of *jihād* against the Wahhābīs. This was published in Bombay in 1307/1889f under the title *al-Risāla al-marḍiyya fī ʾl-radd ʿalā ʾl-Wahhābiyya*, the text of which is also found in a counterrefutation by a later Wahhābī scholar; see Āl Maḥmūd, *Taḥdhīr ahl al-īmān*.

257. Ibn Dāwūd, *al-Ṣawāʿiq wa ʾl-ruʿūd*; on this manuscript, see Ross et al., *Catalogue of the Arabic and Persian Manuscripts in the Oriental Public Library at Bankipore*, 10:87–89. I am grateful to Bernard Haykel for helping me obtain a copy.

258. Ibn Dāwūd, *al-Ṣawāʿiq wa ʾl-ruʿūd*, ff. 1b–4b. This is dated 12 Ṣafar 1210/August ~27, 1795. While *al-Ṣawāʿiq wa ʾl-ruʿūd* is not itself dated, it is likely that Ibn Dāwūd completed his work shortly before this.

time.[259] According to Ibn Dāwūd, it was indeed the ineffectiveness of the refutations that had caused an earlier generation of scholars to cease refuting the Wahhābīs:

> Most of the scholars of the lands wrote refutations of him [i.e., Ibn ʿAbd al-Wahhāb]. . . . Then, when the scholars saw that he was not responding and not returning to the truth . . . and that advising him was unsuccessful, but rather that his terrible acts were only multiplying, they stopped refuting him . . . and they said, "This man is misled, and will only recant when he is overcome by force; nothing will deter him but the sword of the sultan."[260]

Ibn Dāwūd may have agreed with this conclusion, but he decided to write his work anyway out of a sense of religious duty, saying that he was fired by religious zeal (*akhadhatnī ʾl-ghayra al-Islāmiyya*). Furthermore, it was his view that enough time had passed to make a renewal of the refutational effort necessary (*idhā ṭāla ʾl-zamān wajaba ʾl-tajdīd*).[261]

It was not only these reasons that spurred Ibn Dāwūd to write his *al-Ṣawāʿiq wa ʾl-ruʿūd*, however. The more immediate reason was that he wished to respond to an epistle by ʿAbd al-ʿAzīz ibn Muḥammad Āl Suʿūd (r. 1179–1218/1765–1803), the successor to Muḥammad ibn Suʿūd as the leader of the first Saudi state, that was circulating at the time. This epistle, a lengthy polemic against the cult of saints calling on its readers to adopt Wahhābism, was addressed "to whoever sees it among the scholars and judges of the Two Holy Places, al-Shām, Egypt, and Iraq, and all other scholars east and west."[262] Yet while ostensibly written as a response to ʿAbd al-ʿAzīz Āl Suʿūd's epistle, *al-Ṣawāʿiq wa ʾl-ruʿūd* is primarily concerned with disputing the Wahhābīs' use of Ibn Taymiyya and Ibn al-Qayyim. Ibn Dāwūd devotes separate sections (*fuṣūl*; sing. *faṣl*) to Ibn Taymiyya, Ibn al-Qayyim, and Ibn Mufliḥ (d. 763/1362), another student of Ibn Taymiyya's, highlighting what he believes are the main differences between these scholars and Ibn

259. Ibid., f. 13a.

260. Ibid., f. 12a.

261. Ibid., f. 13a.

262. In Ibn Siḥmān, *al-Hadiyya al-saniyya*, 4–28, at 4. The real author of the epistle, according to Ibn Dāwūd, was Ibn Gharīb; see Ibn Dāwūd, *al-Ṣawāʿiq wa ʾl-ruʿūd*, ff. 70a, 192b. This epistle also elicited a short refutation by a certain Muḥammad ibn Muḥammad al-Shāfiʿī al-Qādirī in Aleppo, dated 1211/1796f; see al-Qādirī, *Radd ʿalā risālat ʿAbd al-ʿAzīz ibn Suʿūd*.

ʿAbd al-Wahhāb.[263] While the treatment is longer and more systematic, the approach is generally the same as the previous efforts to rescue Ibn Taymiyya and Ibn al-Qayyim from Wahhābism: namely, that these earlier Ḥanbalīs, though they wrote at length about the dangers of *shirk*, distinguished between *al-shirk al-aṣghar* and *al-shirk al-akbar* and were restrained in their approach to *takfīr*. The rest of *al-Ṣawāʿiq waʾl-ruʿūd* is a line-by-line refutation of ʿAbd al-ʿAzīz's epistle.

Throughout his refutation, Ibn Dāwūd quotes liberally from the works of earlier anti-Wahhābī writers, including Ibn ʿAfāliq, ʿAbdallāh ibn Fayrūz, Ibn al-Ṭayyib al-Maghribī, and Ibn al-Amīr al-Ṣanʿānī. He repeats many of the familiar accusations, including that Ibn ʿAbd al-Wahhāb claims to exercise *ijtihād*, claims prophecy and considers himself infallible, despises the *fiqh* tradition, and resembles the Khārijites. He also accuses the Wahhābī leader of imitating the Prophet Muḥammad, saying, "He imitates the Messenger of God in countless ways."[264] There is only one noticeable addition, however, to the many anti-Wahhābī themes seen before. This is the claim that the Wahhābīs require their followers to shave their heads. Ibn Dāwūd states that they do so as a way of distinguishing themselves from their enemies and that they will kill anyone they come across who is unshaven.[265] He connects this to the Khārijite theme, quoting a *ḥadīth* that predicts the appearance of a group of Muslims (generally assumed to be the Khārijites) whose distinctive characteristic is shaving (*sīmāhum al-taḥlīq*).[266] This claim appears to have been based in fact, as in a letter written about a decade later, ʿAbd al-ʿAzīz Āl Suʿūd's son and successor, Suʿūd ibn ʿAbd al-ʿAzīz (r. 1218–29/1803–14), acknowledges that Wahhābī soldiers do in fact shave their heads as a way of marking them off from those he calls the unbelievers.[267]

The last great refutation of Wahhābism to appear during the first Saudi state was written by ʿAlawī ibn Aḥmad al-Ḥaddād (d. 1232/1817), a Shāfiʿī

263. Ibn Dāwūd, *al-Ṣawāʿiq waʾl-ruʿūd*, ff. 39b–57a (*al-faṣl al-thālith fī mubāyanat Ibn ʿAbd al-Wahhāb liʾbn Taymiyya*), 57a–64a (*al-faṣl al-rābiʿ fī mubāyanat Ibn ʿAbd al-Wahhāb liʾbn al-Qayyim*), 64a–67b (*al-faṣl al-khāmis fī ʾl-radd ʿalayhi min kalām Ibn Mufliḥ*).

264. Ibid., f. 49a.

265. Ibid., f. 21b.

266. Ibid., f. 21a. For the *ḥadīth*, see al-Bukhārī, *Ṣaḥīḥ*, 1444 (*Kitāb al-tawḥīd, bāb qirāʾat al-fājir waʾl-munāfiq wa-aṣwātuhum wa-tilāwatuhum lā tujāwizu ḥanājirahum*, no. 7562).

267. *al-Durar al-saniyya*, 9:290.

from Tarīm in Ḥaḍramawt.[268] Published in Cairo in 1325/1907f, its full title is *Miṣbāḥ al-anām wa-jalāʾ al-ẓalām fī radd shubah al-bidʿī al-Najdī allatī aḍalla bihā ʾl-ʿawāmm* (Enlightening Mankind and Illuminating Darkness in Refutation of the Najdī Innovator's Errors by Which He Misled the Masses).[269] As he indicates within, al-Ḥaddād finished this very long text in Medina in 1215/1801 during a visit to the Ḥijāz.[270] His interest in Wahhābism was sparked, he says, when he witnessed the spread of the movement to parts of ʿUmān and other unidentified places.[271] He set about collecting any and all anti-Wahhābī refutations he could find during his travels across the Middle East, and like Ibn Dāwūd he quotes these repeatedly in his refutation. Al-Ḥaddād had even read and admired Ibn Dāwūd's *al-Ṣawāʿiq wa ʾl-ruʿūd*, which he quotes a part of.[272]

Unlike Ibn Dāwūd's refutation, however, *Miṣbāḥ al-anām* is primarily concerned with defending the cult of saints, which is no surprise coming from a Shāfiʿī Ṣūfī scholar. In this respect, it is quite similar to the earlier Shāfiʿī refutations, such as al-Qabbānī's *Faṣl al-khiṭāb*, the notable difference being that al-Ḥaddād refrains from blaming Wahhābism on Ibn Taymiyya. Perhaps in this regard he had been influenced by Ibn Dāwūd. Al-Ḥaddād states that while everything Ibn ʿAbd al-Wahhāb is preaching is based on the words of Ibn Taymiyya (*jull mā ʿindahu muʿtamad ʿalā aqwāl Ibn Taymiyya al-Ḥanbalī*), the reality is that the Najdī was distinct from the Ḥanbalī scholar. He was closer to being a godless heretic than a follower of Ibn Taymiyya.[273] This was in keeping with the Ḥanbalī position on Ibn ʿAbd al-Wahhāb. As Muḥammad ibn Fayrūz had written, the Najdī reformer's

268. On him, see al-Saqqāf, *Tārīkh al-shuʿarāʾ al-Ḥaḍramiyyīn*, 3:43–47. He was a grandson of the famous Ṣūfī master ʿAbdallāh ibn ʿAlī al-Ḥaddād (d. 1132/1720), on whom, see *EI*³, s.v. "ʿAbdallāh b. ʿAlawī al-Ḥaddād" (Ismail Fajrie Alatas).

269. al-Ḥaddād, *Miṣbāḥ al-anām*. It should be mentioned that *Miṣbāḥ al-anām* reproduces the text of an earlier refutation by a certain ʿAbdallāh ibn Sayyid ʿAlawī al-Ḥuḍarī, the text of which was edited and published in Ebied and Young, "Unpublished Refutation of the Doctrines of the Wahhābis." As al-Ḥaddād explains (*Miṣbāḥ al-anām*, 2), the first four chapters (*fuṣūl*) of his refutation are borrowed from an earlier one, which upon examination turns out to be al-Ḥudarī's refutation.

270. al-Ḥaddād, *Miṣbāḥ al-anām*, 78–79.

271. Ibid., 5.

272. Ibid., 3–4.

273. Ibid., 36.

views were without precedent: "No one dead or alive before him espoused this abominable doctrine of his."[274]

Yet, despite the latter-day efforts of Ibn Dāwūd and al-Ḥaddād to refute the Wahhābīs, the Wahhābī movement was still advancing at the turn of the nineteenth century. Tellingly, just a few years after al-Ḥaddād finished his anti-Wahhābī tract in Medina, the Wahhābīs conquered the city. The earlier opponents of Wahhābism had been right to conclude that the movement would not be defeated by the lash of a pen. What was required was the military intervention of a major power.[275]

Conclusion

As this chapter has shown, the refutations of Ibn ʿAbd al-Wahhāb shed considerable light on the history of early Wahhābism. Several of them reveal when Ibn ʿAbd al-Wahhāb wrote certain of his epistles and letters. As we have seen, the *Kalimāt fī bayān shahādat an lā ilāha illā ʾllāh* and the *Arbaʿ qawāʿid tadūru ʾl-aḥkām ʿalayhā* were written no later than 1155/1742; the epistle to Riyadh and Manfūḥa, no later than 1157/1744; the *Arbaʿ qawāʿid fī ʾl-dīn*, no later than 1158/1745; *Kashf al-shubuhāt*, no later than 1163/1750; and *Mufīd al-mustafīd*, no later than 1170/1757 (though Ibn Ghannām dates it to 1167/1753f). These were some of the *rasāʾil* that Ibn ʿAbd al-Wahhāb used to spread his doctrine and rebut the claims of his enemies, and they illustrate his movement's gradual adoption of violence. Whereas in the al-ʿUyayna period of his preaching he called on Muslims to show hatred and enmity to the so-called polytheists, in the al-Dirʿiyya period he advocated fighting them as well.

While not all the charges leveled against Ibn ʿAbd al-Wahhāb in the refutations are necessarily accurate or illuminating, at least one of them—the claim that he used or abused the teachings of Ibn Taymiyya and Ibn Qayyim al-Jawziyya—is highly instructive. Most of Ibn ʿAbd al-Wahhāb's refuters were either Shāfiʿīs or Ḥanbalīs, and these tended to take a different view of Ibn

274. Ibn Fayrūz, *al-Radd ʿalā man kaffara ahl al-Riyāḍ*, 34.

275. Following the Wahhābī occupation of the Ḥijāz, several scholars further afield, in Morocco and Tunisia, would write refutations of Wahhābism as well. These include the Moroccan Muḥammad al-Ṭayyib ibn Kīrān (d. 1227/1812) and the Tunisian ʿUmar ibn Qāsim al-Maḥjūb (d. 1222/1807), on whose refutations, see, respectively, Heck, "Early Response to Wahhabism from Morocco"; Green, "Tunisian Reply to a Wahhabi Proclamation."

TABLE 1.1. Wahhābī epistles quoted in early refutations

Epistle	Refutation	*Terminus post quem*
Arbaʿ qawāʿid tadūru ʾl-aḥkām ʿalayhā	Ibn ʿAfāliq's *Tahakkum al-muqallidīn*	ca. 1155/1742
Kalimāt fī bayān shahādat an lā ilāha illā ʾllāh	al-Qabbānī's *Faṣl al-khiṭāb*	Mid-1155/ mid-1742
Epistle to Riyadh and Manfūḥa	Ibn Suḥaym's epistle	Rajab 1157/ September 1744
Arbaʿ qawāʿid fī ʾl-dīn	al-Qabbānī's *Naqḍ qawāʿid al-ḍalāl*	Earlier 1158/ earlier 1745
Kashf al-shubuhāt	Ibn ʿAfāliq's letters to Ibn Muʿammar	Ṣafar 1163/ February 1750
Mufīd al-mustafīd	Ibn al-Amīr's *Irshād dhawī ʾl-albāb*	1167/1753f

Taymiyya and Ibn al-Qayyim.[276] The Shāfiʿī refuters, beginning with al-Qabbānī, were concerned above all with defending the legitimacy of the cult of saints, and most of them considered Ibn Taymiyya, along with Ibn al-Qayyim, to be the source of Ibn ʿAbd al-Wahhāb's heretical views in this regard. The Ḥanbalī refuters, for their part, were generally less concerned with defending the legitimacy of the cult of saints. They acknowledged that practices such as *istighātha* could verge toward *shirk* but argued that this was in fact *al-shirk al-aṣghar*, that is, the kind of *shirk* that does not expel one from the community of believers. Furthermore, they claimed that Ibn Taymiyya and Ibn al-Qayyim were hesitant to pronounce *takfīr* on professed Muslims. Ibn al-Amīr al-Ṣanʿānī, in line with the Ḥanbalīs, accused Ibn ʿAbd al-Wahhāb of making poor use of Ibn Taymiyya and Ibn al-Qayyim. Clearly, the ideas of these earlier scholars were critical to what Ibn ʿAbd al-Wahhāb was preaching. It is to their ideas and their influence that we now turn.

276. It is not surprising that the Shāfiʿīs and Ḥanbalīs would be the leaders of the scholarly opposition to Ibn ʿAbd al-Wahhāb in this period, as these were the dominant Sunnī communities in the Arab Middle East and central Arabia, respectively. What is somewhat surprising, however, is how few refutations seem to have been written by Ḥanafī scholars, given the Ottoman Empire's Ḥanafī allegiance. Perhaps there are more refutations by Ḥanafīs that remain to be identified. Others have mentioned refutations sent from the Ḥijāz to the Porte in 1749 and 1793, and perhaps these were authored by Ḥanafīs. For the 1749 refutation, see Qūrshūn, *al-ʿUthmāniyyūn wa-Āl Suʿūd fī ʾl-arshīf al-ʿUthmānī*, 48; and for the 1793 one, see Khoury, "Who Is a True Muslim?" 256.

2

The Doctrine of Ibn ʿAbd al-Wahhāb I

THE TAYMIYYAN BACKGROUND

AS WAS SEEN in the preceding chapter, the names Ibn Taymiyya and Ibn Qayyim al-Jawziyya loomed large in the early debate over Muḥammad ibn ʿAbd al-Wahhāb's movement. From the very beginning these two fourteenth-century Ḥanbalī scholars, and Ibn Taymiyya especially, featured prominently in the refutations of Wahhābism, and for good reason—the influence of their ideas on his preaching was unmistakable. The Shāfiʿīs accused Ibn ʿAbd al-Wahhāb of parroting and reviving Ibn Taymiyya's ideas, while the Ḥanbalīs accused him of misunderstanding and misusing them. To a large degree, the early debate over Wahhābism was a debate over the legitimacy and proper interpretation of Ibn Taymiyya and Ibn al-Qayyim. Was Wahhābism the inevitable outgrowth of Taymiyyan thought, or were Ibn Taymiyya and Ibn al-Qayyim innocent of Wahhābism?

The views of al-Qabbānī, in Basra, are illustrative of the Shāfiʿī perspective. In all three of his refutations, he attributes Wahhābism to the terrible influence of the earlier Ḥanbalī scholar, accusing Ibn ʿAbd al-Wahhāb of adopting the views of Ibn Taymiyya, "your leader and your example" (*imāmuka wa-muqtadāka*), regarding the practices associated with the cult of saints, particularly asking the dead for help (*istighātha*) and using them as a means to God (*tawassul*).[1] The recurrent phrase used to describe this reliance is "reprehen-

1. al-Qabbānī, *Faṣl al-khiṭāb*, f. 104a.

sible emulation" (*al-taqlīd al-radīʾ*).[2] Even Ibn ʿAbd al-Wahhāb's purported exercise of *ijtihād* is described by al-Qabbānī as in reality nothing but *taqlīd* of Ibn Taymiyya (*fa-kāna ʾjtihāduka ʿayn al-taqlīd lahu*).[3] "It is absolutely clear," he writes, "that you have emulated Ibn Taymiyya in prohibiting appealing for intercession to, and seeking the help of, the dead or absent."[4] The scholars are agreed, he asserts, that Ibn Taymiyya's views on these issues are "among his unmentionable faults . . . for which they accused him of unbelief [*qālū bi-kufrihi*]."[5] No one, he argues, should be appealing to such fringe and unacceptable ideas. As he puts it in *Faṣl al-khiṭāb*, speaking of Ibn Taymiyya: "Before this man, did any of the scholars of Islam who are followed in matters of religion declare to be unbelievers those who use the dead as a means to God and who ask the dead for help [*al-mutawassil wa ʾl-mustaghīth*]?"[6] It was this "reprehensible emulation" of Ibn Taymiyya, he says, that led Ibn ʿAbd al-Wahhāb to pronounce *takfīr* on the entire Muslim *umma*.[7] Similarly, the Shāfiʿī Ibn ʿAbd al-Laṭīf, in al-Aḥsāʾ, would portray Wahhābism as rooted in the pernicious ideas of Ibn Taymiyya. In an undated letter to the people of Kuwait, he writes of Ibn ʿAbd al-Wahhāb:

> One should not be misled by those relied on by this ignorant man, who laps up follies in the bitterest of pools, such as Ibn Taymiyya and his followers. . . . Eminent scholars [*aʾimma aʿlām*] unleashed their tongues against him. . . . The scholars of his time and the leading lights and stars of his time demanded that the sultan either kill or subdue him, and he was imprisoned till his death.[8]

The memory of Ibn Taymiyya was alive and well in the Shāfiʿī communities of Iraq and the Arabian Peninsula, and the memory was dark.

The Ḥanbalī opponents of Wahhābism, for their part, made light of the controversial nature of Ibn Taymiyya's and Ibn al-Qayyim's views. The two Ḥanbalī greats could not be conceded to the Wahhābīs. Even Ibn ʿAfāliq, the

2. See, for example, ibid., f. 52b (four instances); al-Qabbānī, *Kashf al-ḥijāb*, ff. 107b (two instances), 109b (two instances).

3. al-Qabbānī, *Kashf al-ḥijāb*, f. 109b.

4. Ibid., f. 108b.

5. Ibid., ff. 108b–9a; cf. al-Qabbānī, *Faṣl al-khiṭāb*, f. 52b.

6. al-Qabbānī, *Faṣl al-khiṭāb*, f. 53a.

7. al-Qabbānī, *Kashf al-ḥijāb*, f. 109a; cf. al-Qabbānī, *Faṣl al-khiṭāb*, ff. 52b–53a.

8. al-Nuwayṣir, *al-Muʿāraḍa*, 221.

Ḥanbalī luminary in al-Aḥsāʾ who initially criticized Ibn ʿAbd al-Wahhāb for relying on Ibn Taymiyya's views on the cult of saints, later joined the Ḥanbalī chorus in defense of Ibn Taymiyya and Ibn al-Qayyim. In his letters to ʿUthmān ibn Muʿammar, he writes that Ibn ʿAbd al-Wahhāb has falsely attributed things to the scholars of Islam (*iftarā ʿalā ahl al-ʿilm*), including Ibn al-Qayyim,[9] and he argues that Ibn ʿAbd al-Wahhāb has read Ibn Taymiyya and Ibn al-Qayyim selectively, picking and choosing from their views as he sees fit:

> What brought this man into this terrible abyss is that he looks at the books of Ibn al-Qayyim and takes from them what suits his fancy, disregarding what contradicts it; he takes from the beginning of a chapter and disregards the end of it. We will relate for you the entirety of Ibn al-Qayyim's words and those of his teacher, Ibn Taymiyya, so that you know that Ibn ʿAbd al-Wahhāb has gone astray and led people astray.[10]

Sulaymān ibn ʿAbd al-Wahhāb, the brother of the Wahhābī founder, would make the same point about selective reading. In his refutation he writes of Ibn Taymiyya and Ibn al-Qayyim, addressing the Wahhābīs: "You have taken from their words what is agreeable to you to the exclusion of what is not."[11] Likewise, the Ḥanbalī ʿAbd al-ʿAzīz al-Razīnī (d. 1179/1765), from Uthayfiya in al-Washm, would assert that Ibn ʿAbd al-Wahhāb had taken Ibn Taymiyya and Ibn al-Qayyim out of context and used their words to mislead his followers. Having fled to al-Aḥsāʾ to study with the Ḥanbalī community there, he wrote in a letter to his hometown in Uthayfiya concerning Ibn ʿAbd al-Wahhāb:

> O servants of God, this idol [*ṭāghūt*] misled a number of people with the words of these two shaykhs early on. He would find words of theirs that were uttered in respect of Jahm ibn Ṣafwān and Bishr al-Marīsī, and their followers from among the Jahmiyya and the Muʿtazila, reciting this to those ignorant commoners around him so they would think the Sunnīs were intended by it. Thus he led them away from their religion, causing their words to carry a meaning that they do not bear.[12]

9. Ibn ʿAfāliq, *Risāla* II, f. 64b.
10. Ibn ʿAfāliq, *Risāla* I, ff. 45b–46a.
11. Ibn ʿAbd al-Wahhāb, *al-Ṣawāʿiq al-ilāhiyya*, 6.
12. al-Bassām, "Min asbāb al-muʿāraḍa," 62–63. On al-Razīnī, see Ibn Fayrūz, *Tarājim*, f. 78a; Ibn Ḥumayd, *al-Suḥub al-wābila*, 2:540–44.

Jahm ibn Ṣafwān (d. 128/745f) and Bishr al-Marīsī (d. 218/833) are prominent heretics in Sunnī Muslim heresiography. While it is true that Ibn Taymiyya frequently condemned these scholars, al-Razīnī is wrong to suggest that Ibn Taymiyya did not target a great number of Sunnī scholars in his polemics. In fact, Ibn Taymiyya accused many of his scholarly opponents, who were Sunnī Muslims, of being Jahmiyya. Al-Razīnī, then, was downplaying the controversial nature of Ibn Taymiyya's doctrine, as were the other Ḥanbalī refuters.

The differences between the Shāfiʿī and Ḥanbalī refuters were certainly great, but there was one thing that they agreed upon: Ibn Taymiyya and Ibn al-Qayyim were central to what Ibn ʿAbd al-Wahhāb was preaching, regardless of whether his use of them was legitimate. As the nineteenth-century Ḥanbalī *muftī* of Mecca Muḥammad ibn Ḥumayd (d. 1295/1878) remarked, in a statement that all the refuters would have agreed with, Ibn ʿAbd al-Wahhāb treated the words of Ibn Taymiyya and Ibn al-Qayyim as scripture: "He saw their words as a proof text not admitting of interpretation [*naṣṣan lā yaqbalu ʾl-taʾwīl*]," that is, not admitting of any interpretation besides his own.[13] All agreed that Ibn ʿAbd al-Wahhāb's use of Ibn Taymiyya and Ibn al-Qayyim was critical to his venture.

Given the widely perceived centrality of Ibn Taymiyya and Ibn al-Qayyim to Wahhābism, it stands to reason that the necessary starting point for examining Ibn ʿAbd al-Wahhāb's doctrine is the religious thought of these two scholars. As Michael Cook has observed, no one has been able to identify a more proximate intellectual influence on Ibn ʿAbd al-Wahhāb than Ibn Taymiyya and Ibn al-Qayyim.[14] Indeed, as this and the following chapter aim to show, Wahhābism can hardly be understood without recourse to its Taymiyyan background. This is not to dismiss the originality of Ibn ʿAbd al-Wahhāb's thought or to discount the contestation surrounding the proper interpretation of Ibn Taymiyya and Ibn al-Qayyim. In the following chapter, we will examine the main tenets of Ibn ʿAbd al-Wahhāb's doctrine, including the ways in which he departed from these two scholars. Here we are concerned with understanding the religious thought of Ibn Taymiyya and Ibn al-Qayyim themselves and with some of the ways in which Ibn ʿAbd al-Wahhāb appealed to their authority.

That Ibn ʿAbd al-Wahhāb drew heavily on the ideas of Ibn Taymiyya and Ibn al-Qayyim is of course not a novel claim. Scholars of Islam have taken note of

13. Ibn Ḥumayd, *al-Suḥub al-wābila*, 2:678.

14. Cook, "On the Origins of Wahhābism," 201.

this fact since at least the time of Ignaz Goldziher, who wrote in his *Vorlesungen über den Islam* (1910): "It was the influence of Ibn Taymīya's teachings that called forth, around the middle of the eighteenth century, one of the recent religious movements in Islam: that of the Wahhābīs."[15] However, the relationship between Taymiyyan and Wahhābī thought has not been rigorously studied before and remains poorly understood. Since Henri Laoust's seminal work on Ibn Taymiyya's thought, *Essai sur les doctrines sociales et politiques de Taḳī-d-Dīn Aḥmad b. Taimīya* (1939), there have been great advances in the research on Ibn Taymiyya and Ibn al-Qayyim,[16] yet the Wahhābī connection has remained neglected. These two chapters may be seen as an effort to fill this research gap.

Ibn Taymiyya and His *Jamāʿa*

Taqī al-Dīn Aḥmad ibn Taymiyya (661–728/1263–1328) was a Ḥanbalī theologian and jurist who lived most of his life in Damascus under the Mamlūk Sultanate of Egypt and Syria (648–922/1250–1517).[17] Widely admired, even by his enemies, for the extraordinary breadth of his knowledge, he was a prodigious author who contributed monumental tomes in several fields. Many of his works were expositions of creed and polemics in the tradition of the refutation (*radd*). It was these, in addition to his contrarian legal opinions, that made him controversial and aroused the ire of the leading Sunnī scholars of Cairo and Damascus, including his fellow Ḥanbalīs. Not only did Ibn Taymiyya take on such groups as the Shīʿa and the philosophers in his writings, but he took aim at the prevailing currents and institutions of Sunnī Islam as well. To these he counterposed his own unique approach to Islamic theology and law, cast as an attempt to recover "the doctrine of the ancestors" (*madhhab al-salaf*) through a return to the Qurʾān, the *sunna* (the Prophet's normative practice), and the words and deeds of the *salaf* (the first three generations of Muslims). For his views, his outspokenness, and his unwillingness to bend to authority, he would spend more than a decade on trial or in prison.

15. Goldziher, *Introduction to Islamic Theology and Law*, 241.

16. See, in particular, Hoover, *Ibn Taymiyya*; Rapoport and Ahmed, *Ibn Taymiyya and His Times*; Bori and Holtzman, eds., "Scholar in the Shadow"; Krawietz and Tamer, *Islamic Theology, Philosophy and Law*.

17. On his life and career, see Laoust, *Essai sur les doctrines sociales et politiques de Taḳī-d-Dīn Aḥmad b. Taimīya*, 7–150; Hoover, *Ibn Taymiyya*. And for a more succinct account of his life, with references to further sources, see Hoover, "Ibn Taymiyya."

Ibn Taymiyya's primary field was creed or theology (*ʿaqīda, iʿtiqād*), also known as the foundations of the religion (*uṣūl al-dīn*). This is the domain of first principles, of obligatory beliefs and practices, and as such it tends to be contentious. Unlike the more latitudinarian domain of Islamic jurisprudence, which generally allows for multiple positions on issues of dispute, in theology there can be only one correct position. While theology was not Ibn Taymiyya's only concern, it was here that he expended the better part of his literary efforts and created the most trouble for himself. The reason for this focus on theology was that he felt, as Jon Hoover has stated, "that God was no longer worshipped and spoken of correctly" in his time.[18] Ibn Taymiyya saw the mainstream beliefs and practices of contemporary Sunnī Islam as having been corrupted—by the influence of the Ashʿarīs, the Ṣūfīs, the Shīʿa, the philosophers, the Christians and Jews, and the Mongols, among others. He therefore authored a seemingly endless series of theological treatises and polemics, "introduc[ing] a new current of theology unprecedented in the Ḥanbalī school and not found elsewhere in medieval Islam" and provoking an uproar thereby.[19]

Ḥanbalī Theology

Not every aspect of Ibn Taymiyya's theology was unprecedented. Much of his religious thought was in fact consistent with the principles that had underlain Ḥanbalism for centuries. The Ḥanbalī approach to theology, as many scholars have observed, was a distinctive one. Unlike their Sunnī counterparts in the Shāfiʿī, Mālikī, and Ḥanafī schools of law, the Ḥanbalīs were largely united in their rejection of what is often called speculative theology (*ʿilm al-kalām*, or simply *kalām*). *Kalām* is a rationalist school of thought that employs a dialectical technique and philosophical terminology (e.g., *body, accident, substance*) to address theological questions and investigate the meaning of the foundational Islamic texts. *Kalām* had become a regular feature of Sunnī Islam beginning around the eleventh century and was popular in the Mamlūk Sultanate as elsewhere.[20]

In earlier periods of Islamic history, the practitioners of *kalām*, or the *mutakallimūn*, were identified with several theological schools. One of the most popular was Muʿtazilism, though this gradually died out in Sunnī Islam.

18. Hoover, "Ḥanbalī Theology," 634.

19. Ibid.

20. This date is suggested in Leaman, "Developed *Kalām* Tradition," 81.

The *kalām* approach later regained strength among Sunnīs in the form of two new theological schools, Ashʿarism and Māturīdism, named for Abū ʾl-Ḥasan al-Ashʿarī (d. 324/935) and Abū Manṣūr al-Māturīdī (d. 333/944), respectively. Over time the three principal law schools of Sunnī Islam, Shāfiʿism, Ḥanafism, and Mālikism, came to be associated with one of these theological schools—Ashʿarism in the case of the Shāfiʿīs and Mālikīs, and Māturīdism in the case of the Ḥanafīs.[21]

In traditional Islamic scholarship, the opponents of *kalām* were known as "the people of *ḥadīth*" (*ahl al-ḥadīth*), while in Western scholarship they have been described as "traditionalists."[22] The traditionalists were associated with the Ḥanbalī *madhhab*. Unlike the *mutakallimūn*, the traditionalists sought to ground Islamic belief in nothing more than the Qurʾān, the *ḥadīth*, and the views and practices of the *salaf*. Their statements of creed thus consist largely of basic affirmations followed by quotations from these sources. For them, any sort of rationalist inquiry into matters of belief was considered anathema. While the Shāfiʿī, Ḥanafī, and Mālikī legal schools could still count among them a number of traditionalists, only Ḥanbalism, the smallest of the four Sunnī legal schools, was defined by its staunch traditionalism.[23] Ḥanbalism was "alone," as George Makdisi observed, "in being at the same time both a legal and a theological school."[24] This was to say, it united the Ḥanbalī legal tradition with theological traditionalism. Members of the other Sunnī legal schools looked on Ḥanbalism as the preserve of traditionalist theology. Thus non-Ḥanbalīs by legal affiliation sometimes identified as Ḥanbalīs in theology, meaning that they were averse to *kalām*.[25]

One area over which the traditionalists and the rationalist *mutakallimūn* frequently clashed was the approach to God's attributes (*ṣifāt*), in particular the humanlike features and characteristics attributed to God in the Qurʾān and the *ḥadīth*. These attributes include descriptions of God as having hands

21. Law school affiliation, however, remained more important to one's social identity than theological affiliation. On this point, see Cook, *Commanding Right and Forbidding Wrong in Islamic Thought*, 339; Eichner, "Handbooks in the Tradition of Later Eastern Ashʿarism," 496.

22. For the traditionalists as the *ahl al-ḥadīth*, see Makdisi, "Hanbalite Islam," 239.

23. There were some exceptions, however, including such eminent Ḥanbalīs as Abū Yaʿlā Ibn al-Farrāʾ (d. 458/1066), Abū ʾl-Wafāʾ Ibn ʿAqīl (d. 513/1119), and Abū ʾl-Faraj Ibn al-Jawzī (d. 597/1201), all of whom applied *kalām* argumentation to varying degrees; see Hoover, "Ḥanbalī Theology," 630–33.

24. Makdisi, "Hanbalite Islam," 239.

25. Hoover, "Ḥanbalī Theology," 627.

and eyes, sitting upon the throne, and descending to the lower heavens. For most rationalist theologians, particularly the Muʿtazila, such anthropomorphic descriptions of God were to be either rejected or reinterpreted metaphorically—that is, subjected to *taʾwīl*. Thus God's hand (*yad*) was to be interpreted as His power (*qudra*), and His sitting upon the throne (*istiwāʾ*) was to be interpreted as His dominion (*istīlāʾ*). The traditionalists rejected the rationalist approach as divesting God of His attributes. Generally speaking, they argued that it was necessary to affirm the attributes as true while avoiding inquiry into their modality or meaning. In this way, they sought to avoid the accusation, frequently leveled at them by the rationalists, that they were likening God to creatures or committing anthropomorphism (*tashbīh*). In the view of the rationalists, many of the traditionalists were crass anthropomorphists who imagined God to have a face and body like those of humans and to move and laugh like them.[26]

Like most Ḥanbalīs before him, Ibn Taymiyya was deeply hostile to *kalām*. The particular target in his case was the Ashʿarī *kalām* of the Damascene Shāfiʿīs, who were a prominent and powerful group of scholars in his day. The *salaf*, Ibn Taymiyya argued, along with the eponyms of the four schools of law, categorically abjured speculative inquiry in matters of theology, and they had harsh words for those who dabbled in it. "Whosoever seeks [knowledge of] religion by means of *kalām* has become a heretic" (*man ṭalaba ʾl-dīn biʾl-kalām tazandaqa*), goes a phrase that he frequently cited, attributed to the proto-Ḥanafī jurist Abū Yūsuf (d. 182/798).[27] For Ibn Taymiyya, the use of *kalām* in theology was a terrible innovation, among the other terrible innovations of the Ashʿarīs.

Ibn Taymiyya, however, was no mere ordinary traditionalist. In his critical engagement with the *mutakallimūn* and others, he did not just stick to the traditionalist line. Rather, he made several important emendations to traditional Ḥanbalī theology.

The first of these concerned the proper approach to the interpretation of God's attributes. As noted above, the traditionalist Ḥanbalī approach to the anthropomorphic descriptions of God in the revealed texts involved affirming the attributes while avoiding inquiry into their modality (*kayfiyya*) or meaning (*maʿnā*). The traditionalists affirmed the attributes, but with the caveats of *bi-lā*

26. *EI*[3], s.v. "Anthropomorphism" (Livnat Holtzman); Holtzman, *Anthropomorphism in Islam*, chap. 4; Hoover, "Early Mamlūk Ashʿarism Against Ibn Taymiyya."

27. See, e.g., Ibn Taymiyya, *Majmūʿ fatāwā*, 16:473.

kayf (lit. "without how," or without inquiring into modality) and *imrār* (lit. "passing over," in the sense of passing over the attributes without comment and without inquiry into their meanings). This was in contrast with the metaphorical reinterpretation (*ta ʾwīl*) favored by the rationalists. Like other Ḥanbalīs, Ibn Taymiyya was a fierce opponent of *ta ʾwīl,* describing the exponents of metaphorical interpretation as Jahmiyya and *mu ʿaṭṭila.* The term *Jahmiyya* refers to Jahm ibn Ṣafwān (d. 128/745f), an anti-Umayyad activist and theologian remembered for spreading the doctrine of *nafy* or *ta ʿṭīl*—the denial or stripping away of God's attributes—among other alleged innovations.[28] Hence the second term, *mu ʿaṭṭila,* meaning "those who strip God of His attributes." For Ibn Taymiyya, the practitioners of *ta ʾwīl* were engaging in the same innovation as Jahm by interpreting away God's attributes, and so he described them as Jahmiyya. Often he used the term in reference to the Ash ʿarīs.[29]

Yet while polemicizing against rationalist *ta ʾwīl,* Ibn Taymiyya also took issue with the noncognitivism or noninterventionism that characterized the traditionalist Ḥanbalī approach. For Ibn Taymiyya, the problem with this approach was that it made out the Prophet and the early generations of Muslims to be ignorant of the meanings of the attributes, which could not have been true. In his view, the attributes of God were not to be likened to the attributes of creatures, but they nonetheless evoked meanings that should be understood in their plain senses and in ways that befit God's majesty. As Khaled El-Rouayheb has explained it, "We do, Ibn Taymiyya insisted, know the meaning of words such as *yad* [hand] or *wajh* [face] or *istawā* [sit] or *yanzilu* [descend]. What we do not know is what it is like for God to have a hand or face, or to sit or descend."[30] The basic idea of Ibn Taymiyya's approach was that it was wrong and unbefitting of God to affirm the attributes in complete ignorance of their meanings. Like his traditionalist predecessors, he adhered to the *bi-lā kayf* doctrine, agreeing that it was impossible to know the modality of the attributes. But he drew a distinction between modality and meaning, such that the meanings of the attributes were opened to linguistic inquiry.[31]

28. On Jahm and his theology, see Schöck, "Jahm b. Ṣafwān (d. 128/745–6) and the 'Jahmiyya,'" esp. 56–67.

29. It is worth noting that the Ash ʿarīs did not universally favor *ta ʾwīl;* they also allowed, and in some cases even preferred, *tafwīḍ,* or delegating the meanings of the attributes to God; see Hoover, "Early Mamlūk Ash ʿarism Against Ibn Taymiyya."

30. El-Rouayheb, "From Ibn Ḥajar al-Haytamī to Khayr al-Dīn al-Ālūsī," 279.

31. In Hoover's phrase, Ibn Taymiyya's approach involved "denying knowledge of the *kayfiyya* and affirming knowledge of the *ma ʿnā,*" even though the boundary line between *kayfiyya*

Another of Ibn Taymiyya's emendations to traditional Ḥanbalī theology was his insistence on the necessary congruence of reason (*ʿaql*) and revelation (*naql*), a theme that permeates his writings and lends a distinctively rationalist character to his theological discourse.[32] His lengthiest treatment of the subject is found in his massive *Darʾ taʿāruḍ al-ʿaql wa'l-naql* (Averting Conflict Between Reason and Revelation), which he wrote in refutation of the Ashʿarī "Universal Principle" (*al-qānūn al-kullī*) formulated by the scholar Fakhr al-Dīn al-Rāzī (d. 606/1210).[33] The gist of the Universal Principle is that reason-based proofs ought to take precedence over revealed proofs in the case of perceived conflict, for reason is the means by which the veracity of revealed proofs is established. In Ibn Taymiyya's view, from this principle sprang many of the Ashʿarīs' theological errors, including their willingness to interpret God's attributes metaphorically. In refuting it, he asserts that reason and revelation, properly understood, never conflict. Underlying his assertion was the conviction that revelation was itself rational, the revealed texts bearing within them rational proofs and arguments that establish the foundations of the religion. In fact, Ibn Taymiyya claimed, revelation was eminently more rational than the rationalist theology of the Ashʿarīs, which drew false conclusions and led people astray. Unlike most Ḥanbalī theologians before him, Ibn Taymiyya was thus not opposed to engaging in reason-based arguments when it came to theology or borrowing the very conceptual frameworks and terminology of the rationalist theologians. Much as he made room in Ḥanbalī theology for investigating the meanings of God's attributes, he widened its scope to include rationalist argumentation, allowing him to clarify and translate the meanings of the revealed texts into another idiom and to engage his theological opponents on their own terms.[34]

---

and *maʿnā* was not always clear; see Hoover, "Early Mamlūk Ashʿarism Against Ibn Taymiyya," 201. And see further Hoover, "Hanbali Theology," 637–38; Hoover, *Ibn Taymiyya*, 109–17; El-Rouayheb, "From Ibn Ḥajar al-Haytamī to Khayr al-Dīn al-Ālūsī," 271–87.

32. See Özervarlı, "Qur'ānic Rational Theology of Ibn Taymiyya"; Hoover, *Ibn Taymiyya's Theodicy*, 29–32.

33. For detailed studies of this work, see El-Tobgui, *Ibn Taymiyya on Reason and Revelation*; Qadhi, "Reconciling Reason and Revelation in the Writings of Ibn Taymiyya."

34. Hoover, *Ibn Taymiyya*, 113–18; Hoover, "Theology as Translation," 47–53; Özervarlı, "Qur'ānic Rational Theology of Ibn Taymiyya." Related to all this was Ibn Taymiyya's notion of the natural constitution (*fiṭra*), which he took to mean mankind's inherent inclination to monotheism. It is on account of *fiṭra*, Ibn Taymiyya says, that human beings may come to know about God by means of the faculty of reason. Likewise, *fiṭra* obviates the need to prove the existence

A third emendation forged by Ibn Taymiyya was his vision of God as perpetually creative and temporally dynamic.[35] Drawing on and responding to certain aspects of the *kalām* tradition and Avicennan philosophy, Ibn Taymiyya posited a God who has been acting and creating from eternity (in the sense of time without beginning) and on behalf of wise purposes, a position he argues is supported both by revelation and by reasoning about God's perfection. For him, God's perfection consists in perpetual dynamism. God's acts subsist in His essence in an infinite regress, and they unfold in temporal sequence. Here Ibn Taymiyya rejects the *kalām* view of a world created by God ex nihilo and the Avicennan cosmology of the emanation of an eternal world. His view of God's continuous creation of the world from eternity was foreign not only to Ḥanbalī traditionalism but also to other currents of medieval Islam.[36]

The idea that God acts on behalf of wise purposes was also invoked in relation to the question of human acts. In contrast with the Ashʿarīs, who rejected the idea that God creates for the sake of a purpose or a cause (*ʿilla*), Ibn Taymiyya contended that God's creative activity is in fact tied to wise purposes subsisting in His essence. A God who acts without regard for wise purposes would be a capricious God unworthy of the highest praise. God, Ibn Taymiyya believed, has created a good and perfect world in accordance with His wise purposes. In such a world, however, why did God create human beings who commit evil deeds and disobey Him? In Ibn Taymiyya's view, God is just to hold humans responsible for the acts that they commit, even if these acts are ultimately God's creation, for God has wise purposes in everything He creates. Without acknowledging the paradox, Ibn Taymiyya insists on the compatibility of God's creation of all human acts with human responsibility for those acts. He explains his position as the golden mean (*wasaṭ*) between the exponents of free will (*qadariyya*) and the exponents of hard determinism (*jabriyya*). Human agency is real in that humans are freely choosing, but at the same time God is the creator of both their will and their acts. This compatibilist approach was not necessarily inconsistent with earlier

of God by means of *kalām*, since knowledge of God is innate. See Hoover, *Ibn Taymiyya's Theodicy*, 39–44; *EI*[3], s.v. "Fiṭra" (Jon Hoover); Özervarlı, "Divine Wisdom, Human Agency and the *Fiṭra* in Ibn Taymiyya's Thought"; Holtzman, "Human Choice, Divine Guidance and the *Fiṭra* Tradition."

35. The word *emendation* admittedly understates the conceptual novelty and sophistication that this entailed.

36. Hoover, "Ḥanbalī Theology," 638–41; Hoover, *Ibn Taymiyya*, 118–23; Hoover, "God's Wise Purposes in Creating Iblīs," 116–20.

Ḥanbalī traditionalism, but it was expressed and articulated in a different and more sophisticated idiom.[37]

Ṣūfī Monism and the Cult of Saints

Not every feature of Ibn Taymiyya's theology had an equal impact on Wahhābism. The Taymiyyan approach to the issue of God's attributes, for instance, though it would be adopted by the Wahhābīs, was not of immediate concern to what Ibn ʿAbd al-Wahhāb was preaching. Similarly, though one sees the influence of Ibn Taymiyya's insistence on the compatibility of reason and revelation in Wahhābī writings, this was not a major theme in Wahhābī discourse. The Taymiyyan notion of a perpetually creative God who acts on behalf of wise purposes was even further from Ibn ʿAbd al-Wahhāb's concerns.

The most significant feature of Ibn Taymiyya's theology, insofar as Wahhābism is concerned, was his approach to certain aspects of Ṣūfism and particularly the cult of saints. As is now well known, Ibn Taymiyya was not an opponent of Ṣūfism, the mystical dispensation in Islam, as such. His writings do not betray a categorical hostility to Ṣūfism, and there is even some evidence, as George Makdisi has shown, that he was initiated into the Qādirī Ṣūfī order.[38] In one of his *fatwās*, Ibn Taymiyya describes the early mystical tradition in Basra as "the path of worship and asceticism" (*ṭarīq al-ʿibāda waʾl-zuhd*), praising this as "the Ṣūfism of truths" (*ṣūfiyyat al-ḥaqāʾiq*).[39] At the same time, however, Ibn Taymiyya was by no means wildly enthusiastic about Ṣūfism, criticizing those who lavished excessive praise on Ṣūfīs and considered the Ṣūfī path superior to all other spiritual paths.[40] He was highly intolerant of two dimensions of popular Ṣūfī belief and practice in particular, against which he polemicized frequently and at great length.

37. Hoover, *Ibn Taymiyya's Theodicy*, 133–76; Holtzman, "Debating the Doctrine of *Jabr*," 61–63; cf. Gimaret, "Théories de l'acte humain." See further, on the issue of the golden mean, an idea frequently espoused by Ibn Taymiyya in his theological writings, Swartz, "Seventh-Century (A.H.) Sunnī Creed," 95–97, 115n31. I should point out that I disagree with Swartz's characterization of the golden mean as a way of fostering "conciliation" and "openness" with other sects. It is plainly a device used by Ibn Taymiyya to position his own (correct) views as intermediate between two sets of deviant views. The Wahhābīs would employ it in this way as well.

38. Makdisi, "Ibn Taimīya." The evidence is contested, however. See Hoover, *Ibn Taymiyya*, 70–73; Sarrió, "Spiritual Anti-elitism," 276–77; Picken, "Quest for Orthodoxy," 247, 257–58.

39. Ibn Taymiyya, *Majmūʿ fatāwā*, 11:16–19.

40. Ibid., 11:13–14.

The first of these dimensions was the monistic cosmology associated with the teachings of the Andalusian-born mystic Muḥyī ʾl-Dīn Ibn ʿArabī (d. 638/1240). Ibn ʿArabī's system, as it came to be conceptualized later, centered on the doctrine of the oneness of being (*waḥdat al-wujūd*), whereby all of creation is understood as a mirror to the Creator, all created things being manifestations (*tajalliyāt*) of the divine. Related to this was an antinomian tendency to minimize the importance of the divine law and the daily acts of worship. Ibn Taymiyya stigmatized the partisans of Ibn ʿArabī's monism as the people of indwelling and union (*ahl al-ḥulūl wa ʾl-ittiḥād, al-ḥulūliyya wa ʾl-ittiḥādiyya*), that is, the people of God's indwelling in His creatures and His union with them.[41] He regretted how prominent this system of thought had become, claiming that it was widely adhered to by the modern-day Jahmiyya (*aghlab ʿalā ʿubbād al-Jahmiyya*), which was to say, by the Ashʿarī *mutakallimūn*.[42] In one polemic he asserts that the partisans of this system "permit polytheism and the worshipping of idols unrestrictedly" (*yujawwizūna ʾl-shirk wa-ʿibādat al-aṣnām muṭlaqan*).[43] Another line of attack that he used was to liken the adherents of Ṣūfī monism to Christians. In his book *al-Jawāb al-ṣaḥīḥ li-man baddala dīn al-masīḥ* (The Correct Answer to Those Who Have Changed the Religion of Christ), a polemic against Christianity, Ibn Taymiyya holds up the doctrines and practices of Christianity as the kinds of things being introduced into Islam by a host of heretics and innovators, including Ṣūfīs. "By knowing the reality of the Christian religion and its falsity," he writes, "one may also know the falsity of the similar views held by the heretics and innovators."[44] One example he gives is Ṣūfī monism and the idea of divine indwelling. This he likens to the Christian deification of Christ, the idea being that both Christians and Ṣūfī monists believe God to be incarnated in this world.

The second aspect of Ṣūfism condemned by Ibn Taymiyya was the cult of saints, which, as noted earlier, is a term referring to the practices associated with visiting the tombs and shrines of saints or prophets. These practices included appealing to the dead for help (*istighātha*) in mundane matters or in matters of the hereafter (i.e., asking a saint to cure a disease or protect a traveler

41. See, for example, ibid., 2:295, 414.

42. Ibid., 2:296, 298.

43. Ibid., 2:296.

44. Ibn Taymiyya, *al-Jawāb al-ṣaḥīḥ*, 1:98; translation borrowed from Hoover, "Ibn Taymiyya," 835.

or asking a saint to intercede with God on the Day of Judgment), as well as using the dead as a means to God (*tawassul*), usually in the sense of making requests of God while invoking the high station (*jāh*) of the deceased. These rites of *ziyāra* were widespread in the Islamic world of Ibn Taymiyya's day, including in the areas of the Mamlūk Sultanate, where they had grown in popularity in tandem with the kind of esoteric Ṣūfism advocated by Ibn ʿArabī and others.[45] In Ibn Taymiyya's eyes, these were innovations smacking of the worst kind of polytheism. While he considered the visitation of graves to be permissible in principle, this was only so long as the visitor's purpose was to beseech God on behalf of the dead (*al-duʿāʾ lil-mayyit*), as he argued was the example of the Prophet and his Companions. The visitation rites that had become institutionalized in Islam, however, were in his view of another kind entirely. It had become customary for visitors to make requests not of God on behalf of the dead but of the dead themselves—to call upon them for help in worldly affairs and appeal to them to intercede with God on the Day of Judgment.[46] According to Ibn Taymiyya, making these requests of the dead amounted to assigning partners to God (*shirk*), as such requests implied that the dead share in God's divine power. Here again, Ibn Taymiyya accused his contemporary Sunnī Muslims of following the path of the Christians in adopting certain innovations in belief and practice from Christianity. In his book *Iqtiḍāʾ al-ṣirāṭ al-mustaqīm li-mukhālafat aṣḥāb al-jaḥīm* (The Necessity of the Straight Path in Distinction from the People of Hellfire), a protracted admonition against imitating unbelievers, he accuses certain heretical Ṣūfīs (*ḍullāl al-mutaʿabbida waʾl-mutaṣawwifa*) of imitating Christians by displaying excessive devotion to prophets and righteous persons (*al-ghuluww fī ʾl-anbiyāʾ waʾl-ṣāliḥīn*).[47] He further accuses them of imitating Jews by worshipping at

45. On the cult of saints in Islam, see *EI*[3], s.v. "Grave Visitation/Worship" (Richard McGregor); and on the connection between the cult of saints and esoteric Ṣūfism, see El Shamsy, *Rediscovering the Islamic Classics*, 41–54, 191–99. For discussions of the cult of saints and Ibn Taymiyya's (and Ibn al-Qayyim's) views, see Taylor, *In the Vicinity of the Righteous*, 171–94; Meri, *Cult of Saints Among Muslims and Jews in Medieval Syria*, 130–38.

46. Ibn Taymiyya, *Majmūʿ fatāwā*, 1:165–66. It is important to note that Ibn Taymiyya did draw a distinction between *istighātha*, which he believed amounted to *shirk*, and *tawassul*, which he disapproved of but regarded as a matter of legitimate dispute; see 1:202–11. Ibn ʿAbd al-Wahhāb took the same approach; see Ibn Ghannām, *Tārīkh*, 1:503–4. Generally, when they polemicized against the cult of saints, they were talking about *istighātha* and *duʿāʾ* (i.e., appealing to created beings directly for things that only God can provide), not mere *tawassul*.

47. Ibn Taymiyya, *Iqtiḍāʾ al-ṣirāṭ al-mustaqīm*, 1:89.

graves, God having cursed the Jews for taking the graves of prophets as places of worship.[48]

So hostile indeed was Ibn Taymiyya to the cult of saints that he called for demolishing the physical structures associated with visitation, namely, the elevated graves and tombs built around them. "These places of worship built upon the graves of prophets, righteous men, kings, and others," he writes in *Iqtiḍāʾ al-ṣirāṭ al-mustaqīm*, "it is an individual duty to destroy them [*yataʿayyanu izālatuhā*] by knocking them down or otherwise. On this I know of no disagreement among the reputable scholars."[49] The reason Ibn Taymiyya was so harsh on the matter of tombs was that he considered them a means or avenue (*dharīʿa*) to *shirk*.[50] He thus justified their destruction in terms of the legal principle of *sadd al-dharāʾiʿ*, or "blocking the means." One had to be especially careful in guarding against this means, he wrote, as the great sin of the people of Noah (*qawm Nūḥ*) was taking the graves of righteous men as places of worship.[51] Ibn Taymiyya's opposition to *ziyāra* even extended to the Prophet's grave in Medina, his view being that one should not set out on trips (*shadd al-riḥāl*, lit. "fasten the saddles") for the purpose of visiting it. He regretted that the Prophet's grave had become part of the Prophet's Mosque and dismissed as forgeries those *ḥadīth*s encouraging Muslims to visit it.[52]

Unlike other of his theological positions, Ibn Taymiyya's views on Ṣūfī monism and the cult of saints are not necessarily to be considered emendations to traditional Ḥanbalī theology, as the Ḥanbalī school admitted of a range of opinions on these matters. Certain Ḥanbalī scholars had taken a similarly harsh stance on the cult of saints. These included Ibn Baṭṭa al-ʿUkbarī (d. 387/997) and Abū ʾl-Wafāʾ Ibn ʿAqīl (d. 513/1119), both of Baghdad. Ibn Baṭṭa considered the building of structures upon graves (*al-bināʾ ʿalā ʾl-qubūr*) and the setting out on trips to visit them (*shadd al-riḥāl ilā ziyāratihā*) to be blameworthy innovations.[53] Likewise, Ibn ʿAqīl condemned the veneration of graves (*taʿẓīm al-qubūr*), setting out on trips to them (*shadd al-riḥāl ilayhā*), and asking the dead to fulfill worldly needs (*khiṭāb al-mawtā biʾl-ḥawāʾij*), deeming such practices to be contrary to God's law (*sharʿ*) and describing

48. Ibid., 2:185–87.

49. Ibid., 2:187.

50. Ibn Taymiyya, *Majmūʿ fatāwā*, 1:164, 179.

51. Ibid., 1:167–68.

52. Ibid., 27:26, 1:233–35.

53. Ibn Baṭṭa, *al-Sharḥ waʾl-ibāna*, 273.

those engaged in them as unbelievers (*wa-hum ʿindī kuffār*).[54] One of Ibn ʿAqīl's Ḥanbalī students in Baghdad, Abū ʾl-Faraj Ibn al-Jawzī (d. 597/1200), was critical of both the cult of saints and Ṣūfī monism (*ḥulūl, ittiḥād*).[55] To that extent he anticipated Ibn Taymiyya's positions, the difference being that Ibn al-Jawzī was categorically hostile to Ṣūfism, considering it to be a school that had gone well beyond mere ascetiscm (*wa ʾl-taṣawwuf madhhab maʿrūf yazīdu ʿalā ʾl-zuhd*).[56] Its adherents, he complained, had come to adopt such innovative practices as listening to music and dancing.[57] In contrast with Ibn Baṭṭa, Ibn ʿAqīl, and Ibn al-Jawzī, the Damascus-based jurist Ibn Qudāma al-Maqdisī (d. 620/1223) took a noticeably favorable view of the cult of saints. In one of his works, he speaks highly of the fact that worshippers are visiting the graves of saints and righteous persons (*al-awliyāʾ wa ʾl-ṣāliḥūn*) and calling on them and seeking their intercession with God, adding that their appeals shall be answered and their adversity assuaged (*wa-yustajābu ʾl-duʿāʾ wa-yukshafu ʾl-balāʾ*).[58] In his monumental work on jurisprudence, *al-Mughnī*, Ibn Qudāma cites Ibn ʿAqīl's view that visiting tombs and shrines is prohibited (*lā yubāḥu*) but notes that the correct view is that it is permitted (*al-ṣaḥīḥ ibāḥatuhu*).[59] Thus, Ibn Taymiyya's approach to these matters was neither in line nor out of step with a preexisting Ḥanbalī consensus.

Controversies and Tribulations

According to one of his contemporary biographers, Shams al-Dīn al-Dhahabī, Ibn Taymiyya's predilection for theological polemic had a polarizing effect on the Sunnī scholarly community to which he belonged. While some hated and anathematized him, others admired and celebrated him. Opinion was divided (*ʿalā alwān*):

> To one group of scholars he was a devil, a liar, and an unbeliever. To other learned and esteemed men he was an excellent and skilled innovator. To others he was a dark and sinister figure. To the great majority of his followers

54. Quoted in Ibn al-Qayyim, *Ighāthat al-lahfān*, 1:352–53.

55. Ibn al-Jawzī, *Kitāb talbīs Iblīs*, 944.

56. Ibid., 953.

57. Ibid., 919–20.

58. Ibn Qudāma, *Taḥrīm al-naẓar fī kutub al-kalām*, 40.

59. Ibn Qudāma, *al-Mughnī*, 3:117.

he was the guardian of the realm of the religion, the bearer of the banner of Islam, and the protector of the prophetic *sunna*.[60]

Among the many scholars who felt antagonized by Ibn Taymiyya were some of the leading Sunnī *ʿulamāʾ* of the day. They did not shy away from refuting him.

The most prolific in this regard was the Shāfiʿī *qāḍī* in Damascus Taqī al-Dīn al-Subkī (d. 756/1355).[61] Some of his criticisms anticipate those that would be leveled against Ibn ʿAbd al-Wahhāb. Ibn Taymiyya, according to al-Subkī, failed to acquire knowledge from a teacher (*lam yajid shaykhan yahdīhi, lam yatahadhdhab bi-shaykh*), deviated from the community of Islam (*shadhdha ʿan jamāʿat al-Muslimīn*), and distorted true Islamic beliefs (*shawwasha ʿaqāʾid al-Muslimīn*).[62] His student Ibn al-Qayyim, he added, encouraged the masses to pronounce *takfīr* on those Muslims of different theological persuasions (*takfīr kull man siwāhu wa-siwā ṭāʾifatihi*).[63] Furthermore, much as Ibn ʿAbd al-Wahhāb's critics saw his doctrine as having deeper roots in the pernicious thought of Ibn Taymiyya, al-Subkī saw Ibn Taymiyya's doctrine as rooted in the larger tradition of the Ḥashwiyya.[64] The latter term was a pejorative used by some of the *mutakallimūn* to stigmatize traditionalists in theology as vulgar anthropomorphists.[65]

A number of Sunnī scholars would write refutations of Ibn Taymiyya's views regarding the cult of saints. The Egyptian Shāfiʿī Nūr al-Dīn al-Bakrī (d. 724/1324), for instance, attacked Ibn Taymiyya for his position on *istighātha*, particularly *istighātha* of the Prophet. Ibn Taymiyya returned fire in a refutation known as *al-Istighātha fī ʾl-radd ʿalā al-Bakrī*.[66] Some fifteen years later, in 728/1328, a similar exercise was carried out with another Egyptian scholar, a prominent Mālikī jurist named Taqī al-Dīn al-Ikhnāʾī (d. 750/1349). The latter played a role in having Ibn Taymiyya arrested and tried over the question of visiting graves and then wrote a refutation of his views on the subject. Ibn Taymiyya was in prison in Damascus when he wrote his response,

60. al-Dhahabī, *Bayān zaghl al-ʿilm*, 87; translation borrowed in part from Bori, "Ibn Taymiyya *wa-Jamāʿatu-hu*," 38.

61. On him, see al-Subkī, *Ṭabaqāt al-Shāfiʿiyya al-kubrā*, 10:139–339.

62. al-Subkī, *al-Rasāʾil al-Subkiyya*, 195, 85, 151, 85.

63. Ibid., 85.

64. Ibid., 84.

65. See *EI*³, s.v. "Ḥashwiyya" (Jon Hoover); Holtzman, *Anthropomorphism in Islam*, 201, 328–39. One possible meaning of *Ḥashwiyya* is "those who stuff things."

66. Ibn Taymiyya, *al-Istighātha*.

a blistering refutation known as *al-Ikhnāʾiyya*, or *al-Radd ʿalā ʾl-Ikhnāʾī*.[67] For this Ibn Taymiyya was stripped of his pen.[68]

Ibn Taymiyya wrote numerous other theological polemics on controversial issues, but it was not only in the theological arena that he courted controversy. He also caused a disturbance in the realm of law by issuing legal judgments that departed from the consensus of the four Sunnī law schools. His willingness to issue such judgments stemmed from his peculiar legal methodology. As Yossef Rapoport has explained, Ibn Taymiyya, who had no qualms about using independent legal reasoning (*ijtihād*), played down the importance of law school affiliation, opposed the passive imitation (*taqlīd*) of any one scholar or school, and rejected as a source of law the consensus (*ijmāʿ*) of any group or generation of scholars after the Companions of the Prophet.[69] While Ibn Taymiyya did not oppose *taqlīd* as such, he held that every judgment ought to be buttressed by reference to the revealed sources of the Qurʾān and the *sunna*. His most controversial legal rulings had to do with divorce oaths (i.e., oaths sworn on pain of divorce) and the triple repudiation (i.e., the pronunciation of three divorce repudiations at once). He held that violating a divorce oath should not entail divorce and that the triple repudiation should not constitute irrevocable divorce.[70]

Ibn Taymiyya's polemics and his legal judgments earned him not only notoriety but also prosecution by the authorities and multiple stints in prison, both in Egypt and in Syria. The first of his various trials or tribulations (*miḥan*; sing. *miḥna*) dates to 698/1298, when he was summoned before the chief *qāḍī* in Damascus to defend his approach to God's attributes as he had elaborated it in one of his statements of creed, *al-Ḥamawiyya al-kubrā*. The three principal *miḥan* that would define his career started a few years later.[71] The first of these lasted from 705/1306 to 709/1310 and involved numerous court proceedings in Damascus and Cairo. It began when the Mamlūk sultan sent a letter to the governor of Damascus demanding that Ibn Taymiyya be tried on account of complaints received about his theological views. The *miḥna* would center on his statements concerning God's attributes in his creedal work known as

67. Ibn Taymiyya, *al-Ikhnāʾiyya*.

68. Hoover, *Ibn Taymiyya*, 36–38.

69. Rapoport, "Ibn Taymiyya's Radical Legal Thought."

70. On these rulings, see Rapoport, "Ibn Taymiyya on Divorce Oaths," 191–217.

71. Murad, "Ibn Taymiyya on Trial." My summary of the *miḥan* is based on this source as well as on Ibn Rajab, *al-Dhayl ʿalā Ṭabaqāt al-Ḥanābila*, 4:491–529.

al-ʿAqīda al-Wāsiṭiyya.[72] Ibn Taymiyya spent some eighteen months in prison in Cairo. After another court proceeding, this time regarding his views on Ibn ʿArabī, he spent an additional sixteen months or so in prison, partly in Cairo and partly in Alexandria. The second *miḥna,* which took place in Damascus, centered on the question of divorce oaths. It lasted from 718/1318 to 721/1321 and saw Ibn Taymiyya imprisoned for five months. The third *miḥna,* which also took place in Damascus, began in 726/1326 and ended with Ibn Taymiyya's death in 728/1328 in the Damascus Citadel, where he had been imprisoned for approximately two years and three months. The subject this time was the cult of saints.

Students and Followers

One of al-Subkī's anti-Taymiyyan works was written after Ibn Taymiyya's death. In it al-Subkī notes that while he would have preferred not to write it, he found himself compelled to do so as Ibn Taymiyya still had followers (*atbāʿ*) who espoused his ideas.[73] Indeed, during his lifetime Ibn Taymiyya attracted a close circle of disciples, described in contemporary sources as his community (*jamāʿa*).[74] This was a group of men who studied with him, collected his works, and embraced his controversial views, especially those regarding theology. The notoriety of Ibn Taymiyya's *jamāʿa* persisted into the later fourteenth century. In 784/1382 the Mamlūk sultan wrote the following in a decree: "It has reached us that in Damascus there is a group of Shafiʿīs, Mālikīs, and Ḥanbalīs manifesting innovations and the doctrine of the Taymiyyans [*madhhab al-Taymiyyīn*]."[75] As is seen here, while some of the *jamāʿa*'s members belonged to the Ḥanbalī school, others belonged to the other legal schools of Sunnī Islam. Their allegiance to Ibn Taymiyya transcended legal school boundaries, something made easier by the fact that Ibn Taymiyya's concerns were more theological than legal. One could adopt his more important views on proper belief and practice without having to agree with his every legal judgment.

72. On the proceedings in Damascus, see Jackson, "Ibn Taymiyyah on Trial in Damascus."

73. al-Subkī, *al-Rasāʾil al-Subkiyya,* 195.

74. Bori, "Ibn Taymiyya *wa-Jamāʿatu-hu.*"

75. Ibn Qāḍī Shuhba, *Tārīkh Ibn Qāḍī Shuhba,* 1:89; noted in Bori, "Ibn Taymiyya (14th to 17th Century)," 93.

Ibn Taymiyya's closest disciple was the Ḥanbalī Shams al-Dīn Ibn Qayyim al-Jawziyya (d. 751/1350), a prolific author who elaborated his teacher's theological and legal views in a great number of treatises and books.[76] Ibn Taymiyya's only pupil to be imprisoned along with him, Ibn al-Qayyim served time in the Damascus Citadel from 726/1326 until his master's death for espousing the same critical view of the cult of saints. Upon his release he was flogged and paraded on a donkey as further punishment.[77] Ibn al-Qayyim was not cowed by this experience, however. Though he led a far less public life than his teacher, he did not shy away from controversy. Many of his works are even more emphatically critical of popular trends in Sunnī Islam than Ibn Taymiyya's. One of his most famous literary products, *al-Kāfiya al-shāfiya fī ʾl-intiṣār lil-firqa al-nājiya* (The Sufficient and Healing [Poem] in Support of the Saved Sect), is a versified Taymiyyan creed of nearly six thousand lines rhyming in the letter *nūn*.[78] The poem is both an allegory for his master's trials and "a raging attack against the Ashʿarīs," as Livnat Holtzman has described it.[79] The fact that al-Subkī wrote a lengthy refutation of it, his *al-Sayf al-ṣaqīl fī ʾl-radd ʿalā ʾbn Zafīl* (The Burnished Sword in Refutation of Ibn Zafīl), shows that the Shāfiʿī scholars in Damascus were still concerned with the spread of Ibn Taymiyya's ideas after he was gone.[80]

Among Ibn Taymiyya's other disciples was the Shāfiʿī ʿImād al-Dīn Ibn Kathīr (d. 774/1373), whose famous commentary on the Qurʾān begins with a long excerpt from Ibn Taymiyya's essay on the principles of Qurʾānic exegesis.[81] Other members of the circle included Ibn Taymiyya's two brothers Badr al-Dīn (d. 717/1318) and Sharaf al-Dīn (d. 727/1327); his Ḥanbalī biographers

76. For his biography, see Bori and Holtzman, "Scholar in the Shadow," 13–31; for an overview of his canon, see Holtzman, "Ibn Qayyim al-Jawziyyah." His name can be rendered either "Ibn Qayyim al-Jawziyya" (the son of the superintendent of the Jawziyya) or "Ibn al-Qayyim" (the son of the superintendent), but not "Ibn Qayyim."

77. Bori and Holtzman, "Scholar in the Shadow," 21.

78. On the poem, see Holtzman, "Accused of Anthropomorphism"; Holtzman, "Insult, Fury, and Frustration."

79. Holtzman, "Accused of Anthropomorphism," 585.

80. See al-Subkī, *al-Rasāʾil al-Subkiyya*, 81–147.

81. Ibn Kathīr, *Tafsīr al-Qurʾān al-ʿaẓīm*, 1:7–14 (= Ibn Taymiyya, *Majmūʿ fatāwā*, 13:363–75). Ibn Kathīr does not attribute the excerpted text, perhaps out of fear of being associated with Ibn Taymiyya. On Ibn Taymiyya's *ḥadīth*-centered approach to exegesis, see Saleh, "Ibn Taymiyya and the Rise of Radical Hermeneutics." And see further Mirza, "Ibn Taymiyya as Exegete"; Mirza, "Was Ibn Kathīr the 'Spokesperson' for Ibn Taymiyya?"

Ibn ʿAbd al-Hādī (d. 744/1343) and ʿUmar al-Bazzār (d. 749/1349); the Ḥanbalīs Aḥmad ibn Ibrāhīm al-Wāsiṭī (d. 711/1311), Sharaf al-Dīn Ibn al-Munajjā (d. 724/1324), Shihāb al-Dīn Ibn Murrī (d. 725/1324f), Taqī al-Dīn Ibn Shuqayr (d. 744/1343), and Shams al-Dīn Ibn Mufliḥ (d. 763/1362); the Shāfiʿīs ʿAlam al-Dīn al-Birzālī (d. 739/1339) and Ibn Shākir al-Kutubī (d. 764/1362); and the Mālikī Ibn Rushayyiq (d. 749/1348). Some of them went on to transmit Ibn Taymiyya's teachings to another generation of religious scholars. For instance, the Ḥanafī Damascene scholar Ibn Abī ʾl-ʿIzz (d. 792/1390) was a student of Ibn al-Qayyim's and Ibn Kathīr's.[82] His commitment to Ibn Taymiyya's theology is on full display in his commentary on the early Ḥanafī creed of Abū Jaʿfar al-Ṭaḥāwī (d. 321/933).[83] In addition to Ibn Taymiyya's own works, Ibn al-Qayyim's books, Ibn Kathīr's Qurʾānic exegesis, and Ibn Abī ʾl-ʿIzz's commentary on al-Ṭaḥāwī's creed would be popular with the Wahhābīs.

In addition to these stalwart followers, a number of scholars occupied a position on the outer rim of Ibn Taymiyya's circle, having been his early disciples but later distancing themselves from him to some degree. In this group may be counted the two famous Shāfiʿī *ḥadīth* scholars al-Mizzī (d. 742/1341f) and al-Dhahabī (d. 748/1348), both traditionalists in theology who were persecuted for their association with Ibn Taymiyya. A scholar from the next generation who occupied a similar position was Ibn Rajab (d. 795/1393), a Ḥanbalī *ḥadīth* scholar who admired Ibn Taymiyya but was also quite critical of him, seeing him as overly preoccupied with theological polemic and unconstrained by the traditional judgments of the Ḥanbalī law school.[84]

Summoning Ibn Taymiyya

Ibn ʿAbd al-Wahhāb made no secret of his admiration for Ibn Taymiyya and Ibn Qayyim al-Jawziyya. He quoted their works, adopted their language and ideas, and appealed to their example as fearless champions of the truth who stood up to the scholarly establishment of their day. At the same time, he was careful not to overstate his dependence on Ibn Taymiyya and his followers. Ibn ʿAbd al-Wahhāb did not wish to give the impression that he was a

82. For their influence on him, see the editors' introduction in Ibn Abī ʾl-ʿIzz, *Sharḥ al-ʿAqīda al-Ṭaḥāwiyya*, 1:63–64.

83. Ibid., passim. On this text, see Shiliwala, "Constructing a Textual Tradition."

84. Bori, "Ibn Taymiyya *wa-Jamāʿatu-hu*," 33–36.

follower of any one scholar or school. In one of his letters, for example, he insists that he is not calling on people to follow the teachings of any particular mystic, jurist, theologian, or *imām*, including those he most admires. In saying this, however, he identified some of the scholars he most revered, naming Ibn al-Qayyim, al-Dhahabī, and Ibn Kathīr.[85] Later on in the same letter, he adds that the best scholars of later generations (*al-muta ʾakhkhirīn*) in terms of knowledge and piety include Ibn al-Qayyim, al-Dhahabī, Ibn Kathīr, and Ibn Rajab and praises them for their severe condemnation of the people of their day (*qad ishtadda nakīruhum ʿalā ahl ʿaṣrihim*).[86] Similarly, in another early letter, he claims that his doctrine is in accord with the views of the best scholars of later generations (*sādāt al-muta ʾakhkhirīn wa-qādatuhum*), including Ibn Taymiyya, Ibn al-Qayyim, Ibn Rajab, al-Dhahabī, and Ibn Kathīr, noting that all of them wrote prolifically in condemnation of polytheism.[87] Thus, while Ibn ʿAbd al-Wahhāb did not harp on his reliance on Ibn Taymiyya and his followers—at times he even seems to be avoiding Ibn Taymiyya's name—it is clear from his writings that he admired them greatly and was inspired by their example, which he saw as worthy of emulation.

Here we will look at just two aspects of the Taymiyyan example to which Ibn ʿAbd al-Wahhāb appealed: (1) his disregard for scholarly authority and (2) his disapproval of the cult of saints. In the next chapter we will examine in greater detail the more specific ideas of Ibn Taymiyya and Ibn al-Qayyim that Ibn ʿAbd al-Wahhāb borrowed and built upon.

Rabbis and Monks

During the Damascus trials of 705/1306, convened to consider his creed known as *al-ʿAqīda al-Wāsiṭiyya,* Ibn Taymiyya displayed a level of confidence bordering on arrogance as he defended himself before a jury of his fellow scholars.[88] Rejecting the notion that his creed should be understood as the creed of the Ḥanbalī school, he asserted that it was in fact "the creed of the ancestors" (*ʿaqīdat al-salaf*) and "the creed of Muḥammad" (*ʿaqīdat*

85. Ibn Ghannām, *Tārīkh,* 1:248 (letter to ʿAbdallāh ibn ʿAbd al-Laṭīf).

86. Ibid., 1:248–49.

87. Ibid., 1:446 (letter to ʿAbd al-Wahhāb ibn ʿĪsā).

88. For his own account of these trials, see Ibn Taymiyya, *Majmūʿ fatāwā,* 3:160–93; and see the translation in Jackson, "Ibn Taymiyyah on Trial in Damascus."

Muḥammad).[89] In saying this, he challenged the jury to find a single consonant (*ḥarf wāḥid*) in the words of the *salaf* that contradicted what he had written, saying that in that event he would gladly rescind the creed. He proposed that they be given three years to try.[90]

This irreverent performance is a good illustration of Ibn Taymiyya's approach to religious authority—namely, that his colleagues had none over him. True authority for him was vested in the foundational Islamic texts, and he believed in drawing directly from these rather than emulating (*taqlīd*) living or dead scholars. His view was that in a given matter one should go directly to the proof texts rather than to the opinions of any person or school, so long as one was capable of doing so.

One of the Qurʾānic verses that Ibn Taymiyya cited in making this argument was Q. 9:31, in which God condemns the Christians for deifying their religious leaders ("their rabbis and their monks"), accusing them of treating these as "lords" above men. In the verse, God says of the Christians: "They have taken their rabbis and their monks [*aḥbārahum wa-ruhbānahum*] as lords apart from God [*arbāban min dūni ʾllāhi*], and the Messiah, Mary's son—and they were commanded to worship but One God; there is no god but He; glory be to Him, above that they associate." In one of his *fatwās*, Ibn Taymiyya cites this verse in writing that no religious leader (*imām*) should be elevated to the status of the Prophet (*manzilat al-nabī*), for that would be to commit the same error as the Christians who took their religious leaders as lords.[91] In another of his works, a book of creed known as *Kitāb al-īmān*, Ibn Taymiyya argues that the Christian deification of "their rabbis and their monks" is tantamount to worship and therefore it constitutes *shirk*. He quotes the *ḥadīth* of ʿAdī ibn Ḥātim, an early Muslim convert from Christianity who, before his conversion, heard the Prophet reciting Q. 9:31. Upon hearing the verse, ʿAdī says to the Prophet, "We have not taken them as lords," to which the Prophet responds, "Do they not forbid what God has permitted, so you forbid it, and permit what God has forbidden, so you permit it?" ʿAdī replies, "Indeed," and the Prophet says, "Then that is worshiping them" (*fa-tilka ʿibādatuhum*).[92] What this indi-

89. Ibn Taymiyya, *Majmūʿ fatāwā*, 3:169 (=Jackson, "Ibn Taymiyyah on Trial in Damascus," 64).

90. Ibn Taymiyya, *Majmūʿ fatāwā*, 3:169.

91. Ibid., 20:216.

92. Ibid., 7:67. For the *ḥadīth* as quoted here, see al-Ṭabarānī, *al-Muʿjam al-kabīr*, 17:92 (no. 218); cf. al-Tirmidhī, *Sunan*, 5:278 (*Kitāb tafsīr al-Qurʾān, bāb wa-min sūrat al-tawba*, no. 3095).

cates, according to Ibn Taymiyya, is that the Christians' obedience to their religious leaders in forbidding what is permitted and permitting what is forbidden amounted to illicit worship, and therefore the Christians were committing *shirk* with respect to their leaders.[93] Ibn Taymiyya's implicit accusation here was that Muslims ought not to treat their religious leaders in a similar way, as to do so would be to commit *shirk*. Excessive deference to one's religious scholars could lead to polytheism and unbelief.

Ibn ʿAbd al-Wahhāb was likewise fond of citing these proof texts in the context of religious authority, noting that these were proofs used by Ibn Taymiyya. In two of his letters, he refers to or quotes Ibn Taymiyya's use of Q. 9:31 in *Kitāb al-īmān*.[94] In one of these he tells a fellow Najdī that the verse is one of Ibn Taymiyya's proofs (*min adillatihi*) that shows the error of deferring to living religious authorities, to "those whom you think are scholars" (*alladhīna taẓunnūna annahum ʿulamāʾ*).[95] Ibn ʿAbd al-Wahhāb goes on to inveigh against the entire educational institution surrounding Islamic jurisprudence (*fiqh*). Quoting the verse, he says: "The Messenger of God and the *imāms* after him understood it as referring to this that you call *fiqh*, which is what God called *shirk* and the taking of them as lords."[96] As is clear from this comment, for Ibn ʿAbd al-Wahhāb, the tradition of *fiqh* had developed into an entirely illegitimate religious institution; *fiqh* education had become a factory for the production of slavish emulators, pseudo-scholars who treated their highly flawed religious authorities as lords. Similarly, in his letter to ʿAbdallāh ibn ʿAbd al-Laṭīf, a Shāfiʿī scholar in al-Aḥsāʾ who had criticized him, Ibn ʿAbd al-Wahhāb accuses his opponents of following "what God censured and called *shirk*, which is the taking of their scholars as lords."[97]

A similar comment is found in *Kitāb al-tawḥīd*, in a chapter that bears a title drawn from Q. 9:31 and the *ḥadīth* of ʿAdī ibn Ḥātim—"Those Who Obey Scholars and Rulers in Forbidding What God Has Permitted or Permitting What God Has Forbidden Have Taken Them as Lords Apart from God."[98] In this chapter Ibn ʿAbd al-Wahhāb quotes the *ḥadīth* of ʿAdī ibn Ḥātim and

93. Ibn Taymiyya, *Majmūʿ fatāwā*, 7:67.

94. Ibn Ghannām, *Tārīkh*, 1:444 (letter to ʿAbdallāh ibn ʿĪsā), 446 (letter to ʿAbd al-Wahhāb ibn ʿĪsā).

95. Ibid., 1:446.

96. Ibid.

97. Ibid., 1:255.

98. Ibn ʿAbd al-Wahhāb, *Kitāb al-tawḥīd*, 259.

applies it to the religious environment of his own day. One of the matters (*masāʾil*) to be extracted from this *ḥadīth*, he writes, is "the changing of circumstances [*taghayyur al-aḥwāl*] to the point where for most people worshipping monks is among the most virtuous of acts, being called friendship, and worshipping rabbis is knowledge and *fiqh*."[99] Ibn ʿAbd al-Wahhāb here interprets the monks (*ruhbān*) of Q. 9:31 as Ṣūfī saints and the rabbis (*aḥbār*) as scholars of *fiqh*, both of whom are being treated as lords by his contemporaries. What he means to say, in other words, is that the method of drawing close to a saint constitutes worship, as does the manner in which students are learning from jurists. Yet Ibn ʿAbd al-Wahhāb is more critical still. "Then the situation changed," he continues in the same chapter of *Kitāb al-tawḥīd*, "to the point where those who are not righteous are being worshipped, and in the second case those who are ignorant are being worshipped."[100] The idea here is that the saints being venerated in Najd and elsewhere—men such as Tāj, Shamsān, and Yūsuf—are not even righteous men to begin with, while the jurisprudents being shown deference and respect are not even knowledgeable. While Ibn Taymiyya was critical of those who deferred unthinkingly to living religious authorities, his criticism was not as extreme as Ibn ʿAbd al-Wahhāb's.[101] Ibn Taymiyya never went so far as to condemn the entire scholarly establishment as the epitome of *shirk*.

Ibn ʿAbd al-Wahhāb also found support from Ibn al-Qayyim in his approach to scholarly authority. The source on which he drew the most in this regard was Ibn al-Qayyim's massive book on the conduct of *muftīs*, *Iʿlām al-muwaqqiʿīn ʿan rabb al-ʿālamīn* (Informing Those in Charge About the Master of the Worlds).[102] While works in this genre typically counsel *taqlīd* and caution against *ijtihād* (except for those with supreme knowledge of the sources and the legal tradition),[103] Ibn al-Qayyim's book is distinguished by its numerous broadsides against *taqlīd*. God, he writes, "did not enjoin us to practice *taqlīd*" (*lam yukallifnā bi ʾl-taqlīd*).[104] Pointing to Q. 9:31, he notes that God condemned the *taqlīd* of our fathers and leaders (*taqlīd al-ābāʾ wa ʾl-ruʾasāʾ*),

99. Ibid., 261.

100. Ibid.

101. Ibn Taymiyya, *Majmūʿ fatāwā*, 27:67.

102. On this text, see Krawietz, "Transgressive Creativity in the Making"; Mustafa, *On Taqlīd*.

103. See EI^3, s.v. "Adab al-muftī" (Muhammad Khalid Masud).

104. Ibn al-Qayyim, *Iʿlām al-muwaqqiʿīn*, 3:569.

urging us to follow the foundational sources (*al-taslīm lil-uṣūl*).[105] It is thus the *muftī*'s duty to issue rulings on the basis of the Qur'ān and the *sunna*, not to imitate his predecessors, even if this renders him alone in his judgment. The true consensus (*ijmā'*) is the scholar who possesses knowledge (*al-'ālim ṣāḥib al-ḥaqq*), even if he is alone in his judgment and the entire world is against him.[106] It is also the duty of lay Muslims, Ibn al-Qayyim says, not just those with scholarly training, to seek knowledge in the sources of revelation insofar as they are able.[107]

Ibn 'Abd al-Wahhāb would refer to Ibn al-Qayyim's *I'lām al-muwaqqi'īn* often. In his letter to 'Abdallāh ibn 'Abd al-Laṭīf, for instance, in which he defends himself against the charge of engaging in *ijtihād*, he cites Ibn al-Qayyim's book in emphasizing the idea that it is every believer's obligation to interface directly with the texts of revelation. The greatest specious argument (*shubha*) of his opponents, he says, is their claim that only a *mujtahid* is qualified to engage with the foundational texts:

> You are saying, "We are not capable of it [i.e., following the path of the Messenger and his Companions], and only the *mujtahid* is capable of it." You have decided that only the *mujtahid* can benefit from the words of God and the words of His Messenger. You are saying, "It is prohibited for someone else to seek guidance from the words of God, the words of His Messenger, and the words of his Companions."[108]

Nowhere, Ibn 'Abd al-Wahhāb retorts, does the Qur'ān stipulate that one must be a *mujtahid* to refer directly to God's words. To the contrary, it condemns in the plainest terms the slavish emulation of one's forefathers. After quoting the *ḥadīth* of 'Adī ibn Ḥātim, Ibn 'Abd al-Wahhāb directs his correspondent to Ibn al-Qayyim's *I'lām al-muwaqqi'īn*, telling him precisely where it can be found in al-Aḥsā'.[109]

Another proof text cited by Ibn al-Qayyim in the context of religious authority, and one that Ibn 'Abd al-Wahhāb would similarly invoke, is the *ḥadīth* about Islam's beginning as something strange and returning as such. The

105. Ibid., 3:452–53.

106. Ibid., 5:388.

107. Ibid., 4:13. The apparent difference between Ibn Taymiyya and Ibn al-Qayyim on this score is noted in Haykel, "On the Nature of Salafi Thought and Action," 45–46.

108. Ibn Ghannām, *Tārīkh*, 1:256.

109. Ibid., 1:250–51.

ḥadīth reads: "Islam began as something strange and will return as something strange as it began, so blessed be the strangers" (*bada ʾa ʾl-Islām gharīban wa-sa-ya ʿūdu gharīban kamā bada ʾa fa-ṭūbā lil-ghurabā ʾ*).[110] The word *gharīb*, translated here as "strange," may perhaps be better rendered as "estranged" or "alien," as the sense that it conveys is of a religion that was foreign in the environment in which it arose. What the *ḥadīth* means is that just as Islam began as a minority religion, the number of true believers being very small relative to the population, in the future Islam will again be in the minority, the number of true believers again being very small relative to the population. Presumably, this will come about because Islam has succumbed to corruption and innovation. In several of his books, Ibn al-Qayyim uses this *ḥadīth* to argue that Islam has returned to being strange. In *I ʿlām al-muwaqqi ʿīn*, he quotes it in the context of lamenting the fact that religious knowledge is contracting (*al- ʿilm yaqillu*), the books of the emulators (*kutub al-muqallidīn*) having steadily gained in popularity.[111] In another of his books, a work of prophetic biography titled *Zād al-ma ʿād fī hady khayr al- ʿibād* (Provisions for the Hereafter from the Guidance of the Best of Mankind), he alludes to the *ḥadīth* in a comment concerning the cult of saints, observing that "the strangeness of Islam has grown severe" (*ishtaddat ghurbat al-Islām*).[112] In yet another book, a commentary on a Ṣūfī spiritual manual, Ibn al-Qayyim notes that the majority of people (*akthar al-nās*) consider the strangers (*ghurabā ʾ*) to be deviants and innovators (*ahl shudhūdh wa-bid ʿa*), when in fact they are those who remain committed to the *sunna* and *tawḥīd*.[113] Islam, he further asserts here, has returned to being strange: "True Islam as practiced by the Prophet and his Companions is today stranger than it was at the time of its first appearance [*ashadd ghurbatan minhu fī awwal ẓuhūrihi*]."[114] "True Islam [*al-Islām al-ḥaqīqī*]," he reiterates, "is very strange [*gharīb jiddan*], and its adherents are strangers among people."[115] Ibn al-Qayyim appears to have seen himself and his fellow scholars in Ibn Taymiyya's circle as the strangers (*ghurabā ʾ*) prophesied to represent true Islam upon its later return.

110. Muslim, *Ṣaḥīḥ*, 1:130 (*Kitāb al-īmān, bāb bayān anna ʾl-Islām bada ʾa gharīban*, no. 232).

111. Ibn al-Qayyim, *I ʿlām al-muwaqqi ʿīn*, 3:526.

112. Ibn al-Qayyim, *Zād al-ma ʿād*, 3:443.

113. Ibn al-Qayyim, *Madārij al-sālikīn*, 4:3167.

114. Ibid., 4:3168.

115. Ibid. Ibn Taymiyya, in contrast with Ibn al-Qayyim, does not appear to have applied the label *ghurabā ʾ* to himself and his followers. For his discussion of the *ḥadīth* of the *ghurabā ʾ*, see Ibn Taymiyya, *Majmū ʿ fatāwā*, 18:291–305.

Following Ibn al-Qayyim's lead, Ibn ʿAbd al-Wahhāb argues throughout his works that Islam has once again become strange, suggesting that he and his followers are the prophesied *ghurabāʾ*. In one of his letters, for example, he quotes Ibn al-Qayyim's remark in *Zād al-maʿād* about the strangeness of Islam having become severe on account of the cult of saints, and he writes: "[T]he religion of Islam, that is, true Islam [*dīn al-Islām al-ṣirf*], is today among the strangest of things [*min aghrab al-ashyāʾ*]."[116] Similarly, in his letter to Ibn ʿAbd al-Laṭīf, he mentions Ibn al-Qayyim's discussion of the "strangers" *ḥadīth* in *Iʿlām al-muwaqqiʿīn*, saying: "If Islam is supposed to return as it began, then how ignorant is the one who appeals to the majority of people as evidence!"[117] For Ibn ʿAbd al-Wahhāb, as for Ibn al-Qayyim, being in the minority was nothing to be ashamed of.

Also like Ibn al-Qayyim, Ibn ʿAbd al-Wahhāb would argue that it is the obligation of all Muslims, scholars and laypeople alike, to interface with the foundational texts of revelation and understand the basics of the religion through them. As he writes in his epistle to Riyadh and Manfūḥa, it is a duty (*farḍ lāzim*) for both knowledgeable and ignorant, men and women, to study and learn the foundations of the religion themselves.[118] It is probably for this reason that some of Ibn ʿAbd al-Wahhāb's epistles take the form of catechisms setting out the very basics of Islam. The most elementary of his catechisms is known as *al-Uṣūl al-thalātha* (The Three Foundations), in which the three foundations correspond to the three questions prophesied to be put to believers on the Day of Resurrection, namely, "Who is your Lord?" "What is your religion?" "And who is your Prophet?" For each of these questions, Ibn ʿAbd al-Wahhāb provides an extended answer, weaving in the main points of his doctrine, including the emphasis on *tawḥīd* and the requirement of dissociation from *shirk* and its adherents (*al-barāʾa min al-shirk wa-ahlihi*).[119]

As was seen in chapter 1, Ibn ʿAbd al-Wahhāb was frequently accused by his critics of engaging in *ijtihād*, and in response he denied the accusation outright. Indeed, he never claimed to be a *mujtahid*. His argument in this regard was that the question of *ijtihād* and *taqlīd* was beside the point, that those accusing him of claiming *ijtihād* failed to grasp what his message was really about, which was *tawḥīd*. The question of *ijtihād* and who was qualified to

116. Ibn Ghannām, *Tārīkh*, 1:351, 359 (letter to ʿAbdallāh ibn Suḥaym).

117. Ibid., 1:251.

118. Ibid., 1:404. Cf. ibid., 1:251; *al-Durar al-saniyya*, 1:169–70.

119. *al-Durar al-saniyya*, 1:125–36, at 129, 133.

practice it was in his view a red herring, for his central concern was theology, not law. Islam, in his view, had become unmoored from its theological foundations, and his objective was to reestablish them. This required refocusing Muslims on the foundational texts of revelation, teaching them the basics of the religion anew. This was not, in his view, a project of *ijtihād*, and to suggest otherwise was deliberately misleading. The idea that only an omnicompetent *mujtahid* could interface directly with the Qurʾān and the *sunna*, extracting and summarizing core Islamic principles, was insupportable. Such an argument was indicative of just how far removed Islam had become from the religion revealed to the Prophet. The scholars—and particularly the scholars of *fiqh*—had come to be treated as lords, posing as the gatekeepers of the foundational texts. Ibn ʿAbd al-Wahhāb saw himself as breaking open the gates.

Intermediaries

Another recurring theme in the early refutations of Wahhābism was Ibn ʿAbd al-Wahhāb's use of a certain line of Ibn Taymiyya's concerning the cult of saints. The line is drawn from the Ḥanbalī legal manual *al-Iqnāʿ* by al-Ḥajjāwī, where it is found as follows in the chapter concerned with apostasy (*bāb ḥukm al-murtadd*): "Said the shaykh . . . '[Whosoever] sets up intermediaries [*wasāʾiṭ*] between himself and God, relying on them, calling on them, and asking [things] of them [*yatawakkalu ʿalayhim wa-yadʿūhum wa-yasʾaluhum*] [has disbelieved] as a matter of consensus.'"[120] The phrase comes in a list of numerous things that render one an apostate, some of which are attributed to Ibn Taymiyya (i.e., "the shaykh") and others of which are not. It is a good example of Ibn Taymiyya's hostility to the rites of *ziyāra*.

The origin of this phrase is a *fatwā* in which Ibn Taymiyya responds to a question regarding a debate between two men over the necessity of taking an intermediary (*wāsiṭa*) between oneself and God.[121] Ibn Taymiyya interprets the question as being about the cult of saints, responding that the only legitimate intermediaries (*wasāʾiṭ*) between human beings and God are the messengers (*rusul*).[122] If what one has in mind is an intermediary for the purpose of deriving benefits and alleviating harms (*jalb al-manāfiʿ wa-dafʿ al-maḍārr*), he continues, then that is the worst form of polytheism, the kind that the pagan

120. al-Ḥajjāwī, *al-Iqnāʿ*, 4:285.

121. Ibn Taymiyya, *Majmūʿ fatāwā*, 1:121–38.

122. Ibid., 1:121.

Arabs committed when they took allies and intercessors apart from God.[123] He sums up the matter in the following words, from which the phrase in *al-Iqnāʿ* is derived: "Whosoever sets up the angels and prophets as intermediaries, calling on them, relying on them, and asking them to bestow benefits and alleviate harms [*yadʿūhum wa-yatawakkalu ʿalayhim wa-yasʾaluhum jalb al-manāfiʿ wa-dafʿ al-maḍārr*], such as asking them to pardon a sin, to guide hearts, to relieve hardships, and to relieve poverty, is an unbeliever according to the consensus of the Muslims."[124] Though he talks specifically here about angels and prophets, Ibn Taymiyya's criticism pertains to any kind of intermediary, including saints. His point, as he goes on to clarify, is not that all forms of supplication (*duʿāʾ*) are prohibited. Rather, it is that Muslims must make their appeals to God alone, not addressing them to intermediaries. A person's relying, supplicating, asking, and requesting (*tawakkuluhu wa-duʿāʾuhu wa-suʾāluhu wa-raghbatuhu*), he says, should be directed to God and never to anyone else.[125]

To bolster his argument, Ibn Taymiyya constructs an analogy between God and His creation and kings and their subjects. In the case of a king, he says, if a person desires something from him, it may make sense to petition his chamberlains or gatekeepers (*ḥujjāb*) as opposed to petitioning the king directly. This is because the gatekeepers are near the king and are able to bring petitions to him. But the same is not permissible in the realm of the divine. Whosoever sets up intermediaries to God in such a way is an unbelieving polytheist who must be asked to repent, and if he does not repent, then he ought to be killed.[126] In another passage, Ibn Taymiyya makes the analogy again, saying, "Whosoever sets up intermediaries between God and His creation, such as the intermediaries between kings and their subjects, is a polytheist. Indeed, that is the religion of polytheist idol-worshippers."[127]

Ibn Taymiyya's line about not taking intermediaries that appears in *al-Iqnāʿ* was an abridgment of the one quoted above in the *fatwā* on the cult of saints. It first appeared in this abridged form in a legal text by one of Ibn Taymiyya's students, the Ḥanbalī Ibn Mufliḥ,[128] and it would appear in the same form in a compilation of Ibn Taymiyya's legal opinions prepared by the later Ḥanbalī

123. Ibid., 1:123.
124. Ibid., 1:124.
125. Ibid., 1:131.
126. Ibid., 1:126.
127. Ibid., 1:134–35.
128. Ibn Mufliḥ, *Kitāb al-furūʿ*, 10:188.

ʿAlāʾ al-Dīn al-Baʿlī (d. 803/1401).[129] From here it seems to have found its way into al-Ḥajjāwī's book, which is where Ibn ʿAbd al-Wahhāb likely encountered it for the first time. As Ibn ʿAbd al-Wahhāb's opponents noted, it was a line that he quoted often. One finds it, in a slightly modified form, in Ibn ʿAbd al-Wahhāb's epistle known as "the nullifiers of Islam" (*nawāqiḍ al-Islām*), a list of ten things that eject one from the faith. The second nullifier reads: "Whosoever sets up intermediaries between himself and God, calling on them, asking them for intercession, and relying on them has disbelieved as a matter of consensus."[130] The phrase is also invoked in an early letter by Ibn ʿAbd al-Wahhāb to several scholars in al-Dirʿiyya. Urging them to pronounce *takfīr* on the saints of Najd, he tells them: "Look at the text of *al-Iqnāʿ* in *bāb ḥukm al-murtadd*. Does it not state clearly that whosoever sets up intermediaries between himself and God, calling on them, is an unbeliever by the consensus of the community?"[131] In condemning the cult of saints, then, Ibn ʿAbd al-Wahhāb was appealing directly to the words and authority of Ibn Taymiyya, and this led to controversy among his scholarly opponents.

Not all of these opponents objected to Ibn ʿAbd al-Wahhāb's use of this phrase in the same way. Indeed, they handled it quite differently, depending on their views of Ibn Taymiyya and *ziyāra*. One approach was to dismiss Ibn Taymiyya's phrase as a peculiar and flawed opinion. This was the view espoused by the Ḥanbalī Ibn ʿAfāliq in his *Tahakkum al-muqallidīn*, where he argued that Ibn Taymiyya's words constituted a minority judgment that got him into a great deal of trouble.[132] At least in this refutation, Ibn ʿAfāliq clearly disagreed with Ibn Taymiyya that supplicating saints and prophets amounted to *shirk*. He even sought to show that al-Ḥajjāwī, though he included this line in his book, actually did not endorse it. "It is outrageous," Ibn ʿAfāliq writes,

> that he [i.e., Ibn ʿAbd al-Wahhāb] draws on his statement in *al-Iqnāʿ*, "Whosoever sets up intermediaries between himself and God. . . ." For *al-Iqnāʿ* quoted this from the shaykh Ibn Taymiyya, and it is stated in the opening passage of *al-Iqnāʿ*, "And sometimes I will attribute a statement to its author as a way of not endorsing it." So how can he use as evidence

129. al-Baʿlī, *al-Akhbār al-ʿilmiyya*, 443.

130. *al-Durar al-saniyya*, 2:361–62; cf. 10:91–93.

131. Ibn Ghannām, *Tārīkh*, 1:415–17, at 417.

132. Ibn ʿAfāliq, *Tahakkum al-muqallidīn*, f. 52a.

> words that he [i.e., al-Ḥajjāwī] attributed in *al-Iqnāʿ* to the shaykh when it was said in the opening passage that attributions are done in order not to endorse?[133]

At the beginning of his book, al-Ḥajjāwī indeed notes that he will sometimes attribute an opinion to its speaker so as not to endorse it himself (*khurūjan min tabiʿatihi*).[134] It is not at all clear, however, that al-Ḥajjāwī was seeking to distance himself from Ibn Taymiyya's opinion in this case, as he frequently cited the shaykh's many other, less controversial opinions as well. In any event, Ibn ʿAfāliq's approach here was to discredit Ibn Taymiyya's view of the cult of saints and to suggest that it was not the accepted opinion of the Ḥanbalī *madhhab*.

A second approach, also taken by the Ḥanbalī refuters, was to try and read Ibn Taymiyya's words restrictively as opposed to repudiating them. Ibn ʿAbd al-Wahhāb's brother, Sulaymān, exemplified this approach in his extant refutation, where he claims that Ibn Taymiyya's words do not mean what the Wahhābīs have taken them to mean. "If you consider the phrase fully," he says to his Wahhābī correspondent, "you will know that you have interpreted the phrase incorrectly."[135] Sulayman focuses here on the word *and* in Ibn Taymiyya's line, arguing that the shaykh was careful to say *and* as opposed to *or* in the phrase "relying on them, calling on them, and asking [things] of them" (*yatawakkalu ʿalayhim wa-yadʿūhum wa-yasʾaluhum*). For Ibn Taymiyya, he claims, the use of *and* indicates that one had to commit all three acts—reliance (*tawakkul*), supplication (*duʿāʾ*), and request (*suʾāl*)—to fall into disbelief. Addressing the Wahhābīs, he writes: "And now you are declaring people to be unbelievers on account of asking alone [*bi'l-suʾāl waḥdahu*]!"[136] Yet, however sincere Sulaymān may have been in making this argument, it is simply not a plausible interpretation of Ibn Taymiyya's words in the *fatwā* on intermediaries quoted above. Ibn Taymiyya's point was that all forms of worship must be directed to God alone (*tawakkuluhu wa-duʿāʾuhu wa-suʾāluhu wa-raghbatuhu*), the implication being that any one of them being directed elsewhere constitutes *shirk*. The approach of Sulaymān was to interpret Ibn Taymiyya's phrase to suit a more tolerant view of the cult of saints than the one Ibn Taymiyya

133. Ibid., f. 52b.

134. al-Ḥajjāwī, *al-Iqnāʿ*, 1:4.

135. Ibn ʿAbd al-Wahhāb, *al-Ṣawāʿiq al-ilāhiyya*, 9.

136. Ibid.

actually espoused. A similarly apologetic tactic was adopted by the Shāfiʿī al-Ṭandatāwī, who refers to Ibn Taymiyya's opinion as the opinion of the Ḥanbalīs (*qawl al-Ḥanābila*) and claims that it does not mean what it appears to. The true meaning of these words, he says, is not that those who take intermediaries to God have disbelieved but, rather, that those who take intermediaries to God "as though they are gods" (*ʿalā annahum āliha*) have disbelieved. And no one, whether from the elite or the masses, is taking intermediaries in this way.[137]

Another kind of restrictive reading of Ibn Taymiyya's phrase was offered by the Ḥanbalī ʿAbdallāh ibn Fayrūz, who acknowledges that the acts described by Ibn Taymiyya amount to *shirk* but claims that Ibn Taymiyya was speaking only about certain heretical Ṣūfīs (*nās min mulḥidī ʾl-ṣūfiyya*), not the ignorant masses. The masses, he writes, believe that saints (*ahl al-ṣalāḥ*) are able to answer supplication (*mustajābūn al-daʿwa*), and while this is not permissible, they must be educated that this is incorrect rather than being immediately subjected to *takfīr*. Those of them who do not repent ought to be detained, and if they persist in their errant belief and there exists a legitimate ruler (*imām*) to enforce the law, then they ought to be killed.[138] In contrast with Sulaymān's reading, Ibn Fayrūz's interpretation is entirely plausible, since Ibn Taymiyya was in fact much more forgiving of the masses than Ibn ʿAbd al-Wahhāb, as will be seen in the next chapter.

The different approaches of Ibn ʿAfāliq, Sulaymān, and Ibn Fayrūz to Ibn Taymiyya's line concerning the cult of saints—condemnation, distortion, and qualification—seem to reflect the different ways in which the Ḥanbalī community of eighteenth-century Arabia was handling the scholar's controversial legacy. While the degree of Ibn Taymiyya's influence on the Ḥanbalī *madhhab* has been called into question,[139] the fact is that he had come to be seen, in the centuries following his death, as the chief authority figure in Ḥanbalism, widely dubbed "the shaykh" in Ḥanbalī legal texts. Previously this term had been reserved for Ibn Qudāma al-Maqdisī (d. 620/1223), but by the time al-Ḥajjāwī was writing in the sixteenth century it was used to refer to Ibn Taymi-

137. Traboulsi, "Early Refutation," 401. It does not appear that al-Ṭandatāwī knew that this line belonged to Ibn Taymiyya.

138. Ibn Dāwūd, *al-Ṣawāʿiq wa ʾl-ruʿūd*, ff. 196b–97a.

139. See Melchert, "Relation of Ibn Taymiyya and Ibn Qayyim al-Jawziyya to the Ḥanbalī School of Law"; El-Rouayheb, "From Ibn Ḥajar al-Haytamī to Khayr al-Dīn al-Ālūsī," 299.

yya exclusively.[140] And yet, the Ḥanbalīs of Arabia did not adopt each and every one of Ibn Taymiyya's views as orthodoxy.[141]

With regard to the cult of saints, none of Ibn ʿAbd al-Wahhāb's Ḥanbalī opponents embodied Ibn Taymiyya's fierce opposition to the institution, and some of them seem not to have fully understood or appreciated his position. In contrast with Ibn Taymiyya and his followers, the Ḥanbalī scholars of eighteenth-century Arabia appear to have looked on the cult of saints either approvingly or with passive disapproval. In this regard, the Ḥanbalī community of Ibn ʿAbd al-Wahhāb's day was not nearly as disputatious and provocative as Ibn Taymiyya and his followers had been. Ibn Taymiyya's harsh words concerning the taking of intermediaries reflected a more or less neglected aspect of his legacy, and it was this aspect in particular that Ibn ʿAbd al-Wahhāb was seizing on and seeking to revive.

Conclusion

As we have seen in this chapter, Ibn Taymiyya's religious thought was to a large degree consistent with traditional Ḥanbalī theology, particularly as regards the rejection of speculative theology (*kalām*). Yet to this he made several emendations, including his more affirmative approach to God's attributes, his insistence on the agreement of reason and revelation, and his conception of God as purposive and perpetually creative. His religious thought was also distinctive in its severe opposition to Ṣūfī monism and the cult of saints.

It is of course true, as some have pointed out, that Ibn ʿAbd al-Wahhāb and his followers did not have access to the full range of Ibn Taymiyya's corpus, and thus they may not have been aware of every dimension of his thought. One must be careful not to overstate this point, however. As we have already seen, the Wahhābī founder was familiar with many of Ibn Taymiyya's and Ibn al-Qayyim's works, as he quotes and refers to them throughout his letters and epistles. It is simply not the case, as has recently been alleged, that "[t]he followers of Ibn ʿAbd al-Wahhāb accessed Ibn Taymiyya's ideas primarily through

140. Al-Matroudi, *Ḥanbalī School of Law and Ibn Taymiyya*, 151.

141. Cf. the case of a group of seventeenth- and eighteenth-century Ḥanbalīs in Syria associated with the Khalwatī Ṣūfī order, who likewise did not feel compelled to adopt Ibn Taymiyya's views wholesale; they studied the works of Ibn ʿArabī and had no difficulty accepting the monist concept of *waḥdat al-wujūd*. See El-Rouayheb, *Islamic Intellectual History in the Seventeenth Century*, 263–65.

the lens of Ibn al-Qayyim's polemical theological poem *al-Nūniyya*, which was widely known in Najd."[142] The early Wahhābīs had access to far more texts by Ibn Taymiyya and Ibn al-Qayyim than this.[143] Moreover, the distinctive theological ideas of Ibn Taymiyya and Ibn al-Qayyim are reiterated throughout these two scholars' corpuses, so lack of access to certain works did not preclude access to their most important ideas.

Of all the features of Ibn Taymiyya's religious thought that would manifest in Wahhābism—and most of them would—none was more significant than his hostility to the cult of saints. In this respect, mainstream Ḥanbalism had ceased to embody the controversial and aggressive Taymiyyan spirit. Ibn ʿAbd al-Wahhāb, by contrast, would, and he would seek to channel that spirit in service of his theopolitical campaign. In doing so, however, he was not merely imitating Ibn Taymiyya and Ibn al-Qayyim, as some of his detractors alleged. Rather, he was modifying their views in substantial ways, putting forward a doctrine that was unmistakably Taymiyyan in origin and inspiration but also significantly more extreme in some of its conclusions.

142. El Shamsy, *Rediscovering the Islamic Classics*, 184.

143. These include, in addition to numerous texts published in Ibn Taymiyya's *Majmūʿ fatāwā*, his *Iqtiḍāʾ al-ṣirāṭ al-mustaqīm*, *al-Istighātha fī ʾl-radd ʿalā ʾl-Bakrī*, and *Minhāj al-sunna al-nabawiyya* and Ibn al-Qayyim's *Iʿlām al-muwaqqiʿīn*, *Zād al-maʿād*, *Madārij al-sālikīn*, and *Ighāthat al-lahfān*. This is not an exhaustive list. For a sense of the works by Ibn Taymiyya and Ibn al-Qayyim available in central Arabia, both during and before the Wahhābī period, see al-Māniʿ, *Nāsikhū ʾl-makhṭūṭāt al-Najdiyyūn*; Āl Furayyān, *al-Wirāqa fī minṭaqat Najd*. Also noteworthy in this regard is a text preserved by the Wahhābī tradition that is described as Ibn ʿAbd al-Wahhāb's excerpts and summaries of some of Ibn Taymiyya's writings; see Ibn ʿAbd al-Wahhāb, *Muʾallafāt al-shaykh*, *qism* 7 (*Masāʾil lakhkhaṣahā ʾl-shaykh al-imām Muḥammad ibn ʿAbd al-Wahhāb min kalām shaykh al-Islām*).

3

The Doctrine of Ibn ʿAbd al-Wahhāb II

THE KEY COMPONENTS

LIKE IBN TAYMIYYA before him, Ibn ʿAbd al-Wahhāb set out to enforce the boundaries between what he saw as *tawḥīd* and *shirk* in a provocative fashion. Yet, as incendiary as Ibn Taymiyya and his followers could be, Ibn ʿAbd al-Wahhāb was more incendiary still. Whereas Ibn Taymiyya sought to promote his views as a legitimate, if iconoclastic, member of the scholarly class of the Mamlūk Sultanate, Ibn ʿAbd al-Wahhāb dismissed the scholarly class of his environment as beyond the pale, and he launched a movement that would ultimately upend the religious and political status quo in Arabia. Both were nonconformists, but whereas Ibn Taymiyya was an iconoclast, Ibn ʿAbd al-Wahhāb was a revolutionary.

The preceding chapter considered the main lines of Ibn Taymiyya's religious thought and further examined some of the ways in which Ibn ʿAbd al-Wahhāb appealed to the Taymiyyan legacy. The present chapter looks more closely at some of the ideas that Ibn ʿAbd al-Wahhāb borrowed and the ways in which he recast and/or modified them. It examines four of the most critical components of his doctrine and their relationship to the religious thought of Ibn Taymiyya and Ibn al-Qayyim. These four components are (1) *tawḥīd,* (2) *takfīr,* (3) *al-walāʾ wa ʾl-barāʾ*, and (4) *jihād.* The chapter looks at the origins of these components in the thought of Ibn Taymiyya and Ibn al-Qayyim, the ways in which Ibn ʿAbd al-Wahhāb made use of them, and the modifications that he introduced. As will be seen, Ibn ʿAbd al-Wahhāb not only borrowed from Ibn Taymiyya and Ibn al-Qayyim but also adapted and reformulated some of their ideas, taking their thought in a more radical direction.

Tawḥīd

There is nothing more important in Ibn ʿAbd al-Wahhāb's doctrine than the concept of *tawḥīd*. Indeed, Ibn ʿAbd al-Wahhāb's notion of *tawḥīd* may be seen as the starting point from which all else follows. As one of his refuters, ʿAbdallāh ibn Dāwūd al-Zubayrī, observed of the early Wahhābīs, "All they talk about is *tawḥīd*, to the point where nine-tenths of what they say is *tawḥīd tawḥīd*!"[1] In several of his epistles, Ibn ʿAbd al-Wahhāb asserts that *tawḥīd* is more obligatory than performing the prayer and paying the *zakāt*, among other of the five pillars of Islam.[2] For him, one had to get *tawḥīd* right before the ritual acts of devotion would even begin to count.

While often translated as "monotheism" or "God's oneness," *tawḥīd* has the more literal sense of "unifying God" or "making God one." Following Ibn Taymiyya, Ibn ʿAbd al-Wahhāb distinguished two distinct senses of *tawḥīd*, one concerning belief and one concerning practice. In the first sense, *tawḥīd* means simply to believe that God is one. In the second sense, it means to worship God as one.[3] For Ibn ʿAbd al-Wahhāb, the second sense was everything. The fact that a person believed in God counted for almost nothing. What mattered was that worship—all worship—be directed to Him alone.

The Two Tawḥīd*s*

In his theological polemics, Ibn Taymiyya frequently speaks of *tawḥīd* as being of two kinds: *tawḥīd al-rubūbiyya* (the oneness of God's lordship) and *tawḥīd al-ulūhiyya* (the oneness of God's divinity), also rendered *tawḥīd al-ilāhiyya*.[4] According to him, one must meet the conditions of both to satisfy the requirements of Islam.

This schema of two *tawḥīd*s, which Ibn Taymiyya almost certainly originated, was designed with a polemical purpose in mind.[5] For Ibn Taymiyya, the

1. Ibn Dāwūd, *al-Ṣawāʿiq wa ʾl-ruʿūd*, f. 18b.

2. See, for instance, *al-Durar al-saniyya*, 1:159, 2:100.

3. These two senses correspond to the English *monotheism* and *monolatry*, respectively. For more on the latter term, see Lav, "Radical Muslim Theonomy."

4. For earlier treatments of Ibn Taymiyya's division of *tawḥīd*, see Diffelen, *De leer der Wahhabieten*, 3–6; Laoust, *Essai sur les doctrines sociales et politiques de Takī-d-Dīn Aḥmad b. Taimīya*, 472–73, 531–32; Hoover, *Ibn Taymiyya's Theodicy*, 27–39. This section is based mainly on my own reading of the relevant Arabic sources.

5. Ibn Taymiyya was hardly the first Muslim theologian to speak of different forms of *tawḥīd*, even ones like this, but his particular schema and its terminology appear to have originated with

conditions of *tawḥīd al-rubūbiyya* are easily met, while those of *tawḥīd al-ulūhiyya* are not. To confess *tawḥīd al-rubūbiyya* is to espouse a basic monotheism; it is to confess that God alone is the Creator and Sustainer of the universe. To confess *tawḥīd al-ulūhiyya* is more involved; it is to worship God properly as per the dictates of Islam—that is, exclusively and without partner. Put otherwise, *tawḥīd al-rubūbiyya* is monotheism, and *tawḥīd al-ulūhiyya* is the practice of monotheism in accordance with the Islamic revelation. For Ibn Taymiyya, *tawḥīd al-rubūbiyya* is no real achievement, as the existence of the single God is self-evident. *Tawḥīd al-ulūhiyya* is the true measure of Islam. As he puts it in one of his polemics, *tawḥīd al-ulūhiyya* is "the salvific *tawḥīd*" (*al-tawḥīd al-munjī*), in contrast with *tawḥīd al-rubūbiyya*, which "does not save one from hellfire" (*lā yunjī min nār*).[6]

In his exegesis of the opening chapter of the Qurʾān, *al-Fātiḥa*, Ibn Taymiyya derives the terms *rubūbiyya* and *ulūhiyya* from the pairing of the words *rabb* (Lord) and *Allāh* (God) in the second verse: "Praise belongs to God, Lord of the worlds" (*al-ḥamdu lillāhi rabbi ʾl-ʿālamīn*). Here as elsewhere in the Qurʾān, says Ibn Taymiyya, the word *rabb* indicates God in the sense of "the Fosterer" (al-Murabbī), "the Creator" (al-Khāliq), "the Sustainer" (al-Rāziq), "the Bringer of Victory" (al-Nāṣir), and "the Guide" (al-Hādī), while the word *Allāh* refers to "the God who is worshipped" (*al-ilāh al-maʿbūd*)."[7] In this way, Ibn Taymiyya associates the word *rubūbiyya* with the divine power to create and direct the affairs of the world and the word *ulūhiyya* with man's duty to worship God as one. Throughout his corpus, he defines *tawḥīd al-rubūbiyya* as, variously, the affirmation that "there is no creator and no sustainer, no giver and no withholder, but God alone"; that "God is the Lord of all things and their Possessor, and that there is no creator and no sustainer but Him"; or that "He is the Master and the Determiner, the Enabler and the Preventer, the One Who Inflicts Harm and the One Who Confers Benefits, the Lowerer and the Raiser, the Empowerer and the Humbler."[8] Put more simply, *tawḥīd al-rubūbiyya* is the affirmation "that God alone created the Heavens

---

him. Modern Wahhābī theologians are at pains to show that the schema does not begin with Ibn Taymiyya, but there is hardly any precedent for them to point to. For an example of this kind of effort, see al-Badr, *al-Qawl al-sadīd*; the only plausible precedent that al-Badr cites is a certain statement by the Ḥanbalī Ibn Baṭṭa al-ʿUkbarī (d. 387/997), who distinguishes between God's *rabbāniyya* and God's *waḥdāniyya* in a similar way to Ibn Taymiyya's distinction between *tawḥīd al-rubūbiyya* and *tawḥīd al-ulūhiyya* (32).

6. Ibn Taymiyya, *al-Istighātha*, 163.

7. Ibn Taymiyya, *Majmūʿ fatāwā*, 14:12–13.

8. Ibid., 14:379–80, 1:92.

and the Earth."[9] *Tawḥīd al-ulūhiyya* he defines, with far less variation, as "the worship of Him alone without partner" (*ʿibādatuhu waḥdahu lā sharīka lahu*) and the idea "that God be worshipped alone without partner" (*an yuʿbada ʾllāh waḥdahu lā sharīka lahu*).[10]

In his polemics, Ibn Taymiyya repeatedly states regarding his opponents, those whose Islam he believed was flawed, that they may have satisfied the conditions of *tawḥīd al-rubūbiyya* but they have fallen short as regards *tawḥīd al-ulūhiyya*. The *mutakallimūn*, being engrossed in establishing the existence of God by rational proofs, have only understood *tawḥīd* in the sense of *tawḥīd al-rubūbiyya* (*wa-lam yaʿrifū min al-tawḥīd illā tawḥīd al-rubūbiyya*).[11] The Ṣūfīs of the Ibn ʿArabī variety, being obsessed with the mystical experience of God (*shuhūd*), are likewise only concerned with *tawḥīd al-rubūbiyya*.[12] "A man does not become a Muslim by virtue of this *tawḥīd* alone," he writes in an attack on these Ṣūfīs, suggesting that their failure to grasp *tawḥīd al-ulūhiyya* has put them beyond the pale.[13] Likewise, those engaged in the cult of saints are deficient in terms of *tawḥīd al-ulūhiyya*, having introduced a host of polytheistic activities notwithstanding their confession of *tawḥīd al-rubūbiyya*.[14] Even outside a strictly polemical context, it is not unusual to find Ibn Taymiyya digressing into a discussion of the two *tawḥīds*, reminding his reader that "whosoever fails to satisfy it [i.e., *tawḥīd al-ulūhiyya*] is one of the polytheists eternally [*min al-mushrikīn al-khālidīn*]."[15]

A key point that Ibn Taymiyya repeatedly makes in developing his dichotomy of *tawḥīd* concerns the unbelievers in Arabia at the time of the Prophet Muḥammad. In Ibn Taymiyya's view, these pagan Arabs were not in fact polytheists (*mushrikūn*) in the full sense of the word, even though they are described as such in the Qurʾān. Rather, they were monotheists, believers in one God, who failed to worship Him alone. In other words, they confessed *tawḥīd al-rubūbiyya* but not *tawḥīd al-ulūhiyya*. To demonstrate this point,

9. Ibid., 1:155.

10. Ibid., 10:669, 3:101.

11. Ibn Taymiyya, *Minhāj al-sunna al-nabawiyya*, 3:289; cf. Ibn Taymiyya, *Majmūʿ fatāwā*, 3:101, 14:15.

12. Ibn Taymiyya, *Majmūʿ fatāwā*, 3:101 (*ghāyat mā ʿindahum min al-tawḥīd huwa shuhūd hādhā ʾl-tawḥīd*); cf. Ibn Taymiyya, *al-Istighātha*, 156–57 (*wa-yaʿuddūna nihāyat al-ʿārifīn al-fanāʾ fī tawḥīd al-rubūbiyya wa-shuhūd al-qaymūmiyya*).

13. Ibn Taymiyya, *Majmūʿ fatāwā*, 3:103.

14. Ibid., 1:159.

15. Ibid., 14:380.

Ibn Taymiyya adduces several verses of the Qurʾān, in particular Q. 31:25, 29:61, and 23:84–89.[16] In the first of these verses, God says to the Prophet about the polytheists in Arabia: "If you ask them, 'Who created the Heavens and the Earth?' they will say, 'God.'" This verse and the others, says Ibn Taymiyya, show that the pagan Arabs in fact professed a belief in one God and that this did not bring them into the fold of Islam. Where they went wrong was in ascribing partners to God in worship, partners they took as intermediaries (*wasāʾiṭ*) to God in seeking to draw near to Him and as intercessors (*shufaʿāʾ*) who would intercede with Him on the Day of Judgment.[17] As evidence that the pagan Arabs took these partners as intermediaries and intercessors, not as creator gods, Ibn Taymiyya appeals to such verses as Q. 10:18 and 39:3.[18] In the first of these, the polytheists say, "These are our intercessors with God" (*hāʾulāʾi shufaʿāʾunā ʿinda ʾllāh*), and in the second, they say, "We only worship them that they may bring us nigh in nearness to God" (*mā naʿbuduhum illā li-yuqarribūnā ilā ʾllāhi zulfā*). That the early unbelievers in Arabia affirmed *tawḥīd al-rubūbiyya* is a point that Ibn Taymiyya makes frequently in his works.[19] He is particularly emphatic about it when discussing the cult of saints, arguing that those engaged in it are taking dead saints and prophets as intermediaries and intercessors just as the polytheists of Arabia did before them.

As has been seen, Ibn ʿAbd al-Wahhāb's main grievance against the professed Muslims of his day was their participation in the cult of saints, or *ziyāra*. While this was not the only thing for which he took them to task, it was certainly the main one. In his letters and epistles, he frequently deploys Ibn Taymiyya's schema of the two *tawḥīds* in order to condemn those engaged in the cult of saints. This is done so often, in fact, that the schema can be seen as the centerpiece of Ibn ʿAbd al-Wahhāb's doctrine—the principal means by which he distinguishes between Muslims and unbelievers, monotheists and polytheists. In putting it to use, sometimes he employs the terminology of *tawḥīd al-rubūbiyya* and *tawḥīd al-ulūhiyya*, and sometimes he does not. In

16. See, for example, ibid., 1:155.

17. Ibid., 1:155, 311, 3:105.

18. Ibid., 1:155–56.

19. For some examples, see ibid., 1:91, 155, 311, 3:96–98, 101, 289, 7:77, 14:377, 380; Ibn Taymiyya, *Minhāj al-sunna al-nabawiyya*, 3:289, 330–31. Ibn al-Qayyim also elaborates Ibn Taymiyya's *tawḥīd* dichotomy and makes the same point concerning the pagan Arabs; see, for instance, Ibn al-Qayyim, *Madārij al-sālikīn*, 1:328.

both cases, however, his reliance on Ibn Taymiyya's concept of *tawḥīd* could not be more clear.

The Two Tawḥīds *in the* Kalimāt *Epistle*

The *Kalimāt fī bayān shahādat an lā ilāha illā 'llāh*, the Wahhābī epistle that arrived in Basra in 1155/1742, is an example of a work in which Ibn ʿAbd al-Wahhāb elaborates Ibn Taymiyya's schema of the two *tawḥīds* without using the terms *tawḥīd al-rubūbiyya* and *tawḥīd al-ulūhiyya*. It begins with a rehearsal of some of Ibn Taymiyya's (and Ibn al-Qayyim's) arguments for why God must be worshipped exclusively. Ibn ʿAbd al-Wahhāb starts off by stating that the phrase "there is no god but God" (*lā ilāha illā 'llāh*) "is that for which created things were created . . . and that for which the messengers were sent." That is to say, *lā ilāha illā 'llāh* is the purpose of creation and revelation. In this regard, he quotes two verses from the Qurʾān: "I have not created the *jinn* and mankind except to worship me" (Q. 51:56) and "Indeed, We sent forth among every nation a messenger, saying, 'Worship you God, and eschew idols'" (Q. 16:36).[20] The pairing of these verses comes from Ibn Taymiyya. In a *fatwā* on the subject of worship, for instance, Ibn Taymiyya states that God "created creation for it" and "sent all of the messengers because of it," and he quotes Q. 51:56 and Q. 16:36.[21]

After having established the purpose of creation and revelation, Ibn ʿAbd al-Wahhāb goes on to state that "the phrase [i.e., *lā ilāha illā 'llāh*] comprises negation and affirmation [*nafy wa-ithbāt*]: the negation of the divinity of all but God, and the affirmation of it entirely for God alone without partner." The concept of divinity (*ilāhiyya*), he explains, relates to worship, and so to affirm the divinity of God means to direct all worship to God alone.[22] He then enumerates some of the forms of worship (*anwāʿ al-ʿibāda*) that must be directed only to God. These include slaughter (*dhabḥ*), prostration (*sujūd*), and, most important for his argument, supplication (*duʿāʾ*). It is not permissible, he says, for one to slaughter for other than God, to prostrate to other than God, or to

20. al-Qabbānī, *Faṣl al-khiṭāb*, f. 28a (= *al-Durar al-saniyya*, 2:102).

21. Ibn Taymiyya, *Majmūʿ fatāwā*, 10:150. Cf. ibid., 3:94, 11:51–52; Ibn al-Qayyim, *Ighāthat al-lahfān*, 1:119.

22. al-Qabbānī, *Faṣl al-khiṭāb*, ff. 28b–29a (= *al-Durar al-saniyya*, 2:102–3, with minor differences).

supplicate other than God.[23] All of this is likewise Taymiyyan in origin. In the same *fatwā* as before, Ibn Taymiyya states that the confession of faith requires that a believer negate the divinity of all but God and affirm the divinity of God.[24] He also goes through some of the forms of worship (*khaṣāʾiṣ ilāhiyyat Allāh*), writing that they are "the fulfillment of the confession that there is no god but God."[25] While he does not mention *duʿāʾ* as one of the forms of worship here, he does so in many other of his writings. In another *fatwā* on worship, for instance, Ibn Taymiyya lists among the forms of worship supplication (*duʿāʾ*), seeking help (*istighātha*), fear (*khashya*), hope (*rajāʾ*), and reliance (*tawakkul*), among other things.[26] Similarly, in one of his books, he writes that "the reality of *tawḥīd* is that we ought to worship God alone, such that none is supplicated but Him, none is dreaded and none is feared but Him, and none is relied on but Him."[27]

Thus far, Ibn ʿAbd al-Wahhāb has established the purpose of creation and revelation as the proper worship of God; he has construed *lā ilāha illā ʾllāh* as the affirmation of God's divinity and the negation of the divinity of all else; he has linked the concept of divinity (*ilāhiyya*) to worship (*ʿibāda*), emphasizing that all forms of worship are owed exclusively to God; and he has identified supplication (*duʿāʾ*) as one of the forms of worship. All of this has its origins in the writings of Ibn Taymiyya.

Next in the epistle, Ibn ʿAbd al-Wahhāb laments the fact that the *duʿāʾ* of other than God has become widespread in the Islamic world, citing the examples of those who visit the tombs of the Shamsān in Najd and ʿAbd al-Qādir al-Jīlānī in Baghdad.[28] The particular complaint here relates to *istighātha*, or the seeking of help from these saints in worldly affairs—namely, help with some sort of difficulty or affliction. Ibn Taymiyya, as we saw in the previous chapter, also decried such petitioning of the dead. In one relevant *fatwā*, for instance, he condemns the practices of supplicating the dead, seeking their intercession with God, and asking things of them (*duʿāʾ al-mayyit*

23. al-Qabbānī, *Faṣl al-khiṭāb*, ff. 29a, 30b–31a, 33a (= *al-Durar al-saniyya*, 2:103–4).

24. Ibn Taymiyya, *Majmūʿ fatāwā*, 10:225. Cf. ibid., 13:199; Ibn al-Qayyim, *Badāʾiʿ al-fawāʾid*, 3:926.

25. Ibn Taymiyya, *Majmūʿ fatāwā*, 10:225.

26. Ibid., 1:74.

27. Ibn Taymiyya, *Minhāj al-sunna al-nabawiyya*, 3:490; cf. Ibn al-Qayyim, *al-Dāʾ wa ʾl-dawāʾ*, 312–16, 457.

28. al-Qabbānī, *Faṣl al-khiṭāb*, ff. 33b–34a (= *al-Durar al-saniyya*, 2:104).

wa ʾl-istishfāʿ bihi wa ʾl-istighātha), speaking in particular of prophets and saints (*al-anbiyāʾ wa ʾl-ṣāliḥīn*).[29]

In the next part of the *Kalimāt*, Ibn ʿAbd al-Wahhāb turns to the objections of a hypothetical polytheist (*mushrik*). The *mushrik* contends that his supplicating of righteous persons does not amount to *shirk* but in fact delivers him from it. Ibn ʿAbd al-Wahhāb instructs his reader to respond by saying that the pagan Arabs likewise believed in one God but failed to worship Him exclusively. Where they went astray was in seeking the intercession (*shafāʿa*) of other beings with God: "The idol-worshippers whom the Messenger of God fought and whose property, sons, and women he seized all believed that God is the One Who Inflicts Harm, the One Who Confers Benefits, and the One Who Arranges the Affair; all that they sought is what you have sought, namely, intercession with God."[30] What Ibn ʿAbd al-Wahhāb is saying, in other words, is that the pagan Arabs confessed *tawḥīd al-rubūbiyya*; they acknowledged that God is the sole creator God and master of the universe, yet they appealed to other beings in seeking intercession and nearness to God. It was this failure to direct their worship to God alone that made their blood and property licit. Ibn ʿAbd al-Wahhāb follows this comment with four quotations from the Qurʾān (Q. 10:18, 39:3, 10:31, and 23:84–89), which together are used to demonstrate that the pagan Arabs confessed *tawḥīd al-rubūbiyya* and worshipped their idols only for the purpose of attaining intercession with and nearness to God.[31] In the first verse, the pagan Arabs say, "These are our intercessors with God" (Q. 10:18), and in the second they say, "We only worship them that they may bring us nigh in nearness to God" (Q. 39:3). These verses illustrate the points of intercession and drawing close to God, respectively. The next two verses are intended to show that the pagan Arabs believed that Allāh is the one almighty God. The first reads: "Say: 'Who provides you out of heaven and earth, or who possesses hearing and sight, and who brings forth the living from the dead and brings forth the dead from the living, and who directs the affair?' They [i.e., the pagan Arabs] will surely say, 'God'" (Q. 10:31). The second reads: "Say: 'Whose is the earth, and whosoever is in it, if you have knowledge?' They will say, 'God's'" (Q. 23:84–85).

29. Ibn Taymiyya, *Majmūʿ fatāwā*, 1:160.

30. al-Qabbānī, *Faṣl al-khiṭāb*, f. 34a–b (= *al-Durar al-saniyya*, 2:104, with one minor difference).

31. al-Qabbānī, *Faṣl al-khiṭāb*, ff. 39a–40a (= *al-Durar al-saniyya*, 2:105, which quotes two more verses to the same effect: Q. 29:61 and Q. 29:63).

All of this admits of a Taymiyyan precedent. Even the idea that the Prophet fought the pagan Arabs despite their confession of *tawḥīd al-rubūbiyya* is a point that Ibn Taymiyya made several places. In a *fatwā* on the cult of saints, for instance, he writes:

> The polytheists from among the Arabs, whom the Messenger of God condemned as unbelievers and fought, and whose blood and property he deemed licit, did not say that their gods shared with God in creating the heavens and the earth and the universe. Rather, they affirmed that God alone is the Creator of the heavens and the earth and the universe. . . . What their worship of them consisted of was supplicating them and taking them as intermediaries, channels, and intercessors.[32]

Like Ibn ʿAbd al-Wahhāb, Ibn Taymiyya was also fond of pairing the verses Q. 10:18 and 39:3 in order to make the point that the early unbelievers took their intermediaries for the purpose of intercession and drawing close to God. As he writes in an epistle, "They [i.e., the pagan Arabs] would say, 'We only worship them that they may bring us nigh in nearness to God' (Q. 39:3) and 'These are our intercessors with God' (Q. 10:18)."[33] He was also fond of citing Q. 10:31 and 23:84–89, among other verses, in the context of demonstrating that the pagan Arabs confessed *tawḥīd al-rubūbiyya*.[34]

In the very next part of the *Kalimāt* epistle, Ibn ʿAbd al-Wahhāb entertains another objection from the hypothetical *mushrik*. This is the claim that the pagan Arabs "believed in idols of stone and wood [*ḥijāra wa-khashab*], whereas we have believed only in righteous persons [*al-ṣāliḥīn*]."[35] Ibn ʿAbd al-Wahhāb retorts that the distinction is irrelevant, telling the reader to respond by saying: "Among the unbelievers there were also those who believed in righteous persons, such as the angels and Jesus son of Mary, and in saints such as al-ʿUzayr [*sic*] and some of the *jinn*."[36] As evidence of this, he quotes, among other verses, Q. 17:57, in which God explains that the pagan Arabs supplicated people who were God-fearing: "Those they call upon are themselves seeking

32. Ibn Taymiyya, *Jāmiʿ al-masāʾil*, 3:150–51; cf. Ibn Taymiyya, *Majmūʿ fatāwā*, 1:155.

33. Ibn Taymiyya, *Majmūʿ fatāwā*, 3:396. Cf. ibid., 1:88, 117; Ibn Taymiyya, *Minhāj al-sunna al-nabawiyya*, 3:330.

34. See, for instance, Ibn Taymiyya, *Majmūʿ fatāwā*, 8:101–2; cf. 1:155–56.

35. al-Qabbānī, *Faṣl al-khiṭāb*, f. 40a (= *al-Durar al-saniyya*, 2:106, with a minor difference).

36. al-Qabbānī, *Faṣl al-khiṭāb*, f. 40a (= *al-Durar al-saniyya*, 2:106, which also mentions *al-Lāt waʾl-ʿUzzā*). ʿUzayr is a man described by the Jews as the son of God in Q. 9:30; he is usually identified with the biblical Ezra.

the means to come to their Lord, which of them shall be nearer; they hope for His mercy, and fear His chastisement."[37] This is followed by a tradition attributed to a party of the ancestors (*ṭā ʾifa min al-salaf*), which has it that "there were groups who called upon the angels, Jesus, and al-ʿUzayr [*sic*], and God said to them: 'Those are my servants, as you are my servants.'"[38] All of these are proof texts that Ibn Taymiyya quotes when discussing the different kinds of intermediaries taken by the pagan Arabs, from the sun and the moon to the *jinn* and certain righteous persons.[39] Recapitulating the main argument of his epistle, Ibn ʿAbd al-Wahhāb asks his reader to ponder the fact that the pagan Arabs only worshipped those whom they worshipped in order to achieve nearness to God and intercession with him (*al-taqarrub ilā ʾllāh wa ʾl-shafā ʿa*).[40] The point about nearness and intercession is one that Ibn Taymiyya makes repeatedly. As he writes in one place: "And the polytheists, who took other gods alongside Him, affirmed that their gods were created, but they took them as intercessors and sought to be near to Him by worshipping them."[41]

In the *Kalimāt* epistle, then, Ibn ʿAbd al-Wahhāb is closely following Ibn Taymiyya's argumentation as regards the two *tawḥīds*—from the basics down to the very evidence selected and the language used—even though he does not mention the terms *tawḥīd al-rubūbiyya* and *tawḥīd al-ulūhiyya*.

The Schema on Display

Ibn ʿAbd al-Wahhāb was not always averse, however, to using the terms *tawḥīd al-rubūbiyya* and *tawḥīd al-ulūhiyya* in some of his letters and epistles. Sometimes he would even spell out the distinction between the two terms, urging his readers to appreciate the difference. In one of his epistles, for instance, he writes:

> *Tawḥīd* is of two kinds: *tawḥīd al-rubūbiyya* and *tawḥīd al-ulūhiyya*. As for *tawḥīd al-rubūbiyya*, it is what the unbelievers affirmed and were not Mus-

37. al-Qabbānī, *Faṣl al-khiṭāb*, f. 50b (= *al-Durar al-saniyya*, 2:107).

38. al-Qabbānī, *Faṣl al-khiṭāb*, f. 50b (= *al-Durar al-saniyya*, 2:107, with one minor difference).

39. See, for instance, Ibn Taymiyya, *Majmūʿ fatāwā*, 1:157–58. Cf. Ibn Taymiyya, *Minhāj al-sunna al-nabawiyya*, 3:396; Ibn Taymiyya, *Jāmiʿ al-masāʾil*, 3:147.

40. al-Qabbānī, *Faṣl al-khiṭāb*, f. 51a (= *al-Durar al-saniyya*, 2:107).

41. Ibn Taymiyya, *Majmūʿ fatāwā*, 1:155.

> lims thereby. It is the affirmation that God is the Creator and the Sustainer, the Giver of Life and the Bringer of Death, the Arranger of All Affairs. . . . As for *tawḥīd al-ulūhiyya,* it is directing worship in all its forms to God exclusively [*ikhlāṣ al-ʿibāda kullihā bi-anwāʿihā lillāh*].[42]

Nearly identical language is found throughout his *rasāʾil.* For instance, in one letter to an unidentified correspondent, Ibn ʿAbd al-Wahhāb writes: "*Tawḥīd al-rubūbiyya* is what the unbelievers affirmed. . . . As for *tawḥīd al-ulūhiyya,* it is directing worship exclusively to God."[43] In another of his epistles, he states: "[*Tawḥīd*] is of two kinds: *tawḥīd al-rubūbiyya* and *tawḥīd al-ulūhiyya.* As for *tawḥīd al-rubūbiyya,* it is what the unbeliever and the Muslim [both] affirmed. As for *tawḥīd al-ulūhiyya,* it is the distinction between unbelief and Islam. It is necessary for every Muslim to distinguish between the one and the other."[44]

Ibn ʿAbd al-Wahhāb is sometimes seen in his writings urging the people of Najd to learn the difference between the two *tawḥīds* and to take action on that basis. One letter shows him responding to a certain Ḥasan, who had written that it was difficult for him (*yushkilu ʿalayya*) to accept the idea that the pagan Arabs confessed *tawḥīd al-rubūbiyya.*[45] Ibn ʿAbd al-Wahhāb does his best to explain the two terms again. In another letter, addressed to a certain preacher in Tharmadāʾ, Ibn ʿAbd al-Wahhāb notes that his correspondent has understood the difference between the two *tawḥīds* but has failed to act on it. He praises the correspondent for having written, correctly, that "the polytheists whom the Prophet fought affirmed *tawḥīd al-rubūbiyya* . . . he fought them only on behalf of *tawḥīd al-ulūhiyya.* One does not enter into Islam by virtue of *tawḥīd al-rubūbiyya* unless it is joined with *tawḥīd al-ulūhiyya.*"[46] But Ibn ʿAbd al-Wahhāb complains that the correspondent has failed to show enmity to those who refuse to acknowledge this.[47] "Why have you not shown them enmity [*li-ayy shayʾ lam tuẓhir ʿadāwatahum*]," he asks, "and [declared] that they are apostate unbelievers [*wa-annahum kuffār*

42. *al-Durar al-saniyya,* 1:137–38.
43. Ibn Ghannām, *Tārīkh,* 1:480.
44. *al-Durar al-saniyya,* 2:125.
45. Ibn Ghannām, *Tārīkh,* 1:488.
46. Ibid., 1:335 (letter to Muḥammad ibn ʿAbbād).
47. Ibid., 1:335–36.

murtaddūn]?"[48] In this letter, the entire religious struggle in Najd appears as one revolving around the distinction between the two *tawḥīd*s and the necessity of acting on it.[49]

Far less frequently, Ibn ʿAbd al-Wahhāb speaks of a third form of *tawḥīd*, which in subsequent generations of Wahhābism (and Salafism) would come to be known as *tawḥīd al-asmāʾ wa ʾl-ṣifāt* (the oneness of God's names and attributes). This third form of *tawḥīd* is little more than a byword for the Taymiyyan approach to God's attributes. While Ibn Taymiyya himself does not appear to have written about God's attributes as a form *tawḥīd*—though he speaks of *al-tawḥīd fī ʾl-ṣifāt* at one point[50]—at least one member of his *jamāʿa* did. This was the Ḥanafī Ibn Abī ʾl-ʿIzz, who may have been the first to enumerate the forms of *tawḥīd* as three rather than two.[51] On one occasion, Ibn ʿAbd al-Wahhāb does the same, writing that "*tawḥīd* is three principles [*thalāthat uṣūl*]: *tawḥīd al-rubūbiyya, tawḥīd al-ulūhiyya*, and *tawḥīd al-dhāt wa ʾl-asmāʾ wa ʾl-ṣifāt*."[52] However, in this *risāla* he devotes far more space to the first two forms than he does to the third. Indeed, in his preaching in general, Ibn ʿAbd al-Wahhāb does not attach much importance to *tawḥīd al-asmāʾ wa ʾl-ṣifāt*. In one of his letters, responding to a question about the three forms of *tawḥīd*, his only comment on the third is to say: "As for the *tawḥīd* of the attributes, *tawḥīd al-rubūbiyya* and *tawḥīd al-ulūhiyya* are not sound without the affirmation of the attributes. But the unbelievers are wiser than those who deny the attributes [*aʿqal mimman ankara al-ṣifāt*]."[53] The matter of God's attributes simply was not a major concern to Ibn ʿAbd al-Wahhāb and his mission. While it would become standard in Wahhābism to define *tawḥīd* as three—as a trio, not a duo—this was not the case early on in Wahhābism.

48. Ibid., 1:336.

49. Interestingly, the anti-Wahhābī refuters do not seem to have devoted much attention to refuting the two *tawḥīd*s thesis. The exception is Ibn Dāwūd al-Zubayrī, who wrote that "if Muḥammad had been sent to us to explain the meaning of the two *tawḥīd*s to us, then he, and not the one who claims [to know its meaning], would have explained it clearly" (*al-Ṣawāʿiq wa ʾl-ruʿūd*, f. 101a). This is somewhat ironic as Ibn Dāwūd was well versed in the ideas of Ibn Taymiyya and Ibn al-Qayyim (which he was seeking to defend) and presumably would have known how much importance these scholars attached to this distinction.

50. Ibn Taymiyya, *Majmūʿ fatāwā*, 3:3 (*al-Tadmuriyya*).

51. Ibn Abī ʾl-ʿIzz, *Sharḥ al-ʿAqīda al-Ṭaḥāwiyya*, 1:140.

52. *al-Durar al-saniyya*, 2:67–68.

53. Ibn Ghannām, *Tārīkh*, 1:481.

The Flourishes

In what has been discussed thus far, Ibn ʿAbd al-Wahhāb has not been seen to have distorted or mispresented Ibn Taymiyya's division of *tawḥīd* in any way. He has even been seen using it for a similar purpose, namely, to condemn those who venerate saints and prophets by supplicating them at grave sites. In deploying Ibn Taymiyya's schema of the two *tawḥīds*, however, Ibn ʿAbd al-Wahhāb did in fact add a few additional arguments of his own. These were intended to anticipate certain objections and magnify the schema's polemical effect. These additions, or flourishes, are twofold.

The first flourish involves the assertion that the pagan Arabs took different types of intermediaries and intercessors, both persons and objects, and that the Prophet fought them all without distinction—that is, without regard to the nature of the intermediary or intercessor taken.[54] The types of objects that Ibn ʿAbd al-Wahhāb refers to include trees (*shajar*), stone (*ḥajar*), and wood (*khashab*), while the kinds of people that he mentions include prophets (*anbiyāʾ*), righteous persons (*ṣāliḥīn*), and saints (*awliyāʾ*).[55] Ibn ʿAbd al-Wahhāb likely developed this distinction in response to his opponents' argument, seen above, that they believed in righteous persons whereas the pagan Arabs believed in idols. This first flourish is similar to a distinction drawn by Ibn Taymiyya between *shirk* with regard to persons and *shirk* with regard to celestial objects, for example, the stars, the sun, and the moon (*al-kawākib wa ʾl-shams wa ʾl-qamar*).[56] However, Ibn ʿAbd al-Wahhāb's distinction is mainly one between persons and earthly objects, and Ibn Taymiyya does not appear to have made the point that the Prophet fought all unbelievers equally regardless of the kind of intermediaries that they worshipped.

Ibn ʿAbd al-Wahhāb's second flourish is to assert that the polytheists of the present day (*al-mushrikūn fī zamāninā*) are qualitatively worse than the polytheists of Arabia whom the Prophet fought.[57] This is for two reasons. The first is that the *shirk* of the earlier polytheists was intermittent, whereas that

54. For some examples, see *al-Durar al-saniyya*, 2:25, 34, 39, 41, 106; Ibn Ghannām, *Tārīkh*, 1:268–69.

55. See, for example, *al-Durar al-saniyya*, 2:107.

56. The first type, he says, corresponds to the *shirk* of the people of Noah; the second, to the *shirk* of the people of Abraham. See, e.g., Ibn Taymiyya, *Majmūʿ fatāwā*, 1:157.

57. For some examples, see *al-Durar al-saniyya*, 1:160, 167, 2:26, 120; Ibn Ghannām, *Tārīkh*, 1:319–20.

of the present-day polytheists is constant. The earlier polytheists, he says, committed *shirk* only sometimes: in times of comfort (*fī 'l-rakhā'*) they would call upon their intermediaries, but in times of hardship (*fī 'l-shidda*) they would leave their intermediaries and direct worship squarely to God. The polytheists of today, on the other hand, always commit *shirk*: they call upon their intermediaries in times of both comfort and hardship. The second reason that the earlier polytheists were better, according to Ibn ʿAbd al-Wahhāb, is that while they worshipped righteous persons who were truly righteous, the present-day polytheists worship the most contemptible of persons: people who commit adultery, steal, and neglect prayer, among other things.[58] Those he has in mind here are of course the Najdī saints of al-Kharj, such as Tāj, Shamsān, and Yūsuf.

Returning to the *Kalimāt*, we can now see how Ibn ʿAbd al-Wahhāb combines the ideas borrowed from Ibn Taymiyya with one of his flourishes in putting together his full argument concerning *tawḥīd*. He does this toward the end of the epistle, where he sums up his argument in a declaration of two points, or "two statements" (*kalimatayn*). After explaining that the pagan Arabs worshipped their intermediaries only to achieve nearness to God and intercession with Him, he writes:

> All of this revolves around two points. The first is that you know that the unbelievers knew that God is the Creator, the Sustainer, and the One Who Directs the Affair; all that they sought by this [i.e., supplicating intermediaries] was nearness to God by means of them. The second point is that there were people who believed in prophets, such as Jesus, and saints, such as al-ʿUzayr [*sic*], and they were the same as those who believed in idols, trees, and rocks. When the Messenger of God fought them, he did not distinguish between those who believed in idols of wood and stone and those who believed in prophets and righteous persons.[59]

This may seem like a lot of words for two points, but the ideas can be simplified further. Put differently, the first point is that the pagan Arabs confessed *tawḥīd al-rubūbiyya* and committed *shirk* when they took intermediaries to achieve nearness to God. The second point is the first flourish, which is the idea that the Prophet fought all kinds of polytheists without distinction.

58. The flourish appears most fully, with both parts, in Ibn Ghannām, *Tārīkh*, 1:272–73 (*Kashf al-shubuhāt*); and *al-Durar al-saniyya*, 2:31.

59. al-Qabbānī, *Faṣl al-khiṭāb*, ff. 52b–53b (= *al-Durar al-saniyya*, 2:107–8).

In another early piece of writing, a letter addressed to the preachers of several Najdī towns, Ibn ʿAbd al-Wahhāb again breaks down his main ideas concerning *tawḥīd* into two points, here described as "two principles" (*qāʿidatayn*). This time, however, the first point is that the pagan Arabs whom the Prophet fought recognized that God is the Creator and the Sustainer, and the second is that they sought intermediaries to God in order to achieve nearness to Him. The two points here comprehend everything in the first point of the *Kalimāt*. After enumerating these points, Ibn ʿAbd al-Wahhāb expounds the second flourish, which is that the present-day polytheists are worse than the earlier ones:

> The polytheists in our time are more misguided than the unbelievers at the time of the Messenger of God, in two respects. The first is that the [earlier] unbelievers only supplicated prophets and angels in times of comfort, whereas in times of hardship they would direct worship to God. . . . The second is that the polytheists of our time supplicate persons who do not compare to Jesus and the angels.[60]

In other words, the present-day unbelievers are worse than the earlier unbelievers on account of the constancy of their unbelief and the inferiority of their intermediaries. Soon Ibn ʿAbd al-Wahhāb would bring together all of these ideas—the distinction between the two *tawḥīd*s and the two flourishes—in one epistle. This was the *Arbaʿ qawāʿid fī ʾl-dīn*.

The Arbaʿ Qawāʿid *Epistle*

While Ibn Taymiyya was a brilliant scholar whose intellectual abilities far surpassed those of Ibn ʿAbd al-Wahhāb, the latter may have been the more gifted communicator. Unlike Ibn Taymiyya, whose writing can appear disorganized and meandering, Ibn ʿAbd al-Wahhāb was a prolific author of *rasāʾil* that took the form of catechisms, namely, short statements of creed intended to be easily understood and digested, even by those with little or no education. In his writings, Ibn ʿAbd al-Wahhāb frequently reduces his ideas into memorable units of thought variously termed *qawāʿid* (principles; sing. *qāʿida*), *masāʾil* (matters; sing. *masʾala*), *kalimāt* (statements; sing. *kalima*), and *uṣūl* (foundations; sing. *aṣl*). His catechisms thus tend to be known by such titles as *al-Uṣūl al-thalātha* (The Three Foundations), *Khams masāʾil* (Five Matters), and

60. Ibn Ghannām, *Tārīkh*, 1:319–20.

al-Uṣūl al-sitta (The Six Foundations). As has been seen, this method of condensing his doctrine into points is on display in many of his *rasāʾil*. Muḥammad ibn Fayrūz, one of his Ḥanbalī refuters, ridiculed this method of enumeration in a poem refuting Ibn ʿAbd al-Wahhāb: "You established a religion on nine matters / and foundations also, the principles being seven."[61] Yet, however unappealing Ibn Fayrūz and his allies may have found it, this method of communicating the Wahhābī doctrine was highly effective.

At some point in the course of his early preaching, Ibn ʿAbd al-Wahhāb settled on four points (*qawāʿid*) as the ideal number for communicating his ideas concerning *tawḥīd*. There would be numerous versions of this four-point epistle known as *Arbaʿ qawāʿid fī ʾl-dīn*, which came to be one of his most popular catechisms. While the different versions admit of some variation, they mostly cover the same ground, namely, Ibn Taymiyya's ideas behind the two *tawḥīd*s and Ibn ʿAbd al-Wahhāb's flourishes.

The earliest extant version of this epistle is the one that arrived in Basra in 1158/1745. As was seen in chapter 1, this version is unique in that it comprises two sets of four points, the first set pertaining to the pagan Arabs and the second to the present-day polytheists. To achieve numeric symmetry, Ibn ʿAbd al-Wahhāb draws out the ideas of the first set in more points than might seem necessary. In the first set, point 1 is that the pagan Arabs confessed *tawḥīd al-rubūbiyya*; point 2 is that they believed in angels, prophets, and saints because these were close to God; point 3 is that they believed in these intermediaries in order to draw close to God and obtain intercession with Him; and point 4 is that they were part-time in their unbelief (part of the second flourish).[62] In the second set, point 1 is that the present-day polytheists are worse than the pagan Arabs (part of the second flourish); point 2 is that the idols (*ṭawāghīt*) in al-Kharj approve of and even invite the polytheistic behavior of those supplicating them and giving them votive offerings; point 3 is that relations have been severed and a state of mutual enmity and *takfīr* has set in between the monotheists (*muwaḥḥidīn*) and the polytheists (*mushrikīn*) in Najd; and point 4 is that some in al-ʿĀriḍ are claiming that the Wahhābīs are in error and have declared Muslims to be unbelievers.[63] This double-barreled version of the *Arbaʿ qawāʿid* epistle may very well have been an early experiment, one that Ibn ʿAbd al-Wahhāb eventually discarded in favor of a single

61. Āl Maḥmūd, *Taḥdhīr ahl al-īmān*, 40.

62. al-Qabbānī, *Naqḍ qawāʿid al-ḍalāl*, ff. 42a–45a.

63. Ibid., ff. 47a–b, 57a, 58b, 62a.

set of four points.[64] It does not survive in this form in the Wahhābī tradition, though the latter preserves a version of the *Arbaʿ qawāʿid* that is almost identical to the first half of this earlier one.[65]

The version of the *Arbaʿ qawāʿid* that was to become the most common has a somewhat different structure.[66] In this version, point 1 is that the earlier polytheists confessed *tawḥīd al-rubūbiyya*; point 2 is that they gave partners to God only in seeking nearness to and intercession with Him; point 3 is that they worshipped different kinds of things, but the Prophet fought them all equally (the first flourish); and point 4 is that the present-day polytheists are worse than the earlier polytheists, since the *shirk* of the earlier polytheists was intermittent whereas that of today's polytheists is constant (part of the second flourish). This is how the four points appear in this most common version of the *Arbaʿ qawāʿid*, omitting the Qurʾānic evidence that follows each point:

> The first point is that the unbelievers whom the Messenger of God fought affirmed that God is the Creator and the Sustainer, the Giver of Life and the Bringer of Death, and the Arranger of All Affairs, and that this did not bring them into Islam. . . .
>
> The second point is that they were saying, "We have not called on them and turned to them except in seeking nearness and intercession [*al-qurba wa ʾl-shafāʿa*]. We seek [these] from God and not from them, yet by means of their intercession and by drawing close to God through them." . . .
>
> The third point is that the Prophet appeared among people who were diverse in what they worshipped. Among them were those who worshipped the sun and the moon, those who worshipped the angels, those who worshipped prophets and righteous persons, and those who worshipped trees and stones. The Messenger of God fought them all and did not distinguish between them. . . .
>
> The fourth point is that the polytheists of our time are more severe in polytheism [*aghlaẓ shirkan*] than the early ones, as the early ones directed worship to God in times of hardship and gave partners to God in times of

64. Cook, "Written and Oral Aspects," 174.

65. See *al-Durar al-saniyya*, 2:27–30. Cook calls this the "rare version" ("Written and Oral Aspects," 169).

66. See the three similar versions in *al-Durar al-saniyya*, 2:23–26, 33–35, 36–39; the first of these is the most common of all.

comfort, whereas the polytheism of the polytheists of our time obtains both in times of hardship and in times of comfort.[67]

This version of the *Arbaʿ qawāʿid*, with some variations in wording but not in the basic structure, would circulate widely during the first Saudi state. The Yemeni historian Luṭf Allāh Jaḥḥāf records in his chronicle that it was being transmitted orally in late eighteenth-century ʿAsīr.[68] In his entry for the year 1212/1797f, he describes how ʿAsīr's ruler solicited from the ruler in al-Dirʿiyya a text to instruct his people in the Wahhābī creed. The text that he received was the *Arbaʿ qawāʿid*. The scholars of ʿAsīr were expected to study and teach it, while the masses were expected to memorize it. The *Arbaʿ qawāʿid* was put to similar use during the Wahhābī conquest of Mecca in 1218/1803. In a brief account of the conquest and subsequent occupation of Mecca, Ibn ʿAbd al-Wahhāb's son ʿAbdallāh recounts how the Wahhābīs provided the scholars in Mecca with some writings on *tawḥīd*, including a shorter work to be taught to the masses (*risāla mukhtaṣara lil-ʿawāmm*).[69] This latter epistle, which ʿAbdallāh reproduces in his account, was the *Arbaʿ qawāʿid*.[70]

In sum, Ibn ʿAbd al-Wahhāb did not fundamentally alter Ibn Taymiyya's schema of the two *tawḥīds*. Like Ibn Taymiyya, he deployed it in the context of the cult of saints, emphasizing the similarity between those professed Muslims who pray at grave sites and the pagan Arabs who took various intermediaries and intercessors to God. His main point was that the participants in the cult of saints were failing to meet the conditions of *tawḥīd al-ulūhiyya*, just as

67. Ibid., 2:24–26.

68. Jaḥḥāf, *Durar nuḥūr al-ḥūr al-ʿīn*, 653–56; discussed in Cook, "Written and Oral Aspects," 168, 170, 172, 176.

69. *al-Durar al-saniyya*, 1:225–26. See further Peskes, "ʿAbdallāh b. Muḥammad b. ʿAbdalwahhāb."

70. For some reason, the version of ʿAbdallāh's account in *al-Durar al-saniyya* (1:222–41) omits the text of the *Arbaʿ qawāʿid*. However, at least two manuscript copies of the account include it. For the first, see Āl al-Shaykh, *Risālat ʿAbdallāh ibn Muḥammad ibn ʿAbd al-Wahhāb*; and on this manuscript, see Muṭīʿ al-Raḥmān and ʿĪd, *al-Fihris al-mukhtaṣar*, 1:376 (no. 1518). For the second, see Āl al-Shaykh, *Risālat al-shaykh ʿAbdallāh Āl al-Shaykh*; and on this manuscript, see Ellis and Edwards, *Descriptive List*, 14. The latter manuscript belonged to a British official in India named James O'Kinealy, who published a fairly good translation of it in 1874; see O'Kinealy, "Translation of an Arabic Pamphlet."

the pagan Arabs had failed to meet the conditions of *tawḥīd al-ulūhiyya*. The novelty of Ibn ʿAbd al-Wahhāb's approach to *tawḥīd* consisted in his recasting of Ibn Taymiyya's schema in didactic form and in supplementing it with his own flourishes. Hence the content of some of his catechisms, especially the *Arbaʿ qawāʿid fī ʾl-dīn*. Yet Ibn ʿAbd al-Wahhāb also used the schema in a way that Ibn Taymiyya probably would not have approved, declaring a great many of the world's Muslims to be unbelievers on its basis.

Takfīr

The practice of *takfīr*, of charging people with unbelief (*kufr*) or declaring them to be unbelievers (*kuffār*; sing. *kāfir*), has generally been discouraged in the history of Sunnī Islam. The dominant tendency among Sunnī Muslim scholars has been to discourage the practice in light of the societal danger that it poses and in view of the Prophet's apparent warning against it.[71] As would be noted in many of the anti-Wahhābī refutations, there are several *ḥadīths* in which the Prophet appears to warn against the unintended consequences of false charges of *kufr*. As he remarks in one of these, "If a man says to his brother, 'O unbeliever [*yā kāfir*],' it redounds upon one of them."[72] Ibn ʿAbd al-Wahhāb, however, was not deterred by such admonitions. For him it was of the utmost importance to draw a sharp line between Islam and *kufr*, and to that end *takfīr* was essential. In this he felt that Ibn Taymiyya was on his side. It is almost certainly with Ibn Taymiyya's *jamāʿa* in mind that Ibn ʿAbd al-Wahhāb speaks admiringly, in one of his letters, of "the scholars [who] in their time pronounced a judgment of *kufr* and *shirk* on many of the people of their time."[73] Ibn ʿAbd al-Wahhāb saw himself as doing something similar, believing that his approach to *takfīr* was no different from Ibn Taymiyya's. As will be seen, however, he was forced to contend with numerous accusations that his approach was in fact less nuanced and less discriminating. A careful look at the two approaches bears these accusations out. While Ibn ʿAbd al-Wahhāb's rationale for *takfīr*—the failure to meet the conditions of *tawḥīd al-ulūhiyya* by engaging in the

71. For an excellent introduction to issues of *takfīr* and apostasy, see the introduction in Adang et al., *Accusations of Unbelief in Islam*; and see also Friedmann, *Tolerance and Coercion in Islam*, chap. 4.

72. For the *ḥadīth*, see Muslim, *Ṣaḥīḥ*, 1:79 (*Kitāb al-īmān, bāb bayān ḥāl īmān man qāla li-akhīhi ʾl-Muslim yā kāfir*, no. 111). Al-Qabbānī cites this in his *Naqḍ qawāʿid al-ḍalāl*, f. 59b.

73. Ibn Ghannām, *Tārīkh*, 1:397 (letter to Sulaymān ibn Suḥaym).

practices related to the cult of saints—was borrowed from Ibn Taymiyya, the latter was significantly more hesitant to pronounce *takfīr* on specific individuals and especially lay Muslims.

Ibn Taymiyya's Restraint

Before looking at the differences in their approaches, it is first important to acknowledge the apparent similarities. Ibn Taymiyya could be severe in condemning those he deemed innovators in religion. When speaking of the participants in the cult of saints, for example, he was given to distinguishing large groups of "innovators," using such phrases as "the innovators from among the Muslims" (*mubtadiʿat al-Muslimīn, al-mubtadiʿūn min al-Muslimīn*) and "the innovators of this community" (*mubtadiʿat hādhihi ʾl-umma*).[74] In many places, he describes such innovators as having fallen into unbelief. Here are two examples: "Whosoever calls on created beings among the dead and the absent and seeks their help . . . is an innovator in religion, an ascriber of partners to the Lord of the Worlds, a follower not of the path of the believers"; "Those who call upon prophets and righteous men after their death, at their graves and elsewhere, are among the polytheists who call upon other than God."[75] On the surface, these do not seem like the words of a man reluctant to pronounce *takfīr* on the innovators in question.

Ibn al-Qayyim could be even harsher when it came to issuing such pronouncements, even seeming to condemn the majority of the people of the world as polytheists. For instance, in his book *Ighāthat al-lahfān*, he repeatedly states that the majority of humankind are idol-worshipping unbelievers:

> In sum, most people on earth [*akthar ahl al-arḍ*] have been captivated by the worship of idols, and only the *ḥunafāʾ* [sing. *ḥanīf*], the followers of the religion of Abraham, are safe from it. . . . Sufficient for knowing their multitude and that they are most people on earth is what is related as sound from the Prophet that "the number of those who will be resurrected to hellfire is, for every thousand, nine hundred ninety-nine." And He says, "But most people refuse but unbelief" (Q. 17:89); and He says, "If you obey most people on earth, they will lead you astray from the path of God"

74. Ibn Taymiyya, *Majmūʿ fatāwā*, 1:179, 161, 174.
75. Ibid., 1:312, 1:178.

> (Q. 6:116); and He says, "But most people, though you earnestly desire it, are not believers" (Q. 12:103).[76]

Those intended by Ibn al-Qayyim's words were no doubt the majority of the professed Muslims of his age. Shortly after this passage, he writes of the so-called idol-worshippers: "They hear the reports about the nations who were captivated by worshipping them [i.e., idols] and their immediate punishment that this led to, and yet this dissuades them not from worshipping them."[77] The idol-worshippers in question are those Muslims who participate in the cult of saints. They have heard the reports (*akhbār*) in the Qur'ān of the peoples who worshipped idols, but these stories have failed to dissuade them from persisting in their error. Similarly, Ibn al-Qayyim writes in his book *Zād al-ma'ād*, speaking of the execrable practices associated with the cult of saints:

> Polytheism has taken possession of most people [*akthar al-nufūs*], on account of the appearance of ignorance and the disappearance of knowledge. Right has become wrong, and wrong has become right; normative practice has become innovation, and innovation has become normative practice. The young are raised amid this, and the old grow decrepit amid it. The guideposts have been obliterated; the strangeness of Islam has grown severe [*wa 'shtaddat ghurbat al-Islām*].[78]

Here Ibn al-Qayyim relates his view about the majority of mankind being engrossed in polytheism to the notion of the strangeness of Islam (*ghurbat al-Islām*), a notion that, as was seen in the previous chapter, Ibn 'Abd al-Wahhāb adopted as well. This entire passage, in fact, appears in one of Ibn 'Abd al-Wahhāb's letters.[79]

From such statements it is possible to conclude, as Ibn 'Abd al-Wahhāb phrased it, that Ibn Taymiyya and his *jamā'a* were scholars who "pronounced a judgment of *kufr* and *shirk* on many of the people of their time." However,

76. Ibn al-Qayyim, *Ighāthat al-lahfān*, 2:976–77. For the *ḥadīth*, see al-Bukhārī, *Ṣaḥīḥ*, 1251 (*Kitāb al-riqāq, bāb qawlihi 'azza wa-jalla anna zalzalat al-sā'a shay' 'aẓīm*, no. 6530); Muslim, *Ṣaḥīḥ*, 1:201 (*Kitāb al-īmān, bāb qawlihi yaqūlu 'llāh li-Ādam akhrij ba'th an-nār*, no. 379). For the understanding of *ba'th al-nār* as "the number of those who will be resurrected to hellfire" (*miqdār mab'ūth al-nār*), see Ibn Ḥajar al-'Asqalānī, *Fatḥ al-bārī*, 11:389 (no. 6530).

77. Ibn al-Qayyim, *Ighāthat al-lahfān*, 2:977.

78. Ibn al-Qayyim, *Zād al-ma'ād*, 3:443.

79. Ibn Ghannām, *Tārīkh*, 1:359 (letter to 'Abdallāh ibn Suḥaym).

despite the severity and sweeping nature of some of their statements, Ibn Taymiyya and Ibn al-Qayyim in fact exhibited restraint when it came to issuing judgments of *kufr* on individuals. For all that they were inclined to point out the presence of *shirk* in everyday beliefs and practices, they were hesitant to excommunicate people without due process. For both men, those committing polytheistic acts, especially laypeople, were to be excused their errors on the basis of ignorance, a principle known as *al-ʿudhr biʾl-jahl* (excusing on the basis of ignorance). If they continue to commit such acts after the evidence that these constitute polytheism has been presented to them, a process called *iqāmat al-ḥujja* (presenting the proof), then, and only then, were they to be judged unbelievers. In this way, the principles of *al-ʿudhr biʾl-jahl* and *iqāmat al-ḥujja* functioned as powerful restraints on the *takfīr* of individuals committing acts that Ibn Taymiyya and Ibn al-Qayyim deemed polytheistic.

In one of his *fatwā*s, Ibn Taymiyya explains how an ignorant person (*jāhil*) might be excused for saying something that constitutes unbelief:

> [As for] statements that one commits unbelief by uttering, it may be that a man has not received the proof texts [*nuṣūṣ*] necessary for knowing the truth; it may be that he has them but they have not been demonstrated to him [*lam tuthbat ʿindahu*] or he has not been able to understand them; and it may be that he has been presented with specious arguments [*shubuhāt*] for which God will excuse him.[80]

Here Ibn Taymiyya shows himself to be much more careful in the practice of *takfīr* than some of his other comments might suggest. An ignorant person is not to be declared an unbeliever before he has been presented with the evidence showing that his actions—or his words, in this case—are tantamount to unbelief. Even if that the evidence has reached the person in question—that is, even if *iqāmat al-ḥujja* has taken place—the person can still be excused if he is unable to understand the evidence or has been misled by a misconception. In another passage on *takfīr*, this one in a letter to some of his supporters, Ibn Taymiyya emphasizes the importance of exercising restraint. He begins by stressing his commitment to *iqāmat al-ḥujja*: "I am one of those most forbidding of subjecting an individual to *takfīr* [*min aʿẓam al-nās nahyan an yunsaba muʿayyan ilā takfīr*], a judgment of great sin, or a judgment of disobedience to God, unless it is known that the scriptural proof [*al-ḥujja al-risāliyya*] whose contravention makes one an unbeliever sometimes, a great sinner other times, has been

80. Ibn Taymiyya, *Majmūʿ fatāwā*, 23:346.

presented."[81] Ibn Taymiyya goes on to underline the important distinction between generalization (*iṭlāq*) and specification (*taʿyīn*) when it comes to *takfīr*. To say that an act constitutes unbelief is a form of generalization; it does not mean that all those who commit the act described are ipso facto unbelievers. This is because of *al-ʿudhr bi ʾl-jahl* and *iqāmat al-ḥujja*. The same principles might apply to someone who rejects something said by the Prophet. "A man who is new to Islam [*ḥadīth ʿahd bi-Islām*]," he explains, "or grew up in a remote desert [*nashaʾa bi-bādiya baʿīda*], or something like this, the like of him does not become an unbeliever by rejecting what he rejects until the proof is presented to him [*ḥattā taqūma ʿalayhi ʾl-ḥujja*]."[82] Another illustration of Ibn Taymiyya's restraint in *takfīr* comes in a *fatwā* on supplicating the dead. He speaks specifically here about the *shirk* pertaining to the cult of saints:

> This *shirk*, if the proof of it is presented to him [i.e., the one committing it] and he does not desist, then he must be killed, as the likes of him among the polytheists are to be killed. He is not to be buried in the cemeteries of Muslims and he is not to be prayed over. But if he is ignorant [*idhā kāna jāhilan*], knowledge not having reached him, and he does not know the truth about the *shirk* that was the basis upon which the Prophet fought the polytheists, then he is not to be judged an unbeliever, especially since this *shirk* has become widespread among those affiliated with Islam [*wa-lā siyyamā wa-qad kathura hādhā ʾl-shirk fī ʾl-muntasibīn ilā ʾl-Islām*].[83]

This passage is particularly important, as it shows that Ibn Taymiyya believed in applying the principles of *iqāmat al-ḥujja* and *al-ʿudhr bi ʾl-jahl* to those seeking the help and intercession of the dead. It shows him emphasizing restraint in *takfīr* on the grounds that *shirk*, in the form of the cult of saints, "has become widespread" (*kathura*). The ubiquity of this form of *shirk* was, in his view, cause for prudence and caution in actually pronouncing *takfīr* on those who commit it.

Ibn al-Qayyim likewise emphasizes the importance of *al-ʿudhr bi ʾl-jahl* and *iqāmat al-ḥujja* in certain places in his work.[84] Thus in those passages where

81. Ibid., 3:229.

82. Ibid., 3:231.

83. Ibn Taymiyya, *Jāmiʿ al-masāʾil*, 3:151.

84. See, for instance, Ibn al-Qayyim, *Madārij al-sālikīn*, 1:909–10; Ibn al-Qayyim, *Ṭarīq al-hijratayn*, 2:896ff. It is perhaps significant, however, that Ibn al-Qayyim's statements in this regard are less frequent and less pronounced.

he states that "most people" have embraced polytheism, what he seems to mean is that most people practice polytheism but are not necessarily to be judged unbelievers on an individual basis. As Ibn ʿAbd al-Wahhāb's brother, Sulaymān, remarks in his refutation, despite what Ibn al-Qayyim wrote about *shirk* having filled the earth, he did not treat the lands of ordinary Muslims as lands of unbelief; nor did any of the scholars of his generation.[85] With respect to Ibn al-Qayyim at least, this was indeed true. Sulaymān also pointed to Ibn Taymiyya's and Ibn al-Qayyim's statements in favor of restraint in *takfīr* where they emphasized the concepts of *al-ʿudhr bi'l-jahl* and *iqāmat al-ḥujja*.[86]

Ibn ʿAbd al-Wahhāb's Lack of Restraint

From his perception that *shirk* had spread widely in the Muslim community, Ibn ʿAbd al-Wahhāb drew the opposite conclusion of the one drawn by Ibn Taymiyya and Ibn al-Qayyim. For him, the diffusion of *shirk* was justification not for discretion but for urgent action in the all-important pursuit of eradicating *shirk*. Thus Ibn ʿAbd al-Wahhāb generally did not display the same qualms about condemning everyday Muslims as unbelievers.[87]

When it came to justifying his approach to *takfīr*, Ibn ʿAbd al-Wahhāb was particularly fond of citing Ibn al-Qayyim. Channeling his words, Ibn ʿAbd al-Wahhāb frequently claimed that the majority of the world's Muslims had fallen into unbelief.[88] Yet Ibn ʿAbd al-Wahhāb could be even more explicit in making such condemnations. In one version of the *Arbaʿ qawāʿid* epistle, for instance, he states: "Polytheism is what has filled the earth, and people call it belief in righteous persons [*al-iʿtiqād fī 'l-ṣāliḥīn*]."[89] In another epistle, he writes: "The beliefs in righteous persons and others that most people profess today are *shirk*."[90] In several other such statements, it is clear that he is speaking not merely about Najd but about the Islamic world more broadly. In one of these Ibn ʿAbd al-Wahhāb refers to *shirk* as "what most people of the earth profess

85. Ibn ʿAbd al-Wahhāb, *al-Ṣawāʿiq al-ilāhiyya*, 41–42.

86. Ibid., 18–28.

87. An excellent account of Ibn ʿAbd al-Wahhāb's approach to *takfīr* is Crawford, *Ibn 'Abd al-Wahhab*, 61–66, from which some of my conclusions are drawn. See also Sirriyeh, "Wahhābīs, Unbelievers, and the Problems of Exclusivism"; Firro, "Political Context of Early Wahhabi Discourse of *Takfir*."

88. See, e.g., *al-Durar al-saniyya*, 2:89–90; Ibn Ghannām, *Tārīkh*, 1:359.

89. *al-Durar al-saniyya*, 1:159.

90. Ibn Ghannām, *Tārīkh*, 1:409.

[*mā ʿalayhi akthar ahl al-arḍ*], from east to west [*min al-mashriq ilā ʾl-maghrib*]."[91] And in another he remarks: "That which is being performed in the Ḥijāz, Basra, Iraq, and Yemen . . . this is *shirk*."[92] Ibn Ghannām, in his history, goes even further in depicting the majority of the Islamic world as being sunken in *shirk*. The book's first section describes in detail the alleged polytheistic rites that were being practiced in Najd, al-Aḥsāʾ, the Ḥijāz, Yemen, Egypt, Iraq, and Syria, among other places, before the rise of Ibn ʿAbd al-Wahhāb's movement.[93] The majority of the people in these lands are made out to be unbelieving polytheists on account of their participation in the cult of saints. In his characteristically florid language, Ibn Ghannām states: "The majority of the people in his [i.e., Ibn ʿAbd al-Wahhāb's] time were smeared with filth and covered with the dirt of impurities, such that they had become engrossed in *shirk*. . . . They turned to the worship of saints and righteous persons and cast off the tie of *tawḥīd* and religion."[94] This was not hyperbole. The presumption in early Wahhābism was very much so that the majority of the world's professed Muslims were unbelieving polytheists who ought to be treated as such.

This more expansive approach to *takfīr* was in part rooted in a different approach to the concepts of *al-ʿudhr bi ʾl-jahl* and *iqāmat al-ḥujja*. Ibn ʿAbd al-Wahhāb acknowledged these concepts but did not appreciate their restraining power on *takfīr*. His dismissive view of them comes through most clearly in a letter to two Najdī men who had expressed reservations about excommunicating those who venerate the so-called *ṭawāghīt* of Najd. Ibn ʿAbd al-Wahhāb was writing to them for the purpose of disabusing them of the notion that *iqāmat al-ḥujja* is relevant to the case at hand. In the letter he distinguishes three categories of people who have not had the proof presented to them (*alladhī lam taqum ʿalayhi ʾl-ḥujja*) and for whom, therefore, *iqāmat al-ḥujja* is necessary before *takfīr* can legitimately be pronounced. The three categories are those who are "new to Islam" (*ḥadīth ʿahd bi ʾl-Islām*), those who "grew up in a remote desert" (*nashaʾa bi-bādiya baʿīda*), and those whose *shirk* concerns "an obscure matter" (*masʾala khafiyya*).[95] As examples of a *masʾala khafiyya*, Ibn ʿAbd al-Wahhāb mentions two forms of sorcery (*ṣarf* and *ʿaṭf*). In the case of the people concerned, however—that is, those who supplicate the saints in

91. *al-Durar al-saniyya*, 1:166.

92. Ibid., 10:7.

93. Ibn Ghannām, *Tārīkh*, 1:171–89.

94. Ibid., 1:171.

95. Ibid., 1:457–58 (letter to ʿĪsā ibn Qāsim and Aḥmad ibn Suwaylim).

Najd—Ibn ʿAbd al-Wahhāb rejects the idea that *iqāmat al-ḥujja* is a necessary condition of *takfīr*, since the polytheists in Najd are not new to Islam, did not grow up in a remote desert, and are not committing *shirk* in an obscure matter. Rather, as he asserts, their *shirk* pertains to the foundations of the religion (*uṣūl al-dīn*). The Qurʾān, he insists, constitutes the proof (*ḥujja*) that has to be presented to them, and doubtless they have already received it. "When it comes to the foundations of the religion that God clarifies and establishes in His Book," he writes, "God's proof is the Qurʾān, so anyone it has reached, the proof has reached [*fa-man balaghahu fa-qad balaghathu ʾl-ḥujja*]."[96] What is more, he adds, it is not necessary for those who have received the Qurʾān to understand it; they need only to have received it. "The source of your confusion [*aṣl ishkālikum*]," he tells his correspondents,

> is that you have not distinguished between presenting the proof and understanding the proof [*bayna qiyām al-ḥujja wa-bayna fahm al-ḥujja*]. Most of the unbelievers and hypocrites [mentioned in the Qurʾān] did not understand God's proof, despite its being presented to them. As God says, "Or do you think that most of them listen and understand? They are but as cattle; nay, they are further astray from the way" (Q. 25:44). Being presented with the proof and being reached by the proof are one thing; the understanding of it by them is another. Their unbelief occurs upon its reaching them; if they do not understand it, that is another matter.[97]

Thus for Ibn ʿAbd al-Wahhāb, the requirement of *iqāmat al-ḥujja* was in practice no impediment to *takfīr* at all. If one has been exposed to the Qurʾān—as all people in the Arabian Peninsula presumably had been—then *iqāmat al-ḥujja* has taken place. Anyone who visits the dead and performs the rites of *ziyāra* is to be considered an unbeliever and treated as such. Ignorance is no safeguard against *takfīr*, since it does not matter whether one understands the proof that is being presented or not.

While Ibn ʿAbd al-Wahhāb does not address the issue of *al-ʿudhr bi ʾl-jahl* explicitly in this letter, he does so elsewhere, usually to dismiss it as a barrier to *takfīr*. For instance, he writes in *Kashf al-shubuhāt*: "A person may become an unbeliever by a word spoken by his tongue. He might say it while being ignorant, but he is not excused on the basis of ignorance [*wa-qad yaqūluhā*

96. Ibid., 1:458.
97. Ibid.

wa-huwa jāhil fa-lā yuʿdharu bi ʾl-jahl]."[98] This was not Ibn Taymiyya's view at all. As was seen above, he held that someone who is unable to understand the proof should not be declared an unbeliever until the proof has been both presented to him *and* explained to him. And he specifically stated that those who venerate saints are not to be subjected to *takfīr* until they are taught that their actions constitute *shirk*.

Ibn ʿAbd al-Wahhāb's view that *iqāmat al-ḥujja* need only apply in the event of a *masʾala khafiyya* was important to his reasoning. As per usual, he seems to have based this view on certain words of Ibn Taymiyya's. This is apparent from *Mufīd al-mustafīd*, in which he quotes Ibn Taymiyya to show that the latter was restrained in *takfīr* only in the case of "obscure doctrines" (*al-maqālāt al-khafiyya*), suggesting that when it came to "clear matters" (*al-umūr al-ẓāhira*) he did not believe that *iqāmat al-ḥujja* was necessary prior to *takfīr*.[99] The relevant quotation of Ibn Taymiyya comes from a *fatwā* in which he accuses many of the scholars of the *mutakallimūn* of having committed unbelief. The theological errors that the leading scholars among the *mutakallimūn* commit, he says, do not concern "obscure doctrines" but, rather, "clear matters known by the masses and the elite of the Muslims to be a part of the religion of the Muslims . . . such as God's command to worship God alone without partner."[100] In *Mufīd al-mustafīd*, Ibn ʿAbd al-Wahhāb seeks to draw attention to Ibn Taymiyya's distinction between *kufr* in "obscure doctrines" and *kufr* in "clear matters," the idea being that the latter does not require *iqāmat al-ḥujja*. Ibn Taymiyya's words indeed seem to suggest as much, but in other places, as we have seen, he is clear in excusing on the basis of ignorance those Muslims who visit graves and supplicate the dead before the proof has been presented to them. A more plausible interpretation of Ibn Taymiyya's quotation, then, rests on a distinction between Muslim scholars and the laity. Ibn Taymiyya was talking about scholars who embrace *kalām* theology; these men, in his view, should not be excused on the basis of ignorance when it comes to *kufr* in clear matters, such as worshipping saints, because as scholars they are well informed. As for ignorant lay Muslims, however, they ought to be excused on the basis of ignorance and presented with proof before being subject to *takfīr*. The critical distinction here is between scholars and laypeople, not those who commit *shirk* in "obscure doctrines" and those who commit *shirk* in "clear matters."

98. *al-Durar al-saniyya*, 1:71.
99. Ibn Ghannām, *Tārīkh*, 2:703–4.
100. Ibn Taymiyya, *Majmūʿ fatāwā*, 4:54.

As was seen in chapter 1, the matter of Ibn ʿAbd al-Wahhāb's and Ibn Taymiyya's different approaches to *takfīr* was a recurring theme in the early controversy over Wahhābism. It is one of the main themes of *Mufīd al-mustafīd,* in which Ibn ʿAbd al-Wahhāb combats at length the accusation that Ibn Taymiyya was restrained in pronouncing *takfīr* on individuals (*takfīr al-muʿayyan*). He describes this claim as "the specious argument that the enemies are relating" and identifies its source as Ibn Taymiyya's statement that he is "one of those who are most against subjecting an individual to *takfīr*."[101] To debunk this claim, Ibn ʿAbd al-Wahhāb quotes some passages of Ibn Taymiyya's that appear to show him pronouncing *takfīr* on individuals, including the one about the scholars of the *mutakallimūn* noted above. Another passage shows Ibn Taymiyya urging people not to eat animals slaughtered by certain ignorant persons (*jāhilūn*) in Mecca on the grounds that they are apostates (*murtaddīn*).[102] While Ibn ʿAbd al-Wahhāb does well to show Ibn Taymiyya at his least restrained in *takfīr,* the weight of the evidence does not support his argument. The Wahhābī founder was never able to prove that Ibn Taymiyya was as extreme in *takfīr* as he was, because the claim was unfounded.[103] For Ibn Taymiyya and Ibn al-Qayyim, the lay Muslim participants in the cult of saints were to be treated prima facie as Muslims; they were to be corrected and educated, not immediately denounced as unbelievers. It is of course possible that Ibn ʿAbd al-Wahhāb did not have access to some of the texts in which Ibn Taymiyya most clearly elaborates his position on *iqāmat al-ḥujja* and *al-ʿudhr biʾl-jahl,* but this does not change the fact that he repeatedly dismissed as irrelevant those statements of Ibn Taymiyya's emphasizing restraint in *takfīr.*

Takfīr *as a Duty*

A further aspect of Ibn ʿAbd al-Wahhāb's approach to *takfīr* is the way he imposed it on his followers as a duty. One of the conditions of Islam, he frequently states, is to declare unbelievers to be unbelievers—that is, to pronounce *takfīr* on those who, in his eyes, are unbelievers by virtue of committing *shirk.* Ibn ʿAbd al-Wahhāb speaks of this duty in his letter to Riyadh and

101. Ibn Ghannām, *Tārīkh,* 2:703–4.

102. Ibid., 2:700 (= Ibn Taymiyya, *Iqtiḍāʾ al-ṣirāṭ al-mustaqīm,* 2:64–65).

103. For another example of Ibn ʿAbd al-Wahhāb rebutting the charge that Ibn Taymiyya exercised restraint in *takfīr,* see Ibn Ghannām, *Tārīkh,* 1:431–40 (letter to Aḥmad ibn ʿAbd al-Karīm).

Manfūḥa, where he writes concerning the saints of Najd: "The religion of Islam is not sound without dissociating from them and pronouncing *takfīr* on them, as God says, 'So whoever rejects idols [*fa-man yakfur bi 'l-ṭāghūt*] and believes in God has lain hold of the firmest bond' (Q. 2:256)."[104] The duty of *takfīr* was not something that he derived from Ibn Taymiyya and Ibn al-Qayyim. Unlike Ibn ʿAbd al-Wahhāb, these scholars were not seeking to divide society by demanding declarations of *takfīr* against those perceived as worshipping the dead.

As is seen from the previous example, the Wahhābī requirement of *takfīr* is often linked to Q. 2:256 and particularly the phrase "So whoever rejects idols" (*fa-man yakfur bi 'l-ṭāghūt*). For Ibn ʿAbd al-Wahhāb, the word *ṭāghūt* (pl. *ṭawāghīt*), translated here as "idols," has the general meaning of anything that is worshipped apart from God (*al-ṭāghūt ʿāmm fī kull mā ʿubida min dūn Allāh*).[105] As was seen in chapter 1, he frequently applied this term to the Najdī saints, such as Tāj, Shamsān, and Yūsuf. In several of his epistles, he explains that while there are many different kinds of *ṭawāghīt*, there are five chief forms: (1) Satan, (2) a person who allows himself to be worshipped (*man ʿubida wa-huwa rāḍin*), (3) a person who claims knowledge of the unseen, (4) a person who calls people to worship him, and (5) a person who judges not according to what God has revealed.[106] There is some variation in his enumeration of these five chief forms, but always included is the figure of a person who allows himself to be worshipped.[107] The *ṭawāghīt* of Najd, in his view, fit this description: not only were they being worshipped by their devotees, but they welcomed being worshipped.[108]

Critical to Ibn ʿAbd al-Wahhāb's understanding of *ṭāghūt* was a definition provided by Ibn al-Qayyim in *Iʿlām al-muwaqqiʿīn*. Here Ibn al-Qayyim defines *ṭāghūt* as

> every manner of thing in which man exceeds the proper limits, whether in terms of being worshipped, being followed, or being obeyed. The *ṭāghūt* of every people is thus the one whom they appeal to for judgment apart from God and His Messenger, or the one whom they worship apart from God, or

104. Ibid., 1:404.

105. *al-Durar al-saniyya*, 1:161.

106. Ibid., 1:136.

107. See, e.g., ibid., 1:161–63.

108. He is probably referring to the way they allegedly accepted votive offerings while they were still alive.

the one whom they follow without sure knowledge from God, or the one whom they obey in matters they do not know God requires obedience.[109]

For Ibn al-Qayyim, the issue of *ṭāghūt* was not an abstraction. Similar to the way he viewed most of mankind as having reverted to *shirk*, he viewed most people on earth as having taken their respective *ṭawāghīt* in an ungodly way. Most people on earth, he asserts in *I ʿlām al-muwaqqi ʿīn*, have turned away from the worship of God "to the worship of *ṭāghūt*, from appealing for judgment to God and His Messenger to appealing for judgment to *ṭāghūt*, and from obeying Him and following His Messenger to obeying *ṭāghūt* and following it."[110] In condemning the so-called *ṭawāghīt* of Najd and elsewhere, Ibn ʿAbd al-Wahhāb was no doubt drawing on this understanding of *ṭāghūt* put forward by Ibn al-Qayyim. However, his understanding of *takfīr* as a duty was not drawn from Ibn al-Qayyim.

As alluded to above, the duty of *takfīr* is one that Ibn ʿAbd al-Wahhāb derived from the concept of rejecting idols (*al-kufr bi ʾl-ṭāghūt*) in Q. 2:256. In this verse, the verbal noun *kufr* carries the meaning of rejection, not *takfīr*, though the two terms are linguistically related. In an epistle on the meaning of *ṭāghūt*, Ibn ʿAbd al-Wahhāb invokes Q. 2:256 to make the point that God has mandated that all believers pronounce *takfīr* on the *ṭawāghīt* and those who worship them. Referring to the verse, he states that "the first thing that God imposed on mankind was *al-kufr bi ʾl-ṭāghūt* and belief in God." The meaning of *al-kufr bi ʾl-ṭāghūt* is "that you believe that worshipping other than God is wrong, that you eschew it and hate it, and that you pronounce *takfīr* on those who do it and show them enmity." A bit later in the epistle, he clarifies that none of this is optional. "Know," he states, "that a person does not become a Muslim without rejecting *ṭāghūt*."[111] Notably, this radical interpretation of *al-kufr bi ʾl-ṭāghūt* is not buttressed by quotations from earlier scholars.

As can be seen from this example, Ibn ʿAbd al-Wahhāb also interpreted *al-kufr bi ʾl-ṭāghūt* as requiring the display of hatred and enmity to polytheists. Here as elsewhere, he included *takfīr* among other elements that make up the

109. Ibn al-Qayyim, *I ʿlām al-muwaqqi ʿīn*, 2:92. Ibn ʿAbd al-Wahhāb quotes this definition in *al-Durar al-saniyya*, 1:136, and paraphrases it at 1:161. For a similar definition of *ṭāghūt* by Ibn Taymiyya, see Ibn Taymiyya, *Majmūʿ fatāwā*, 28:200–201. This understanding of *ṭāghūt* seems to have been common in Sunnī Islamic thought. A similar definition is provided by the early exegete Abū Jaʿfar al-Ṭabarī (d. 310/923) in his Qurʾānic exegesis; see al-Ṭabarī, *Tafsīr*, 4:558.

110. Ibn al-Qayyim, *I ʿlām al-muwaqqi ʿīn*, 2:93.

111. *al-Durar al-saniyya*, 1:161–63; cf. 2:121–22.

larger duty of confronting polytheists. Another good example of this is the following short statement in which Ibn ʿAbd al-Wahhāb summarizes his doctrine as a statement of two commands (*amrān*):

> The foundation of Islam and its principle are two commands. The first is the command to worship God alone without partner, to agitate for this, to show loyalty for the sake of it, and to pronounce *takfīr* on those who do not practice it. The second is to warn against the association of other beings in the worship of God, to be harsh in this, to show enmity for the sake of it, and to pronounce *takfīr* on those who practice it.[112]

The duty of *takfīr* was thus part of Ibn ʿAbd al-Wahhāb's more general demand that Muslims confront polytheists and condemn them. Often the duty of *takfīr* was omitted in such articulations of the required confrontation, but in such cases it was implied.

A further part of Ibn ʿAbd al-Wahhāb's duty of *takfīr* relates to those who refrain from carrying it out. Ibn ʿAbd al-Wahhāb required his followers to pronounce *takfīr* not only on unbelievers—in the sense of those who commit *shirk* by worshipping other than God—but also on those who fail or hesitate to pronounce *takfīr* on these alleged unbelievers. In his study of Ibn ʿAbd al-Wahhāb, Michael Crawford refers to this secondary requirement as, appropriately, "secondary *takfīr*."[113] Ibn ʿAbd al-Wahhāb's most famous statement in this regard comes in his epistle known as "the ten nullifiers of Islam," where it appears as the third nullifier: "Whosoever does not pronounce *takfīr* on the polytheists, or is doubtful about their unbelief, or affirms the validity of their doctrine is an unbeliever by consensus."[114] The reason Ibn ʿAbd al-Wahhāb was so insistent on this point, it seems, was that he wished to enforce a sharp boundary line between his followers and all others. In the fight over his doctrine there was to be no middle ground, no possibility for neutrality. If a person did not agree with him that the *ṭawāghīt* of Najd were unbelievers, and that those perceived as worshipping them were unbelievers, then that person was to be regarded as an unbeliever in turn.

In theory at least, the notion of secondary *takfīr* was fairly well established in Sunnī Islamic thought. Ibn ʿAbd al-Wahhāb likely was influenced by what he read about it in al-Ḥajjāwī's *al-Iqnāʿ*, and indeed the third nullifier was

112. Ibid., 2:202, 204–5 (broken up because it is being commented on); cf. 1:153.

113. Crawford, *Ibn 'Abd al-Wahhab*, 66.

114. *al-Durar al-saniyya*, 10:91.

derived from this source. In his letter to Riyadh and Manfūḥa, for instance, Ibn ʿAbd al-Wahhāb refers to a passage in *al-Iqnāʿ* that is very similar in construction to the third nullifier.[115] Another influence seems to have been Ibn Taymiyya, who is quoted in *al-Iqnāʿ* articulating a duty of secondary *takfīr* in the specific case of ʿAlī ibn Abī Ṭālib, the fourth caliph in Sunnī Islam. Of anyone claiming that ʿAlī is a god or a prophet, he writes, "there is no doubt about his unbelief; nay, there is no doubt about the unbelief of those who temporize [*tawaqqafa*] in pronouncing *takfīr* on him."[116] The idea behind secondary *takfīr* was thus by no means a Wahhābī innovation.[117] What was unusual was the emphasis Ibn ʿAbd al-Wahhāb placed on it in his preaching and the context in which he was doing so. The Najdī preacher was urging Muslims to pronounce *takfīr* on those who failed to pronounce *takfīr*, all in an ostensibly Sunnī Muslim context.

Downplaying Takfīr

While Ibn ʿAbd al-Wahhāb's statements concerning *takfīr* are consistently extreme, there are some notable exceptions to this pattern. In these exceptional passages, he is seen downplaying his approach to *takfīr*, saying that he does not pronounce *takfīr* on those who have not been presented with proof. One of these statements is found in a letter to a scholar in al-Washm, in which Ibn ʿAbd al-Wahhāb writes: "As for what the enemies have related about me that I pronounce *takfīr* on the basis of supposition and on the basis of loyalty [*annī ukaffiru bi ʾl-ẓann wa ʾl-muwālāt*], or that I pronounce *takfīr* on an ignorant person who has not been presented with the proof [*aw ukaffiru ʾl-jāhil alladhī lam taqum ʿalayhi ʾl-ḥujja*], this is a great lie."[118] Another example comes in an epistle in which he

115. al-Ḥajjāwī, *al-Iqnāʿ*, 4:286.

116. Ibid., 4:289 (= Ibn Taymiyya, *al-Ṣārim al-maslūl*, 3:1108).

117. Recent debates within the Islamic State (aka ISIS) over Ibn ʿAbd al-Wahhāb's third nullifier have yielded numerous quotations of Muslim scholars who endorsed some version of secondary *takfīr*, including Abū Bakr ibn ʿAyyāsh (d. 193/809), al-Qāḍī ʿIyāḍ (d. 544/1149), and al-Nawawī (d. 676/1277), among others. See al-Maqdisī, *al-Bāʿith ʿalā itmām al-nāqiḍ al-thālith*, 10ff. The purpose of these earlier scholars' espousal of secondary *takfīr* seems to have been to emphasize the *kufr* of the unbelieving group in question. Thus when Ibn Taymiyya writes, concerning the Druze, "[W]hoever doubts their unbelief is an unbeliever like them" (*Majmūʿ fatāwā*, 35:162), his point is to make clear that their status as unbelievers is unquestionable.

118. Ibn Ghannām, *Tārīkh*, 1:338 (letter to Muḥammad ibn ʿĪd).

addresses the charge that he has excommunicated all those who fail to emigrate to Wahhābī territory. In rebutting the charge, he writes:

> If we do not pronounce *takfīr* on those who worship the idol above [the grave of] ʿAbd al-Qādir and the idol above the grave of Aḥmad al-Badawī and the likes of them, on account of their ignorance and the absence of someone able to inform them [*li-ajl jahlihim wa-ʿadam man yunabbihuhum*], then how could we pronounce *takfīr* on those who have not committed polytheism when they do not emigrate to us, or those who have not disbelieved and taken up arms [against us]?[119]

In these examples, Ibn ʿAbd al-Wahhāb seems to be saying that he does not pronounce *takfīr* on those who visit and supplicate saints but, rather, that he excuses them on the basis of ignorance. This stands in stark contrast to what we have seen of his views on *takfīr* elsewhere. What is one to make of this?

The most reasonable explanation for these kinds of comments is that Ibn ʿAbd al-Wahhāb was simply not consistent in expounding his doctrine, his approach perhaps changing over time or according to context. It may be that at the beginning of his mission he was more restrained in *takfīr* or that he spoke about *takfīr* in different ways before different audiences. It should be underscored that these examples of moderation in *takfīr*, though they are quoted often by modern Wahhābīs seeking to play down the severity of the Wahhābī doctrine, are few and far between in Ibn ʿAbd al-Wahhāb's corpus. Far more often we find him dismissing *al-ʿudhr bi'l-jahl* and *iqāmat al-ḥujja* as impediments to *takfīr* and urging people to excommunicate those who supplicate the dead.

The existence of comments such as these was a source of confusion even for the Wahhābīs. One of Ibn ʿAbd al-Wahhāb's great-grandsons, Isḥāq ibn ʿAbd al-Raḥmān Āl al-Shaykh (d. 1319/1901), in a short essay on the subject of *takfīr*, instructs the reader not to be concerned with such statements: "His refraining [from *takfīr*] in some of his responsa should be understood as having been for a certain purpose [*li-amr min al-umūr*]."[120] Ibn ʿAbd al-Wahhāb's refraining (*tawaqquf*) from *takfīr* in certain writings, then, was not to be taken as normative, for everywhere else his message was that we must pronounce *takfīr* on

119. *al-Durar al-saniyya*, 1:104. Aḥmad al-Badawī (d. 674/1276) is the namesake of the Aḥmadiyya order; his grave is in Ṭanṭā, Egypt. See *EI*³, s.v. "al-Badawī, al-Sayyid" (Catherine Mayeur-Jaouen).

120. Āl al-Shaykh, *Ḥukm takfīr al-muʿayyan*, 19.

those who commit polytheism, whether they are ignorant or not, as "those who have been reached by the Qurʾān have had the proof presented to them" (*man balaghahu ʾl-Qurʾān fa-qad qāmat ʿalayhi ʾl-ḥujja*).[121] This was a reference to Ibn ʿAbd al-Wahhāb's letter quoted above, in which he claims that the Qurʾān constitutes the proof and that it need not be understood prior to *takfīr*. A similar approach was taken by ʿAbdallāh ibn ʿAbd al-Laṭīf Āl al-Shaykh (d. 1339/1920), Ibrāhīm ibn ʿAbd al-Laṭīf Āl al-Shaykh (d. 1329/1911), and Sulaymān ibn Siḥmān (d. 1349/1930), who in a *fatwā* quote the same letter of Ibn ʿAbd al-Wahhāb's. The three scholars explain that people at the beginning of Ibn ʿAbd al-Wahhāb's *daʿwa* were living in a period when there was little trace of Islam left or knowledge of the prophetic message (*fi zaman fatra wa-ʿadam ʿilm bi-āthār al-risāla*), and thus initially Ibn ʿAbd al-Wahhāb did not pronounce *takfīr* on them before presenting them with the proof and preaching to them (*lam yukaffir al-nās ibtidāʾan illā baʿd qiyām al-ḥujja waʾl-daʿwa*). Yet that approach was confined to a specific period in time and was not to be taken as normative. Quoting Ibn ʿAbd al-Wahhāb's letter, the authors insist that *takfīr* of a person who commits *shirk* is a duty, even if that person does not understand the proof (*wa-in lam yafhamūhā*), the proof being the Qurʾān.[122]

Another approach occasionally used by Ibn ʿAbd al-Wahhāb, in downplaying his views on *takfīr*, was to say that he was not pronouncing *takfīr* on most of the Muslim *umma*. In a letter to an Iraqi scholar, for example, he sought to give the impression that the targets of his *takfīr* were quite limited and certainly did not extend to the *umma* at large. "As for *takfīr*," he writes, "I pronounce *takfīr* on those who have known the religion of the Messenger and who subsequently revile it, forbid people from observing it, and show enmity to those who practice it. These are the people I declare to be unbelievers. The majority of the *umma* [*akthar al-umma*], praise be to God, are not like that [*laysū kadhālika*]."[123] In saying this, Ibn ʿAbd al-Wahhāb was seeking to rebut the accusation that he was engaging in generalized or indiscriminate *takfīr* (*al-takfīr biʾl-ʿumūm*), a charge that he frequently denied.[124] Evidently, he was worried about the per-

121. Ibid., 19–20.

122. Āl Ḥamad, *Ijmāʿ ahl al-sunna al-nabawiyya*, 155–61, at 160. Cf. the view of the occasionally more moderate ʿAbd al-Laṭīf ibn ʿAbd al-Raḥmān Āl al-Shaykh (d. 1293/1876), who does take one of these statements of Ibn ʿAbd al-Wahhāb's as normative (Āl al-Shaykh, *Miṣbāḥ al-ẓalām*, 84).

123. Ibn Ghannām, *Tārīkh*, 1:414 (letter to Ibn al-Suwaydī).

124. See, e.g., *al-Durar al-saniyya*, 1:63, 104, 10:131.

ception of him as someone who rashly dismissed professed Muslims as unbelievers, even if this was precisely what he was doing. One possible explanation for this kind of statement is that the *umma*, for Ibn ʿAbd al-Wahhāb, consisted only of the *ghurabāʾ*, those "strangers" who adhered to his doctrine; therefore to say that he was not declaring most of the *umma* to be unbelievers was not to say very much at all, and indeed it was misleading, as it concealed the fact that in his view most professed Muslims had fallen into polytheism. Similarly, Ibn ʿAbd al-Wahhāb was fond of saying that he did not pronounce *takfīr* on Muslims. As he writes in his letter to Riyadh and Manfūḥa, "We have not pronounced *takfīr* on Muslims; rather, we have only pronounced *takfīr* on polytheists [*mā kaffarnā illā ʾl-mushrikīn*]."[125] While these words are intended to signal restraint in *takfīr*, they in fact mean something different. What Ibn ʿAbd al-Wahhāb is really saying is that all those we declare to be unbelievers are just that—unbelievers—and so we cannot possibly be accused of having excommunicated Muslims.[126] Muḥammad ibn Fayrūz takes note of this lexical sleight of hand in one of his refutations, where he writes: "It is known that if one criticizes Ibn ʿAbd al-Wahhāb and his followers for pronouncing *takfīr* on Muslims, they will say: 'We have not pronounced *takfīr* on a Muslim!'"[127] Some of Ibn ʿAbd al-Wahhāb's more moderate-sounding comments on *takfīr* ought to be read in this light. They were intended not to clarify the nature of his approach but, rather, to obscure and make light of it.

Ibn Taymiyya and Ibn al-Qayyim were prone to using harsh, even anathemizing language to condemn and criticize those groups of Sunnī Muslims they regarded as innovators in religion, including the participants in the cult of saints. On closer examination, however, they were not necessarily pronouncing *takfīr* on the individuals in these groups, particularly the unlearned among them, emphasizing the restraints of *al-ʿudhr bi ʾl-jahl* and *iqāmat al-ḥujja*. Ibn ʿAbd al-Wahhāb, for his part, generally ignored these restraints in the context of those he regarded as polytheists, arguing that if these people had been exposed to the Qurʾān, they had been presented with proof. Also unlike Ibn Taymiyya and Ibn al-Qayyim, he made it a point of his predicatory campaign

125. Ibn Ghannām, *Tārīkh*, 1:404.
126. Crawford describes this sort of response as "glib" (*Ibn ʿAbd al-Wahhab*, 61).
127. Ibn Fayrūz, *al-Radd ʿalā man kaffara ahl al-Riyāḍ*, 60.

to demand that Muslims pronounce *takfīr* on those he regarded as polytheists, and he further argued that those who failed to pronounce *takfīr* on these polytheists were themselves to be denounced as unbelievers.

Al-Walāʾ waʾl-Barāʾ

In the writings of Ibn Taymiyya and Ibn al-Qayyim, pronouncing *takfīr* on unbelievers does not often appear as a duty incumbent upon Muslims. The matter of *al-walāʾ waʾl-barāʾ*, of association and dissociation, is different. Ibn Taymiyya and Ibn al-Qayyim would present the different elements of *al-walāʾ waʾl-barāʾ*—showing loyalty to God and fellow Muslims and dissociating from unbelievers—as conditions of the proper worship of God, that is, of *tawḥīd al-ulūhiyya*. Ibn ʿAbd al-Wahhāb would do the same.

The Requirements of Tawḥīd al-ulūhiyya

Statements to the effect that the elements of *al-walāʾ waʾl-barāʾ* form a part of *tawḥīd al-ulūhiyya* abound in Ibn Taymiyya's works. As he writes in one place, "This *tawḥīd* [i.e., *tawḥīd al-ulūhiyya*] is the worship of God alone without partner. . . . It comprises obeying Him and obeying His Messenger and showing loyalty to His allies and showing enmity to His enemies [*wa-muwālāt awliyāʾihi wa-muʿādāt aʿdāʾihi*]."[128] Elsewhere, he states similarly that "*al-tawḥīd al-ilāhī* [i.e., *tawḥīd al-ulūhiyya*] . . . is the worship of Him alone without partner, obeying Him and obeying His Messenger, commanding what he commanded and forbidding what he forbade, and loving for His sake and hating for His sake [*waʾl-ḥubb fīhi waʾl-bughḍ fīhi*]."[129] The words *loyalty* (*muwālāt*), *enmity* (*muʿādāt*), *love* (*ḥubb*), and *hatred* (*bughḍ*) are indicative of the concept of *al-walāʾ waʾl-barāʾ*. In other of Ibn Taymiyya's writings, these words appear among the forms of worship that constitute *tawḥīd al-ulūhiyya*, along with such things as supplication (*duʿāʾ*) and reliance (*tawakkul*).[130]

The phrase *al-walāʾ waʾl-barāʾ*, meaning "association and dissociation" or "loyalty and disavowal," is the term used by modern Salafīs and Wahhābīs to capture the duties in question. It is only in the last century or so that this phrase came to be widely adopted in Sunnī Islam. The exact phrase *al-walāʾ*

128. Ibn Taymiyya, *Majmūʿ fatāwā*, 14:378.

129. Ibid., 2:457.

130. See, e.g., ibid., 8:370.

wa ʾl-barāʾ is not common in Ibn Taymiyya's and Ibn al-Qayyim's writings, but the concept was always there, even if it fell under a different designation.[131] The Sunnī aversion to the phrase and its variants (e.g., *al-walāya wa ʾl-barāʾa*) stems from the fact that historically this pairing of terms was closely identified with Khārijism and Imāmī Shīʿism. Each of these sects developed a doctrine of *al-walāʾ wa ʾl-barāʾ* related to the outcome of the first Islamic civil war in 37/657, which pitted the followers of Muʿāwiya against those of ʿAlī. For the Khārijites, who rejected both Muʿāwiya and ʿAlī and claimed Islamic rule for themselves, the phrase was used to signify association with the Khārijite *imāms* and fellow Khārijites, on the one hand, and dissociation from all non-Khārijite Muslims, particularly the followers of Muʿāwiya and ʿAlī, on the other.[132] For the Shīʿa, who were loyal to ʿAlī and considered him to be the first true caliph, *al-walāʾ wa ʾl-barāʾ* entailed association with the Shīʿī *imāms* and dissociation from all perceived enemies of the family of the Prophet (*ahl al-bayt*).[133] The Sunnī movement (*ahl al-sunna wa ʾl-jamāʿa*), as it emerged in the early centuries of Islam, condemned these versions of *al-walāʾ wa ʾl-barāʾ* as heretical, including the associated phraseology. Aḥmad ibn Ḥanbal is reported to have said that the term *dissociation* (*barāʾa*) is a religious innovation (*bidʿa*).[134]

While Ibn Taymiyya did not employ the phrase *al-walāʾ wa ʾl-barāʾ*—nor, for that matter, did Ibn ʿAbd al-Wahhāb[135]—he wrote about the concept at length under several headings, including *al-walāya wa ʾl-ʿadāwa* (association and enmity) and *maḥabba* (love).[136] As he commonly explains it, the concept

131. Ibn al-Qayyim uses the phrase at least once (*Madārij al-sālikīn*, 1:513); Ibn Taymiyya nearly uses it in his *Qāʿida fī ʾl-maḥabba*, 163 (*fa-lā walāʾa lillāh illā bi ʾl-barāʾa min ʿaduww Allāh wa-rasūlihi*).

132. On the concept in Khārijism, and its Ibāḍī subsect in particular, see Ennāmi, *Studies in Ibāḍism*, 193–225.

133. On the concept in Shīʿism, see Kohlberg, "*Barāʾa* in Shīʿī Doctrine."

134. Wagemakers, "Transformation of a Radical Concept," 85. Despite early Sunnī rejection of the terminology, a concept of *al-walāʾ wa ʾl-barāʾ* has long obtained in Sunnism, though it has not received much attention in Western scholarship. Abū Ḥāmid al-Ghazzālī (d. 505/1111), for example, though without using the exact phrase, devotes space to it in his *Iḥyāʾ ʿulūm al-dīn* (2:157–72). The history of *al-walāʾ wa ʾl-barāʾ* in Sunnī Islamic thought bears further study; it does not begin with Ibn Taymiyya as is sometimes alleged.

135. The phrase is found in an epistle attributed to him (*al-Durar al-saniyya*, 1:117), but ʿAbdallāh al-ʿUthaymīn has rightly disputed the epistle's attribution (*Buḥūth wa-taʿlīqāt fī tārīkh al-Mamlaka al-ʿArabiyya al-Suʿūdiyya*, 37).

136. Ibn Taymiyya, *Majmūʿ fatāwā*, 28:19; Ibn Taymiyya, *Qāʿida fī ʾl-maḥabba*.

of *al-walāʾ wa ʾl-barāʾ* is the duty to associate with and show love to fellow Muslims and to dissociate from and show hatred and enmity to unbelievers. It thus combines a positive aspect (association and love) and a negative aspect (hatred and enmity). The key words in Ibn Taymiyya's approach to the concept are, in its positive aspect, *muwālāt/walāya/walāʾ* (association or loyalty) and *ḥubb/maḥabba* (love) and, in its negative aspect, *muʿādāt/ʿadāwa/ʿadāʾ* (enmity) and *bughḍ/baghḍāʾ* (hatred). *Muwālāt* corresponds to and is rooted in *ḥubb*, while *ʿadāwa* corresponds to and is rooted in *bughḍ*.[137] As Ibn Taymiyya explains it, "Association is against enmity. The origin of association is love and nearness [*aṣl al-walāya al-maḥabba wa ʾl-qurb*], while the origin of enmity is hatred and distance [*wa-aṣl al-ʿadāwa al-bughḍ wa ʾl-buʿd*]."[138] All of these words come together in a *ḥadīth* commonly cited in discussions of the concept. In this *ḥadīth*, the Prophet states: "The firmest of the bonds of faith [*awthaq ʿurā ʾl-īmān*] is showing loyalty for the sake of God and showing enmity for the sake of God [*al-muwālāt fī ʾllāh wa ʾl-muʿādāt fī ʾllāh*], and loving for the sake of God and hating for the sake of God [*wa ʾl-ḥubb fī ʾllāh wa ʾl-bughḍ fī ʾllāh*]."[139] From *ḥadīths* such as this and certain Qurʾānic verses comes the distinctive language of *al-walāʾ wa ʾl-barāʾ*. Such phrases as "association for the sake of God" (*al-muwālāt fī ʾllāh*) and "love for the sake of God" (*al-ḥubb fī ʾllāh*), on the one side, and "enmity for the sake of God" (*al-muʿādāt fī ʾllāh*) and "hatred for the sake of God" (*al-bughḍ fī ʾllāh*), on the other, all point in one way or another to the concept of *al-walāʾ wa ʾl-barāʾ*. The term *barāʾ/barāʾa*, meaning "dissociation" or "disavowal," also appears in the company of *hatred* and *enmity* and is close in meaning. According to Ibn Taymiyya, what *al-walāʾ wa ʾl-barāʾ* requires is that Muslims love that which God loves and associate with that with which God associates; conversely, it requires them to hate that which God hates and show enmity to that to which God shows enmity.[140] Ibn Taymiyya speaks harshly of those who would neglect these requirements or show love or hatred in the wrong direction. As he notes in a *fatwā*, "One should know that a believer must be shown loyalty even if he wrongs you and oppresses you, and an unbeliever must be shown enmity

137. Ibn Taymiyya, *Qāʿida fī ʾl-maḥabba*, 273.

138. Ibn Taymiyya, *Majmūʿ fatāwā*, 11:161–62.

139. For the *ḥadīth* as worded, see al-Albānī, *Silsilat al-aḥādīth al-ṣaḥīḥa*, 2:698–700 (no. 998). The more common version is simply *awthaq ʿurā ʾl-īmān al-ḥubb fī ʾllāh wa ʾl-bughḍ fī ʾllāh*.

140. Ibn Taymiyya, *Qāʿida fī ʾl-maḥabba*, 162.

even if he gives to you and is kind to you."[141] Ibn al-Qayyim's language in this regard could be equally severe. In his book *Madārij al-sālikīn*, after condemning the polytheism of the cult of saints, he writes: "None is saved from the snare of this greater polytheism [*sharak hādhā ʾl-shirk al-akbar*] save for he who devotes his *tawḥīd* exclusively to God, shows enmity to the polytheists for the sake of God, draws near to God by hating them, takes God as his sole protector and deity and object of worship, and thus devotes his love exclusively to Him."[142] When it comes to Muslim sinners, Ibn Taymiyya and Ibn al-Qayyim were much less harsh. As Ibn Taymiyya says, a sinner deserves loyalty "in proportion to the good that is in him" (*bi-qadr mā fīhi min al-khayr*) and enmity "in proportion to the bad that is in him" (*bi-qadr mā fīhi min al-sharr*).[143]

Another key phrase in Ibn Taymiyya's approach to *al-walāʾ wa ʾl-barāʾ* is *millat Ibrāhīm* (the religion of Abraham), a Qurʾānic term that he associates with the negative aspect of the concept.[144] In the Qurʾān, Abraham appears as the paradigmatic example of condemning and dissociating from unbelievers. The most oft-cited verse in this regard is Q. 60:4, in which God declares: "You have had a good example in Abraham, and those with him, when they said to their people, 'We dissociate from you and that which you worship apart from God [*innā buraʾāʾ minkum wa-mimmā taʿbūdūna min dūn Allāh*]. We reject you, and between us and you enmity and hatred [*al-ʿadāwa wa ʾl-baghḍāʾ*] have shown themselves forever, until you believe in God alone.'" Given that the Prophet Abraham was "a good example" (*uswa ḥasana*) of the duty to dissociate from, hate, and show enmity to unbelievers, Ibn Taymiyya occasionally associated the duty with the phrase *millat Ibrāhīm*. "God commanded him," Ibn Taymiyya writes of Abraham, "to dissociate from everything that is worshipped apart from Him. This is the religion of Abraham, the friend [of God]."[145] As Ibn Taymiyya saw it, dissociation on the model of Abraham was a key part of *tawḥīd al-ulūhiyya*; Abraham had "fulfilled," or put into action, "this *tawḥīd*" (*ḥaqqaqa hādhā ʾl-tawḥīd*).[146] Importantly, he emphasized that *millat Ibrāhīm* entails dissociation not only from what is worshipped but also from those doing the worshipping, as Q. 60:4 indicates

141. Ibn Taymiyya, *Majmūʿ fatāwā*, 28:209.
142. Ibn al-Qayyim, *Madārij al-sālikīn*, 2:929.
143. Ibn Taymiyya, *Majmūʿ fatāwā*, 28:209.
144. See, for example, ibid., 16:546, 28:32; Ibn Taymiyya, *Qāʿida fī ʾl-maḥabba*, 158.
145. Ibn Taymiyya, *Majmūʿ fatāwā*, 16:546.
146. Ibn Taymiyya, *Minhāj al-sunna al-nabawiyya*, 5:350.

("We dissociate from you and that which you worship apart from God"). He thus writes in one of his books that "this dissociation from it [i.e., polytheism] includes the polytheists," not just polytheism.[147] Ibn al-Qayyim makes the same point in one of his books, stating that dissociation from *shirk* requires "dissociation from them [i.e., polytheists] and from that which they worship."[148] The idea that Muslims are required to dissociate from polytheism and polytheists, and to show them hatred and enmity, was one frequently espoused by Ibn Taymiyya and Ibn al-Qayyim, rooted in their concept of *tawḥīd al-ulūhiyya*.

Preaching Confrontation

Following these scholars, Ibn ʿAbd al-Wahhāb also conceived of the duties of *al-walāʾ waʾl-barāʾ* as requirements stemming from *tawḥīd al-ulūhiyya*. While he sometimes spoke about the importance of love and loyalty, his emphasis was almost always on *al-walāʾ waʾl-barāʾ* in its negative aspect. Those who failed to show hatred and enmity to polytheists, he would repeatedly say, have failed to meet the conditions of *tawḥīd al-ulūhiyya* and thus of Islam. One of his favorite passages to cite in this regard was Ibn al-Qayyim's statement quoted above that "[n]one is saved from the snare of this greater polytheism save for he who devotes his *tawḥīd* exclusively to God, [and] shows enmity to the polytheists for the sake of God." There was no clearer statement from Ibn Taymiyya or Ibn al-Qayyim to the effect that showing hatred and enmity to polytheists was an absolute must. In *Mufīd al-mustafīd*, Ibn ʿAbd al-Wahhāb quotes this passage and remarks: "So reflect on the fact that Islam is not sound without showing enmity to the partisans of this polytheism [*lā yaṣiḥḥu illā bi-muʿādāt ahl hādhā ʾl-shirk*]. If a person does not show them enmity, then he belongs to them [*fa-in lam yuʿādihim fa-huwa minhum*]."[149] In saying this, Ibn ʿAbd al-Wahhāb was urging his readers to confront the partisans of the cult of saints by showing them enmity, which appears to have meant, in the first place, verbally denouncing them. True Muslims were required to dissociate from, hate, and show enmity to the polytheists around them (i.e., the opponents of Wahhābism).

For Ibn Taymiyya and Ibn al-Qayyim, the duty of showing hatred and enmity appears to have been something of an abstraction. They were not sending out epistles calling on people to confront certain communities of

147. Ibid.

148. Ibn al-Qayyim, *Madārij al-sālikīn*, 1:512.

149. Ibn Ghannām, *Tārīkh*, 2:710; cf. *al-Durar al-saniyya*, 10:107.

Sunnī Muslims seen as wayward. Ibn ʿAbd al-Wahhāb, by contrast, made this duty a key part of his mission. It was a duty he invoked frequently in his letters and epistles, urging his readers to confront and antagonize polytheists and warning that failure to do so jeopardized their status as Muslims. In his telling, this was a theological imperative of the highest order, bound up with *tawḥīd al-ulūhiyya* and predicated on the examples of the Prophets Abraham and Muḥammad.

The earliest datable articulation of the duty of *al-walāʾ wa ʾl-barāʾ* in Ibn ʿAbd al-Wahhāb's writings is found in the *Kalimāt* epistle. Here, as in most of his writings on the subject, he emphasizes only the negative aspect of the concept—enmity, hatred, and dissociation. After explaining the ideas related to *tawḥīd al-ulūhiyya* and *tawḥīd al-rubūbiyya*, and suggesting that the present-day polytheists are worse than the pagan Arabs, he demands action. It is not sufficient to agree with what I am saying regarding *tawḥīd* and *shirk*, he says, but, rather, you must demonstrate your agreement by showing hatred and enmity to idols and the idolaters who worship them:

> Do not think if you say, "This is the truth. I follow it and I abjure all that is against it, but I will not confront them [*lā ataʿarraḍuhum*] and I will say nothing concerning them," do not think that that will profit you. Rather, it is necessary to hate them [*lā budda min bughḍihim*], to hate those who love them [*wa-bughḍ man yuḥibbuhum*], to revile them [*wa-masabbatihim*], and to show them enmity [*wa-muʿādātihim*].[150]

Immediately after spelling out this duty, Ibn ʿAbd al-Wahhāb seeks to show that it is grounded in the example of the messengers (*rusul*), those prophets sent with a divine revelation,[151] and particularly the example of Abraham and Muḥammad. The first proof text that he cites is Q. 60:4, in which Abraham and his followers are seen telling their polytheistic community, "We dissociate from you and that which you worship apart from God. We reject you, and between us and you enmity and hatred have shown themselves forever, until you believe in God alone."[152] After this he seeks to illustrate that the Prophet

150. al-Qabbānī, *Faṣl al-khiṭāb*, f. 65a–b (= *al-Durar al-saniyya*, 2:109, where *lā ataʿarraḍuhum* is *lā ataʿarraḍu lil-mushrikīn*). For similar passages, see *al-Durar al-saniyya*, 2:119–22.

151. Ibn ʿAbd al-Wahhāb distinguishes between prophets in general (*anbiyāʾ*; sing. *nabī*) and prophets who are messengers (*rusul*; sing. *rasūl*), who are those sent by God with a revealed message that they are commanded to spread; see, e.g., *al-Durar al-saniyya*, 1:133–34. All of the *rusul*, in Ibn ʿAbd al-Wahhāb's understanding, were entrusted with the mission of condemning and confronting *shirk* and the *mushrikūn*.

152. al-Qabbānī, *Faṣl al-khiṭāb*, f. 65b (= *al-Durar al-saniyya*, 2:109).

Muḥammad confronted his community in the same manner, writing, "If a person were to have said [at the rise of Islam], 'I follow Muḥammad, and he has the truth, but I will not confront [*lā ata ʿarraḍu*] al-Lāt, al-ʿUzzā, Abū Jahl, and the likes of them; I have no obligation concerning them [*mā ʿalayya minhum*],' then his Islam would not be sound."[153] Al-Lāt and al-ʿUzzā were pagan deities in Mecca; Abū Jahl was one of the Prophet's fiercest opponents in Mecca during the early period of his preaching. The point of these examples was thus to show that without confronting (*taʿarruḍ*) these false idols and their worshippers—without showing them hatred and enmity—a person's Islam was not sound. Such was the example, in the view of Ibn ʿAbd al-Wahhāb, of the Prophet Muḥammad during the Meccan period of his preaching. Ibn ʿAbd al-Wahhāb was telling his followers to confront the present-day polytheists in the way that the early Muslims had confronted the pagan Arabs of Mecca. This did not involve violence, as *jihād* in the sense of warfare had not yet been allowed or prescribed for the early Muslims. In the *Kalimāt* epistle, then, it was verbal confrontation, not *jihād*, that Ibn ʿAbd al-Wahhāb was enjoining his followers to carry out.

This was not the only place where Ibn ʿAbd al-Wahhāb invoked the Prophet's conduct in Mecca to illustrate the duty of *al-walāʾ wa ʾl-barāʾ*. Another example comes in his epistle known as *Sittat mawāḍiʿ min al-sīra* (Six Episodes from the Prophetic Biography), which recounts six episodes intended to show the Prophet's emphasis on distinguishing between monotheists and polytheists.[154] The second episode concerns the moment when the Prophet began preaching openly in Mecca. According to the Islamic tradition, after the Prophet received his first revelation in 610, he preached in Mecca in a secretive fashion for approximately three years. Then, with the revelation of Q. 15:94, "Proclaim that which you are commanded and turn away from the polytheists," he came out openly with his message. In doing so, he began to disparage the religion of the pagan Meccans, who previously had been tolerant of the Prophet's preaching but now grew angry.[155] This is how Ibn ʿAbd al-Wahhāb relates the story:

> The second episode is that when he [i.e., the Prophet] began to warn them [i.e., the people of Mecca] against *shirk* and commanded them to observe

153. Ibid.

154. *al-Durar al-saniyya*, 8:111–19.

155. See the standard account in Ibn Hishām, *al-Sīra al-nabawiyya*, 1:262–65.

> the contrary of it, namely, *tawḥīd*, they did not detest this and they deemed it to be fine, speaking among themselves about joining it. This was until he began openly to revile their religion and declare their learned ones to be ignorant [*ilā an ṣarraḥa bi-sabb dīnihim wa-tajhīl ʿulamāʾihim*]. It was then that they rose up against him and his supporters in enmity, and said, "He has belittled our minds, disparaged our religion, and reviled our gods [*saf-faha aḥlāmanā wa-ʿāba dīnanā wa-shatama ālihatanā*]."[156]

What this episode illustrates, says Ibn ʿAbd al-Wahhāb, is that it is necessary for Muslims to antagonize the polytheists around them, just as the Prophet antagonized the polytheists of Mecca. Though his doing so meant that the Meccan notables would persecute him, the Prophet did not relent. "When you have come to know this matter," Ibn ʿAbd al-Wahhāb writes, "then you will know that a person's religion and Islam are not sound, even if he professes *tawḥīd* and eschews *shirk* [*wa-law waḥḥada ʾllāh wa-taraka ʾl-shirk*], unless he shows enmity to the polytheists and openly professes enmity and hatred of them [*illā bi-ʿadāwat al-mushrikīn wa ʾl-taṣrīḥ lahum bi ʾl-ʿadāwa wa ʾl-baghḍāʾ*]."[157] This line is followed by a partial quotation of Q. 58:22, which warns against showing love to the enemies of Islam: "You will not find any people who believe in God and the Last Day who love those who oppose God and His Messenger." In Ibn ʿAbd al-Wahhāb's view, then, if a person truly seeks to profess Islam, he must "openly profess enmity and hatred" of polytheists, even though doing so is likely to incur their wrath as it did in the case of the Prophet in Mecca. In many other places in his writings, he would similarly hold up the Prophet's preaching in Mecca as an instance of the normative display of hatred and enmity.[158]

It is possible that Ibn ʿAbd al-Wahhāb was influenced by Ibn al-Qayyim in seeing the Prophet's Meccan example in this way. In his book *Zād al-maʿād*, Ibn al-Qayyim similarly describes the Prophet's initial act of public preaching as the display of enmity. In Mecca, Ibn al-Qayyim writes, the Prophet "came out openly with his mission and openly confronted his people with enmity [*aʿlana ṣ bi ʾl-daʿwa wa-jāhara qawmahu bi ʾl-ʿadāwa*]."[159] This picture of the Prophet exhibiting enmity to the polytheists in Mecca does not

156. *al-Durar al-saniyya*, 8:113.

157. Ibid.

158. See, for instance, ibid., 9:376–77; Ibn ʿAbd al-Wahhāb, *Mukhtaṣar sīrat al-rasūl*, 21.

159. Ibn al-Qayyim, *Zād al-maʿād*, 1:84.

appear to have been a common portrayal of his early preaching, so it is possible that Ibn ʿAbd al-Wahhāb was led to see it this way by Ibn al-Qayyim. We know that Ibn ʿAbd al-Wahhāb read and appreciated *Zād al-maʿād*, as he quotes it throughout his prophetic biography and even composed an abridgment of it.[160] In any event, for Ibn al-Qayyim as for Ibn ʿAbd al-Wahhāb, the story of the Prophet's preaching in Mecca was not a story about enduring unwarranted persecution, as it is sometimes depicted, but, rather, a story about the obligation to be assertive and confrontational in professing Islam.

As noted before, Ibn ʿAbd al-Wahhāb was focused on the negative side of *al-walāʾ wa ʾl-barāʾ*. While he did occasionally refer to the other side of the formula, urging his followers to show love and loyalty to one another,[161] he was far more concerned that they show hatred and enmity to those seen as polytheists. Often when he brought up the issue of love and loyalty, it was to discourage showing these to any but true Muslims. In some of his writings, we find him emphasizing the prohibition against any such displays of affection to the enemies of Wahhābism, describing this behavior as *kufr*. As he warns Sulaymān ibn Suḥaym in a letter, "To show loyalty to the unbelievers is unbelief" (*muwālāt al-kuffār kufr*).[162] Ibn ʿAbd al-Wahhāb underscores a similar point in his epistle on the ten nullifiers of Islam, where the eighth nullifier appears as "supporting the polytheists and helping them against the Muslims" (*muẓāharat al-mushrikīn wa-muʿāwanatuhum ʿalā ʾl-Muslimīn*).[163] The word *Muslims* of course refers to the Wahhābīs.

Hijra

Related to the concept of *al-walāʾ wa ʾl-barāʾ* is the duty of *hijra* (emigration). Ibn ʿAbd al-Wahhāb was sometimes accused of requiring his followers to perform *hijra* to the territories under Wahhābī control, thus equating the area of the first Saudi state with the domain of Islam (*dār al-Islām*) and considering all other lands to be the domain of unbelief (*dār al-kufr*). In traditional Islamic jurisprudence, Muslims are indeed required, barring certain obstacles, to emigrate from *dār al-kufr* to *dār al-Islām*, the former defined as those lands in which the

160. Ibn ʿAbd al-Wahhāb, *Mukhtaṣar sīrat al-rasūl*, passim; Ibn ʿAbd al-Wahhāb, *Muʾallafāt al-shaykh*, *qism* 4 (*Mukhtaṣar Zād al-maʿād*).

161. See, e.g., *al-Durar al-saniyya*, 2:119.

162. Ibn Ghannām, *Tārīkh*, 1:394.

163. *al-Durar al-saniyya*, 10:92.

laws of unbelief (*aḥkām al-kufr*) predominate and the latter as those in which the laws of Islam (*aḥkām al-Islām*) predominate.[164] In his epistle *al-Uṣūl al-thalātha,* Ibn ʿAbd al-Wahhāb defines *hijra* as "migrating from the land of polytheism to the land of Islam" (*al-intiqāl min balad al-shirk ilā balad al-Islām*), adding that it "will remain [as a duty] until the arrival of the Hour."[165] While Ibn ʿAbd al-Wahhāb did not make *hijra* a sticking point in his preaching, it is clear that many of his followers did undertake *hijra* in the sense of leaving the domain of unbelief for the domain of Islam. One finds Ibn ʿAbd al-Wahhāb encouraging them to do so in his letters. In one of these, for example, he chides a correspondent in al-Aḥsāʾ for harboring doubts about leaving "the land of the polytheists" (*balad al-mushrikīn*), stating that the only acceptable excuse for not leaving is compulsion (*ikrāh*). Yet the compulsion, he says, must be truly onerous to acquit one of the obligation of *hijra.*[166]

The key issue for Ibn ʿAbd al-Wahhāb when it came to *hijra* was whether a person in the lands of unbelief or polytheism was able to manifest the religion (*iẓhār al-dīn*). As he writes in one of his epistles, a Muslim is permitted to stay in the domain of unbelief so long as he is able to manifest the religion, and the idea that he, Ibn ʿAbd al-Wahhāb, imposes *hijra* on those who are able to do so is a lie.[167] Exactly what is meant by *iẓhār al-dīn* is not fully explained, but in the context it is clear that he is referring to the mandatory display of hatred and enmity to polytheists. This understanding of *iẓhār al-dīn* is also suggested by Ibn ʿAbd al-Wahhāb in a brief commentary on Q. 10:104–5, in which God commands the Prophet, "[B]e thou not of the polytheists." Here Ibn ʿAbd al-Wahhāb underscores the importance of dissociating from polytheists and refers to the fact that it is necessary to perform *hijra* if one is unable to state openly that one is at war with the *ṭawāghīt* of one's land.[168] In other words, if a person cannot state clearly to the *ṭawāghīt* that he disapproves of them and is their enemy, then it is incumbent on him to perform *hijra.*

Subsequent generations of Wahhābī scholars would articulate this concept of *iẓhār al-dīn* more clearly. A good example comes in a *fatwā* by Ibn ʿAbd al-Wahhāb's sons Ḥusayn and ʿAbdallāh, who respond to a question about a

164. These were the dominant views of *hijra* and *dār al-kufr*/*dār al-Islām* in Sunnī Islamic jurisprudence; see Abou El Fadl, "Islamic Law and Muslim Minorities."

165. *al-Durar al-saniyya,* 1:134.

166. Ibn Ghannām, *Tārīkh,* 1:432–33 (letter to Aḥmad ibn ʿAbd al-Karīm).

167. *al-Durar al-saniyya,* 1:104.

168. Ibn Ghannām, *Tārīkh,* 1:598.

man who purports to love the religion but has failed to perform *hijra* on the grounds that doing so would be burdensome. The two scholars respond by saying that the person in question is still a Muslim "if he is able to manifest his religion in front of them [i.e., the polytheists], dissociating from them and the religion they profess and manifesting his rejection of them and his enmity for them." But if he cannot do so, and "if he is able to perform *hijra* but fails to do so, and dies among the polytheists, then we fear" that he has died an unbeliever.[169] Put otherwise, if the person in question is able to manifest the religion (*iẓhār al-dīn*) in the sense of showing hatred and enmity to the polytheists around him, then he need not perform *hijra*; but if he cannot manifest the religion in this way, then *hijra* is required.

Unlike Ibn ʿAbd al-Wahhāb and the later Wahhābī scholars, Ibn Taymiyya and Ibn al-Qayyim did not speak of *hijra* as a duty to be performed by Muslims living in areas where allegedly polytheistic practices were predominant and where Muslims were unable to show hatred and enmity to the perceived polytheists. To a large extent, this is because Ibn Taymiyya and Ibn al-Qayyim were more reluctant to pronounce *takfīr* on the individual professed Muslims in these areas, notwithstanding the presence of the cult of saints or other practices considered by them to be polytheistic. They did not dismiss broad swaths of professed Sunnī Muslims as unbelievers by dint of association with the cult of saints. Ibn ʿAbd al-Wahhāb and his followers did, and thus they demanded that Muslims exhibit hatred and enmity to these "polytheists" or else perform *hijra*.

In elaborating his concept of *al-walāʾ waʾl-barāʾ*, Ibn ʿAbd al-Wahhāb was influenced by the thinking and some of the words of Ibn Taymiyya and Ibn al-Qayyim, but his approach was distinct in its almost exclusive focus on the negative aspect of the concept and in its divisive method of implementation. The fact that he placed so much emphasis on the requirement to confront and antagonize so-called polytheists underscores the activist nature of his mission. From the very beginning it was a movement aimed at disrupting and unsettling the established order of things. Telling the people of Najd that their local saints were in fact *ṭawāghīt* and that those who venerated them were *mushrikūn* was provocative enough; urging his followers to show hatred

169. *al-Durar al-saniyya*, 12:455.

and enmity to them was even more incendiary. Ibn ʿAbd al-Wahhāb's ambition was revolutionary: he was seeking to demolish the religious status quo in Najd and reestablish in its place a commitment to true Islam as he understood it.

At the beginning of his mission, when he was preaching in Ḥuraymilāʾ and al-ʿUyayna, the required display of hatred and enmity took the form of verbal denunciation. To satisfy the requirement of showing hatred and enmity to polytheists, one had to confront them by verbally denouncing them, as Ibn ʿAbd al-Wahhāb believed was the example set by the Prophet Muḥammad in his early preaching in Mecca. Once Ibn ʿAbd al-Wahhāb's mission became enmeshed with the political project of the first Saudi state, however, the necessary confrontation with polytheists would involve *jihād* as well.

Jihād

While the literal meaning of *jihād* is "struggle," in the Islamic tradition it has long carried the sense of religious war against unbelievers. Ibn ʿAbd al-Wahhāb used it in this sense in calling for *jihād* against the opponents of the first Saudi state, the intention being to fight and conquer these unbelievers standing in the state's path and convert them to Islam. In this way, Ibn ʿAbd al-Wahhāb justified the *jihād* of the first Saudi state as a war for the purpose of spreading *tawḥīd* and eradicating *shirk*.

Jihād may be the component of Ibn ʿAbd al-Wahhāb's doctrine that owes the least to Ibn Taymiyya and Ibn al-Qayyim. However, there was one aspect of Ibn Taymiyya's approach to *jihād* that Ibn ʿAbd al-Wahhāb noticeably seized on. This was an argument made by Ibn Taymiyya in favor of *jihād* against the Mongols, an argument used to justify waging *jihād* against self-described Muslims.

Ibn Taymiyya and the Anti-Mongol Jihād

Much of what Ibn Taymiyya wrote about *jihād* was conventional. Consistent with the prevailing theory in Sunnī Islam at the time,[170] he distinguished two forms of *jihād*: (1) offensive *jihād* (*jihād al-ṭalab*) for the purpose of extending the realm of the faith and (2) defensive *jihād* (*jihād al-dafʿ*) for the purpose of defending Muslim territory from invading unbelievers. The former

170. Crone, *God's Rule*, 297–98, 363–73.

was understood as a collective duty (*farḍ kifāya*) for the Muslim *umma*, meaning that as long as some members of the *umma* were carrying it out, others were dispensed from it; the latter was understood as an individual duty (*farḍ ʿayn*), meaning that it was binding on all Muslims in or around the territory concerned. In his book *al-Siyāsa al-sharʿiyya* (Sharīʿa-Guided Policy), Ibn Taymiyya sets out this dichotomy in fairly conventional terms, calling offensive *jihād* war of choice (*qitāl ikhtiyār*) and defensive *jihād* war of necessity (*qitāl iḍṭirār*). Both, he states, are required by the faith.[171]

What is distinctive about his discussion of *jihād* here is the argument that Ibn Taymiyya makes for fighting those who refuse to observe one or more of the laws of Islam (*al-mumtaniʿīn ʿan baʿḍ al-sharāʾiʿ*).[172] "Any recalcitrant group [*ṭāʾifa mumtaniʿa*] that associates with Islam," he argues, "and refuses to observe one or more of its manifest and well-established laws [*wa ʾmtanaʿat ʿan baʿḍ sharāʾiʿihi ʾl-ẓāhira al-mutawātira*] must be opposed with *jihād* [*yajibu jihāduhā*], according to the general agreement of the Muslims, until the religion is God's entirely, as Abū Bakr al-Ṣiddīq and all of the Companions fought the withholders of the *zakāt*."[173] The term "withholders of the *zakāt*" (*māniʿū ʾl-zakāt*) refers to those professed Muslims in Arabia who, in the years following the death of the Prophet Muḥammad, refused to pay the *zakāt* to the Caliph Abū Bakr. Their argument was that with the death of the Prophet, it was no longer binding on them to pay the *zakāt* to the Muslim ruler in Medina. As Ibn Taymiyya relates, Abū Bakr deemed it necessary to fight these *zakāt* withholders despite their profession of Islam. Another example of a recalcitrant group (*ṭāʾifa mumtaniʿa*) mentioned by Ibn Taymiyya here is the Khārijites, whose recalcitrance consisted in their refusal to recognize ʿAlī as the legitimate caliph after ʿUthmān.[174] The point that Ibn Taymiyya was underscoring here is that these recalcitrant groups, though they professed Islam, were nonetheless legitimate targets of *jihād*. Summing up his discussion, he writes: "It is established by the Book, the *sunna*, and the consensus of the *umma* that those who depart from the Sharīʿa of Islam [*man kharaja ʿan sharīʿat al-Islām*] are to be fought, even if they pronounce the confession of faith."[175]

171. Ibn Taymiyya, *al-Siyāsa al-sharʿiyya*, 163–64; cf. Ibn al-Qayyim, *al-Furūsiyya al-Muḥammadiyya*, 121–24.

172. Ibn Taymiyya, *al-Siyāsa al-sharʿiyya*, 163.

173. Ibid., 160–61.

174. Ibid., 161–62.

175. Ibid., 162.

While Ibn Taymiyya does not say so here, his emphasis on the duty to wage *jihād* against these recalcitrant groups was closely related to his argument for *jihād* against the Mongols, an issue that preoccupied him and on which he wrote at length. In the years 699–702/1299–1303, the Mongol Īlkhānid dynasty, led by Ghāzān Khān (r. 694–703/1295–1304), staged three invasions of Syria, occupying Damascus for several months in 699–700/1300. A final invasion took place in 712/1312–13, during the reign of Öljeitü (r. 703–16/1304–16). Ibn Taymiyya was highly active in encouraging the Mamlūk Sultanate's resistance to these invaders, at one point traveling to Egypt to plead for reinforcements and at another preaching among soldiers and even taking up arms himself. In three extant *fatwās*, he provided extensive religious justification for waging *jihād* against the Mongols.[176] The reason such justification was necessary was that the Mongols had recently embraced Islam, and in Islamic law it is generally forbidden to wage *jihād* against fellow Muslims. In 694/1295, Ghāzān Khān converted to Islam, and with his accession the Īlkhānate became a Sunnī Muslim state. His campaigns were even carried out in the name of Islam. All of this made some Mamlūk soldiers uneasy about fighting the Mongol army. Ibn Taymiyya's response was that these reservations were unfounded, as the Mongols did not sufficiently adhere to Islam.

In the first of these three *fatwās*, which was written in response to the first series of Mongol invasions, Ibn Taymiyya argues that the Mongols are not fighting on behalf of Islam but, rather, on behalf of the Īlkhānate, and he accuses them of neglecting many or most of the laws of Islam (*kathīran min sharāʾiʿ al-Islām aw akhtarahā*).[177] Without getting into the specifics regarding what they have neglected, he casts the Mongols as a recalcitrant group (*ṭāʾifa mumtaniʿa*), asserting that such a group must be fought when it fails to observe one or more of the manifest and well-established obligations of Islam (*baʿḍ wājibāt al-Islām al-ẓāhira al-mutawātira*), such as prayer, paying the *zakāt*, observing the Ramaḍān fast, and judging according to the Book and the *sunna*, among other things.[178] He goes on to compare the Mongols with the withholders of the *zakāt* and the Khārijites.[179] With regard to the withholders of the *zakāt*, he relates a story about ʿUmar ibn al-Khaṭṭāb's dispute

176. Ibn Taymiyya, *Majmūʿ fatāwā*, 28:544–53, 501–8, 509–43 (chronological order). On Ibn Taymiyya and the Mongols, including these *fatwās*, see Hoover, *Ibn Taymiyya*, 12–18, 30–31.

177. Ibn Taymiyya, *Majmūʿ fatāwā*, 28:551, 544.

178. Ibid., 28:545.

179. Ibid., 28:545–46.

with Abū Bakr over the legitimacy of fighting them. In this story, ʿUmar, who would succeed Abū Bakr as caliph, objected to fighting those withholding the *zakāt* on the grounds that the Prophet had said: "I was commanded to fight people until they say, 'there is no god but God.' Whosoever says it secures his property and his person from me except as required by Islam, and his accounting will be with God." To this Abū Bakr retorts that the *zakāt* is required by Islam. Thereupon ʿUmar concedes the point, acknowledging that Abū Bakr is right and that fighting those who withhold the *zakāt* is allowed and necessary.[180] After relating this story, Ibn Taymiyya turns to the story of ʿAlī and the Khārijites, explaining that ʿAlī fought the Khārijites despite their profession of Islam. On the analogy with the withholders of the *zakāt* and the Khārijites, Ibn Taymiyya asserts, the Mongols ought to be opposed in *jihād*, for the Mongols are in fact worse than these other recalcitrant groups, being even more in breach of the Sharīʿa (*aʿẓam khurūjan ʿan sharīʿat al-Islām*).[181] Whoever doubts that the Mongols should be fought, he concludes, is among the most ignorant of people concerning the religion (*ajhal al-nās bi-dīn al-Islām*).[182]

In the second anti-Mongol *fatwā*, also written in response to the first series of invasions, Ibn Taymiyya makes many of the same arguments, describing the Mongols as being in revolt against Islam (*khārijūn ʿan al-Islām*) and placing them in the same category as the withholders of the *zakāt* and the Khārijites.[183] He is more specific this time, however, in describing those aspects of Islam that they have allegedly neglected. The Mongols, he writes,

> do not wage *jihād* against the unbelievers, they do not impose the poll tax [*al-jizya*] or humiliation on the People of the Book, they do not prohibit any of their soldiers from worshipping what they please of the sun, the moon, or other things. . . . Most of them do not observe the religious obligations [*al-wājibāt*], neither prayer, nor the *zakāt*, nor the *ḥajj*, nor other things, and they do not judge among themselves in accordance with the judgment of God; rather they judge according to their customs [*bi-awḍāʿ lahum*] that sometimes accord with Islam and sometimes contradict it.[184]

180. al-Bukhārī, *Ṣaḥīḥ*, 273 (*Kitāb al-zakāt, bāb wujūb al-zakāt*, nos. 1399–1400). There are numerous narrations of this *ḥadīth*; Ibn Taymiyya only paraphrases it here.

181. Ibn Taymiyya, *Majmūʿ fatāwā*, 28:546.

182. Ibid.

183. Ibid., 28:503–4.

184. Ibid., 28:505.

In the third *fatwā*, which was written during the later Mongol invasion of 712/1312–13, Ibn Taymiyya again condemns the Mongols for failing to apply the Sharīʿa and using their own legal code. This local code he identifies by name—the *yāsā*. The Mongols, he states, are observing "the laws of the polytheists, such as the *yāsā* of Genghis Khān, king of the polytheists" (*aḥkām al-mushrikīn ka-yāsā Jankaskhān malik al-mushrikīn*).[185] While he does not delve into the content of the *yāsā*, he indicates that it is specific to Genghis Khān and that the Mongols are fighting people to bring them into accord with it.[186] This third *fatwā*, in addition to being the most detailed of the three in its legal argumentation, is also the harshest in its judgment concerning the Mongols generally. Ibn Taymiyya provides some personal observations of Mongol iniquity and irreligiosity, describing how the Mongol army neither prays nor has preachers among it.[187] He also indicates that the Mongols are apostates from Islam. While he does not say this outright, he compares them, as before, with the withholders of the *zakāt*, whom he states here were apostates (*murtaddīn*) given that they did not have a valid excuse (*shubha sāʾigha*) for refusing to pay the *zakāt*.[188] Later he reinforces the point, noting that the earliest Muslim (*salaf*) called the withholders of the *zakāt* apostates.[189] All of this strongly suggests that Ibn Taymiyya put the Mongols in the same category. Whatever the case, his vision of a Mongol-dominated Middle East was a dark one indeed. If the Mongol campaigns were to succeed, he concludes, it would mean "the decline of Islam and the obliteration of its laws" (*zawāl dīn al-Islām wa-durūs sharāʾiʿihi*).[190] The Mongols may have professed Islam, but as far as Ibn Taymiyya was concerned they represented a threat to Islam and the Sharīʿa, and so it was incumbent on true Muslims to fight them.

One of Ibn Taymiyya's students, Ibn Kathīr, likewise condemned the Mongols for adopting the *yāsā*, though he was even clearer in pronouncing *takfīr* on them. His condemnation comes in his exegesis of the Qurʾān, in a commentary on Q. 5:50, "Is it the judgment of pagan ignorance that they are seeking [*a-fa ḥukm al-jāhiliyya yabghūna*]? Yet who is fairer in judgment than God,

185. Ibid., 28:530. For the correct reading of the Arabic text (as *ka-yāsā*, not *kanāʾis*), see Michot, "Un important témoin," 346.

186. Ibn Taymiyya, *Majmūʿ fatāwā*, 28:522.

187. Ibid., 28:520.

188. Ibid., 28:519.

189. Ibid., 28:530–31.

190. Ibid., 28:531.

for a people having sure faith?" Here Ibn Kathīr identifies the *yāsā* as a modern-day example of the "judgment of pagan ignorance" (*ḥukm al-jāhiliyya*) mentioned in the Qur'ān. The Mongols, he writes, "give priority to it [*yuqaddimūnahā*] over judging by God's Book and the *sunna* of His Messenger. Whosoever does this among them is an unbeliever who must be fought until he returns to the judgment of God and His Messenger."[191] Ibn Kathīr's basis for fighting the Mongols was thus their refusal to judge by God's law. Ibn Taymiyya's rationale included this but was broader. For him, the basis for *jihād* against the Mongols was not only their adherence to the *yāsā* but also their refusal to comply with any of the "manifest and well-established" obligations of the faith, which included prayer and paying the *zakāt*.

Invoking the Anti-Mongol Jihād

Ibn ʿAbd al-Wahhāb's approach to *jihād* would change over time, depending on the circumstances. At the very beginning of his mission, he did not advocate *jihād* against his opponents, rather, calling for verbal confrontation with them; then, upon moving to al-Dirʿiyya, he justified *jihād* against them as defensive warfare, arguing that the Wahhābīs were only fighting in self-defense; later on, he called for offensive *jihād* against his opponents, seeing this as legitimate warfare for promoting *tawḥīd* and eradicating *shirk*.[192] In the final stage, his endorsement of offensive *jihād* was effectively an endorsement of the expansion of the first Saudi state. It was in justifying this that he drew on some of Ibn Taymiyya's arguments for fighting the Mongols, in particular the argument concerning Abū Bakr and the withholders of the *zakāt*. What was attractive to him about this was the justification it provided for fighting those who affirm their faith in Islam.

In *Mufīd al-mustafīd*, the epistle that he wrote in 1167/1753f in the lead-up to the conquest of Ḥuraymilāʾ, Ibn ʿAbd al-Wahhāb would paraphrase several parts of Ibn Taymiyya's third anti-Mongol *fatwā*. In doing so, his purpose was to show that Ibn Taymiyya, contrary to the claims of anti-Wahhābī refuters, pronounced *takfīr* on professed Muslims and endorsed *jihād* against them. Those parts of the *fatwā* that he paraphrases include the story of Abū Bakr making the case for fighting the withholders of the *zakāt*,[193] Ibn Taymiyya's

191. Ibn Kathīr, *Tafsīr al-Qurʾān al-ʿaẓīm*, 3:131.

192. For more on this progression, see chapter 4.

193. Ibn Ghannām, *Tārīkh*, 2:713; cf. Ibn Taymiyya, *Majmūʿ fatāwā*, 28:519.

argument that the withholders of the *zakāt* were fought on account of their refraining from one of the obligations of the faith,[194] and his statement that the *salaf* called the Mongols apostates.[195] Ibn ʿAbd al-Wahhāb does not reproduce any of Ibn Taymiyya's exact words, meaning possibly that he did not have a copy of the *fatwā* at hand. Nonetheless, he faithfully paraphrases these parts of the *fatwā*, the difference being that he places more emphasis on the apostasy of the withholders of the *zakāt* than Ibn Taymiyya did. He even attributes to Ibn Taymiyya the following words: "Their unbelief and their inclusion among the apostates was established by the general agreement of the Companions in accordance with the proof texts of the Book and the *sunna*."[196] Ibn Taymiyya did not write this, but he did refer twice to the apostasy of the withholders of the *zakāt* in his *fatwā*. That may have left an impression on Ibn ʿAbd al-Wahhāb, who considered the case of Abū Bakr and the withholders of the *zakāt* strong evidence in favor of his approach to *takfīr* and *jihād*.[197]

This was hardly the only time Ibn ʿAbd al-Wahhāb referred to the case of Abū Bakr and the withholders of the *zakāt* in justifying his approach to *jihād*. Another example comes in an epistle that takes the form of a brief history of the struggle between Islam and unbelief, from Adam to the time of the Mongol invasions.[198] The case of Abū Bakr and the withholders of the *zakāt* is the first of several examples that he cites as part of an effort to prove that it can be perfectly legitimate to excommunicate and fight those who profess Islam. This was meant as a rebuke to his scholarly enemies who contended that those who say "there is no god but God" are Muslims whose blood and property are safe.[199] The last of the examples that he cites in this text is the story of the Mongols (*qiṣṣat al-tatār*). Though the Mongols converted to Islam, Ibn ʿAbd al-Wahhāb writes, "they did not act in accordance with their religious obligations and they manifested things indicating their departure from the Sharīʿa [*wa-aẓharū*

194. Ibn Ghannām, *Tārīkh*, 2:713 (*al-mubīḥ lil-qitāl mujarrad al-manʿ lā jaḥd al-wujūb*); cf. Ibn Taymiyya, *Majmūʿ fatāwā*, 28:519 (*wa-hum yuqātalūnu ʿalā manʿihā wa-in aqarrū biʾl-wujūb*).

195. Ibn Ghannām, *Tārīkh*, 2:713 (*wa-sammūhum jamīʿahum ahl al-ridda*); cf. Ibn Taymiyya, *Majmūʿ fatāwā*, 28:530–31 (*kāna ʾl-salaf qad sammū māniʿī ʾl-zakāt murtaddīn*).

196. Ibn Ghannām, *Tārīkh*, 2:713.

197. Ibid.

198. *al-Durar al-saniyya*, 9:353–96, at 384–86. This epistle also appears as the preface to Ibn ʿAbd al-Wahhāb's prophetic biography; see Ibn ʿAbd al-Wahhāb, *Mukhtaṣar sīrat al-rasūl*, 3–35.

199. *al-Durar al-saniyya*, 9:386.

ashyā' min al-khurūj 'an al-sharī'a]."[200] For this reason, even though they uttered the confession of faith and prayed, "the scholars pronounced *takfīr* on them, fought them, and raided them until God removed them from the lands of the Muslims."[201] The scholars mentioned here are not identified by Ibn 'Abd al-Wahhāb, but one can safely assume that Ibn Taymiyya and Ibn Kathīr were foremost in mind.

The case of the Mongols, to be clear, was not a prominent theme in Ibn 'Abd al-Wahhāb's arguments for *jihād*. It was not often that he invoked Ibn Taymiyya's anti-Mongol *fatwās*,[202] though he did often bring up the case of Abū Bakr and the withholders of the *zakāt* as evidence in favor of fighting those who profess Islam.[203] For this he was indebted to Ibn Taymiyya.

Eradicating Shirk

Ibn 'Abd al-Wahhāb's greater rationale for waging *jihād* against his opponents, the enemies of the first Saudi state, was that it was justified as part of a general campaign for the eradication of *shirk*. The Qur'ānic verse that he frequently cited in this regard is Q. 8:39: "And fight them till there is no *fitna* and the religion is God's entirely" (*wa-qātilūhum ḥattā lā takūna fitna wa-yakūna 'l-dīn kulluhu lillāh*). The Arabic word *fitna* admits of a number of meanings, including "trial" and "temptation," but the one that Ibn 'Abd al-Wahhāb and his followers would emphasize is *shirk*. As Ibn Kathīr notes in his Qur'ān commentary, a number of the early exegetes understood the phrase "till there is no *fitna*" (*ḥattā lā takūna fitna*) in Q. 8:39 to mean "till there is no *shirk*" (*ḥattā lā yakūna shirk*).[204] In line with this view, Ibn 'Abd al-Wahhāb and his followers would gloss *fitna* as *shirk*, interpreting Q. 8:39 as a license to wage *jihād* for the purpose of eliminating polytheism wherever it is found. An example of this reading is found in a response to a question

200. Ibid., 9:394.

201. Ibid.

202. I know of no other case of him doing so besides *Mufīd al-mustafīd*. His grandson Sulaymān ibn 'Abdallāh Āl al-Shaykh (d. 1233/1818) would quote from the second of Ibn Taymiyya's anti-Mongol *fatwās* in his commentary on *Kitāb al-tawḥīd*; see Āl al-Shaykh, *Taysīr al-'azīz al-ḥamīd*, 1:295–96.

203. For further examples, see Ibn Ghannām, *Tārīkh*, 1:435 (letter to Aḥmad ibn 'Abd al-Karīm); *al-Durar al-saniyya*, 1:98, 2:47.

204. Ibn Kathīr, *Tafsīr al-Qur'ān al-'aẓīm*, 4:56.

about what the Wahhābīs are prohibiting their enemies from doing. Ibn ʿAbd al-Wahhāb answers: "We have prohibited them from committing *shirk* [*nahaynāhum ʿan al-shirk*] . . . and we are fighting them on account of it [*wa-nuqātiluhum ʿalayhi*], as God says, 'And fight them till there is no *fitna*,' that is, *shirk*, 'and the religion is God's entirely' (Q. 8:39)."[205] In several other *rasāʾil*, Ibn ʿAbd al-Wahhāb invokes Q. 8:39 in this way.[206] The next generations of Wahhābīs would likewise emphasize the meaning of *fitna* as *shirk* in discussions of the purpose of *jihād*. For example, Sulaymān ibn ʿAbdallāh Āl al-Shaykh, in a brief explanation of Q. 8:39 in his commentary on *Kitāb al-tawḥīd*, writes that "*fitna* here is *shirk*; thus [God] indicates that if *shirk* exists, fighting persists . . . even if they say 'there is no god but God.'"[207]

Interestingly, the Wahhābī reading of *fitna* as *shirk* in Q. 8:39 does not seem to come from Ibn Taymiyya. The latter does not appear to have emphasized this reading,[208] which makes sense given his view that unbelief alone is not a sufficient justification for *jihād*. As he writes in *al-Siyāsa al-sharʿiyya*: "Fighting is to be done against those who fight us when we seek to manifest God's religion. . . . Those who do not prevent the Muslims from establishing God's religion, their unbelief is a harm only to themselves."[209] While Ibn Taymiyya certainly endorsed the idea of offensive *jihād*, he did not make this out to be warfare for the purpose of eliminating *shirk*. Rather, offensive *jihād* in his view was warfare for the purpose of establishing God's religion, that is, expanding the area of the world under the rule of God's law. So long as unbelievers did not interfere with this, they were not to be fought. The Wahhābī approach to *jihād* was more proactive. Those who manifested *shirk* were to be fought on that basis; no further rationale was needed.

205. *al-Durar al-saniyya*, 1:95–96 (letter to Aḥmad al-Bakbalī, co-authored with ʿAbd al-ʿAzīz ibn Muḥammad Āl Suʿūd).

206. See, e.g., Ibn Ghannām, *Tārīkh*, 1:339 (letter to Muḥammad ibn ʿĪd), 426 (letter to Aḥmad ibn Ibrāhīm).

207. Āl al-Shaykh, *Taysīr al-ʿazīz al-ḥamīd*, 1:291.

208. One exception is Ibn Taymiyya, *Qāʿida fī ʾl-maḥabba*, 158–59.

209. Ibn Taymiyya, *al-Siyāsa al-sharʿiyya*, 158–60. For a more elaborate argument in this regard, see Ibn Taymiyya, *Qāʿida mukhtaṣara fī qitāl al-kuffār*. The attribution of this text has been contested, but the editor demonstrates that nearly every argument made here regarding *jihād* can be found in Ibn Taymiyya's other works. For more on this text, see al-Kharāshī, *Aqwāl al-ʿulamāʾ*; Crone, "No Compulsion in Religion," 141–42; Zaman, *Modern Islamic Thought in a Radical Age*, 265–66, 304–5.

The Escalation of Enmity

In addition to justifying offensive *jihād* in terms of eliminating *shirk*, Ibn ʿAbd al-Wahhāb also justified it as part of the duty to manifest hatred and enmity to polytheists. In his *Kalimāt* epistle, written before the introduction of *jihād* into his movement, he describes the duty to confront polytheists in terms of the Prophet's confrontation of the pagan Arabs—that is, verbal confrontation. But as the first Saudi state expanded, this duty to confront polytheists broadened to include physical confrontation as well. In other words, the duty to show polytheists hatred and enmity now encompassed waging *jihād* against them.

The first indication of the escalation of enmity to the level of *jihād* is found in *Mufīd al-mustafīd*, in which Ibn ʿAbd al-Wahhāb presents *al-walāʾ waʾl-barāʾ* and *jihād* as complementary duties. In one passage, he brings enmity and *jihād* together, saying, "The essence of the divine revelation and the prophetic mission is unifying God through worshipping Him alone without partner and destroying idols [*wa-kasr al-awthān*]; and it is well known that destroying them is not sound without displaying severe enmity and drawing the sword [*illā bi-shiddat al-ʿadāwa wa-tajrīd al-sayf*]."[210] Later on, stressing the importance of showing enmity to polytheists, he remarks: "May God have mercy on him who considers and reflects upon the command received by Muḥammad from God to show enmity to those who commit *shirk*, near or far, to pronounce *takfīr* on them, and to fight them 'till the religion is God's entirely' (Q. 8:39)."[211] Ibn ʿAbd al-Wahhāb was thus presenting *jihād* as a fundamental duty, together with *takfīr* and the display of enmity. These were the ways that God had commanded the Prophet to confront the unbelievers of his time, and so they were the ways that the Wahhābīs must confront their polytheist enemies. Another good example of Ibn ʿAbd al-Wahhāb linking the duty of *ʿadāwa* and *jihād* comes in an epistle discussing what the Wahhābīs command and prohibit. Outlining the duties incumbent on Muslims, he quotes Q. 60:4, the verse concerning Abraham's dissociation from his people, and puts a violent spin on it:

> One should know that if [a believer] is to follow the Messenger, then incumbent on him are dissociating from this [i.e., *shirk*], directing worship

210. Ibn Ghannām, *Tārīkh*, 2:699.

211. Ibid., 2:711.

> exclusively to God, rejecting it and those who commit it, condemning those who practice it, showing them hatred and enmity, and waging *jihād* against them until the religion becomes God's entirely, as He says, "You have had a good example in Abraham, and those with him, when they said to their people, 'We dissociate from you and that which you worship apart from God'" (Q. 60:4).[212]

Here Ibn ʿAbd al-Wahhāb reads into the "good example" of Abraham a call to arms, *jihād* being the natural extension of showing hatred and enmity. The distinction between *ʿadāwa* and *jihād* is effectively collapsed.

These examples give the lie to the idea that the Wahhābī founder was exclusively concerned with *al-walāʾ wa ʾl-barāʾ* in a social sense. While it has been argued that Ibn ʿAbd al-Wahhāb's emphasis on the "principle of separation" (that is, *al-walāʾ wa ʾl-barāʾ* in its negative aspect) was restricted to the social sphere and that it was later Wahhābī scholars who extended it to the political sphere,[213] in fact Ibn ʿAbd al-Wahhāb's emphasis on showing hatred and enmity was both social and political. While it is true that at the very beginning of his movement he was focused only on disrupting Najdī religious culture, this was rife with political implications, and his movement quickly took on a political dimension. For most of his career, he was preaching the necessity of showing hatred and enmity to polytheists, and fighting them in *jihād*, in the context of supporting the first Saudi state. A similar argument holds that Ibn ʿAbd al-Wahhāb "was essentially apolitical" and that his movement was "manipulated toward political ends" by the Āl Suʿūd.[214] This idea seems to derive from the fact that Ibn ʿAbd al-Wahhāb seldom wrote about politics explicitly, yet it ignores the fact that he wrote frequently about *jihād*. There is no evidence to suggest that he was being manipulated into promoting the interests of the Saudi state, which he believed was spreading the message of true Islam across Arabia. Indeed, as will be seen in the next chapter, there is no reason to believe that the Āl Suʿūd were motivated only by secular political ambition.

The generations of Wahhābī scholars after Ibn ʿAbd al-Wahhāb would similarly blur the line between *ʿadāwa* and *jihād* in their writings, and sometimes they would even equate the two terms. Sulaymān ibn ʿAbdallāh Āl

212. *al-Durar al-saniyya*, 1:146.

213. Wagemakers, "Enduring Legacy of the Second Saudi State," 95.

214. Dallal, *Islam Without Europe*, 35, 6; cf. Dallal, "Origins and Objectives of Islamic Revivalist Thought," 349–50.

al-Shaykh, for example, in his commentary on *Kitāb al-tawḥīd*, explains the meaning of showing enmity for the sake of God (*al-muʿādāt fīhi*) as "manifesting enmity in deed [*iẓhār al-ʿadāwa bi ʾl-fiʿl*], such as *jihād* against the enemies of God and dissociation from them [*ka ʾl-jihād li-aʿdāʾ Allāh wa ʾl-barāʾa minhum*]."[215] His cousin ʿAbd al-Raḥmān ibn Ḥasan Āl al-Shaykh took the same approach. In a brief commentary on one of Ibn ʿAbd al-Wahhāb's epistles, he quotes some of the Qurʾānic verses enjoining *jihād* in explaining the duty to show enmity:

> His words, "and showing enmity for the sake of it [i.e., *tawḥīd*]": As God says, "then kill them wherever you find them, and take them, and confine them, and lie in wait for them at every place of ambush" (Q. 9:5). The verses concerning this are many in number, such as His words, "And fight them till there is no *fitna* and the religion is God's entirely" (Q. 8:39), *fitna* meaning *shirk*.[216]

This statement may be seen as the epitome of the Wahhābī approach to *jihād*: *fitna* glossed as *shirk*, and *ʿadāwa* glossed as *jihād*.[217]

It should be noted that Ibn Taymiyya does anticipate this understanding of *ʿadāwa* as *jihād* in at least one of his writings, a short work published as *Qāʿida fī ʾl-maḥabba* (A Principle Concerning Love). Here he writes that *jihād* is one of the duties that stems from the larger duty to love God, in addition to showing hatred and enmity to the enemies of God. For Ibn Taymiyya, then, the concept of *al-walāʾ wa ʾl-barāʾ* did encompass *jihād*. As he writes, "[T]he love of God requires *jihād* in the way of Him,"[218] and from the context it is clear that he is talking about *jihād* as warfare. At one point he even explains Abraham's dissociation from his people and their *shirk* by quoting Q. 8:39, thus clearly linking Abraham's display of hatred and enmity to fighting.[219] It is possible that Ibn ʿAbd al-Wahhāb was influenced by reading this text or another like it, but more likely he came to connect *ʿadāwa* to *jihād* on his own. *Qāʿida fī ʾl-maḥabba* is a rare text, and Ibn Taymiyya does

215. Āl al-Shaykh, *Taysīr al-ʿazīz al-ḥamīd*, 2:962.

216. *al-Durar al-saniyya*, 2:205.

217. For an extensive treatment of the relationship between *ʿadāwa* and *jihād* in traditional Wahhābī thought, which has informed my views here, see al-Sanad, *Juhūd ʿulamāʾ Najd fī taqrīr al-walāʾ wa ʾl-barāʾ*, 334–431.

218. Ibn Taymiyya, *Qāʿida fī ʾl-maḥabba*, 165, 162.

219. Ibid., 158.

not seem to have drawn this connection elsewhere.[220] Perhaps the connection between *ʿadāwa* and *jihād* was not such a great conceptual leap.

———

In their approach to *jihād,* Ibn ʿAbd al-Wahhāb and his followers were not following the lead of Ibn Taymiyya. While Ibn ʿAbd al-Wahhāb found some inspiration in Ibn Taymiyya's anti-Mongol *fatwās,* especially with regard to the example of Abū Bakr fighting the withholders of the *zakāt,* for the most part he was not reciting Ibn Taymiyya's views on *jihād* or expanding on them. The main feature of his approach to *jihād* was the view that wherever *shirk* is found, *jihād* is warranted. The perceived existence of *shirk* in a given place gave the Wahhābīs carte blanche to wage offensive *jihād.* This is not something that Ibn Taymiyya's words would seem to support. Nor was the escalation of enmity a view that he commonly espoused.

Conclusion

As the foregoing has sought to show, Ibn ʿAbd al-Wahhāb's doctrine cannot be understood without reference to Ibn Taymiyya and Ibn al-Qayyim. The four main components of Ibn ʿAbd al-Wahhāb's doctrine depended, albeit to varying degrees, on the ideas of these scholars. Ibn ʿAbd al-Wahhāb adopted Ibn Taymiyya's conception of two *tawḥīds, tawḥīd al-rubūbiyya* and *tawḥīd al-ulūhiyya,* as the means for distinguishing between true and false Muslims. He pronounced *takfīr* on those participating in the cult of saints on the grounds that they failed to meet the conditions of *tawḥīd al-ulūhiyya.* Ibn ʿAbd al-Wahhāb also followed Ibn Taymiyya in conceiving of the different elements of *al-walāʾ wa ʾl-barāʾ* as conditions of *tawḥīd al-ulūhiyya,* and in this way he argued that those who fail to show hatred and enmity to polytheists have not sufficiently professed Islam. With regard to *jihād,* he borrowed Ibn Taymiyya's example of Abū Bakr and the withholders of the *zakāt,* which was intended to show that professed Muslims could indeed be fought in *jihād.* But for the most part, his approach to *jihād* was not Taymiyyan in inspiration. Some of Ibn ʿAbd

220. As far as I have been able to tell, Ibn al-Qayyim did not make this connection. It is perhaps significant, however, that Ibn Rajab did. See Ibn Rajab, *Majmūʿ rasāʾil,* 3:322 (*al-jihād fī sabīl Allāh . . . min tamām muʿādāt aʿdāʾ Allāh alladhī tastalzimuhu ʾl-maḥabba*); noted in al-Sanad, *Juhūd ʿulamāʾ Najd fī taqrīr al-walāʾ wa ʾl-barāʾ*, 334.

al-Wahhāb's doctrinal views, it should be noted, seem to derive solely from Ibn al-Qayyim. These include Ibn ʿAbd al-Wahhāb's view of himself and his followers as the *ghurabāʾ*, his view that the masses (*ʿāmma*) ought to learn the basics of the religion from the sources of revelation directly, and his view that the Prophet's public preaching in Mecca was exemplary of the display of hatred and enmity.

But as much as Ibn ʿAbd al-Wahhāb depended on Ibn Taymiyya and Ibn al-Qayyim in formulating his doctrine, he also departed from them in significant ways. In the case of *tawḥīd*, he added his own polemical flourishes to Ibn Taymiyya's two-*ṭawḥīd* schema, and he put all these ideas together in catechisms fit for mass consumption and even memorization. With respect to *takfīr*, unlike Ibn Taymiyya and Ibn al-Qayyim, he rejected *iqāmat al-ḥujja* and *al-ʿudhr bi ʾl-jahl* as inapplicable in the case of the cult of saints, resulting in a greater willingness to pronounce *takfīr* on individuals seen as committing *shirk*. As regards *al-walāʾ wa ʾl-barāʾ*, he followed Ibn Taymiyya and Ibn al-Qayyim in emphasizing that true Muslims must show hatred and enmity to polytheists, but unlike them he believed that Muslims ought to show hatred and enmity to the participants in the cult of saints, regarding such worshippers as unbelievers who are not excused on the basis of ignorance. Finally, regarding *jihād*, he conceived of the basis of offensive *jihād* as the eradication of *shirk*—something Ibn Taymiyya's words do not appear to support—and he went his own way in extending the duty of enmity to a duty of *jihād*.

As one can see, all of Ibn ʿAbd al-Wahhāb's departures from Ibn Taymiyya and Ibn al-Qayyim were in a more radical direction. The most significant of these was his more expansive approach to *takfīr*, which had implications for *ʿadāwa* and *jihād* as well. The unhindered practice of *takfīr* meant that Ibn ʿAbd al-Wahhāb, unlike Ibn Taymiyya and Ibn al-Qayyim, judged vast swaths of professed Muslims to be unbelievers, and this allowed him to brandish *ʿadāwa* and *jihād* at a much wider set of targets than Ibn Taymiyya and Ibn al-Qayyim ever did. Though he could be misleading or inconsistent in explaining his approach to *takfīr*, there is no question that Ibn ʿAbd al-Wahhāb indulged the practice to a degree unsupported by his Ḥanbalī forebears.

Excursus: Wahhābism and Early Modern Islamic Revivalism

Wahhābism emerged in a relatively remote environment and does not appear to have been inspired by any other contemporary movement in Islam. It has nonetheless been a common practice for historians to compare Wahhābism with other revivalist or reformist Islamic movements of the early modern period, namely, the seventeenth to eighteenth centuries. This was a period when a number of Muslim scholars were seeking to revive or reform Islam in various locales: Shāh Walī Allāh (d. 1176/1762) in India, Ibn al-Amīr al-Ṣanʿānī (d. 1182/1769) and Muḥammad ibn ʿAlī al-Shawkānī (d. 1250/1839) in Yemen, ʿUsman dan Fodio (d. 1232/1817) in Nigeria, and Muḥammad ʿAlī al-Sanūsī (d. 1276/1859) in Algeria, among others.

In the debate over Wahhābism's relationship to these other movements, the prevailing view has shifted dramatically in the last few decades. Previously, it was common for academics to assume that Wahhābism belonged to a broader revivalist trend, one that it both inaugurated and typified. Marshall Hodgson, for example, the great American historian of Islam, writes to this effect in his *The Venture of Islam*, claiming that Wahhābism "inspired a number of other movements in other areas. Numerous pilgrims who came to Arabia during its ascendancy learned of its principles and were enthused by its militancy."[221] This thesis was lent further support in the 1970s by the work of John Voll, who sought to establish the connections between these movements by tracing their scholarly networks. Ibn ʿAbd al-Wahhāb, he concluded, was part of a broader network of revivalist scholars: "[O]ne can place the founder of the Wahhābī movement in a world of Islamic revivalism that stretches from Indonesia to Africa."[222] The basis of this conclusion was not so much the assumed doctrinal affinities between them but, rather, the existence of teacher-student relationships. For instance, Voll made much of the fact that Muḥammad Ḥayāt al-Sindī in Medina was a teacher of Ibn ʿAbd al-Wahhāb's. He even discerned a link between Ibn ʿAbd al-Wahhāb and the Indian reformer Shāh Walī Allāh on the grounds that the latter had studied with one of al-Sindī's teachers.[223] Voll's theory was weak, however, and it soon came under attack.

The idea of a broader revivalist trend inspired by Wahhābism was thoroughly refuted in the 1990s by Ahmad Dallal, who regretted that this thesis had "gained wide currency among scholars of modern Islam."[224] In a detailed study of the ideas of four revivalist thinkers—Walī Allāh, Dan Fodio, al-Sanūsī, and Ibn ʿAbd al-Wahhāb—he showed that each man represented a more or less distinct intellectual trend, rightly dismissing the idea that common links

221. Hodgson, *Venture of Islam*, 3:161.

222. Voll, "Muḥammad Ḥayyā al-Sindī and Muḥammad ibn ʿAbd al-Wahhāb," 39.

223. Ibid.

224. Dallal, "Origins and Objectives of Islamic Revivalist Thought," 342n12.

among teachers and pupils are indicative of intellectual affinities. The work of several other scholars strengthened Dallal's critique. Bernard Haykel, in a book on al-Shawkānī, warned against lumping together different scholars as part of a single phenomenon, emphasizing that broader conclusions about early modern Islam require first understanding these thinkers in their own contexts.[225] Khaled El-Rouayheb has shown that al-Sindī represented not a broader revivalist movement but, rather, a distinct a group of *ḥadīth*-oriented Ṣūfīs working to upset the "established tradition of jurisprudence and theology."[226] Dallal himself reaffirmed his argument in a chapter in *The New Cambridge History of Islam,* adding to his previous analysis studies of Ibn al-Amīr al-Ṣanʿānī and al-Shawkānī.[227]

It was not the intention of these studies to deny that there were resemblances between the various revivalist movements around the eighteenth century or that they shared some ideas. Dallal acknowledged the similarities between the various revivalist movements, but he stopped at Wahhābism. Wahhābism, according to Dallal, was in a category all its own, having nothing in common with the other movements. "Ibn ʿAbd al-Wahhāb," he claimed, "shared none of the concerns of other eighteenth-century thinkers."[228] Moreover, "Wahhābism lacks intellectual complexity and thus does not lend itself to much intellectual analysis."[229]

These conclusions go too far in the other direction. However different Wahhābism was from other contemporary revivalist movements—and it certainly was different—it is a stretch to say that Ibn ʿAbd al-Wahhāb shared *none* of their concerns. In fact, he shared with Ibn al-Amīr and al-Shawkānī a concern over the cult of saints (and to a lesser extent a concern over legal school partisanship), and all of them condemned the cult of saints on the same grounds—the ones provided by Ibn Taymiyya. Like Ibn ʿAbd al-Wahhāb, Ibn al-Amīr and al-Shawkānī adopted Ibn Taymiyya's ideas concerning *tawḥīd* and *shirk* and compared the participants in the cult of saints with the pagan Arabs, arguing that the latter were in reality monotheists.[230]

225. Haykel, *Revival and Reform in Islam,* 12–15.

226. El-Rouayheb, "From Ibn Ḥajar al-Haytamī to Khayr al-Dīn al-Ālūsī," 303.

227. Dallal, "Origins and Early Development of Islamic Reform"; see further his *Islam Without Europe.*

228. Dallal, "Origins and Early Development of Islamic Reform," 113; cf. Dallal, *Islam Without Europe,* 24ff.

229. Dallal, "Origins and Early Development of Islamic Reform," 111.

230. al-Amīr, *Taṭhīr al-iʿtiqād,* 35–38; al-Shawkānī, *al-Durr al-naḍīd,* 65–71.

Just like the Wahhābīs, Ibn al-Amīr adopted Ibn Taymiyya's two forms of *tawḥīd*.[231]

Another near contemporary of Ibn ʿAbd al-Wahhāb's with similar religious concerns was the Indian reformer Shāh Ismāʿīl ibn ʿAbd al-Ghanī al-Shahīd (d. 1246/1831), the intellectual founder of the Ṭarīqa-yi Muḥammadiyya in India.[232] The Ṭarīqa-yi Muḥammadiyya was a movement that wielded significant influence over the greater Ahl-i Ḥadīth movement taking shape in nineteenth-century India. Like Wahhābism, it was highly critical of perceived saint worship and drew on Ibn Taymiyya's ideas. In his Urdu manifesto *Taqwiyat al-īmān*, Shāh Ismāʿīl compares the participants in the cult of saints with the pagan Arabs, arguing that the latter were in fact monotheists who failed to profess *tawḥīd al-ulūhiyya*.[233] This is the exact same argument Ibn ʿAbd al-Wahhāb was making, and like the Najdī reformer Shāh Ismāʿīl argued that *shirk* had spread far and wide in the Muslim community.[234] The similarities between the Tarīqa-yi Muḥammadiyya and Wahhābism were not lost on contemporary Muslim observers. In a little-known Arabic refutation of *Taqwiyat al-īmān*, written in approximately 1240/1824f, an obscure Indian author accuses Shāh Ismāʿīl of following "the Najdī Khārijites" (*al-khawārij al-Najdiyya*) in the practice of *takfīr*.[235] Following the refutation is a series of encomia by eight prominent scholars in Mecca and Medina.[236] The effort is reminiscent of al-Ṭandatāwī's anti-Wahhābī refutation back in 1156/1743, which also acquired the encomia of several prominent Ḥijāzī scholars.

All this is simply to show that Wahhābism should not be seen as sui generis, as having nothing whatsoever in common with the other revivalist movements of the early modern period. Wahhābism did not necessarily inspire these other movements; nor did they share an intellectual origin in a

231. al-Amīr, *Taṭhīr al-iʿtiqād*, 34–35. He calls them *tawḥīd al-rubūbiyya* and *tawḥīd al-ʿibāda*.

232. On Shāh Ismāʿīl, see Gaborieau, *Le Mahdi incompris*, 93–115; and on the Ṭarīqa-yi Muḥammadiyya generally, see Pearson, *Islamic Reform and Revival in Nineteenth-Century India*.

233. al-Shahīd, *Risālat al-tawḥīd*, 20.

234. Ibid., 16. Gaborieau has argued that Shāh Ismāʿīl came to these views through exposure to the works of al-Shawkānī, not those of the Wahhābīs; see Gaborieau, *Le Mahdi incompris*, 112–13.

235. ʿAbd al-Waḥīd, *Hidāyat ʿawāmm al-muʾminīn*, f. 4a. The manuscript is undated, but one of the encomia is dated 1240/1824f (f. 40b). On this manuscript, see Muṭīʿ al-Raḥmān and ʿĪd, *al-Fihris al-mukhtaṣar*, 1:494 (no. 2049).

236. ʿAbd al-Waḥīd, *Hidāyat ʿawāmm al-muʾminīn*, ff. 40a–45b.

network of *ḥadīth*-oriented scholars in the Ḥijāz. But at the very least Wahhābism belonged to a wider grouping of movements that drew on the ideas of Ibn Taymiyya and Ibn al-Qayyim in similar ways. The Wahhābīs' approach to *takfīr* and *jihād* may have been unique; they were far quicker to excommunicate and fight professed Muslims than the adherents of other movements. But the similarities between Wahhābism and other contemporary Islamic reform movements should not be ignored. The existence of these affinities helps to explain how later generations of Wahhābīs could form intimate ties with scholars in such places as India and Iraq beginning in the nineteenth century.

4

The Warpath of Early Wahhābism

THE FIRST SAUDI STATE (1741–1818)

HAVING DETERMINED that *shirk* was widespread in both Arabia and the broader Islamic world and that a renewed focus on *tawḥīd* was necessary, Ibn ʿAbd al-Wahhāb could have followed more than one path. He could have settled into a life of quiet scholarship or left Najd in search of a more religiously palatable setting. What he chose to do, however, was to launch a movement that would upend the political and religious environment of Arabia, culminating in the rise of a state, the first Saudi state, to imperial heights. Was this the direction in which he intended his movement to go from the beginning? Did he ever imagine that he would give rise to a vast empire that, by the mid-1210s/early 1800s, would span most of the Arabian Peninsula and reach the doorstep of the Fertile Crescent? These are the questions that this chapter explores.

It is first important to emphasize that the emergence of the first Saudi state was in many ways an improbable occurrence. There was no indication that anything like it was on the horizon. In the eighteenth century and for many centuries before, Najd was a politically weak and fractious region; located in a fairly remote part of the southern Middle East, it had few endowments in terms of natural resources or fertile farmland conducive to large-scale state formation. The last time it played host to a large-scale state-building enterprise was in the ninth–eleventh centuries, and there was little reason to expect that it would suddenly do so again. Indeed, it is difficult to detect much if any change in the basic patterns of social, political, and economic life in Najd in the centuries preceding the rise of the first Saudi state.[1] While it has been

1. Vassiliev, *History of Saudi Arabia*, 29–63; Cook, "Expansion of the First Saudi State," 675–79.

hypothesized that the settled population (*ḥaḍar*) of the region had been growing relative to the nomadic population, and that the Saudi state was in some way a response to this development,[2] this and similar theories are difficult to substantiate, as they rely to a large degree on extrapolation from meager and ambiguous sources.[3] As Michael Cook has observed, concerning the idea that "long-term historical change" was responsible for the emergence of the first Saudi state, "[W]e are perhaps on solider ground in regarding the event as an act of God."[4] This was to say, it is safer to conclude that religion was the crucial factor in the state's rise, that it was the religious conviction of Ibn ʿAbd al-Wahhāb and his followers that made the difference in reversing the historical pattern and overturning the status quo.

Ibn ʿAbd al-Wahhāb may have had choices initially, but once he came out openly with his mission (*aʿlana biʾl-daʿwa*), as Ibn Bishr puts it, calling on his followers to show hatred and enmity to the perceived polytheists around them, the range of possible outcomes of his preaching narrowed. Many of his scholarly opponents wanted him killed, a fate that he escaped thanks in part to the absence of strong political structures in Najd, as well as the fact that no foreign power, including the Ottoman Empire, exerted much control over the region. To that extent, Najd was favorable terrain for launching a controversial movement, a place where he could preach without exposing himself to too much danger. It also helped that the people of Najd, for whatever reason—perhaps simmering resentment toward the local cult of saints—were highly receptive to his message. Within just a few years, Ibn ʿAbd al-Wahhāb seems to have been able to convince most of the people of al-ʿĀriḍ that the Islam they had been practicing was *shirk*, and the movement continued to grow. Then, by a stroke of luck, he managed to form an alliance with the leader of al-Dirʿiyya, Muḥammad ibn Suʿūd, who offered him protection and agreed to promote his doctrine as the basis of his emirate's expansion. Gradually, the minor emirate developed into the first Saudi state. This was by no means an inevitable outcome, but it is one that was to some degree determined by the divisive nature of Ibn ʿAbd

2. Al Juhany, *Najd Before the Salafi Reform Movement*, 159–63; Al-Dakhil, "Social Origins of the Wahhabi Movement," esp. 13–19. A related idea concerns a hypothesized process of detribalization among the settled population of Najd, on which, see Al-Fahad, "'Imama vs. the 'Iqal." Cf. the discussion in Crawford, *Ibn 'Abd al-Wahhab*, 89–91.

3. Cook, "Expansion of the First Saudi State," 675–79. Cook's argument, which is addressed to Al Juhany's thesis, applies equally well to Al-Dakhil's.

4. Ibid., 679.

al-Wahhāb's doctrine. With its emphasis on showing hatred and enmity to those Muslims seen as polytheists, Wahhābism necessarily entailed the polarization of Najdī society, and in practice this would mean the polarization of Najdī politics as well.

This chapter looks at how and why Ibn ʿAbd al-Wahhāb's movement progressed as it did, examining its development into the first Saudi state and the state's subsequent trajectory. While it does not intend to solve all the mysteries of the state's emergence and expansion, it does argue that the Wahhābī movement followed a natural course of sorts. This was the warpath of early Islam and the early Islamic state, which the Wahhābī movement's development recalls. The chapter therefore begins with a brief examination of the Prophet Muḥammad's career and the rise of his state, highlighting the resemblances with the career of Ibn ʿAbd al-Wahhāb and the rise of the first Saudi state. Next it examines the development of Ibn ʿAbd al-Wahhāb's movement from one that was essentially nonviolent into one that advocated *jihād*. From there it considers the first Saudi state's progress in the years after Ibn ʿAbd al-Wahhāb's passing, years that saw the state grow increasingly aggressive and ambitious. The Saudi rulers, as will be seen, threatened to invade Iraq and Syria with reference to the Prophet's ultimatum to the ruler of Byzantium. Finally, it examines the demise of the first Saudi state in 1233/1818 at the hands of the Egyptian army and the implications of this defeat for the subsequent history of Wahhābism.

The Prophet's Path

In the traditional account of his career, the Prophet Muḥammad passes through several stages as regards preaching and warfare. In the first stage, in Mecca, the Prophet began to receive divine revelation but preached only in a secretive fashion. This began in approximately 610 and lasted two or three years. Thereafter, when the number of converts to the new religion had grown, God commanded him to preach openly. As Muḥammad ibn Isḥāq (d. 150/767), one of the earliest biographers of the Prophet, relates: "Three years of his mission, according to what I have been told, elapsed from the time the Messenger of God hid and concealed his divine command until God commanded him to manifest His religion [*bi-iẓhār dīnihi*]. Then God said: 'Proclaim that which you are commanded and turn away from the polytheists' (Q. 15:94)."[5] The Prophet's public preaching in this stage involved disparaging

5. Ibn Hishām, *al-Sīra al-nabawiyya*, 1:262 (cf. Guillaume, *Life of Muhammad*, 117).

the religion of the pagan Arabs, which earned him the wrath of the people of Mecca, the Quraysh. According to Ibn Isḥāq,

> When the Messenger of God publicly declared Islam to his people and proclaimed it as he was commanded by God, his people did not withdraw from him or reject him in any way, according to what I have been told, until he spoke of their gods and denounced them [*ḥattā dhakara ālihatahum wa-ʿābahā*]. When he did so they took great exception to it and resolved to oppose him and show him enmity [*wa-ajmaʿū khilāfahu wa-ʿadāwatahu*].[6]

In Ibn Isḥāq's account, some of the leading men of Quraysh confronted the Prophet's uncle and protector, Abū Ṭālib, telling him: "Your nephew has reviled our gods, denounced our religion, derided our traditional values, and told us that our forefathers were misguided."[7] Yet the Prophet was undeterred: "The Messenger of God continued as he was, proclaiming the religion of God and calling to it [*yuẓhiru dīn Allāh wa-yadʿū ilayhi*]."[8] As was seen in chapter 3, Ibn Qayyim al-Jawziyya interpreted the Prophet's disparagement of the pagan Arabs' religion in this stage as the display of enmity, and Ibn ʿAbd al-Wahhāb would do so as well. This stage of the Prophet's career, which might be described as peaceful but assertive preaching, lasted ten years and ended with the emigration (*hijra*) of the Prophet and his followers to Medina in 622, corresponding to year 1 of the Islamic calendar.

It was in Medina that *jihād* in the sense of armed struggle was introduced, marking the beginning of yet another phase in Muḥammad's career. Before this time, God had prohibited the Prophet from using force; now he would be given permission to fight his enemies. The sources allow for more than one reading of the stages of his career concerning *jihād*. In the reading favored by Ibn Taymiyya and Ibn al-Qayyim, and by Ibn ʿAbd al-Wahhāb after them, the stages of *jihād* were three. Ibn al-Qayyim gives a clear rundown of these stages in his book *Zād al-maʿād*, which Ibn ʿAbd al-Wahhāb quotes in his prophetic biography. The first of these stages began with the initial granting of permission to fight, which was revealed in Q. 22:39: "Permission is granted to those who are fought against in that they were wronged."[9] With the revelation of this verse

6. Ibn Hishām, *al-Sīra al-nabawiyya*, 1:264 (cf. Guillaume, *Life of Muhammad*, 118).

7. Ibn Hishām, *al-Sīra al-nabawiyya*, 1:265 (cf. Guillaume, *Life of Muhammad*, 119).

8. Ibn Hishām, *al-Sīra al-nabawiyya*, 1:264 (cf. Guillaume, *Life of Muhammad*, 119).

9. Ibn al-Qayyim, *Zād al-maʿād*, 3:63 (= Ibn ʿAbd al-Wahhāb, *Mukhtaṣar sīrat al-rasūl*, 106). The variant reading of *yuqātalūna* (as *yuqātilūna*) does not appear to be relevant here.

the Muslims were permitted, but not obligated, to fight in self-defense. The next stage began when fighting in self-defense became obligatory. The verse held to have inaugurated this stage is Q. 2:190: "And fight in the path of God those who fight you."[10] This stage came to an end with the revelation of those verses calling for offensive *jihād*, the Muslims being commanded to fight polytheists proactively. One of the verses in this regard, according to Ibn ʿAbd al-Wahhāb, was Q. 9:36: "And fight the polytheists altogether, as they fight you altogether."[11] It was on the basis of offensive *jihād* that the city-state of Medina expanded into the early caliphate. The Muslims captured Mecca in the year 8/630, and thereafter the Arab tribes sent delegations to Medina recognizing Muḥammad as their prophet and ruler.

A helpful summation of the stages of the Prophet's career concerning *jihād* is provided by Ibn Taymiyya. As he writes in *al-Jawāb al-ṣaḥīḥ*,

> In the beginning, the Prophet was commanded to struggle against the unbelievers with his tongue, not his hand. . . . [H]e was commanded to refrain from fighting them on account of his and the Muslims' inability to do so. When he emigrated to Medina and acquired supporters, *jihād* was made permissible for him. When they gathered strength, fighting was prescribed for them. . . . When God conquered Mecca . . . God commanded him to fight all the unbelievers.[12]

In *Zād al-maʿād*, Ibn al-Qayyim summarizes the progression similarly:

> He spent ten and some years [in Mecca] warning by means of calling without fighting and without [taking] the poll tax; he was commanded to refrain, to be patient, and to turn away. Then he was permitted to emigrate and he was permitted to fight. Then [God] commanded him to fight those fighting him, and to refrain from those not fighting him. Then God commanded him to fight the polytheists "until the religion is God's entirely" (Q. 8:39).[13]

Elsewhere in *Zād al-maʿād*, Ibn al-Qayyim captures the progressive legitimation of *jihād* even more succinctly, saying: "It was forbidden, then permitted,

10. Ibn al-Qayyim, *Zād al-maʿād*, 3:64 (= Ibn ʿAbd al-Wahhāb, *Mukhtaṣar sīrat al-rasūl*, 106).

11. Ibn ʿAbd al-Wahhāb, *Mukhtaṣar sīrat al-rasūl*, 106.

12. Ibn Taymiyya, *al-Jawāb al-ṣaḥīḥ*, 1:237.

13. Ibn al-Qayyim, *Zād al-maʿād*, 3:143 (= Ibn ʿAbd al-Wahhāb, *Mukhtaṣar sīrat al-rasūl*, 57).

then prescribed against those initiating hostilities against them, then prescribed against all the polytheists."[14]

The Prophet died in the year 11/632, by which time the Islamic state was beginning to grow into an ever-larger polity. There was no expansion beyond Arabia during the Prophet's lifetime, but tradition holds that he entertained designs on lands further afield. This is brought out in a series of letters that the Prophet is said to have sent to the rulers of neighboring empires, including Heraclius (Hiraql) of the Byzantine Empire. In the letter to Heraclius, reproduced by Ibn al-Qayyim in *Zād al-maʿād*, the Prophet writes:

> In the name of God, the Merciful, the Compassionate. From Muḥammad, the Messenger of God, to Heraclius, the ruler of the Romans. Peace be upon whoever follows right guidance! To proceed: I summon you with the summons of Islam. Submit, and you shall be safe, and God shall reward you twice over. But, if you turn away, the sin of the husbandmen shall be upon you.[15]

As will be seen, this letter would be quoted by the Wahhābīs after Ibn ʿAbd al-Wahhāb's death, when they began raiding into Iraq and Syria.

Returning to the stages of the Prophet's career, in the telling of Ibn Taymiyya and Ibn al-Qayyim, and of Ibn ʿAbd al-Wahhāb as well, there were five stages in total. These were (1) secretive preaching, (2) public preaching, (3) voluntary defensive *jihād*, (4) obligatory defensive *jihād*, and (5) offensive *jihād*.[16] The trend is in the direction of greater assertiveness and greater use of force.

The career of Ibn ʿAbd al-Wahhāb, according to the Wahhābī tradition, followed a similar trajectory. As was seen in chapter 1, in Basra and Ḥuraymilāʾ, Ibn ʿAbd al-Wahhāb preached his doctrine of *tawḥīd* in secretive fashion, not seeking to stir up trouble for himself. He did not preach his doctrine openly until after his father died in 1153/1741, when he began disparaging the religion of those around him as polytheism and invoking the Prophet's example in

14. Ibn al-Qayyim, *Zād al-maʿād*, 3:64.

15. Ibid., 3:600–601. This version of the letter is based on al-Bukhārī, *Ṣaḥīḥ*, 656 (*Kitāb al-jihād wa ʾl-siyar, bāb daʿwat al-yahūd wa ʾl-naṣārā*, no. 2941); Muslim, *Ṣaḥīḥ*, 3:1396 (*Kitāb al-jihād wa ʾl-siyar, bāb kitāb al-nabī ṣ ilā Hiraql yadʿūhu ilā ʾl-Islām*, no. 1773); cf. al-Ṭabarī, *Tārīkh al-Ṭabarī*, 2:649. My translation is partly borrowed from al-Ṭabarī, *History of al-Ṭabarī*, 104. On the historicity of this letter, see Bashear, "Mission of Diḥya al-Kalbī and the Situation in Syria."

16. For a somewhat different set of stages as interpreted by Reuven Firestone, see his "Disparity and Resolution in the Qurʾānic Teachings on War."

Mecca. As his early biographers are keen to emphasize, he was not advocating violence at this stage. According to Ibn Ghannām, when Ibn ʿAbd al-Wahhāb started his public campaign, "he was calling to the path of guidance and disputing the people of vileness in the better way."[17] The phraseology here is borrowed from Q. 16:125, "Call you to the way of your Lord with wisdom and good admonition, and dispute with them in the better way," one of the Qurʾānic verses associated with the Prophet's public preaching in Mecca. In another reference to this verse, Ibn Gharīb states that Ibn ʿAbd al-Wahhāb was at this stage "calling to the way of his Lord with wisdom and good admonition."[18] At this point in his career, then, according to the Wahhābī tradition, Ibn ʿAbd al-Wahhāb was engaged in peaceful but assertive preaching, as the Prophet had been at the beginning of his public preaching in Mecca. Warfare was not part of his campaign at this stage. That would change only after Ibn ʿAbd al-Wahhāb moved to al-Dirʿiyya in approximately 1157/1744f. As will be detailed in what follows below, Ibn ʿAbd al-Wahhāb first characterized the warfare of the nascent Saudi state as defensive in nature, only later justifying it as offensive *jihād* for the purpose of eradicating *shirk*. The Wahhābī tradition thus provides us with a picture of Ibn ʿAbd al-Wahhāb's career that resembles that of the Prophet, a career that passes through stages of secretive preaching, public preaching, defensive *jihād*, and offensive *jihād*. This portrayal may have been the result of a deliberate effort on the part of the biographers to liken Ibn ʿAbd al-Wahhāb to the Prophet, but it is a portrayal that nonetheless appears accurate.

The question raised by all this is to what extent Ibn ʿAbd al-Wahhāb was consciously following in the footsteps of the Prophet. The prophetic path described above was of course well known to Ibn ʿAbd al-Wahhāb, and he regarded the Prophet's conduct as worthy of emulation. As he writes in one of his letters: "I know of nothing better for drawing close to God than adhering to the way of God's Messenger in a time of alienation."[19] It is unlikely that the resemblance between his career and the Prophet's was entirely coincidental. As Ibn ʿAbd al-Wahhāb saw it, he was modeling his behavior after the Prophet's, and similar to the Prophet he found himself preaching in an environment steeped in *shirk*. Islam had returned to being "strange," and it was his objective to preach the correct understanding of *tawḥīd* to the polytheists around him. A successful outcome would naturally have meant coming together with his

17. Ibn Ghannām, *al-ʿIqd al-thamīn*, 24–25.

18. Ibn Gharīb, *al-Tawḍīḥ*, 1:229.

19. Ibn Ghannām, *Tārīkh*, 1:422 (letter to ʿAbdallāh ibn Suwaylim).

supporters in a religiopolitical community, and an even more successful outcome would have seen that community's expansion, to include fighting and conquering those deemed recalcitrant polytheists. While Ibn ʿAbd al-Wahhāb could not have anticipated his far-reaching success, he knew what success looked like, as he knew the Prophet's path and where it led.

One major difference between Ibn ʿAbd al-Wahhāb's career and the Prophet's is that Ibn ʿAbd al-Wahhāb was never a head of state. He was not a politician, only a preacher and scholar. In the few places where Ibn ʿAbd al-Wahhāb addresses matters of politics in his writings, he usually does not stray far from traditional Sunnī Muslim dogma, with its emphasis on deference to established authority. In an undated creed, for instance, he stresses the duty of obedience to rulers, whether they are pious or impious, so long as they do not command people to sin.[20] In one of his epistles, he invokes the *ḥadīth* in which the Prophet states that obedience to a ruler is required even if he be an Ethiopian slave.[21] Yet Ibn ʿAbd al-Wahhāb was by no means passive about politics. He believed that Muslim scholars ought to play a significant advisory role in the political realm. In a fragment of writing describing the proper relationship between scholars and rulers, he states that the ruler (*amīr*) ought to take scholars (*ʿulamāʾ*) as his advisers and consultants (*mishwaratahu wa-ahl majlisihi*), adding that it is the duty of the scholars to rally support for the ruler and overlook his flaws.[22] Here, then, is a rare glimpse of Ibn ʿAbd al-Wahhāb's view on the role of scholars (such as himself) in politics. Unlike the Prophet and his successors, the caliphs, Ibn ʿAbd al-Wahhāb would not seek to assume the headship of state, but he would seek to exercise a significant influence in political affairs. Indeed, he played a much larger role in the first Saudi state than is commonly recognized.

Defensive *Jihād*

As noted in chapter 1, the first phase of Ibn ʿAbd al-Wahhāb's career as the leader of a predicatory movement (*daʿwa*) began in 1153/1741, shortly after his father died. This was in Ḥuraymilāʾ, where he began to preach about *tawḥīd* and the requirement of showing hatred and enmity to polytheists. He gathered followers there before relocating to his hometown of al-ʿUyayna, ruled by

20. *al-Durar al-saniyya*, 1:33.

21. Ibid., 1:173.

22. Ibid., 9:6.

ʿUthmān ibn Muʿammar, where his movement continued to gain followers. Then, in approximately 1157/1744f, he moved from al-ʿUyayna to al-Dirʿiyya, bringing many of his followers with him. In al-Dirʿiyya, he found a welcoming supporter in the town's ruler, Muḥammad ibn Suʿūd (r. 1139–79/1726f–65), who agreed to support the Wahhābī *daʿwa* on the condition that Ibn ʿAbd al-Wahhāb not abandon al-Dirʿiyya for another town. The alliance paid early dividends for both parties, as the towns of al-ʿĀriḍ were won over to Wahhābism and accepted the authority of Ibn Suʿūd as their overlord. The lone holdout was the town of Riyadh, ruled by Dahām ibn Dawwās, which soon entered into a long war with al-Dirʿiyya. Two years passed between Ibn ʿAbd al-Wahhāb's arrival in al-Dirʿiyya and the outbreak of hostilities with Riyadh, in approximately 1159/1746f. According to Ibn Ghannām, the war started when Riyadh attacked the nearby town of Manfūḥa, which had recently adopted Wahhābism and accepted the writ of al-Dirʿiyya. The war between al-Dirʿiyya and Riyadh would last, with some interruptions, nearly thirty years, coming to an end only in 1187/1773 with Riyadh's final submission.

In the early years of the war, Ibn ʿAbd al-Wahhāb maintained that the military operations of al-Dirʿiyya were strictly defensive in nature, portraying them as defensive *jihād*. In a letter to an Iraqi scholar, for example, responding to a question about why the Wahhābīs fight, he writes: "To this day we have not fought anybody except to defend ourselves and [our] women [*dūn al-nafs wa ʾl-ḥurma*]." "They are the ones," he adds, "who came to us in our lands and left [us] no choice [*atawnā fī diyārinā wa-lā abqaw mumkinan*]."[23] Ibn Ghannām, in his history, likewise indicates that the Wahhābīs' use of military force was defensive at the beginning of the movement. Ibn ʿAbd al-Wahhāb, he writes, did not order the use of violence until his enemies pronounced *takfīr* on him and deemed his blood licit: "He gave no order to spill blood or to fight against the majority of the heretics and the misguided until they started judging that he and his followers were to be killed and subject to *takfīr*."[24]

Whether it was true or not, the Wahhābīs claimed that the enemies of their movement were the ones to initiate both the fighting and the practice of *takfīr*. As Ibn ʿAbd al-Wahhāb says in a passage of his Qurʾānic exegesis: "They are the ones who started pronouncing *takfīr* on us and fighting us" (*hum alladhīna badaʾūnā bi ʾl-takfīr wa ʾl-qitāl*).[25] Similarly, in an undated epistle to some of

23. Ibn Ghannām, *Tārīkh*, 1:415 (letter to Ibn al-Suwaydī).

24. Ibid., 1:220.

25. Ibid., 1:532.

his opponents, responding to the complaint that the Wahhābīs were fighting and pronouncing *takfīr* on the people of al-ʿĀriḍ, he writes: "[W]e did not come to you with *takfīr* and warfare" (*naḥnu mā jiʾnākum fī ʾl-takfīr wa ʾl-qitāl*).[26] It may well be true that the enemies of Wahhābism, and more specifically Dahām ibn Dawwās, were the first to engage in warfare. The memory of Riyadh striking first against al-Dirʿiyya is ingrained in Wahhābī tradition. ʿAbd al-Raḥmān ibn Ḥasan Āl al-Shaykh, in his account of his grandfather's life, describes Dahām as the first person to launch a military attack on the Wahhābīs (*awwal man shanna ʾl-ghāra ʿalayhim*), portraying it as unprovoked.[27] However, the claim that the opponents of Wahhābism were the first to engage in *takfīr* is not believable at all. It seems to be based on the idea that Ibn ʿAbd al-Wahhāb made only vague accusations of *takfīr* at the beginning of his mission, whereas his enemies made specific ones. This is how Ibn Ghannām justifies it in his history.[28]

In any event, in this early period of the Saudi expansion, the warfare of the embryonic state was being cast as defensive *jihād*. In 1159/1746f, according to ʿAbd al-Raḥmān ibn Ḥasan Āl al-Shaykh, the towns of al-ʿĀriḍ tendered their allegiance to Ibn Suʿūd and accepted Wahhābism as their official version of Islam. These included al-ʿUyayna, Ḥuraymilāʾ, al-ʿAmmāriyya, and Manfūḥa, the only exception being Riyadh.[29] Ibn Ghannām gives us a sense of what it meant for a town to enter the Saudi-Wahhābī fold. First, a town's ruler would give *bayʿa*, the traditional Islamic contract of allegiance between ruler and ruled, to both Ibn Suʿūd and Ibn ʿAbd al-Wahhāb.[30] As Ibn Ghannām relates in one example, in 1160/1747f, ʿUthmān ibn Muʿammar, who was suspected of treachery, visited al-Dirʿiyya to renew his *bayʿa* to both men (*wa-ʿāhada ʾl-shaykh wa-Muḥammad ibn Suʿūd*).[31] The impression given is that Ibn Suʿūd and Ibn ʿAbd al-Wahhāb were functioning almost as corulers, though this is never said explicitly. Similarly, in 1171/1757f, the two men are depicted as jointly installing the new ruler of the subjugated town of Ḥuraymilāʾ.[32] Occasionally,

26. Ibid., 1:409.

27. Āl al-Shaykh, *al-Maqāmāt*, 79.

28. Ibn Ghannām, *Tārīkh*, 1:221.

29. Mengin, *Histoire de l'Égypte*, 2:451–53.

30. See *EI*[3], s.v. "Bayʿa" (Andrew Marsham). Ibn Ghannām uses *bayʿa* and *ʿahd* interchangeably. I render the verb *bāyaʿa* as "to give *bayʿa* to," but it should be borne in mind that the pledge is a reciprocal one.

31. Ibn Ghannām, *Tārīkh*, 2:680–81.

32. Ibid., 2:749–50.

Ibn ʿAbd al-Wahhāb is even seen making political decisions on his own. In 1163/1750, for instance, when Ibn Muʿammar was assassinated in al-ʿUyayna, Ibn ʿAbd al-Wahhāb was the one who traveled there to restore order and appoint a new ruler.[33] Likewise, in 1167/1753f, Ibn ʿAbd al-Wahhāb was the one who ordered the execution of a man spreading the anti-Wahhābī writings of his brother in al-ʿUyayna.[34]

A town's conversion to Wahhābism also involved welcoming a Wahhābī preacher to instruct the townspeople in the Wahhābī doctrine and to implement Islamic law. In 1170/1756f, when the town of Thādiq in the subregion of al-Miḥmal was conquered, not only did Ibn ʿAbd al-Wahhāb appoint a new local ruler, but he also sent a scholar to give instruction in *tawḥīd* and to judge in accordance with the law of Islam.[35] Similarly, in 1167/1753f, when Dahām adopted Wahhābism temporarily (one of several times he would do so), he requested that Ibn ʿAbd al-Wahhāb send a preacher to Riyadh to issue judgments and impart Wahhābī dogma. The preacher, we are told, was sent and proceeded to judge in accordance with the rules of Islam and to provide instruction in *tawḥīd*.[36]

As is seen here, Ibn ʿAbd al-Wahhāb sought not only to impose his doctrine of *tawḥīd* on subjugated territories but also to ensure a strict application of Islamic legal norms. As he writes in his letter to the Iraqi scholar, regarding both his own role in al-Dirʿiyya and the requirements and prohibitions he has instituted,

> I have a position in my town and my word is obeyed [*anā ṣāḥib manṣib fī qaryatī masmūʿ al-kalima*]. Some rulers have condemned this as it contravenes a custom that they grew up with. Also, I have required those under my rule to perform the prayer and pay the *zakāt*, among other of God's ordinances [*farāʾiḍ Allāh*], and I have forbidden them from engaging in usury, drinking intoxicants, and other kinds of prohibited things.[37]

Another requirement he imposed was communal prayer five times a day, all men being expected to pray together in the mosque.[38] According to ʿAbd

33. Ibid., 2:687–88.
34. Ibid., 2:695–96.
35. Ibid., 2:745.
36. Ibid., 2:695.
37. Ibid., 1:412–13 (letter to Ibn al-Suwaydī).
38. Ibid., 2:910.

al-Raḥmān ibn Ḥasan Āl al-Shaykh, the legal norms imposed by Ibn ʿAbd al-Wahhāb also included prohibitions on smoking tobacco and wearing silk.[39] Instituting Islamic law thus figured prominently in his mission, though the main thrust of his teaching was doctrinal as opposed to legal. The first thing he has prohibited, he tells his Iraqi correspondent, is *shirk*.[40]

Offensive *Jihād*

Exactly when the transition from defensive *jihād* to offensive *jihād* in Wahhābism took place is difficult to say, but we can be sure that the transition was taking place no later than 1165/1752, which is when the town of Ḥuraymilāʾ committed what Ibn Ghannām calls apostasy (*ridda*). Ḥuraymilāʾ had initially submitted to al-Dirʿiyya no later than 1160/1747, when it is described as fighting alongside the other Wahhābī towns in that year's hostilities with Riyadh.[41] But in 1165/1752, a group of anti-Wahhābī conspirators inspired by Ibn ʿAbd al-Wahhāb's brother, Sulaymān, arranged a coup and installed a new ruler opposed to the Saudi-Wahhābī order. War between Ḥuraymilāʾ and al-Dirʿiyya followed, ending in Ḥuraymilāʾ's submission two and a half years later, in 1168/1755.[42]

As is clear from the text of *Mufīd al-mustafīd*, Ibn ʿAbd al-Wahhāb justified the war to reconquer Ḥuraymilāʾ in terms of offensive *jihād*. In this epistle, which he wrote to the people of al-ʿUyayna shortly after the so-called apostasy of Ḥuraymilāʾ, his main objective was to justify the *jihād* being prosecuted against Ḥuraymilāʾ as well as to dispute the anti-Wahhābī arguments being circulated by his brother. The inhabitants of Ḥuraymilāʾ are described here as polytheists and apostates who must be fought until they profess *tawḥīd* and eschew *shirk*. They are to be fought, Ibn ʿAbd al-Wahhāb argues, on the same basis that Abū Bakr fought the withholders of the *zakāt* in the wars of apostasy in early Islam, which was that they had failed to adhere to Islam in full.[43] In saying this, he quotes or alludes to several of the verses indicative of offensive *jihād*, including Q. 9:73: "O Prophet, struggle against the unbelievers and the hypocrites and be harsh with them." The latter verse is described as one of the unambiguous verses (*al-āyāt al-muḥkamāt*) revealed in connection with the

39. Mengin, *Histoire de l'Égypte*, 2:452.

40. Ibn Ghannām, *Tārīkh*, 1:412.

41. Ibid., 2:679.

42. Ibid., 2:691–94.

43. Ibid., 2:713.

duty to wage *jihād* against those who commit *shirk* and apostasy.[44] By this point, then, in 1167/1753f when *Mufīd al-mustafīd* was written, al-Dirʿiyya was on an aggressive war footing. It was not Ibn ʿAbd al-Wahhāb's argument that the Wahhābīs were fighting in self-defense. His argument, rather, was that they were fighting for the purpose of defeating apostasy and eradicating *shirk*. A town that had submitted to al-Dirʿiyya was not permitted to exit the Saudi-Wahhābī fold.

Later Wahhābī epistles are even clearer in establishing the basis of al-Dirʿiyya's *jihād* as the elimination of *shirk*, as when Ibn ʿAbd al-Wahhāb writes in one of his letters: "We have prohibited them [our enemies] from committing *shirk* [*nahaynāhum ʿan al-shirk*] . . . and we are fighting them on account of it [*wa-nuqātiluhum ʿalayhi*], as God says, 'And fight them till there is no *fitna*,' that is, *shirk*, 'and the religion is God's entirely' (Q. 8:39)."[45] Here and in *Mufīd al-mustafīd*, Ibn ʿAbd al-Wahhāb is no longer defensive about the fact that the Wahhābīs' are excommunicating and fighting their enemies. Whereas before he claimed that these acts were reactive or defensive in nature, he now supported them unapologetically. This is the approach taken in several other of his *rasāʾil*. Ibn ʿAbd al-Wahhāb would indeed become fond of saying that his enemies agreed with him on the issues of *tawḥīd* and *shirk* but opposed him on the issues of *takfīr* and *qitāl*, proceeding, in these discussions, to justify his proactive approach.[46]

In addition to illustrating the transition from defensive to offensive *jihād*, the Wahhābī war on Ḥuraymilāʾ reveals the Wahhābīs' growing military capabilities. The scale of the fighting described by Ibn Ghannām is larger than anything to have gone before. The military commander in this venture was Ibn Suʿūd's son, ʿAbd al-ʿAzīz ibn Muḥammad Āl Suʿūd, who was emerging as the principal leader of military operations against the opponents of Wahhābism and the Saudi state. According to Ibn Ghannām, ʿAbd al-ʿAzīz commanded a force of eight hundred men, alongside an additional two hundred men under the command of the deposed ruler of Ḥuraymilāʾ. In a surprise attack, ʿAbd al-ʿAzīz's army quickly took control of the town, killing one hundred men and losing seven.[47] While the number of fatalities may not seem large, it is high

44. Ibid., 2:724.

45. *al-Durar al-saniyya*, 1:95–96.

46. See, for example, Ibn Ghannām, *Tārīkh*, 1:338–39 (letter to Muḥammad ibn ʿĪd); *al-Durar al-saniyya*, 10:8.

47. Ibn Ghannām, *Tārīkh*, 2:736–37.

compared with the number killed in preceding battles.[48] The Wahhābīs were now capable of wielding much larger armies than before, and they were using this capacity to make an example of the town at the center of anti-Wahhābī propaganda in Najd.

The conquest of Ḥuraymilāʾ in 1168/1755 marked the submission of the Najdī subregion al-Shaʿīb. The area of al-Miḥmal fell shortly thereafter with the conquest of the town of Thādiq in 1170/1756f.[49] Things did not proceed all that quickly from this point onward, however; the expansion was slow and uneven. There were numerous reversals and setbacks, mainly in the form of so-called apostasy (*ridda*). What is meant by *ridda* in this context is a town's annulling of the *bayʿa* to Ibn Suʿūd and its expulsion or murder of the Wahhābī preacher or preachers.[50] Such acts of *ridda* were frequent in the first thirty years or so of the state's expansion. Even in 1168/1755, the conquest of Ḥuraymilāʾ was offset by the loss of Riyadh, which apostatized after a brief conversion.[51] The decades-long wavering of Dahām's Riyadh is exemplary of the difficulties faced by the Wahhābīs in their bid to pacify Najd. At the time of his ultimate defeat in 1187/1773, Dahām had embraced Wahhābism three times (ca. 1158/1746f, 1167/1753f, and 1177/1763f) and apostatized three times (1159/1746f, 1168/1755, and 1178/1764). His conversion to Wahhābism never lasted more than a year and was almost certainly insincere. Ibn Ghannām records that the nearly thirty-year war between al-Dirʿiyya and Riyadh cost four thousand lives—1,700 Wahhābīs (*Muslimīn*) and 2,300 non-Wahhābīs (*ḍullāl*).[52]

The greatest military setback suffered by the Wahhābīs during this early period was the invasion of Najd in 1178/1764 by the Ismāʿīlī Shīʿa of Najrān, a region in southwestern Arabia. A great battle took place with the Ismāʿīlīs near the town of al-Ḥāʾir, south of Riyadh, in Rabīʿ II 1178/September–October 1764. It was a decisive defeat for the Wahhābīs, who lost some four hundred men.[53] Meanwhile the leader of the Banū Khālid in al-Aḥsāʾ, ʿUrayʿir ibn Dujayn, seized the opportunity to mount his own invasion of

48. The most lethal operation before this was an assault on Tharmadāʾ, led by ʿUthmān ibn Muʿammar, in which some seventy from Tharmadāʾ are said to have been killed (ibid., 2:684).

49. Ibid., 2:745.

50. See, for example, ibid., 2:694 (the apostasy of Manfūḥa).

51. Ibid., 2:737–38.

52. Ibid., 2:799.

53. Ibid., 2:767–71.

Najd. Most of the towns that had previously submitted to al-Dirʿiyya abandoned it in favor of the invaders. There followed a siege of the Wahhābī capital in which the forces of Sudayr, al-Washm, Riyadh, and Manfūḥa all participated. The defenders of al-Dirʿiyya lost fifty men but managed to retain control of the town.[54]

Despite these difficulties, the Wahhābī expansion in Najd was never permanently reversed. When the Ismāʿīlīs and the forces of the Banū Khālid left Najd, al-Dirʿiyya quickly recovered, reimposing its authority on the rebellious towns. After another couple of decades, the expansion finally succeeded. The area of al-Washm fell completely in 1181/1767f.[55] The entirety of al-ʿĀriḍ was secured in 1187/1773 with the final submission of Riyadh. The conquest of Sudayr was completed by 1196/1781f, and that of al-Kharj in 1199/1784f.[56] To the north, in al-Qaṣīm, opposition was stamped out in 1196/1781f, though there was lingering resistance in ʿUnayza until 1202/1787f.[57] Farther north, in Ḥāʾil, a majority of the people (*ghālib ahl tilka ʾl-bilād*) submitted in 1201/1786f at the behest of a Wahhābī army sent from al-Qaṣīm.[58] By the 1190s/1780s, the Wahhābīs had conquered the greater part of Najd. They began to set their sights on al-Aḥsāʾ and the Ḥijāz.

In prosecuting their war, the Wahhābīs generally seem to have observed the traditional Islamic rules of offensive *jihād* that require a summons (*daʿwa*) to Islam to be issued before the commencement of hostilities. In a *fatwā* attributed to some of Ibn ʿAbd al-Wahhāb's sons, the authors refer explicitly to the matter of the summons, saying that while issuing it is not obligatory, it is preferred. In any event, they claim that the summons has been delivered far and wide in their *jihād* against the polytheists of Arabia and elsewhere: "Everyone we have fought has received our summons [*wa-kull man qātalnāhu fa-qad balaghathu daʿwatunā*]. Indeed, what we are certain of and what we believe is that the people of Yemen, the Tihāma, the Ḥijāz, al-Shām, and Iraq have received our summons."[59] This was to say, the people of these adjacent lands were fully aware of what the Wahhābīs were preaching, and so fighting them was allowed without the issuance of a more specific *daʿwa*.

54. Ibid., 2:771–76.

55. Ibid., 2:784; Cook, "Expansion of the First Saudi State," 670.

56. Ibn Ghannām, *Tārīkh*, 2:845–47, 855.

57. Ibid., 2:837–45, 2:873–74.

58. Ibid., 2:865.

59. *al-Durar al-saniyya*, 9:253.

A brief word is in order about the submission of the nomadic tribes to the first Saudi state and their conversion to Wahhābism. Ibn ʿAbd al-Wahhāb demonstrated a pronounced hostility to nomadic peoples or bedouin (*badw*), regarding them as even further removed from Islam than the typical town dwellers. In one epistle, for instance, he disputes the claim that the bedouin are Muslims, describing them as many times more unbelieving than the Jews (*kufr hāʾulāʾi aghlaẓ min kufr al-yahūd bi-aḍʿāf muḍāʿafatan*).[60] His reasoning was that they observed none of the rites of Islam but, rather, adhered to the religious customs of their forefathers. And yet, as Ibn Ghannām's account shows, a tribe, like a town, could convert to Wahhābism and accept the writ of al-Dirʿiyya, and this frequently happened. In the year 1176/1762f, for example, ʿAbd al-ʿAzīz led a raid southward against the Subayʿ tribe, who had, we are told, annulled their *bayʿa* (*naqaḍū ʾl-ʿahd*).[61] This means that the tribe had previously submitted to al-Dirʿiyya. In 1200/1785f, the Wahhābīs raided the Qaḥṭān tribe with the support of the Ẓafīr, who presumably had adopted Wahhābism as part of the process of fighting in the *jihād*.[62] While it is not fully spelled out what adopting Wahhābism meant for the tribes, it is evident that they could be accorded the status of Muslims and fight alongside the Saudi forces without abandoning nomadism. Even if Wahhābism was mainly a movement of townspeople and had the effect of curbing the excesses of the bedouin by imposing a new order in Najd, the bedouin were still capable of joining in al-Dirʿiyya's military campaigns.

New Obligations, Clarified Roles

As is apparent from Ibn Ghannām's history, a Najdī town's adoption of Wahhābism entailed a military commitment of some kind to the emirate of al-Dirʿiyya. Thus in approximately 1159/1746f, al-ʿUyayna is seen taking part in the early military response to Riyadh, Ibn Muʿammar and Ibn Suʿūd leading a raid together; the next year, in 1160/1747f, al-ʿUyayna, Ḥuraymilāʾ, al-Dirʿiyya, and Manfūḥa jointly staged an assault on Riyadh.[63] Another indication of the military requirement is found in Ibn Ghannām's account of the events of the year 1188/1774f, which saw the submission of Ḥarma and

60. Ibid., 8:118.

61. Ibn Ghannām, *Tārīkh*, 2:764.

62. Ibid., 2:858–59.

63. Ibid., 2:677–79.

al-Majmaʿa in Sudayr. Following their defeat, the towns' leaders are seen giving *bayʿa* to ʿAbd al-ʿAzīz and Ibn ʿAbd al-Wahhāb and requesting a two-year respite from being required to participate in the *jihād* (*ʿadam al-muṭālaba bi ʾl-jihād*).[64] The implication is that under normal conditions they would be obligated to contribute forces to the military efforts of al-Dirʿiyya. ʿAbd al-ʿAzīz ibn Muḥammad Āl Suʿūd hints at the same obligation in an undated letter to a correspondent in Yemen. When the ruler of a town wishes to give *bayʿa* to the Wahhābīs, he explains, we give *bayʿa* to each other and explain the religion to the town's leader; then we command him to establish the religion in his territory, call people to it, and wage *jihād* against those who oppose it. In the same letter, he remarks that Wahhābī military forces (*al-juyūsh wa ʾl-ajnād*) levied in the area of al-ʿĀriḍ are commanded to fight those who have received the summons to Islam and refuse to accept it.[65] It is evident from what he says here that propagating the religion by means of warfare was by now part and parcel of Wahhābism. A town or a people could not join the Wahhābī movement without participating in the Saudi state's expansionary *jihād*.

A town's adherence to Wahhābism also appears to have entailed a financial obligation to al-Dirʿiyya. While Ibn Ghannām is mostly silent on this matter, Ibn Bishr reports that wealth in the form of the *zakāt*, a fifth of the war spoils, and other forms of value flowed to al-Dirʿiyya during the reigns of ʿAbd al-ʿAzīz (r. 1179–1218/1765–1803) and his son Suʿūd (r. 1218–29/1803–14).[66] Previously, the Najdī towns levied noncanonical taxes (*mukūs*) on their people, while the more powerful bedouin tribes extracted tribute (*khuwa*) from the towns.[67] These practices were abolished by the Wahhābīs, but the loss in revenue was more than compensated for by the plentiful supply of war spoils resulting from the Saudi state's expansion.

In 1179/1765, Muḥammad ibn Suʿūd died, and thereafter his son, ʿAbd al-ʿAzīz, was given the *bayʿa* as his successor. Ibn Ghannām describes an elaborate scene with numerous people visiting al-Dirʿiyya from across Najd to give *bayʿa* to ʿAbd al-ʿAzīz, the affair being overseen by Ibn ʿAbd al-Wahhāb.[68]

64. Ibid., 2:804.

65. *al-Durar al-saniyya*, 9:244–45 (letter to Muḥammad ibn Aḥmad al-Ḥifẓī). For more on the army of the first Saudi state, see Vassiliev, *History of Saudi Arabia*, 132–35.

66. Ibn Bishr, *ʿUnwān al-majd*, 1:269. See further Vassiliev, *History of Saudi Arabia*, 112–18.

67. Al-Fahad, "'Imama vs. the 'Iqal," 41–42.

68. Ibn Ghannām, *Tārīkh*, 2:780.

Gradually, ʿAbd al-ʿAzīz came to assume the traditional role of *imām*, that is, of a Muslim political leader. It does not appear that ʿAbd al-ʿAzīz's father ever quite played this role. Throughout Ibn Ghannām's history, Muḥammad ibn Suʿūd and Muḥammad ibn ʿAbd al-Wahhāb are referred to by the titles *amīr* and *shaykh*, respectively. ʿAbd al-ʿAzīz, by contrast, from the time of the *bayʿa* ceremony in 1179/1765 onward, is described as the *imām*, or "the *imām* of the Muslims" (*imām al-Muslimīn*).[69] During Abd al-ʿAzīz's reign, Ibn ʿAbd al-Wahhāb would continue to perform his role as the religious leader—the *shaykh*—and occasionally he is still depicted as active in politics as well, receiving the *bayʿa* along with ʿAbd al-ʿAzīz.[70] But his political role is noticeably diminished after the death of Muḥammad ibn Suʿūd.[71] Ibn ʿAbd al-Wahhāb's last major act in affairs of state was in 1202/1787f, when, according to Ibn Ghannām, he ordered the Wahhābīs to give *bayʿa* to Suʿūd, ʿAbd al-ʿAzīz's son, as heir apparent.[72]

When Ibn ʿAbd al-Wahhāb died a few years later, in 1206/1792,[73] at the age of about ninety, there was no longer any ambiguity as to who held the reins of power in al-Dirʿiyya. ʿAbd al-ʿAzīz was the supreme leader of the Muslim community, the *imām*, and the *imāmate* was vested in the Āl Suʿūd. On his death in 1218/1803, ʿAbd al-ʿAzīz was succeeded by his son Suʿūd, a dynastic form of succession having been established.[74] Meanwhile, the religious establishment became the preserve of the family of Ibn ʿAbd al-Wahhāb, known as the Āl al-Shaykh.[75] In the first decades of the Saudi state, the division between the religious and political establishments had been less clear, but now the roles

69. See, for instance, ibid., 2:780, 816, 866. He is also described as the *imām* at the beginning of the book, where Ibn Ghannām speaks of the *imām* requesting him to write it (1:168).

70. See, for instance, ibid., 2:810, 813, 844.

71. According to Ibn Bishr, Ibn ʿAbd al-Wahhāb effectively retired from politics following the submission of Riyadh in 1187/1773, entrusting his political portfolio to ʿAbd al-ʿAzīz (*ja ʿala ʾl-shaykh al-amr bi-ʿAbd al-ʿAzīz wa-fawwaḍa umūr al-Muslimīn wa-bayt al-māl ilayhi*; *ʿUnwān al-majd*, 1:93); noted in Rentz, *Birth of the Islamic Reform Movement in Saudi Arabia*, 137–38. I agree with Rentz's view that his "retirement" was likely a more gradual process than this account suggests.

72. Ibn Ghannām, *Tārīkh*, 2:875.

73. Ibid., 2:900–904.

74. It may be noted that there is no basis for this in the classical theory of the *imāmate*, though dynastic succession is common in Islamic history.

75. That a particular family should have a monopoly on religious leadership also has no normative basis in Islam.

of the Āl Suʿūd and the Āl al-Shaykh were clarified.[76] The Āl Suʿūd were the masters of the state, while the Āl al-Shaykh, together with other Wahhābī scholars, were first and foremost preachers who sought to enforce conformity with the Wahhābī creed and Islamic law. Four of Ibn ʿAbd al-Wahhāb's sons served as scholars of note. These were Ḥusayn (d. 1224/1809),[77] ʿAbdallāh (d. 1242/1826f),[78] ʿAlī (d. 1245/1829f),[79] and Ibrāhīm (fl. 1251/1835f).[80] According to Ibn Bishr, who attended a study circle with one of these sons in al-Dirʿiyya, the blind Ḥusayn was the chief *qāḍī* in al-Dirʿiyya (*al-qāḍī fī balad al-Dirʿiyya*) and the first successor to Ibn ʿAbd al-Wahhāb (*al-khalīfa baʿd abīhi*).[81] Following Ḥusayn's death in 1224/1809, ʿAbdallāh took charge as successor to his brother (*al-khalīfa baʿd akhīhi Ḥusayn*).[82] Like their father, the sons would leave behind a corpus of writings to their name, ʿAbdallāh being the most prolific. In addition to numerous *fatwās*, he authored a long refutation of a Zaydī critic of Wahhābism and a biography of the Prophet.[83]

Upon Ibn ʿAbd al-Wahhāb's death, some of his scholarly opponents celebrated his passing with exclamations of joy and relief. In Bahrain, ʿUthmān ibn Jāmiʿ (d. 1240/1824f),[84] a student of Muḥammad ibn Fayrūz's, marked the occasion by writing: "The damned one has died and joy has come" (*māta ʾl-shaqī wa-jāʾa ʾl-faraj*), an Arabic sentence with the numerical value of 1206, the year of his death.[85] Another student of Ibn Fayrūz's, the Zubayr-based

76. This analysis accords with Crawford's view that the so-called pact of al-Dirʿiyya, wherein these roles are said to have been specified, is back-projection (*Ibn 'Abd al-Wahhab*, 36).

77. On him, see Ibn Bishr, *ʿUnwān al-majd*, 1:204, 290–91; Āl al-Shaykh, *Mashāhīr*, 43; Āl Bassām, *ʿUlamāʾ Najd*, 2:63–65.

78. On him, see Ibn Bishr, *ʿUnwān al-majd*, 1:205; Āl al-Shaykh, *Mashāhīr*, 48–69; Āl Bassām, *ʿUlamāʾ Najd*, 1:169–79; al-Qāḍī, *Rawḍat al-nāẓirīn*, 1:421–24.

79. On him, see Ibn Bishr, *ʿUnwān al-majd*, 1:206; Āl al-Shaykh, *Mashāhīr*, 70–71; Āl Bassām, *ʿUlamāʾ Najd*, 5:284–86; al-Qāḍī, *Rawḍat al-nāẓirīn*, 2:135–37.

80. On him, see Ibn Bishr, *ʿUnwān al-majd*, 1:206; Āl al-Shaykh, *Mashāhīr*, 72; Āl Bassām, *ʿUlamāʾ Najd*, 1:417–18. Both Āl al-Shaykh and Āl Bassām report that he was alive in 1251/1835f, but this is on the authority of a rather late source—ʿAbd al-Raḥmān ibn Qāsim (d. 1392/1972).

81. Ibn Bishr, *ʿUnwān al-majd*, 1:204, 206. This is the first example of many blind scholars in Wahhābī history.

82. Ibid., 1:205.

83. See *Majmūʿat al-rasāʾil wa ʾl-masāʾil al-Najdiyya*, 4:47–221 (*Kitāb jawāb ahl al-sunna al-nabawiyya*); Āl al-Shaykh, *Mukhtaṣar sīrat al-rasūl*.

84. On him, see Ibn Fayrūz, *Tarājim*, f. 78b; Ibn Sanad, *Sabāʾik al-ʿasjad*, 216–18; Ibn Ḥumayd, *al-Suḥub al-wābila*, 2:701–2; Āl Bassām, *ʿUlamāʾ Najd*, 5:109–12.

85. al-ʿAtīqī, *Tuwuffiya rukn al-ḍalāl*.

Ṣāliḥ ibn Sayf al-ʿAtīqī (d. 1223/1808),[86] put the sentence into verse in a letter to Ibn Jāmiʿ:

With the death of the evil one, the *imām* of error,
the bedrock of corruption, the leader unto crookedness,
The Musaylima of al-ʿĀriḍ, the aggressor,
the one who will pass unto hellfire and there be enfolded,
The good news reached me and you recorded:
"The damned one has died and joy has come."[87]

Yet the men's celebration, in 1206/1792, was premature. Wahhābism was not going to die with its founder. Not only had Ibn ʿAbd al-Wahhāb cultivated a new generation of Wahhābī scholars who would continue to preach his doctrine and refine it in certain ways, but his movement was now embodied in a state, the first Saudi state, that had yet to reach its zenith.

Expansion Beyond Najd

Following the submission of Najd in the 1190s/1780s, the expansion of the Saudi state continued beyond central Arabia: to the east in al-Aḥsāʾ, to the west in the Ḥijāz, and finally north and south. The expansion was not consistent in approach, the biggest contrast being seen between east and west. While the Wahhābīs were generally violent and aggressive in al-Aḥsāʾ, in the Ḥijāz they exhibited a significant level of restraint. The difference seems to owe to the heavy concentration in al-Aḥsāʾ of Imāmī Shīʿa, whom the Wahhābīs were seeking to annihilate. Such anti-Shīʿī hostility is unsurprising given Ibn ʿAbd al-Wahhāb's views on the Shīʿa, or the Rejectionists (*rāfiḍa*), as he called them. As he wrote in one of his letters, the Rejectionists, who were the first to bring *shirk* into the Muslim community (*awwal man adkhala ʾl-shirk fī hādhihi ʾl-umma*), had abandoned Islam altogether (*khārijūn ʿan al-sunna bal ʿan al-milla*).[88] Mundane power politics likely played a role as well in motivating the

86. On him, see Ibn Fayrūz, *Tarājim*, f. 78b; Ibn Sanad, *Sabāʾik al-ʿasjad*, 268–70; Ibn Ḥumayd, *al-Suḥub al-wābila*, 2:429–30; Āl Bassām, *ʿUlamāʾ Najd*, 2:474–77.

87. al-ʿAtīqī, *Tuwuffiya rukn al-ḍalāl* (meter = *mutaqārib*).

88. Ibn Ghannām, *Tārīkh*, 1:412 (letter to Ibn al-Suwaydī); Ibn ʿAbd al-Wahhāb, *Muʾallafāt al-shaykh*, 7:42 (*Risāla fī ʾl-radd ʿalā ʾl-rāfiḍa*). *Rāfiḍa* is a derogatory term for the Shīʿa that refers either to the Shīʿa's alleged rejection of Islam or to their rejection of the first two (in the Sunnī view) rightly guided caliphs, Abū Bakr and ʿUmar.

Wahhābī approach in the east. The rulers of al-Aḥsāʾ had pushed Ibn ʿAbd al-Wahhāb out of al-ʿUyayna back in 1157/1744f, they had launched a campaign against al-Dirʿiyya in 1172/1758f,[89] and they had taken advantage of the Ismāʿīlī invasion of Najd in 1178/1764 to launch another invasion. Al-Aḥsāʾ was thus perceived as both a religious and a political threat, and it was also a potential source of revenue as a trading hub and a rich date palm oasis.

Al-Aḥsāʾ

The first of the Wahhābī incursions into al-Aḥsāʾ took place before the consolidation of Wahhābī power in Najd. In 1176/1762f, ʿAbd al-ʿAzīz Āl Suʿūd led a raid into the area, beginning with al-Muṭayrifī, a small town north of the central oases, then making his way south to al-Mubarraz. Ibn Ghannām, who, it should be recalled, was from al-Aḥsāʾ, describes this as a particularly bloody affair. In the first town, the Wahhābīs attacked the inhabitants by surprise, entering homes and killing all the polytheists (*mushrikīn*) they could find. The dead numbered some seventy. Turning to al-Mubarraz, they killed a group of farmers working in the palm groves.[90]

The next raids into al-Aḥsāʾ, which began in 1198/1783f and were led by Suʿūd ibn ʿAbd al-ʿAzīz Āl Suʿūd, are depicted by Ibn Ghannām as similarly merciless rampages.[91] Later, during a raid in 1203/1788f, the Wahhābīs killed more than three hundred inhabitants of the town of al-Fuḍūl, near al-Hufūf. The victims, described as heretics (*ahl al-zaygh wa ʾl-shirk*), are said to have called on their gods to protect them (*daʿaw ālihatahum*) only to be killed like cattle (*qutilū qatl al-naʿam*).[92] Far greater carnage followed in 1206/1791f, during another Suʿūd-led raid that extended all the way to the coastal city of al-Qaṭīf. The people there, Ibn Ghannām records, "had built a lighthouse for Rejectionism" (*rafaʿū lil-rifḍ manāran*) and worshipped their gods day and night. Al-Qaṭīf held off the invaders, but the nearby town of Sayhāt was not so lucky. In a single day, 1,500 of its inhabitants were struck down, and the Wahhābīs destroyed Shīʿī places of worship (*kanāʾis al-rifḍ wa ʾl-ṭughyān*)

89. Ibn Ghannām, *Tārīkh*, 2:751–53.

90. Ibid., 2:762–63. Ibn Ghannām's tone is boastful in describing these campaigns in al-Aḥsāʾ.

91. Ibid., 2:849–50.

92. Ibid., 2:882.

and burned Shīʿī books.[93] The numbers may be exaggerated, but no doubt these were highly traumatic events for the Shīʿī population of the east.

In 1207/1792f, the Wahhābīs signaled their intention to annex the province, not just raid it. That year, after leading a raid that killed six hundred of the Banū Khālid, the ruling tribe in the area, Suʿūd dispatched two messengers to the people of al-Aḥsāʾ, urging them to submit to the rule of al-Dirʿiyya and accept Islam and warning of the consequences of not doing so.[94] This was in mid-Shaʿbān 1207/late March 1793. Probably hoping to fend off further offensives, the inhabitants returned a favorable response. In Ramaḍān 1207/April 1793, Suʿūd arrived in al-Aḥsāʾ and was welcomed there as ruler, receiving the *bayʿa* from the area's inhabitants (*ʿāhadūhu ʿalā ʾl-Islām*). Ibn Ghannām describes him as overseeing a drastic religious transformation during his short presence. The actions taken included destroying grave sites (*al-maʿbadāt wa ʾl-qubab wa ʾl-qubūr*) and places of Shīʿī ritual (*kanāʾis al-rifḍ wa ʾl-bidaʿ*), imposing communal prayer (*iẓhār al-ṣalawāt fī ʾl-masājid*), and banning a number of practices contrary to Islamic law (*ibṭāl mā khālafa ʾl-sharʿ min al-aḥkām*), such as usury (*al-ribā*) and noncanonical taxes (*al-ʿushūr wa ʾl-amkās*).[95] Subsequent events show that a number of Wahhābī preachers were brought to al-Aḥsāʾ to impart the Wahhābī doctrine and maintain the new religious dispensation.

The early imposition of Wahhābism in al-Aḥsāʾ, however, did not take. Not long after Suʿūd's departure, a revolt broke out against the new Wahhābī masters, led by a group described as Shīʿī heretics and miscreants (*rafaḍa wa-fujjār*). In early Shawwāl 1207/mid-May 1793, they attacked and killed the several Wahhābī preachers sent by al-Dirʿiyya, as well as certain other representatives of the Saudi state. The total killed was close to thirty.[96] Three months later, in Muḥarram 1208/August 1793, Suʿūd and his forces returned to the area with a vengeance. After several fierce battles, sieges, and punitive raids, including one battle that killed some sixty fighters from the town of al-Mubarraz, the leader of the Banū Khālid, Barrāk ibn ʿAbd al-Muḥsin, sued for peace. Barrāk assured Suʿūd that the people of al-Aḥsāʾ would reenter the faith, and Suʿūd agreed to return to Najd on the condition that Barrāk oversee the conversion. The agreement reached, Barrāk set about suppressing dissent in the various towns, receiving the *bayʿa*—sometimes by force—on behalf of

93. Ibid., 2:899–900.
94. Ibid., 2:906–9.
95. Ibid., 2:909–10.
96. Ibid., 2:912–13.

the ruler in al-Dirʿiyya, and ordering that the religious principles of Wahhābism be observed.[97]

There was to be one more attempt at revolt in al-Aḥsāʾ, in 1210/1796, but this time the conspirators were thwarted before they could strike. As Ibn Ghannām relates, when a Wahhābī commander caught wind of what was afoot, he quickly put sixty of the suspected conspirators to death. It was the beginning of a brief campaign of exceptional cruelty aimed at stamping out any last signs of rebellion. In Dhū ʾl-ḥijja 1210/June–July 1796, Suʿūd himself arrived to lead the effort. After having the people renew the *bayʿa* in public, he proceeded to retaliate by meting out punishments (*iqāmat al-qiṣāṣ wa ʾl-ḥudūd*) to all those involved in this "second apostasy" (*al-ridda al-thāniya*). He ordered some of the miscreants to be beheaded (*afnā ruʾūs dhawī ʾl-sharr wa ʾl-fasād*) and exiled the rest (*wa-azāḥa bāqiyahum ʿan al-bilād*). The executions continued for days as more suspects were rounded up. In addition, Suʿūd ordered the destruction of more shrines, forced people to give up their weapons on pain of death, ordered the walls and towers surrounding the different towns of al-Aḥsāʾ torn down, and built a massive fort with a permanent contingent of forces. Ibn Ghannām ends his description of these events by quoting Q. 8:60: "And make ready for them what you can of strength and troops of forces, to strike terror."[98] The conquest of al-Aḥsāʾ was complete, though challenges remained.

The next two years saw two major efforts to expel the Wahhābīs from al-Aḥsāʾ, neither of which would succeed. The first was a campaign led by Thuwaynī ibn ʿAbdallāh (d. 1212/1797), chief of the Muntafiq tribe of southern Iraq, acting at the behest of the Ottoman governor of Baghdad. The British traveler John Jackson, who passed through Iraq in the late 1790s, describes "Sheik Twyney" as "a very powerful Arab prince; having under his government the whole of the right banks of the Euphrates, from nearly as high as Hilla down to Bussora."[99] In 1211/1796f, the Ottoman governor of Baghdad, Sulaymān Bāshā (d. 1217/1802),[100] recruited Thuwaynī to prepare a large-scale operation to oust the Wahhābīs from al-Aḥsāʾ. According to Ibn Ghannām's account, when Thuwaynī stopped in Basra to gather additional forces, some of the anti-Wahhābī scholars there wrote poems for him encouraging the effort. One of these scholars was Muḥammad ibn Fayrūz. Thuwaynī collected his army and

97. Ibid., 2:915–22.

98. Ibid., 2:931–46.

99. Jackson, *Journey from India*, 51–52.

100. For a brief biography, see al-Karkūklī, *Dawḥat al-wuzarāʾ*, 218–19.

set out in Sha'bān 1211/February 1797; two months later, Su'ūd left Najd with his forces to meet the enemy. Thuwaynī's campaign came to an abrupt end with his assassination at the hands of a Wahhābī slave in Muḥarram 1212/June–July 1797. His army fell into disarray and was quickly beaten back.[101]

Another challenge came the following year, when Sulaymān Bāshā ordered his deputy governor, 'Alī Kahyā (fl. 1222/1807), to lead a second expedition against the Wahhābī presence in al-Aḥsā'. 'Alī set out from Baghdad with his forces in Rabī' II 1213/October 1798, but returned in Ṣafar 1214/July 1799 after inconclusive military operations.[102] Thereafter, a Wahhābī envoy visited Baghdad to ratify a truce. The ceremony was observed by Harford Jones Brydges, the British resident political adviser in Baghdad, who was invited to attend the reception at Sulaymān Bāshā's palace. His account is worth quoting at length as it illustrates the Wahhābī view of the Ottomans at this time. "[T]he envoy proceeded towards the foot of the staircase which led into the room," writes Jones Brydges,

> and . . . with great gravity and dignity unsupported marched up the stairs, entered the room, and before any further ceremony could take place, sat himself down at a small distance immediately opposite the paçha, and addressed him in Arabic as follows:—"Hoy Suleiman! peace be upon all those who think right. Abdul Aziz has sent me to deliver to you this letter, and to receive from you the ratification of an agreement made between his son, Saoud, and your servant Ally; let it be done soon, and in good form; and the curse of God be on him who acts treacherously. If you seek instruction, Abdul Aziz will afford it." Thus ended, the envoy, to the utter astonishment and apparent confusion of the paçha, rose, and departed.[103]

The phrase "peace be upon all those who think right" is almost certainly Jones Brydges's translation of *al-salām 'alā man ittaba'a 'l-hudā* (peace be upon whoever follows right guidance), the phrase with which the Prophet is said to

101. Ibn Ghannām, *Tārīkh*, 2:947–63, 1017–23. Cf. Ibn Sanad, *Maṭāli' al-su'ūd*, 293–95; al-Karkūklī, *Dawḥat al-wuzarā'*, 204–5. For the date of Thuwaynī's assassination, see Ibn Bishr, *'Unwān al-majd*, 1:236.

102. al-Karkūklī, *Dawḥat al-wuzarā'*, 205–10. Cf. Ibn Sanad, *Maṭāli' al-su'ūd*, 313–21; Ibn Bishr, *'Unwān al-majd*, 1:252–55. Al-Karkūklī and Ibn Sanad provide elaborate truce terms, but a copy of the truce preserved in the Ottoman archive, dated 4 Jumādā II 1214, stipulates simply that the parties not attack one another; see the text in Ibn Sanad, *Maṭāli' al-su'ūd*, 319n2.

103. Jones Brydges, *Account of the Transactions of His Majesty's Mission to the Court of Persia*, 2:24–26; cf. Vassiliev, *History of Saudi Arabia*, 95–96, where part of this is quoted.

have addressed his non-Muslim adversaries. The Wahhābī envoy thus strode nonchalantly into the Ottoman governor's palace in Baghdad, addressed him as an infidel, and offered to provide him instruction in Islam. Sulaymān Bāshā was shocked at such behavior. The truce, as we shall see, did not last long.

The Ḥijāz

Unlike in the east, the Wahhābī expansion in the west was preceded by respectful scholarly overtures. As the seat of Islam's two holiest sites, the Ḥijāz evidently required a more delicate approach than al-Aḥsāʾ. On two occasions, in 1185/1771f and 1204/1789f, the Wahhābī scholar ʿAbd al-ʿAzīz al-Ḥuṣayyin (d. 1237/1822)[104] was sent to Mecca to explain Wahhābism to its ruler, the *sharīf*, and to engage the scholars of the city in debate. The first mission was preceded by correspondence with the Sharīf Aḥmad ibn Saʿīd (r. 1184–86/1770–73). Ibn Ghannām preserves a letter, respectful in tone, from ʿAbd al-ʿAzīz Āl Suʿūd and Ibn ʿAbd al-Wahhāb to the *sharīf*.[105] The debate in Mecca between the local scholars and al-Ḥuṣayyin that followed, according to Ibn Ghannām, revolved around the issues of generalized *takfīr* (*al-takfīr biʾl-ʿumūm*), the destruction of tombs at grave sites, and the supplication of righteous persons, including asking them for help (*istighātha*) and asking them for intercession (*shafāʿa*). Al-Ḥuṣayyin denied that the Wahhābīs engaged in generalized *takfīr* but was adamant that tombs be destroyed and that supplication amounted to *shirk*. Ibn Ghannām claims that the scholars of Mecca were convinced by his arguments,[106] a claim that strains credulity. According to another account of this event, by the Meccan-based Shāfiʿī scholar Zaynī Daḥlān (d. 1304/1886), the Meccan scholars scoffed at the Wahhābī scholar's performance.[107] Al-Ḥuṣayyin's second mission to Mecca was less eventful than the first. Ibn Ghannām relates that he was sent after the Sharīf Ghālib ibn Musāʿid (r. 1202–28/1788–1813) requested a scholar to explain the truth about Wahhābism. Al-Ḥuṣayyin arrived with a letter from Ibn ʿAbd al-Wahhāb to

104. On him, see Ibn Bishr, *ʿUnwān al-majd*, 1:414–17; Āl al-Shaykh, *Mashāhīr*, 206–11. The Wahhābī tradition preserves a polemic on *tawassul* by him (*al-Durar al-saniyya*, 2:173–202).

105. Ibn Ghannām, *Tārīkh*, 2:790.

106. Ibid., 2:789–91.

107. Daḥlān, *Khulāṣat al-kalām*, 228. He also claims that a group of Wahhābī scholars came to Mecca for the same purpose during the first reign of Sharīf Masʿūd ibn Saʿīd (r. 1145–65/1732–52) and that this had similarly failed.

the *sharīf*. This time, the scholars of Mecca refused to debate or meet with him.[108] This kind of mission to Mecca would be repeated one more time by another Wahhābī scholar, Ḥamad ibn Muʿammar (d. 1225/1811),[109] who came to Mecca at the request of the *sharīf* in 1211/1796f. Ḥamad performed the *ʿumra* (the secondary pilgrimage to Mecca), and a debate was held with the city's scholars. At its conclusion, they asked Ḥamad to put his arguments into writing, which he did.[110]

By the time of this third mission, the Wahhābīs and the *sharīf* were engaged militarily. The two sides first came to blows in 1205/1790f, when Ghālib launched a months-long offensive against Najd.[111] According to Daḥlān, this was a preemptive attack aimed at preventing the Wahhābīs from gaining control of the Ḥijāz.[112] It was not successful, however, as every year the Wahhābīs gained more followers among the *sharīf*'s tribal allies. In 1210/1795f, Ghālib's forces suffered a defeat in the desert at the hands of the Wahhābīs and these tribes.[113] By 1212/1797f, the majority of the tribes in the vicinity of the Ḥijāz had allied with al-Dirʿiyya.[114] During that year, after a crushing battle at al-Khurma, the *sharīf* and ʿAbd al-ʿAzīz Āl Suʿūd reached a truce that allowed the Wahhābīs to participate in the *ḥajj*, which they were previously forbidden from doing. Suʿūd set out for Mecca and performed his first *ḥajj* in 1214/1800.[115]

By this point, Ghālib's position vis-à-vis the Wahhābīs had grown considerably weaker, though the truce remained in place until 1217/1803. That year, Ghālib was betrayed by one of his commanders, ʿUthmān al-Muḍāyifī, in an event that led to the first Wahhābī occupation of Mecca. After visiting al-Dirʿiyya and giving *bayʿa* to ʿAbd al-ʿAzīz, ʿUthmān al-Muḍāyifī gathered an army and besieged the city of al-Ṭāʾif in Dhū ʾl-qaʿda 1217/February–March 1803. By all accounts, the siege ended in a massacre. Ibn Bishr records

108. Ibn Ghannām, *Tārīkh*, 2:886–87.

109. On him, see Ibn Bishr, *ʿUnwān al-majd*, 1:303–4; Āl al-Shaykh, *Mashāhīr*, 202–5; Āl Bassām, *ʿUlamāʾ Najd*, 2:121–28; al-Qāḍī, *Rawḍat al-nāẓirīn*, 3:111–13. He coauthored some *fatwā*s with Ibn ʿAbd al-Wahhāb and others with his sons, available in *al-Durar al-saniyya*.

110. Ibn Ghannām, *Tārīkh*, 2:967–72. For Ibn Muʿammar's treatise (*al-Fawākih al-ʿidhāb fī ʾl-radd ʿalā man lam yuḥkim al-sunna wa ʾl-kitāb*), see ibid., 2:972–1016.

111. Ibid., 2:888–95.

112. Daḥlān, *Khulāṣat al-kalām*, 228.

113. Ibn Ghannām, *Tārīkh*, 2:929–30.

114. Ibid., 2:1032–33. This is the point at which Ibn Ghannām's chronicle ends; I rely mainly on Ibn Bishr's account for what follows.

115. Ibn Bishr, *ʿUnwān al-majd*, 1:245, 255–56.

that nearly two hundred were killed in the streets and in their homes, while Daḥlān describes an even more gruesome scene without specifying the number of casualties.[116] A month later, during the *ḥajj*, Su'ūd and his forces appeared outside Mecca, prompting Ghālib to withdraw to Jeddah. Guaranteeing the security and safety of its people, Su'ūd entered Mecca and set about destroying tombs with his followers. Before leaving, he stationed troops in a fort outside the city walls and appointed Ghālib's brother, 'Abd al-Mu'īn ibn Musā'id, as Mecca's ruler. Su'ūd remained in the city for two or three weeks.[117]

This first Wahhābī occupation of Mecca was short-lived. In Rabī' I 1218/ July 1803, Ghālib regained control of Mecca, but his hold would last only a few years. After an extended blockade of the city imposed by Su'ūd's allies, Ghālib relented in Dhū 'l-qa'da 1220/February 1806, agreeing to terms with Su'ūd, who was now the head of the Saudi state. This time, Wahhābism would be instituted in Mecca. This meant that the scholars were required to teach Ibn 'Abd al-Wahhāb's writings, communal prayer was mandated, and tobacco was banned, among other measures. In agreeing to these terms, Ghālib was allowed to remain as the city's nominal ruler.[118] Earlier in the year (i.e., 1220/1805), Medina fell to the Wahhābīs as well, and a similar campaign of tomb destruction ensued.[119] The massacre at al-Ṭā'if notwithstanding, the conquest of the Ḥijāz had taken place with far less bloodshed than the conquest of al-Aḥsā'.

South and North

According to Ibn Bishr, al-Dir'iyya was able to conquer Mecca in 1220/1806 because the surrounding areas were already under Wahhābī sway. Najd, 'Asīr, Yemen, and the rest of the Ḥijāz were already part of Su'ūd's realm, which allowed him to close the roads leading to Mecca and impose a siege.

When it came to 'Asīr and Yemen, the Wahhābī expansion proceeded in much the same way as it did among the tribes in the Ḥijāz: The rulers of these areas saw momentum going the Wahhābīs' way, and they threw their lot in accordingly. An example of this is the case of Abū Nuqṭa (d. 1224/1809), the

116. Ibid., 1:258–59; Daḥlān, *Khulāṣat al-kalām*, 273–75.

117. Ibn Bishr, *'Unwān al-majd*, 1:260–61 (twenty days); Daḥlān, *Khulāṣat al-kalām*, 275–79 (fourteen days).

118. Ibn Bishr, *'Unwān al-majd*, 1:279–80; Daḥlān, *Khulāṣat al-kalām*, 292–93.

119. Ibn Bishr, *'Unwān al-majd*, 1:280–81.

ruler of ʿAsīr, who adopted Wahhābism sometime in 1211–12/1796–97f.[120] Joining the Wahhābīs made particularly good sense to him, as he and Ghālib were fierce rivals. Abū Nuqṭa would be a dependable ally, though al-Dirʿiyya's influence in the southwest of Arabia does not appear to have been very strong otherwise. Farther to the south, in Jīzān, Abū Mismār, the ruler of the town of Abū ʿArīsh, embraced Wahhābism in the early nineteenth century. But though nominally a vassal of al-Dirʿiyya, he defied Suʿūd's orders to attack Sanaa in 1224/1809, prompting Suʿūd to launch a campaign against Abū Mismār.[121] Unlike in al-Aḥsāʾ and the Ḥijāz, in the southern regions Wahhābī control remained mostly weak and uncertain.

To the north of Najd, beyond the region of Jabal Shammar, the Wahhābīs never managed even this level of control. Their commitment to northward expansion was nonetheless strong. In the 1210s/1790s, they began carrying out raids against the towns and tribes of lower Iraq and Syria. Wahhābī raiding in southern Iraq began in 1212/1798, when Suʿūd led an expedition to the towns of Sūq al-Shuyūkh and al-Samāwa.[122] Further operations were likely held off on account of the aforementioned truce reached with Sulaymān Bāshā, the governor of Baghdad, in 1214/1799, but this did not prove a hindrance for long. Less than two years later, Suʿūd and his forces entered the Shīʿī holy city of Karbalāʾ and committed what is perhaps the most infamous atrocity of the first Saudi state. According to Ibn Bishr, Suʿūd arrived outside the city in Dhū ʾl-qaʿda 1216/March–April 1802, whereupon

> the Muslims gathered against it, climbed its walls, and entered it by force. They killed most of its people in the markets and homes; they destroyed the tomb erected above the grave of al-Ḥusayn (as claimed by those who believe in it); they took what was inside and around the shrine; and they took the monument that was placed above the grave and studded with emeralds, rubies, and jewels. They took all the various possessions that they found in the place—weapons, vestments, household effects, gold, silver, heavy manuscripts, and other things—such that cannot be counted. They remained there only one morning, leaving with all the possessions before midday. 2,000 of its inhabitants were killed.[123]

120. Jaḥḥāf, *Durar nuḥūr al-ḥūr al-ʿīn*, 635.

121. Ibn Bishr, *ʿUnwān al-majd*, 1:292–94.

122. Ibid., 1:244.

123. Ibn Bishr, *ʿUnwān al-majd*, 1:257; cf. Vassiliev, *History of Saudi Arabia*, 98. "Al-Ḥusayn" refers to Ḥusayn ibn ʿAlī (d. 11/632), the third *imām* in Twelver Shīʿism, who was killed at Karbalāʾ in a battle with the Umayyads.

In May 1804, the French Orientalist and diplomat Jean-Baptiste Louis Rousseau, who was based in Iraq, published a report on the sacking of Karbalāʾ in a French periodical. His account, the earliest to have been written, dates the event to April 20, 1802, and puts the death toll at 4,500.[124] In describing the Wahhābīs and their attack, Rousseau's account seems to reflect the concerns of the rulers in Baghdad. The Wahhābīs, he states, are a group of radical Muslims lusting after martyrdom. They are a people "who regard death with such contempt as to go in search of it, who are animated by an extraordinary fanaticism, who believe they are making themselves martyrs by fighting against foreign nations." In his view, the Wahhābīs' raiding in Iraq portended further territorial expansion northward. "There is no doubt," he writes, "that if the Wahabis continue in the same way as they began, they will gradually subdue all of Arabia, and even extend their possessions to Mesopotamia and part of Syria."[125] In Rajab 1218/November 1803, ʿAbd al-ʿAzīz Āl Suʿūd was killed in al-Dirʿiyya by an assassin. The assailant was rumored to be a Shīʿī from Karbalāʾ, who had journeyed to Najd to take vengeance for the atrocity in his town.[126]

The attack on Karbalāʾ was not the last Wahhābī raid in the north. Two months before Rousseau's May 1804 report, Suʿūd was back in Iraq leading his forces against Basra and Zubayr. The Wahhābīs besieged Zubayr for twelve days, destroying the shrines outside its walls, including the tombs of al-Ḥasan al-Baṣrī and Ṭalḥa ibn al-Zubayr.[127] The year 1220/1805f saw another round of raiding, this one targeting not only Basra and Zubayr but also Najaf and al-Samāwa. Ibn Bishr describes a series of skirmishes with minimal casualties.[128] A few years later, in Jumādā I 1223/June–July 1808, Suʿūd returned to Karbalāʾ. However, finding it better fortified, he retreated, plundering several villages around Basra and Zubayr along the way.[129] In Rabīʿ II 1225/May–June 1810, Suʿūd led his forces into southern Syria for the first time, raiding in the vicinity of the towns of Buṣrā and al-Muzayrīb and allegedly inspiring dread in the

124. Rousseau, "Notice sur la horde des Wahabis." Cf. al-Karkūklī, *Dawḥat al-wuzarāʾ*, 217 (same date as Ibn Bishr, death toll of around one thousand); Ibn Sanad, *Maṭāliʿ al-suʿūd*, 333 (year 1216, no death toll given). On the authorship of Rousseau's report, which is unsigned, see Bonacina, *Wahhabis Seen Through European Eyes*, 54.

125. Rousseau, "Notice sur la horde des Wahabis," 1102.

126. Ibn Bishr, *ʿUnwān al-majd*, 1:261–62. Cf. al-Karkūklī, *Dawḥat al-wuzarāʾ*, 227; Jaḥḥāf, *Durar nuḥūr al-ḥūr al-ʿīn*, 848–49.

127. Ibn Bishr, *ʿUnwān al-majd*, 1:273–75.

128. Ibid., 1:281–82.

129. Ibid., 1:287.

Ottoman governor of Damascus.[130] Whether these northern raids were paving the way for territorial expansion into Iraq and Syria, as Rousseau feared, is unclear. The letters from Suʿūd to the Ottoman governors of Baghdad and al-Shām, however, strongly suggest that this was the Wahhābīs' intention.

The Letters of Suʿūd ibn ʿAbd al-ʿAzīz Āl Suʿūd

During his lifetime, Ibn ʿAbd al-Wahhāb had played the role of chief author of letters and epistles setting out the Wahhābī doctrine and calling people to Islam. After his death, some of this responsibility devolved on ʿAbd al-ʿAzīz Āl Suʿūd. In approximately 1210/1795, as was seen in chapter 1, ʿAbd al-ʿAzīz addressed a long epistle "to whoever sees it among the scholars and judges of the Two Holy Places, al-Shām, Egypt, and Iraq, and all other scholars east and west."[131] He would dispatch at least one more epistle like it, this one addressed "to whoever sees it among the people of the lands of the *ʿajam* and the *rūm*."[132] From the way these epistles are addressed, it is clear that the Wahhābī ruler believed it was necessary to bring Wahhābism not only to the inhabitants of Arabia but to all the world's nominal Muslims. ʿAbd al-ʿAzīz viewed the expansion of Wahhābism and the Saudi state as ordained by God. His second epistle struck a triumphalist chord. As he wrote of the opponents of Wahhābism, "God has given us victory over them and bequeathed to us their land, territories, and possessions. This is God's practice and His custom with the messengers and those who follow them, until the Day of Resurrection."[133]

When ʿAbd al-ʿAzīz died in 1218/1803, his son Suʿūd inherited the job of writing such letters. Suʿūd's letters were far more menacing than anything ʿAbd al-ʿAzīz or Ibn ʿAbd al-Wahhāb had written, as well as clearer in conveying the Wahhābīs' territorial designs north of Arabia. Three extant letters of his are worth highlighting. The first is a response to a letter from the governor of Baghdad, ʿAbdallāh Bāshā (r. 1225–28/1810–13), who like many governors of Baghdad during this period enjoyed a rather short reign.[134] In his letter,

130. Ibid., 1:298–99.

131. Ibn Siḥmān, *al-Hadiyya al-saniyya*, 4–28, at 4.

132. *al-Durar al-saniyya*, 1:258–64, at 258. The words *ʿajam* and *rūm* appear to mean the non-Arabs of Persia and Anatolia, respectively.

133. Ibid., 1:262. ʿAbd al-ʿAzīz also wrote letters to individuals; see 1:265–84, 2:166–69, 9:244–46.

134. Ibid., 9:264–89. In his letter, which is undated, Suʿūd identifies his correspondent only as *wazīr Baghdād*. We can identify him as ʿAbdallāh Bāshā, however, as Suʿūd refers to two

written sometime in 1225–27/1810–12, Suʿūd refers to many of the events that had transpired between the Saudi state and Ottoman Iraq, including the Wahhābī attack on Karbalāʾ. He takes great pride in the massacre there: "Your statement that we took Karbalāʾ, slaughtered its people, and took its property—praise belongs to God, Lord of the Worlds! We make no apology for this, and we say, 'the unbelievers shall have the likes thereof' (Q. 47:10)."[135] Speaking more generally of the Wahhābīs' predilection for *jihād*, he writes: "As for what you mentioned that we kill the unbelievers, this is something for which we make no apology and that we do not minimize. We shall do more of it, God willing. . . . We abase the unbelievers, shed their blood, and make booty of their property, by the might and power of God." This statement is followed by several Qurʾānic verses related to offensive *jihād*, including Q. 9:5: "Then, when the sacred months are drawn away, slay the polytheists wherever you find them, and take them, and confine them, and lie in wait for them at every place of ambush." Suʿūd continues by noting that "the verses and *ḥadīth*s concerning *jihād* and encouraging it are countless; we have no labor but *jihād* [*wa-lā lanā daʾba illā ʾl-jihād*], and we have no appetite save for the possessions of the unbelievers [*wa-lā lanā maʾkala illā min amwāl al-kuffār*]."[136]

Suʿūd's intentions regarding his correspondent's territory were just as evident as his violent ardor. His hope was that God would soon replace the *shirk* in ʿAbdallāh Bāshā's lands with Wahhābī Islam: "We will eradicate the falsehood from it and establish the truth in it, God willing."[137] Suʿūd goes on to ridicule ʿAbdallāh for never having performed the *ḥajj* and being unable to do so given Wahhābī control of Mecca, and he further scorns ʿAbdallāh with reference to the latter's Christian slave origins: "I hope that you die upon your Christian religion and are among the pigs of hellfire."[138] "If you desire salvation and the safety of [your] realm," Suʿūd continues, "then I summon you to Islam, as [the Prophet] said to Heraclius, king of the Romans, 'Submit, and you shall be

---

biographical details: the *wazīr*'s Christian birth and the fact that he was purchased as a slave by Sulaymān Bāshā (r. 1194–1217/1780–1802). See 9:286–87. ʿAbdallāh Bāshā is the only governor of Baghdad from this time who fits this description; see Longrigg, *Four Centuries of Modern Iraq*, 227.

135. *al-Durar al-saniyya*, 9:284. We can be sure that the letter was written around 1225–27/1810–12 because it refers to the fact that Mecca is still under Saudi control (9:285–86); ʿAbdallāh Bāshā's reign began in 1225/1810, and Saudi control of Mecca ended in 1227/1812.

136. Ibid., 9:280–82.

137. Ibid., 9:282.

138. Ibid., 9:286.

safe, and God shall reward you twice over. But, if you turn away, the sin of the husbandmen shall be upon you.'"[139] This was a quotation from the Prophet's letter to Heraclius that had preceded the Islamic expansion into Iraq and Syria in the seventh century. By quoting it, Suʿūd was indicating that a similar fate was in store for the Ottomans should they fail to accept Wahhābism. There was to be no truce (*muhādana*) between al-Dirʿiyya and Baghdad. One outcome was for ʿAbdallāh to accept Islam, but "if you refuse, then we say to you as God says, 'but if they turn away, then they are clearly in schism; God will suffice you for them; He is the All-hearing, the All-knowing' (Q. 2:137)."[140] This was to say, the Wahhābīs would continue to fight the Ottomans in Baghdad until they converted peacefully or were made to convert.

In another letter, this one dated Rajab 1225/July–August 1810, Suʿūd issued a similar threat, this one to the Ottoman governor of al-Shām, again quoting the Prophet's summons to Heraclius and Q. 2:137.[141] The date of the letter is significant, as this was around the time that the Wahhābīs were beginning to conduct raids in southern Syria. Addressed to Yūsuf Bāshā (r. 1222–25/1807–10), the letter begins with the phrase "peace be upon whoever follows right guidance" and proceeds: "I summon you to God alone without partner, as the Prophet said in his letter to Heraclius, 'Submit, and you shall be safe, and God shall reward you twice over.'"[142] After a brief explanation of the Wahhābī position on *shirk*, Suʿūd offers to send scholars (*maṭāwiʿa*) to Syria for a debate (*munāẓara*), also offering to host Yūsuf's scholars for a debate in Najd. He warns of the consequences of rejecting the summons and continuing to profess unbelief.[143] The reply to this letter came not from Yūsuf but from his successor as Ottoman governor of al-Shām, Sulaymān Bāshā (r. 1225–27/1810–12).[144] In this letter, dated mid-Rajab 1225/mid-August 1810, Sulaymān does little to hide his contempt for the Wahhābī ruler, expressing outrage that Suʿūd would deign to address Muslims as unbelievers. "We are in fact Muslims!" he retorts. Rejecting the offer to debate with the Wahhābī scholars, he notes that such a futile exercise has been tried by others before.

139. Ibid., 9:287.

140. Ibid., 9:288.

141. See the letter in Mardam, "Majmūʿa makhṭūṭa"; drawn to my attention by Commins, *Islamic Reform*, 23.

142. Mardam, "Majmūʿa makhṭūṭa," 65.

143. Ibid., 65–66.

144. Ibid., 66–69. This Sulaymān Bāshā is not to be confused with the Sulaymān Bāshā who previously ruled in Baghdad.

He ends by telling Suʿūd that the Wahhābīs are Khārijites rebelling against the authority of the Ottoman sultan (*khawārij ʿan . . . al-ṭāʿa al-sulṭāniyya*) and that they ought to go back to where they came from.[145]

Several months later, in mid-Dhū ʾl-qaʿda 1225/mid-December 1810, Suʿūd sent a reply to Sulaymān.[146] In this follow-up letter, he shows even greater hostility than before. Suʿūd disputes the claim that Sulaymān and his people are in fact Muslims, referring to the manifestations of unbelief and polytheism that predominate in al-Shām, Iraq, Egypt, and elsewhere, namely, tombs and the visitation practices associated with them.[147] Speaking of the tombs in al-Shām, he writes: "If you are truthful in your claim to belong to the religion of Islam and to follow the Messenger, then destroy all those idols and level them to the ground and repent to God!"[148] He calls on Sulaymān to prohibit his subjects from directing worship to anything apart from God and to impose the legal obligations of Islam (*shaʿāʾir al-Islām*), saying, "[I]f you do that, then you will be our brothers." However, he threatens, "if you continue in this current state of yours, and if you do not repent of the polytheism that you practice and do not adhere to the religion of God . . . then we will continue fighting you until you return to God's true religion."[149] He then quotes Q. 8:39 and 9:5, as he also did in the letter to ʿAbdallāh Bāshā.[150] Appended to this letter are the endorsements of several scholars in Mecca and Medina, as well as that of the Meccan *sharīf*, Ghālib ibn Musāʿid. One can only assume that most of these men had no choice but to provide their endorsements.[151]

From the content of these letters, there can be little doubt that Suʿūd was a committed and zealous Wahhābī who wished to extend his realm beyond the northern frontier of Arabia. It is also likely that he expected to succeed. Why, indeed, would he not have expected to? In the space of little more than fifty years, the petty oasis town of al-Dirʿiyya had grown into the capital of an empire spanning most of the Arabian Peninsula, including the holiest sites in Islam. Following the warpath of the early Islamic state, the next stop was northward to Iraq and Syria. That Suʿūd was conscious of this precedent is made clear by his

145. Ibid., 67–69.

146. *al-Durar al-saniyya*, 1:287–313.

147. Ibid., 1:293.

148. Ibid., 1:312.

149. Ibid.

150. Ibid., 1:313.

151. Ibid., 1:314–17. The endorsements can also be seen in a manuscript copy of the letter held at Dārat al-Malik ʿAbd al-ʿAzīz in Riyadh; see the photo in *al-Aṭlas al-tārīkhī*, 77.

multiple references to the Prophet's letter to Heraclius that foreshadowed the conquest of Byzantium. The Ottoman rulers, however, were not going to share in the fate of their Byzantine forebears.

The Destruction of the First Saudi State

In 1225/1810, the Porte entrusted Muḥammad ʿAlī, the Macedonian-born ruler of Egypt, with the mission of recovering the holy cities of Mecca and Medina.[152] The Wahhābī occupation of the holy cities was an embarrassment for Constantinople, and after decades of ignoring the Wahhābī threat, the Ottomans were determined to restore order in the Ḥijāz. The initial campaign was led by Muḥammad ʿAlī's son, Ṭūsūn Bāshā, who arrived in Yanbuʿ in late 1226/late 1811. Within a year his army captured Medina, and in 1228/1812 Mecca fell without a fight. Despite some military difficulties over the next two years, including the resistance of ʿAsīr and of some of the tribes of the Ḥijāz, Ṭūsūn's forces were soon in control of the entirety of the Red Sea coast.

In 1229/1814, Suʿūd ibn ʿAbd al-ʿAzīz Āl Suʿūd died of illness in al-Dirʿiyya, being succeeded by his son ʿAbdallāh (r. 1229–33/1814–18). Meanwhile, Muḥammad ʿAlī's military mission in Arabia had evolved. No longer was his objective the eviction of the Wahhābīs from the holy cities of Mecca and Medina. Muḥammad ʿAlī now resolved to destroy the Saudi state in its entirety. Recalling Ṭūsūn to Egypt, he entrusted the command of this larger expedition to another son, Ibrāhīm Bāshā, who began "a slow but irresistible" advance into Najd.[153] The expeditionary force had the advantage of modern European military training—some of the commanders had been trained in France—and matériel, including artillery and seemingly endless supplies and reinforcements. The Wahhābīs were no match. By early 1233/late 1817, Ibrāhīm had penetrated into al-Qaṣīm and was threatening al-Washm and Sudayr. In Dhū ʾl-qaʿda 1233/September 1818, after a months-long siege, al-Dirʿiyya finally submitted to the invaders. Ibrāhīm remained in Najd for nine more months, razing al-Dirʿiyya to the ground before his departure. The devastation was captured by George Foster Sadleir, an Irish captain in the army of the East India Company who passed through al-Dirʿiyya in August 1819. Sadleir, who was pursuing Ibrāhīm's army in hopes of forming an alliance with the Egyptians, described the former

152. al-Jabartī, *ʿAjāʾib al-āthār*, 4:119. On the Egyptian campaign in Arabia generally, see Vassiliev, *History of Saudi Arabia*, 140–55; Commins, *Wahhabi Mission*, 32–39.

153. Vassiliev, *History of Saudi Arabia*, 153.

Saudi capital as an uninhabited collection of ruins: "These ruins are very extensive. . . . [T]he walls of the fortification have been completely razed by the Pacha [i.e., Ibrāhīm], and the date plantations and gardens destroyed. I did not see one man during my search through these ruins."[154]

ʿAbdallāh Āl Suʿūd did not enjoy a long or prosperous rule. Upon the capture of al-Dirʿiyya, he surrendered to the invaders and was taken to Cairo and then Istanbul, where he was publicly beheaded.[155] Other members of the Āl Suʿūd were sent into exile in Cairo, as were members of the Āl al-Shaykh, including three of Ibn ʿAbd al-Wahhāb's sons.[156] One member of the Āl al-Shaykh who was not spared execution was Sulaymān ibn ʿAbdallāh Āl al-Shaykh (d. 1233/1818), one of Ibn ʿAbd al-Wahhāb's grandsons and a rising star in the Wahhābī religious establishment.[157] He was executed shortly after the fall of al-Dirʿiyya. According to Ibn Bishr, Sulaymān was forced to listen to music before being brought to a cemetery and shot by a firing squad.[158] That he was singled out for such treatment may have been related to his unflinching commitment to the Wahhābī doctrine and fierce opposition to the Egyptian invasion.

The Wahhābī tradition preserves a short book by Sulaymān from this period known as *al-Dalāʾil fī ḥukm muwālāt ahl al-ishrāk* (The Proofs Concerning the Judgment of Showing Loyalty to Polytheists). The theme of this work is the importance of *al-walāʾ waʾl-barāʾ* and *jihād* in the face of the Egyptian threat, or, as Sulaymān puts it, "the command to show enmity to the polytheists, to hate them, to wage *jihād* against them, and to separate from them."[159] The background to this book was the advance into Najd of Ibrāhīm's army, described by Sulaymān as "the soldiers of polytheism and tombs" (*junūd al-shirk waʾl-qibāb*),[160] and the defection of a growing number of Najdī towns

154. Sadleir, *Diary of a Journey Across Arabia*, 65–66.

155. The execution took place in Ṣafar 1234/December 1818. For more on ʿAbdallāh's journey and execution, see Crawford and Facey, "ʿAbd Allāh Al Saʿūd and Muḥammad ʿAlī Pasha."

156. For a list of those taken to Cairo, as well as those who died during the invasion, see Commins, *Wahhabi Mission*, 42, 225–27.

157. On him, see Ibn Bishr, *ʿUnwān al-majd*, 1:384–85; Āl al-Shaykh, *Mashāhīr*, 44–47; Āl Bassām, *ʿUlamāʾ Najd*, 2:341–49; al-Qāḍī, *Rawḍat al-nāẓirīn*, 3:162–64. Among other works, Sulaymān wrote an influential commentary on *Kitāb al-tawḥīd*; see Āl al-Shaykh, *Taysīr al-ʿazīz al-ḥamīd*.

158. Ibn Bishr, *ʿUnwān al-majd*, 1:384–85.

159. Āl al-Shaykh, *Majmūʿ al-rasāʾil*, 56.

160. Ibid., 41.

and tribes. In condemning this backsliding, Sulaymān emphatically rejects the view that fear (*khawf*) is a legitimate excuse for allying with the Egyptians. The only valid excuse for exhibiting approval of polytheists, he says, is compulsion (*ikrāh*), and the bar for this is steep. A person who is subject to compulsion (*mukrah*) "is one whom the polytheists have captured, saying to him, 'Disbelieve,' or 'Do this or else we will do [such and such] to you and kill you,' or one whom they take and torture until he shows his agreement with them."[161] Throughout the book, Sulaymān repeatedly emphasizes torture as a key condition of *ikrāh*, saying at one point that a person "has not suffered compulsion until the polytheists have tortured him" (*lā yakūnu mukrahan ḥattā yu ʿadhdhibahu ʾl-mushrikūn*).[162] The excuse that people were giving for withdrawing their allegiance to al-Dirʿiyya and accepting the authority of Ibrāhīm, namely, that they were afraid, is therefore invalid. Until they are tortured, Muslims have a duty to show enmity to polytheists and to fight them in *jihād*. For Sulaymān, the obligation of manifesting hatred and enmity was to be maintained even in the face of almost certain death.

Unlike earlier Wahhābī scholars writing on *al-walāʾ waʾl-barāʾ* and *jihād*, Sulaymān was writing at a time when the Wahhābī movement was in retreat. His goal was not only to keep the Saudi state afloat but also to preserve Wahhābism from external attack and internal corruption. In this way, his book set the stage for the next phase of Wahhābī history, during which the Wahhābī scholars were adamant about maintaining a posture of enmity and *jihād* vis-à-vis the greater Islamic world, frequently condemning those who adopted a more relaxed or more flexible position.

Conclusion

Contrary to the claims of his critics, Ibn ʿAbd al-Wahhāb did not see himself as a prophet. He and his followers did see themselves, however, as following in the Prophet's footsteps. In their understanding, they had begun by preaching in a nonviolent but assertive manner, exhibiting enmity to the polytheists around them as the Prophet had done in Mecca. Then, after being attacked, they fought their enemies in defensive *jihād* before progressing to offensive *jihād* for the purpose of eliminating *shirk* and expanding the realm of the faith. After Ibn ʿAbd al-Wahhāb's death, his successors continued to see themselves

161. Ibid., 42.

162. Ibid., 44, 58.

as soldiers on the prophetic warpath, as evinced by Suʿūd's intended expansion to Iraq and Syria and invocation of the Prophet's menacing letter to Heraclius. In a sudden reversal, however, the leaders of the first Saudi state were unable to follow the course of the early Islamic caliphate to its end point.

In subsequent decades, the Wahhābī scholars had to come to terms with the destruction of their foundational polity. Why had God visited His wrath upon the first Saudi state? Obviously, in their view, it was not because the Wahhābī movement had been flawed in conception. The answer, given by one of the leading scholars of the second Saudi state, Ḥamad ibn ʿAtīq, was simple. The Egyptian invasion had been a divine test (*ibtilāʾ*), similar to the test faced by the Muslims of Ibn Taymiyya's age in the Mongol invasions. "The people of Islam [i.e., the Wahhābīs]," he wrote, "were tested with things resembling what the Shaykh al-Islām Ibn Taymiyya, may God have mercy on him, mentioned concerning the occasion of the appearance of the Tatars [i.e., the Mongols]." The empowerment of the unbelieving Ottomans (*al-turk al-kuffār*) over Najd was a result of the wisdom and justice of God (*min ḥikmat Allāh waʿadlihi*), being punishment for the sins (*dhunūb*) of the people of Najd.[163] Such thinking allowed the Wahhābī scholars of subsequent generations to avoid any kind of critical reassessment of their doctrine. There was nothing wrong with what they had been preaching or the way their state had been functioning. What was needed, then, was to reestablish the Wahhābī *daʿwa* and to reestablish the theopolitical order of the first Saudi state. To do so, the scholars believed, they would have to abide by their doctrinal principles with the same commitment and tenacity as before. Their efforts to do so form the next chapter in the history of Wahhābism.

163. Ibn ʿAtīq, *Sabīl al-najāt wa ʾl-fikāk*, 26. For similar arguments, see Āl al-Shaykh, *al-Maqāmāt*, 110ff.; Ibn Siḥmān, *Minhāj ahl al-ḥaqq wa ʾl-ittibāʿ* (al-Furqān ed.), 18.

5

The Reassertion of Enmity

THE SECOND SAUDI STATE (1823–1887)

FOLLOWING THE DEMISE of the first Saudi state in 1233/1818 and the destruction of al-Dirʿiyya at the hands of Ibrāhīm Bāshā, it was not long before the Āl Suʿūd managed to stage a comeback in Najd. The leader of the Saudi restoration was Turkī ibn ʿAbdallāh Āl Suʿūd (r. 1238–49/1823–34), a grandson of Muḥammad ibn Suʿūd's. He is regarded as the founder of what came to be known as the second Saudi state (1238–1305/1823–87).[1] Unlike his many relatives who were forced into exile in Cairo, Turkī evaded capture amid the fall of al-Dirʿiyya and was able to remain in Najd. In 1238/1823, he made a bid for power, attacking the Egyptian garrisons in Riyadh and Manfūḥa with his supporters. At the time, the garrisons were nearly all that remained of Egyptian military power in Najd.

While the Egyptians continued to occupy parts of Arabia for several decades from their base in the Ḥijāz, their hold on central Arabia was precarious from the beginning. Difficult to supply and lacking in resources, Najd was not a priority for the Egyptians. Far more important was maintaining control over the Ḥijāz. Turkī was able to rally support among the various Najdī towns, entering Riyadh, which he made his capital, with his forces in 1240/1824. In a short span of time he succeeded in recovering much of the ancestral Saudi domain. Within a year, according to Ibn Bishr, all of Najd had submitted to his rule, and by 1245/1830 he had gained control of al-Aḥsāʾ as well.[2] The Ḥijāz, however, never came under the sway of the second Saudi state.[3]

1. All major subsequent Saudi rulers have been descendants of Turkī.

2. Ibn Bishr, *ʿUnwān al-majd*, 2:32, 60–62.

3. On these events and the second Saudi state more generally, see Vassiliev, *History of Saudi Arabia*, 160–203; Winder, *Saudi Arabia in the Nineteenth Century*.

In 1249/1834, at the height of his powers, Turkī was assassinated in Riyadh. The plot was hatched by a rival member of the Āl Suʿūd, Mishārī ibn ʿAbd al-Raḥmān, who was killed in the ensuing turmoil. The headship of state passed to Turkī's son Fayṣal, who had been exiled to Cairo but returned to Najd in 1243/1827f. Fayṣal's reign (1249–54/1834–38, 1259–82/1843–65) was to last some three decades, interrupted by a five-year interval during which he again found himself in exile in Cairo (1254–59/1838–43).

The second Saudi state saw the renewal of the alliance between the Āl al-Shaykh and the Saudi rulers. The chief scholarly authority during the reigns of Turkī and Fayṣal was ʿAbd al-Raḥmān ibn Ḥasan Āl al-Shaykh (d. 1285/1869), one of Ibn ʿAbd al-Wahhāb's grandsons.[4] Born in al-Dirʿiyya in 1193/1779f, ʿAbd al-Raḥmān was taken to Cairo after the fall of al-Dirʿiyya but managed to return to Najd in 1241/1825f after an interval of seven or eight years. In Cairo he is said to have studied with a number of Egyptian scholars at al-Azhar, but this does not seem to have induced any moderation in his religious thinking. His approach to Wahhābism was no different from the approach of the scholars of the first Saudi state, being focused on *tawḥīd*, the duty of showing enmity and hatred to polytheists, and, in the right circumstances, fighting them in *jihād*. In Riyadh he served as chief *qāḍī* of the reconstituted Saudi realm, as well as the principal teacher of the next generation of Wahhābī scholars. Like his cousin Sulaymān ibn ʿAbdallāh Āl al-Shaykh, ʿAbd al-Raḥmān authored an extensive commentary on *Kitāb al-tawḥīd*, among numerous other works.[5]

Like its predecessor, the second Saudi state expanded across Arabia on the basis of extending the domain of *tawḥīd* and eradicating *shirk*. The Wahhābī rationale for the state's expansion is reflected in some of ʿAbd al-Raḥmān's writings, including an epistle coauthored with Fayṣal ibn Turkī. Calling on the people of Najd to direct worship exclusively to God, the authors underscore the duties of dissociation and *jihād*:

> God has made it obligatory for the monotheists to cut off relations with the polytheists and to wage *jihād* against them [*muqāṭaʿat al-mushrikīn wa-jihādahum*], as in His words, "Fight those who believe not in God and the

4. On him, see Ibn Bishr, *ʿUnwān al-majd*, 2:33–42; Āl al-Shaykh, *Mashāhīr*, 78–92; Āl Bassām, *ʿUlamāʾ Najd*, 1:180–201; al-Qāḍī, *Rawḍat al-nāẓirīn*, 1:269–73; Āl ʿAbd al-Muḥsin, *Tadhkirat ulī ʾl-nuhā*, 1:173–82; and see further al-Ghunaym, *al-Mujaddid al-thānī*.

5. See Āl al-Shaykh, *Fatḥ al-majīd li-sharḥ Kitāb al-tawḥīd*.

> Last Day . . ."—the verse (Q. 9:29). And He says, "slay the polytheists wherever you find them" (Q. 9:5). The verses commanding *jihād* against them and *jihād* against their hypocrite brethren are numerous. He has made *jihād* against them and dissociation from them [*jihādahum wa ʾl-barāʾa minhum*] obligatory in most of the chapters of the Qurʾān.[6]

The situation was not entirely the same as before, however, given that the people of Najd had already embraced Wahhābism before and the cult of saints in Najd had largely been eliminated. Thus the leaders of the second Saudi state did not regard the majority of Najdīs prima facie as unbelievers. In a letter to Fayṣal, ʿAbd al-Raḥmān counsels the ruler to wage *jihād* against those who refuse to adhere to *tawḥīd* (*man abā an yaltazima ʾl-tawḥīd*), bedouin and settled peoples alike. But not everyone in Najd, he explains, needs to be fought, given that Wahhābism is already the faith of the majority of its people. Even the majority of the nomads, he says, require only an instructor (*wa-akthar bādiyat Najd yakfī fīhim al-muʿallim*).[7] Most people in Najd, then, according to the leading Wahhābī religious authority at the outset of the second Saudi state, were not to be approached with enmity and *jihād*. Wahhābism was in need of reinforcement, not reimplantation. In this effort, however, there would be struggles.

This chapter is about the attempt to reinforce the Wahhābī doctrine during the second Saudi state. It focuses on the Wahhābī scholars' repeated efforts to underscore the obligation to evince hatred and enmity to those seen as polytheists and to resist any kind of compromise in this regard. As would be the case in later periods as well, during the second Saudi state the leading Wahhābī scholars found themselves engaged in bouts of verbal combat with those who would seek to dilute Wahhābism and tone down its militant and separatist tendencies. The chapter begins by examining the scholars' efforts during the second Egyptian occupation of Najd (1253–59/1837–43), a six-year period during which the Egyptian army returned to central Arabia. It then looks at the scholars' activities during a period known as the Saudi civil war (1282–1305/1865–87), a time of political turmoil following the death of Fayṣal ibn Turkī. Finally, it examines their determination to confront a new anti-Wahhābī scholarly challenge in the areas north of Riyadh, where commitment to Wahhābism did not run deep.

6. *al-Durar al-saniyya*, 14:137.

7. Ibid., 14:67.

The Second Egyptian Occupation

In 1252/1836, Egypt's ruler, Muḥammad ʿAlī, decided to reestablish Egyptian authority in central Arabia, fearing the growing power of Riyadh. In that year he dispatched an army led by Ismāʿīl Bey, the former head of the Cairo police, to Najd for the purpose of removing Fayṣal from power. Unlike before, Cairo would seek to rule Najd indirectly through a member of the Āl Suʿūd, Khālid ibn Suʿūd, who had been exiled to Egypt upon the fall of al-Dirʿiyya. Khālid and Ismāʿīl Bey marched on Riyadh in 1253/1837, whereupon Fayṣal, who was unable to put up an effective resistance, fell back to al-Aḥsāʾ. A year later, in 1254/1838, he was captured in southern Najd and forced back into exile in Cairo. During this period Khālid was the ruler in Riyadh, though the real power in Najd was a man named Khūrshīd Bāshā, Muḥammad ʿAlī's former governor in the Ḥijāz, who oversaw Egyptian military operations in Najd from his base in al-Qaṣīm.[8]

During this second Egyptian occupation of Najd (1253–59/1837–43), the leading Wahhābī scholars sought refuge south of Riyadh, particularly in the towns of al-Ḥawṭa and al-Ḥarīq in the district of al-Furaʿ.[9] ʿAbd al-Raḥmān ibn Ḥasan Āl al-Shaykh and his allies portrayed their flight from Egyptian-ruled territory as *hijra* away from a land ruled by polytheists, and they encouraged their coreligionists either to emigrate with them or to resist the foreign invaders by means of *jihād*.

ʿAbd al-Raḥmān's chief scholarly ally in this regard was Ḥamad ibn ʿAtīq (d. 1301/1884), a young and fiery scholar who had been his student in Riyadh.[10] Born in 1227/1812f in al-Zilfī, a town just north of Sudayr, Ibn ʿAtīq was one of the most influential scholars of his generation, known for his hostility to the enemies of Wahhābism and his uncompromising approach to the Wahhābī doctrine. Much of his life was spent in southern Najd, where he served as the *qāḍī* of al-Kharj, al-Ḥawṭa, and al-Aflāj, successively, and taught many students.

In their writings from this period, ʿAbd al-Raḥmān and Ibn ʿAtīq argued that it was necessary to make *hijra* from the areas under Egyptian control and,

8. On this period, see Vassiliev, *History of Saudi Arabia*, 158–73; Winder, *Saudi Arabia in the Nineteenth Century*, 60–148.

9. Ibn Bishr, *ʿUnwān al-majd*, 2:123, 148, 157; Vassiliev, *History of Saudi Arabia*, 171; Commins, *Wahhabi Mission*, 46. The term "second Egyptian occupation" is borrowed from Commins.

10. On him, see Āl al-Shaykh, *Mashāhīr*, 244–54; Āl Bassām, *ʿUlamāʾ Najd*, 2:84–95; al-Qāḍī, *Rawḍat al-nāẓirīn*, 1:115–17; Āl ʿAbd al-Muḥsin, *Tadhkirat ulī ʾl-nuhā*, 1:282–87.

to the greatest extent possible, to oppose the occupation with *jihād*. This was not the position of all or even most of the people in Najd, however, many of whom believed that it was not necessary to fight the invaders or to withdraw to more remote areas. Those who argued for a more passive approach in the face of the Egyptian occupation included some members of the Wahhābī scholarly class. ʿAbd al-Raḥmān and Ibn ʿAtīq engaged the advocates of this approach in a series of polemics.

The first series of polemics concerned an obscure Najdī by the name of Ibn Nabhān.[11] The ordeal of Ibn Nabhān, as revealed in ʿAbd al-Raḥmān's refutation of him,[12] began after Ibn ʿAtīq wrote an epistle inveighing against those he saw as giving loyalty to the Egyptian occupiers. In this epistle, Ibn ʿAtīq adduced a number of Qurʾānic verses and *ḥadīth*s in support of the obligations of *hijra* and *jihād* and against showing loyalty to unbelievers (*muwālāt al-kuffār*). Ibn Nabhān responded with an epistle of his own, in which he refuted Ibn ʿAtīq's views and argued that neither *hijra* nor *jihād* was binding on the people of Najd in the present circumstances. *Hijra* is not necessary, he argues, as the people of Najd are still perfectly capable of manifesting the religion (*iẓhār al-dīn*) in the presence of the occupiers, and furthermore *jihād* would not be legitimate as there is no recognized *imām* (*imām muttabaʿ*) to lead it.[13] Neither of these epistles is extant, but we learn much about the exchange from the refutation of Ibn Nabhān by ʿAbd al-Raḥmān.

In his refutation, ʿAbd al-Raḥmān reprimands Ibn Nabhān for approving of the new state of affairs in Najd (*istiḥsān hādhihi ʾl-ḥāla*) and neglecting the duties of *hijra* and *jihād* (*tark al-farḍayn*), and he suggests that Ibn Nabhān may have committed apostasy thereby. Ibn Nabhān and those like him, he writes, are arguing that there is no land of Islam to make *hijra* to and that there is no *imām* to rally around; but in this they are ignoring the fact that "God has made it a duty to dissociate from polytheism and polytheists, to reject them, to show them enmity and hatred, and to wage *jihād* against them." He thus rejects Ibn Nabhān's claim regarding *iẓhār al-dīn*, arguing that one who fails to show hatred and enmity to polytheists has not in fact manifested the religion.[14] Regarding the argument that *jihād* is legitimate only in the presence

11. The case of Ibn Nabhān, about whom we know nothing apart from his name, is discussed briefly in Al-Fahad, "From Exclusivism to Accommodation," 499–500.

12. *al-Durar al-saniyya*, 8:167–204.

13. Ibid., 8:198–99.

14. Ibid., 8:190–98.

of a recognized *imām*, ʿAbd al-Raḥmān responds by stressing the overriding nature of the duty of *jihād* (*ʿumūm farḍ al-jihād*). Whenever there exists a group with some strength (*manʿa*), he says, it is obligatory for that group to wage *jihād* for the sake of God, whether there be an *imām* or not. To posit that there can be no *jihād* without an *imām* is to put things in exactly the wrong order, as it is only through *jihād* that an *imām* can emerge.[15] At the end of his refutation, ʿAbd al-Raḥmān notes that the point regarding an *imām* is moot anyway, for after some time (*baʿd al-farāgh*) God has again blessed the Wahhābīs with an *imām* who is waging *jihād* and calling people to Islam.[16]

The *imām* to whom ʿAbd al-Raḥmān refers here is likely ʿAbdallāh ibn Thunayyān Āl Suʿūd, a cousin of Fayṣal ibn Turkī's who briefly succeeded Khālid ibn Suʿūd as ruler in Riyadh. When Muḥammad ʿAlī's empire started to collapse in 1255/1840, the Egyptian ruler ordered the withdrawal of all his forces from Arabia. There followed a chaotic year during which Khālid ibn Suʿūd and ʿAbdallāh ibn Thunayyān fought for control of Najd. The latter prevailed in 1257/1841, and two years later, in 1259/1843, Fayṣal returned from Cairo and resumed his reign. The polemics with Ibn Nabhān thus appear to have begun just before the withdrawal of Egyptian forces from Najd.

Following ʿAbd al-Raḥmān's refutation, Ibn ʿAtīq authored his own refutation of Ibn Nabhān, which he titled *Sabīl al-najāt wa ʾl-fikāk min muwālāt al-murtaddīn wa ʾl-atrāk* (The Path of Deliverance and Disengagement from Showing Loyalty to the Apostates and the Turks).[17] This is one of the better-known Wahhābī epistles of the second Saudi state, though its relationship to the episode of Ibn Nabhān is not generally understood. In *Sabīl al-najāt wa ʾl-fikāk*, Ibn ʿAtīq does not refer to Ibn Nabhān by name, but we can gather that it is about him as Ibn ʿAtīq describes his earlier epistle and ʿAbd al-Raḥmān's refutation of the unnamed opponent (*hādhā ʾl-muʿāriḍ*) in the introduction. While he writes that ʿAbd al-Raḥmān's refutation was a sufficient response to this antagonist, Ibn ʿAtīq clearly felt compelled to treat the issues in question at greater length. His objective, as he says, is to clarify some of the issues that many professed Muslims, including many supposed scholars, have erred in,

15. Ibid., 8:199, 202–3.

16. Ibid., 8:203.

17. Ibn ʿAtīq, *Sabīl al-najāt wa ʾl-fikāk*. Some modern Saudi editors replace the word *atrāk* in the title with the euphemism *ahl al-ishrāk* (the people of polytheism). For the author's rendering of the title, see 24; and see also the titles of the various manuscripts in al-Māniʿ, *al-Āthār al-makhṭūṭa*, 173.

including the requirement of showing enmity to unbelievers and polytheists and cutting ties with them, the requirement of *hijra*, and the matter of manifesting the religion. The lengthy *Sabīl al-najāt wa 'l-fikāk* is a locus classicus for the Wahhābī doctrine of *al-walā ʾ wa 'l-barā ʾ* and the related issues of *hijra* and *iẓhār al-dīn*. Those scholars who hold the wrong views on these matters are described as the opposition (*al-mu ʿāraḍa*). Among the people of Najd, Ibn ʿAtīq says, there are two misguided groups, one that approves of "the ignorant and wayward opposition" (*al-mu ʿāraḍa al-jāhila al-ḍālla*) and one that disapproves of the opposition but fails to condemn it.[18]

Throughout the book, Ibn ʿAtīq lays great emphasis on the requirement of showing enmity to unbelievers and polytheists and the prohibition against showing them loyalty. "Whosoever shows loyalty to the unbelievers belongs not to God in anything" (*wa-man yuwāli 'l-kāfirīn fa-laysa min Allāh fī shay ʾ*), he warns, "and whosoever shows loyalty to the Turks is himself a Turk" (*wa-man tawallā 'l-turk fa-huwa turkī*), the word *Turks* being Ibn ʿAtīq's term for the Egyptian-led invaders.[19] In making his argument, he quotes at length here from Sulaymān ibn ʿAbdallāh's *al-Dalā ʾil fī ḥukm muwālāt ahl al-ishrāk*, which admonishes Muslims for associating with and showing support to polytheists.[20]

Most of *Sabīl al-najāt wa 'l-fikāk* is standard Wahhābī doctrine, though Ibn ʿAtīq does make a few original points concerning *al-walā ʾ wa 'l-barā ʾ* and *hijra* that would become enduring themes in Wahhābī scholarly literature. The first point he makes is that dissociation from polytheists is more important than dissociation from the things that they worship—otherwise put, that it is more important to dissociate from the *people* who worship false gods than it is to dissociate from the *false gods* themselves. He derived this view from the example of Abraham in Q. 60:4, where Abraham is quoted as saying, "[W]e dissociate from you and that which you worship apart from God" (*innā bura ʾā ʾ minkum wa-mimmā ta ʿbūdūna min dūn Allāh*). Ibn ʿAtīq notes that *barā ʾa* from the polytheists here precedes *barā ʾa* from their idols. The lesson here is that it is insufficient to dissociate from idols alone; it is above all necessary to dissociate from, and to show hatred and enmity to, the idol-worshippers. "How many are those," he writes, "who do not commit polytheism yet fail to show enmity to

18. Ibn ʿAtīq, *Sabīl al-najāt wa 'l-fikāk*, 22–23.
19. Ibid., 31–35.
20. Ibid., 78–83.

those who do! The one who does this is not a Muslim, as he has abandoned the religion of all the messengers!"[21]

The second original point that Ibn ʿAtīq makes concerns the difference between enmity (*ʿadāwa*) and hatred (*bughḍ*). In Q. 60:4, as Ibn ʿAtīq notes, *ʿadāwa* precedes *bughḍ* in Abraham's phrase, "We reject you, and between us and you enmity has shown itself, and hatred forever" (*kafarnā bikum wa-badā baynanā wa-baynakum al-ʿadāwa waʾl-baghḍāʾ abadan*). What this shows, he says, is that *ʿadāwa* is more important than *bughḍ*. For Ibn ʿAtīq, *bughḍ* is something internal—a feeling or emotion—where *ʿadāwa* is outward—the expression or manifestation of *bughḍ*. "A person might hate the polytheists but not show them enmity," he writes disapprovingly. "[Such a person] has not met his obligation until enmity and hatred are demonstrated by him, and the enmity and hatred must be evident, manifest, and clear [*bādiyatayn ẓāhiratayn bayyinatayn*]." Hatred borne in the heart, he goes on to say, "is of no benefit until its signs are manifested and its effects are made clear, and that will happen only when it is joined by enmity and separation [*al-ʿadāwa waʾl-muqāṭaʿa*]."[22]

On the question of *hijra*, Ibn ʿAtīq provides a useful clarification regarding its relationship to *iẓhār al-dīn*. Up to this point, the Wahhābī scholars, beginning with Ibn ʿAbd al-Wahhāb, had linked the duty of *hijra* to the ability to manifest the religion (*iẓhār al-dīn*), suggesting that the latter entails showing hatred and enmity to the unbelievers in a given area. Ibn ʿAtīq is more explicit in equating *iẓhār al-dīn* with the display of hatred and enmity. Many people, he writes in *Sabīl al-najāt waʾl-fikāk*, believe that *iẓhār al-dīn* means uttering the confession of faith and performing the prayers and the other ritual obligations, when in fact *iẓhār al-dīn* means for one openly to express enmity to the unbelieving group in a particular area (*al-taṣrīḥ . . . lahā bi-ʿadāwatihi*).[23] "A man has not manifested his religion [*lā yakūnu muẓhiran li-dīnihi*]," he states, "until he dissociates from the unbelievers who are in his midst and states plainly to them that they are unbelievers and that he is their enemy. If that has not happened, the religion has not been manifested."[24] For Ibn ʿAtīq, *iẓhār al-dīn* in this sense is the condition of *hijra*. One is not dispensed from the duty of emigrating from a land of unbelief unless one can manifest the religion—either that or a person must be suffering compulsion (*ikrāh*). Like the Wahhābī

21. Ibid., 44.
22. Ibid., 44–45.
23. Ibid., 92.
24. Ibid., 95.

scholars before him, Ibn ʿAtīq defines *ikrāh* as severe physical agony, namely, torture (*taʿdhīb*). Many people in Najd are mistaken, he writes, quoting Sulaymān ibn ʿAbdallāh, in believing that fear is a valid excuse for acting friendly toward the polytheist invaders and submitting to their rule.[25]

During the short reign of ʿAbdallāh ibn Thunayyān (r. 1257–59/1841–43), there transpired a similar episode between the Wahhābī scholars and another obscure Najdī. This was a man from al-Kharj who objected, in an epistle, to the idea that *hijra* and *jihād* were binding on him during the second Egyptian occupation. ʿAbd al-Raḥmān authored a refutation of him known by the title *al-Mawrid al-ʿadhb al-zulāl fī kashf shubah ahl al-ḍalāl* (The Pleasing and Pure Pool Exposing the Specious Arguments of the People of Error).[26] In the introduction, he describes coming across an unsigned epistle (*risāla*) that he believed was written by a man from al-Kharj.[27] The author of the epistle had complained about the conduct of Ibn Thunayyān, in particular his seizure of property as spoils of war, and the undue influence of the Āl al-Shaykh over him.[28] The man had further argued that there was never any obligation on him to perform *hijra* when the Egyptians were in Najd (*lammā kāna ahl Miṣr bi-bilād Najd*).[29]

ʿAbd al-Raḥmān's main concern in his response is with this last point. The man from al-Kharj and those like him, he says, have been spreading specious arguments (*shubuhāt*) to justify their previous inaction in the face of the Egyptian occupation.[30] At the beginning of *al-Mawrid*, he reiterates the main themes of the Wahhābī doctrine, including the worship of God exclusively (*ikhlāṣ al-ʿibāda*), dissociation from polytheism and polytheists (*waʾl-barāʾa min al-shirk wa-ahlihi*), and fighting the latter until there is no *fitna*, glossed as *shirk* (*wa-qitāluhum ḥattā lā takūna fitna ay shirk*).[31] The anonymous man from al-Kharj presumably needed to be reminded of all this, in particular the points

25. Ibid., 90–91, 95.

26. See *al-Durar al-saniyya*, 11:298–349; *Majmūʿat al-rasāʾil waʾl-masāʾil al-Najdiyya*, 4:287–318. An early manuscript of *al-Mawrid* bears a copy date of 1261/1845; see Āl al-Shaykh, *al-Mawrid al-ʿadhb al-zulāl*, 32. It is likely that the refutation was written earlier than this, as this episode preceded the next one concerning Ibn Duʿayj, as we shall see below.

27. *al-Durar al-saniyya*, 11:299.

28. Ibid., 11:323–35, 322.

29. Ibid., 11:328.

30. Ibid., 11:333–34.

31. Ibid., 11:310.

regarding *barāʾa* and *qitāl*. Abd al-Raḥmān says of the purveyors of *shubuhāt* (*al-mushabbiha*) such as the man from al-Kharj:

> God commanded them to fight the polytheists and they fought alongside them; He commanded them to stay away from them and they gave them sanctuary and drew near to them; He commanded them to show them enmity and they showed them loyalty; He commanded them to show them hatred and they showed them love; and He commanded them to give support to the Muslims and they gave support to the unbelievers against them.[32]

These people, according to ʿAbd al-Raḥmān, put worldly interest above divine command, abandoning their religious duties and their Muslim brethren in a time of need. There was no excuse (*ʿudhr*) for them to remain among polytheists. Worse than their eschewal of *hijra*, however, was their support for the invaders (*muẓāharatuhum wa-muʿāwanatuhum*), which they are now seeking to justify retroactively.[33]

Another Najdī who defended himself against accusations of failing to perform *hijra* during the second Egyptian occupation was Aḥmad ibn Duʿayj (d. 1268/1851f). Unlike Ibn Nabhān and the man from al-Kharj, Ibn Duʿayj was a member of the Wahhābī scholarly class, and thus his views garnered special attention from ʿAbd al-Raḥmān and Ibn ʿAtīq.[34] Born in 1190/1776f in the town of Marāt in al-Washm, Ibn Duʿayj served as the town's *qāḍī* for decades. His commitment to the Wahhābī doctrine appears to have been unquestionable. After the fall of the first Saudi state, he wrote a long poem praising the Āl Suʿūd and decrying the invasion of Najd by the forces of Ibrāhīm Bāshā.[35] Yet, like many others in Najd during the second Egyptian occupation, he was outraged by the accusation that he was betraying Islam by not emigrating from Egyptian-occupied territory.

The immediate cause of the dispute with Ibn Duʿayj, which occurred around 1261/1845,[36] about two years after Fayṣal's return to power, was a short rhetorical *fatwā* that he wrote on the issue of *hijra*. In the *fatwā*, Ibn Duʿayj states that

32. Ibid., 11:344–45.

33. Ibid., 11:334, 343.

34. On him, see Āl Bassām, *ʿUlamāʾ Najd*, 1:497–501; al-Qāḍī, *Rawḍat al-nāẓirīn*, 1:89–90; and see further the editor's introduction in Ibn Duʿayj, *Tārīkh*, 204–20.

35. This is the *Tārīkh* mentioned in the previous note.

36. One of the texts in question is dated this year, as will be seen.

he is inquiring about a matter (*innī sāʾil ʿan masʾala*) that has been discussed far and wide and aroused great controversy. This is the view of the ignorant (*qawl al-juhhāl*) that "everyone who resides in a town that has been overcome by the military forces [of Egypt] and does not emigrate from there is an unbeliever."[37] According to Ibn Duʿayj, this view is unfounded, as the new masters did not command any of the residents of the towns in question to abandon their religion (*al-rujūʿ ʿan dīnihi*), nor did they compel them to act in a way contrary to the faith. Even were the opposite the case, he says, it would still be wrong to pronounce *takfīr* on those who failed to emigrate, since the Prophet deemed it permissible to commit an act of unbelief in the event of compulsion (*wa-abāḥa ʾl-kufr idhā ukriha ʿalayhi*). Moreover, he insists, the people of Najd continued to harbor hatred toward the occupying forces and only granted the invaders access to their lands in order to protect themselves, their property, and their children. He ends by warning that whoever pronounces *takfīr* on a Muslim has himself become an unbeliever (*wa-man kaffara Musliman fa-huwa kāfir*).[38]

Ibn Duʿayj's *fatwā* was refuted by at least three scholars, including ʿAbd al-Raḥmān, Ibn ʿAtīq, and Ṣāliḥ ibn Muḥammad al-Shathrī (d. 1309/1891f).[39] ʿAbd al-Raḥmān, in his refutation, rejects the suggestion that anyone is pronouncing *takfīr* on those who failed to perform *hijra*. This is a charge that Ibn Duʿayj has invented in order to vindicate himself and to justify his own failure in this regard.[40] In doing so, he has misrepresented one of the foundations of the religion.[41] While it is true, ʿAbd al-Raḥmān concedes, that one need not undertake *hijra* in the event of compulsion, the claim that Ibn Duʿayj and others like him were enduring compulsion is to be rejected (*daʿwāhu ʾl-ikrāh mamnūʿa*). They were not imprisoned or put in shackles, he says, nor was there

37. Ibn ʿAtīq, *al-Difāʿ ʿan ahl al-sunna*, 6.

38. Ibid., 6–7.

39. See Āl al-Shaykh, *al-Maṭlab al-ḥamīd*, 101–50; Ibn ʿAtīq, *al-Difāʿ ʿan ahl al-sunna*; al-Shathrī, *Radd ʿalā ṣāḥib al-risāla al-maʿrūf bi ʾbn Duʿayj*; al-Shathrī, *Radd ʿalā ʾbn Duʿayj*. On al-Shathrī, see Āl Bassām, *ʿUlamāʾ Najd*, 2:533–35. His refutation is discussed in Commins, *Wahhabi Mission*, 47–49. While al-Shathrī's refutation adds little to the discussions of ʿAbd al-Raḥmān and Ibn ʿAtīq, it is helpful in that it quotes Āl al-Shaykh's *al-Mawrid al-ʿadhb al-zulāl*, likely indicating that the episode concerning Ibn Duʿayj followed the episode concerning the man from al-Kharj.

40. Āl al-Shaykh, *al-Maṭlab al-ḥamīd*, 123. Ibn Duʿayj is identified (as Aḥmad ibn ʿAlī al-Marāʿī) at 122. The editor of this volume titles ʿAbd al-Raḥmān's refutation *Irshād ṭālib al-hudā li-mā yubāʿidu ʿan al-radā*. For another version, see *al-Durar al-saniyya*, 8:204–72.

41. Āl al-Shaykh, *al-Maṭlab al-ḥamīd*, 129, 127.

a police presence barring egress from their towns.[42] On the contrary, Ibn Duʿayj willingly made peace with and showed love to those who sought to destroy the religion, as did many others among the notables of Najd (*aʿyān ahl Najd*).[43]

Ibn ʿAtīq makes many of the same points in his own refutation of Ibn Duʿayj, dated Rabīʿ I 1261/March–April 1845.[44] Many of the arguments in *Sabīl al-najāt wa ʾl-fikāk* regarding *al-walāʾ wa ʾl-barāʾ*, *hijra*, and *iẓhār al-dīn* are repeated here. As before, Ibn ʿAtīq distinguishes between hatred and enmity, writing that "hatred of the polytheists requires showing them enmity . . . hatred that is not accompanied by manifest enmity is profitless [*al-bughḍ alladhī lā tuqārinuhu ʾl-ʿadāwa al-ẓāhira lā yanfaʿu*]."[45] "Manifesting the religion," he states, "means openly expressing enmity to the unbelievers [*al-taṣrīḥ lil-kuffār bi ʾl-ʿadāwa*]," and there is no possible way that Ibn Duʿayj was manifesting the religion during this period.[46] To the contrary, he asserts, Ibn Duʿayj, who was aligned with the Wahhābīs (*inqāda li-ahlihi*) when they were in power, inclined toward the unbelievers (*al-ṭāʾifa al-khārija ʿalā ʾl-Islām*) when they took over, seeking to ingratiate himself with Khūrshīd Bāshā.[47] The reason he is so sure that Ibn Duʿayj did not evince enmity to the Egyptian forces is that Ibn Duʿayj was not persecuted by them. When a Muslim living among unbelievers is truly manifesting the religion, he states, the unbelievers will not leave him to practice his religion (*lā yatrukuhu ahl al-kufr ʿalā dīnihi*) but, rather, will show him enmity in response to the enmity that he is showing them. Thus for Ibn ʿAtīq, manifesting the religion in a land overrun by unbelievers inevitably entails a hostile response from them.[48] Peaceful coexistence with occupying unbelievers is in effect not possible, because manifesting the religion necessarily elicits their hostility and persecution.

As the three cases of Ibn Nabhān, the man from al-Kharj, and Ibn Duʿayj show, during the second Egyptian occupation the leading Wahhābī scholars were intent on reasserting enmity as a condition of faith. This was in contrast to the proponents of a more passive approach to the Egyptian occupation, who saw themselves as suffering compulsion and who argued that there was

42. Ibid., 131.
43. Ibid., 125; cf. 132, 140.
44. Ibn ʿAtīq, *al-Difāʿ ʿan ahl al-sunna*, 35.
45. Ibid., 30–31.
46. Ibid., 15.
47. Ibid., 18.
48. Ibid., 30–32.

no choice but to accept the rule of the foreign occupiers. For ʿAbd al-Raḥmān ibn Ḥasan Āl al-Shaykh and Ḥamad ibn ʿAtīq, this position was a betrayal of the basic principles of Wahhābism, which require Muslims either to antagonize and agitate against unbelievers or else to separate from them and flee their territory. According to the Wahhābī doctrine, as they repeatedly argued, one cannot practice Islam in a passive way; one must maintain a posture of hostility to unbelievers except in the case of *ikrāh*, meaning torture.

The Saudi Civil War

The second part of Fayṣal ibn Turkī's reign (1259–82/1843–65) was the most stable and prosperous period of the second Saudi state. Fayṣal reimposed the state's authority over all the districts of Najd and in al-Aḥsāʾ to the east. The period following his reign, however, was one of unending turmoil. After Fayṣal's death in Rajab 1282/December 1865, Najd was beset by a protracted civil war that would eventually bring the second Saudi state to ruin. The war began as a contest between Fayṣal's sons ʿAbdallāh (r. 1282–88/1865–71, 1292–1305/1875–87) and Suʿūd (r. 1288–91/1871–75). ʿAbdallāh, the heir apparent, assumed power upon his father's death. For some five years he ruled in Riyadh, while his brother plotted a coup; in 1288/1871 ʿAbdallāh was forced to flee when Suʿūd launched a campaign to take the Saudi capital with the support of several towns and tribes.

The previous year, in 1287/1870f, ʿAbdallāh had appealed to the Ottoman authorities in Iraq for military assistance against Suʿūd. While ʿAbdallāh was generally seen as the more committed to the Wahhābī creed of the two brothers, this did not prevent him from appealing for help to those regarded as polytheists by the Wahhābī scholars. The appeal led the Ottomans to occupy al-Aḥsāʾ in late 1287/early 1871, but it did not yield sufficient assistance to forestall Suʿūd's advance. Suʿūd would rule in Riyadh for several years, dying of illness in Dhū ʾl-ḥijja 1291/January 1875. Thereafter, Riyadh was briefly ruled by a third son of Fayṣal's, ʿAbd al-Raḥmān, before ʿAbdallāh regained power in a tenuous alliance with his surviving brothers and the sons of Suʿūd. The arrangement lasted until 1305/1887, when Suʿūd's sons ousted ʿAbdallāh, prompting the intervention of the Āl Rashīd in Ḥāʾil and effectively bringing the second Saudi state to an end.[49]

49. On these events, see Vassiliev, *History of Saudi Arabia*, 174–209; Winder, *Saudi Arabia in the Nineteenth Century*, 229–78; Crawford, "Civil War."

While the Wahhābī scholars were not particularly active in the Saudi civil war—they duly gave *bayʿa* to the new leader in Riyadh whenever a change in power occurred—there was one matter to which they devoted a good deal of attention. This was ʿAbdallāh ibn Fayṣal's appeal to the Ottomans for help against his brother Suʿūd, a request understood by the scholars as seeking help from polytheists (*al-istiʿāna biʾl-mushrikīn*). When the appeal was made, ʿAbd al-Raḥmān ibn Ḥasan Āl al-Shaykh was no longer alive. He had died in Dhū ʾl-qaʿda 1285/February 1869, about year and a half before ʿAbdallāh's request. Ḥamad ibn ʿAtīq was still active, however, as was ʿAbd al-Raḥmān's son ʿAbd al-Laṭīf. It was the latter who took the lead in addressing the issue of *al-istiʿāna biʾl-mushrikīn*.

Born in al-Dirʿiyya in 1225/1810f, ʿAbd al-Laṭīf ibn ʿAbd al-Raḥmān Āl al-Shaykh (d. 1293/1876) played the leading role in the Wahhābī scholarly establishment after his father's death.[50] He was among the many Najdīs exiled to Cairo in 1233/1818 after the fall of the first Saudi state, though for reasons that are unclear he stayed in Egypt for much longer than his father, returning to Najd only in 1264/1847f, after a stay of more than thirty years.[51] The biographies relate that he pursued religious studies at al-Azhar and in Alexandria during this period and that upon his return to Arabia he worked as a preacher in al-Aḥsāʾ for two years before settling in Riyadh. The English traveler Palgrave, who met him in Riyadh in the early 1860s, observed that ʿAbd al-Laṭīf spoke with an Egyptian accent; he also could appear tolerant and worldly for a Wahhābī scholar, "bearing in his manners a sensible dash of Egyptian civilization."[52] As one might expect, ʿAbd al-Laṭīf's decades-long experience in Egypt and elite Islamic education seem to have inculcated in him a more cosmopolitan outlook relative to his Wahhābī peers. Occasionally, one detects signs of doctrinal moderation in his writings, and sometimes he draws a contrast with Ibn ʿAtīq as a more moderate thinker and preacher. In one of his letters, for instance, ʿAbd al-Laṭīf rebukes Ibn ʿAtīq for the severity (*ghilẓa*) of his preaching and counsels him to take a softer approach, suggesting that he begin with gentleness (*līn*) and move toward severity only if necessary and

50. On him, see Āl al-Shaykh, *Mashāhīr*, 93–121; Āl Bassām, *ʿUlamāʾ Najd*, 1:202–14; al-Qāḍī, *Rawḍat al-nāẓirīn*, 1:399–403; Āl ʿAbd al-Muḥsin, *Tadhkirat ulī ʾl-nuhā*, 1:243–57; and see further Āl al-Shaykh, *al-Shaykh al-imām ʿAbd al-Laṭīf ibn ʿAbd al-Raḥmān ibn Ḥasan Āl al-Shaykh*.

51. The timing of his return may have had something to do with the end of Muḥammad ʿAlī's reign in 1264/1848.

52. Palgrave, *Narrative of a Year's Journey*, 2:20–21.

practicable.[53] Another noteworthy difference concerns the obligation of showing enmity. In one of his *fatwās*, ʿAbd al-Laṭīf writes that a Muslim may be excused for failing to manifest enmity (*iẓhār al-ʿadāwa*) to polytheists in the event of weakness and fear (*al-ʿajz waʾl-khawf*), describing the existence of enmity (*wujūd al-ʿadāwa*) as the necessary condition of faith.[54] Ibn ʿAtīq, as we have seen, argued the opposite of this, claiming that to harbor hatred in one's heart was insufficient and that the necessary condition of faith was *ʿadāwa* in the sense of the outward display of hatred and enmity. Another contrast is found in their views on the status of Mecca. In a rather infamous *fatwā*, Ibn ʿAtīq strongly suggests that Mecca has become part of *dār al-kufr* on the grounds that *shirk* is widespread in the city.[55] ʿAbd al-Laṭīf, in one of his writings, rejects the idea that the Ḥijāz can fall under that designation.[56]

One should be careful, however, not to exaggerate the extent of ʿAbd al-Laṭīf's ostensible moderation.[57] In Palgrave's view, "[S]uch liberal semblance is merely a surface whitewash; the tongue may be the tongue of Egypt, but the heart and brain are ever those of Najd." Having attended some of ʿAbd al-Laṭīf's teaching sessions, Palgrave concluded that the Wahhābī scholar was no more tolerant than his Wahhābī colleagues. Rather, he was one who "hates the progress he has witnessed, and in which he has to a certain degree participated."[58] This judgment seems to have been correct. Despite the occasional flashes of moderation, ʿAbd al-Laṭīf was in most cases firmly committed to the Wahhābī doctrine as expounded by the earlier scholars. Like them, he believed that the majority of the nominal Islamic world was not Muslim, on account of the ubiquity of the cult of saints and other innovations. "Belief in stones and trees is the religion of most people in these times [*ghālib al-nās fī hādhihi ʾl-awqāt*]," he writes in one of his books, referring in particular to Persia and Transoxania but noting that the observation applies to all lands, both desert and sown.[59] Furthermore, when it came to the most consequential doctrinal disputes of

53. Āl al-Shaykh, *ʿUyūn al-rasāʾil*, 1:474–75. This source comprises the extant letters and epistles of ʿAbd al-Laṭīf as arranged by his student Sulaymān ibn Siḥmān.

54. *al-Durar al-saniyya*, 8:359–60.

55. Ibid., 9:259–64.

56. Āl al-Shaykh, *Miṣbāḥ al-ẓalām*, 84.

57. Steinberg (*Religion und Staat in Saudi-Arabien*, 75) is likewise skeptical of ʿAbd al-Laṭīf's, or his father's, purported moderation (*Mäßigung*), citing the severity (*Heftigkeit*) of their writings.

58. Palgrave, *Narrative of a Year's Journey*, 2:21–22.

59. Āl al-Shaykh, *Miṣbāḥ al-ẓalām*, 221.

his day, ʿAbd al-Laṭīf firmly upheld the traditional principles of militant Wahhābism. We thus find him routinely emphasizing the importance of showing hatred and enmity to polytheists, not just harboring them deep in one's heart.

On the issue of *al-istiʿāna bi ʾl-mushrikīn,* ʿAbd al-Laṭīf's stance was not that of a moderate, and he and Ibn ʿAtīq shared the same general view. By his own account, ʿAbd al-Laṭīf confronted ʿAbdallāh ibn Fayṣal and chastised him for appealing to the Ottomans. As he relates in a letter, "I addressed him with speech of condemnation and dissociation [*fa-khāṭabtuhu shifāhan bi ʾl-inkār wa ʾl-barāʾa*], and I was severe in saying that this amounted to the destruction of the foundations of Islam [*wa-aghlaẓtu lahu bi ʾl-qawl inna hādhā hadm li-uṣūl al-Islām*]." Upon being confronted in this way, according to ʿAbd al-Laṭīf, ʿAbdallāh repented and sought the scholar's forgiveness.[60]

Whatever else the scholars may have said to ʿAbdallāh ibn Fayṣal is not recorded. As far as one can tell, they did not write refutations of him, rather relating their condemnations in private. The written reaction to ʿAbdallāh's appeal to the "polytheist" Ottomans had more to do with a certain Wahhābī scholar who had given his approval of the move. This was Muḥammad ibn ʿAjlān (d. 1293/1876f), the *qāḍī* of al-Kharj, who at some point composed an epistle defending ʿAbdallāh's request.[61] The epistle is unfortunately lost, as are the refutations of it by ʿAbd al-Laṭīf and Ibn ʿAtīq. It is possible, however, to reconstruct the arguments of the two sides from the contents of ʿAbd al-Laṭīf's subsequent letters.[62]

In one of these letters, ʿAbd al-Laṭīf refers to Ibn ʿAjlān's epistle as "the devil's snare" (*ḥibālat al-shayṭān*), describing it as "a passageway leading to the legitimization of showing loyalty to the polytheists and seeking their support against the Muslims." The epistle's main point, he states, was that "bringing idol-worshippers to the land of Islam and seeking their help against one who has rebelled against the authority [of the *imām*] are not a sin." ʿAbd al-Laṭīf indicates that many people in Najd were persuaded by what Ibn ʿAjlān had

60. Āl al-Shaykh, *ʿUyūn al-rasāʾil,* 2:920.

61. On Ibn ʿAjlān, see Āl Bassām, *ʿUlamāʾ Najd,* 5:469–71; and for his death date, see Āl Musallam, "Min ʿulamāʾ wa-quḍāt Ḥawṭat Banī Tamīm wa ʾl-Ḥarīq."

62. See, in particular, Āl al-Shaykh, *ʿUyūn al-rasāʾil,* 1:237–45 (letter to Muḥammad ibn ʿAlī Āl Mūsā), 277–84 (letter to Ibn ʿAjlān), 436–44 (letter to Zayd ibn Muḥammad Āl Sulaymān), 2:871–81 (letter to ʿAbd al-Raḥmān ibn Ibrāhīm). Cf. the discussion in Crawford, "Civil War," 237–38; Al-Fahad, "From Exclusivism to Accommodation," 501–4; Commins, *Wahhabi Mission,* 64.

written, noting that the epistle was circulating and being read in public spaces.[63] In another letter, he notes that upon first encountering the epistle, "I drew attention to the conspicuous error and the disgraceful ignorance that it contained, and I hid from people the first copy that came to us lest it spread and circulate among the commoners and the riffraff." In short order, however, "it spread in al-Kharj and al-Furaʿ, and [another] copy arrived in our town [i.e., Riyadh]."[64]

From what ʿAbd al-Laṭīf relates, Ibn ʿAjlān's argument appears to have been twofold: first, that all Muslims have a duty to obey the *imām* (in this case ʿAbdallāh ibn Fayṣal) and to strive for unity and, second, that seeking the help of polytheists (*al-istiʿāna biʾl-mushrikīn*) is a legal issue admitting of legitimate disagreement (*masʾala khilāfiyya*), meaning that the evidence is ambiguous enough to allow for more than one view.[65] Yet, despite the characterization of the issue as a *masʾala khilāfiyya*, it is clear that Ibn ʿAjlān favored the view that *al-istiʿāna biʾl-mushrikīn* is permissible. According to ʿAbd al-Laṭīf, in making his argument, Ibn ʿAjlān cited a *ḥadīth* in which the Prophet and Abū Bakr employed a polytheist from Quraysh during the *hijra* to Medina.[66] As further evidence for his view, Ibn ʿAjlān claimed that Ibn Taymiyya, in the wars against the Mongols, sought the help of the people of Egypt and al-Shām despite the fact that they were unbelievers (*wa-hum ḥīnaʾidhin kuffār*).[67] Ibn ʿAjlān was thus still writing from a Wahhābī perspective; he was not arguing that the Ottomans were Muslims. His claim, rather, was that it may be permissible for Muslims to seek the help of polytheists. Even so, he indicated a certain degree of sympathy for the Ottoman military elite, noting that the leaders of the invading Ottoman forces (*akābir al-ʿaskar*) in al-Aḥsāʾ were pious people (*ahl taʿabbud*), even if the soldiery were not.[68]

ʿAbd al-Laṭīf's refutation of Ibn ʿAjlān seems to have consisted of four chief points. The first was that, though the question of *al-istiʿāna biʾl-mushrikīn* is indeed a *masʾala khilāfiyya*, the evidence that it is forbidden is stronger than the evidence that it is permitted. This is because the opinion in favor of it is

63. Āl al-Shaykh, *ʿUyūn al-rasāʾil*, 2:874.

64. Ibid., 1:438.

65. Ibid., 1:279, 441.

66. Ibid., 1:279. For the *ḥadīth* (*... wa-staʾjara rasūl Allāh ṣ wa-Abū Bakr rajulan min banī ʾl-Dīl ...*), see al-Bukhārī, *Ṣaḥīḥ*, 741–42 (*Kitāb al-maghāzī, bāb hijrat al-nabī ṣ wa-aṣḥābihi ilā ʾl-Madīna*, no. 3905).

67. Āl al-Shaykh, *ʿUyūn al-rasāʾil*, 1:280.

68. Ibid.

based on a *mursal ḥadīth* (i.e., one whose chain of transmission is incomplete), whereas the opinion against it is founded on a sound *ḥadīth*. In the sound *ḥadīth*, the Prophet declares that he will not seek the help of a polytheist (*fa-lan astaʿīna bi-mushrik*).[69] ʿAbd al-Laṭīf dismissed as irrelevant the *ḥadīth* showing Muḥammad and Abū Bakr hiring a polytheist during the *hijra*, arguing that hiring (*istiʾjār*) and seeking help (*istiʿāna*) are not the same.[70] The second point was that the scholars who deemed *al-istiʿāna biʾl-mushrikīn* permissible did so only conditionally. They stipulated as a condition of its permissibility that the unbelievers not possess power and strength (*shawka wa-ṣawla*) in the assembled army and that they not take part in the decision-making with the Muslims. Such was not the case with the invited Ottoman forces, says ʿAbd al-Laṭīf, since they had gone on to occupy eastern Arabia.[71] His third point was that *al-istiʿāna biʾl-mushrikīn* is only a *masʾala khilāfiyya* in a scenario in which Muslims are fighting polytheists. Suʿūd, however, was not a polytheist but, rather, a Muslim rebel (*bāghī*). As ʿAbd al-Laṭīf writes, while some scholars have deemed it permissible to seek the aid of a polytheist against another polytheist (*al-intiṣār biʾl-mushrik ʿalā ʾl-mushrik*), no reputable scholar has deemed it permissible to seek the aid of a polytheist against a Muslim rebel (*al-intiṣār biʾl-mushrik ʿalā ʾl-bāghī*).[72] The fourth and most important point was that the whole question of ʿAbdallāh's appeal for help went well beyond the issue of *al-istiʿāna biʾl-mushrikīn*. This was because the appeal had led directly to the handing over of Muslim land (i.e., al-Aḥsāʾ) to polytheists (*tawliyatihim wa-jalbihim wa-tamkīnihim min dār Islāmiyya*).[73] Because of ʿAbdallāh's request, he writes, "polytheism, unbelief, and Shīʿism [*rifḍ*] are being manifested openly in those lands."[74]

As for Ibn ʿAjlān's other arguments, namely, those concerning Ibn Taymiyya and the alleged piety of the Ottoman military commanders, ʿAbd al-Laṭīf dismisses them outright. The notion that the people of Egypt and al-Shām

69. Ibid., 1:281–82, 443. For the *mursal ḥadīth* (*... anna ʾl-nabī ṣ ashama li-qawm min al-yahūd qātalū maʿahu ...*), see al-Tirmidhī, *Sunan*, 4:127–28 (*Kitāb al-siyar, bāb mā jāʾa fī ahl al-dhimma yaghzūna maʿa ʾl-Muslimīn hal yushamu lahum*, no. 1558); and for the *ṣaḥīḥ ḥadīth*, see Muslim, *Ṣaḥīḥ*, 3:1449–50 (*Kitāb al-jihād waʾl-siyar, bāb karāhat al-istiʿāna fī ʾl-ghazw bi-kāfir*, no. 1817).

70. Āl al-Shaykh, *ʿUyūn al-rasāʾil*, 1:279.

71. Ibid., 1:443, 283.

72. Ibid.

73. Ibid., 1:281.

74. Ibid., 1:439–40.

were unbelievers during Ibn Taymiyya's age, he says, is false, as is the assertion that Ottoman military leaders in al-Aḥsāʾ are pious people. Even if the latter were in fact God-fearing people, he says, this would not confer on them the status of Muslims. For Ibn ʿArabī, Ibn Sabʿīn, and Ibn al-Fāriḍ were all simultaneously pious and among the most unbelieving people on earth.[75]

From ʿAbd al-Laṭīf's letters we learn much less about Ibn ʿAtīq's refutation of Ibn ʿAjlān, though it is clear that Ibn ʿAtīq was similarly focused on the issue of yielding Muslim territory to polytheists (*taslīm bilād al-Muslimīn ilā ʾl-mushrikīn*).[76] We also learn that Ibn ʿAtīq, unlike ʿAbd al-Laṭīf, pronounced *takfīr* on Ibn ʿAjlān, accusing him of flagrant apostasy (*ridda ṣarīḥa*). This was a bridge too far for ʿAbd al-Laṭīf, though he nonetheless defended Ibn ʿAtīq against the objections of certain detractors who accused Ibn ʿAtīq of being ignorant. Acknowledging that Ibn ʿAtīq had erred in condemning Ibn ʿAjlān as an unbeliever (*ṣadara minhu baʿḍ al-khaṭaʾ fī ʾl-taʿbīr*), ʿAbd al-Laṭīf nonetheless praises him as an esteemed champion of Islam and enemy of polytheism and polytheists.[77]

ʿAbdallāh ibn Fayṣal, it should be noted, was not the only party to the Saudi civil war who sought and received some form of assistance from the Ottomans. By the end of the war, as Michael Crawford has observed, all four sons of Fayṣal (ʿAbdallāh, Suʿūd, ʿAbd al-Raḥmān, and Muḥammad) were in some way "compromised by association with the Ottomans."[78] These other questionable associations, however, do not appear to have been accompanied by the kind of scholarly support that Ibn ʿAjlān gave to ʿAbdallāh's appeal and thus did not give rise to the same level of condemnation. The reason ʿAbdallāh's appeal invited so much controversy was that it was justified by one of the Wahhābī scholars. By arguing that Muslims are permitted to seek the help of polytheists, Ibn ʿAjlān was perceived to be corrupting the Wahhābī doctrine, and thus ʿAbd al-Laṭīf and Ibn ʿAtīq took swift action to prevent his views from gaining currency among the faithful.

The conduct of the Wahhābī scholars during the Saudi civil war may seem to point in two opposing directions. On the one hand, the scholars betrayed a measure of realism and flexibility in their willingness to adapt to a frequently changing political environment. When Suʿūd ousted ʿAbdallāh, ʿAbd al-Laṭīf

75. Ibid., 1:280.

76. Ibid., 1:441.

77. Ibid., 1:438.

78. Crawford, "Civil War," 242.

gave his imprimatur to the new ruler in Riyadh on the traditional Islamic grounds that an *imām*, however flawed, is necessary for the thriving and prospering of Islam.[79] He would just as quickly offer his support to ʿAbdallāh when the latter resumed power in 1292/1875, despite ʿAbdallāh's earlier request for help from the Ottomans. Ostensibly, these were the acts of a pragmatic scholar concerned for the well-being of his community, not an uncompromising religious radical. On the other hand, the scholars were deeply disturbed by ʿAbdallāh's request to the Ottomans and were unwilling simply to look the other way. If ʿAbd al-Laṭīf's account is to be believed, he castigated the *imām* for making his appeal, and ʿAbdallāh duly repented. Ibn ʿAtīq, meanwhile, representing the more hard-line tendency among the Wahhābī scholars, pronounced *takfīr* on Ibn ʿAjlān for justifying the request.

The scholars were thus united in their rejection and condemnation of ʿAbdallāh ibn Fayṣal's entreaty to the Ottomans, and they were not shy in putting their views into writing. It would be wrong describe them as being politically quietist in this period, even if they showed considerable deference to whoever was in power in Riyadh at a given time. For the Wahhābī scholars, there were doctrinal red lines that the Āl Suʿūd dared not cross without suffering consequences in terms of scholarly support. Seeking the help of so-called polytheists was one of them. It is significant that ʿAbdallāh repented of his sinful request in the presence of ʿAbd al-Laṭīf upon returning to power in Riyadh. He understood that doing so was necessary if he wished to have the full support of the Wahhābī scholarly class.

The Ottoman Occupation of al-Aḥsāʾ

After its seizure by Ottoman forces in 1287/1871, the eastern region of al-Aḥsāʾ never again came under the control of the second Saudi state. Beset by civil war, Riyadh was too weak ever to mount a serious challenge to the Ottomans in the east. This did not stop ʿAbd al-Laṭīf ibn ʿAbd al-Raḥmān Āl al-Shaykh, however, from advocating *jihād* against the Ottoman rulers there, as he did repeatedly during this period. Most of his work in this regard took place during the reign of Suʿūd (1288–91/1871–75).[80]

Al-Aḥsāʾ was a land that ʿAbd al-Laṭīf knew well, having worked there as a preacher for two years when it was still controlled by Riyadh. In his view,

79. Ibid., 235.
80. Ibid., 238–39.

the Ottoman presence there was an abomination. The Ottoman Empire was "the unbelieving and iniquitous state" (*al-dawla al-kāfira al-fājira*),[81] and in al-Aḥsāʾ it was empowering the Shīʿa and other polytheists and sinners. The region, ʿAbd al-Laṭīf declares in a letter, had become "a land in which polytheism and unbelief are ascendant, Shīʿism and the religion of the Europeans [*al-rifḍ wa-dīn al-ifranj*] are manifest . . . and Islam and *tawḥīd* are being destroyed."[82] In two famous poems, he would evoke all these horrors and more. In the first of these he writes:

The Rejectionists and polytheists have acquired power,
 and by them the market of wickedness and wrong has been erected.
With them centers for sodomy and fornication
 have returned, to which every sinner makes his way.
The unity of the religion has come undone, its bond has been severed,
 and has become lost amid the forces of the greatest evil . . .
The signs of guidance and Qurʾāns are cast aside,
 and villages are ruled by positive law.[83]

The reference to positive law (*qānūn*) in this poem is worth highlighting, as it stands out as a new Wahhābī grievance in ʿAbd al-Laṭīf's writings. ʿAbd al-Laṭīf refers to it again in his second poem lamenting the conditions in al-Aḥsāʾ, where he writes: "Nay, the law of the Christians [*qānūn al-naṣārā*] reigns there / apart from any proof text found in the Qurʾān."[84] In his letters he likewise condemns the European laws (*al-qawānīn al-ifranjiyya*) that the Ottomans have allegedly introduced in al-Aḥsāʾ.[85] Before ʿAbd al-Laṭīf, no Wahhābī scholar appears to have inveighed against *qānūn* or identified it as a feature of the regnant polytheism of the Islamic world. Hereafter, the charge that *qānūn*, as opposed to the Sharīʿa, is being implemented in Ottoman-controlled lands is one that becomes common in Wahhābī writings. It is unsurprising that ʿAbd al-Laṭīf would be the first Wahhābī scholar to draw attention to *qānūn*, given his long experience in Egypt, where he would have become aware of the importation of European-style legal codes to the Islamic world.

81. Āl al-Shaykh, *ʿUyūn al-rasāʾil*, 2:920.
82. Ibid., 1:210–11; cf. 1:220–21.
83. Ibid., 2:571–72 (meter = *ṭawīl*).
84. Ibid., 2:913 (meter = *rajaz*).
85. Ibid., 1:256.

The presence of *qānūn* in al-Aḥsāʾ, however, was only one reason among many that ʿAbd al-Laṭīf believed that *jihād* against the Ottoman presence there was necessary. The main reason he would give was that this was a case of unbelievers invading and seizing a Muslim territory. Therefore defensive *jihād* was necessary for the purpose of recovering the land, and participation in the *jihād* was an individual obligation (*farḍ ʿayn*) on all Muslims concerned.[86] Unfortunately for ʿAbd al-Laṭīf, his words failed to provoke Suʿūd, or any other Saudi ruler, to action. Worse still was that many adherents of Wahhābism continued to live in and visit al-Aḥsāʾ, despite the Wahhābī prohibition on living in an area where one is unable to manifest the religion.

Throughout his letters, ʿAbd al-Laṭīf is seen refuting the idea that living in and visiting al-Aḥsāʾ is permissible, urging people to perform *hijra* to the areas under Wahhābī control.[87] In one letter, he describes traveling to al-Aḥsāʾ as tantamount to visiting an enemy's military encampment (*muʿaskar al-ʿaduww al-ḥarbī*).[88] His basic argument is that Muslims are required to perform *hijra* in the event that they are unable to manifest the religion (*iẓhār al-dīn*), meaning showing hatred and enmity to the unbelievers around them, and in the present circumstances this is not possible in the area in question. "Our scholars have stated," he writes in one letter, "that it is prohibited to live in and visit a land in which a person is incapable of manifesting his religion [*yuʿjazu fīhā ʿan iẓhār dīnihi*]."[89] *Iẓhār al-dīn*, he writes, is not possible and is not happening (*mutaʿadhdhir ghayr ḥāṣil*) in al-Aḥsāʾ, as no one can go there without indulging the unbelievers and showing them loyalty (*al-rukūn wa ʾl-muwālāt wa ʾl-mudāhana*).[90] In one letter, he complains that people have traveled to al-Aḥsāʾ only to return to Najd with a favorable impression of the occupiers.[91] This was even more reason that such travel ought to be prohibited.

ʿAbd al-Laṭīf's position here was practically no different from the position of earlier Wahhābī scholars during the first and second Egyptian occupations of Najd, and indeed ʿAbd al-Laṭīf was appealing to their authority. Like Sulaymān ibn ʿAbdallāh, and like ʿAbd al-Raḥmān ibn Ḥasan Āl al-Shaykh

86. See, for instance, ibid., 1:223–24, 239, 276, 458.

87. Ibid., 1:465; cf. 2:572, where the same point is made in verse (*fa-hājir ilā rabbi ʾl-bariyyati ṭāliban / riḍāhu wa-rāghim bi ʾl-hudā kulla jāʾirī*).

88. Ibid., 1:239.

89. Ibid., 1:214.

90. Ibid., 1:221–22.

91. Ibid., 1:228–29.

and Ḥamad ibn ʿAtīq, he was worried that Ibn ʿAbd al-Wahhāb's teachings were being cast aside in favor of normalization with polytheists, and he was determined to prevent any such development. As he states in one of his letters,

> The call of our shaykh [i.e., Ibn ʿAbd al-Wahhāb] to the *tawḥīd* of God, to believe in Him, to direct all worship to Him, and to dissociate from His enemies and to wage *jihād* against them must . . . be clung to stubbornly, and must not be replaced with loyalty to the enemies of God and His messengers, retreating to their state, and satisfaction with their rule.[92]

"The foundation of the religion is not sound and is not stable," he writes in the same letter, "without cutting off relations with the enemies of the religion, making war on them, waging *jihād* against them, and dissociating from them."[93] With words like these, ʿAbd al-Laṭīf was taking a strong stance against those who, in his view, were seeking to dilute and corrupt the Wahhābī doctrine.

The *jihād* in the east, despite all of ʿAbd al-Laṭīf's pleading, never materialized. The Saudi rulers never succeeded in unifying around a strong leader who could reestablish authority in Najd, let alone recapture al-Aḥsāʾ. When ʿAbd al-Laṭīf died in Dhū ʾl-qaʿda 1293/November–December 1876, the second Saudi state, to which he had returned from Egypt thirty years earlier, was in a state of interminable decline. Yet before then, ʿAbd al-Laṭīf would be involved in other, perhaps even more pressing challenges to the authority of the kind of Wahhābism that he and his colleagues represented.

Anti-Wahhābī Activism in Najd

In addition to the second Egyptian occupation, the Saudi civil war, and the Ottoman occupation of al-Aḥsāʾ, the Wahhābī scholars of the second Saudi state were also concerned about the adverse influence of two anti-Wahhābī scholars in Najd. These were Dāwūd ibn Jirjīs and ʿUthmān ibn Manṣūr. For the most part, the activities of these men did not impinge on politics and warfare—the exception being when Ibn Jirjīs allegedly accompanied Ottoman forces to al-Aḥsāʾ in 1287/1871[94]—but the threat that they posed was still seri-

92. Ibid., 1:268.
93. Ibid., 1:265.
94. Ibid., 2:922.

ous enough to warrant the sustained attention of the Wahhābī scholars, who wrote a series of refutations of them between the 1260s/1840s and the 1290s/1870s. That they devoted so much time and energy to refuting these men speaks to the insecurity of Wahhābism in Najd during this period. While Wahhābism remained the official religion of the second Saudi state, it was not universally accepted, and the scholars were keen to defend their version of Islam lest the arguments against it gain traction.

Dāwūd ibn Sulaymān ibn Jirjīs (d. 1299/1881) was a Shāfiʿī scholar from Iraq and a leader of the Khālidī branch of the Naqshabandī order there.[95] Born into a scholarly family in Baghdad in 1231/1815f, he spent many years studying in Iraq as well as in other locales, including the Ḥijāz and Syria. At some point in his thirties, his studies brought him to ʿUnayza, one of the two main towns of al-Qaṣīm, where he sought a credential in Ḥanbalī *fiqh*. His teacher there was the Wahhābī scholar ʿAbdallāh ibn ʿAbd al-Raḥmān Abā Buṭayn (d. 1282/1865).[96] One of the more distinguished Wahhābī scholars of his generation, Abā Buṭayn was born in Sudayr in 1194/1780. He served as the *qāḍī* of several towns, including al-Ṭāʾif in the Ḥijāz and Shaqrāʾ in al-Washm, his final post being ʿUnayza, where he lived from 1248/1832f to 1270/1853f.

It was Abā Buṭayn who was the first Wahhābī scholar to refute Ibn Jirjīs. In a later refutation, Abā Buṭayn explains the events that led him to write against his former student. Ibn Jirjīs had come to ʿUnayza in the 1260s/1840s. During this stay he caused no trouble, studying in hopes of obtaining an *ijāza* in the Ḥanbalī *madhhab*. Some four years later, however, when he returned to ʿUnayza en route to Mecca for the *ḥajj*, he brought with him a piece of writing (*waraqa*) that stoked controversy. The writing consisted of quotations by Ibn Taymiyya intended to show that he was more tolerant of the cult of saints than the Wahhābīs made him out to be. Abā Buṭayn met with Ibn Jirjīs to discuss the matter, after which the senior scholar wrote a lengthy rebuttal of the Iraqi's

95. On him, see *EI*³, s.v. "Dāwūd b. Jirjīs" (Itzchak Weismann); al-Baghdādī, *Nubdha laṭīfa fī tarjamat shaykh al-Islām*; Āl ʿAbd al-Muḥsin, *Tadhkirat ulī ʾl-nuhā*, 1:276–78. And see further Commins, "Why Unayza?" 3–4; Weismann, "Naqshabandiyya-Khâlidiyya and the Salafî Challenge in Iraq," 236–38.

96. On him, see Ibn Ḥumayd, *al-Suḥub al-wābila*, 2:626–33; Āl al-Shaykh, *Mashāhīr*, 235–38; Āl Bassām, *ʿUlamāʾ Najd*, 4:225–44; al-Qāḍī, *Rawḍat al-nāẓirīn*, 1:432–36; Āl ʿAbd al-Muḥsin, *Tadhkirat ulī ʾl-nuhā*, 1:178–81; and see further al-ʿAjlān, *al-Shaykh al-ʿallāma ʿAbdallāh ibn ʿAbd al-Raḥmān Abā Buṭayn*. The long alif in *Abā* is a fixed vowel (al-ʿAjlān, *al-Shaykh al-ʿallāma ʿAbdallāh ibn ʿAbd al-Raḥmān Abā Buṭayn*, 5n1).

waraqa.[97] This rebuttal came to be known as *al-Intiṣār li-ḥizb Allāh al-muwaḥḥidīn wa ʾl-radd ʿalā ʾl-mujādil ʿan al-mushrikīn* (Support for the Monotheist Partisans of God and Refutation of the One Disputing on Behalf of the Polytheists). As Abā Buṭayn writes in it, a certain person (i.e., Ibn Jirjīs) was claiming that supplicating the dead (*duʿāʾ al-amwāt*) did not constitute *shirk* and that this was Ibn Taymiyya's view.[98] *Al-Intiṣār* is a detailed exposition of the Wahhābī doctrine that occasionally jibes at Ibn Jirjīs for his reading of Ibn Taymiyya.

Ibn Jirjīs's *waraqa* may have been an early draft of a longer work that he completed in 1273/1856, titled *Ṣulḥ al-ikhwān min ahl al-īmān wa-bayān al-dīn al-qayyim fī tabriʾat Ibn Taymiyya wa ʾbn al-Qayyim* (Conciliating the Brothers of Faith and Explaining the Right Religion in Vindication of Ibn Taymiyya and Ibn al-Qayyim).[99] This book was devoted to defending Ibn Taymiyya and Ibn al-Qayyim against the charge that they pronounced *takfīr* on those participating in the cult of saints. It is mainly a collection of quotations from their books and *fatwās*. ʿAbd al-Laṭīf ibn ʿAbd al-Raḥmān Āl al-Shaykh would write a line-by-line refutation of it.[100] Neither the *waraqa* nor *Ṣulḥ al-ikhwān* was an explicitly anti-Wahhābī tract; both were focused on Ibn Taymiyya and Ibn al-Qayyim. Yet Ibn Jirjīs's interpretation of these scholars' views was rightly perceived as an indirect attack on Wahhābism. Ibn Jirjīs was portraying Ibn Taymiyya and Ibn al-Qayyim as almost entirely tolerant of the cult of saints—a highly selective and misleading interpretation of their words and by far the most forgiving interpretation of them to be advanced by an anti-Wahhābī writer thus far.

Another theme in Ibn Jirjīs's work that aroused the ire of the Wahhābī scholars was his defense of the Ṣūfī poem *al-Burda* and its author, al-Būṣīrī. As has been seen, the Wahhābīs were highly critical of al-Būṣīrī since the time of Ibn ʿAbd al-Wahhāb, who had condemned al-Būṣīrī for the line in his poem that reads: "O most noble of creation [i.e., the Prophet], none have I to seek

97. Abā Buṭayn, *Taʾsīs al-taqdīs fī kashf talbīs Dāwūd ibn Jirjīs*, 19. The date of his arrival appears here as the 1260s (*fī athnāʾ ʿashr sittīn baʿd al-miʾatayn*).

98. Abā Buṭayn, *al-Intiṣār li-ḥizb Allāh al-muwaḥḥidīn*, 45–46.

99. See Ibn Jirjīs, *Ṣulḥ al-ikhwān*. For the completion date, see Brockelmann, *Geschichte der arabischen Litteratur*, SII, 790.

100. Āl al-Shaykh, *Minhāj al-taʾsīs wa ʾl-taqdīs fī kashf shubuhāt Dāwūd ibn Jirjīs*. It was completed in or before 1280/1863f, the date of the earliest known manuscript; see al-Mānīʿ, *al-Āthār al-makhṭūṭa*, 62.

refuge in / but you. . . ."[101] Abā Buṭayn would be alerted by some of his students in al-Qaṣīm that Ibn Jirjīs had written a poetic elaboration (*tashṭīr*) of *al-Burda*. In a letter responding to them, Abā Buṭayn criticizes Ibn Jirjīs for ascribing divine powers to the Prophet, suggesting that the Iraqi is deifying Muḥammad in the way that the Christians deify Jesus.[102] We can be sure that Abā Buṭayn's letter was written no later than 1269/1853, for in that year Ibn Jirjīs, who was in Mecca, composed a refutation of it.[103] Abā Buṭayn would respond with two more refutations of Ibn Jirjīs.[104] The dispute also attracted the attention of ʿAbd al-Raḥmān ibn Ḥasan Āl al-Shaykh in Riyadh, who authored at least one tract refuting Ibn Jirjīs and supporting Abā Buṭayn.[105]

What seems to have elicited this flurry of refutations was the receptive hearing that Ibn Jirjīs's views were receiving in al-Qaṣīm. During the second Saudi state, the Wahhābī scholars in al-ʿĀriḍ viewed al-Qaṣīm as a district where Wahhābism had never quite taken root and where opponents of the movement were welcome. Their perceptions seem to have been valid. In an undated letter to the people of ʿUnayza, ʿAbd al-Laṭīf complains bitterly about the town's stubborn persistence in hosting Ibn Jirjīs (*ikrām Dāwūd al-ʿIrāqī*) despite his well-known hostility to Wahhābism and open support for the cult of saints (*ʿadāwat al-tawḥīd wa-ahlihi wa ʾl-taṣrīḥ bi-ibāḥat duʿāʾ al-ṣāliḥīn*).[106] "This man is getting to be familiar with your town and is becoming accustomed to visiting it," he writes, "and some of its notables and leaders hold him in high regard, associate with him, and support him." He suggests that some of the people of al-Qaṣīm hate Wahhābism, seeing it as an imposition from al-ʿĀriḍ.[107] The English traveler Charles Doughty, who visited Arabia in the

101. al-Qabbānī, *Faṣl al-khiṭāb*, f. 82b (= *al-Durar al-saniyya*, 2:111).

102. This correspondence is found in *Majmūʿat al-rasāʾil wa ʾl-masāʾil al-Najdiyya*, 2:235–44.

103. Ibn Jirjīs, *Naḥt ḥadīd al-bāṭil*, 16. See the completion date at 96.

104. An edition of the first response is found in al-ʿAjlān, *al-Shaykh al-ʿallāma ʿAbdallāh ibn ʿAbd al-Raḥmān Abā Buṭayn*, 358–429, where it is titled *al-Radd ʿalā ʾl-Burda*; the second, which is much longer, has been published as Abā Buṭayn, *Taʾsīs al-taqdīs fī kashf talbīs Dāwūd ibn Jirjīs*.

105. The first, known as *Bayān al-maḥajja fī ʾl-radd ʿalā ʾl-lajja*, is found in *al-Durar al-saniyya*, 11:121–213; *Majmūʿat al-rasāʾil wa ʾl-masāʾil al-Najdiyya*, 4:223–85. While some sources say that this was a response to Muḥammad ibn Ḥumayd (d. 1295/1878), the Ḥanbalī *muftī* in Mecca, the contents suggest that it was directed at Ibn Jirjīs. The second tract is known as *Kashf mā alqāhu Iblīs min al-bahraj wa ʾl-talbīs ʿalā qalb Dāwūd ibn Jirjīs*.

106. Āl al-Shaykh, *ʿUyūn al-rasāʾil*, 1:288.

107. Ibid., 1:295.

years 1876–78, would similarly describe ʿUnayza as a place where Wahhābism was not firmly established. In his *Travels in Arabia Deserta,* he recalls: "I found it a reproach in Aneyza to be named *Waháby* . . . a mocking word in the mouths of the eyyâl [i.e., young men] which they bestowed on any lourdane ill-natured fellow."[108] According to one ʿUnayzan man he met, a merchant of anti-Wahhābī bent, only "an half of this townspeople are Wahábies," which was still too many for the merchant, who preferred spending his time in Basra, away from "Waháby straitness and fanaticism."[109] The existence of opposition to Wahhābism in al-Qaṣīm can be attributed at least partly to the area's status as a trading hub and routine stop on the pilgrimage route from Iraq. At the time of Doughty's visit, Burayda, the other principal town of al-Qaṣīm, was, in the traveler's words, "a small and weak principality," whereas ʿUnayza was home to a number of prominent merchant families.[110] These families were ill-disposed to Wahhābī restrictions on travel to places such as Iraq and al-Aḥsāʾ that would interfere with commerce and trade.

Al-Qaṣīm was not the only site of anti-Wahhābī activism in Najd during this period. The district of Sudayr also had something of this reputation, as the case of Ibn Manṣūr demonstrates. ʿUthmān ibn ʿAbd al-ʿAzīz ibn Manṣūr (d. 1282/1865) was born in the town of al-Farʿa in al-Washm in approximately 1211/1796f, though he lived most of his life in Sudayr.[111] Before the fall of al-Dirʿiyya, he fled to Iraq, where he continued his education in Basra, Zubayr, and Baghdad. The biographies note that in Iraq he studied with a number of anti-Wahhābī scholars of Najdī origin, including Muḥammad ibn Sallūm (d. 1246/1831), who are said to have influenced his anti-Wahhābī views. Ibn Manṣūr's case is quite distinct from that of Ibn Jirjīs, as the former was not an avowed anti-Wahhābī but presented himself as a bona fide Wahhābī scholar for most of his life. He was also not initially an opponent of the Wahhābī movement.

It was during his time in Iraq that Ibn Manṣūr seems to have developed his anti-Wahhābī views. At first, he evinced no hostility to Wahhābism whatsoever. At the beginning of his stay in Iraq, in 1232/1816f or just afterward, he

108. Doughty, *Travels in Arabia Deserta,* 2:455.

109. Ibid., 2:368.

110. Ibid., 2:455.

111. On him, see Āl Bassām, *ʿUlamāʾ Najd,* 5:89–106; al-Qāḍī, *Rawḍat al-nāẓirīn,* 2:113–17; al-Hindī, *Zahr al-khamāʾil,* 36–37; al-Rudayʿān, *Manbaʿ al-karam,* 147–65; and see further the editors' introduction in Ibn Manṣūr, *Fatḥ al-ḥamīd fī sharḥ al-tawḥīd,* 1:45–129. Cf. the discussion in Al-Fahad, "From Exclusivism to Accommodation," 507–8; Commins, *Wahhabi Mission,* 60–61.

wrote a verse refutation of ʿUthmān ibn Sanad (d. 1242/1827), a Najdī scholar in Basra who had written a poem critical of Ibn Taymiyya and Ibn ʿAbd al-Wahhāb. While mainly a defense of Ibn Taymiyya, Ibn Manṣūr's poem also mentions Ibn ʿAbd al-Wahhāb favorably, as in the line "Explain to me the error of the shaykh so that I may respond to you / was it in his destroying of idols? For the truth he did follow."[112] Over the course of the next decade, however, Ibn Manṣūr's outlook on Wahhābism changed, as he came to see Ibn ʿAbd al-Wahhāb and the devotees of his doctrine as modern-day Khārijites. This is apparent from his book-length treatment of Khārijism, titled *Manhaj al-maʿārij li-akhbār al-khawārij biʾl-ishrāf ʿalāʾl-isrāf min dīnihim al-mārij* (The Lofty Path to the Reports About the Khārijites Gazing Down upon the Extremism of Their Disordered Religion), which brings together the many traditions concerning the historical Khārijites.[113] While the book is mostly what it purports to be, at times Ibn Manṣūr uses the term *Khārijites* as code for the Wahhābīs, as when he complains that the Khārijites excommunicate and fight Muslims on the grounds that the latter have not satisfied the confession of faith. The historical Khārijites were known for practicing *takfīr* on the basis of major sins (*kabāʾir*), the Wahhābīs being the ones who excommunicated and fought professed Muslims on the grounds of not satisfying the confession of faith. Elsewhere in the book, in an oblique reference to Ibn ʿAbd al-Wahhāb, Ibn Manṣūr states that a true Muslim renewer (*mujaddid*) would not pronounce *takfīr* on the *umma* (*yaḥkumu ʿalayhā biʾl-kufr*). Such a comment makes no sense in the context of the historical Khārijites.[114]

Upon his return to Najd, in approximately 1242/1826f, Ibn Manṣūr concealed his anti-Wahhābī views, even posing as a loyal Wahhābī scholar. In 1252/1836, he completed an extensive commentary on Ibn ʿAbd al-Wahhāb's *Kitāb al-tawḥīd*,[115] the contents of which were sound enough to merit the endorsement (*taqrīẓ*) of ʿAbd al-Raḥmān ibn Ḥasan Āl al-Shaykh, whose only complaint was that the author had mentioned Ibn Sallūm favorably in the

112. Ibn Manṣūr, *al-Radd al-dāmigh*, 114 (meter = *ṭawīl*). For the date of the poem, see the editor's introduction at 77.

113. Ibn Manṣūr, *Manhaj al-maʿārij*. Ibn Manṣūr notes that he drafted part of the book (*kuntu sawwadtu baʿḍahu*) in Basra in 1240/1824f and completed the fair copy (*thumma ʿanna lī . . . an ubayyiḍahu*) in Najd in 1255/1839f (f. 104a).

114. These examples are noted in the editors' introduction in Ibn Manṣūr, *Fatḥ al-ḥamīd fī sharḥ al-tawḥīd*, 1:69–71.

115. Ibid., 1:154.

introduction.[116] Ibn Manṣūr served for some two decades as the *qāḍī* of Sudayr and thereafter, for approximately five years, as the *qāḍī* of Ḥāʾil. Around 1270/1853f, he retired to Sudayr, where he remained until his death. It was only after his death that the full extent of his anti-Wahhābism became known, though there had been suspicions that something was amiss.

Toward the end of his life, rumors began to circulate that Ibn Manṣūr was not the proper Wahhābī that he was pretending to be. Both ʿAbd al-Raḥmān and ʿAbd al-Laṭīf wrote to him to express their dismay at the reports they were hearing, appealing to him to return to the truth. In his letter, ʿAbd al-Raḥmān states that he has it on good authority from visitors to Sudayr that Ibn Manṣūr does not adhere to the Wahhābī doctrine. The visitors, ʿAbd al-Raḥmān tells him, thought that you knew the truth of Wahhābism (*ṣiḥḥat al-daʿwa*) but they saw the opposite of this. Effectively retracting his endorsement of Ibn Manṣūr's commentary on *Kitāb al-tawḥīd*, he states that upon careful examination Ibn Manṣūr's stance on *tawḥīd al-ulūhiyya* is no different from that of ʿAbdallāh al-Muways, one of the early opponents of Ibn ʿAbd al-Wahhāb. "What I have found in you is deception" (*mā laqītu fīka ḥīla*), he concludes.[117] ʿAbd al-Laṭīf, in his letter to Ibn Manṣūr, likewise draws attention to the troubling rumors surrounding his correspondent's creed, complaining of reports that he is on friendly terms with both the Wahhābīs and their opponents in Sudayr.[118] For the leading Wahhābī scholars in Riyadh, of course, one could not be a good Muslim without separating from and denouncing the opponents of Wahhābism.

Upon his death in 1282/1865, Ibn Manṣūr's anti-Wahhābī writings would be discovered. As ʿAbd al-Raḥmān recounts in one of his refutations, when Ibn Manṣūr died his books were collected to be sold, and among them were found two works that caused a storm.[119] The first was a short poem (some thirty-five lines) in praise of Ibn Jirjīs; the second was a long prose refutation of Ibn ʿAbd al-Wahhāb. According to ʿAbd al-Raḥmān, Ibn Manṣūr had hidden his true nature (*wa-kāna yukhfī amrahu hādhā*), but the newfound texts laid bare the truth.[120]

116. Ibid., 1:170.

117. *al-Durar al-saniyya*, 12:43–45.

118. Ibid., 12:294–96 (= Āl al-Shaykh, *ʿUyūn al-rasāʾil*, 2:637–39).

119. *al-Durar al-saniyya*, 11:512, 579.

120. Ibid., 11:554.

The poem praising Ibn Jirjīs, which refers to the Iraqi by name and mentions one of his refutations of Abā Buṭayn, ends with a note encouraging him to keep standing up to the Wahhābīs, who are described in Khārijite terms (*shīʿat jund al-Nahrawān*).[121] Several Wahhābī scholars, including ʿAbd al-Raḥmān, ʿAbd al-Laṭīf, and Ibn ʿAtīq, would refute the poem in verse, describing Ibn Manṣūr and Ibn Jirjīs as partners in crime.[122] The second work by Ibn Manṣūr, titled *Jalāʾ al-ghumma ʿan takfīr hādhihi ʾl-umma* (Removing the Darkness from the Excommunication of This Community), is preserved almost entirely in the refutation of it by ʿAbd al-Laṭīf.[123] *Jalāʾ al-ghumma* was not Ibn Manṣūr's only polemic against Wahhābism, as he refers in it to two others,[124] though it appears to be the only one that survived. As the title suggests, the book is an attack on Ibn ʿAbd al-Wahhāb's approach to *takfīr* and *jihād*, accusing him of excommunicating the *umma*, fighting Muslims as unbelievers, and deeming their lands to be *bilād kufr*.[125] In making his case that Ibn ʿAbd al-Wahhāb was guilty of these things, Ibn Manṣūr quotes from several of Ibn ʿAbd al-Wahhāb's epistles, including *Sittat mawāḍiʿ min al-sīra*, *Kashf al-shubuhāt*, and the *Kalimāt*. Many of the charges are the same as those brought by earlier refuters, though Ibn Manṣūr mentions none of their works; he does, however, attribute some of his knowledge of Wahhābism to his teachers in Iraq.[126] Like many of his predecessors, Ibn Manṣūr brings Ibn Taymiyya and Ibn al-Qayyim to bear against Ibn ʿAbd al-Wahhāb, claiming that, unlike the Wahhābīs, they were hesitant to pronounce *takfīr* against professed Muslims.[127] Ibn Manṣūr did not go so far as Ibn Jirjīs in claiming that they were tolerant of the cult of saints, but like the Iraqi he did come to the defense of the author of *al-Burda*, arguing that Ibn ʿAbd al-Wahhāb had failed to understand the poem.[128]

121. Ibid., 12:331–33.

122. For ʿAbd al-Laṭīf's poem, see ibid., 12:333–36. A manuscript copy of all these poems (copied in 1283/1867), which I have not been able to access, is described in al-Wazzān and al-Basīmī, "Manhaj al-shaykh ʿUthmān ibn Manṣūr," 53–54.

123. Āl al-Shaykh, *Miṣbāḥ al-ẓalām*. For the title of Ibn Manṣūr's work, see 43, 25.

124. The titles are found ibid., 64. The first is *Ghasl al-daran ʿammā rakibahu hādhā ʾl-rajul min al-miḥan*; the second is *Tabṣirat ulī ʾl-albāb*.

125. See, for instance, ibid., 44, 52.

126. Ibid., 44.

127. See, for instance, ibid., 300–301.

128. Ibid., 307–9.

The case of Ibn Manṣūr was not a minor ordeal in the eyes of the Wahhābī scholars in Riyadh. The fact that ʿAbd al-Raḥmān and ʿAbd al-Laṭīf wrote more than a dozen refutations of him after his death is indicative of a serious level of concern,[129] perhaps a worry that his views were catching on in parts of Najd. In a brief letter to a man in al-Ḥarīq, a town south of Riyadh, ʿAbd al-Laṭīf, refuting some of Ibn Manṣūr's claims, instructs his correspondent to read the letter aloud in public lest anyone be misled by Ibn Manṣūr's ignorance and error (*an yaghtarra bi-jahālatihi wa-ḍalālatihi*).[130] Ibn Manṣūr was a well-respected scholar in several regions of Najd, and he had taught numerous men who went on to be important scholars in their own right, including the historian Ibn Bishr. The revelation of his anti-Wahhābī views was a scandal, and the senior Wahhābī scholars were determined to limit the fallout.

With the onset of the Saudi civil war, the perceived threat of Ibn Manṣūr seems to have receded into the background as the scholars became preoccupied with Ibn ʿAjlān, the Ottoman occupation of al-Aḥsāʾ, and political uncertainty in Riyadh. Yet they nonetheless continued to make time to refute Ibn Jirjīs, who in the meantime had not ceased his anti-Wahhābī activism. In 1291/1874f, ʿAbd al-Laṭīf penned a short refutation of a text by Ibn Jirjīs at the request of some students.[131] There was nothing new in what Ibn Jirjīs was saying, ʿAbd al-Laṭīf notes, apart from some additional mendacity (*al-ziyāda min al-kadhib*).[132] In this new tract, the Iraqi was reiterating his claim that Ibn Taymiyya and Ibn al-Qayyim were on his side in the debate over *takfīr* and *ziyāra*. ʿAbd al-Laṭīf's response was to say that this was akin to attributing Abraham to Judaism and Christianity.[133] ʿAbd al-Laṭīf wrote this refutation only two years before his death, in 1293/1876, at the age of about sixty-five. Shortly thereafter, a Wahhābī scholar living in Mecca, Aḥmad ibn Ibrāhīm ibn ʿĪsā (d. 1329/1911), wrote another refutation of a work by Ibn Jirjīs, also on the

129. These include ʿAbd al-Laṭīf's *Miṣbāḥ al-ẓalām* and ʿAbd al-Raḥmān's *al-Maqāmāt*, mentioned in chapter 1. See also, by ʿAbd al-Raḥmān, *al-Durar al-saniyya*, 5:267–82, 11:512–33, 533–46, 547–51, 554–74, 575–86, 12:45–46; and, by ʿAbd al-Laṭīf, 4:73–104, 5:287–304, 12:296–98, 298–331, 336–37.

130. Āl al-Shaykh, *ʿUyūn al-rasāʾil*, 2:742.

131. Āl al-Shaykh, *Tuḥfat al-ṭālib wa ʾl-jalīs fī kashf shubah Dāwūd ibn Jirjīs*; originally printed as *Dalāʾil al-rusūkh fī ʾl-radd ʿalā ʾl-manfūkh*. For the completion date, see Āl al-Shaykh, *Dalāʾil al-rusūkh*, 55.

132. Āl al-Shaykh, *Tuḥfat al-ṭālib wa ʾl-jalīs fī kashf shubah Dāwūd ibn Jirjīs*, 36.

133. Ibid.

subject of Ibn Taymiyya and Ibn al-Qayyim.[134] Ibn Jirjīs died a few years later, in 1299/1882.

The writings of Ibn Jirjīs and Ibn Manṣūr in this period were to some extent a reprise of the early refutations of Wahhābism in the time of Ibn ʿAbd al-Wahhāb. The two scholars accused the Wahhābīs of pronouncing *takfīr* on Muslims and fighting them as unbelievers, defended the practices associated with the cult of saints, and claimed that Ibn Taymiyya and Ibn al-Qayyim were in fact on their side on these issues. The response of the Wahhābī scholars, who rejected all of this, was similar to the response of Ibn ʿAbd al-Wahhāb to his early critics. There was, in short, little new to this debate, apart from Ibn Manṣūr's deception and Ibn Jirjīs's strained argument that Ibn Taymiyya and Ibn al-Qayyim fully tolerated the cult of saints. What the activities of Ibn Jirjīs and Ibn Manṣūr show is that the main themes of the earlier debate had not changed and that in Najd there were still scholarly holdouts to the dominant Wahhābī dispensation. Perhaps there were many others, like Ibn Manṣūr, who camouflaged themselves in a Wahhābī guise while secretly criticizing Wahhābism. ʿAbd al-Raḥmān and ʿAbd al-Laṭīf surely worried that this was the case.

Conclusion

During the second Saudi state, the leaders of the Wahhābī scholarly establishment were keen to reassert the spirit of manifest enmity that had defined Wahhābism during the previous era. The leading Wahhābī scholars of the period, beginning with ʿAbd al-Raḥmān ibn Ḥasan Āl al-Shaykh and Ḥamad ibn ʿAtīq, contended with a series of challenges to the Wahhābī doctrine. The common theme of these challenges was the argument that Wahhābī Muslims were not obligated to leave a territory occupied by unbelievers and that Wahhābīs were not necessarily obligated to show them hatred and enmity. The Wahhābī scholars were determined to prevent such a view from gaining hold, emphasizing the importance of *iẓhār al-dīn* and its meaning as the ability to show hatred and enmity to unbelievers. In their view, there was no excuse, apart from *ikrāh*, for one who failed to perform *hijra* away from Egyptian-dominated Najd during the second Egyptian occupation. The same went for those who

134. Ibn ʿĪsā, *al-Radd ʿalā shubuhāt al-mustaghīthīn bi-ghayr Allāh*. The completion date is 1294/1877 (see 102–3). On Ibn ʿĪsā, see Āl Bassām, *ʿUlamāʾ Najd*, 1:436–52; al-Qāḍī, *Rawḍat al-nāẓirīn*, 1:91–94.

failed to leave Ottoman-dominated al-Aḥsāʾ decades later. Appealing to the polytheist Ottomans for help in the Saudi civil war was likewise anathema to the scholars, indicating a lack of commitment to the Wahhābī creed. Meanwhile, the scholars took aim at the opponents of Wahhābism in and around Najd in refutation after refutation, concerned that criticism of Wahhābism was becoming acceptable in certain parts of Najd.

It should be noted that the political leaders of the second Saudi state, the Āl Suʿūd, do not appear to have been the Wahhābī stalwarts that their forebears had been during the first Saudi state. Turkī ibn ʿAbdallāh Āl Suʿūd and his descendants were more disposed to realpolitik and less motivated by religious fervor than their predecessors. There were no menacing letters to the governors of Syria and Iraq in this period and no bids to conquer the Ḥijāz, let alone expand beyond the Arabian Peninsula. On the contrary, there is some evidence that the Saudi rulers paid tribute to the Ottomans and the Egyptians, a fact that might have been kept hidden from the scholars.[135] Fayṣal ibn Turkī, as R. Bayly Winder put it, was "[f]arsighted enough to realise that he could not convert the whole world to Wahhabism, and that if he tried he would again bring ruin on his people and himself. . . . He was a devout Wahhabi, but, instead of attacking Karbala, he received a British diplomat in his capital."[136] The Āl Suʿūd of the second Saudi state may not have been religious zealots, but they were still a more dependable ally for the Wahhābī scholars than the next dynasty that would rule in central Arabia—the Āl Rashīd.

135. Winder, *Saudi Arabia in the Nineteenth Century*, 206–7; Vassiliev, *History of Saudi Arabia*, 163.

136. Winder, *Saudi Arabia in the Nineteenth Century*, 228. The diplomat was Lewis Pelly (d. 1892), the British resident in the Persian Gulf, who visited Riyadh with a delegation in 1865.

6

The Persistence of Enmity

THE RASHĪDĪ INTERREGNUM (1887–1902)

THE ORIGINS of the Rashīdī emirate of Jabal Shammar can be traced to the triumph of ʿAbdallāh ibn ʿAlī ibn Rashīd over his rival, Ṣāliḥ ibn ʿAbd al-Muḥsin ibn ʿAlī, in a struggle for control of Ḥāʾil in 1251/1835. The two men were representatives of Ḥāʾil's leading families, the Āl Rashīd and the Āl ʿAlī, respectively. Following ʿAbdallāh ibn Rashīd's consolidation of power, Ḥāʾil and the surrounding areas would remain under the control of the Āl Rashīd for nearly ninety years. From its capital of Ḥāʾil, the Rashīdī emirate expanded north and west into Syria and the Ḥijāz, and in the late nineteenth century it would challenge Riyadh for political supremacy in Najd. Unlike the case of the Saudi states, the Rashīdī expansion was undertaken not in the name of Islam but, rather, in the name of the Shammar tribe to which the Āl Rashīd belonged. Tribal solidarity, rather than religion, was the source of the Āl Rashīd's political legitimacy.[1]

The Āl Rashīd did not identify with and support Wahhābism in the same way as the Āl Suʿūd had, but generally they were not opposed to it either. Given that Wahhābism was fairly well established in Jabal Shammar, the Rashīdī rulers showed a certain deference to Wahhābī sensibilities. As in al-Qaṣīm, however, in Jabal Shammar the outside world beckoned. Ḥāʾil was a regional trading and pilgrimage hub, and the Āl Rashīd were not inclined to enforce Wahhābī prohibitions on travel to non-Wahhābī lands. In fact they encouraged transregional commerce, welcoming traders and pilgrims from all backgrounds and denominations, including Shīʿa. The English traveler

1. Al-Rasheed, *Politics in an Arabian Oasis*, 89. On the history of the Rashīdī emirate, see ibid., passim; Vassiliev, *History of Saudi Arabia*, 192–209.

William Palgrave, who visited Ḥāʾil in 1862 during the reign of Ṭalāl ibn ʿAbdallāh ibn Rashīd (r. 1263–84/1847–68), describes the "dexterous prudence" with which the Rashīdī emir navigated the religious politics of the capital:

> Merchants from Baṣrah, from Meshid 'Alee and Wāsiṭ, shopkeepers from Medinah and even from Yemen, were invited by liberal offers to come and establish themselves in the new market of Ḥā'yel. . . . Many of these traders belonged to the Shiya'a sect, hated by all good Sonnites, doubly hated by the Wahhabees. But Ṭelāl affected not to perceive their religious discrepancies, and silenced all murmurs by marks of special favour towards these very dissenters, and also by the advantages which their presence was not long in procuring for the town.[2]

According to Palgrave, the *qāḍī* of Ḥāʾil at this time was likewise a man of practical outlook: "a tolerable representative of what may here be called the moderate party, neither participating in the fanaticism of the Wahhabee, nor yet, like the most of the indigenous chiefs, hostile to Mahometanism; he takes his cue from the court direction, and is popular with all factions because belonging properly to none."[3] To the extent that Wahhābism was observed in Ḥāʾil, it manifested in the rejection of the cult of saints and the enforcement of public prayer. As the Finnish traveler George Wallin wrote of his visit to Ḥāʾil in 1845 during the reign of ʿAbdallāh ibn ʿAlī ibn Rashīd (r. 1251–63/1835–47),

> The two principal tenets of the Wahhâby doctrine, to which the Shammar still unalterably adhere, are the rejection of all saints, even the Prophet himself, as mediator between God and man; and 2ndly, the necessity of saying the prayers publicly in a mosque, in common with a congregation, and not alone at home. . . . [T]here were in Hâil many instances of 'Abd Allah [ibn Rashīd]'s having severely punished several men for default of attending to that service.[4]

2. Palgrave, *Narrative of a Year's Journey*, 130–31, partially quoted in Al-Rasheed, *Politics in an Arabian Oasis*, 101.

3. Palgrave, *Narrative of a Year's Journey*, 158, quoted in Al-Rasheed, *Politics in an Arabian Oasis*, 92. The *qāḍī*, who is named by Palgrave as "Moḥammed-el-Ḳāḍee," can likely be identified as Muḥammad ibn Saʿd (d. no earlier than 1280/1863f), on whom, see al-Hindī, *Zahr al-khamāʾil*, 38; al-Rudayʿān, *Manbaʿ al-karam*, 162–65.

4. Wallin, "Narrative of a Journey," 184, quoted in Al-Rasheed, *Politics in an Arabian Oasis*, 91.

However, when it came to Wahhābī prohibitions on such things as tobacco, silk, music, and "friendly intercourse" with non-Wahhābī Muslims, Wallin wrote, "[T]he people of Hail told me, not without a certain sneer of derision, that the subjects of the Sa'oods still submitted [to them] more or less; but they have long since been declared void, or at least, greatly modified among Shammars, to whom the continued intercourse with 'Irâk, Higâz, Egypt, and the strangers that visit their land, has imparted a greater liberality of opinions."[5]

Wallin was writing at a time when the second Saudi state was still more powerful than the Rashīdī emirate. ʿAbdallāh ibn Rashīd professed his loyalty to Riyadh, though even at this time his allegiance appears to have been mostly nominal. Over time, as the power of the Rashīdī emirate grew and that of the second Saudi state weakened, Ḥāʾil distanced itself from Riyadh and aligned itself more with the Ottoman Empire. Thus by the time of Palgrave's visit to Ḥāʾil in 1862, the Rashīdī emir styled himself a vassal of the Ottoman sultan, not a loyal subject of Fayṣal ibn Turkī Āl Suʿūd. As Palgrave writes, "[T]he name of the Sultan, with its pompous appendix of now unmeaning titles, is proclaimed every Friday with a loud voice in the public prayer of Ḥā'yel, and profession is made that Ṭelāl is only his vicegerent, and from him derives all authority."[6] Ḥāʾil did not pay tribute to the Ottomans, but the Ottoman sultan was regarded as the overlord of the Rashīdī emirate. Those devout Wahhābīs who disapproved of this arrangement were forced to hold their tongues. As Palgrave remarks, speaking of the Ottoman sultan, "[T]hough Wahhabees call him an 'infidel,' and the men of Shomer 'a Turkish mule,' such courteous sayings can only be uttered in private."[7]

Following Ṭalāl, the next member of the Āl Rashīd to enjoy a long and stable rule was Muḥammad ibn ʿAbdallāh ibn Rashīd (r. 1288–1315/1872–97), who oversaw the expansion of the Rashīdī emirate to Najd amid the collapse of the second Saudi state. In 1305/1887, he entered Riyadh with his forces and installed a man named Sālim ibn Sabhān as ruler of the subdued Saudi capital, effectively ending the reign of ʿAbdallāh ibn Fayṣal Āl Suʿūd. Ibn Rashīd returned to Ḥāʾil with ʿAbdallāh and several more members of the Āl Suʿūd, holding them as unofficial prisoners. ʿAbdallāh would be allowed to return to Riyadh only in the days before his death in 1307/1889. His brother ʿAbd al-Raḥmān ibn Fayṣal Āl Suʿūd was allowed to return as well and soon would

5. Wallin, "Narrative of a Journey," 183.

6. Palgrave, *Narrative of a Year's Journey*, 1:133.

7. Ibid.

lead one final challenge to the rule of the Āl Rashīd in Najd. Following complaints about Sālim ibn Sabhān and his heavy-handed policies (he had chased down and killed several of Suʿūd ibn Fayṣal's sons), Muḥammad ibn Rashīd appointed ʿAbd al-Raḥmān as governor of Riyadh. With the support of some of the people of al-Qaṣīm and a section of the Muṭayr tribe, ʿAbd al-Raḥmān staged a revolt in Najd. His challenge culminated in the battle of al-Mulaydāʾ near al-Qaṣīm in 1308/1891, in which the Āl Rashīd won a decisive victory, prompting ʿAbd al-Raḥmān to seek refuge in Kuwait. More than a decade would pass before a member of the Āl Suʿūd would challenge the Āl Rashīd for control of Riyadh.

Amid the fall of the second Saudi state in 1305/1887, the Wahhābī scholars in Najd found themselves with no choice but to profess their allegiance to the ruler in Ḥāʾil. While the Āl Rashīd were a less than ideal political ally, the scholars neither resisted their rule nor pronounced *takfīr* on them. Their approach to politics during the Rashīdī interregnum—that is, between the fall of the second Saudi state in 1305/1887 and the rise of the third Saudi state in 1319/1902—was for the most part pragmatic. Even so, the scholars did not soften their resolve in the face of the enemies of Wahhābism; nor did they tolerate efforts to dilute Wahhābī exclusivism and militancy. Indeed, they placed no less emphasis on the foundational Wahhābī principles as the scholars of the previous era. The Rashīdī interregnum coincided with the appearance of the first printed anti-Wahhābī texts, a challenge they were determined to meet by publishing their own works defending the Wahhābī movement and its doctrine. It also coincided with the rise of a group of scholars in al-Qaṣīm who advocated a toned-down version of Wahhābism, one that limited the practice of *takfīr* and condemned those who prohibited travel to neighboring regions. These challenges, and the scholars' response to them, are the subject of this chapter.

Scholars of the Next Generation

When the second Saudi state came to an end in 1305/1887, the leading scholars of the Wahhābī religious establishment had just given way to the next generation. ʿAbd al-Laṭīf ibn ʿAbd al-Raḥmān Āl al-Shaykh and Ḥamad ibn ʿAtīq had recently passed away, in 1293/1876 and 1301/1884, respectively. The Rashīdī interregnum thus came at a time when a new group of Wahhābī scholars were beginning to fill their shoes. The leaders of this new cohort were the duo of ʿAbdallāh ibn ʿAbd al-Laṭīf Āl al-Shaykh, a son of the late ʿAbd al-Laṭīf, and Sulaymān ibn Siḥmān.

ʿAbdallāh ibn ʿAbd al-Laṭīf (d. 1339/1920) was born in the eastern Arabian town of al-Hufūf in 1265/1848f, during his father's short stint as a preacher in al-Aḥsāʾ.[8] Like his brothers Muḥammad, ʿAbd al-ʿAzīz, and Ibrāhīm, he was groomed from an early age for a career as a religious scholar. He pursued his studies in Riyadh under his father until the latter's death in 1293/1876, whereupon he moved south to the town of al-ʿAmmār in al-Aflāj. As was the case during the second Egyptian occupation, during the political turmoil of the Saudi civil war the southern areas of Najd served as something of a refuge for the Wahhābī scholars. In al-Aflāj, ʿAbdallāh became a devoted student of Ibn ʿAtīq's, along with Sulaymān ibn Siḥmān, who was already there.

Sulaymān ibn Siḥmān (d. 1349/1930) was born around the same time as ʿAbdallāh, in approximately 1266/1849f, but on the opposite side of the Arabian Peninsula.[9] His birthplace was the small village of al-Suqqā on the mountainous outskirts of Abhā, in the western province of ʿAsīr. His father, a government official and Qurʾān instructor in al-Suqqā named Siḥmān ibn Muṣliḥ, relocated the family to Riyadh in 1280/1863f. There the young Ibn Siḥmān studied under ʿAbd al-Raḥmān ibn Ḥasan Āl al-Shaykh and his son ʿAbd al-Laṭīf, staying there for approximately seven years. With the outbreak of the Saudi civil war in 1287/1870, Siḥmān moved the family south to al-ʿAmmār, seeking out the relative tranquility of al-Aflāj. For the next fifteen years and more, Ibn Siḥmān studied with Ibn ʿAtīq, being joined by ʿAbdallāh ibn ʿAbd al-Laṭīf in 1293/1876.

8. On him, see Āl al-Shaykh, *Mashāhīr*, 129–41; Āl Bassām, *ʿUlamāʾ Najd*, 1:215–30; al-Qāḍī, *Rawḍat al-nāẓirīn*, 1:459–70; Āl ʿAbd al-Muḥsin, *Tadhkirat ulī ʾl-nuhā*, 2:290–314; and see further Āl al-Shaykh, *al-Shaykh ʿAbdallāh ibn ʿAbd al-Laṭīf*.

9. On him, see Āl al-Shaykh, *Mashāhīr*, 290–322; Āl Bassām, *ʿUlamāʾ Najd*, 2:399–412; al-Qāḍī, *Rawḍat al-nāẓirīn*, 1:168–72; Ibn Ḥamdān, *Tarājim*, 16–24; Āl ʿAbd al-Muḥsin, *Tadhkirat ulī ʾl-nuhā*, 3:256–66; and see further al-ʿAmrawī, *Qalāʾid al-jumān fī bayān sīrat Āl Suḥmān*. This last title raises the question of the vocalization of the Siḥmān name. As can be seen, al-ʿAmrawī prefers "Suḥmān," a choice described to me by one Saudi scholar as groundless (interview with ʿAbd al-Raḥmān al-Shuqayr, Riyadh, August 25, 2015). Another Saudi academic, Sulaymān al-Kharāshī, who has edited some of Ibn Siḥmān's books, told me that the typographic standard is "Saḥmān" (interview with Sulaymān al-Kharāshī, Riyadh, August 30, 2015). According to Ismāʿīl ibn Saʿd ibn ʿAtīq, a great-grandson of Ḥamad ibn ʿAtīq, "Siḥmān" was the preferred vocalization of the Siḥmān family (interview with Ismāʿīl ibn Saʿd ibn ʿAtīq, via Muḥammad ibn Suʿūd al-Ḥamad, Riyadh, September 7, 2015). For this reason, and because "Siḥmān" is the most common pronunciation I have heard, I have opted for "Siḥmān." This is also the choice of Al-Fahad in his "From Exclusivism to Accommodation" and "The ʿImama vs. the ʿIqal."

Following the death of Ibn ʿAtīq in 1301/1884, and the death of Siḥmān the same year (i.e., 1301/1883f), Ibn Siḥmān and ʿAbdallāh returned to Riyadh. This was during the second reign of the *imām* ʿAbdallāh ibn Fayṣal (1292–1305/1875–87) and only a few years before the conquest of Riyadh by Muḥammad ibn Rashīd. In Riyadh, ʿAbdallāh assumed the role of the head of the Wahhābī religious establishment and principal instructor of religious students. Ibn Siḥmān served as the *imām*'s personal scribe (*kātib*), though his principal vocation, as we shall see, was as the author of numerous refutations of the enemies of Wahhābism.

Upon the fall of the second Saudi state, ʿAbdallāh and Ibn Siḥmān were both forced to spend time in Ḥāʾil. On the orders of Ibn Rashīd, ʿAbdallāh was sent to the Rashīdī capital for a period of one year beginning in 1308/1891, during which time he worked as a preacher and instructor. Ibn Siḥmān spent some four years in Ḥāʾil, accompanying the *imām* ʿAbdallāh there during the latter's brief exile in 1305–7/1887–89 and staying another two years. He returned to Riyadh in 1309/1891f. The biographies indicate that he was not in Ḥāʾil by choice and that he spent much of his time copying manuscripts. Unlike ʿAbdallāh, he does not appear to have been much of a teacher. Both men are said to have forged a strong connection with the scholars of Ḥāʾil, including especially Ṣāliḥ ibn Sālim Āl Bunayyān (d. 1330/1912), a hard-line Wahhābī scholar in Jabal Shammar who later served as the *qāḍī* of Ḥāʾil.[10] Ṣāliḥ was closely aligned with the scholars in Riyadh and participated, through his writings, in the era's religious conflicts with the opponents of Wahhābism.

ʿAbdallāh and Ibn Siḥmān were not the only prominent Wahhābī scholars of this period. Others included Saʿd ibn Ḥamad ibn ʿAtīq, a son of Ḥamad ibn ʿAtīq, and Isḥāq ibn ʿAbd al-Raḥmān Āl al-Shaykh, a brother of ʿAbd al-Laṭīf Āl al-Shaykh. The careers of Saʿd and Isḥāq illustrate a new development during this period, which was the pursuing of religious studies beyond Najd, particularly in India. Toward the end of the second Saudi state and during the Rashīdī interregnum, more than twenty Najdīs pursued religious studies in India.[11] Driving this development, in addition to the political instability in Najd, was the rise in India of an intellectual movement known as the Ahl-i Ḥadīth.[12] The scholars of the Ahl-i Ḥadīth were, as their

10. On him, see al-Hindī, *Zahr al-khamāʾil*, 57–61; al-Rudayʿān, *Manbaʿ al-karam*, 212–31; Āl Bassām, *ʿUlamāʾ Najd*, 2:462–65; al-Qāḍī, *Rawḍat al-nāẓirīn*, 1:228–37.

11. al-Mudayhish, "Min ʿulamāʾ Najd alladhīna raḥalū ilā ʾl-Hind li-ṭalab al-ʿilm."

12. See *EI*[3], s.v. "Ahl-i Ḥadīth" (Claudia Preckel).

name indicates, focused on the study of the *ḥadīth* corpus, and like the Wahhābīs they were hostile to the cult of saints and enamored of the teachings of Ibn Taymiyya. The Wahhābīs and the Ahl-i Ḥadīth were thus natural allies to a certain extent, and during this period they would come to see each other as such.

One of the first Najdī scholars to study in India was Sa'd ibn 'Atīq (d. 1349/1930).[13] Born in al-Ḥawṭa, in the southern district of al-Fura', in 1267/1850f, Sa'd set out for India in 1301/1884 and stayed there for some nine years. Most of his time appears to have been spent in Bhopal, where he studied with scholars associated with the Ahl-i Ḥadīth, including Ṣiddīq Ḥasan Khān al-Qannawjī (d. 1307/1890),[14] Muḥammad Bashīr al-Sahsawānī (d. 1323/1905),[15] and the Yemeni-born Ḥusayn ibn Muḥsin al-Anṣārī (d. 1327/1909),[16] among others. He also studied in Delhi with the renowned *ḥadīth* scholar Nadhīr Ḥusayn al-Dihlawī (d. 1320/1902).[17] Before returning to Najd, where he would succeed his father as the *qāḍī* of al-Aflāj, Sa'd spent more than a year studying in Mecca.

Isḥāq ibn 'Abd al-Raḥmān Āl al-Shaykh (d. 1319/1901) was another well-traveled Wahhābī scholar who spent time studying in India.[18] Born in Riyadh in 1276/1859f, Isḥāq was more than fifty years younger than his brother 'Abd al-Laṭīf and ten years younger than his nephew 'Abdallāh ibn 'Abd al-Laṭīf. In 1308/1891, following the Rashīdī conquest of Riyadh, Isḥāq left for India, where he stayed for three years, studying in Bombay, Delhi, Bhopal, and Machhali Shahar with a number of Ahl-i Ḥadīth scholars, including the aforementioned Nadhīr Ḥusayn, Muḥammad Bashīr, and Ḥusayn ibn Muḥsin. After a few more years studying in Cairo and Mecca, Isḥāq finally returned to Riyadh, where he worked as a teacher. He died only a few years later, in 1319/1901, aged

13. On him, see Āl al-Shaykh, *Mashāhīr*, 323–28; Āl Bassām, *'Ulamā' Najd*, 2:220–27; al-Qāḍī, *Rawḍat al-nāẓirīn*, 1:144–49; Ibn Ḥamdān, *Tarājim*, 106–14. On his India trip, see the editor's introduction in Ibn 'Atīq, *Kitāb al-majmū' al-mufīd*, 9–16.

14. On him, see *EI*[3], s.v. "Khān, Ṣiddīq Ḥasan" (Claudia Preckel); al-Ḥasanī, *al-I'lām*, 8:1246–50. Before and during Sa'd's trip, Ḥamad ibn 'Atīq carried on a correspondence with Ṣiddīq Ḥasan Khān, complaining in one letter of the dearth of Islamic texts in Najd; see Āl al-Shaykh, *Mashāhīr*, 245–54.

15. On him, see al-Ḥasanī, *al-I'lām*, 8:1352–53.

16. On him, see ibid., 8:1391–93.

17. On him, see ibid., 8:1212–14.

18. On him, see Āl al-Shaykh, *Mashāhīr*, 122; Āl Bassām, *'Ulamā' Najd*, 1:557–64; al-Qāḍī, *Rawḍat al-nāẓirīn*, 1:98–99; and see further al-Ghunaym, *Juhūd al-shaykh Isḥāq ibn 'Abd al-Raḥmān*.

just over forty, his premature death preventing him from assuming a more prominent role in the Wahhābī scholarly establishment.

That these young Wahhābī scholars would choose to pursue religious studies abroad, in India and elsewhere, can seem somewhat puzzling given Wahhābī opposition to the idea of travel to areas seen as lands of polytheists. Both Saʿd and Isḥāq, as we shall see, would subsequently argue strongly against the permissibility of travel to lands dominated by polytheists. How they squared this position with their own travel to Hindu- and British-dominated India is difficult to say. Perhaps they believed themselves to be uniquely capable of manifesting the religion in places where *shirk* was prevalent, or perhaps they considered certain communities in India, such as in Bhopal, to be Islamic lands unto themselves. Whatever the case, the international experience of these young men helped the Wahhābīs form alliances with like-minded scholars in foreign locales, including the Ahl-i Ḥadīth in India and the al-Ālūsī family in Baghdad.[19] A member of the al-Ālūsī family played a key role in the production of the first printed Wahhābī text.

Confronting Anti-Wahhābism in Print

The al-Ālūsī scholars shared with the Wahhābīs a predilection for Taymiyyan theology, including hostility toward the cult of saints, and like them harbored a particular disdain for the anti-Wahhābī Dāwūd ibn Jirjīs. The two factions saw themselves as aligned in the literary war on the Iraqi scholar. Nuʿmān ibn Maḥmūd al-Ālūsī (d. 1317/1899) composed a refutation of Ibn Jirjīs in 1275/1859,[20] and later Maḥmūd Shukrī al-Ālūsī (d. 1342/1924) undertook to complete an unfinished refutation of Ibn Jirjīs by ʿAbd al-Laṭīf Āl al-Shaykh.[21] In the 1280s/1860s, ʿAbd al-Laṭīf was corresponding with another

19. On them, see *EI*[3], s.v. "al-Alūsī Family" (Edouard Méténier). And see further Abu-Manneh, "Salafiyya and the Rise of the Khālidiyya in Baghdad in the Early Nineteenth Century"; Weismann, "Genealogies of Fundamentalism." The alleged influence of the Wahhābīs on this group of scholars, mentioned in both of these articles, bears further investigation. My sense is that the al-Ālūsī scholars gravitated toward Taymiyyan theology independently of the Wahhābīs, as was the case with Ibn al-Amīr al-Ṣanʿānī in Yemen, the Ahl-i Ḥadīth in India, and others.

20. al-Ālūsī, *Shaqāʾiq al-Nuʿmān fī shaqāshiq Ibn Sulaymān*, ff. 2a–27a. This was written in response to an epistle by Ibn Jirjīs refuting Nuʿmān's father, Abū ʾl-Thanāʾ Maḥmūd al-Ālūsī (d. 1270/1854). Ibn Jirjīs's refutation of Abū ʾl-Thanāʾ was printed as *Risāla fī ʾl-radd ʿalā ʾl-marḥūm al-sayyid Maḥmūd afandī al-Ālūsī*.

21. al-Ālūsī, *Fatḥ al-mannān tatimmat Minhāj al-taʾsīs radd Ṣulḥ al-ikhwān*.

member of the al-Ālūsī clan, ʿAbd al-Raḥmān al-Ālūsī (d. 1284/1867), praising him for manifesting Islam in the proper way and combating the so-called preachers of error (*al-duʿāt ilā ʾl-ḍalāl*).[22] In 1305/1887f, one of ʿAbd al-Laṭīf's refutations of Ibn Jirjīs, known as *Dalāʾil al-rusūkh fī ʾl-radd ʿalā ʾl-manfūkh* (Firmly Established Evidence in Refutation of the Inflated One), was printed in Egypt with the help of the al-Ālūsī family; it bore the endorsements of several Iraqi scholars, who likewise saw themselves as ideologically aligned with the Wahhābīs.[23] In a letter, Nuʿmān al-Ālūsī reported to Isḥāq ibn ʿAbd al-Raḥmān Āl al-Shaykh that "we have published it in Egypt" (*fa-ṭabaʿnāhu fī Miṣr*).[24] *Dalāʾil al-rusūkh* appears to have been the earliest Wahhābī text to appear in print. It was in India, however, where the publication of Wahhābī texts really took off, a development facilitated by the growing links between the Wahhābīs and the Ahl-i Ḥadīth.

In the 1300s/1890s, a number of publishing houses in India, mainly in Bombay but also in Delhi and Amritsar, began producing lithographs of Wahhābī texts in cooperation with the scholars in Najd. These included Ibn ʿAbd al-Wahhāb's *Kitāb al-tawḥīd* (Delhi, 1308/1890f),[25] ʿAbd al-Raḥmān ibn Ḥasan's commentary thereon (Delhi, 1311/1893f),[26] two refutations by ʿAbd al-Laṭīf ibn ʿAbd al-Raḥmān (Bombay, n.d.; Bombay, 1310/1892f),[27] the Wahhābī compendium *Majmūʿat al-tawḥīd* (Delhi, 1895),[28] and, somewhat later, Ibn Ghannām's history (Bombay, 1337/1918).[29] Another early publication was a short book by Ibn Siḥmān titled *al-Bayān al-mubdī li-shanāʿat al-Qawl al-mujdī* (The Clear Explanation of the Abomination of the Helpful Word). This was published in Amritsar in 1897. The story of this book illustrates the impetus behind much of the Wahhābī publishing in India—namely, to respond to the printed refutations of Wahhābism with printed counterrefutations.

22. *al-Durar al-saniyya*, 14:188–90.

23. Āl al-Shaykh, *Dalāʾil al-rusūkh*, *alif–hāʾ* (pagination in Arabic letters). *Dalāʾil al-rusūkh* was later reprinted as *Tuḥfat al-ṭālib wa ʾl-jalīs fī kashf shubah Dāwūd ibn Jirjīs*.

24. al-Ghunaym, *Juhūd al-shaykh Isḥāq ibn ʿAbd al-Raḥmān*, 50–51.

25. Khān, *Muʿjam al-maṭbūʿāt*, 400.

26. Ibid., 280.

27. Ibid., 300–301.

28. Fulton and Ellis, *Supplementary Catalogue*, cols. 627–29.

29. Khān, *Muʿjam al-maṭbūʿāt*, 136. To my knowledge, the earliest Wahhābī publication in India was a shorter compendium of Wahhābī texts titled *Raghbat al-muwaḥḥidīn fī taʿallum aṣl al-dīn*, dated 1306/1889; on this, see the editor's introduction in the new edition, al-Kamālī, *Raghbat al-muwaḥḥidīn*, 12–16.

Ibn Siḥmān's *al-Bayān al-mubdī* is a refutation of a Shāfiʿī scholar in Mecca named Muḥammad Saʿīd Bābṣayl, but its story begins with Bābṣayl's teacher Aḥmad ibn Zaynī Daḥlān (d. 1304/1886), a prominent Shāfiʿī scholar in Mecca and the author of several anti-Wahhābī works.[30] His book *al-Durar al-saniyya fī ʾl-radd ʿalā ʾl-Wahhābiyya* (The Splendid Pearls in Refutation of the Wahhābīs), published in Cairo in 1299/1882, was widely read and aroused the ire of the Wahhābī scholars in Najd.[31] *Al-Durar al-saniyya* takes the form of a response to a request to assemble the *ḥadīths*, Qurʾānic verses, and other evidence in favor of visiting the Prophet's tomb and using him as a means to God (*ziyārat al-nabī ṣ wa ʾl-tawassul bihi*).[32] After fulfilling this request, Daḥlān goes on in the book to cover the evidence in favor of *ziyāra* more generally, before turning to a long and detailed critique of Wahhābism, including the movement's history and doctrine. In this section, Daḥlān quotes from some of the early anti-Wahhābī refutations, repeating some of the early accusations such as that Ibn ʿAbd al-Wahhāb claimed prophecy and professed that Muslims ceased to exist six hundred years ago.[33] Showing his familiarity with the Wahhābī doctrine, Daḥlān dismisses the distinction between *tawḥīd al-ulūhiyya* and *tawḥīd al-rubūbiyya*, correctly identifying this as the basis for the Wahhābīs' approach to *takfīr*.[34] Like some of the early refuters, he quotes the contemporary opponents of Ibn Taymiyya, such as Taqī al-Dīn al-Subkī and Ibn Ḥajar al-Haytamī,[35] suggesting that the Wahhābīs are the heirs of the dreaded fourteenth-century Ḥanbalī scholar.[36]

Al-Durar al-saniyya was the first refutation of Wahhābism to appear in print, and as such it generated a fervent response from the Wahhābī scholars. Ibn Siḥmān was the first to refute it, doing so in a work titled *al-Mawāhib al-*

30. Ibn Siḥmān, *al-Bayān al-mubdī*. For the date, see Fulton and Ellis, *Supplementary Catalogue*, cols. 827–28.

31. On him, see *EI*³, s.v. "Daḥlān, Aḥmad b. Zaynī" (Esther Peskes). For a contemporary portrait, see Hurgronje, "Some of My Experiences with the Muftis of Mecca."

32. Daḥlān, *al-Durar al-saniyya*, 2.

33. Ibid., 24–25, 33–35. The early anti-Wahhābī refutations that he quotes are Ibn Sulaymān al-Kurdī's *risāla*, Ibn ʿAfāliq's *Tahakkum al-muqallidīn*, and ʿAlawī al-Ḥaddād's *Miṣbāḥ al-anām*.

34. Daḥlān, *al-Durar al-saniyya*, 25–26.

35. See, for instance, ibid., 3, 7, 11.

36. Ibid., 21. Daḥlān never uses *Wahhābī* or any of its variants in this book (the title is not his), though he does so frequently in his history of Mecca; see Daḥlān, *Khulāṣat al-kalām*, 227ff. (this section of the book is in some places identical to *al-Durar al-saniyya*).

rabbāniyya fī ʾl-intiṣār lil-ṭāʾifa al-Muḥammadiyya al-Wahhābiyya wa-radd aḍālīl al-shubah al-Daḥlāniyya (The Divine Gifts in Support of the Muḥammadan Wahhābī Sect and in Refutation of the Erroneous Specious Arguments of Daḥlān), which he completed in 1302/1884f.[37] With the exception of a brief prose introduction, *al-Mawāhib al-rabbāniyya* is written entirely in verse. This was in keeping with Ibn Siḥmān's fondness for poetry. While by no means the first Wahhābī poet, he indulged the genre more than any Wahhābī scholar before him.[38] In *al-Mawāhib al-rabbāniyya*'s nearly five hundred lines, he rebuts Daḥlān's anti-Wahhābī charges, accusing him of quoting spurious *ḥadīth*s and misinterpreting others and chiding him for relying on al-Subkī and al-Haytamī. The appearance of *Wahhābī* in the title shows that the scholars were beginning to adopt the *Wahhābī* epithet for themselves.[39] Two other Wahhābī scholars, Ṣāliḥ al-Shathrī (d. 1309/1891f) and Zayd ibn Muḥammad Āl Sulaymān (d. 1307/1889), authored refutations of Daḥlān's *al-Durar al-saniyya*, in 1304/1887 and 1306/1889, respectively.[40]

37. Ibn Siḥmān, *al-Mawāhib al-rabbāniyya*. This manuscript, though incomplete, is helpful in confirming the author's choice of title (f. 1a). For the full text of the refutation (sans the original introduction), see Ibn Siḥmān, *ʿUqūd al-jawāhir* (al-Rushd ed.), 1:193–228. The author's original copy, complete with date, is held at Maktabat al-Midhnab al-ʿĀmma. See the photo of the colophon in al-Ṣamʿānī, *al-Shaykh Sulaymān ibn Siḥmān*, 120.

38. At the beginning of the poem, he explains his choice of medium, saying that poetry possesses greater power than the sword: *fa-qultu mujīban bi ʾl-qarīḍi li-annahū / ashaddu ʿalā ʾl-aʿdā mina ʾl-ṣārimi ʾl-hindī* (meter = *ṭawīl*); see Ibn Siḥmān, *ʿUqūd al-jawāhir* (al-Rushd ed.), 1:197; cf. 1:183.

39. Ibn Siḥmān seems to have been inspired in this by an obscure pro-Wahhābī scholar named Mullah ʿImrān ibn Riḍwān (d. 1280/1863f), from the Arabic-speaking coastal town of Bandar Lengeh (Ar., Lanja) in the far south of Iran on the Persian Gulf. In a poem with which Ibn Siḥmān was familiar, Mullah ʿImrān proudly takes up the "Wahhābī" label, writing: "If the follower of Aḥmad [i.e., the Prophet] is described as Wahhābī / then I affirm that I am Wahhābī" (*in kāna tabiʿu Aḥmadin mutawahhiban / fa-anā ʾl-muqirru bi-annanī Wahhābī*; meter = *ṭawīl*); see Ibn Riḍwān, *Mukhtārāt*, 83. On Mullah ʿImrān, who appears to have been ethnically Arab, see the editor's introduction at 13–17. Mullah ʿImrān may have been the first Wahhābī to identify as such, but Ibn Siḥmān was responsible for popularizing the practice. A Shāfiʿī, Mullah ʿImrān may have been influenced by al-Shāfiʿī's famous line in which he proclaims himself a *rāfiḍī*: *in kāna rifḍan ḥubbu Āli Muḥammadin / fa ʾl-yashhadi ʾl-thaqalāni annī rāfiḍī*. See al-Subkī, *Ṭabaqāt al-Shāfiʿiyya al-kubrā*, 1:299.

40. See al-Shathrī, *Taʾyīd al-malik al-mannān fī naqḍ ḍalālāt Daḥlān*, 142; Āl Sulaymān, *Fatḥ al-mannān fī naqḍ shubah al-ḍāll Daḥlān*, 187. Al-Shathrī was mentioned above as one of the refuters of Ibn Duʿayj.

None of these refutations of *al-Durar al-saniyya* was published, though two Ahl-i Ḥadīth scholars in India authored refutations of Daḥlān that did appear in print. The titles of their works were *Ṣiyānat al-insān ʿan waswasat al-shaykh Daḥlān* (Safeguarding Mankind from the Whispers of Shaykh Daḥlān), by ʿAbdallāh ibn ʿAbd al-Raḥmān al-Sindī, and *al-Ḥaqq al-mubīn fī ʾl-radd ʿalā ʾl-luhābiyya al-mubtadiʿīn* (The Clear Truth in Refutation of the Zealous [?] Innovators), by ʿAbd al-Karīm ibn Fakhr al-Dīn. Both books were published in Delhi in 1890.[41] The names of both authors were pseudonyms, though the identity of the first was later revealed as Muḥammad Bashīr al-Sahsawānī, one of the teachers of Saʿd ibn ʿAtīq and Isḥāq ibn ʿAbd al-Raḥmān in Bhopal.[42] It was likely Muḥammad Bashīr's contact with these students and other Wahhābīs that allowed him to procure the original Wahhābī sources that he quotes throughout the book, including Ibn Ghannām's history. While largely a refutation of Daḥlān, *Ṣiyānat al-insān* is also a defense of Wahhābism.

When these refutations were printed in Delhi, Daḥlān had already been dead for several years. His anti-Wahhābī role would be assumed by one of his students in Mecca, Muḥammad Saʿīd Bābṣayl (d. 1330/1912), a scholar of Yemeni origin who succeeded Daḥlān as the Shāfiʿī *muftī* of Mecca. In 1309/1891, Bābṣayl took it upon himself to respond to the two Indian refutations of *al-Durar al-saniyya* in a work of his own.[43] Titled *al-Qawl al-mujdī fī ʾl-radd ʿalā ʿAbdallāh ibn ʿAbd al-Raḥmān al-Sindī* (The Helpful Word in Refutation of ʿAbdallāh ibn ʿAbd al-Raḥmān al-Sindī), it was published as a lithograph in Jakarta in 1309/1892.[44] In *al-Qawl al-mujdī*, Bābṣayl devotes most of his attention to Ibn Taymiyya, whom he assails as the source of the Wahhābīs' corruption and innovation (*manbat shajarat al-fasād wa ʾl-bidʿa*).[45] The error and corruption of Ibn ʿAbd al-Wahhāb, he writes, are the outgrowth of Ibn Taymiyya's (*ḍalāl wa-fasād mutafarriʿ ʿalā ḍalāl wa-fasād*).[46]

Ibn Siḥmān responded to Bābṣayl in *al-Bayān al-mubdī li-shanāʿat al-Qawl al-mujdī*, a prose refutation that, as was mentioned above, was published in

41. Fulton and Ellis, *Supplementary Catalogue*, cols. 6, 56–57. The first book is widely available online; the second, which I have not been able to access, is rare.

42. al-Sahsawānī, *Ṣiyānat al-insān*. The identity of the second author is unclear.

43. On him, see "Bābṣayl muftī ʾl-Shāfiʿiyya." The biographical dictionaries with which I am familiar say next to nothing about him.

44. See Bābṣayl, *al-Qawl al-mujdī*. I am grateful to the National Library of Israel for lending me a copy of this rare lithograph.

45. Ibid., 4.

46. Ibid., 17.

Amritsar in 1897. Ibn Siḥmān was likely in Ḥāʾil when he wrote it, as following the main text is an endorsement by the Ḥāʾil-based Ṣāliḥ ibn Sālim Āl Bunayyān, who praises Ibn Siḥmān as the eloquent author of numerous refutations.[47] As in most of his prose refutations, Ibn Siḥmān follows here the standard procedure of commenting line by line on his opponent's text. In marshaling his evidence, he quotes at length from Ibn Ghannām's history, including the epistles and letters of Ibn ʿAbd al-Wahhāb therein.[48] Defending Ibn Taymiyya, he dismisses Bābṣayl's and Daḥlān's sources—namely, al-Subkī and al-Haytamī—and quotes a number of Shāfiʿīs who had a favorable view of Ibn Taymiyya, including Ibn Kathīr, al-Dhahabī, al-Mizzī, ʿAfīf al-Dīn al-Yāfiʿī (d. 768/1367), Ibrāhīm al-Kūrānī (d. 1101/1690), ʿAlī al-Suwaydī (d. 1237/1822), Nuʿmān al-Ālūsī, and Maḥmūd al-Ālūsī.[49] *Al-Bayān al-mubdī* was the first of more than a dozen works by Ibn Siḥmān, most of them refutations, that would be published in India over the next twenty years. The majority of the early Wahhābī publications in India were in fact Ibn Siḥmān's refutations.[50] In publishing these, it is clear that Ibn Siḥmān was driven by a concern with the large number of anti-Wahhābī tracts that were appearing in print at this time, beginning with Daḥlān's *al-Durar al-saniyya*. His concern is on display in an undated poem that he wrote in a letter to a man in Qatar, asking him for assistance in publishing his refutations. The correspondent, ʿAbdallāh ibn Muḥammad ibn Khāṭir (d. 1326/1908f), was

47. Ibn Siḥmān, *al-Bayān al-mubdī*, 150–58.

48. In this instance he suggests that the interested reader consult Ibn Ghannām's book directly (*fa-ʿalayhi bi-muṭālaʿat Rawḍat al-afkār wa'l-afhām*); see ibid., 67.

49. Ibid., 71–83.

50. For a list of Ibn Siḥmān's Indian publications, see Khān, *Muʿjam al-maṭbūʿāt*, 192–93; al-Ḍubayb, "Ḥarakat iḥyāʾ al-turāth baʿd tawḥīd al-jazīra," 46–47, 59–60. They include *al-Bayān al-mubdī li-shanāʿat al-qawl al-mujdī* (1897), *Taʾyīd madhhab al-salaf wa-kashf shubuhāt man ḥādda wa'nḥarafa* (1323/1905), *Kashf al-shubhatayn ʿan risālat Yūsuf ibn Shabīb wa'l-qaṣīdatayn* (1327/1909f), *Kashf al-awhām wa'l-iltibās ʿan tashbīh baʿḍ al-aghbiyāʾ min al-nās* (1328/1910), *Tamyīz al-ṣidq min al-mayn fī muḥāwarat al-rajulayn* (printed with *Kashf al-awhām wa'l-iltibās*), *Iqāmat al-ḥujja wa'l-dalīl wa-īḍāḥ al-maḥajja wa'l-sabīl* (1332/1913), *al-Ṣawāʿiq al-mursala al-shihābiyya ʿalā'l-shubah al-dāḥiḍa al-Shāmiyya* (1335/1916), *Tabriʾat al-shaykhayn al-imāmayn min tazwīr ahl al-kadhib wa'l-mayn* (printed with *al-Ṣawāʿiq al-mursala*), *Kashf al-shubuhāt allatī awradahā ʿAbd al-Karīm al-Baghdādī fī ḥill dhabāʾiḥ al-ṣulb wa-kuffār al-bawādī* (printed with *al-Ṣawāʿiq al-mursala*), *Taḥqīq al-kalām fī mashrūʿiyyat al-jahr bi'l-dhikr baʿd al-salām* (printed with *al-Ṣawāʿiq al-mursala*), *al-Dīwān al-musammā bi-ʿUqūd al-jawāhir* (1337/1919), *al-Asinna al-ḥidād fī radd shubuhāt ʿAlawī al-Ḥaddād* (n.d.), *al-Ḍiyāʾ al-shāriq fī radd shubuhāt al-mādhiq al-māriq* (printed with *al-Asinna al-ḥidād*), *Kashf ghayāhib al-ẓalām ʿan awhām Jalāʾ al-awhām* (n.d.), and *Irshād al-ṭālib ilā ahamm al-maṭālib* (printed with *Kashf ghayāhib al-ẓalām*).

presumably a businessman with resources and connections in India. In the poem, Ibn Siḥmān complains that the enemies of Wahhābism have been printing their works in great numbers:

> And how much they have done corruption in the land with the books that
> they have spread in the east and the west!
> They have published of them, by my life, [so many] publications
> and cast them into every country and place.[51]

The anti-Wahhābī books hitting the market, in addition to Daḥlān's *al-Durar al-saniyya* (1299/1882), included Ibn Jirjīs's *Ṣulḥ al-ikhwān* (1306/1888f), Sulaymān ibn ʿAbd al-Wahhāb's *al-Ṣawāʿiq al-ilāhiyya* (1306/1888f), and ʿAlawī al-Ḥaddād's *Miṣbāḥ al-anām* (1325/1907f), as well as refutations by the Syrians Muḥammad ʿAṭāʾ Allāh ibn Ibrāhīm al-Kasm (1901) and Mukhtār ibn Aḥmad al-ʿAẓamī (1330/1912) and the Iraqi Jamīl Ṣiqdī al-Zahāwī (1323/1905). Ibn Siḥmān composed long refutations of most of these, among other works in prose and in verse.

The early Wahhābī printing in India was thus largely motivated by an interest in responding to the enemies of Wahhābism, whose works were circulating in print for the first time, and it was made possible by the growing collaboration between the Wahhābīs and the Ahl-i Ḥadīth. Yet while Ibn Siḥmān and his allies were occupied with refuting these anti-Wahhābī authors and publishing their refutations, they were also busy with what they perceived to be a gathering threat to Wahhābism back in Najd.

The *Fitna* in al-Qaṣīm

Amid the decline of the Saudi state and the corresponding rise of the Rashīdī emirate, a group of dissident scholars in al-Qaṣīm came to the fore to challenge the authority of the scholars in Riyadh. Most of them were living in Burayda. While these men professed their fidelity to the Wahhābī movement, in their view the Wahhābī doctrine did not require the kinds of prohibitions on travel and interaction with non-Wahhābī Muslims advocated by previous Wahhābī scholars. What they sought to introduce, in other words, was a more moderate version of Wahhābism. To ʿAbdallāh ibn ʿAbd al-Laṭīf and Ibn Siḥmān, this

51. Ibn Siḥmān, *ʿUqūd al-jawāhir* (al-Rushd ed.), 2:139–41, at 141 (meter = *ṭawīl*).

was a gross distortion of the teachings of Muḥammad ibn ʿAbd al-Wahhāb and his successors, and it needed to be confronted and put down.

The dissident faction in al-Qaṣīm was led by the scholarly duo of Ibrāhīm ibn Jāsir (d. 1338/1919) and ʿAbdallāh ibn ʿAmr (d. 1326/1908f), both from Burayda. Ibn Jāsir, the senior partner of the pair, was born in 1241/1825f,[52] while Ibn ʿAmr was born much later, in 1287/1870f.[53] Both are said to have studied in Iraq and Syria, where they were exposed to anti-Wahhābī views. In the developing controversy over their approach to Wahhābism, it was Ibn ʿAmr who played the role of chief antagonist of the scholars in Riyadh, writing refutations of them and complaining about them to the ruler in Ḥāʾil. Whether these men were truly committed to the doctrine of Ibn ʿAbd al-Wahhāb, or whether they were masquerading as Wahhābīs à la ʿUthmān ibn Manṣūr, is difficult to determine. At one point, Ibn Jāsir is known to have held a positive view of the cult of saints, as he himself acknowledged in a statement announcing his "return to the truth" (*al-rujūʿ ilā ʾl-ḥaqq*).[54] Yet, apart from Ibn Jāsir's onetime support for *ziyāra*, there is little indication that either he or Ibn ʿAmr was opposed to Ibn ʿAbd al-Wahhāb's basic views concerning *tawḥīd* and *shirk*. They may well have seen themselves as the genuine heirs of Ibn ʿAbd al-Wahhāb, believing that the Wahhābī doctrine, properly understood, entailed a much more moderate approach to *takfīr* and *al-walāʾ wa ʾl-barāʾ* than was being advocated by ʿAbdallāh and Ibn Siḥmān.

In Burayda, the dissident faction was opposed by another group of scholars aligned with the scholars in Riyadh. This opposing faction was headed by two members of the Āl Salīm family, the cousins Muḥammad ibn ʿUmar ibn Salīm (d. 1308/1890)[55] and Muḥammad ibn ʿAbdallāh ibn Salīm (d. 1326/1908).[56] The chief representatives of the Āl Salīm, both had studied with ʿAbdallāh Abā

52. On him, see Āl Bassām, *ʿUlamāʾ Najd*, 1:277–93; al-ʿUmarī, *ʿUlamāʾ Āl Salīm*, 203–4; al-ʿUbūdī, *Muʿjam usar Burayda*, 3:54–98.

53. On him, see Āl Bassām, *ʿUlamāʾ Najd*, 4:324–34; al-ʿUmarī, *ʿUlamāʾ Āl Salīm*, 357; al-ʿUbūdī, *Muʿjam usar Burayda*, 15:613–37. Cf. the discussion of Ibn ʿAmr in Steinberg, *Religion und Staat in Saudi-Arabien*, 106–7, 172–75; Al-Fahad, "From Exclusivism to Accommodation," 508–10; Commins, *Wahhabi Mission*, 68–69, 73.

54. Ibn Jāsir, *Rujūʿ al-shaykh Ibrāhīm ibn Jāsir*, 177–80. This may have been written around 1303/1886, which is mentioned by Ibn Jāsir here as the year when his views were corrected.

55. On him, see Āl al-Shaykh, *Mashāhīr*, 255–57; Āl Bassām, *ʿUlamāʾ Najd*, 6:340–48; al-Qāḍī, *Rawḍat al-nāẓirīn*, 2:260–63; al-ʿUmarī, *ʿUlamāʾ Āl Salīm*, 53–63.

56. On him, see Āl al-Shaykh, *Mashāhīr*, 258–59; Āl Bassām, *ʿUlamāʾ Najd*, 6:150–59; al-Qāḍī, *Rawḍat al-nāẓirīn*, 2:264–67; al-ʿUmarī, *ʿUlamāʾ Āl Salīm*, 20–52.

Buṭayn in ʿUnayza and ʿAbd al-Raḥmān ibn Ḥasan Āl al-Shaykh and his son ʿAbd al-Laṭīf in Riyadh. The ideological division in Burayda, and in al-Qaṣīm more generally, was thus seen at the time as one between the followers of the Āl Salīm and the followers of Ibn Jāsir and Ibn ʿAmr.[57] In the polemical parlance of the day, the followers of the Āl Salīm were "the rabid dogs" (*al-maghālīth*), while the followers of Ibn Jāsir and Ibn ʿAmr were "the opposition" (*al-ḍidd*).[58] Years later, Muḥammad ibn ʿAbd al-Laṭīf Āl al-Shaykh (d. 1367/1948), a younger brother of ʿAbdallāh ibn ʿAbd al-Laṭīf, summarized the nature of the struggle between the two sides. The people of al-Qaṣīm, he wrote,

> came to be two parties and two groups [*ḥizbayn wa-farīqayn*]. One group believed that the Ottoman state [*al-dawla al-ʿUthmāniyya*] and the grave-worshippers resembling them were Muslims, not apostates; they did not believe in the necessity of showing them enmity and dissociating from them; they deemed traveling to their lands permissible; and they did not believe in the necessity of emigrating away from them. The second group opposed them and professed the contrary of what they believed. Between them there arose a great struggle and conflict.[59]

As is indicated here, the dispute in al-Qaṣīm revolved around the related issues of *takfīr*, *al-walāʾ wa ʾl-barāʾ*, *hijra*, and the permissibility of travel to lands seen as dominated by grave-worshippers, in particular Ottoman lands. Ibn Jāsir and Ibn ʿAmr denied that the inhabitants of the Ottoman Empire were polytheists and argued that traveling to their lands, for business or otherwise, was permissible. Their view was that manifesting the religion could be achieved by fulfilling the basic religious obligations of prayer and fasting, and therefore travel to any land in which that was possible was allowed. The Āl Salīm, by contrast, in line with the scholars in Riyadh, maintained that the Ottoman Empire was an infidel state where polytheism reigned and that travel to the lands under its control was forbidden. They understood manifesting the religion to mean showing

57. It may seem surprising that Burayda was the scene of this struggle rather than ʿUnayza, with its greater reputation for anti-Wahhābism. It is possible that ʿUnayza did not have a sufficient number of strict Wahhābīs for there to be much of a contest there.

58. al-ʿUbūdī, *Muʿjam usar Burayda*, 3:60. These terms occasionally appear in the chronicle of Ibrāhīm Āl ʿAbd al-Muḥsin, who was from Burayda; see, e.g., Āl ʿAbd al-Muḥsin, *Tadhkirat ulī ʾl-nuhā*, 1:372, 2:38.

59. Quoted in Ibn ʿAqīl al-Ẓāhirī, *Masāʾil min tārīkh al-jazīra al-ʿarabiyya*, 60.

hatred and enmity to the unbelievers in the land concerned, and thus they considered travel to lands in which this was not possible to be prohibited. This second position was of course consistent with the views of the Wahhābī scholars of the second Saudi state, as was seen in the preceding chapter.

The dispute in al-Qaṣīm seems to have been ongoing for some time, though it did not attract the attention of the scholars in Riyadh until 1313/1895f, when Ibn Siḥmān fired the opening salvo in what was to be a long series of refutations between himself and Ibn ʿAmr. That year, Ibn Siḥmān wrote a stern letter to a group of men in Burayda, including Fawzān Āl ʿAlī, Sābiq ibn Fawzān, and ʿAbdallāh Āl Ḥusayn, reprimanding them for what he understood to be their view that travel to the so-called lands of polytheists was permitted.[60] Ibn Siḥmān begins his letter by expressing his disappointment in what he has learned about the men's views:

> What has become widely known about some of the brothers has reached me. It has saddened my heart and provoked much grief, caused anguish where there was tranquility, and turned happiness to sorrow. This is that they claim that living among the polytheists is permissible for those who pray and fast, that travel is permissible to the lands of polytheists and idol-worshippers [*bilād al-mushrikīn wa-ʿubbād al-aṣnām*], and that those who forbid these things and prohibit them are fearmongering extremists [*min al-mushaddidīn al-munaffirīn*].[61]

Ibn Siḥmān continues by positing two possible sources of these brothers' misguidedness. Either they harbor doubt about the foundations of the Wahhābī *daʿwa* (*shakk fī aṣl hādhihi ʾl-daʿwa*), or they have been led astray by the falsehoods and distortions of certain people seeking to promote interaction with all and sundry (*maʿa kull man habba wa-daraja*).[62] The latter, he suggests, is more likely, adding that this is the less dangerous (*aqall khaṭaran*) of the two possibilities. The certain people said to be disseminating falsehoods are not mentioned by name but would surely include Ibn Jāsir and Ibn ʿAmr. Ibn Siḥmān warns his correspondents about the likes of them, saying: "Be not deceived by falsehood and the distortions and lies told by every ignoramus."[63]

60. See Ibn Siḥmān, *ʿUqūd al-jawāhir* (al-Rushd ed.), 2:51–58.
61. Ibid., 2:51.
62. Ibid., 2:51–52.
63. Ibid., 2:52.

The rest of the letter is a poem of some seventy lines in which Ibn Siḥmān spells out the Wahhābī position on travel to polytheist lands, complete with explanations of *al-walāʾ wa ʾl-barāʾ* and *iẓhār al-dīn*. Following his predecessors, he defines *iẓhār al-dīn* as the manifestation of hatred and enmity to unbelievers, describing this as the condition that must be met for one to be able to travel to lands of unbelief. Harking back to Abraham's example in the Qurʾān, he urges the men to adhere to the religion of Abraham (*millat Ibrāhīm*):

The religion of Abraham, follow its path
and show enmity to those to whom he showed enmity, if you are Muslim,
And show loyalty to those to whom he showed loyalty, and beware being foolish, lest you be brought low and have regret.
Is it part of the religion, o you, to live together with the enemies
in a land where unbelief has grown oppressive and severe,
And not to manifest, when you are in the land of unbelief,
your religion among people, openly and publicly?
From what Book and from what *sunna*
did you take a sound proof text for this?
Whosoever does not manifest the religion openly,
you have permitted for him this forbidden residence,
If he fasts or prays and harbors hatred,
and in his heart has enmity for the blind unbelievers.
May your mother be bereft of you! Have you thought to yourself even once
about the religion of Abraham, or do you wish to destroy it?[64]

At the end of the letter, Ibn Siḥmān requests a response from his correspondents, asking them either to recant their views and affirm the truth of what he has written or else to present their evidence against it.[65] Ibn Siḥmān's letter has been published in his poetry collection, or *dīwān*, though it is thanks to a manuscript in Ḥāʾil that we know the year it was sent—1313/1895f.[66] What

64. Ibid., 2:54 (meter = *ṭawīl*).

65. Ibid., 2:58.

66. Ibn Siḥmān, *Risāla ilā ʾl-ikhwān* (unnumbered folios). An unsigned epistle in Mecca, also in manuscript form, likewise dates the outbreak of the conflict between Ibn ʿAmr and the scholars in Riyadh to 1313; see *Risāla li-muʾallif majhūl*, 164.

transpired after this poem is knowable only because of a manuscript in Riyadh that contains Ibn Siḥmān's refutations of Ibn ʿAmr and, within them, several more texts that form part of the exchange.[67]

The letter by Ibn Siḥmān to the men in Burayda did not elicit a favorable response, rather angering one of its recipients, Sābiq ibn Fawzān. Sābiq authored a critical response and sent this to Riyadh, requesting that one of the Āl al-Shaykh provide clarification on the matters in question. As one can tell from the ensuing refutations, Sābiq was deeply offended by the suggestion that he and the other addressees of Ibn Siḥmān's letter had forsaken the religion of Abraham, believing that Ibn Siḥmān had pronounced *takfīr* on him and his associates. Sābiq further believed that Ibn Siḥmān's position on travel, as expressed in his letter, was extreme and groundless and hoped that a member of the Āl al-Shaykh would set the perceived fanatical scholar straight.[68]

Unfortunately for Sābiq, the leading Wahhābī scholar in Riyadh at the time was Ibn Siḥmān's friend ʿAbdallāh ibn ʿAbd al-Laṭīf, who did not hesitate to defend Ibn Siḥmān against Sābiq's indictment.[69] ʿAbdallāh begins his letter to Sābiq by stating that he knows Sābiq to be a man of sound creed (*ḥasan al-iʿtiqād*), though later he regrets that Sābiq and his companions have been led astray by certain heretics in al-Qaṣīm who have sought to permit what is forbidden.[70] This has given rise to a tribulation (*fitna*) that has only grown in severity. At first, according to ʿAbdallāh, the *fitna* was concerned with the permissibility of shunning those who mix with unbelievers and travel to their lands (*mashrūʿiyyat al-hajr wa-tark al-salām ʿalā ʾl-mukhāliṭīn wa ʾl-musāfirīn*).[71] The practice of shunning (*hajr*) entailed not speaking to a person, inviting him to one's home,

67. This is Ibn Siḥmān's *al-Radd ʿalā ʿAbdallāh ibn ʿAmr*, held at Dārat al-Malik ʿAbd al-ʿAzīz. The collection comprises two refutations of Ibn ʿAmr, both the original copies in the author's hand. The first (ff. 0b–122b), described in the margin as *al-Radd al-kabīr*, is also known as *al-Jawāb al-fāʾiḍ li-Arbāb al-qawl al-rāʾid*; the second (ff. 123b–201b) has no known title. I am grateful to Dārat al-Malik ʿAbd al-ʿAzīz for providing me with a copy of the collection. For an unpublished edition of *al-Radd al-kabīr*, made from two copies that depart somewhat from the original, see Ibn Siḥmān, "al-Jawāb al-fāʾiḍ."

68. Ibn Siḥmān, *al-Radd ʿalā ʿAbdallāh ibn ʿAmr*, ff. 1b–2a, 3b, 9a–b, 29a.

69. ʿAbdallāh's letter to Sābiq is partially preserved ibid., ff. 0b–122b (i.e., Ibn Siḥmān's *al-Radd al-kabīr*). A copy of the letter, to which I have not had access, is held at Jāmiʿat al-Imām Muḥammad ibn Suʿūd al-Islāmiyya in Riyadh; see Āl al-Shaykh, *al-Shaykh ʿAbdallāh ibn ʿAbd al-Laṭīf*, 72–75.

70. Ibn Siḥmān, *al-Radd ʿalā ʿAbdallāh ibn ʿAmr*, ff. 10a, 35a.

71. Ibid., ff. 31b, 33a.

or responding to his greetings for a limited time.[72] Then the *fitna* developed into a broader rejection of the foundations of the religion and of the religious obligations (*jaḥd al-uṣūl wa-inkār al-wājibāt*).[73] The instigators of this *fitna*, ʿAbdallāh says, are seeking to convince the people of al-Qaṣīm that their view in favor of mixing with polytheists and traveling to their lands is consistent with the principles of Islam as elaborated by the Wahhābī scholars. They profess to hold Ibn ʿAbd al-Wahhāb in high regard and to belong to his movement (*wa-yuẓhirūna taʿẓīmahu waʾl-intimāʾ ilā ṭarīqatihi*), but in reality this is only a tactic used to mislead those with little knowledge.[74] Much as Ibn Jirjīs and Ibn Manṣūr distorted the words of Ibn Taymiyya, he says, so these men have distorted the words of Ibn ʿAbd al-Wahhāb.[75] While ʿAbdallāh refrains here from identifying any of these misleaders by name, he surely has Ibn ʿAmr and Ibn Jāsir foremost in mind.

As regards the issue of travel, ʿAbdallāh tells Sābiq that mixing with unbelievers (*ikhtilāṭ al-Muslim biʾl-kāfir*) is one of the greatest causes of corruption on earth (*min aʿẓam al-fasād fī ʾl-arḍ*), emphasizing the obligation to show enmity to unbelievers and the prohibition against showing them loyalty (*muʿādāt al-kuffār waʾl-nahy ʿan muwālātihim*).[76] In classic Wahhābī fashion, he cites the examples of Abraham and Muḥammad as illustrative of the duty of manifesting enmity. Regarding Abraham's dissociation from his people and what they worshipped, he says: "This dissociation is the supreme condition without which Islam is not sound [*al-sharṭ al-akbar allatī lā yaṣiḥḥu ʾl-Islām illā bihā*], and its nonexistence is invalidating of the foundation of Islam."[77] What further testifies to this, he continues, is that "if a man in the time of the Prophet had said, 'I follow Muḥammad, and what he professes is true, but I will not fight Abū Jahl and I will not confront any of the people [*lā uqātilu Abā Jahl wa-lā ataʿarraḍu li-aḥad min al-nās*],' do you think that he would be a Muslim despite this?"[78] The matter of travel to the lands of unbelievers, ʿAbdallāh continues in his letter, is not an obscure matter, and it is well estab-

72. al-ʿUbūdī, *Muʿjam usar Burayda*, 15:613.

73. Ibn Siḥmān, *al-Radd ʿalā ʿAbdallāh ibn ʿAmr*, f. 33a.

74. Ibid., f. 54b.

75. Ibid., f. 92a.

76. Ibid., f. 11a.

77. Ibid., f. 20a.

78. Ibid., f. 23a. This statement of ʿAbdallāh's is very similar to Ibn ʿAbd al-Wahhāb's in the *Kalimāt* epistle, where he writes: "If a person were to have said, 'I follow Muḥammad, and he has the truth, but I will not confront al-Lāt, al-ʿUzzā, Abū Jahl, and the likes of them; I have no

lished that traveling to and residing in such lands are forbidden for those unable to manifest the religion.[79] As for the meaning of manifesting the religion, what it entails is stating clearly to them that one does not profess their religion (*al-taṣrīḥ lahum annahu laysa ʿalā millatihim*) and showing them enmity (*iẓhārihi ʾl-ʿadāwa lahum*).[80] To manifest the religion is not merely to pray and to fast and to harbor enmity and hatred for polytheists in one's heart; rather, it is to condemn polytheists for the *shirk* that they believe in and practice (*al-inkār ʿalayhim fīmā ʿtaqadūhu wa-faʿalūhu min al-shirk*). Such condemnation, ʿAbdallāh asserts, is simply not being undertaken by the travelers to and residents of the lands of polytheists today.[81]

Turning to Ibn Siḥmān's letter to the brothers in Burayda, ʿAbdallāh reproaches Sābiq for misinterpreting Ibn Siḥmān's words and blowing them out of proportion.[82] Ibn Siḥmān was not charging him and his companions with unbelief, ʿAbdallāh explains, but, rather, was speaking in general terms about those who contradict divine proofs and permit what is forbidden. He was seeking to give advice (*naṣīḥa*) and to begin a scholarly exchange (*mudhākara*), not to single any one person out as an unbeliever.[83]

As one can see here, ʿAbdallāh was trying his best to be diplomatic, where Ibn Siḥmān had been intentionally provocative. While it is true that Ibn Siḥmān had not pronounced *takfīr* on Sābiq and his companions, it was also the case that ʿAbdallāh was understating the severity of what Ibn Siḥmān had said. The latter's letter was meant to be offensive and unsettling, suggesting as it did that the recipients failed to understand and observe the foundational principles of Islam. ʿAbdallāh's letter, by contrast, while supporting Ibn Siḥmān's positions, was intended to placate and repair relations with the aggrieved men. The contrasting approaches of the two scholars do well in illustrating their respective roles as the chief representative of the Wahhābī establishment and the foremost refuter of the enemies of Wahhābism, respectively. Ibn Siḥmān's tendency was to be aggressive and uncompromising, and in this way he took after the fiery Ḥamad ibn ʿAtīq. ʿAbdallāh was trying to

---

obligation concerning them,' then his Islam would not be sound." See al-Qabbānī, *Faṣl al-khiṭāb*, f. 65b (= *al-Durar al-saniyya*, 2:109).

79. Ibn Siḥmān, *al-Radd ʿalā ʿAbdallāh ibn ʿAmr*, ff. 57a, 58a.

80. Ibid., f. 95a.

81. Ibid., ff. 102b, 103b.

82. Ibid., f. 35a.

83. Ibid.

compensate for his friend's overzealousness, and in this way he was more akin to his father, the occasionally moderate-seeming ʿAbd al-Laṭīf.

Around the same time as ʿAbdallāh was responding to Sābiq, another of the scholars in Riyadh, Isḥāq ibn ʿAbd al-Raḥmān Āl al-Shaykh, was replying to a similar query from a man in Burayda. This was ʿAbdallāh ibn Aḥmad Āl Rawwāf (d. 1359/1940), who had written to Isḥāq asking about the permissibility of traveling to the lands of polytheists.[84] In his question, Āl Rawwāf notes that al-Qaṣīm is divided between those who permit such travel and those who prohibit it (*māniʿ wa-mujīz*).[85] In his response, Isḥāq argues at length that the prohibitors are correct and the permitters are wrong, making many of the same points as Ibn Siḥmān and ʿAbdallāh. In order to be able to travel to such lands, he explains, one must be able to manifest the religion, which he defines in terms of Abraham's example in the Qurʾān of enunciating enmity and hatred (*al-qawl bi'l-lisān maʿa 'l-ʿadāwa wa'l-baghḍāʾ*).[86] "Hatred of the unbeliever is a condition of faith" (*bughḍ al-kāfir mashrūṭ fī 'l-īmān*), he asserts.[87] Without specifying any lands in particular, he refers to the manifest unbelief and the rule by positive law (*al-kufr al-jalī al-bawwāḥ wa'l-ḥukm bi'l-qawānīn*) that predominate there as evidence of their polytheistic status. Those who reside in such places, he adds, are more sinful than those who merely visit them, but visiting is still prohibited.[88] Preceding Isḥāq's response are the endorsements of seven Wahhābī scholars in Najd, including ʿAbdallāh and Saʿd ibn ʿAtīq.[89] One of these is dated Muḥarram 1314/June 1896, which suggests that Isḥāq's work was written around this time.[90]

Meanwhile, in response to these writings prohibiting travel, Ibn ʿAmr was busy sending letters to the emir in Ḥāʾil, Muḥammad ibn Rashīd, accusing the scholars in Riyadh of promoting extremism. In one of these letters, dated Ramaḍān 1314/February 1897, Ibn ʿAmr mentions Ibn Siḥmān's letter to the men in Burayda, noting that it includes a pronouncement of *takfīr* on a number of people (*fīhā takfīr jamāʿa*). He also refers to ʿAbdallāh's letter to Sābiq, describing ʿAbdallāh as responsible for "the extremism that has spread in

84. On him, see Āl Bassām, *ʿUlamāʾ Najd*, 4:28–31.

85. Āl al-Shaykh, *al-Ajwiba al-samʿiyyāt li-ḥall al-asʾila al-Rawwāfiyyāt*, 66.

86. Ibid., 84.

87. Ibid., 82.

88. Ibid., 98.

89. Ibid., 47–61.

90. The date appears only in the earlier edition of the text; see Āl al-Shaykh, *Sulūk al-ṭarīq al-aḥmad*, 15.

Najd" (*al-ghuluww alladhī shāʿa fī Najd*). The extremism of ʿAbdallāh and his ilk, he states, can be found in every Najdī town and has been embraced by the majority of the scholars of Najd (*akthar ṭalabat al-ʿilm fī Najd*). Their doctrine consists in judging all lands to be lands of unbelief, forbidding travel there, and pronouncing *takfīr* on all who disagree with them. The first to give expression to these extremist views, he claims, was Ḥamad ibn ʿAtīq, who stipulated conditions for travel that are simply impossible to meet (*yataʿadhdharu wujūduhā*). Ibn ʿAmr asks Ibn Rashīd for help in correcting the views of the extremist scholars, saying: "We hope that God returns them to the truth by means of you." The contents of the letter suggest that this was not Ibn ʿAmr's first such appeal to Ibn Rashīd, as he refers to the positive response that an earlier complaint of his elicited.[91]

While ʿAbdallāh may have been the bigger target in Ibn ʿAmr's sights, it was Ibn Siḥmān who suffered most from Ibn ʿAmr's complaints to Ibn Rashīd. Around this time, Ibn Siḥmān found himself personally threatened by the emir, who had been appalled by the contents of Ibn Siḥmān's letter to Sābiq (at least as conveyed to him by Ibn ʿAmr). In an extant letter to Ibn Rashīd, Ibn Siḥmān pleads with the ruler to show forbearance (*musāmaḥa*) and to rescind his reproach (*izālat mashrūhikum*).[92] "Shaykh ʿAbdallāh [ibn ʿAbd al-Laṭīf] has told me of your reproaching me for the letter and poem that I wrote to the brothers in al-Qaṣīm," he writes. "If I had received some previous instruction from you, or heard from you that I ought to avoid this matter, I would not have thought to speak about it with even one word . . . for hearing and obeying are incumbent on me [*fa ʾl-wājib ʿalaynā ʾl-samʿ wa ʾl-ṭāʿa*]."[93] The letter to Ibn Rashīd was accompanied by an apologetic poem, in which Ibn Siḥmān praises the ruler and asks for forgiveness. Ibn Siḥmān was careful not to confess to having committed any particular offense, however, claiming that his words had been misrepresented by slanderers (i.e., Ibn ʿAmr):

> Slanderers [*al-wāshūn*] have distorted my words, and I am not
> the first to be wronged by a slanderous accuser . . .
> By God and by God, I am truthful
> and I am not regretful [*ghayr nādim*] for what I wrote.[94]

91. Ibn ʿAmr, *Risāla ilā ʾl-amīr Muḥammad ibn Rashīd*, 168–71.

92. See the letter in al-Bassām, "Min juhūd al-malik ʿAbd al-ʿAzīz fī tawḥīd kalimat al-ʿulamāʾ," 177–80.

93. Ibid., 177.

94. Ibid., 179 (meter = *ṭawīl*).

Despite this apology, Ibn Siḥmān appears to have remained on Ibn Rashīd's bad side. For several years, he refrained from writing on the issues in question, at least under his own name, and later would say that Ibn Rashīd had threatened to kill him if he spoke out.

In the meantime, Ibn ʿAmr took an additional step in his effort to cast the scholars in Riyadh as dreadful extremists. Having found two earlier poems by Ibn Siḥmān on the subject of travel, he composed a critical response (*jawāb*) to each of these, making Ibn Siḥmān out to be far outside the Islamic (and Wahhābī) mainstream. The first of Ibn Siḥmān's poems to be subjected to Ibn ʿAmr's critical appraisal had been written some twenty years earlier.[95] It takes the form of a rhetorical question about whether it is permissible for a Muslim to live in a land ruled by unbelievers:

A question! Is there a *muftī* who will compose
 and write an answer to this question,
in prose or in rows of poetry as he likes,
 clarifying and explaining the meaning of the evidence . . .
Is it permitted by the religion for one to reside
 in a land that has been occupied and settled by unbelievers? . . .
By God, what is the judgment concerning a resident of their land
 and what is the manner of manifesting the religion amid them?[96]

The poem continues in the voice of the fictitious questioner, who asks whether the proper understanding of *iẓhār al-dīn* is the religion of Abraham (*millat Ibrāhīm*) or whether it is prayer and fasting and bearing hatred for the unbelievers in one's heart.[97] The implicit answer is that *iẓhār al-dīn* is to be equated with *millat Ibrāhīm* in the sense of manifesting hatred and enmity to unbelievers. As the recipient of the poem was living in Mecca, Ibn Siḥmān seems to have been implying that Mecca was a place overrun by unbelievers and where Muslims should not reside.

In his *jawāb* to the poem, Ibn ʿAmr disputes Ibn Siḥmān's understanding of *millat Ibrāhīm* as a religious requirement equivalent to *iẓhār al-dīn*. "The poor man does not know," Ibn ʿAmr writes, "that the religion of Abraham is the foundation of Islam, that it is worshipping God and eschewing the worship

95. Noted by Isḥāq Āl al-Shaykh in his *Īḍāḥ al-maḥajja wa ʾl-sabīl*, 27.
96. Ibn Siḥmān, *ʿUqūd al-jawāhir* (al-Rushd ed.), 2:95–96 (meter = *ṭawīl*).
97. Ibid., 2:96.

of what is apart from him."[98] The correct understanding of *iẓhār al-dīn,* he says, is the ability to carry out one's religious obligations (*an yatamakkana ʾl-insān min adāʾ wājibāt dīnihi*), which he defines as believing in God and His Prophet, performing the daily prayers, and fasting during Ramaḍān. While verbal condemnation of unbelievers (*al-inkār bi ʾl-lisān*) is ideal, he says, it is not required for one to achieve *iẓhār al-dīn.*[99]

When Ibn ʿAmr's *jawāb* made its way to Riyadh, it was refuted by Isḥāq ibn ʿAbd al-Raḥmān, whose contempt for Ibn ʿAmr is palpable. In his refutation, Isḥāq makes clear that "this ignorant moron" (*hādhā ʾl-ghabī al-jāhil*), meaning Ibn ʿAmr, is no scholar at all (*laysa min ahl al-ʿilm*).[100] This is evident, he explains, from the man's misconstrual of *millat Ibrāhīm* and his failure to understand its relationship to *iẓhār al-dīn.* The fact of the matter is that *iẓhār al-dīn* is the equivalent of *millat Ibrāhīm* (*iẓhār al-dīn huwa millat Ibrāhīm*), the latter being a byword for the requirements of *al-walāʾ wa ʾl-barāʾ*. *Millat Ibrāhīm* consists in "confronting the enemies of God with enmity and hatred, dissociating from them and what they worship, loving for the sake of God and hating for the sake of God, showing loyalty for His sake and showing enmity for His sake, and dissociating from polytheism and polytheists."[101] That *millat Ibrāhīm* possesses this meaning, Isḥāq says, has been well established by the scholars of the Wahhābī *daʿwa* (*ahl hādhihi ʾl-daʿwa al-ḥanīfiyya*).[102] For Ibn ʿAmr to fail to understand this is revealing of who he really is, which is an opponent of the *daʿwa* of Ibn ʿAbd al-Wahhāb, not its representative.[103]

The second of Ibn Siḥmān's poems that Ibn ʿAmr would dig up and criticize was written in 1305/1887f. As Ibn Siḥmān would later explain, it was a poem that he had written in response to a man in al-Aḥsāʾ who claimed to be able to manifest the religion there.[104] In the poem, Ibn Siḥmān retorts that this is impossible, referring to the many disturbing features of al-Aḥsāʾ: positive law, sodomy, fornication, drinking, smoking, music, Shīʿism, and the

98. Āl al-Shaykh, *Īḍāḥ al-maḥajja wa ʾl-sabīl,* 8. Ibn ʿAmr's *jawāb* is partially preserved in this source.

99. Ibid., 36, 43.

100. Ibid., 8.

101. Ibid., 10.

102. Ibid., 12.

103. Ibid., 14–15.

104. See Ibn Siḥmān, *al-Radd ʿalā ʿAbdallāh ibn ʿAmr,* f. 123b.

general oppression of the unbelievers.[105] He then proceeds to lay out the proper understanding of *iẓhār al-dīn*:

And the love and the hatred that are our religion,
    and enmity for the sake of God that is the measure,
And likewise loyalty on behalf of His majesty,
    if one examines the matter carefully,
Are something impossible in a place governed by an oppressor [*amr muḥāl fī wilāyat man ṭaghā*].
    If [a land] is truly so, residing [there] would not occur to you . . .
Manifesting this religion is clearly pronouncing to them
    that they are unbelievers, for indeed they are an unbelieving people,
And evident enmity and manifest hatred,
    this is manifesting [the religion] and [proper] condemnation.
By God, such is not what is apparent among you.
    O those with understanding, have you no notice?
This, and not enough is bearing hatred in the heart
    and love in it—this is not the measure.
Rather, the measure is to bear it
    openly and clearly, for they have gone astray.[106]

In his *jawāb*, Ibn ʿAmr again disputes this understanding of *iẓhār al-dīn* as the ability to manifest hatred and enmity.[107] He further assails Ibn Siḥmān for suggesting that one cannot truly be a Muslim in a land governed by an oppressive ruler (*man ṭaghā*). This, he writes, is a great calamity (*ṭāmma kubrā*), regretting that such abominable extremism (*al-ghuluww al-shanīʿ*) is the view of a great many people in Najd.[108]

Whereas Isḥāq ibn ʿAbd al-Raḥmān had authored the response to Ibn ʿAmr's first *jawāb*, the scholar in Riyadh who responded to this second *jawāb* was none other than Ibn Siḥmān himself.[109] This would not have been apparent to Ibn ʿAmr, however, as Ibn Siḥmān refrained from writing it under his own name, given the threat issued by Ibn Rashīd. Seeking to give the impression that the author was someone else, Ibn Siḥmān refers to himself here in

105. Ibn Siḥmān, *ʿUqūd al-jawāhir* (al-Rushd ed.), 1:319–20.
106. Ibid., 1:320–21 (meter = *rajaz*).
107. Ibn ʿAmr, *Jawāb*, 175.
108. Ibid., 172–74.
109. See Ibn Siḥmān, *al-Juyūsh al-rabbāniyya*.

the third person (e.g., *manẓūmat Ibn Siḥmān*).[110] In this short refutation, Ibn Siḥmān defends himself against the charge of extremism while reaffirming that the man in al-Aḥsāʾ was incapable of manifesting the religion. Had the man been able to do so, he says, the polytheists there would not have let him be but would have either killed or expelled him—the same understanding of *iẓhār al-dīn* that was elaborated by Ḥamad ibn ʿAtīq. This is the meaning of the poem's assertation that *al-walāʾ wa'l-barāʾ* is impossible (*muḥāl*) in al-Aḥsāʾ, he explains, maintaining that such remains the case in al-Aḥsāʾ to this day.[111] As for the matter of an oppressive ruler, the poem was not referring to all kinds of oppressive rulers, he clarifies, but, rather, to the oppressive rulers of the Ottoman Empire, whose unbelief should be apparent to everyone familiar with it.[112]

The back-and-forth between Ibn ʿAmr and the scholars in Riyadh did not end here. There would be at least one more exchange of refutations. Upon seeing Ibn Siḥmān's unsigned refutation of the *jawāb*, Ibn ʿAmr composed a counterrefutation of it, and at some point during this period he also composed a refutation of ʿAbdallāh's letter to Sābiq.[113] In these works, Ibn ʿAmr again elaborates his view of *iẓhār al-dīn* as the ability to perform the ritual acts of worship, accusing ʿAbdallāh and Ibn Siḥmān of extremism—indeed, of pronouncing *takfīr* on virtually everyone on the planet (*takfīr man ʿalā wajh al-arḍ*).[114] Turning to insults, he describes Ibn Siḥmān as a mere poet (*wa-mā huwa illā shāʿir*) and as ʿAbdallāh's servant (*khādimuka*).[115] Ibn Siḥmān would later respond to each of Ibn ʿAmr's refutations with one of his own.

In Rajab 1315/November 1897, amid Ibn ʿAmr's campaign against the scholars, Muḥammad ibn Rashīd died. His cousin and successor, ʿAbd al-ʿAzīz ibn Mutʿib ibn Rashīd (r. 1315–24/1897–1906), was even less tolerant of the likes of Ibn Siḥmān than his predecessor. The new emir in Ḥāʾil dismissed many of the scholars in al-Qaṣīm from their positions, including Muḥammad ibn ʿAbdallāh ibn Salīm, the *qāḍī* of Burayda, who was exiled with one of his sons to the nearby town of al-Nabhāniyya. Another of his sons was exiled to another

110. Ibid., 95.

111. Ibid., 104.

112. Ibid., 107–8.

113. These works are reproduced in Ibn Siḥmān, *al-Radd ʿalā ʿAbdallāh ibn ʿAmr*. To add to the confusion, Ibn ʿAmr wrongly attributes Ibn Siḥmān's unsigned refutation to Ibrāhīm ibn ʿAbd al-Laṭīf Āl al-Shaykh (ff. 123b–24a).

114. Ibid., f. 37b.

115. Ibid., ff. 127b, 25a.

nearby town, al-Bukayriyya.[116] The reign of ʿAbd al-ʿAzīz ibn Rashīd is remembered as a particularly oppressive time for the Wahhābīs, both for the scholars and for anyone suspected of harboring anti-Rashīdī sympathies. Ibn ʿAmr's complaints thus fell on very receptive ears during his reign. The scholars in Riyadh appear to have been intimidated into silence, ceasing to speak out against Ibn ʿAmr on the controversial issue of travel. But they were the ones who would have the last word.

When Ibn Siḥmān finally did respond to Ibn ʿAmr, it was after the founding in 1319/1902 of the third Saudi state, which restored a sense of security to the scholars in Riyadh. No longer worried about the possible repercussions of writing on the issues of *al-walāʾ wa ʾl-barāʾ* and travel, Ibn Siḥmān was comfortable enough to describe the Āl Rashīd as "oppressive kings" (*al-mulūk al-ẓalama*), accusing them of having helped Ibn ʿAmr spread his heresy (*ḍalāl*).[117] In these final two refutations, Ibn Siḥmān explains the circumstances that forced him into silence, recounting how Ibn ʿAmr wrote to Ibn Rashīd to complain about the contents of his letter to the men in Burayda. In one of the refutations, he claims that Ibn ʿAmr misled the emir into thinking that "we were pronouncing *takfīr* on him and pronouncing *takfīr* on those who travel to the lands of polytheists," which led Ibn Rashīd to issue a threat against him (*jāʾanā minhu tahdīd wa-waʿīd*) and to prohibit him from writing on the issues in question. It was in response to this, he says, that he wrote the apologetic poem to the ruler in Ḥāʾil, though in doing so he had been careful to employ a certain ambiguity (*nawʿ min al-taʾwīl*) so as not really to apologize.[118] In his other final refutation, Ibn Siḥmān explains how the rulers in Ḥāʾil helped and supported Ibn ʿAmr in his malicious campaign (*fa-sāʿadahu ʾl-mulūk wa-aʿānūhu*), claiming that their hearts and their agendas were one (*tashābahat arwāḥuhum wa ʾttaḥada maqṣūduhum*).[119] He also explains why he hid his identity as the author of the earlier refutation, saying that he did so "out of fear that he [i.e., Ibn ʿAmr] and his companions would seek to harm

116. Āl ʿAbd al-Muḥsin, *Tadhkirat ulī ʾl-nuhā*, 1:342, 2:38.

117. Ibn Siḥmān, *al-Radd ʿalā ʿAbdallāh ibn ʿAmr*, f. 1b; cf. f. 29a. The two refutations that make up *al-Radd ʿalā ʿAbdallāh Ibn ʿAmr* are Ibn Siḥmān's final refutations of Ibn ʿAmr. The first, known as *al-Radd al-kabīr* (ff. 0b–122b), was written in response to Ibn ʿAmr's refutation of ʿAbdallāh's letter to Sābiq; the second, not known by any title and left unfinished by the author (ff. 123b–201b), was written in response to Ibn ʿAmr's refutation of Ibn Siḥmān's unsigned refutation of Ibn ʿAmr's *jawāb*.

118. Ibid., f. 118b.

119. Ibid., f. 191a.

me as they were seeking to do us harm earlier and were complaining about us, until such time as God was kind to us [*ḥattā laṭafa ʾllāh binā*]."[120] The kindness of God here is likely a reference to the rise of the third Saudi state, which saved the scholars from the yoke of the Āl Rashīd and provided them with the freedom to speak and write openly. In all likelihood, these last refutations by Ibn Siḥmān were written around 1323/1905, as in one of them Ibn Siḥmān refers to an event that transpired that year. This was the occupation of Burayda and ʿUnayza by Ottoman forces following the towns' brief capture by the Āl Suʿūd.[121] Ibn ʿAmr played a role in meeting with the leaders of the Ottoman forces as a messenger on behalf of the ruler of Burayda.[122] Ibn Siḥmān refers to Ibn ʿAmr's mediating role in the event, writing that "when those unbelieving enemies of God and His Messenger came to al-Qaṣīm, they were met by the leader of those despicable cretins [*zaʿīm hāʾulāʾi ʾl-ṣaʿāfiqa al-ḥamqā*] and the author of this refutation, ʿAbdallāh ibn ʿAmr. . . . He facilitated their entry to the lands of the Muslims."[123]

As the last word in the debate between the scholars in Riyadh and Ibn ʿAmr in Burayda, Ibn Siḥmān's refutations comprise what were the orthodox views of early twentieth-century Wahhābism. Here Ibn Siḥmān repeatedly emphasizes the duty to manifest enmity and hatred to polytheists (*iẓhār ʿadāwat al-mushrikīn wa-bughḍihim*), accusing Ibn ʿAmr of failing to understand this duty and its centrality to Wahhābism.[124] Ibn ʿAmr is depicted as the successor to Ibn Jirjīs and Ibn Manṣūr as the main instigator of trouble (*fitna*) and the main disseminator of anti-Wahhābī views in Najd.[125] He is "the tyrant of al-Qaṣīm" (*ṭāghiyat al-Qaṣīm*), similar to how Ibn Jirjīs was "the tyrant of Iraq" (*ṭāghiyat al-ʿIrāq*).[126] In response to the accusation that he was pronouncing *takfīr* on the entire world—an accusation he denies, emphasizing that those who travel to the lands of polytheists are sinners, not necessarily unbelievers—Ibn Siḥmān retorts that Ibn ʿAmr is the one whose approach to *takfīr* is defective. For Ibn ʿAmr and his allies fail to pronounce *takfīr* on the Ottoman Empire (*lā taqūlūna bi-takfīrihim*), they acknowledge its ruler as the leader of Islam

120. Ibid., f. 126a.
121. Vassiliev, *History of Saudi Arabia*, 219.
122. Āl ʿAbd al-Muḥsin, *Tadhkirat ulī ʾl-nuhā*, 2:51.
123. Ibn Siḥmān, *al-Radd ʿalā ʿAbdallāh ibn ʿAmr*, f. 29a.
124. Ibid., f. 1a.
125. Ibid., f. 32a–b.
126. Ibid., f. 47b.

(*wa-sulṭānuhum ʿindakum sulṭān al-Islām*), and they deem its territory to be Islamic lands as opposed to lands of war (*wa-bilāduhum bilād Islām lā bilād ḥarb*).[127] From this it is clear that Ibn Siḥmān considered the entire Ottoman Empire to be an abode of unbelief, meaning that it was a place ruled by unbelievers that ultimately ought to be conquered in *jihād*. He specifies three lands in particular—al-Shām, Egypt, and Iraq—as off-limits to visitors on account of their non-Islamic status. Responding to Ibn ʿAmr's view of *iẓhār al-dīn*, he writes:

> Whoever deems al-Shām, Egypt, Iraq, and other such countries the majority of whose inhabitants supplicate saints and righteous persons and cleave to their graves . . . to be Islamic lands, then speaking with him about *iẓhār al-dīn* and the duty of *hijra* is trouble without benefit. How can one who deems them to be Islamic lands discuss *hijra* and *iẓhār al-dīn*? Only those who judge these countries to be lands of unbelief should be talking about and investigating these issues.[128]

For Ibn Siḥmān, then, al-Shām, Egypt, and Iraq, among other places, were lands of unbelief (*bilād kufr*) on account of the predominance there of the cult of saints. Presumably this was also the view of his scholarly allies in Riyadh, even if they were generally more reluctant to identify particular countries in this way.

The fate of Ibn ʿAmr speaks volumes about which side ultimately prevailed in this long struggle. In 1324/1906, al-Qaṣīm was conquered by the third Saudi state, and two years later, in 1326/1908f, Ibn ʿAmr was executed in Riyadh at the order of the Saudi ruler, ʿAbd al-ʿAzīz ibn ʿAbd al-Raḥmān Āl Suʿūd. The circumstances surrounding his execution are not well attested, but according to one credible account the killing had more to do with Ibn ʿAmr's political machinations than his religious views. Ibn ʿAmr allegedly had journeyed to Iraq in order to plead with Ottoman officials there for further support against the Āl Suʿūd. Upon returning to al-Qaṣīm, he was apprehended by Saudi forces and brought to Riyadh for punishment.[129] Yet while the execution may have had more to do with politics than religion, his death dealt a major blow to the Ibn Jāsir and Ibn ʿAmr faction in Burayda. As one Wahhābī historian remarked on the execution: "God dispersed the wayward and the misleading by means of the rule of the Āl Suʿūd."[130] Ibn Siḥmān and his allies can only have

127. Ibid., f. 37b.

128. Ibid., f. 91a.

129. al-ʿUbūdī, *Muʿjam usar Burayda*, 15:615–16.

130. Āl ʿAbd al-Muḥsin, *Tadhkirat ulī ʾl-nuhā*, 2:96.

been pleased. It was a radical change in fortunes for Ibn ʿAmr. Ten years after successfully inciting the Rashīdī ruler against Ibn Siḥmān, he was put to death by a Saudi ruler aligned with Ibn Siḥmān.

In assessing the challenge that Ibn ʿAmr posed to the authority of the Wahhābī scholars in Riyadh, it should be emphasized again that Ibn ʿAmr postured as a scholar belonging to the Wahhābī tradition. He dismissed as a great lie (*buhtān ʿaẓīm*) the accusation that he was an opponent of the doctrine of Ibn ʿAbd al-Wahhāb,[131] and he disputed the charge that he was, like Ibn Jirjīs and Ibn Manṣūr, permitting *shirk* (*ijāzat al-shirk*).[132] Rather than slandering the founder of Wahhābism as responsible for extremism, Ibn ʿAmr attributed the extremism of his Wahhābī contemporaries to the influence of Ḥamad ibn ʿAtīq. It is possible that Ibn ʿAmr sincerely believed that the principles of Wahhābism had been distorted by Ibn ʿAtīq and those after him. But the reality is that Ibn ʿAmr was the one whose views—on *al-walāʾ wa ʾl-barāʾ*, *hijra*, and *iẓhār al-dīn*—were out of step with the Wahhābī tradition. Whether Ibn ʿAmr was really trying to be faithful to the Wahhābī tradition as he understood it is difficult to say. The charitable view would be that he was simply ignorant of what the Wahhābī doctrine entailed, assuming that it had been radicalized later on. But it is perhaps more likely, as his enemies claimed, that Ibn ʿAmr's professed fidelity to the Wahhābī *daʿwa* was a facade. Whatever the case, the effort to forge a more moderate form of Wahhābism in al-Qaṣīm during the Rashīdī interregnum ended in failure. For Ibn ʿAmr personally, it ended in death.

Conclusion

Like their predecessors in the second Saudi state, the Wahhābī scholars of the Rashīdī interregnum were committed to preserving Wahhābism in its militant, uncompromising state. To a very large degree, their efforts in refuting the movement's opponents in print and confronting the toned-down version of Wahhābism in al-Qaṣīm were an extension of the efforts of ʿAbd al-Raḥmān ibn Ḥasan Āl al-Shaykh, Ḥamad ibn ʿAtīq, and ʿAbd al-Laṭīf ibn ʿAbd al-Raḥmān Āl al-Shaykh before them. It is telling that Ibn Siḥmān would portray ʿAbdallāh ibn ʿAmr as the successor to Dāwūd ibn Jirjīs and ʿUthmān ibn Manṣūr as the foremost domestic antagonist of the Wahhābīs. In his eyes, he was merely continuing his predecessors' work in safeguarding the Wahhābī doctrine from the likes of such enemies. In doing this job, Ibn Siḥmān never

131. Ibn Siḥmān, *al-Radd ʿalā ʿAbdallāh ibn ʿAmr*, f. 54b.

132. Ibid., f. 92b.

ceased to emphasize the Wahhābī requirement of showing hatred and enmity to unbelievers as a condition for living in and traveling to lands beyond Najd. In his writings, the key phrase in this regard was *millat Ibrāhīm*, which he used as a byword for the duty of showing hatred and enmity more than any Wahhābī scholar before him. As he writes in the initial letter to the men in Burayda that touched off the polemics with Ibn ʿAmr, "The religion of Abraham, follow its path / and show enmity to those to whom he showed enmity, if you are Muslim."[133] Ibn Siḥmān would stop at nothing to ensure that the proper understanding of *millat Ibrāhīm* was not forgotten.

Yet while the Rashīdī interregnum was a period when Ibn Siḥmān and his allies held forth on *millat Ibrāhīm*, reasserting their principles and rebuking their opponents, this was only half the story. The other half was the sense of persecution that they suffered at the hands of the Āl Rashīd, who sometimes made it difficult for them to preach their doctrine openly. In this context, Ibn Siḥmān composed an elegiac poem in which he bemoaned the strangeness or alienation of Islam (*ghurbat al-dīn*), accusing the people of Najd of having abandoned the religion of Abraham:

> For the religion let the knowing and the rightly guided weep,
> for its traces have been obliterated from the earth,
> And the attention of the people and their contriving have turned
> to this lower world and the accumulation of *dirhams*,
> And the enhancement of this world of theirs through the corruption of their religion,
> and the satisfaction of their pleasures and their tastes . . .
> The religion of Abraham, its way has been abandoned
> and effaced, and its waymarks have become as obliterated traces.
> Indeed, it has disappeared from among us. How, when before the winds carried it to all regions?
> The religion is not but love and hate and loyalty,
> as well as dissociation from every deviant sinner . . .
> The infallible one [i.e., the Prophet] professed his dissociation from every Muslim
> who lives in the abode of unbelief without showing opposition,
> And without manifesting the religion amid the people of vileness.
> Are we not to shun those who commit crimes?

133. Ibn Siḥmān, *ʿUqūd al-jawāhir* (al-Rushd ed.), 2:54 (meter = *ṭawīl*).

Nay, our living mentality today is
to make peace with every kind of sinner.
How great is the trial of Islam by all who are ignorant!
How few are the supporters [of the religion] among those with knowledge!
This is the time for patience, if you are firm
in religion, so be patient as the most determined of people.[134]

If this poem was really written, as Ibn Siḥmān says, during the Rashīdī interregnum, then the patience he was advising here was sound counsel indeed. The Wahhābīs would not have to wait long from the time the Āl Rashīd seized Riyadh, in 1305/1887, to the time ʿAbd al-ʿAzīz ibn ʿAbd al-Raḥmān Āl Suʿūd made his bid for the lost Saudi capital in 1319/1902. Even though the Wahhābī scholars had proclaimed their loyalty to the Rashīdī emir, this was never done enthusiastically. The scholars never saw the Āl Rashīd as the natural allies of their *daʿwa* in the way they saw the Āl Suʿūd. In retrospect, as Ibn Siḥmān put it, the Āl Rashīd were but "oppressive kings" who served the interests of Ibn ʿAmr and his like. The revival of Saudi power in Najd seemed to mark the revival of the Wahhābī scholars' fortunes. The emerging reality, however, would be more complicated than this picture of militant Wahhābism triumphant.

134. Ibid., 2:329–30 (meter = *ṭawīl*).

7

The Decline of Enmity

THE RISE OF THE THIRD SAUDI STATE (1902–1932)

FOLLOWING THE BATTLE of al-Mulaydā ʾ in 1308/1891, which saw the triumph of the Āl Rashīd over rebel forces aligned with ʿAbd al-Raḥmān ibn Fayṣal Āl Suʿūd, the defeated Saudi leader fled to the desert with his family, ultimately settling in Kuwait. The Kuwaiti ruler gave him sanctuary in cooperation with the Ottoman government, which paid ʿAbd al-Raḥmān a monthly stipend of sixty liras. With him in Kuwait was his young son, ʿAbd al-ʿAzīz ibn ʿAbd al-Raḥmān Āl Suʿūd. Born in Riyadh in approximately 1292/1875f, ʿAbd al-ʿAzīz was about fifteen years of age when his family fled Riyadh to the desert. Just over a decade later, in Shawwāl 1319/January 1902, he returned to Riyadh with a band of his followers, capturing the city in a surprise attack in which the Rashīdī governor and his guards were killed. ʿAbd al-ʿAzīz's capture of Riyadh in 1319/1902 marks the beginning of the third Saudi state. When ʿAbd al-Raḥmān arrived in Riyadh a few months later, he saw to it that his son was given the *bayʿa* as the new Saudi ruler. ʿAbd al-ʿAzīz thus served as the state's ruler from the beginning.[1]

Upon learning that ʿAbd al-ʿAzīz had taken Riyadh, the emir in Ḥāʾil, ʿAbd al-ʿAzīz ibn Rashīd, was preoccupied with an ongoing military conflict with Kuwait. He nonetheless gathered his forces and made south for Riyadh. The Saudi leader successfully fended off the attack. Soon after, he managed to extend his rule to the rest of al-ʿĀriḍ and al-Kharj, and within months he was threatening to take al-Qaṣīm as well. In response to these developments, and

1. On these events and the early period of the third Saudi state, see Vassiliev, *History of Saudi Arabia*, 210–86; Al-Rasheed, *History of Saudi Arabia*, 37–68.

at the urging of Ibn Rashīd, the Ottomans dispatched thousands of troops to al-Qaṣīm in 1322/1904. ʿAbd al-ʿAzīz's army fought a series of battles against the combined Ottoman and Rashīdī forces. In Ṣafar 1324/April 1906, during one of these battles, Ibn Rashīd was killed and decapitated. Six months later, the Ottomans abandoned the effort in Najd, and the newfound Saudi state annexed al-Qaṣīm. Meanwhile, the emirate of Jabal Shammar was beset by a dynastic crisis from which it would never recover. The next fifteen years saw the rise and fall of more than a dozen emirs and regents in Ḥāʾil, many of whom were murdered. The Ottomans, for their part, following the Young Turk Revolution in 1326/1908, were plunged into a political crisis of their own, coinciding with a prolonged military conflict in the Balkans. The situation redounded to the benefit of ʿAbd al-ʿAzīz, who conquered Ottoman-controlled al-Aḥsāʾ in 1331/1913 with only a few thousand forces. By this point, Riyadh was clearly the rising power in Arabia.

While ʿAbd al-ʿAzīz restored the historic alliance with Wahhābism and the Āl al-Shaykh, there appears to have been little emphasis on religion during the first decade of his rule. According to the historian Alexei Vassiliev, ʿAbd al-ʿAzīz did not initially give much weight to Wahhābism, "whether as a means of legitimizing his power, strengthening people's loyalty or lending dynamism to his campaigns of conquest."[2] Nonetheless, the Wahhābī scholars in Najd saw ʿAbd al-ʿAzīz as their natural ally and depicted him as a Muslim warrior in the classic Wahhābī mold, one who was waging *jihād* for the sake of expanding the ambit of *tawḥīd* and defeating *shirk*. Sulaymān ibn Siḥmān, for instance, in a book written around the time of the consolidation of Saudi rule in al-Qaṣīm, praises ʿAbd al-ʿAzīz as "the leader of the Islamic armies" (*qāʾid al-juyūsh al-Islāmiyya*).[3] For the scholars, ʿAbd al-ʿAzīz was the legitimate Islamic ruler, the *imām*, and he was renewing the Saudi-Wahhābī religiopolitical enterprise of old. It was a role that he would embrace.

In the 1330s/1910s, the Islamic character of the state was enhanced by the rise of the Ikhwān movement. The Ikhwān (Brothers) were former bedouin tribesmen who, at the behest of the new Saudi ruler, abandoned their nomadic lifestyle in favor of permanent settlement in agricultural camps. The tens of thousands of fighting-age men in the settlements, known for their religious zeal, formed the shock troops of ʿAbd al-ʿAzīz's army, leading the Saudi campaigns against Jabal Shammar and the Ḥijāz in the 1340s/1920s. With the conquests

2. Vassiliev, *History of Saudi Arabia*, 227.

3. Ibn Siḥmān, *al-Ḍiyāʾ al-shāriq*, 143, 136.

of Ḥāʾil in 1340/1921 and Mecca in 1343/1924, the Saudi state reached the limits of its territorial expansion.

The military campaigns of the Ikhwān were undertaken as *jihād* against unbelievers and were portrayed as such by the Wahhābī scholars. Ibn Siḥmān, for instance, in a poem written in 1337/1918 celebrating an Ikhwān raid on the outskirts of Ḥāʾil, urges the Saudi ruler to continue waging *jihād* against the infidel Rashīdī forces: "So struggle for God as is His due / for they are an army of intrusive unbelievers."[4] Similarly, in an undated letter to some of the Ikhwān, ʿAbdallāh ibn ʿAbd al-Laṭīf Āl al-Shaykh urges them to fight the Āl Rashīd and their supporters on account of their unbelief. He says of the Rashīdīs that there is no doubt regarding their *kufr*, claiming that they have shown enmity to the people of *tawḥīd*, have sought the aid of unbelievers (i.e., the Ottomans), and have failed to obey the *imām*, meaning ʿAbd al-ʿAzīz.[5] In a longer justification of *jihād*, one of the Wahhābī scholars (perhaps Ibn Siḥmān, but his name is not recorded) expounds three reasons why *jihād* against the people of Ḥāʾil is among the most virtuous forms of *jihād* (*min afḍal al-jihād*).[6] The first is that the people of Ḥāʾil are in a state of rebellion against the *imām* (*al-khurūj ʿan ṭāʿat walī amr al-Muslimīn*) and therefore must be fought until they obey his commands; the second is that they have failed to pronounce *takfīr* on the polytheists of the Ottoman Empire and elsewhere (*ʿadam takfīr al-mushrikīn*); and the third is that they have given support to polytheists (*muẓāharat al-mushrikīn*), meaning the Ottomans, and supported them in waging war against Muslims. Presumably, this refers to the help, meager as it was, provided by the Āl Rashīd to the Ottomans during World War I.[7] The arguments for *jihād* proffered by the scholars thus centered on the status of the people of Ḥāʾil as unbelievers, their failure to condemn the Ottomans and others as unbelievers, and their failure to obey the *imām* (i.e., ʿAbd al-ʿAzīz), even if they had never recognized him as such. In saying this, the Wahhābī scholars were lending their support to the Ikhwān-led campaign in the north.

The Saudi expansion in Arabia was not as Islamically pure as the scholars may have believed, however, for in fact the emergent Saudi state enjoyed the financial and military support of the British Empire. While much attention has

4. Ibn Siḥmān, *Tahniʾa lil-imām ʿAbd al-ʿAzīz*, 95 (meter = *ṭawīl*).

5. *al-Durar al-saniyya*, 9:82–85, at 83.

6. Ibid., 9:289–93, at 292.

7. The Wahhābī scholars in Ḥāʾil, it should be mentioned, objected to the idea that *jihād* against Jabal Shammar was religiously valid; see al-Rudayʿān, *Manbaʿ al-karam*, 91–93.

been paid by historians to the British role in promoting the "Arab revolt" of the Sharīf Ḥusayn in the Ḥijāz, the British support for ʿAbd al-ʿAzīz was of more lasting consequence. In Ṣafar 1334/December 1915, ʿAbd al-ʿAzīz and the British political resident in the Persian Gulf, Percy Cox, signed an accord known as the Anglo-Saudi Treaty. In exchange for Saudi agreement not to attack Bahrain or Kuwait, and a Saudi pledge not to have dealings with other foreign powers, the British agreed to recognize ʿAbd al-ʿAzīz as the legitimate ruler of Najd and al-Aḥsāʾ. Beginning the following year, they provided him with regular arms shipments and a monthly subsidy of £5,000, a sum that he collected until his incursion into the Ḥijāz a decade later.

The Wahhābī scholars can only have looked with disapproval on the matter of British financial assistance, if they were even aware of it. Several years before the arrangement with the British was made official, Ibn Siḥmān denied in a book the accusation that the Saudi ruler had received support from the British, dismissing the charge as unfounded. Addressing his Iraqi opponent, he writes:

> Indeed, we have not inclined toward them [i.e., the British] or appealed to them for support in any of the things that you have claimed. Nor, indeed, have we taken them as allies. Surely you know that no flag of theirs is to be found in our lands, and that we have not appointed consulates or adopted their laws [*qawānīnahum*] in our territories, putting them before the law of God and His Messenger. We dissociate before God from them and from you.[8]

Once the alliance with Great Britain was reached, approximately a decade after this was written, none of the Wahhābī scholars appears to have condemned it, at least not publicly. Ibn Siḥmān's remarks show that they certainly would not have approved. For Ibn Siḥmān, and presumably for his colleagues as well, the idea that a Saudi ruler would form an alliance with unbelievers was unconscionable, being entirely at odds with the Wahhābī duty to show hatred and enmity to unbelievers. In a *fatwā* written in Shaʿbān 1333/June 1915, Ibn Siḥmān presents the Christian powers of Europe as an enemy, even though he considered the Ottomans to be worse.[9]

8. Ibn Siḥmān, *al-Ḍiyāʾ al-shāriq*, 651.

9. Ibn Siḥmān, *Fatwā fī ʾl-dawla al-turkiyya wa ʾl-naṣārā*. This is a *fatwā* responding to the question of which side Muslims ought to hope will prevail in World War I. Ibn Siḥmān replies that in principle a Christian victory is to be preferred, as the Ottomans are polytheists (*ʿabadat al-awthān wa ʾl-aṣnām*) while the Christians are people of the book (*ahl al-kitāb*), and "the

ʿAbd al-ʿAzīz was not overly concerned with the scholars' views on matters of state. While he treated them with respect and conferred with them regularly, he did not defer to them when it came to important political decisions. If the scholars had their way, the third Saudi state would have looked a lot more like the first Saudi state—a state that, to paraphrase Ibn Siḥmān, would not deign to fly Christian flags or host Christian embassies, let alone form an alliance with a Christian power. That, however, was not to be the nature of the state that ʿAbd al-ʿAzīz was building.

This chapter considers the waxing and waning of militant Wahhābism during the early years of the third Saudi state (1319–51/1902–32). It examines the saga of the Ikhwān from the standpoint of the scholars, who enjoyed a difficult relationship with the zealous Wahhābī warriors, and it explores the scholars' similarly uneasy relationship with the Islamic modernist scholar Rashīd Riḍā, who emerged as a key promoter of the Wahhābīs in the 1440s/1920s, publishing many of their works in Cairo. It begins, however, with a look at the scholars' efforts at the beginning of this period to enforce a hard-line approach to Wahhābism. As during the Rashīdī interregnum, at the beginning of the third Saudi state the scholars found themselves contending with a version of Wahhābism seen as too lenient, this time in eastern Arabia. Unlike before, the proponent of this moderate form of Wahhābism was a member of the Āl al-Shaykh—Ḥusayn ibn Ḥasan Āl al-Shaykh (d. 1329/1911).

Debating *Takfīr* in Trucial ʿUmān

Ḥusayn ibn Ḥasan Āl al-Shaykh was born in Riyadh in 1284/1867f.[10] He was the son of Ḥasan ibn Ḥusayn Āl al-Shaykh (d. 1340/1922), a well-regarded Wahhābī scholar who served as the *qāḍī* of several towns and cities, including Riyadh, during the Rashīdī interregnum. Little information about Ḥusayn has come down to us apart from the fact that he relocated to eastern Arabia in approximately 1325/1907f. It was in his adopted home of al-Jazīra al-Ḥamrāʾ (also known as Jazīrat al-Zaʿāb), a small island town in modern-day Raʾs al-

unbelief of the apostate from Islam is more severe than the unbelief of the original unbeliever" (*wa-kufr al-murtadd ʿan al-Islām aghlaẓ min kufr al-kāfir al-aṣlī*). His hope, however, is that God will pit them against each other in a long-drawn-out war. See ibid., 137. The *fatwā* was endorsed by ʿAbdallāh ibn ʿAbd al-Laṭīf and his brother Muḥammad ibn ʿAbd al-Laṭīf.

10. On him, see Āl al-Shaykh, *Mashāhīr*, 127; Āl Bassām, *ʿUlamāʾ Najd*, 2:59–60; al-Qāḍī, *Rawḍat al-nāẓirīn*, 1:106–7.

Khayma in the United Arab Emirates, that he came to the attention of the scholars in Najd. From messages sent to Riyadh from the townspeople of al-Jazīra al-Ḥamrāʾ, the scholars learned that Ḥusayn was advocating an excessively tolerant approach to those identified as Jahmiyya and Ibāḍīs.

The Ibāḍīs are the moderate Khārijite sect that has long formed the majority of the population south of the ʿUmān promontory, in what is today the Sultanate of ʿUmān. *Jahmiyya*, as has been seen before, is a derogatory term used by the Wahhābīs to denote the adherents of *kalām* theology, the accusation being that they take after Jahm ibn Ṣafwān in denying God's attributes, among other innovations. The Jahmiyya in question were the Mālikī Muslims in eastern Arabia, who were seen by the Wahhābīs as adhering to Ashʿarī *kalām*, and interpreting God's attributes allegorically. It was also the view of the Wahhābīs that the Mālikīs, as well as the Ibāḍīs, were adherents of the cult of saints. In the early twentieth century, the population of Trucial ʿUmān, to borrow the contemporary British term for the area that is now the United Arab Emirates, was divided between Wahhābī Ḥanbalīs and non-Wahhābī Mālikīs. Al-Jazīra al-Ḥamrāʾ was a Wahhābī enclave;[11] the Wahhābīs there were taught to regard the Mālikīs as Jahmiyya unless they acknowledged Wahhābī theology.[12] Ḥusayn ibn Ḥasan Āl al-Shaykh came with a different view.

The views of Ḥusayn are captured in a number of surviving texts written by him and his allies. One of these allies was an obscure Ḥanbalī scholar named Yūsuf ibn Shabīb, who was born in Kuwait but lived in Amritsar, India. In 1325/1907f, Ibn Shabīb published a book in Amritsar titled *Naṣīḥat al-muʾminīn fī ʾl-dhabb ʿan takfīr al-Muslimīn* (Advice to the Believers in Opposition to the Excommunication of Muslims), which was viewed by the scholars of Riyadh as representing the ideas of Ḥusayn.[13] In the book, Ibn Shabīb does not evince outright hostility to Wahhābism, but his arguments are implicitly aimed at Wahhābī orthodoxy concerning *takfīr*. He begins by decrying the fact that certain unnamed persons are devoting all their time and energy to denigrating and pronouncing *takfīr* on professed Muslims, addressing them with such phrases as "O unbeliever" (*yā kāfir*), "O polytheist" (*yā mushrik*), "O innovator" (*yā mubtadiʿ*), and "O Jahmī" (*yā Jahmī*), all of which is misguided and counterproductive. The proper way to perform *daʿwa* and to command right and forbid

11. Lorimer, *Gazetteer of the Persian Gulf, 'Omān, and Central Arabia*, 2:1437–38, 1936.

12. This is my understanding from the documents produced in the ensuing controversy.

13. Ibn Shabīb, *Naṣīḥat al-muʾminīn*. The cover page describes the author as *al-Amritsarī maskanan wa ʾl-Kuwaytī waṭanan wa ʾl-Ḥanbalī madhhaban*.

wrong, he says, is not with antagonism and hostility but, rather, "with friendliness, compassion, kindliness, gentleness, and patience" (*bi ʾl-rifq wa ʾl-shafaqa wa ʾl-iḥsān wa ʾl-talaṭṭuf wa ʾl-ṣabr*). This, he says, was the example of the Prophet.[14] With regard to *takfīr*, he claims that Ibn Taymiyya's approach, which is the right one, was marked by restraint.[15]

Ibn Shabīb's book was not received well in Najd, where it was immediately refuted by Ibn Siḥmān in a book titled *Kashf al-shubhatayn* (Exposing the Two Specious Arguments), published in Bombay in 1326/1908f.[16] The two specious arguments that he refutes here are (1) the idea that the Jahmiyya and the Ibāḍīs are Muslims who should not be excluded from the faith and (2) the idea that the appropriate kind of *daʿwa* in their case is one that involves kindliness and patience. Ibn Siḥmān notes at the beginning of his work that he has been in contact with certain brothers (*ikhwān*) in Trucial ʿUmān (*al-sāḥil min arḍ ʿUmān*) and that they have complained to him about deviant scholars there who are defending and associating with the Jahmiyya, the Ibāḍīs, and grave-worshippers.[17] The brothers, he explains, are the Muslims (i.e., Wahhābīs) in the area who rightly insist on showing enmity to these groups and who urge Muslims not to sit with or greet them or any who show them loyalty.[18] It is the intention of Ibn Shabīb and his ilk, writes Ibn Siḥmān, to have normal relations with all and sundry (*an tamshiya ʾl-ḥāl maʿa man habba wa-daraja*), and in pursuing this terrible end they have wrongly condemned the brothers as extremists in *takfīr*.[19]

As Ibn Siḥmān explains in *Kashf al-shubhatayn*, the deviant groups in question, the Jahmiyya and the Ibāḍīs, are unquestionably unbelievers on account of their errant beliefs. Numerous scholars, including Aḥmad ibn Ḥanbal, Ibn Taymiyya, and Ibn al-Qayyim, he says, agreed that the Jahmiyya have left Islam entirely on account of their doctrine of stripping God of His attributes.[20] The Ibāḍīs are likewise unbelievers, he asserts, both because they deny God's attributes like the Jahmiyya and because they have become grave-worshippers.[21]

14. Ibid., 3–4.

15. Ibid., 12–21.

16. See the editor's introduction in Ibn Siḥmān, *Kashf al-shubhatayn*, 4. The original edition was published by Maṭbaʿat Kulzār Ḥasanī.

17. Ibid., 7.

18. Ibid., 63.

19. Ibid., 69, 24.

20. Ibid., 18–22.

21. Ibid., 62–63.

These are not the kinds of people Ibn Taymiyya had in mind, Ibn Siḥmān argues, when he cautioned restraint in *takfīr*.[22] The Jahmiyya and the Ibāḍīs are not to be excused on the basis of ignorance, for what they believe is contrary to obligatory Islamic beliefs (*ḍarūriyyāt al-Islām*), and the proof of their error has been presented to them over a long period of time (*al-ḥujja balaghathum mundhu azmān*).[23] Speaking in particular about "the Jahmiyya of Dubai and Abu Dhabi" (*Jahmiyyat Dubuy wa-Abi Ḍabī*), whom he accuses of saint-worship in addition to stripping God of His attributes, he states:

> These two lands have been reached by the proof. The proof is the Qur'ān, the *ḥadīth*, and the creeds of the four *imāms*. Our scholars have debated with them numerous times, and they have only grown more stubborn and recalcitrant in their insistence on Jahmism, supplicating other than God, and slaughtering for other than God, as has been well known about them for years and years.[24]

As for the view that these groups ought to be preached to with kindliness and patience, Ibn Siḥmān retorts that they ought to be treated with "harshness, severity, and manifest enmity" (*bi 'l-ghilẓa wa 'l-shidda wa 'l-mu'ādāt al-ẓāhira*), this being the true example of the Prophet. The Prophet, he explains, was only commanded to use "gentleness and friendliness" (*al-līn wa 'l-rifq*) with unbelievers at the beginning of Islam (*fī awwal al-Islām*).[25] This approach came to an end when God revealed Q. 15:94: "Proclaim that which you are commanded and turn away from the polytheists." Thereafter the Prophet openly reviled their religion and showed them enmity.[26] Later on, when the Muslims gathered strength, God revealed Q. 9:73, "O Prophet, fight the unbelievers and the hypocrites and be harsh with them," among other verses commanding the Prophet and his followers to wage *jihād* against unbelievers.[27] The revelation of these verses, according to Ibn Siḥmān, abrogated (*nasakha*) the gentle approach.[28] The right approach, then, is to show hatred and enmity to unbelievers and to wage *jihād* against them, pursuant to the Prophet's

22. Ibid., 64–68, 72–73, 82–84.
23. Ibid., 63, 60.
24. Ibid., 72, 84.
25. Ibid., 27, 56.
26. Ibid., 57–58.
27. Ibid., 27.
28. Ibid., 39.

example: "May he who advises himself and who seeks salvation solicit God's favor by showing enmity to the enemies of God and His Messenger; and may he know that the foundation of belief is not sound or firm without breaking ties with the enemies of God, waging *jihād* against them, dissociating from them, and seeking nearness to God by hating them and reviling them."[29]

It was after the publication of *Kashf al-shubhatayn* that Ḥusayn ibn Ḥasan Āl al-Shaykh entered the picture more clearly. In response to Ibn Siḥmān's book, Ḥusayn composed a brief poem defending Ibn Shabīb, depicted as a venerable scholar, and ridiculing Ibn Siḥmān, described as a mere poet who ought to abstain from discussions of Islamic law.[30] He also wrote to Muḥammad ibn ʿAbd al-Laṭīf Āl al-Shaykh (d. 1367/1948),[31] a brother of ʿAbdallāh ibn ʿAbd al-Laṭīf, who was taking a larger role in the Wahhābī religious establishment at this time. In his letter, Ḥusayn contends that there are two acceptable positions concerning the Jahmiyya: (1) that they are unbelievers and (2) that they are not unbelievers. While he claims that his own view is that the Jahmiyya are unbelievers, he disagrees that those who believe otherwise ought to be subjected to *takfīr*. This was a reference to Ibn ʿAbd al-Wahhāb's third nullifier of Islam, "Whosoever does not pronounce *takfīr* on the polytheists, or is doubtful about their unbelief, or affirms the validity of their doctrine is an unbeliever by consensus," which Ḥusayn was arguing did not apply in the case of the so-called Jahmiyya of Trucial ʿUmān.[32] In a related poem and letter, Ḥusayn would make the case that *takfīr* should not take place until after the proof has been presented and clarified to the one who is committing *kufr*. He thus believed that the commoners or laypeople (*ʿawāmm*) associated with the Jahmiyya ought to be excused on the basis of ignorance.[33]

Around this time, in 1325/1907f, the scholars in Riyadh received a query from a man in Trucial ʿUmān that sheds much light on the situation there concerning Ḥusayn.[34] The questioner, a Wahhābī opponent of Ḥusayn, explained

29. Ibid., 52.

30. Āl Ḥamad, *Ijmāʿ ahl al-sunna al-nabawiyya*, 30: *wa-mā anta illā shāʿirun dhū qaṣāʾidin / fa-daʿ ʿanka fī ʾl-aḥkāmi mā anta jāhilū* (meter = *ṭawīl*).

31. On him, see Āl al-Shaykh, *Mashāhīr*, 146–47; Āl Bassām, *ʿUlamāʾ Najd*, 6:134–39; al-Qāḍī, *Rawḍat al-nāẓirīn*, 2:311–14; and see further Āl al-Shaykh, *al-Shaykh Muḥammad ibn ʿAbd al-Laṭīf*.

32. Āl Ḥamad, *Ijmāʿ ahl al-sunna al-nabawiyya*, 23–26.

33. Ibid., 110, 127.

34. Ibid., 155–65. The questioner is identified by Ibn Siḥmān as the Qaṭarī Muḥammad ibn Ḥasan al-Marzūqī (d. 1354/1935). See ibid., 134; and on al-Marzūqī, see the introduction in al-Jābir, *al-Luʾluʾ al-naqī*.

how when Ḥusayn arrived in al-Jazīra al-Ḥamrāʾ he caused a disturbance by claiming that there were two legitimate views (*qawlān*) concerning the Jahmiyya. The Jahmiyya, in the questioner's eyes, were most of the people of Dubai, Abu Dhabi, and nearby areas. When the local preacher in al-Jazīra al-Ḥamrāʾ, a certain Ibrāhīm, rejected Ḥusayn's plea to cease rebuking (*dhamm*) the Jahmiyya in public, Ḥusayn withdrew from the congregation and formed a new one with half the townspeople supporting him. He thus divided the people of al-Jazīra al-Ḥamrāʾ around the issue of whether the Jahmiyya, understood as most of the people of Trucial ʿUmān, could legitimately be seen as Muslims. The questions that the questioner posed to the Najdī scholars were whether Ḥusayn was right in claiming that there were two legitimate views concerning the Jahmiyya and whether a person who says so may serve as an *imām* (i.e., a prayer leader).

The answer of the scholars to both questions was of course no.[35] The response was authored by the trio of ʿAbdallāh ibn ʿAbd al-Laṭīf Āl al-Shaykh, his brother Ibrāhīm ibn ʿAbd al-Laṭīf (d. 1329/1911), and Ibn Siḥmān. There is only one valid position regarding the Jahmiyya, they write in their *fatwā*, and that is that they are *kuffār*, the proof having been presented to them. As the questioner noted, Ḥusayn was appealing to some of Ibn ʿAbd al-Wahhāb's statements indicative of a more restrained approach to *takfīr*. To this the respondents state that the shaykh's comments were made during a particular period in time early in his career and are not to be taken as normative. The later and normative position of Ibn ʿAbd al-Wahhāb, they explain, is that concerning the foundational matters of belief there is no excuse of ignorance and the proof has been presented in the form of the Qurʾān. They also emphasize that there are Wahhābī preachers in the area of Trucial ʿUmān who have been spreading the true Islamic message for some time. The fact that the proof has been presented to the unbelieving Jahmiyya there is thus unquestionable.

Several years later, in 1328/1910, Ibn Siḥmān would publish a refutation of Ḥusayn under the title *Kashf al-awhām wa ʾl-iltibās ʿan tashbīh baʿḍ al-aghbiyāʾ min al-nās* (Uncovering the Illusions and Confusion Concerning the Misleading of One of the Idiots of Mankind).[36] Toward the beginning he explains how he had initially resisted the urge to write a refutation of Ḥusayn out of respect for the latter's father, who claimed that Ḥusayn's views were being distorted. But after seeing Ḥusayn's own writings, Ibn Siḥmān was determined to

35. Āl Ḥamad, *Ijmāʿ ahl al-sunna al-nabawiyya*, 155–65.

36. See ibid., 21–117. The original edition was published in Bombay by al-Maṭbaʿa al-Muṣṭafawiyya.

respond.[37] The book-length refutation of Ḥusayn is similar to the *fatwā* coauthored with ʿAbdallāh and Ibrāhīm, though here Ibn Siḥmān accuses Ḥusayn of trying to promote normal relations with all and sundry (*an tamshiya ʾl-ḥāl maʿa man habba wa-daraja*), just as he had accused Ibn Shabīb.[38] Contrary to what "this stupid ignoramus" (*hādhā jāhil al-ghabī*) claims, Ibn Siḥmān writes, the scholars do not have more than one position on the status of the Jahmiyya; rather, there has been broad agreement that they are unbelievers. The beliefs that they reject, such as God's being above the created world and His sitting upon the throne, are among those clear and unambiguous matters that God has clarified in His book. It does not matter whether the Jahmiyya have adopted their views out of a failure to understand the proof texts, for "whosoever has heard the Qurʾānic verses and the prophetic *ḥadīth* has had the proof presented to him, even if he has not understood them [*wa-in lam yafhamhā*]." In saying this, he quotes Ibn ʿAbd al-Wahhāb's statement that it does not matter whether the unbelievers have understood the proof or not, for "their unbelief occurs upon its reaching them."[39] The only area where a legitimate dispute might obtain concerns the ignorant followers (*muqallidūn*) among the Jahmiyya. In principle, he concedes, there may be followers of a Jahmī scholar who can be excused on the basis of ignorance, but he does not credit the possibility in the present circumstances.[40]

What happened next in the dispute over *takfīr* in al-Jazīra al-Ḥamrāʾ is unknown. Ḥusayn ibn Ḥasan Āl al-Shaykh died in 1329/1911, a year after the publication of Ibn Siḥmān's *Kashf al-awhām wa ʾl-iltibās*. The cause of death is not recorded in any of the biographies. It is possible that the controversy in al-Jazīra al-Ḥamrāʾ ended with his death, the split in the congregation being resolved in favor of the more hard-line preacher.

What is noteworthy about this episode is the concerted effort that the scholars in Riyadh put into refuting the dissident Ḥusayn. As before in the case of Ibn ʿAmr in al-Qaṣīm, the Wahhābī scholars were intent on putting a stop to any attempt to dilute the Wahhābī doctrine of its exclusivist principles. In both cases, Ibn Siḥmān accused the dissident scholar in question of seeking to normalize relations with "all and sundry" (*man habba wa-daraja*), meaning all kinds of Muslims regardless of whether they adhere to the Wahhābī creed. To

37. Ibid., 31.
38. Ibid., 28.
39. Ibid., 114–17.
40. Ibid., 55–66.

him, such an idea was anathema, being antithetical to the mission begun by Ibn ʿAbd al-Wahhāb. The notion that the Islamic mainstream in Abu Dhabi and Dubai would be legitimized by a self-identified Wahhābī scholar was a threat to everything Wahhābism stood for. The responses to Ḥusayn ibn Ḥasan Āl al-Shaykh are also noteworthy in revealing the scholars' position on issues of *takfīr* and particularly *al-ʿudhr bi ʾl-jahl*. From their discussions, it is clear that Ibn ʿAbd al-Wahhāb's unforgiving approach to *al-ʿudhr bi ʾl-jahl* was still the accepted view of the leading Wahhābī scholars in Najd. While some of Ibn ʿAbd al-Wahhāb's statements might seem to support restraint in *takfīr*, the view of these scholars was that such statements were not authoritative. All those who had received the Qurʾān, even if they failed to understand it, were the proper targets of *takfīr* if they failed to adhere to the foundational Islamic principles as the Wahhābīs understood them.[41]

The Ikhwān

If Ḥusayn ibn Ḥasan Āl al-Shaykh was a case of undue leniency in the application of Wahhābī principles, the Ikhwān were a case of undue extremism. The origins of the Ikhwān movement can be traced to the efforts of ʿAbd al-ʿAzīz Āl Suʿūd to encourage the various nomadic tribal groupings in Najd to settle permanently in agricultural camps.[42] In doing so, his motive was twofold: first, to bring the bedouin under his control, thus preventing them from fomenting instability and disorder, and second, to exploit their warlike spirit for the purpose of expanding the territory under his control. ʿAbd al-ʿAzīz gave the bedouin money, building supplies, and agricultural equipment as an inducement to settle in the camps, which were known as *hujar* (sing. *hijra*). The latter term was a nod to the duty of *hijra*, or emigration from a land of unbelief

41. It may be noted here that not all acts of scholarly dissent in this period took the form of efforts to tone down the Wahhābī doctrine. One Wahhābī scholar in al-Qaṣīm, ʿĪsā ibn Muḥammad al-Malāḥī (d. 1353/1934f), was accused of excessive zeal in *takfīr*, and in a refutation of him Ibn Siḥmān refers to the presence in Riyadh of extremists like him. See Ibn Siḥmān, *ʿUqūd al-jawāhir* (al-Muṣṭafawiyya ed.), 130. The controversy began when al-Malāḥī, a scholar from Jabal Shammar living in al-Qaṣīm, was accused of pronouncing *takfīr* on the people of Jabal Shammar in a poem written in 1324/1906f, though he denied that this was the meaning of his words. On this episode, see al-Rudayʿān, *Manbaʿ al-karam*, 72–90; al-ʿUbūdī, *Muʿjam usar Burayda*, 21:170–97.

42. On the Ikhwān, see Habib, *Ibn Sa'ud's Warriors*; Kostiner, "On Instruments and Their Designers."

to a land of Islam. By abandoning nomadism and settling in the *hujar*, the relocating nomads believed that they were abandoning their previous state of pagan ignorance and adopting Islam for the first time. Most of the *hujar* were built in the vicinity of existing towns, the first being built in the area of al-Arṭāwiyya, in the north of Sudayr, in 1331/1913. Over the next fifteen years the number of *hujar* would grow to more than two hundred, each of them being associated with one or more of the nomadic tribes.[43] Al-Arṭāwiyya, for instance, was dominated by the Muṭayr, while al-Ghaṭghaṭ, to the west of Riyadh, was the province of the ʿUtayba.

The religious zeal and belligerency of the Ikhwān recalled the spirit of the early Wahhābī warriors who fought to expand the borders of the first Saudi state. The Ikhwān acquired a reputation for zealotry and violence by committing atrocities in the Ḥijāzī towns of Turaba in 1337/1919 and al-Ṭāʾif in 1343/1924 and for destroying tombs and shrines wherever they went.[44] To the Lebanese American Ameen Rihani, who visited Najd in 1341/1922–23, the Ikhwān appeared a dreadful band of religious zealots bent on conquest and martyrdom:

> [T]he Ikhwan, the roving, ravening Bedu of yesterday, the militant Wahhabis of to-day, are the white terror of Arabia. . . . [F]rantically fanatical Unitarians; Puritan Copperheads! And the Sultan Abd'ul-Aziz is a Cromwell in the sense that he has made these people and fired them with unextinguishable enthusiasm for Allah and for Najd. He has imbued them with the spirit of conquest; he has led them to battle and taught them sacrifice. About them are related, by friend and foe, strange heroic deeds and rare stoic achievements. Also unspeakable atrocities. . . . It is their faith, a living, glowing, flaming faith, which makes the blood of a brother fallen in battle sacred in their eyes. Through it they behold Al-Jannat [paradise]. . . . They are all fond seekers—seekers of Al-Jannat and the houris [virgins].[45]

The unbridled militancy of the Ikhwān would ultimately pose a serious problem for ʿAbd al-ʿAzīd. As Rihani goes on to explain, not all the Ikhwān were under the *imām*'s control, as some had been reported embarking on unsanctioned

43. Habib, *Ibn Sa'ud's Warriors*, 58; Vassiliev, *History of Saudi Arabia*, 227.

44. Habib, *Ibn Sa'ud's Warriors*, 93–94, 113–14. For a contemporary description of some of the destruction in the Ḥijāz, see Rutter, *Holy Cities of Arabia*, 1:270ff.

45. Rihani, *Ibn Sa'oud of Arabia*, 208–9.

raids. Reflecting on this, he wrote: "[T]he Ikhwan are a power, a terrible power, which needs to be regulated and put under a modern system of administrative control. Otherwise, such raids as have taken place on the borders of Iraq and Trans-Jordania will always recur much to the discredit of the Government of Najd."[46] A few years earlier, in 1337/1919, a British military officer made a similar observation about the operational independence of the Ikhwān. In a report to the India Office, Captain Norman Bray registered his concern that ʿAbd al-ʿAzīz had created an army that he might not be able to control. "[T]he horse of religious ferment," he wrote, "has exceeded his expectation in its power and the rider finds it harder to control than he had anticipated."[47] ʿAbd al-ʿAzīz would indeed struggle to rein in the Ikhwān, whose rebelliousness would ultimately lead to a violent showdown with the Saudi ruler in 1347/1929. For the time being, however, they served a valuable purpose.

As with ʿAbd al-ʿAzīz, the Wahhābī scholars saw their relationship with the Ikhwān deteriorate over time. Early on, the two sides enjoyed a close and collaborative partnership. ʿAbdallāh ibn ʿAbd al-Laṭīf was responsible for sending preachers to the *hujar* for the purpose of instructing the newly settled bedouin in the Wahhābī doctrine.[48] The scholars saw the Ikhwān as their ideological children, men who were helping to re-create the puritanical Wahhābī order of old. Their zealotry was to be celebrated, not condemned. In a poem written in 1337/1918, Ibn Siḥmān praises the Ikhwān thus:

They are the purest of brothers in honesty and fidelity,
  and they have waged *jihād* for the sake of God against the wicked.
They performed *hijra* and settled down in buildings in the villages,
  and they have been as the strongholds of the partisans of the
    religion.[49]

In another poem, Ibn Siḥmān defends the Ikhwān against the charge of extremism (*ghuluww*), noting that certain people have mischaracterized them as Khārijites.[50] While acknowledging that the Ikhwān have committed mistakes, he insists that they do not, like the historical Khārijites, pronounce *takfīr* on sinners, and he praises them for dealing harshly with those who travel

46. Ibid., 213–14.
47. Habib, *Ibn Sa'ud's Warriors*, 80.
48. Āl al-Shaykh, *al-Shaykh ʿAbdallāh ibn ʿAbd al-Laṭīf*, 94–96.
49. Ibn Siḥmān, *Tahniʾa lil-imām ʿAbd al-ʿAzīz*, 94 (meter = *ṭawīl*).
50. Ibn Siḥmān, *ʿUqūd al-jawāhir* (al-Rushd ed.), 2:88–91.

to the lands of polytheists by shunning them and showing them enmity. If the Ikhwān are to be considered Khārijites, he writes, then so should he:

> If shunning [*hijrān*] sinners and hating them,
> and the religion of Abraham with its pillars,
> Of loving and hating and showing enmity and showing loyalty,
> are rebellion [*khurūjan*] like the act of the withdrawing renegades,
> Then we bear witness to you, nay, but to God, that
> that is what we profess to God before the worlds.[51]

From Ibn Siḥmān's words it would appear that all was well between the scholars and the Ikhwān, that the two were entirely doctrinally aligned. Tensions, however, had been building from the beginning.

Within just a few years of the establishment of the first *hijra*, conflict arose over a set of doctrines unique to the Ikhwān and to which the scholars, including Ibn Siḥmān, strongly objected. Influenced by their own cadre of religious specialists, some of whom had studied with the scholars in Riyadh, the Ikhwān began to show less deference to the scholarly authorities in the Saudi capital, accusing them of compromising core Wahhābī principles at the behest of the Saudi ruler. While there was some validity to this perception, it was also true that the Ikhwān had taken up positions that were peculiar and more extreme than anything the scholars had ever countenanced.

While there are no documents in which the ideas of the Ikhwān are clearly set out and recorded, their views can be gleaned from some of the refutations by the Wahhābī scholars. The earliest of these is a book by Ibn Siḥmān in which he responds to a series of questions put to him by one of the Ikhwān. Completed in Shaʿbān 1335/June 1917, it was published in Cairo as *Irshād al-ṭālib ilā ahamm al-maṭālib* (Guiding the Seeker to the Most Important Subjects).[52] From the answers he gives, it is clear that Ibn Siḥmān was deeply worried about the Ikhwān's approach to *takfīr* and ostracism (*hajr*), the latter being the practice of shunning those who commit sins by avoiding them and ceasing to greet them for some period of time. These are matters, Ibn Siḥmān states at the outset of the book, that only the scholars should be speaking

51. Ibid., 2:90 (meter = *ṭawīl*).

52. Ibn Siḥmān, *Irshād al-ṭālib* (al-Khizāna ed.), 109. It was first published in Bombay by al-Maṭbaʿa al-Muṣṭafawiyya (within Ibn Siḥmān's *Kashf ghayāhib al-ẓalām ʿan awhām Jalāʾ al-awhām*) and subsequently in Cairo by Maṭbaʿat al-Manār in 1340/1921f.

about (*lā yatakallamu fīhā illā 'l-ʿulamāʾ*), warning the Ikhwān against launching into *takfīr* and *hajr* without first consulting the scholars.[53]

In *Irshād al-ṭālib,* Ibn Siḥmān does not directly address what is problematic about the Ikhwān's approach to *takfīr,*[54] but we learn a great deal about their approach to *hajr.* As Ibn Siḥmān explains, while *hajr* is rightfully performed against sinners (*ʿuṣāt*), for example, those who neglect obligatory duties such as prayer, it should not be performed in a way that is excessive or counterproductive.[55] The degree of *hajr* should be commensurate with the offense: "The sinner is to be shunned in proportion to the sin he has committed." Furthermore, the period of *hajr* should not last beyond the point at which the sinner seeks repentance. Ibn Siḥmān notes that certain Ikhwān have refused to accept the repentance of sinners, continuing to shun them and to show them enmity. Of this he strongly disapproves, warning the Ikhwān against needlessly alienating Muslims and urging them to be mindful of the costs and benefits of their behavior.[56]

Another peculiar feature of the Ikhwān described in *Irshād al-ṭālib* had to do with their preferred headgear. Some of the Ikhwān's preachers, Ibn Siḥmān explains, believe that wearing a turban (*ʿimāma*) is necessary and insist on shunning those who persist in wearing the more common cord (*ʿiqāl*) around the headdress. These preachers believe that the turban was the Prophet's preferred headgear and thus that all the Ikhwān ought to wear it as a sign that they have adopted Islam and repudiated their nomadic past. For Ibn Siḥmān, this preference for the turban (*faḍl al-ʿimāma*) was an innovation. The Prophet and his Companions said nothing about it, and neither did Ibn ʿAbd al-Wahhāb. The preachers among the Ikhwān, he claims, are misinterpreting certain *ḥadīth*s regarding the turban, which in truth is nothing but an Arab custom.[57] In saying this, Ibn Siḥmān notes that he has the support of ʿAbdallāh ibn ʿAbd al-Laṭīf, claiming that the latter spoke harshly on these matters with some of the Ikhwān.[58] ʿAbdallāh had apparently been ignored.

53. Ibid., 31–32.

54. He merely responds to a question about the types of *kufr* that expel one from the community and those that do not; see ibid., 34–45.

55. Ibid., 58–59.

56. Ibid., 65–66.

57. Ibid., 68–109.

58. Ibid., 78.

In the summer of 1337/1919, some of the Ikhwān leaders came to Riyadh to discuss issues of controversy in the presence of ʿAbd al-ʿAzīz and the scholars. The issues raised by ʿAbd al-ʿAzīz were six in number, including *takfīr*, *hajr*, and the turban. As the scholars would recall in a letter addressed to the Ikhwān (*kāffat al-ikhwa min ahl al-hujar*), ʿAbd al-ʿAzīz raised the issues in the form of six questions:

1. Are the ostensibly Muslim bedouin (*bādiyat al-Muslimīn*) to be condemned as unbelievers?
2. Is there a difference between a person who wears a turban and one who wears a cord when they are of the same creed?
3. Is there a difference between people who settled earlier (*al-ḥaḍar al-awwalīn*) and those who emigrated later to the *hujar* (*al-muhājirīn al-ākhirīn*)?
4. Is there a difference between the slaughtered animals of the bedouin and the slaughtered animals of the settled peoples and emigrants?
5. Do the emigrants have the authority to attack, beat, threaten, or discipline those who have not performed *hijra*, seeking to force them to do so?
6. Does one have the right to shun (*an yahjura*) someone, be he a bedouin or a settled person, for a reason that is not clear (*bi-ghayr amr wāḍiḥ*) without the permission of the ruler or a judge (*bi-ghayr idhn walī ʾl-amr aw al-ḥākim al-sharʿī*)?[59]

The scholars' answers to all these questions were summarized in a single sentence: "All these matters are contrary to God's law [*mukhālifa lil-sharʿ*]," and anyone engaging in one of the practices described ought to be reprimanded.[60] The Ikhwān, as is seen here, referred to themselves by the term *emigrants* (*muhājirūn*), that is, people who have performed *hijra*. They believed that those bedouin who failed to perform *hijra* (i.e., who failed to abandon nomadism and settle in one of the *hujar*) were unbelievers who ought to be compelled to do so. Meanwhile, their slaughtered animals were not permissible. With regard to the turban, the Ikhwān were again told that it was in no way

59. al-Tuwayjirī, *Li-surāt al-layl hatafa ʾl-ṣabāḥ*, 243–44 (letter from ʿAbdallāh ibn ʿAbd al-Laṭīf, Ḥasan ibn Ḥusayn, Saʿd ibn ʿAtīq, ʿUmar ibn Salīm, ʿAbdallāh al-ʿAnqarī, Sulaymān ibn Siḥmān, Muḥammad ibn ʿAbd al-Laṭīf, ʿAbdallāh ibn Bulayhid, and ʿAbd al-Raḥmān ibn Sālim).

60. Ibid., 244.

superior to the cord, and they were instructed to seek the permission of the *imām* or a scholar before engaging in *hajr*, unless the intended *hajr* was for a clear and obvious reason.

The following year, in Shawwāl 1338/June 1920, ʿAbdallāh ibn ʿAbd al-Laṭīf and several other scholars would note in a letter that their advice had convinced some Ikhwān but not others, the people of al-Arṭāwiyya being the most intransigent.[61] In the letter, they further complain that the Ikhwān are disparaging the rulers and the scholars, especially the latter. A month later, ʿAbdallāh penned a short epistle to the Ikhwān warning them against promoting extremism and division.[62] Here he refers again to the disrespect that the Ikhwān are showing the rulers and the scholars, noting that the scholars are being accused of compromising their views (*mudāhana*) on behalf of the rulers. In a sign that the allegiance of some of the Ikhwān was now in doubt, ʿAbdallāh underscores the Islamic prohibition on fighting against one's rulers (*al-manʿ min qitāl al-aʾimma*) in the absence of flagrant unbelief. Being faithful to one's *bayʿa* to the *imām* and obeying him, ʿAbdallāh writes, are among the foundations without which Islam is not sound (*al-uṣūl allatī lā yaqūmu ʾl-Islām illā bihā*).[63] Henceforward, this was a theme that the scholars would repeatedly stress in their correspondence with the Ikhwān. This letter by ʿAbdallāh is also significant in being one of his last contributions as a scholar, as he would die a few months later, in Rabīʿ I 1339/November 1920. Thereafter his brother, Muḥammad ibn ʿAbd al-Laṭīf, would assume the role of the head of the Wahhābī religious establishment.

Around this time, Ibn Siḥmān wrote a follow-up to *Irshād al-ṭālib* responding to some additional questions put to him by one of the Ikhwān. This second set of responses, published as *Minhāj ahl al-ḥaqq wa ʾl-ittibāʿ fī mukhālafat ahl al-jahl wa ʾl-ibtidāʿ* (The Way of the People of Truth and Adherence in Opposition to the People of Ignorance and Innovation), helps reveal some of the more specific arguments being made by the Ikhwān's preachers.[64] According

61. Ibid., 247–51 (letter from ʿAbdallāh ibn ʿAbd al-Laṭīf, Ḥasan ibn Ḥusayn, Saʿd ibn ʿAtīq, and Muḥammad ibn ʿAbd al-Laṭīf to ʿAbdallāh ibn Salīm, ʿAbd al-Raḥmān ibn ʿAbd al-Laṭīf, and ʿAbdallāh ibn ʿAtīq).

62. *al-Durar al-saniyya*, 9:88–94. For the completion date, see Āl al-Shaykh, *Risāla ilā man yarāhu min al-ikhwān*, f. 1b. This epistle was also published under the title *Risāla fī ʾl-ittibāʿ wa-ḥaẓr al-ghuluww fī ʾl-dīn*, in *Majmūʿat rasāʾil wa-fatāwā fī masāʾil muhimma*, 1–11.

63. *al-Durar al-saniyya*, 9:91–93.

64. Ibn Siḥmān, *Minhāj ahl al-ḥaqq wa ʾl-ittibāʿ* (al-Furqān ed.). It was first published in Cairo by Maṭbaʿat al-Manār in 1340/1921f, together with *Irshād al-ṭālib*.

to Ibn Siḥmān, these preachers, repeatedly described here as ignorant (*juhhāl*), maintain that the bedouin who have not settled in *hujar* are unbelievers. The basis for their view is a set of passages in Ibn ʿAbd al-Wahhāb's epistles in which the shaykh clearly pronounces *takfīr* on the bedouin. One example is a passage in *Sittat mawāḍiʿ min al-sīra*, where Ibn ʿAbd al-Wahhāb declares the *kufr* of the bedouin to be exponentially worse than that of the Jews (*aghlaẓ min kufr al-yahūd bi-aḍʿāf muḍāʿafatan*).[65] According to the questioner, the preachers are reading such lines aloud before the Ikhwān, seeking to convince them that the scholars are wrong in considering the bedouin to be Muslims.[66] Ibn Siḥmān's response is to say that Ibn ʿAbd al-Wahhāb's words no longer apply. After the Wahhābī *daʿwa* spread during the first Saudi state, he explains, the people of Najd, settled and nomadic alike, adopted Islam, abandoning their polytheistic practices, and since then they have not been as they were before. He cites ʿAbd al-Raḥmān ibn Ḥasan Āl Shaykh's statement, written at the beginning of the second Saudi state, that the majority of the people of Najd are Muslims who need not be fought and that most of the bedouin need only an instructor.[67] The questioner also reports that the preachers among the Ikhwān have abused and insulted the scholars, claiming that they have compromised God's religion (*dāhanū fī dīn Allāh*) for the sake of the ruler and concealed and buried *millat Ibrāhīm* (*katamūhā wa-dafanūhā*). One of the Ikhwān preachers' chief complaints was that ʿAbd al-ʿAzīz had decreed that they no longer be allowed to preach among the bedouin, that task being reserved for preachers appointed by the ruler.[68] Ibn Siḥmān does not countenance the idea that the scholars have been compromising the religion, citing his long record of propounding the doctrine of *millat Ibrāhīm* in the face of numerous opponents. The misguided Ikhwān, he retorts, have indulged extremism and innovations, in particular pronouncing *takfīr* on all nomads who have not settled and shunning all who refuse to don the turban. They have also gone too far in punishing sinners, he states, noting the case of a man who was beaten to death for failing to attend prayer.[69] The tone and substance of *Minhāj ahl al-ḥaqq wa ʾl-ittibāʿ* indicate that the Ikhwān were drifting into the category of deviant rebels. Dug in on

65. *al-Durar al-saniyya*, 8:118.

66. Ibn Siḥmān, *Minhāj ahl al-ḥaqq wa ʾl-ittibāʿ* (al-Furqān ed.), 14.

67. Ibid., 16–20.

68. Ibid., 86.

69. Ibid., 88–90.

their doctrinal eccentricities, they had ceased to see the *imām* or the scholars as their natural allies.

Why did some of the Ikhwān insist that the scholars were compromising the religion, even burying *millat Ibrāhīm*? Since we do not possess any of the writings of the Ikhwān themselves, we are unfortunately unable to understand their thinking in full. There is one issue that the scholars indeed appear to have changed their tune on, however, as revealed by Ibn Siḥmān's *Minhāj ahl al-ḥaqq wa ʾl-ittibāʿ*. This is the issue of travel to the lands of polytheists. In the book, Ibn Siḥmān maintains that it is still the scholars' position that such travel is prohibited, referring to his lengthy polemics against Ibn ʿAmr on the subject, but he concedes that the scholars no longer support the practice of *hajr* of those who travel to such lands. The reason, he says, is that people simply were not deterred from traveling, and shunning travelers was only stoking division among Muslims.[70] This was a rare admission by Ibn Siḥmān that the scholars had succumbed to reality on an issue near and dear to their hearts. Previously, in his refutations of Ibn ʿAmr, Ibn Siḥmān had explicitly endorsed *hajr* of travelers to so-called polytheist lands, citing examples of the Prophet shunning people for having engaged in similarly sinful behavior.[71] While the scholars would continue to hold that traveling to neighboring lands was prohibited, they no longer believed in imposing consequences on those who did so. It is likely that ʿAbd al-ʿAzīz pushed the scholars in this direction.

For another half decade or so, ʿAbd al-ʿAzīz continued to tolerate the excesses of the Ikhwān, as they were still helping him expand his realm. Once the entirety of the Ḥijāz was incorporated into his domains in 1344/1925, however, relations with the Ikhwān began to sour. In part this was due to the Ikhwān's disappointment in not being granted a political role in the Ḥijāz. Fayṣal al-Dawīsh (d. 1349/1930), the leader of the Muṭayr tribe, had hoped to be appointed governor of Medina, while Sulṭān ibn Bijād (d. 1351/1932), the head of the ʿUtayba, had wished to be made governor of al-Ṭāʾif.[72] ʿAbd al-ʿAzīz, however, wanted the Ikhwān to stay far away from the Ḥijāz, where they had exhibited destructive tendencies and were deeply unpopular with non-Wahhābī Muslims. Another source of tension was ʿAbd al-ʿAzīz's signing of agreements with the British on final borders with Iraq and Transjordan. These agreements, signed in Rabīʿ II 1344/November 1925, stipulated that

70. Ibid., 101–6.

71. Ibn Siḥmān, *al-Radd ʿalā ʿAbdallāh ibn ʿAmr*, ff. 33b–34a.

72. Vassiliev, *History of Saudi Arabia*, 272–73.

cross-border raids would be considered acts of aggression; the Ikhwān henceforth were prohibited from waging *jihād* north of the newly demarcated boundaries.[73] Additional grievances voiced by leaders of the Ikhwān included ʿAbd al-ʿAzīz's sending his sons to Egypt and London; his use of the telegraph, telephone, and automobiles; his alleged levying of noncanonical taxes in Najd and the Ḥijāz; and his tolerance of the Shīʿa in al-Aḥsāʾ.[74]

The last major effort to mend relations with the Ikhwān took place in 1345/1927, when ʿAbd al-ʿAzīz convened a large conference in Riyadh. Among the attendees were Fayṣal al-Dawīsh and Sulṭān ibn Bijād. The scholars, who were present as well, issued a *fatwā* following the conference, jointly signed by more than fifteen of them, including Muḥammad ibn ʿAbd al-Laṭīf, Saʿd ibn ʿAtīq, and Ibn Siḥmān.[75] The *fatwā*, dated Shaʿbān 1435/February 1927, indicates that the issues discussed during the conference included the telegraph; positive laws (*qawānīn*); the annual Egyptian *ḥajj* procession, which included a show of military force and a ceremonial palanquin (*maḥmal*); noncanonical taxes; the Shīʿa in al-Aḥsāʾ; and the matter of the *imām*'s authority in *jihād*. The scholars responded by saying that the telegraph was something that was not understood well enough to judge on it one way or another; that positive laws in the Ḥijāz, if they existed, ought to be replaced by the Sharīʿa; that the Egyptian *ḥajj* procession ought not to be granted entry into Mecca; that noncanonical taxes should not be levied, though their continued levy would not be grounds for rebellion; that the Shīʿa ought to cease practicing polytheism and embrace Islam and should be expelled if they refuse to convert; and that the *imām* was to be deferred to in matters pertaining to *jihād*. As can be seen, on some of these questions the scholars sided with the Ikhwān. They too wanted to see the Shīʿa converted or expelled from al-Aḥsāʾ, and they too wanted to eradicate positive laws and noncanonical taxes, though they did not acknowledge that these were present. Unlike the Ikhwān, however, the scholars believed that the *imām* had authority when it came to warfare, that he was to decide when and where *jihād* would be waged.

Once again, the scholars' collective opinion did not persuade. The Ikhwān grew increasingly rebellious. Beginning in Jumādā I 1346/November 1927, the Ikhwān of the Muṭayr undertook extensive raids into Iraq and Kuwait, prompt-

73. Ibid., 264.

74. Wahba, *Jazīrat al-ʿarab fī ʾl-qarn al-ʿashrīn*, 318.

75. Ibid., 319–21; cf. al-Tuwayjirī, *Li-surāt al-layl hatafa ʾl-ṣabāḥ*, 366–69. For a translation of this *fatwā* (by Guido Steinberg), see Amin et al., *Modern Middle East*, 57–61.

ing the British to respond with airpower. Rather than launching an outright rebellion against ʿAbd al-ʿAzīz, the Ikhwān focused their energy on carrying out additional raids in Iraq, hoping to demonstrate the Saudi leader's feckless-ness and betrayal of Wahhābī militancy. Meanwhile, the rebel leaders plotted for a post-Saudi future. Al-Dawīsh hoped to become the ruler of all of Najd, while Ibn Bijād sought to rule in the Ḥijāz. A third leader, Ḍaydān ibn Ḥithlayn (d. 1347/1929) of the ʿUjmān, intended to be the ruler of al-Aḥsāʾ.

The flagrant disobedience of the Ikhwān had the opposite of the intended effect, galvanizing support for ʿAbd al-ʿAzīz among those who feared the chaos and lawlessness of an Ikhwān-ruled Arabia. In Shawwāl 1347/March 1929, the rebel factions of the Ikhwān, led by al-Dawīsh and Ibn Bijād, met an army of ʿAbd al-ʿAzīz's forces in an area near al-Arṭāwiyya called al-Sabala. At the battle of al-Sabala, the Ikhwān were dealt a major defeat, al-Dawīsh being wounded and Ibn Bijād being captured and taken to Riyadh. This did not end the rebellion, however, as ʿAbd al-ʿAzīz opted not to pursue the retreating rebels. The remaining Ikhwān regrouped and set out to disrupt the roads connecting Najd to the Ḥijāz and al-Aḥsāʾ. In the fall of 1348/1929, ʿAbd al-ʿAzīz's forces inflicted several more defeats on the Ikhwān, many of whom, including al-Dawīsh, sought refuge in Iraq and Kuwait. In Shaʿbān 1348/January 1930, they finally gave up, surrendering themselves to ʿAbd al-ʿAzīz.

Just before the final submission of the Ikhwān, the scholars, including Muḥammad ibn ʿAbd al-Laṭīf and Ibn Siḥmān, issued a *fatwā* describing the retreating Ikhwān as unbelievers and apostates who ought to be fought by all Muslims.[76] The reasons included that the Ikhwān had excommunicated Muslims and deemed their blood and property licit and that they were seeking refuge in the lands of the enemies of God. With these words, the scholars completed their reversal on the Ikhwān. Having earlier celebrated and promoted them as the vanguard of a militant Wahhābī revival, the scholars now considered the Ikhwān to be rebel apostates—this after the Ikhwān repeatedly dismissed their advice and undermined their authority.

The downfall of the Ikhwān, however, was not an entirely positive development for the scholars, as it also meant the loss of a powerful ideological ally. The Ikhwān and the scholars had their differences, to be sure, but they both wished to see a Saudi state that resembled the original of the eighteenth and early nineteenth centuries. With the Ikhwān's absence, there would be less pressure on ʿAbd al-ʿAzīz to shape the new Saudi polity in accordance with militant

76. *al-Durar al-saniyya*, 9:209–11.

Wahhābī ideals. The scholars would have less leverage over the ruler—ʿAbd al-ʿAzīz would be freer to ignore their complaints and pronouncements—as there was no longer a significant military force driven by Wahhābī fervor.[77]

Rashīd Riḍā

Another problematic ally for the scholars during the early period of the third Saudi state, though one whose support for ʿAbd al-ʿAzīz was unwavering, was Rashīd Riḍā (d. 1354/1935). Riḍā was an Islamic modernist scholar in Cairo who edited the influential journal *al-Manār* and operated a publishing house of the same name. Beginning in the 1340s/1920s, Riḍā used his journal to promote the political cause of ʿAbd al-ʿAzīz, whom he saw as a pan-Islamic leader capable of uniting the Islamic world in the face of Western imperialism. With the abolition of the Ottoman Caliphate in 1342/1924 and the subsequent Saudi conquest of the Ḥijāz, Riḍā would put all his hopes in the ascendant ʿAbd al-ʿAzīz. In the pages of *al-Manār*, he praised the Saudi ruler for his wisdom and discernment, for keeping the European powers at arm's length, and for spreading Wahhābism, portrayed as an enlightened form of Islam.[78]

Riḍā's embrace of Wahhābism was a highly controversial development at the time, as most of the Islamic world still perceived the Wahhābī movement as heretical. Yet while Riḍā's support for Wahhābism was genuine, he advocated what amounted to a toned-down version of it. In the words of his friend Shakīb Arslān (d. 1366/1946), a Lebanese Druze and fellow proponent of pan-Islamism, the kind of Wahhābism that Riḍā supported was "a true Wahhābism, but enlightened and modern" ("un vrai Wahabisme, mais éclairé et moderne").[79] Riḍā regarded some of the Wahhābīs, including the Ikhwān, as extremists.[80] But he denied that they represented the true spirit of Wahhābism, a term that he used neutrally and that he described as a movement of reform and renewal (*al-iṣlāḥ wa ʾl-tajdīd*). Muḥammad ibn ʿAbd al-Wahhāb, he wrote, was a *mujaddid*, a renewer of Islam, who taught the people of Najd the proper

77. This point is made in Steinberg, "Wahhabi Ulama and the Saudi State," 20–24.

78. Riḍā, *al-Wahhābiyyūn wa ʾl-Ḥijāz*. The articles collected here were published in *al-Manār* and in the Egyptian daily *al-Ahrām* in the preceding years.

79. Arslān, "La disparition d'une des plus grandes figures de l'Islam Rachid Ridha," 448–49; noted in Lauzière, *Making of Salafism*, 104. On Riḍā's relations with ʿAbd al-ʿAzīz and the Wahhābī scholars, see Lauzière, *Making of Salafism*, 60–94.

80. Lauzière, *Making of Salafism*, 67.

understanding of *tawḥīd* as expounded by Ibn Taymiyya.[81] Riḍā hoped to rehabilitate the image of the Wahhābīs in the eyes of his Arabic-speaking readers around the world, and for this role ʿAbd al-ʿAzīz considered him a treasured asset. The Wahhābī scholars in Najd, however, had their reservations about Riḍā's "enlightened and modern" Wahhābism, which to them was a foreign concept. They did not entirely trust him, and some, including Ibn Siḥmān, would come to see him as an enemy.

Born in 1282/1865 in Tripoli, in modern-day Lebanon, Riḍā began his intellectual career as a disciple of one of the pioneers of Islamic modernism, the Egyptian Muḥammad ʿAbduh (d. 1323/1905).[82] ʿAbduh and his followers believed that Islam needed to be reformed in accordance with the requirements of the modern, European-led world. Immersed in European philosophy and culture, they departed drastically in some ways from the accumulated theological and legal tradition of Sunnī Islam. ʿAbduh, for instance, wished to do away with the Sunnī legal schools and was skeptical of much of the *ḥadīth* corpus. Shortly after moving to Cairo in 1315/1898, Riḍā sought and obtained ʿAbduh's assistance in establishing his journal, *al-Manār*. He saw himself as a steward of ʿAbduh's intellectual project. Yet Riḍā was always more conservative in his approach to the Islamic textual tradition than his mentor and, unlike him, was deeply sympathetic to the teachings of Ibn Taymiyya and Ibn ʿAbd al-Wahhāb.[83] Even before becoming a full-fledged supporter of ʿAbd al-ʿAzīz and the Wahhābīs, Riḍā evinced a marked sympathy for Ibn Taymiyya and Wahhābism in his editing and publishing activities. In 1327/1909f, he published one of Ibn Taymiyya's polemics against the cult of saints, and a few years later he published one of Ibn al-Qayyim's books, *Madārij al-sālikīn*.[84] In 1338/1919, Riḍā published Ibn ʿAbd al-Wahhāb's *Kashf al-shubuhāt*.[85] All of this was in a way that signaled approval of the texts being published.

81. Riḍā, *al-Wahhābiyyūn wa ʾl-Ḥijāz*, 6.

82. The best introduction to ʿAbduh and Riḍā remains Hourani, *Arabic Thought in the Liberal Age*, chaps. 6 and 9.

83. For ʿAbdūh's view of Ibn Taymiyya, see El-Rouayheb, "From Ibn Ḥajar al-Haytamī to Khayr al-Dīn al-Ālūsī," 311; for his view of the Wahhābīs, see Lauzière, *Making of Salafism*, 62–63.

84. Mutawallī, *Manhaj al-shaykh Muḥammad Rashīd Riḍā*, 196, 200. The treatise by Ibn Taymiyya is known as *Qāʿida jalīla fī ʾl-tawassul wa ʾl-wasīla* (published several times more by al-Manār).

85. Mutawallī, *Manhaj al-shaykh Muḥammad Rashīd Riḍā*, 202.

Beginning in the early 1440s/early 1920s, Riḍā went even further in demonstrating his sympathy for Wahhābism when he made his al-Manār publishing house available for the printing of Wahhābī texts. This was done at ʿAbd al-ʿAzīz's expense and with the collaboration of the Wahhābī scholars, who would send Riḍā both books and compendia to be printed. The first Wahhābī works that he published, in 1340/1921f, were Ibn Siḥmān's two books responding to the Ikhwān, *Irshād al-ṭālib* and *Minhāj ahl al-ḥaqq wa ʾl-ittibāʿ*. These were followed by several more works by Ibn Siḥmān and several compendia of Wahhābī texts, the largest being the four-volume *Majmūʿat al-rasāʾil wa ʾl-masāʾil al-Najdiyya*, published between 1344/1925f and 1349/1930f.[86] Yet while Riḍā's decision to publish the Wahhābī canon signaled his growing approval of the movement, he was not on board with everything the Wahhābī scholars had written, particularly as regards *takfīr*. Riḍā was by no means a neutral or passive publisher but, rather, one willing to register his disapproval when he saw the need to do so. In publishing the Wahhābīs, he sometimes added critical commentary in the form of footnotes, which provoked the ire of the Wahhābī scholars, particularly Ibn Siḥmān.

The most blatant intervention by Riḍā concerned the issue of *takfīr* as discussed by Ibn Siḥmān in his book *Minhāj ahl al-ḥaqq wa ʾl-ittibāʿ*. Even though this book was written in part to refute the overzealous approach to *takfīr* of the Ikhwān, Ibn Siḥmān made some remarks about *takfīr* that struck Riḍā as extreme. In the relevant part of the book, Ibn Siḥmān is seen responding to a question about whether the people of the Arabian Peninsula outside the territory of ʿAbd al-ʿAzīz (*wilāyat imām al-Muslimīn*) are to be considered Muslims or not. His answer is that to all appearances most of them are not Muslims (*al-ẓāhir anna ghālibahum wa-aktharahum laysū ʿalā ʾl-Islām*). As for those inside the Saudi domain, the presumption is that they are Muslims, he continues, before reiterating the point that the presumption regarding most of those outside the territory of ʿAbd al-ʿAzīz is that they are not Muslims (*al-ghālib*

86. The other compendia include *al-Hadiyya al-saniyya wa ʾl-tuḥfa al-Wahhābiyya al-Najdiyya* (1342/1923f), arranged by Ibn Siḥmān, *Majmūʿat al-ḥadīth al-Najdiyya* (1342/1923f), *Majmūʿat rasāʾil wa-fatāwā fī masāʾil muhimma tamussu ilayhā ḥājat al-ʿaṣr* (1346/1927f), and *Majmūʿat al-tawḥīd al-Najdiyya* (1346/1927f), all edited by Riḍā. The other works by Ibn Siḥmān printed by al-Manār include *Tanbīh dhawī ʾl-albāb al-salīma ʿan al-wuqūʿ fī ʾl-alfāẓ al-mubtadiʿa al-wakhīma* (1343/1924f), *Tabriʾat al-shaykhayn al-imāmayn min tazwīr ahl al-kadhib wa ʾl-mayn* (1343/1924f), *al-Ḍiyāʾ al-shāriq fī radd shubuhāt al-mādhiq al-māriq* (1344/1925f), and *Rujum ahl al-taḥqīq wa ʾl-īmān ʿalā mukaffirī Ṣiddīq Ḥasan Khān* (1346/1927f). Most of these are noted in al-Shuqayr, *Ṭibāʿat al-kutub wa-waqfuhā ʿind al-malik ʿAbd al-ʿAzīz*, 56ff.

ʿalā aktharihim mā dhakarnā awwalan min ʿadam al-Islām).[87] In the edition of Ibn Siḥmān's book published by al-Manār, this second phrase does not appear. Instead, the words are replaced with an ellipsis accompanied by a footnote, in which Riḍā writes the following:

> We have deleted here the like of what came before it of the ignorant judgment concerning most of them. The reality is that all the settled people [in Arabia] profess Islam, as do many of the nomads in Yemen. One of our students who traversed their land, traveling from Yemen to the Ḥijāz, informed us that they pray and that he even saw women carrying firewood who, upon the setting of the sun, cast down their firewood, purified themselves with sand, and prayed.[88]

Clearly, Riḍā and Ibn Siḥmān were not on the same page when it came to matters of *takfīr*. Whereas Ibn Siḥmān thought it safe to assume that most of the people of the Arabian Peninsula outside the Saudi realm were *kuffār*, for Riḍā this was an unthinkable proposition.

A few years after the al-Manār edition of *Minhāj ahl al-ḥaqq wa ʾl-ittibāʿ* was published, Ibn Siḥmān decided it was time to respond. As was his wont with those he perceived as the enemies of Wahhābism, he put down his thoughts in the form of a refutation. The untitled refutation of Riḍā, which was completed in Rabīʿ I 1342/October 1924, would go unpublished for nearly a century.[89] In one part of the refutation, Ibn Siḥmān directly addresses Riḍā's handiwork in *Minhāj ahl al-ḥaqq wa ʾl-ittibāʿ*. After describing Riḍā's intervention and quoting the offending footnote, Ibn Siḥmān reaffirms his view that the majority of the people in the areas concerned are unbelieving polytheists (*ghālib ahl hādhihi ʾl-amṣār ʿalā ʾl-kufr bi ʾllāh wa ʾl-ishrāk bihi*), as should be apparent to anyone familiar with those lands and with knowledge of the truth of Islam. He cites as evidence the activities of the grave-worshippers (*ʿubbād al-qubūr*) in those lands and extends his judgment of presumed *kufr* to some of the areas beyond the Arabian Peninsula, including Egypt, Syria, and Iraq. To support his claim, he quotes several pages of Ibn Ghannām's history that describe the many *ziyāra*-related practices on display in Arab lands from the Ḥijāz to Iraq. Only an ignorant and confused person (*jāhil murtāb*), he concludes, would doubt that these people are committing *shirk*. As regards Riḍā's

87. Ibn Siḥmān, *Minhāj ahl al-ḥaqq wa ʾl-ittibāʿ* (al-Furqān ed.), 79.
88. Ibn Siḥmān, *Minhāj ahl al-ḥaqq wa ʾl-ittibāʿ* (al-Manār ed.), 61n1.
89. See Ibn Siḥmān, *Taʿaqqubāt*; for the completion date, see 230.

belief that all the settled population of Arabia adheres to Islam, he replies that one who understands Islam correctly (*man ʿarafa ʾl-Islām ʿalā ḥaqīqatihi*) would not say so, given the large number of settled peoples who supplicate saints and righteous persons there. The suggestion that all these people are Muslims simply because they pronounce the confession of faith and perform the prayer is false.[90] From the view of Ibn Siḥmān, then, Riḍā appeared as an apologist for grave-worshipping polytheists, someone who failed miserably to understand what it meant to be a Muslim according to Wahhābī teachings. While in reality Riḍā was no supporter of the cult of saints—for the Islamic modernists, supplicating saints and asking them for help were considered superstitious—this did not raise his stature in Ibn Siḥmān's eyes. In the refutation, Riḍā is repeatedly identified as an antagonist (*muʿtariḍ*) who does not know the truth of Islam.

Elsewhere in his refutation, Ibn Siḥmān criticizes Riḍā for endorsing the metaphorical interpretation of God's attributes, for asserting that electricity (*kahrabāʾ*) is the basis of the created world, and for declaring that a person does not necessarily apostatize by committing an act indicative of unbelief (*man atā bi-shayʾ yadullu ʿalā ʾl-kufr*), on the grounds that such a person might have done so on the basis of a variant interpretation or out of ignorance (*mutaʾawwilan aw jāhilan*).[91] Somewhat surprisingly, Ibn Siḥmān does not criticize Riḍā here for the latter's comments on the issue of *al-walāʾ wa ʾl-barāʾ*. In his books *Irshād al-ṭālib* and *Minhāj ahl al-ḥaqq wa ʾl-ittibāʿ*, Ibn Siḥmān had quoted Ibn Taymiyya's line that "a believer must be shown loyalty even if he wrongs you and oppresses you, and an unbeliever must be shown enmity even if he gives to you and is kind to you."[92] In both books Riḍā added an explanatory note attempting to show that, contrary to the apparent meaning of Ibn Taymiyya's words, it is possible to have normal relations with unbelievers. As he writes in the first of these notes, "[T]he meaning [of Ibn Taymiyya's words] is not that an unbeliever's kindness must be met with enmity and harm. Islam commands its adherents to be greater than all unbelievers in graciousness and kindness and godliness."[93] In the second of these notes, Riḍā comments similarly that "[the duty of] showing enmity to an unbeliever on account of

90. Ibid., 211–29.

91. Ibid., 141–45, 149–65, 165–211.

92. Ibn Siḥmān, *Irshād al-ṭālib* (al-Khizāna ed.), 53; Ibn Siḥmān, *Minhāj ahl al-ḥaqq wa ʾl-ittibāʿ* (al-Furqān ed.), 21–22, 68.

93. Ibn Siḥmān, *Irshād al-ṭālib* (al-Manār ed.), 25n1.

his unbelief pertains generally to the belligerent unbeliever, especially one who shows enmity to the believers on account of their religion. It does not prohibit showing kindness to others of them."[94] In other words, it is only necessary to show enmity to those unbelievers engaged in hostilities with Muslims or those who are actively showing enmity to Muslims.

Clearly, Riḍā did not agree with the idea—foundational to Wahhābism—that showing hatred and enmity to unbelievers is a condition of faith. In his exegesis of the Qurʾān, he would write similarly that "some religious zealots claim out of ignorance that it is not permissible for a Muslim to exhibit kindness in interacting with or associating with a non-Muslim, or to trust him in any matter at all."[95] Though he speaks here of a group of zealots in Afghanistan, the Wahhābīs would have been just as fitting an example. Whether or not Riḍā understood that he was repudiating a central Wahhābī principle regarding the mandatory display of enmity, it is clear that this was a principle that he could not possibly accept. The project of Islamic modernists like Riḍā was to fashion an enlightened form of Islam capable of flourishing in the modern, Western-dominated world. They emphasized those aspects of Islamic thought most conducive to interfaith tolerance, not the ideas that Ibn Siḥmān harped on in his numerous refutations. Riḍā's embrace of Wahhābism was thus quite difficult to square with his Islamic modernist commitments. He dealt with the problem by downplaying the exclusivist tendencies of the Wahhābīs, sometimes even censoring them.

While Ibn Siḥmān was the most outspoken of Riḍā's critics among the Wahhābī scholars, he was not the only one. In 1340/1922, the ʿUnayza-born Muḥammad ibn ʿAbd al-ʿAzīz ibn Mānīʿ (d. 1385/1965), then serving as the *qāḍī* of Qatar, sent a letter to Ibn Siḥmān criticizing some aspects of Riḍā's thought.[96] In the letter, Ibn Mānīʿ indicates his agreement with Ibn Siḥmān that Riḍā has a corrupted understanding of the Islamic creed (*fasād al-muʿtaqad*), noting in particular Riḍā's tolerance of Shīʿa, Khārijites, Jahmiyya, and grave-worshippers. In Ibn Mānīʿ's view, Riḍā and his ilk were "philosophers and not religious scholars" (*falāsifa laysū bi-ahl dīn*), for they privileged reason over revealed proof texts. "They call themselves reformers," he writes,

94. Ibn Siḥmān, *Minhāj ahl al-ḥaqq wa ʾl-ittibāʿ* (al-Manār ed.), 12n1.

95. Riḍā, *Tafsīr al-Qurʾān al-ḥakīm*, 3:277; cf. the discussion in March, *Islam and Liberal Citizenship*, 229–34, where this passage is quoted.

96. On him, see Āl Bassām, *ʿUlamāʾ Najd*, 6:100–113; al-Qāḍī, *Rawḍat al-nāẓirīn*, 2:338–46.

"but in fact they are corrupters."[97] Two years later, in 1342/1923f, another Najdī scholar wrote to Ibn Siḥmān complaining about Riḍā. This was ʿAbd al-ʿAzīz ibn Ṣāliḥ al-Ṣayrāmī (d. 1345/1927),[98] the *qāḍī* of al-Dilam in al-Kharj, who refers in his letter to "the editor of *al-Manār* and other innovators and misled people."[99] Other Najdī scholars who criticized Riḍā include ʿAbdallāh ibn ʿAlī ibn Yābis (d. 1389/1969) and ʿAbd al-Raḥmān ibn Nāṣir al-Saʿdī (d. 1376/1956).[100] Indeed, that Riḍā was a corrupting influence on Islam seems to have been the common perception of the Wahhābī scholars, though it was not a view that they were willing to articulate publicly. Their reticence was almost certainly due to the close relationship that Riḍā enjoyed with the Saudi ruler, ʿAbd al-ʿAzīz, who saw the Islamic modernist scholar as an important ally—someone crucial to rehabilitating the image of Wahhābism in the eyes of the Islamic world.

Following the conquest of the Ḥijāz, ʿAbd al-ʿAzīz's relationship with Riḍā and the Islamic modernist school would grow even stronger. ʿAbd al-ʿAzīz worked closely with Riḍā to show the world that the Saudis were capable of ruling Mecca and Medina in a responsible manner. As part of this effort, he appointed a number of Riḍā's disciples to important positions as teachers and preachers in the Ḥijāz. Among these were three Egyptians: ʿAbd al-Ẓāhir Abū ʾl-Samḥ (d. 1370/1951), who became the main *imām* at the Grand Mosque in Mecca; Muḥammad Ḥāmid al-Fiqī (d. 1378/1959), who served as a teacher at the Grand Mosque while editing the reformist journal *al-Iṣlāḥ*; and Muḥammad ʿAbd al-Razzāq Ḥamza (d. 1392/1972), who worked as a teacher and *imām* at the Prophet's Mosque in Medina. Riḍā's disciples also included the Syrian Muḥammad Baḥjat al-Bayṭār (d. 1396/1976), who taught at the Grand Mosque in Mecca among other positions, and the Moroccan Taqī al-Dīn al-Hilālī (d. 1407/1987), who taught at the Prophet's Mosque in Medina.[101] Some of these men stayed in the Ḥijāz for only a few years, while others settled there for good. Even if they did not hold the highest official religious positions in the Ḥijāz—the chief judge (*raʾīs al-quḍāt*) for the region was ʿAbdallāh ibn Ḥasan Āl al-Shaykh (d. 1378/1959)—they had more "daily and direct interaction

97. Ibn Māniʿ, *Risāla ilā Sulaymān ibn Siḥmān*; cf. Ibn Siḥmān, *Taʿaqqubāt*, 117–21, where most of this letter is transcribed as part of the editor's introduction.

98. On him, see Āl Bassām, *ʿUlamāʾ Najd*, 3:386–89.

99. Ibn Siḥmān, *Taʿaqqubāt*, 122.

100. Ibid., 91–102

101. Lauzière, *Making of Salafism*, 70–75.

with the population" than the Wahhābī scholars did.[102] Their presence helped to reassure a wary Ḥijāzī populace, and the Islamic world more generally, that Wahhābī rule in the Ḥijāz would not be threatening and unsettling.

In collaboration with Riḍā, ʿAbd al-ʿAzīz hosted a pan-Islamic conference in Mecca during the summer of 1344/1926. For Riḍā, the purpose of this was to lay the foundation for a new league of Muslim states, while for ʿAbd al-ʿAzīz, the objective was more about gaining legitimacy for his rule in the Ḥijāz.[103] Delegates were invited from numerous countries, including Turkey, Egypt, and Iran. Some of the Wahhābī scholars from Najd attended as well, even though attending required them to interact with Muslims from countries they had very recently regarded as lands of unbelief. At the conference, the Wahhābī scholars in attendance insisted on the prohibition of certain "innovations" in the rites of pilgrims, particularly acts of supplication, but their view was not universally endorsed. Unable to resolve the matter, the congress decreed the establishment of a committee of scholars to study it further. While by no means a great success, the congress was a watershed in demonstrating ʿAbd al-ʿAzīz's commitment to bringing Wahhābism into the Islamic mainstream. As Martin Kramer observed of the congress: "So began the modern transformation by which the Saudis were to shed their association with schismatic fanaticism, and become for many Muslims the sole keepers of the orthodox flame."[104]

While it may have irked the Wahhābī scholars, the "enlightened and modern" Wahhābism advocated by Riḍā and his disciples was just the kind that ʿAbd al-ʿAzīz wanted his state to be identified with: an Islam that, while harking back to the Wahhābī tradition, was amenable to the ways of the modern world. Surviving in this world required Wahhābism to loosen restrictions on interacting with non-Muslims and Muslims of non-Salafī theological persuasions. There was little in the Wahhābī tradition to justify such a change, but Riḍā's version of Wahhābism represented the wave of the future.

The Decline of Enmity

In the account of his journey to Najd in 1341/1922f, Ameen Rihani, the Lebanese American quoted above, observed a certain tension between ʿAbd al-ʿAzīz and the Wahhābī scholars. While their relationship was generally one of

102. Ibid., 76.
103. Kramer, *Islam Assembled*, 106–22.
104. Ibid., 108.

"harmony," there were times when "the zealotry of the Ulema" seemed to put the relationship in jeopardy.[105] As with the Ikhwān, ʿAbd al-ʿAzīz found himself having "to keep them in check."[106] While he had used the scholars "to consolidate his State and maintain his control over his subjects," he also had taken care "to keep them in their place . . . to show the people, even if he has to be despotic, that they, the Ulema, are not the supreme power in the State."[107] While ʿAbd al-ʿAzīz's piety—"the sincerity of the Sultan's belief"—was unquestionable, ʿAbd al-ʿAzīz was nonetheless willing to violate the strictures of Wahhābism in pursuit of his political ambitions:

> [T]hough he must be as the Imam of the Wahhabis a strict Unitarian, he knows when and where to relax—when and where to be tolerant in the interest of his country and his people. One of the Ulema, now and then, thus vents his grief: "In days of thine ancestors, O thou-Long-of-Days, the world was not troubled with all these problems." The Sultan smiles and goes ahead towards the fulfilment of his purpose.[108]

ʿAbd al-ʿAzīz's purpose was expanding his state and securing its international recognition. In conversation with him, Rihani questioned whether the Saudi ruler in fact shared the "militant purpose" of the scholars and the Ikhwān, whether he really believed "that it is the duty of the Imam to fight the *mushrekin* everywhere—to wage war against them till they become Unitarians."[109] "No, no," ʿAbd al-ʿAzīz responded. "Take Al-Hasa, for instance. We have there thirty thousand of the Shi'ah, who live in peace and security. No one ever molests them. All we ask of them is not to be too demonstrative in public on their fête-days."[110] A few years later, in 1345/1927, as was seen above, the scholars would rule in their *fatwā* that the Shīʿa in al-Aḥsāʾ must either convert to Islam or be expelled. When it came to judgments such as these, ʿAbd al-ʿAzīz simply ignored them, proceeding ahead "towards the fulfilment of his purpose."

Another judgment of the scholars that ʿAbd al-ʿAzīz ignored concerned the presence of Western businessmen in Arabia who were prospecting for oil. In an undated letter to the ruler, nine of the scholars, including Muḥammad ibn

105. Rihani, *Ibn Sa'oud of Arabia*, 201–2.

106. Ibid., 234.

107. Ibid., 204.

108. Ibid., 234.

109. Ibid.

110. Ibid., 235.

ʿAbd al-Laṭīf, Saʿd ibn ʿAtīq, and Ibn Siḥmān, explain that they have recently learned about the presence of a foreign company in Arabia searching for "mineral resources" (*maʿādin*).[111] "You well understand," the scholars write in the letter, "that collaborating with foreigners who are the subjects of Christian authority and bringing them into Arab lands and Islamic sovereign territory are prohibited. The Sharīʿa does not permit these things." The scholars go on to underscore the corruptions (*mafāsid*), both religious and worldly, that are sure to attend such invitation of and collaboration with foreign guests. "Your polity is an Islamic and religious polity [*wilāya Islāmiyya dīniyya*]," they remind ʿAbd al-ʿAzīz, and as such "it will not be sound without religious governance and the observance of the Muḥammadan Sharīʿa."[112] Once again, the scholars' advice fell on deaf ears. Exactly when this letter was authored is unclear, but it possibly came in response to an oil concession over al-Aḥsāʾ awarded to a British company in Ramaḍān 1341/May 1923.[113] This was the first Saudi oil concession ever awarded, inked during a time when few believed Arabia to have substantial oil reserves. A decade later, the discovery of oil in Bahrain led to the awarding of another major oil concession in Saudi territory, this one to Standard Oil of California. The company began to produce commercial quantities of oil in the late 1350s/late 1930s. Throughout this period, a small number of scholars continued to express their opposition to the presence of Western oil workers, and as before ʿAbd al-ʿAzīz ignored their counsel.[114]

In 1339/1920f, ʿAbd al-ʿAzīz wrote to the scholars to assure them that anyone speaking or judging in a way contrary to the teachings of Ibn ʿAbd al-Wahhāb and his descendants would be "exposed to danger" (*mutaʿarraḍ lil-khaṭar*).[115] In reality, however, his reign did not entail the enforcement of militant Wahhābī principles as contained in the writings of the Wahhābī founder and his successors. The state that he was creating was not to be like the first Saudi state, antagonizing and waging *jihād* against the Islamic world indefinitely. Rather, it was to be another nation-state in the global Westphalian state system. ʿAbd al-ʿAzīz's ambition was to secure a legitimate place in the

111. *al-Durar al-saniyya*, 9:333–34.

112. Ibid.

113. On which, see Keating, *Mirage*, 136.

114. One of these scholars was ʿAbd al-ʿAzīz ibn Bāz (d. 1420/1999), who would become the grand *muftī* of the Saudi kingdom after Muḥammad ibn Ibrāhīm Āl al-Shaykh; see Steinberg, "Wahhabi Ulama and the Saudi State," 24–26.

115. *al-Durar al-saniyya*, 14:379.

system, not to upset and overturn it. The Wahhābī scholars may have disagreed with this vision, but it was one that they would nonetheless have to tolerate. They would also have to tolerate the normalization of relations between Wahhābī Muslims and their non-Wahhābī counterparts, an objective that was crucial to ʿAbd al-ʿAzīz's political ambition. It was in this context that he gave a speech, in Dhū ʾl-qaʿda 1347/May 1929, opposing and rejecting the term *Wahhābism*:

> They call us Wahhābīs and call our doctrine Wahhābī, believing that ours is a particular school [*madhhab khāṣṣ*]. This is a terrible error that arose out of lying propaganda. . . . We are not the adherents of a new school and a new creed. Muḥammad ibn ʿAbd al-Wahhāb introduced nothing new. Our creed is the creed of the pious ancestors that is found in the Book of God and the *sunna* of His Messenger.[116]

While in one sense ʿAbd al-ʿAzīz was merely reiterating a Wahhābī dictum, this being that Wahhābism is nothing but true Islam, he was also pushing back against the idea of Wahhābī separatism. It was important to him that the Wahhābīs shed their self-conception as a sect apart from and hostile to the majority of the Islamic world. Such a change required rejecting the very idea that there was a particular Wahhābī doctrine or creed, and it also required ceasing to self-identify as "Wahhābīs," as Ibn Siḥmān and some of the other scholars had begun to do.

Just a few years later, in Jumādā I 1351/September 1932, ʿAbd al-ʿAzīz issued a royal decree proclaiming the Kingdom of Saudi Arabia (al-Mamlaka al-ʿArabiyya al-Suʿūdiyya). Heretofore the third Saudi state had been known as the Kingdom of the Ḥijāz, Najd, and Its Dependencies (Mamlakat al-Ḥijāz wa-Najd wa-Mulḥaqātihā), a phrase that indicated the kingdom was a mixture of different territories. A newspaper article accompanying the decree explained that the purpose of the change of name was to capture the new sense of national unity (*al-waḥda al-ʿunṣuriyya*) felt by the people of Arabia.[117] That unity would be expressed by the name of the Saudi dynasty, the kingdom being named after the Āl Suʿūd family. The kingdom's subjects would soon refer to themselves as "Saudis" (Suʿūdiyyūn), a designation not previously used by the inhabitants of the Arabian Peninsula. A national identity of Saudiness was thus being cultivated just as Wahhābī particularism was being dis-

116. "Khiṭāb jalālat al-malik."

117. "Taḥwīl ism Mamlakat al-Ḥijāz wa-Najd wa-Mulḥaqātihā."

couraged. King ʿAbd al-ʿAzīz, as he was now known, had given the people of Arabia a new state and a new identity. These were not what the Wahhābī scholars had been looking forward to thirty years earlier when they hailed the conquest of Riyadh.

Conclusion

At the beginning of the third Saudi state, the Wahhābī scholars' approach to their doctrine was entirely unreformed. They still regarded neighboring areas as lands of polytheists whose inhabitants were to be excommunicated and shown hatred and enmity. One member of the Āl al-Shaykh was pilloried for suggesting otherwise. The appearance of the Ikhwān gave the scholars hope that the state being created by ʿAbd al-ʿAzīz would be a polity in the mold of the first Saudi state, but the excesses of the Ikhwān made them an imperfect ally at best and one that the scholars would ultimately turn on and condemn. Meanwhile, the scholars watched as the Saudi ruler grew close to a prominent Islamic modernist in Egypt, Rashīd Riḍā, who condemned some of their views as beyond the pale even as he printed their works. The Saudi ruler was also allowing Christian oilmen into the country over the scholars' stern objections and holding Islamic conferences attended by all kinds of Muslims. As the scholars were slowly but surely learning, the third Saudi state was to be much more a conventional nation-state than a militant Wahhābī one.

The question for the scholars was whether to tolerate all of this or to agitate against the king's rule. The decision was nearly unanimous in accepting the new status quo, even though doing so would require them to modify their approach to the Wahhābī doctrine. Over the past decades, the scholars had come to appreciate the value of political stability, having experienced first the Saudi civil war, then the Rashīdī interregnum, and finally the Ikhwān revolt. In opposing the Ikhwān, they repeatedly stressed the importance of obedience to the ruler, and now they would uphold that ideal themselves, even if the ruler's vision did not match theirs.

In Ṣafar 1349/July 1930, Sulaymān ibn Siḥmān died in Riyadh, and with him something of the spirit of militant Wahhābism died as well. While Ibn Siḥmān never seems to have openly criticized the new political order being built by ʿAbd al-ʿAzīz, he was also the scholar most out of step with it. He was a man from another era. There was no member of the Wahhābī scholarly class who placed greater emphasis on the duty of showing hatred and enmity to polytheists, whom he saw as the majority of the Islamic world, and now that emphasis was to be discouraged. Though Ibn Siḥmān spent decades trying to prevent the normalization of relations with "all and sundry," his work was now being undercut by the ruler in Riyadh, who wanted the Wahhābīs to get along with their non-Wahhābī counterparts and see themselves as part of the larger Islamic world. Despite his efforts, the Wahhābism of the future was going to look a lot more like the versions promoted by Ibn ʿAmr, Ḥusayn ibn Ḥasan Āl al-Shaykh, and Rashīd Riḍā than the version championed by Ibn Siḥmān and his scholarly allies.

Conclusion

THE FALL AND RISE OF MILITANT WAHHĀBISM

IN 1381/1961, the Syrian scholar ʿAlī al-Ṭanṭāwī published a short biography of Muḥammad ibn ʿAbd al-Wahhāb.[1] In its author's conception, it was to be the first of its kind: a balanced and impartial account of the founder of Wahhābism, one that would finally transcend the propaganda war (*ḥarb al-diʿāya*) that had raged since the movement's founding more than two centuries before. Born in Damascus in 1327/1909 and educated in Islamic reformist circles there from a young age, al-Ṭanṭāwī was one of his generation's leading pan-Islamist thinkers and writers, spending most of his career in Saudi Arabia.[2] An adherent of Salafī (i.e., Taymiyyan) theology, he was also deeply influenced by the ideas of Rashīd Riḍā and his disciples. His views on Wahhābism were mixed. There were things that he liked about Ibn ʿAbd al-Wahhāb and things that he disliked. In writing his book, he said, he was not setting out to please either the partisans of Wahhābism or its opponents but, rather, to state the truth as he saw it.[3]

The result was a mildly critical assessment of the founder of Wahhābism, at once praised for preaching the correct understanding of *tawḥīd* and criticized for the manner (*uslūb*) in which he did so. The problem with his *uslūb*, in al-Ṭanṭāwī's view, was that it involved pronouncing *takfīr* on Muslims and fighting them as unbelievers. Ibn ʿAbd al-Wahhāb, he wrote, "observed the manifestations of *shirk* being committed by certain people at graves, and so he

1. al-Ṭanṭāwī, *Muḥammad ibn ʿAbd al-Wahhāb*.

2. For an account of his life, see Dīrāniyya, "Sīrat al-shaykh ʿAlī al-Ṭanṭāwī."

3. al-Ṭanṭāwī, *Muḥammad ibn ʿAbd al-Wahhāb*, 1:11, 40–44.

considered them to be polytheists. He then extended this judgment generally [*ʿammama ʾl-ḥukm*] to every land where these domes and tombs were found. This is to say, he judged Muslims to be apostates en masse [*ḥakama bi-riddat al-Muslimīn jamīʿan*] and deemed their blood and property licit."[4] While this might seem like an unflattering portrayal of the Najdī reformer, al-Ṭanṭāwī was far more concerned with being perceived as an apologist for the Wahhābī movement than he was the reverse.[5] His hope was to be as balanced as possible, but he understood that for many this would look like an apology for Wahhābism.

According to al-Ṭanṭāwī, two factors had converged to make it possible for him to write an objective biography of Ibn ʿAbd al-Wahhāb. The first was a discernible fading of Wahhābī zeal. "The zeal of the Wahhābīs [*ḥamāsat al-Wahhābiyyīn*] in calling to it [i.e., their creed] and their insistence on spreading it have waned [*faturat*]," he wrote. The second factor was a corresponding reduction in anti-Wahhābī sentiment. "Their enemies' zeal [*ḥamāsat khuṣūmihim*] in waging war on it," he wrote, "has [also] waned." While a remnant of scholars on both sides persisted in prosecuting the propaganda war as before, hostilities had relaxed considerably.[6] How this had come to pass al-Ṭanṭāwī does not say explicitly, but at one point he suggests something of an answer. This was that the central issue in the debate over Wahhābism—the cult of saints—was no longer as important as it once was. The cult of saints, in his view, had ceased to enjoy the widespread appeal and legitimacy it once did. The anti-Wahhābī refutations defending the practices associated with *ziyāra*, though they continued to be churned out, had come to possess a timeworn quality. Many now looked at these practices with derision. "Today, we read this talk for entertainment and amusement," he wrote of the texts defending the cult of saints, whereas before "anyone who rejected it would have been considered an innovating Wahhābī deserving of people's disdain and eternal damnation."[7] While the recession of the cult of saints might be overstated here, it is true that the institution was in a decline of sorts, not being on the cutting edge of twentieth-century Islamic culture in the Arab world. For modernist scholars like al-Ṭanṭāwī, saint veneration was mindless superstition incompatible with a renewed and revitalized Islam. The Wahhābī form of Islam, on the

4. Ibid., 1:9–10.

5. Ibid., 1:11.

6. Ibid.

7. Ibid., 1:6.

contrary, stripped of its historical zeal, *was* compatible with their modernist vision, as Riḍā's embrace of it had shown.

Despite having written somewhat critically of Wahhābism, al-Ṭanṭāwī soon found himself living and working in Saudi Arabia. Two years after the book was published, he took up a teaching position in Riyadh at what would later be known as the Imām Muḥammad ibn Suʿūd Islamic University. A few years later, he moved to the Ḥijāz, where he lived and worked until his death in 1420/1999. A decade earlier, in 1410/1990, he received the King Faisal Prize for Service to Islam, the kingdom's highest honor for Islamic service. The not entirely flattering biography of Ibn ʿAbd al-Wahhāb, written some thirty years earlier, had not prevented him from enjoying a highly successful career in the kingdom and even receiving its signature Islamic prize.

While the perceived decline of the cult of saints was one factor helping to reduce tensions between the Wahhābīs and their enemies, even more important were the efforts of King ʿAbd al-ʿAzīz Āl Suʿūd in taming the Wahhābī movement and promoting its incorporation into the Islamic mainstream. In building the Kingdom of Saudi Arabia in the early twentieth century, ʿAbd al-ʿAzīz had harnessed militant Wahhābism to his advantage, but thereafter he moved to corral it. The Wahhābī scholars pined for a polity like the first Saudi state, one that would agitate on behalf of Wahhābism and wage *jihād* against the surrounding polytheists to expand the realm of the faith, but ʿAbd al-ʿAzīz had other ideas. This was a time when the nation-state system was expanding to the non-Western world, including the Middle East, and his ambition was to secure a place in that system. It is a credit to him that he was able to do so while maintaining the loyalty of the scholars, who did not share this vision and occasionally objected to his policies. By keeping the scholars loyal while modernizing the state, ʿAbd al-ʿAzīz effectively paved the way for the rapprochement that was to come between the Wahhābīs and the larger Islamic world. As Eldon Rutter, a British convert to Islam and pilgrim in the Ḥijāz in the mid-1920s, observed, "[W]ere it not for the qualities of personal power, of statesmanship, and of public-spirited justice displayed by Abdul Azîz, the whole of the Muslim world would still detest the Wahhâbîs, as they have been detested, until recently, ever since their movement was started by the Shaykh Muhammad Ibn Abdul Wahhâb."[8]

ʿAbd al-ʿAzīz did not completely marginalize the scholars, however. In exchange for supporting the new regime, they received a great supply of funds

8. Rutter, *Holy Cities of Arabia*, 1:190–91.

for teaching and spreading the Wahhābī creed, and they were granted power to oversee a vast bureaucracy dedicated to commanding right and forbidding wrong (*al-amr bi ʾl-maʿrūf wa ʾl-nahy ʿan al-munkar*), which now became the symbol of the religious establishment's power in Saudi society.[9] In practice, commanding right and forbidding wrong meant enforcing conformity with Islamic law in daily life and ensuring attendance at communal prayer and gender segregation, among other things. While discussed in earlier Wahhābī doctrinal texts, it was not as central to the Wahhābī mission as the duty of showing hatred and enmity to those seen as polytheists. At this point, however, the focus of the Wahhābī scholars was on consolidating their influence in the state's power structure.

At the forefront of this effort was the personage of Muḥammad ibn Ibrāhīm Āl al-Shaykh (d. 1389/1969), a grandson of ʿAbd al-Laṭīf ibn ʿAbd al-Raḥmān Āl al-Shaykh who headed the Wahhābī religious establishment from the 1360s/1940s onward.[10] In 1373/1953, he assumed the new title of "grand *muftī*" (*al-muftī ʾl-akbar*). No scholar played a greater role in helping to build the institutions and networks that would form the backbone of Wahhābī scholarly power in Saudi society for years to come. Beginning in the 1370s/1950s, he laid the foundation of a new, centralized educational system on the model of Egypt's al-Azhar, working to establish educational institutes across the country. In 1374/1955, he formed an organization for issuing *fatwā*s and managing religious affairs (Dār al-Iftāʾ waʾl-Ishrāf ʿalā ʾl-Shuʾūn al-Dīniyya), inspired by the model on offer in nearby Muslim states. The establishment of committees for commanding right and forbidding wrong (later merged into a single committee) preceded these developments by some decades, though the committees would be brought under his authority. Much of the Wahhābī scholars' energy would be channeled into running and nurturing these religious institutions. Thus began what Nabil Mouline has termed the "routinization and institutionalization" of Wahhābism in Saudi Arabia, a process whereby the scholars acquired institutional heft in the framework of the modern Saudi state.[11] The Wahhābī establishment's authority manifested in its ability to cultivate a large contingent of scholars and preachers steeped in the Wahhābī doctrine who would oversee a conservative Islamic society.

9. On the origins of this bureaucracy, see Cook, *Commanding Right and Forbidding Wrong in Islamic Thought*, 180–91.

10. On him, see Āl al-Shaykh, *Mashāhīr*, 169–84; Āl Bassām, *ʿUlamāʾ Najd*, 1:242–63; al-Qāḍī, *Rawḍat al-nāẓirīn*, 3:363–69.

11. Mouline, *Clerics of Islam*, 261; and see further, on this process, 119–70.

This process of "routinization and institutionalization," it should be understood, was not accompanied by any critical reexamination of fundamental Wahhābī principles. The Wahhābī view that most of the world's Muslims were flawed in their beliefs remained standard for years to come; the idea that Muslims ought to show hatred and enmity to polytheism and polytheists continued to be taught. There was change, however, in the way Wahhābī principles were applied. Muḥammad ibn Ibrāhīm Āl al-Shaykh, for instance, though he often recalled the exclusivist principles of traditional Wahhābism, also exhibited a greater tolerance and realism than his predecessors. In one of his *fatwās*, for instance, he writes that the majority of the Islamic world is only nominally Muslim (*Islām al-akthar Islām ismī*), suggesting a willingness to pronounce *takfīr* on most professed Muslims.[12] But he also participated in a Muslim congress in Mecca alongside the Mālikī Shaykh al-Islām of Tunisia and the former chief *muftī* of Egypt, men who certainly did not adhere to the Wahhābī doctrine and whom an earlier generation of Wahhābī scholars would have considered Jahmiyya.[13] In another *fatwā*, Ibn Ibrāhīm is seen discouraging travel to areas where he believes *shirk* and *kufr* to be prevalent, including Beirut, but he also acknowledges that there might be a worthwhile religious interest (*maṣlaḥa dīniyya*) in traveling there, given the opportunities for preaching about *tawḥīd* and warning against *shirk*.[14] This is a noticeable change on the matter of travel to so-called lands of unbelief, as Ibn Ibrāhīm indicates that such travel might actually be productive. For those seeking to travel to and live in lands of unbelief, he still underscores the Wahhābī requirement of manifesting the religion (*iẓhār al-dīn*), which he defines as "openly professing *tawḥīd* and dissociating from what the polytheists believe [*mimmā ʿalayhi ʾl-mushrikūn*]."[15] But it is noteworthy that he omits the duty of dissociating from and showing enmity to the polytheists themselves. The idea that *iẓhār al-dīn* in lands of unbelief inevitably entails a hostile response from the unbelievers, and that therefore it is impossible to travel there while professing Islam—an idea elaborated by Ḥamad ibn ʿAtīq, Sulaymān ibn Siḥmān, and others—was not one that Ibn Ibrāhīm espoused.

By the time Ibn Ibrāhīm's successor as grand *muftī*, ʿAbd al-ʿAzīz ibn Bāz (d. 1420/1999), was responding to similar questions, the Wahhābī perception

12. Āl al-Shaykh, *Fatāwā wa-rasāʾil*, 1:77.

13. Lacroix, *Awakening Islam*, 13–14.

14. Āl al-Shaykh, *Fatāwā wa-rasāʾil*, 1:90–92.

15. Ibid., 1:91–92.

that the Islamic world was steeped in *shirk* had changed. Ibn Bāz did not proceed from the assumption that the Islamic world consisted mainly of polytheist unbelievers. With regard to the issue of travel, he was concerned in his *fatwās* only with travel to the West, which he argued was prohibited given all the terrible things there that could lead Muslims astray. The only exception was the case of preachers, who he said should be permitted to travel in order to spread the message of Islam.[16] Similarly, when writing about the duty to show hatred and enmity to polytheists, Ibn Bāz was doing so mainly in the context of Christians and Jews.[17] In this he was pushing back against the idea of interfaith tolerance, insisting that this was not the true message of Islam. He was not, however, demanding that Wahhābī Muslims confront their non-Wahhābī counterparts, which was the main idea of showing hatred and enmity in the past. Rather than condemning the majority of the Islamic world, the Wahhābī scholars were trying to cultivate influence in it. Ibn Bāz played a leading role in international Islamic organizations, such as the Muslim World League, that promoted Islamic solidarity across nations.

Unlike earlier Wahhābī scholars, Ibn Ibrāhīm and Ibn Bāz were not warning at length about the dangers of traveling to non-Wahhābī lands and interacting with non-Wahhābī Muslims. Where Ibn Ibrāhīm put up a significant fight was over the application of positive laws (*qawānīn*) in the kingdom, attacking the various law codes and courts that he saw as transgressive of the Sharīʿa. He famously summarized his views on *qawānīn* in his 1380/1960 essay, *Risāla fī taḥkīm al-qawānīn* (Treatise Concerning the Application of Positive Laws).[18] But even on this issue he exhibited a degree of realism. Here as elsewhere, the grand *muftī*'s approach was one of "negotiation and compromise," not intransigence.[19] It was this approach that would characterize the Wahhābī scholarly establishment under the Kingdom of Saudi Arabia, the idea being to expand the establishment's influence, not to pick unwinnable fights.

This approach involved a large degree of deference to the Saudi ruler, leading to perceptions that the scholars were compromising their values. As Guido Steinberg has noted, the Wahhābī scholars of the twentieth century proved themselves "ready to submit to the wishes of the king whenever an important political issue was at stake," whether that be allowing Westerners to produce

16. Ibn Bāz, *Majmūʿ fatāwā*, 4:129–30, 192–99.

17. Ibid., 2:173–89.

18. Āl al-Shaykh, *Fatāwā wa-rasāʾil*, 12:284–91 (= *al-Durar al-saniyya*, 16:206–18).

19. Mouline, *Clerics of Islam*, 145.

oil in the kingdom or allowing Western troops access to the country.[20] The act that most starkly revealed the scholars' place in the system was their acquiescence in the decision to invite American troops to be stationed on Saudi soil in 1411/1990 during the first Gulf War. When the Council of Senior Scholars (Hayʾat Kibār al-ʿUlamā) assented to the monarch's decision to invite American troops, it inspired a backlash among religious conservatives and Islamists who saw it as an affront to the country's status as a conservative Islamic state. The scholars who condoned it were seen as lackeys of the state. A broad-based opposition movement calling for a greater application of Islamic law in the country, known as the Awakening (Ṣaḥwa), emerged in the aftermath.[21] While the Ṣaḥwa was heavily influenced by the political ideas and culture of the Muslim Brotherhood in Egypt, it also made appeals to the Wahhābī heritage. Some of its leading voices, including the scholars Salmān al-ʿAwda and Safar al-Ḥawālī, hearkened back to the first Saudi state and the early Wahhābī movement, lamenting how far the kingdom had drifted from its roots.[22] The Saudi activist (and later global *jihādī*) Osama bin Ladin complained that the official scholars were "diluting the doctrine of *tawḥīd* and *al-walāʾ waʾl-barāʾ*,"[23] which was to say, they were promoting a toned-down version of the foundational principles of the Wahhābī doctrine.

This was not the first time that a religious movement inside the kingdom had criticized the Saudi rulers and the scholarly establishment for compromising Wahhābī principles. Years earlier, in the 1390s/1970s, a group known as al-Jamāʿa al-Salafiyya al-Muḥtasiba (The Salafī Group that Commands Right and Forbids Wrong) grew to prominence with a similar message, arguing that the Āl Suʿūd and their supporters had betrayed the Wahhābī heritage. In a pamphlet published in 1398/1978, Juhaymān al-ʿUtaybī (d. 1400/1980), the leader of the group, emphasized the traditional Wahhābī requirements of *al-walāʾ waʾl-barāʾ*, including the duty "to dissociate from polytheism and its practitioners and to manifest enmity to them." He condemned the Āl Suʿūd for "showing loyalty to unbelievers and treating polytheists as brothers."[24] Juhaymān's group was most famous for seizing and occupying the Grand Mosque in Mecca for two weeks in 1400/1979, believing that one of their own

20. Steinberg, "Wahhabi Ulama and the Saudi State," 26.

21. On the Ṣaḥwa generally, see Lacroix, *Awakening Islam*.

22. Fandy, *Saudi Arabia and the Politics of Dissent*, 83, 100–101.

23. Ibn Lādin, *Majmūʿ rasāʾil wa-tawjīhāt*, 168.

24. al-ʿUtaybī, *Rafʿ al-iltibās*, 5, 11.

was the prophesied *mahdī*, or rightly guided one.[25] Before it grew into an apocalyptic movement, however, the main message of Juhaymān's group was that the modern Saudi state had betrayed its Wahhābī roots.

Another movement that has appealed to the authority and heritage of militant Wahhābism is the Sunnī *jihādī* movement, the ideological movement associated with al-Qāʿida and the Islamic State. In Arabic, Sunnī *jihādism* is known variously as the *jihādī* current (*al-tayyār al-jihādī*) or Jihādī Salafism (*al-salafiyya al-jihādiyya*), the latter term indicating the group's adherence to Salafī (and Wahhābī) theology. One of the starting points of the *jihādī* movement is that the modern-day rulers of the Islamic world are apostates on account of their failure to rule by God's law, and thus it is a duty to wage *jihād* against them for the purpose of reestablishing Islamic rule. In this the *jihādīs* were profoundly influenced by the revolutionary thought of Sayyid Quṭb (d. 1386/1966), a member of the Egyptian Muslim Brotherhood who condemned the nominal Muslim rulers of the region for usurping God's sovereignty (*ḥākimiyya*) in their failure to implement the Sharīʿa. Quṭb also argued that Islamic society had abandoned Islam and reverted to a state of pre-Islamic ignorance (*jāhiliyya*), and he called for the creation of a vanguard (*ṭalīʿa*) to lead an Islamic revolution. While Quṭb himself was not influenced by the Wahhābīs (and some of his ideas ran contrary to the Wahhābī doctrine), his followers in the *jihādī* movement were. In the 1400s/1980s, *jihādī* ideologues began to appeal to the Wahhābī heritage as the principal source of their revolutionary ideology, seeing themselves as the heirs of the movement begun by Ibn ʿAbd al-Wahhāb. Gradually, the *jihādī* movement acquired a distinctly Wahhābī character, as Wahhābī texts and concepts became a focal point of *jihādī* ideology.

One of those most responsible for this Wahhābizing trend in the *jihādī* movement was the Palestinian Jordanian ʿIṣām al-Barqāwī, better known as Abū Muḥammad al-Maqdisī.[26] Born in the West Bank village of Burqa in 1378/1959, al-Maqdisī was raised in Kuwait, where he moved with his family as a young child. In Kuwait he become involved in the country's Islamist scene at an early age, visiting and associating with a variety of groups of different orientations and outlooks. These included the Surūrī movement, named for Muḥammad Surūr Zayn al-ʿĀbidīn, a former Muslim Brother who blended Brotherhood activism with the theological purity of Salafism, as well as the

25. Hegghammer and Lacroix, "Rejectionist Islamism in Saudi Arabia."

26. On al-Maqdisī and his thought, see Wagemakers, *Quietist Jihadi*.

Kuwaiti branch of al-Jamāʿa al-Salafiyya al-Muḥtasiba, the group that led the takeover of the Grand Mosque in Mecca in 1979. He did not become seriously involved with the *jihādī* movement until the 1400s/1980s, when he spent time with the *mujāhidīn* in Afghanistan fighting against the Soviets. It was there that he acquired a reputation as a young *jihādī* scholar and one who was deeply influenced by the teachings of Wahhābism.

As al-Maqdisī tells it, his first encounter with the Wahhābī tradition was textual. While pursuing religious studies in Saudi Arabia in the early 1400s/early 1980s, he chanced upon a set of old books in the Prophet's Mosque in Medina titled *al-Durar al-saniyya fī ʾl-ajwiba al-Najdiyya*. This was the main compendium of the writings of the Wahhābī scholars from the time of Ibn ʿAbd al-Wahhāb to the early twentieth century. The encounter with these texts, he would say, "was my first contact with the books of the *imāms* of the Najdī mission."[27] In Saudi Arabia, he would make copies of *al-Durar al-saniyya*, and he would buy every book by the Wahhābī divines that he could get his hands on, studying them and taking careful notes. The result, or "the fruit of this reading," was his first major book, *Millat Ibrāhīm*, which he completed in Kuwait in 1405/1984.[28]

Millat Ibrāhīm (The Religion of Abraham) took the form of an indictment of the ruling regimes of the Middle East and a call to revolution against them in the form of *jihād*. In this it resembled earlier *jihādī* manifestos, such as ʿAbd al-Salām Faraj's *al-Farīḍa al-ghāʾiba* (The Absent Duty), which inspired the assassination of Anwar Sadat in 1401/1981. But *Millat Ibrāhīm* was different in that it made its case for revolution primarily in terms of Wahhābism. In the book, al-Maqdisī produces an endless series of quotations by the leading Wahhābī scholars from the mid-eighteenth to the early twentieth century, arguing that their emphasis on showing hatred and enmity to polytheists, and waging *jihād* against them, ought to apply to modern-day rulers. These rulers were apostates who had failed to rule by God's law, and they had committed *shirk* by making themselves into idols (*ṭawāghīt*) who usurped God's divine prerogatives regarding legislation. While the Wahhābī scholars he quoted only rarely spoke of this sort of legal-political *shirk*, being above all concerned with the *shirk* pertaining to the cult of saints, al-Maqdisī saw no problem in applying their words to his own desired target. The *jihādī* war on legal-political *shirk*, he argued, was merely the latest phase in an age-old war on polytheism more

27. al-Maqdisī, *Wa-lākin kūnū rabbāniyyīn*, 7–8.

28. Ibid., 25.

generally. It just so happened that the most threatening form of *shirk* today was "the *shirk* of appealing to constitutions and man-made laws" (*shirk al-taḥākum ilā 'l-dasātīr wa 'l-qawānīn al-waḍ 'iyya*).[29] In another book, al-Maqdisī makes this point more clearly, where he writes that "every age is afflicted by its own particular tribulation and forms of polytheism." In the age of Aḥmad ibn Ḥanbal, this was "entering into false discourse around God's names and attributes." In the age of Ibn 'Abd al-Wahhāb, it was "the worship of graves, tombs, and saints." In the present age, it is "the application of European laws" (*taḥkīm qawānīn al-faranja*).[30] All forms of *shirk*, however, are fundamentally the same. "There is no difference," he writes elsewhere, "between the polytheism of graves and the polytheism of the written constitution [*shirk al-qubūr wa-shirk al-dustūr*]," that is, between the *shirk* encountered by Ibn 'Abd al-Wahhāb and the legal-political *shirk* of the present age.[31] The remedy in both cases is the same, namely, enmity and *jihād*. To the extent that al-Maqdisī was misappropriating the Wahhābī tradition, it was in making out (apostate) Muslim rulers to be the principal targets of enmity and *jihād*, not the partisans of the cult of saints. There was at least some precedent in the Wahhābī tradition, however, for seeing positive law as a manifestation of *shirk*.

Shortly after completing *Millat Ibrāhīm* in 1405/1984, al-Maqdisī left Kuwait for the Afghanistan-Pakistan border region, where he became one of the many Arab volunteers drawn there by the Soviet occupation of Afghanistan. It was in Peshawar, Pakistan, that *Millat Ibrāhīm* was published for the first time, quickly becoming a hit among the Arab volunteers, the so-called Afghan Arabs. According to al-Maqdisī, the book spread like wildfire in the Afghanistan-Pakistan border area, and soon it was circulating in the Arab world as well, being printed and reprinted numerous times.[32] In the years that followed, *Millat Ibrāhīm* would come to be seen as a manifesto of sorts of the emergent Jihādī Salafī movement, and al-Maqdisī, as one of its leading theorists. In a great many more books and essays, he continued to put the Wahhābī heritage front and center in his ideological campaign against the regimes of the Middle East. Many other writers and activists would follow his lead. Over the next two decades, as the Jihādī Salafīs cohered into a distinct movement, one increasingly Wahhābī in orientation, they distanced themselves from the ideas of Sayyid Quṭb, some of

29. al-Maqdisī, *Millat Ibrāhīm*, 23.

30. al-Maqdisī, *Kashf al-niqāb 'an sharī 'at al-ghāb*, 2–3.

31. al-Maqdisī, *al-Kawāshif al-jaliyya*, 235.

32. al-Maqdisī, *Wa-lākin kūnū rabbāniyyīn*, 27.

whose views were incompatible with Wahhābī theology. As Daniel Lav has noted, "At the end point of the [Jihādī Salafī] school's development, its doctrine no longer made explicit reference to Quṭb."[33] The centrality of *ḥākimiyya*, of the necessity of making God's law supreme, remained, but it was Salafized or Wahhābized, subsumed under the rubric of *tawḥīd al-ulūhiyya*, the idea that all worship is owed to God alone.[34]

The centrality of Wahhābism to the Jihādī Salafī movement became even more evident with the rise of the Islamic State in the 1430s/2010s. When the Islamic State came to the world's attention in 1434/2013, its fidelity to Wahhābism was loudly trumpeted by its official representatives and online supporters. An official preaching van on the streets of Raqqa, Syria, was decked out in Wahhābī catechisms.[35] The recruits in Islamic State training camps were made to study textbooks about Wahhābī creed.[36] In the summer of 1436/2015, the Islamic State's official publishing house began the printing of classic Wahhābī texts, from Ibn ʿAbd al-Wahhāb's *Arbaʿ qawāʿid fī ʾl-dīn* and *Kashf al-shubuhāt* to Sulaymān ibn ʿAbdallāh's *al-Dalāʾil fī ḥukm muwālāt ahl al-ishrāk* and Ḥamad ibn ʿAtīq's *Sabīl al-najāt wa ʾl-fikāk*. The purpose of printing these texts was to inculcate in the new generation of *jihādīs* a proper understanding of Islamic belief, one that was exclusivist and militant. In the introduction to one of these works, the anonymous editor likens the Islamic State to the early Wahhābī *daʿwa*, claiming that the Islamic State "is again renewing *tawḥīd*, *jihād*, and the *sunna*," as the Wahhābīs had done before. The official scholars and wicked preachers in Saudi Arabia (*ʿulamāʾ al-salāṭīn wa-duʿāt al-sūʾ*), by contrast, have forsaken the Wahhābī heritage: "They lyingly ascribe themselves to the *imām* Muḥammad ibn ʿAbd al-Wahhāb, knowing full well that today the Islamic State, its *daʿwa*, and its *jihād* are an extension and embodiment of the mission of *tawḥīd* and *jihād* initiated by the Messenger of God and his companions and renewed by Ibn ʿAbd al-Wahhāb and his descendants."[37] In other words, the Islamic State was to be seen as the rightful heir of the Wahhābī *daʿwa*, not Saudi Arabia and its religious establishment. A similar

33. Lav, *Radical Islam and the Revival of Medieval Theology*, 169.

34. At one point it was common for *jihādīs* to speak of *tawḥīd al-ḥākimiyya*, but gradually this fell out of favor.

35. "Islamic State," *Vice News*, August 2014.

36. This was *Muqarrar fī ʾl-tawḥīd*, produced by the Islamic State's scholarly unit (Hayʾat al-Buḥūth wa ʾl-Iftāʾ) in 1436/2014f.

37. Ibn ʿAbd al-Wahhāb, *Kashf al-shubuhāt* (al-Himma ed.), 5n1.

point was made in an internal Islamic State memo describing the genesis of this series of texts. One of the reasons for publishing them, the document states, is that

> the caliphate is living a reality similar to that of the first Saudi state, which appeared in the Arabian Peninsula amid a sea of *shirk* and *kufr* and was fought on account of the fact that it was renewing *tawḥīd* and the *sunna*. The reality of the early *imāms* of the Najdī *daʿwa* thus resembles what we are living through today in terms of the arraying of *ṭawāghīt* and apostates against us and the severe alienation of Islam.[38]

In their writings, the Wahhābī scholars exhibited "the desired harshness" (*al-shidda al-maṭlūba*) that is appropriate for these times. They were scholars "who were waging *jihād* against apostates affiliated with Islam and the *sunna* and who (i.e., the early *imāms* of the Najdī *daʿwa*) had a state that ruled by what God has revealed and pronounced *takfīr* on polytheists and showed them enmity."[39] Islamic State officials thus believed not only that they were the rightful heirs of the Wahhābī tradition but also that their political project was similar to that of the first Saudi state. It was important to publish the Wahhābī canon not only because it embodied the true doctrine of Islam but also because doing so would cultivate the militant spirit necessary for confronting the onslaught of *kufr* and *shirk* that they were facing.

Similar statements regarding Wahhābism and the first Saudi state were made by the Islamic State's online supporters. In a post on the messaging app Telegram in Ramaḍān 1438/May 2017, a certain Gharīb al-Surūriyya described the Islamic State as "the true heir of the blessed Najdī mission" (*al-warīth al-ḥaqīqī lil-daʿwa al-Najdiyya al-mubāraka*), explaining that "it is supporting *tawḥīd*, eradicating *shirk*, pronouncing *takfīr* on polytheists, and establishing God's law."[40] When a branch of the Islamic State launched a campaign of terrorist attacks on the Shīʿa in eastern Saudi Arabia in 1436/2014, Gharīb al-Surūriyya cited as justification the early Wahhābī attacks on the Shīʿa of al-Aḥsāʾ during the first Saudi state, quoting Ibn Ghannām. The Islamic State, he claimed, was

38. "Taqrīr mukhtaṣar ḥawl silsilat rasāʾil al-ṭawḥīd al-khāliṣ." This undated document was uploaded on September 17, 2018, to the Telegram channel al-Nadhīr al-ʿUryān, which leaked numerous internal Islamic State documents starting in August 2018.

39. Ibid.

40. al-Surūriyya, "al-Dawla al-Islāmiyya imtidād lil-daʿwa al-Najdiyya." See further, on the Islamic State and Saudi Arabia, Bunzel, *Kingdom and the Caliphate*.

following the path of its Wahhābī forebears in seeking to annihilate the Shīʿa.[41] The theme of continuity with Wahhābī history was stressed again by another pseudonymous writer in 1435/2014, who in an essay highlighted the similarities between the Islamic State and the first Saudi state, even likening Islamic State leader Abū Bakr al-Baghdādī to Muḥammad ibn ʿAbd al-Wahhāb. In the essay, he claims that "the Islamic State is an extension of the *daʿwa* and state of the *imām* Muḥammad ibn ʿAbd al-Wahhāb, the first Saudi state."[42]

Meanwhile, in the Kingdom of Saudi Arabia, the Wahhābī religious establishment has seen its power steadily eroded in recent years as a result of the reformist measures of Crown Prince Muḥammad ibn Salmān. Since 1437/2016, the country's religious police force has been neutered, women have been permitted to drive, movie theaters have been opened, and an entertainment authority has been established sponsoring concerts and wrestling matches, among other things that have stirred resentment among religious conservatives. The kingdom is pursuing a religious makeover in the direction of what it calls "moderate Islam." So far this has not involved any kind of overt break with the Wahhābī tradition, but it has meant that the state's Wahhābī origins have been de-emphasized. Thus as militant Wahhābism has reared its head in the form of Jihādī Salafism, the Saudi kingdom has sought to leave it even further behind.

41. al-Surūriyya, "Sīrat aʾimmat al-Islām fī hadm mawāḍiʿ al-shirk waʾl-ṭughyān."

42. al-Nābiʿ, *al-Shaykh al-Baghdādī ʿalā khuṭā ʾl-imām Muḥammad ibn ʿAbd al-Wahhāb*, 2 (originally published by Gharīb al-Ghurabāʾ on the forum *Muntadayāt al-Minbar al-Iʿlāmī al-Jihādī* on June 26, 2014).

APPENDIX

TABLE A.1. Dated or roughly datable early refutations of Wahhābism

Author	Legal Affiliation and Location	Title/Description	Completion Date
Muḥammad ibn ʿAfāliq (d. 1163/1750)	Ḥanbalī, al-Aḥsāʾ	*Tahakkum al-muqallidīn fī muddaʿī tajdīd al-dīn*	ca. 1155/1742
Aḥmad ibn ʿAlī al-Qabbānī (fl. 1159/1746)	Shāfiʿī, Basra	*Faṣl al-khiṭāb fī radd ḍalālāt Ibn ʿAbd al-Wahhāb*	12 Shawwāl 1155/ca. December 10, 1742
ʿAbd al-Wahhāb al-Ṭandatāwī (d. 1156/1743)	Shāfiʿī, Mecca	*Kitāb radʿ al-ḍalāla wa-qamʿ al-jahāla*[a]	6 Muḥarram 1156/ March 2, 1743
Sulaymān ibn Suḥaym (d. 1181/1767f)	Ḥanbalī, Riyadh	Epistle to Muslim scholars[b]	No later than Rajab 1157/ September 1744
al-Qabbānī	Shāfiʿī, Basra	*Kashf al-ḥijāb ʿan wajh ḍalālāt Ibn ʿAbd al-Wahhāb*	Late Rajab 1157/early September 1744
Muḥammad ibn al-Ṭayyib al-Maghribī (d. 1170/1756f)	Mālikī, Medina	Unknown (fragment)[c]	22 Muḥarram 1158/ ca. February 24, 1745
al-Qabbānī	Shāfiʿī, Basra	*Naqḍ qawāʿid al-ḍalāl wa-rafḍ ʿaqāʾid al-ḍullāl*	22 Jumādā I 1158/ca. June 22, 1745
Ibn ʿAfāliq	Ḥanbalī, al-Aḥsāʾ	Letters to ʿUthmān ibn Muʿammar	No later than Ṣafar 1163/ February 1750
Sulaymān ibn ʿAbd al-Wahhāb (d. 1208/1794)	Ḥanbalī, Ḥuraymilāʾ	Letter to Ḥasan ibn ʿĪdān (*al-Ṣawāʿiq al-ilāhiyya fī ʾl-radd ʿalā ʾl-Wahhābiyya*)	ca. 1165/1752f

(continued)

TABLE A.1. *(continued)*

Author	Legal Affiliation and Location	Title/Description	Completion Date
Muḥammad ibn Ismāʿīl al-Amīr al-Ṣanʿānī (d. 1182/1768)	Unaffiliated, Yemen	*Irshād dhawī ʾl-albāb ilā ḥaqīqat Ibn ʿAbd al-Wahhāb*	1170/1757
ʿAbdallāh Afandī al-Rāwī al-Baghdādī (d. 1215/1800f)	Shāfiʿī, Baghdad	Refutation of several works by Muḥammad ibn ʿAbd al-Wahhāb[d]	1194–1203/1780–89
ʿAbdallāh ibn Dāwūd al-Zubayrī (d. 1212/1797f)	Ḥanbalī, Zubayr	*al-Ṣawāʿiq wa ʾl-ruʿūd raddan ʿalā ʾl-shaqī ʿAbd al-ʿAzīz Suʿūd*	ca. 18 Ṣafar 1210/ September 3, 1795
Muḥammad ibn Muḥammad al-Shāfiʿī al-Qādirī	Shāfiʿī, Aleppo	*Radd ʿalā risālat ʿAbd al-ʿAzīz ibn Suʿūd*	1211/1796f
Muḥammad ibn Fayrūz (d. 1216/1801)	Ḥanbalī, al-Aḥsāʾ	*al-Risāla al-marḍiyya fī ʾl-radd ʿalā ʾl-Wahhābiyya*[e]	ca. 1213/1798
ʿAlawī ibn Aḥmad al-Ḥaddād (d. 1232/1817)	Shāfiʿī, Ḥaḍramawt	*Miṣbāḥ al-anām wa-jalāʾ al-ẓalām fī radd shubah al-bidʿī al-Najdī allatī aḍalla bihā ʾl-ʿawāmm*	ca. 12 Rajab 1216/ November 18, 1801

[a] Traboulsi, "Early Refutation," 391–415.

[b] Ibn Ghannām, *Tārīkh*, 1:344–47.

[c] Ibn Dāwūd, *al-Ṣawāʿiq wa ʾl-ruʿūd*, ff. 81b–82b, 113a, 142b–43a.

[d] Ibn Gharīb, *al-Tawḍīḥ*, passim.

[e] Āl Maḥmūd, *Taḥdhīr ahl al-īmān*, 33–46.

TABLE A.2. Undated early refutations of Wahhābism

Author	Legal Affiliation and Location	Title/Description	Time Frame
ʿAbdallāh ibn ʿAbd al-Laṭīf (d. 1181/1767f)	Shāfiʿī, al-Aḥsāʾ	*Tajrīd sayf al-jihād li-muddaʿī ʾl-ijtihād*[a]	al-ʿUyayna period
ʿAbdallāh ibn ʿAbd al-Laṭīf	Shāfiʿī, al-Aḥsāʾ	Response to a question from Kuwait[b]	al-ʿUyayna period (likely)
ʿAbd al-ʿAzīz al-Razīnī (d. 1179/1765)	Ḥanbalī, al-Aḥsāʾ	*Risāla* to the people of Uthayfiya[c]	al-ʿUyayna period (likely)
ʿAbdallāh ibn Fayrūz (d. 1175/1762)	Ḥanbalī, al-Aḥsāʾ	Unknown (fragment)[d]	al-ʿUyayna period (likely)
ʿĪsā ibn Muṭlaq (d. 1198/1783f)	Mālikī, al-Aḥsāʾ	Unknown (fragment)[e]	al-ʿUyayna period (likely)
Muḥammad ibn Aḥmad al-Saffārīnī (d. 1188/1774)	Ḥanbalī, Nābulus	*Fatwā* responding to a question about *ijtihād*[f]	al-ʿUyayna period (likely)
al-Saffārīnī	Ḥanbalī, Nābulus	*al-Ajwiba al-najdiyya ʿan al-asʾila al-Najdiyya*	al-Dirʿiyya period
ʿAbdallāh al-Muways (d. 1175/1761f)	Ḥanbalī, Sudayr	Letter to Ibn ʿAbd al-Wahhāb[g]	al-Dirʿiyya period
Muḥammad ibn Sulaymān al-Kurdī (d. 1194/1780)	Shāfiʿī, Mecca	*Fatwā* in response to questions about Ibn ʿAbd al-Wahhāb[h]	al-Dirʿiyya period
Ṣāliḥ ibn ʿAbdallāh al-Najdī	Unknown (likely Ḥanbalī), Medina	Unknown (fragment)[i]	al-Dirʿiyya period
Muḥammad ibn Fayrūz	Ḥanbalī, al-Aḥsāʾ	*al-Radd ʿalā man kaffara ahl al-Riyāḍ wa-man ḥawlahum min al-Muslimīn*	al-Dirʿiyya period (prior to the conquest of Riyadh in 1187/1773)

[a] Not extant; see the response to it by Ibn ʿAbd al-Wahhāb in Ibn Ghannām, *Tārīkh*, 1:246–62.

[b] al-Nuwayṣir, *al-Muʿāraḍa*, 218–22 (excerpts).

[c] al-Bassām, "Min asbāb al-muʿāraḍa," 62–63, 71–73.

[d] Ibn Dāwūd, *al-Ṣawāʿiq wa ʾl-ruʿūd*, ff. 196b–97b.

[e] al-Ḥaddād, *Miṣbāḥ al-anām*, 62–63.

[f] al-Saffārīnī, *Jawāb*.

[g] al-Bassām, "Min asbāb al-muʿāraḍa," 68.

[h] al-Ḥaddād, *Miṣbāḥ al-anām*, 82–86.

[i] Ibn Dāwūd, *al-Ṣawāʿiq wa ʾl-ruʿūd*, ff. 82b–83a.

GLOSSARY

ʿadāwa enmity, especially in the sense of hatred that is manifested or displayed
ahl al-ḥadīth traditionalist theologians averse to rationalist theology
***ʿālim* (pl. *ʿulamāʾ*)** religious scholar
ʿaqīda* or *iʿtiqād creed, theology (cf. *uṣūl al-dīn*)
Ashʿarism school of rationalist theology, generally associated with Shāfiʿī and Mālikī law schools
barāʾa dissociation; disavowal
***bidʿa* (pl. *bidaʿ*)** blameworthy innovation
bughḍ hatred
dār al-Islām domain of Islam; area where the laws of Islam predominate
dār al-kufr domain of unbelief; area where the laws of Islam do not predominate
daʿwa religious call; predicatory movement; preaching
duʿāʾ supplication; appealing to someone for help or assistance (cf. *istighātha*)
***faqīh* (pl. *fuqahāʾ*)** Muslim jurist
***fatwā* (pl. *fatāwā*)** nonbinding religious judgment issued in response to a query
fiqh Islamic jurisprudence
fitna strife; discord; also can be glossed as *shirk*
ḥadīth transmitted report of the Prophet Muḥammad's sayings or doings; the corpus of such reports
ḥākimiyya divine sovereignty; idea that God is sovereign in matters of legislation
hijra emigration, especially from *dār al-kufr* to *dār al-Islām*
***ḥukm* (pl. *aḥkām*)** legal judgment
ijtihād using independent reasoning to examine the foundational Islamic texts and arrive at legal judgments
īmān belief; faith
iqāmat al-ḥujja (lit. "presenting the proof") presenting the proof to one accused of committing *kufr* that the act or belief in question constitutes *kufr*
istighātha appealing to someone for help or assistance (cf. *duʿāʾ*)
iẓhār al-dīn manifesting the religion; ability to show hatred and enmity to unbelievers in a particular setting
Jahmiyya derogatory term for followers of rationalist theology, particularly as regards the metaphorical interpretation of God's attributes
jihād (lit. "struggle") religious war against unbelievers, either defensive (*jihād al-dafʿ*) or offensive (*jihād al-ṭalab*)

jinn ethereal beings imperceptible to human senses

***kāfir* (pl. *kuffār*)** unbeliever

kalām form of rationalist theology

Khārijism early Islamic sect associated with rebellion and excess in *takfīr*

kufr unbelief

kufr akbar major unbelief, i.e., unbelief that expels one from the faith

kufr aṣghar minor unbelief, i.e., unbelief that does not expel one from the faith

***madhhab* (pl. *madhāhib*)** school of law; doctrine, in the sense of a set of religious teachings

Māturīdism school of rationalist theology, generally associated with Ḥanafī law school

muftī one who issues *fatwās*

mujtahid practitioner of *ijtihād*

***mutakallim* (pl. *mutakallimūn*)** rationalist theologian; practitioner of *kalām*

***muṭawwaʿ* (pl. *maṭāwiʿ*)** local religious scholar or preacher in Najd

***mushrik* (pl. *mushrikūn*)** polytheist; associationist; practitioner of *shirk*

***qāḍī* (pl. *quḍāt*)** religious scholar who issues judgments and adjudicates disputes

qitāl fighting or warfare, usually in the sense of *jihād*

***risāla* (pl. *rasāʾil*)** letter; epistle

salaf ancestors, especially the pious ancestors (*al-salaf al-ṣāliḥ*), the first three generations of Muslims

Salafism purist movement in Sunnī Islam associated with Taymiyyan theology and named for *al-salaf al-ṣāliḥ*, whom Salafīs purport to emulate

shafāʿa intercession, especially intercession with God on behalf of another on the Day of Resurrection

Sharīʿa Islamic law

shirk (lit. "association") association of others with God; polytheism

shirk akbar major polytheism, i.e., polytheism that expels one from the faith

shirk aṣghar minor polytheism, i.e., polytheism that does not expel one from the faith

ṣifāt divine attributes, especially the anthropomorphic divine attributes

sīra prophetic biography; biography

sunna normative practice of the Prophet Muḥammad as embodied in the *ḥadīth*

ṭāghūt idol; that which is worshipped apart from God

takfīr declaring another to be a *kāfir*; excommunication

taqlīd adherence to the teachings of a *madhhab*; emulation; imitation

tawassul using the dead as a means to God, especially making requests of God by invoking the high station (*jāh*) of a saint or prophet

tawḥīd God's oneness; monotheism; monolatry

tawḥīd al-asmāʾ wa ʾl-ṣifāt oneness of God's attributes; Ibn Taymiyya's approach to the divine attributes

tawḥīd al-rubūbiyya oneness of God's lordship; affirmation that God alone is the creator of the universe

tawḥīd al-ulūhiyya oneness of God's divinity; exclusivity of worship; directing all forms of worship to God alone

al-ʿudhr bi ʾl-jahl (lit. "excusing on the basis of ignorance") excusing a person accused of committing *kufr* on grounds of the person's ignorance (i.e., ignorance that the act or belief in question constitutes *kufr*)

umma the global Muslim community

uṣūl al-dīn (lit. "the foundations of the religion") creed, theology (cf. *ʿaqīda*)

Wahhābism predicatory movement (*daʿwa*) named for Muḥammad ibn ʿAbd al-Wahhāb; the movement's doctrinal content

al-walāʾ wa'l-barāʾ association and dissociation; showing love to God and fellow Muslims and showing hatred and enmity to polytheism and polytheists

***walī* (pl. *awliyāʾ*)** saint; friend of God

zakāt obligatory alms

ziyāra (lit. "visitation") rites of visitation at graves of saints and prophets; cult of saints (cf. *duʿāʾ*; *istighātha*; *tawassul*)

BIBLIOGRAPHY

Abā Buṭayn, ʿAbdallāh ibn ʿAbd al-Raḥmān (d. 1282/1865). *al-Intiṣār li-ḥizb Allāh al-muwaḥḥidīn wa ʾl-radd ʿalā ʾl-mujādil ʿan al-mushrikīn*. Ed. al-Walīd ibn ʿAbd al-Raḥmān Āl Furayyān. Riyadh: Dār Ṭayba, 1409/1989.

———. *Taʾsīs al-taqdīs fī kashf talbīs Dāwūd ibn Jirjīs*. Ed. ʿAbd al-Salām ibn Barjas Āl ʿAbd al-Karīm. Beirut: Muʾassasat al-Risāla, 1422/2001.

ʿAbd al-Waḥīd. *Hidāyat ʿawāmm al-muʾminīn fī ʾl-radd ʿalā ḍalāl al-mubtadiʿīn*. Ms. Mecca, Maktabat al-Ḥaram al-Makkī, *ʿĀmm* 2283.

Abou El Fadl, Khaled. "Islamic Law and Muslim Minorities: The Juristic Discourse on Muslim Minorities from the Second/Eighth to the Eleventh/Seventeenth Centuries." *Islamic Law and Society* 1 (1994): 141–87.

Abū Dāwūd al-Sijistānī, Sulaymān ibn al-Ashʿath (d. 275/889). *Sunan Abī Dāwūd*, 4 vols. Ed. Muḥammad Muḥyī ʾl-Dīn ʿAbd al-Ḥamīd. Cairo: Maṭbaʿat Muṣṭafā Muḥammad, 1354/1935.

Abū ʾl-Khayr, ʿAbdallāh ibn Aḥmad Mirdād (d. 1343/1924f). *al-Mukhtaṣar min Kitāb nashr al-nawr wa ʾl-zahr fī tarājim afāḍil Makka min al-qarn al-ʿāshir ilā ʾl-qarn al-rābiʿ ʿashar*, 2nd ed. Jeddah: ʿĀlam al-Maʿrifa, 1406/1986.

Abu-Manneh, Butrus. "Salafiyya and the Rise of the Khālidiyya in Baghdad in the Early Nineteenth Century." *Die Welt des Islams* 43 (2003): 349–72.

Adang, Camilla, Hassan Ansari, Maribel Fierro, and Sabine Schmidtke, eds. *Accusations of Unbelief in Islam: A Diachronic Perspective on* Takfīr. Leiden: Brill, 2016.

Ahlwardt, Wilhelm. *Verzeichnis der arabischen Handschriften*, 10 vols. Hildesheim: George Olms Verlag, 1980.

ʿAjlān, ʿAlī ibn Muḥammad al-. *al-Shaykh al-ʿallāma ʿAbdallāh ibn ʿAbd al-Raḥmān Abā Buṭayn muftī ʾl-diyār al-Najdiyya: ḥayātuhu wa-āthāruhu wa-juhūduhu fī nashr ʿaqīdat al-salaf maʿa taḥqīq risālatihi ʾl-Radd ʿalā ʾl-Burda*. Riyadh: Dār al-Ṣumayʿī, 1422/2001.

Āl ʿAbd al-Laṭīf, ʿAbd al-ʿAzīz ibn Muḥammad. *Daʿāwā ʾl-munāwiʾīn li-daʿwat al-shaykh Muḥammad ibn ʿAbd al-Wahhāb*. Riyadh: Dār Ṭayba, 1409/1989.

———. "Mawqif ʿUthmān ibn Muʿammar min daʿwat al-shaykh Muḥammad ibn ʿAbd al-Wahhāb: murājaʿāt min khilāl risālatay Ibn Muʿammar." *al-Dāra* 32 (1427/2006): 189–200.

Āl ʿAbd al-Muḥsin, Ibrāhīm ibn ʿUbayd (d. 1425/2004). *Tadhkirat ulī ʾl-nuhā wa ʾl-ʿirfān bi-ayyām Allāh al-wāḥid al-rayyān*, 8 vols. Riyadh: Maktabat al-Rushd, 1428/2007.

Āl ʿAbd al-Qādir, Muḥammad ibn ʿAbdallāh (d. 1391/1971). *Tuḥfat al-mustafīd bi-tārīkh al-Aḥsāʾ fī ʾl-qadīm wa ʾl-jadīd*, 2 vols. Riyadh: al-Amāna al-ʿĀmma lil-Iḥtifāl bi-Murūr Miʾat ʿĀm ʿalā Taʾsīs al-Mamlaka, 1419/1999.

Albānī, Muḥammad Nāṣir al-Dīn al- (d. 1419/1999). *Silsilat al-aḥādīth al-ṣaḥīḥa wa-shayʾ min fiqhihā wa-fawāʾidihā*, 7 vols. Riyadh: Maktabat al-Maʿārif, 1415–22/1995–2002.

Āl Bassām, ʿAbdallāh ibn ʿAbd al-Raḥmān (d. 1423/2003), ed. *Khizānat al-tawārīkh al-Najdiyya*, 10 vols. N.p.: n.p., 1419/1998f.

———. *ʿUlamāʾ Najd khilāl thamāniyat qurūn*, 6 vols. Riyadh: Dār al-ʿĀṣima, 1419/1998f.

Āl Bunayyān, Ṣāliḥ ibn Sālim (d. 1330/1912). *Radd ʿalā ʾbn ʿAmr*. Ḥāʾil: Maktabat al-Shaykh Ṣāliḥ ibn Sālim Āl Bunayyān.

Āl Furayyān, al-Walīd ibn ʿAbd al-Raḥmān. *al-Wirāqa fī minṭaqat Najd*. Riyadh: Dārat al-Malik ʿAbd al-ʿAzīz, 1433/2011f.

Algar, Hamid. *Wahhabism: A Critical Essay*. Oneonta, NY: Islamic Publications International, 2002.

Āl Ḥamad, ʿAbd al-ʿAzīz ibn ʿAbdallāh al-Zīr, ed. *Ijmāʿ ahl al-sunna al-nabawiyya ʿalā takfīr al-muʿaṭṭila al-Jahmiyya*. Riyadh: Dār al-ʿĀṣima, 1415/1994f.

Āl Maḥmūd, ʿAbdallāh ibn Saʿd (d. ca. 1340/1921f). *Taḥdhīr ahl al-īmān ʿammā taḍammanathu risālat Ibn Fayrūz min al-buhtān*. Ed. Sulaymān ibn Ṣāliḥ al-Kharāshī. Kuwait: Dār al-Khizāna, 1438/2017.

Āl Musallam, ʿAbdallāh Zayd. "Min ʿulamāʾ wa-quḍāt Ḥawṭat Banī Tamīm waʾl-Ḥarīq." *al-Jazīra*, February 18, 2001.

Āl al-Shaykh, ʿAbdallāh ibn ʿAbd al-Laṭīf (d. 1339/1920). *Risāla ilā man yarāhu min al-ikhwān*. Ms. Riyadh, Maktabat al-Malik Salmān, 343, f. 1a–b.

Āl al-Shaykh, ʿAbdallāh ibn Muḥammad (d. 1242/1826f). *Mukhtaṣar sīrat al-rasūl*, 2nd ed. Cairo: al-Maṭbaʿa al-Salafiyya, 1396/1976.

———. *Risālat ʿAbdallāh ibn Muḥammad ibn ʿAbd al-Wahhāb*. Ms. Mecca, Maktabat al-Ḥaram al-Sharīf, *ʿAqāʾid* 1349.

———. *Risālat al-shaykh ʿAbdallāh Āl al-Shaykh ʿindamā dakhalū Makka*. Ms. London, British Library, Or. 6631.

Āl al-Shaykh, ʿAbd al-Laṭīf ibn ʿAbd al-Raḥmān (d. 1293/1876). *Dalāʾil al-rusūkh fī ʾl-radd ʿalā ʾl-manfūkh*. Cairo: Maṭbaʿat al-Muqtaṭaf waʾl-Laṭāʾif al-Gharrāʾ, 1305/1887f.

———. *Minhāj al-taʾsīs wa ʾl-taqdīs fī kashf shubuhāt Dāwūd ibn Jirjīs*, 2nd ed. Ed. Ismāʿīl ibn Saʿd ibn ʿAtīq. Riyadh: Dār al-Hidāya, 1407/1987.

———. *Miṣbāḥ al-ẓalām fī ʾl-radd ʿalā man kadhaba ʿalā ʾl-shaykh al-imām*. Ed. ʿAbd al-ʿAzīz ibn ʿAbdallāh al-Zīr Āl Ḥamad. Riyadh: Dār al-ʿĀṣima, 1434/2013.

———. *Tuḥfat al-ṭālib wa ʾl-jalīs fī kashf shubah Dāwūd ibn Jirjīs*, 2nd ed. Ed. ʿAbd al-Salām ibn Barjas Āl ʿAbd al-Karīm. Riyadh: Dār al-ʿĀṣima, 1410/1989f.

———. *ʿUyūn al-rasāʾil wa ʾl-ajwiba ʿalā ʾl-masāʾil*, 2 vols. Ed. Ḥusayn Muḥammad Bawā Abū ʿAbd al-Raḥīm. Riyadh: Maktabat al-Rushd, 1420/2000.

Āl al-Shaykh, ʿAbd al-Muḥsin ibn ʿAbd al-ʿAzīz. *al-Shaykh ʿAbdallāh ibn ʿAbd al-Laṭīf ibn ʿAbd al-Raḥmān Āl al-Shaykh muftī ʾl-diyār al-Najdiyya: sīratuhu wa-rasāʾiluhu*. Riyadh: n.p., 1433/2012.

———. *al-Shaykh al-imām ʿAbd al-Laṭīf ibn ʿAbd al-Raḥmān ibn Ḥasan Āl al-Shaykh: sīratuhu wa-rasāʾiluhu*. Riyadh: n.p., 1434/2013.

———. *al-Shaykh Muḥammad ibn ʿAbd al-Laṭīf ibn ʿAbd al-Raḥmān Āl al-Shaykh muftī Najd wa-qāḍī quḍāt al-Washm wa-ʿAsīr wa ʾl-Riyāḍ: sīratuhu wa-rasāʾiluhu*. Riyadh: n.p., 1432/2011.

Āl al-Shaykh, ʿAbd al-Raḥmān ibn ʿAbd al-Laṭīf (d. 1406/1986). *Mashāhīr ʿulamāʾ Najd wa-ghayrihim*, 2nd ed. Riyadh: Dār al-Yamāma, 1394/1974f.

Āl al-Shaykh, ʿAbd al-Raḥmān ibn Ḥasan (d. 1285/1869). *Fatḥ al-majīd li-sharḥ Kitāb al-tawḥīd*, rev. ed. Ed. al-Walīd ibn ʿAbd al-Raḥmān Āl Furayyān. Mecca: Dār ʿĀlam al-Fawāʾid, 1436/2014f.

———. *Kashf mā alqāhu Iblīs min al-bahraj wa ʾl-talbīs ʿalā qalb Dāwūd ibn Jirjīs*. Ed. ʿAbd al-ʿAzīz ibn ʿAbdallāh al-Zīr Āl Ḥamad. Riyadh: Dār al-ʿĀṣima, 1415/1994f.

———. *al-Maqāmāt*. Ed. ʿAbdallāh ibn Muḥammad al-Muṭawwaʿ. Riyadh: Dārat al-Malik ʿAbd al-ʿAzīz, 1426/2005.

———. *al-Maṭlab al-ḥamīd fī bayān maqāṣid al-tawḥīd*. Ed. Ismāʿīl ibn Saʿd ibn ʿAtīq. Riyadh: Dār al-Hidāya, 1411/1991.

———. *al-Mawrid al-ʿadhb al-zulāl*. Ms. Riyadh, Maktabat al-Malik Fahd al-Waṭaniyya, 568.

Āl al-Shaykh, Isḥāq ibn ʿAbd al-Raḥmān (d. 1319/1901). *al-Ajwiba al-samʿiyyāt li-ḥall al-asʾila al-Rawwāfiyyāt*. Ed. ʿĀdil bin Bādī al-Murshidī. Riyadh: Dār Aṭlas al-Khaḍrāʾ, 1425/2005.

———. *Ḥukm takfīr al-muʿayyan wa ʾl-farq bayna qiyām al-ḥujja wa-fahm al-ḥujja*. Ed. Ismāʿīl ibn Saʿd ibn ʿAtīq. Riyadh: Dār Ṭayba, 1409/1988.

———. *Īḍāḥ al-maḥajja wa ʾl-sabīl wa-iqāmat al-ḥujja wa ʾl-dalīl ʿalā man ajāza ʾl-iqāma bayna ahl al-shirk wa ʾl-taʿṭīl*. Ed. Ismāʿīl ibn Saʿd ibn ʿAtīq. Riyadh: Maktabat al-Hidāya, 1415/1994f.

———. *Sulūk al-ṭarīq al-aḥmad*. Ed. Ismāʿīl ibn Saʿd ibn ʿAtīq. Riyadh: Dār al-Hidāya, 1413/1991.

Āl al-Shaykh, Muḥammad ibn Ibrāhīm (d. 1389/1969). *Fatāwā wa-rasāʾil samāḥat al-shaykh Muḥammad ibn Ibrāhīm ibn ʿAbd al-Laṭīf Āl al-Shaykh*, 13 vols. Ed. Muḥammad ibn ʿAbd al-Raḥmān ibn Qāsim. Mecca: Maṭbaʿat al-Ḥukūma, 1399–1405/1979–84.

Āl al-Shaykh, Sulaymān ibn ʿAbdallāh (d. 1233/1818). *Majmūʿ al-rasāʾil*. Ed. al-Walīd ibn ʿAbd al-Raḥmān Āl Furayyān. Mecca: Dār ʿĀlam al-Fawāʾid, 1420/1999f.

———. *Taysīr al-ʿazīz al-ḥamīd fī sharḥ Kitāb al-tawḥīd*, 2 vols. Ed. Usāma ibn ʿAṭāyā al-ʿUtaybī. Riyadh: Dār al-Ṣumayʿī, 1428/2007.

Āl Sulaymān, Zayd ibn Muḥammad (d. 1307/1889). *Fatḥ al-mannān fī naqḍ shubah al-ḍāll Daḥlān*. Ed. ʿAbdallāh ibn Zayd Āl Musallam. Riyadh: Dār al-Tawḥīd, 1426/2005f.

Ālūsī, Maḥmūd Shukrī ibn ʿAbdallāh -al (d. 1342/1924). *Fatḥ al-mannān tatimmat Minhāj al-taʾsīs radd Ṣulḥ al-ikhwān*. Ed. ʿUmar ibn Aḥmad Āl ʿAbbās. Riyadh: Dār al-Tawḥīd, 1430/2009.

Ālūsī, Nuʿmān ibn Maḥmūd -al (d. 1317/1899). *Shaqāʾiq al-Nuʿmān fī shaqāshiq Ibn Sulaymān*. Ms. Princeton, Princeton University, Garrett 2795, ff. 2a–27a.

Amin, Camron Michael, Benjamin C. Fortna, and Elizabeth B. Frierson, eds. *The Modern Middle East: A Sourcebook for History*. Oxford: Oxford University Press, 2006.

Amīr, Muḥammad ibn Ismāʿīl al-Ṣanʿānī al- (d. 1182/1769). *Dīwān al-Amīr al-Ṣanʿānī*. Cairo: Maṭbaʿat al-Madanī, 1384/1964.

———. *Irshād dhawī ʾl-albāb ilā ḥaqīqat aqwāl Ibn ʿAbd al-Wahhāb*. Ed. ʿAbd al-Karīm Aḥmad Jadbān. N.p.: Majālis Āl Muḥammad, 2008.

———. *Taṭhīr al-iʿtiqād ʿan adrān al-ilḥād*. Ed. Muḥammad ibn Jibrīl al-Shaḥrī. Dammāj, Yemen: Maktabat al-Imām al-Wādiʿī, 1430/2009.

ʿAmrawī, ʿUmar ibn Gharāma al-. *Qalāʾid al-jumān fī bayān sīrat Āl Suḥmān*. Riyadh: n.p., 1408/1987f.

Arslān, Shakīb (d. 1366/1946). "La disparition d'une des plus grandes figures de l'Islam Rachid Ridha." *La Nation arabe* 5 (1935): 447–50.

ʿAṣrī, Sayf ibn ʿAlī al-. *al-Qawl al-tamām bi-ithbāt al-tafwīḍ madhhaban lil-salaf al-kirām*. Beirut: Dār al-Bashāʾir al-Islāmiyya, 2009.

ʿAssāfī, Muḥammad ibn Ḥamad al- (d. 1394/1974). *Tarājim al-fuḍalāʾ*. Ms. Riyadh, Jāmiʿat al-Imām Muḥammad ibn Suʿūd al-Islāmiyya, 9164.

Assmann, Jan. *Moses the Egyptian: The Memory of Egypt in Western Monotheism*. Cambridge, MA: Harvard University Press, 1997.

ʿAtīqī, Ṣāliḥ ibn Sayf al- (d. 1223/1808). *Tarjamat Muḥammad ibn Fayrūz*. Ms. Princeton, Princeton University, Garrett 651Y, ff. 75a–76b.

———. *Tuwuffiya rukn al-ḍalāl*. Ms. Princeton University, Garrett 651Y, f. 68a.

al-Aṭlas al-tārīkhī lil-Mamlaka al-ʿArabiyya al-Suʿūdiyya, 2nd ed. Riyadh: Dārat al-Malik ʿAbd al-ʿAzīz, 1421/2000.

ʿAzzāwī, ʿAbbās al- (d. 1391/1971). *Tārīkh al-ʿIrāq bayna ʾḥtilālayn*, 6 vols. Baghdad: Maṭbaʿat Baghdād, 1353–73/1935–54.

Bābānī, Ismāʿīl ibn Muḥammad al- (d. 1399/1920f). *Īḍāḥ al-maknūn fī ʾl-dhayl ʿalā Kashf al-ẓunūn*, 4 vols. Beirut: Dār Iḥyāʾ al-Turāth al-ʿArabī, n.d.

Bābṣayl, Muḥammad Saʿīd ibn Muḥammad (d. 1330/1912). *al-Qawl al-mujdī fī ʾl-radd ʿalā ʿAbdallāh ibn ʿAbd al-Raḥmān al-Sindī*. Jakarta: n.p., 1309/1892.

"Bābṣayl muftī ʾl-Shāfiʿiyya wa-imām maqāmihā biʾl-ḥaram al-Makkī." *Makka al-Mukarrama*, February 5, 2015.

Badr, ʿAbd al-Razzāq ibn ʿAbd al-Muḥsin al-. *al-Qawl al-sadīd fī radd man ankara taqsīm al-tawḥīd*. Riyadh: Dār Ibn al-Qayyim, 1423/2003.

Baghdādī, ʿAbd al-Wahhāb al-Mūsawī al-. *Nubdha laṭīfa fī tarjamat shaykh al-Islām . . . Dāwūd al-Baghdādī*. Bombay: Maṭbaʿat Nukhbat al-Akhbār, 1305/1887.

Baghdādī, Muḥammad Saʿīd al-Rāwī al- (d. 1354/1936). *Tārīkh al-usar al-ʿilmiyya fī Baghdād*. Ed. ʿImād ʿAbd al-Salām Raʾūf. Baghdad: Dār al-Shuʾūn al-Thaqāfiyya al-ʿĀmma, 1997.

Baʿlī, ʿAlāʾ al-Dīn ʿAlī ibn Muḥammad al- (d. 803/1401). *al-Akhbār al-ʿilmiyya min al-ikhtiyārāt al-fiqhiyya li-shaykh al-Islām Ibn Taymiyya*. Ed. Aḥmad ibn Muḥammad al-Khalīl. Riyadh: Dār al-ʿĀṣima, 1418/1998.

Bashear, Suliman. "The Mission of Diḥya al-Kalbī and the Situation in Syria." *Der Islam* 74 (1997): 64–91.

Bassām, ʿAbdallāh ibn Muḥammad al- (d. 1346/1927). *Tuḥfat al-mushtāq fī akhbār Najd wa ʾl-Ḥijāz wa ʾl-ʿIrāq*. Ed. Ibrāhīm al-Khālidī. Kuwait: Sharikat al-Mukhtalif, 2000.

Bassām, Aḥmad ibn ʿAbd al-ʿAzīz al-. "Min asbāb al-muʿāraḍa al-maḥalliyya li-daʿwat al-shaykh Muḥammad ibn ʿAbd al-Wahhāb fī ʿahd al-dawla al-Suʿūdiyya al-ūlā." *al-Dirʿiyya* 14 (1422/2001): 23–77.

———. "Min juhūd al-malik ʿAbd al-ʿAzīz fī tawḥīd kalimat al-ʿulamāʾ wa-qiyādatihim al-dīniyya (Burayda namūdhajan)." *al-ʿUlūm al-insāniyya wa ʾl-ijtimāʿiyya* 6 (1429/2008): 158–207.

Bonacina, Giovanni. *The Wahhabis Seen Through European Eyes (1772–1830): Deists and Puritans of Islam*. Leiden: Brill, 2015.

Bonnefoy, Laurent. Review of *Wahhabi Islam: From Revival and Reform to Global Jihad. The Journal of Islamic Studies* 17 (2006): 371–72.

Bori, Caterina. "Ibn Taymiyya (14th to 17th Century): Transregional Spaces of Reading and Reception." *The Muslim World* 108 (2018): 87–123.

———. "Ibn Taymiyya *wa-Jamā'atu-hu*: Authority, Conflict and Consensus in Ibn Taymiyya's Circle." In *Ibn Taymiyya and His Times*, ed. Yossef Rapoport and Shahab Ahmed, 23–52. Karachi: Oxford University Press, 2010.

Bori, Caterina, and Livnat Holtzman. "A Scholar in the Shadow." *Oriente Moderno*, Nuova Serie, Anno 90 (2010): 11–42.

———, eds. "A Scholar in the Shadow: Essays in the Legal and Theological Thought of Ibn Qayyim al-Ǧawziyyah." Theme issue, *Oriente Moderno*, Nuova Serie, Anno 90 (2010).

Brockelmann, Carl. *Geschichte der arabischen Litteratur*, 2nd ed., 2 vols., 3 supplements. Leiden: Brill, 1996.

Browne, Edward G. *A Supplementary Hand-List of the Muḥammadan Manuscripts in the Libraries of the University and Colleges of Cambridge*. Cambridge: Cambridge University Press, 1922.

Bukhārī, Muḥammad ibn Ismāʿīl al- (d. 256/870). *Ṣaḥīḥ al-Bukhārī*. Ed. Abū Ṣuhayb al-Karmī. Riyadh: Bayt al-Afkār al-Dawliyya, 1419/1998.

Bunzel, Cole. *The Kingdom and the Caliphate: Duel of the Islamic States*. Washington, DC: Carnegie Endowment for International Peace, February 2016.

Burckhardt, Johann Ludwig. *Notes on the Bedouins and Wahábys*, 2 vols. London: Henry Colburn and Richard Bentley, 1830.

———. *Travels in Arabia*, 2 vols. London: Henry Colburn, 1829.

Calder, Norman. "Al-Nawawī's Typology of *Muftīs* and Its Significance for a General Theory of Islamic Law." *Islamic Law and Society* 3 (1996): 137–64.

Collingwood, R. G. *The Idea of History*, rev. ed. Oxford: Oxford University Press, 1994.

Commins, David. "From Wahhabi to Salafi." In *Saudi Arabia in Transition: Insights on Social, Political, Economic and Religious Change*, ed. Bernard Haykel, Thomas Hegghammer, and Stéphane Lacroix, 151–66. Cambridge: Cambridge University Press, 2015.

———. *Islamic Reform: Politics and Social Change in Late Ottoman Syria*. New York: Oxford University Press, 1990.

———. "Traditional Anti-Wahhabi Hanbalism in Nineteenth-Century Arabia." In *Ottoman Reform and Muslim Regeneration: Studies in Honour of Butrus Abu-Manneh*, ed. Itzchak Weismann and Fruma Zachs, 81–96. London: I. B. Tauris, 2005.

———. *The Wahhabi Mission and Saudi Arabia*. London: I. B. Tauris, 2006.

———. "Why Unayza? Ulema Dissidents and Nonconformists in the Second Saudi State." Unpublished paper, n.d.

Cook, Michael. *Ancient Religions, Modern Politics: The Islamic Case in Comparative Perspective*. Princeton: Princeton University Press, 2014.

———. *Commanding Right and Forbidding Wrong in Islamic Thought*. Cambridge: Cambridge University Press, 2000.

———. "The Expansion of the First Saudi State: The Case of Washm." In *The Islamic World from Classical to Modern Times*, ed. C. E. Bosworth, Charles Issawi, Roger Savory, and A. L. Udovich, 661–99. Princeton: The Darwin Press, Inc., 1989.

———. "The Historians of Pre-Wahhābī Najd." *Studia Islamica* 76 (1992): 163–76.

———. "On the Origins of Wahhābism." *Journal of the Royal Asiatic Society*, Series 3, 2 (1992): 191–202.

———. "The Provenance of the *Lam' al-shihāb fī sīrat Muḥammad ibn 'Abd al-Wahhāb*." *Journal of Turkish Studies* 10 (1986): 79–86.

———. "Tales of Arabian Might." *Times Literary Supplement*, April 7, 2006.

———. "Written and Oral Aspects of an Early Wahhābī Epistle." *Bulletin of the School of Oriental and African Studies* 78 (2015): 161–78.

Crawford, Michael J. "Civil War, Foreign Intervention, and the Question of Political Legitimacy: A Nineteenth-Century Saʿūdī Qāḍī's Dilemma." *International Journal of Middle East Studies* 14 (1982): 227–48.

———. "The *Daʿwa* of Ibn ʿAbd al-Wahhāb Before the Āl Saʿūd." *Journal of Arabian Studies* 1 (2011): 147–61.

———. *Ibn 'Abd al-Wahhab*. London: Oneworld, 2014.

Crawford, Michael J., and William Facey. "ʿAbd Allāh Al Saʿūd and Muḥammad ʿAlī Pasha: The Theatre of Victory, the Prophet's Treasures, and the Visiting Whig, Cairo 1818." *Journal of Arabian Studies* 7 (2017): 44–62.

Crone, Patricia. *God's Rule: Government and Islam*. New York: Columbia University Press, 2004.

———. "'No Compulsion in Religion': Q. 2:256 in Mediaeval and Modern Interpretation." In *Le Shi'isme Imamite quarante ans après: Hommage à Etan Kohlberg*, ed. Mohammad Ali Amir-Moezzi, Meir M. Bar-Asher, and Simon Hopkins, 131–78. Turnhout, Belgium: Brepols, 2009.

Cureton, William, and Charles Rieu. *Catalogus codicum manuscriptorum orientalium qui in Museo Britannico asservantur, pars secunda*. London: Impensis Curatorum Musei Britannici, 1846–71.

Daḥlān, Aḥmad ibn Zaynī (d. 1304/1886). *al-Durar al-saniyya fī ʾl-radd ʿalā ʾl-Wahhābiyya*. Cairo: al-Maṭbaʿa al-Bahiyya, 1299/1882.

———. *Khulāṣat al-kalām fī bayān umarāʾ al-balad al-ḥarām*. Cairo: al-Maṭbaʿa al-Khayriyya, 1305/1887f.

Dakhil, Khalid S. Al-. "Social Origins of the Wahhabi Movement." Ph.D. dissertation, University of California, Los Angeles, 1998.

Dallal, Ahmad S. *Islam Without Europe: Traditions of Reform in Eighteenth-Century Islamic Thought*. Chapel Hill: University of North Carolina Press, 2018.

———. "The Origins and Early Development of Islamic Reform." In *The New Cambridge History of Islam*, vol. 6, ed. Michael Cook, 107–47. Cambridge: Cambridge University Press, 2010.

———. "The Origins and Objectives of Islamic Revivalist Thought, 1750–1850." *Journal of the American Oriental Society* 113 (1993): 341–59.

DeLong-Bas, Natana J. *Wahhabi Islam: From Revival and Reform to Global Jihad*. Oxford: Oxford University Press, 2004.

Determann, Jörg Matthias. *Historiography in Saudi Arabia: Globalization and the State in the Middle East*. London: I. B. Tauris, 2014.

Dhahabī, Muḥammad ibn Aḥmad al- (d. 673/1274). *Bayān zaghl al-ʿilm*. Ed. Muḥammad Abū ʿAbdallāh Aḥmad. Medina: Dār al-Maymana, 1434/2013.

Diffelen, Roelof Willem van. *De leer der Wahhabieten*. Leiden: Brill, 1927.

Dīrāniyya, Mujāhid. "Sīrat al-shaykh ʿAlī al-Ṭanṭāwī." *al-Adab al-Islāmī* 9 (1423/2002): 132–38.

Doughty, Charles Montagu. *Travels in Arabia Deserta*, new ed., 2 vols. New York: Random House, 1937.

Ḍubayb, Aḥmad ibn Muḥammad al-. "Ḥarakat iḥyāʾ al-turāth baʿd tawḥīd al-jazīra." *al-Dāra* 1 (1395/1975): 42–60.

al-Durar al-saniyya (see Ibn Qāsim, ʿAbd al-Raḥmān).

Ebied, R. Y., and M.J.L. Young. "An Unpublished Refutation of the Doctrines of the Wahhābis." *Rivista degli studi orientali* 50 (September 1976): 377–97.

EI (see *Encyclopaedia of Islam*).

Eichner, Heidrun. "Handbooks in the Tradition of Later Eastern Ashʿarism." In *The Oxford Handbook of Islamic Theology*, ed. Sabine Schmidtke, 494–514. Oxford: Oxford University Press, 2016.

Ellis, A. G., and Edward Edwards. *A Descriptive List of the Arabic Manuscripts Acquired by the Trustees of the British Museum Since 1894*. London: William Clowes and Sons, 1912.

El-Rouayheb, Khaled. "From Ibn Ḥajar al-Haytamī (d. 1566) to Khayr al-Dīn al-Ālūsī (d. 1899): Changing Views of Ibn Taymiyya Among Non-Ḥanbalī Sunni Scholars." In *Ibn Taymiyya and His Times*, ed. Yossef Rapoport and Shahab Ahmed, 269–318. Karachi: Oxford University Press, 2010.

———. *Islamic Intellectual History in the Seventeenth Century: Scholarly Currents in the Ottoman Empire and the Maghreb*. Cambridge: Cambridge University Press, 2015.

El-Tobgui, Carl Sharif. *Ibn Taymiyya on Reason and Revelation: A Study of Darʾ al-taʿāruḍ al-ʿaql wa-l-naql*. Leiden: Brill, 2020.

Encyclopaedia of Islam, 1st ed. [abbreviated *EI*^{1}], 4 vols., 1 supp. Leiden: Brill, 1908–38.

Encyclopaedia of Islam, 2nd ed. [abbreviated *EI*^{2}], 12 vols. Leiden: Brill, 1960–2004.

Encyclopaedia of Islam, 3rd ed. [abbreviated *EI*^{3}], multiple vols. Leiden: Brill, 2007–.

Ende, Werner. "Religion, Politik und Literatur in Saudi-Arabien: Der geistesgeschichtliche Hintergrund der heutigen religiösen und kulturpolitischen Situation." *Orient* 22 (1981): 377–90 (I); 23 (1982): 21–35 (II), 378–93 (III), 524–39 (IV).

Ennāmi, ʿAmr K. *Studies in Ibāḍism*. Benghazi: University of Libya, 1972.

Fadel, Mohammad. "The Social Logic of *Taqlīd* and the Rise of the *Mukhtaṣar*." *Islamic Law and Society* 3 (1996): 193–233.

Fahad, Abdulaziz H. Al-. "From Exclusivism to Accommodation: Doctrinal and Legal Evolution of Wahhabism." *New York University Law Review* 79 (2004): 485–519.

———. "The ʿImama vs. the ʿIqal: Hadari-Bedouin Conflict and the Formation of the Saudi State." In *Counter-narratives: History, Contemporary Society, and Politics in Saudi Arabia and Yemen*, ed. Madawi Al-Rasheed and Robert Vitalis, 35–75. New York: Palgrave Macmillan, 2004.

———. "Raiders and Traders: A Poet's Lament on the End of the Bedouin Heroic Age." In *Saudi Arabia in Transition: Insights on Social, Political, Economic and Religious Change*, ed. Bernard Haykel, Thomas Hegghammer, and Stéphane Lacroix, 231–62. Cambridge: Cambridge University Press, 2015.

Fākhirī, Muḥammad ibn ʿUmar al- (d. 1277/1860). *Tārīkh al-Fākhirī*. Ed. ʿAbdallāh ibn Yūsuf al-Shibl. Riyadh: al-Amāna al-ʿĀmma lil-Iḥtifāl bi-Murūr Miʾat ʿĀm ʿalā Taʾsīs al-Mamlaka, 1419/1999.

Fandy, Mamoun. *Saudi Arabia and the Politics of Dissent*. New York: St. Martin's Press, 1999.

Fāyiz, ʿAbd al-ʿAzīz ibn Muḥammad al-. "Min nawādir al-wathāʾiq fī baldat al-Dākhila bi-iqlīm Sudayr." *al-Jazīra*, September 21, 2014.

Fihris al-Khizāna al-Taymūriyya, 4 vols. Cairo: Maṭbaʿat Dār al-Kutub al-Miṣriyya, 1367–69/1948–50.

Fihrist-i kutubi-i ʿArabī va-Fārsī va-Ūrdū makhzūneh-yi Kutubkhāneh-yi Āṣafiyyeh-yi Sarkār-i ʿĀlī, 4 vols. Hyderabad: Dār al-Ṭabʿ-i Sarkār-i ʿĀlī, 1333–55/1914f–36f.

Firestone, Reuven. "Disparity and Resolution in the Qurʾānic Teachings on War: A Reevaluation of a Traditional Problem." *Journal of Near Eastern Studies* 56 (1997): 1–19.

Firro, Tarik K. "The Political Context of Early Wahhabi Discourse of *Takfir*." *Middle Eastern Studies* 49 (2013): 770–89.

Friedmann, Yohanan. *Tolerance and Coercion in Islam: Interfaith Relations in the Muslim Tradition*. Cambridge: Cambridge University Press, 2003.

Fulton, Alexander S., and A. G. Ellis. *Supplementary Catalogue of Arabic Printed Books in the British Museum*. London: Oxford University Press, 1926.

Gaborieau, Marc. *Le Mahdi incompris: Sayyid Ahmad Barelwî (1786–1831) et le millénarisme en Inde*. Paris: CNRS Éditions, 2010.

Ghazzālī, Abū Ḥāmid al- (d. 505/1111). *Iḥyāʾ ʿulūm al-dīn*, 4 vols. Beirut: Dār al-Maʿrifa, 1402/1982.

Ghazzī, Kamāl al-Dīn Muḥammad al- (d. 1214/1799). *al-Naʿt al-akmal li-aṣḥāb al-imām Aḥmad ibn Ḥanbal*. Ed. Muḥammad Muṭīʿ al-Ḥāfiẓ and Nizār al-Abāẓa. Damascus: Dār al-Fikr, 1402/1982.

Ghunaym, Khālid ʿAbd al-ʿAzīz al-. *al-Mujaddid al-thānī: ʿAbd al-Raḥmān ibn Ḥasan Āl al-Shaykh wa-ṭarīqatuhu fī taqrīr al-ʿaqīda*. Riyadh: Maktabat al-Rushd, 1418/1997.

Ghunaym, Sulṭān ibn Rāshid al-. *Juhūd al-shaykh Isḥāq ibn ʿAbd al-Raḥmān ibn Ḥasan ibn Muḥammad ibn ʿAbd al-Wahhāb fī taqrīr ʿaqīdat al-salaf*. Riyadh: n.p., 1437/2016.

Gimaret, Daniel. "Théories de l'acte humain dans l'école ḥanbalite." *Bulletin d'études orientales* 29 (1977): 157–78.

Goldziher, Ignaz. "The Cult of Saints in Islam." *The Moslem World* 1 (1911): 302–12.

———. *Introduction to Islamic Theology and Law*. Trans. Andras Hamori and Ruth Hamori. Princeton: Princeton University Press, 1981.

Green, Arnold H. "A Tunisian Reply to a Wahhabi Proclamation: Texts and Contexts." In *In Quest of an Islamic Humanism: Arabic and Islamic Studies in Memory of Mohamed al-Nowaihi*, ed. Arnold H. Green, 155–77. Cairo: The American University in Cairo Press, 1984.

Guillaume, Andrew. *The Life of Muhammad: A Translation of [Ibn] Isḥāq's "Sīrat Rasūl Allāh."* London: Oxford University Press, 1955.

Habib, John S. *Ibn Sa'ud's Warriors of Islam: The Ikhwan of Najd and Their Role in the Creation of the Sa'udi Kingdom, 1910–1930*. Leiden: Brill, 1978.

Ḥaddād, ʿAlawī ibn Aḥmad al- (d. 1232/1817). *Miṣbāḥ al-anām wa-jalāʾ al-ẓalām fī radd shubah al-bidʿī al-Najdī allatī aḍalla bihā ʾl-ʿawāmm*. Cairo: al-Maṭbaʿa al-ʿĀmira al-Sharafiyya, 1325/1907f.

Ḥajjāwī, Mūsā ibn Aḥmad al- (d. 968/1560). *al-Iqnāʿ li-ṭālib al-intifāʿ*, 4 vols. Ed. ʿAbdallāh ibn ʿAbd al-Muḥsin al-Turkī. Riyadh: al-Amāna al-ʿĀmma lil-Iḥtifāl bi-Murūr Miʾat ʿĀm ʿalā Taʾsīs al-Mamlaka, 1423/2002.

Hallaq, Wael B. "Ifta' and Ijtihad in Sunni Legal Theory: A Developmental Account." In *Islamic Legal Interpretation: Muftis and Their Fatwas*, ed. Muhammad Khalid Masud, Brinkley Messick, and David S. Powers, 33–43. Cambridge, MA: Harvard University Press, 1996.

Hartmann, Richard. "Die Wahhābiten." *Zeitschrift der Deutschen Morgenländischen Gesellschaft* 78 (1924): 176–213.

Ḥasanī, ʿAbd al-Ḥayy ibn Fakhr al-Dīn al- (d. 1341/1923). *al-Iʿlām bi-man fī tārīkh al-Hind min al-aʿlām al-musammā bi-Nuzhat al-khawāṭir wa-bahjat al-masāmiʿ waʾl-nawāẓir*, 8 vols. Beirut: Dār Ibn Ḥazm, 1420/1999.

Haykel, Bernard. "On the Nature of Salafi Thought and Action." In *Global Salafism: Islam's New Religious Movement*, ed. Roel Meijer, 33–57. New York: Columbia University Press, 2009.

———. *Revival and Reform in Islam: The Legacy of Muhammad al-Shawkānī*. Cambridge: Cambridge University Press, 2003.

Heck, Paul L. "An Early Response to Wahhabism from Morocco: The Politics of Intercession." *Studia Islamica* 107 (2002): 235–54.

Hegghammer, Thomas, and Stéphane Lacroix. "Rejectionist Islamism in Saudi Arabia: The Story of Juhayman al-ʿUtaybi Revisited." *International Journal of Middle East Studies* 39 (2007): 103–22.

Hindī, ʿAlī ibn Muḥammad al- (d. 1419/1998). *Zahr al-khamāʾil fī tarājim ʿulamāʾ Ḥāʾil*. Ed. Sulṭān ibn Hulayyal al-Mismār. Ḥāʾil: n.p., 1346/2014f.

Hodgson, Marshall G. S. *The Venture of Islam: Conscience and History in a World Civilization*, 3 vols. Chicago: University of Chicago Press, 1974.

Holtzman, Livnat. "Accused of Anthropomorphism: Ibn Taymiyya's *Miḥan* as Reflected in Ibn Qayyim al-Jawziyya's *al-Kāfiya al-Shāfiya*." *The Muslim World* 106 (2016): 561–87.

———. *Anthropomorphism in Islam: The Challenge of Traditionalism (700–1350)*. Edinburgh: Edinburgh University Press, 2018.

———. "Debating the Doctrine of *Jabr* (Compulsion): Ibn Qayyim al-Jawziyya Reads Fakhr al-Dīn al-Rāzī." In *Islamic Theology, Philosophy and Law: Debating Ibn Taymiyya and Ibn Qayyim al-Jawziyya*, ed. Birgit Krawietz and Georges Tamer, 61–93. Berlin: Walter de Gruyter, 2013.

———. "Human Choice, Divine Guidance and the *Fiṭra* Tradition: The Use of Hadith in Theological Treatises by Ibn Taymiyya and Ibn Qayyim al-Jawziyya." In *Ibn Taymiyya and His Times*, ed. Yossef Rapoport and Shahab Ahmed, 163–88. Karachi: Oxford University Press, 2010.

———. "Ibn Qayyim al-Jawziyyah." In *Essays in Arabic Literary Biography II: 1350–1850*, ed. Joseph E. Lowry and Devin J. Stewart, 202–23. Wiesbaden: Harrassowitz Verlag, 2009.

———. "Insult, Fury, and Frustration: The Martyrological Narrative of Ibn Qayyim al-Jawzīyah's *Al-Kāfiyah al-Shāfiyah*." *Mamlūk Studies Review* 17 (2013): 155–98.

Hoover, Jon. "Early Mamlūk Ashʿarism Against Ibn Taymiyya on the Nonliteral Reinterpretation (*Taʾwīl*) of God's Attributes." In *Philosophical Theology in Islam: Later Ashʿarism East and West*, ed. Ayman Shihadeh and Jan Thiele, 195–230. Leiden: Brill, 2020.

———. "God's Wise Purposes in Creating Iblīs: Ibn Qayyim al-Ǧawziyyah's Theodicy of God's Names and Attributes." *Oriente Moderno*, Nuova Serie, Anno 90 (2010): 113–34.

———. "Ḥanbalī Theology." In *The Oxford Handbook of Islamic Theology*, ed. Sabine Schmidtke, 625–46. Oxford: Oxford University Press, 2016.

———. "Ibn Taymiyya." In *Christian-Muslim Relations: A Bibliographical History*, vol. 4, ed. David Thomas and Alex Mallet, 824–78. Leiden: Brill, 2012.

———. *Ibn Taymiyya*. London: Oneworld, 2019.

———. *Ibn Taymiyya's Theodicy of Perpetual Optimism*. Leiden: Brill, 2007.

———. "Islamic Universalism: Ibn Qayyim al-Jawziyya's Salafī Deliberations on the Eternity of Hell-Fire." *The Muslim World* 99 (2009): 181–201.

———, with Marwan Abu Ghazaleh Mahajneh. "Theology as Translation: Ibn Taymiyya's Fatwa Permitting Theology and Its Reception into His *Averting the Conflict Between Reason and Revealed Tradition* (Darʾ Taʿāruḍ al-ʿAql wa-l-Naql)." *The Muslim World* 108 (2018): 40–86.

Hourani, Albert. *Arabic Thought in the Liberal Age, 1798–1939*. Cambridge: Cambridge University Press, 1983.

Hoyland, Robert. *Seeing Islam as Others Saw It: A Survey and Evaluation of Christian, Jewish and Zoroastrian Writings on Early Islam*. Princeton: Darwin Press, 1997.

Hurgronje, Christiaan Snouck. "Some of My Experiences with the Muftis of Mecca (1885)." *Asian Affairs* 8 (2007): 25–37.

Ḥusaynī, Muḥammad Rafīq al-. "Makhṭūṭ nādir min maktabat al-Shaykh Qāsim." *al-Ayyām*, March 11, 2016.

Ibn ʿAbbād, Muḥammad ibn Ḥamad (d. 1175/1761f). *Tārīkh Ibn ʿAbbād*. Ed. ʿAbdallāh ibn Yūsuf al-Shibl. Riyadh: al-Amāna al-ʿĀmma lil-Iḥtifāl bi-Murūr Miʾat ʿĀm ʿalā Taʾsīs al-Mamlaka, 1419/1999.

Ibn ʿAbd al-Wahhāb, Muḥammad (d. 1206/1792). *Kashf al-shubuhāt*. N.p.: Maktabat al-Himma, 1437/2016.

———. *Kitāb al-tawḥīd alladhī huwa ḥaqq Allāh ʿalā ʾl-ʿabīd*, 5th ed. Ed. Daghash ibn Shabīb al-ʿAjmī. Kuwait: Maktabat Ahl al-Athar, 1345/2014.

———. *Muʾallafāt al-shaykh al-imām Muḥammad ibn ʿAbd al-Wahhāb*, multiple vols. Ed. ʿAbd al-ʿAzīz ibn Zayd al-Rūmī et al. Riyadh: Jāmiʿat al-Imām Muḥammad ibn Suʿūd al-Islāmiyya, 1398/1977f. The volumes are classified by part (*qism*) as follows, some *qisms* having more than one volume:

- *qism* 1: *al-ʿAqīda wa ʾl-ādāb al-Islāmiyya*
- *qism* 2: *al-Fiqh* (2 vols.)
- *qism* 3: *Mukhtaṣar sīrat al-rasūl wa ʾl-fatāwā*
- *qism* 4: *al-Tafsīr wa-Mukhtaṣar Zād al-maʿād*
- *qism* 5: *al-Rasāʾil al-shakhṣiyya*
- *qism* 6: *al-Ḥadīth* (5 vols.)
- *qism* 7: *Mulḥaq al-muṣannafāt*

———. *Mufīd al-mustafīd fī kufr tārik al-tawḥīd*, 2nd ed. Ed. Ḥamad ibn Aḥmad al-ʿAṣlānī. Riyadh: Maktabat al-Rushd, 1432/2011.

———. *Mukhtaṣar sīrat al-rasūl*. Ed. Muḥammad Ḥāmid al-Fiqī. Cairo: Maṭbaʿat al-Sunna al-Muḥammadiyya, 1375/1956.

Ibn ʿAbd al-Wahhāb, Sulaymān (d. 1208/1794). *al-Ṣawāʿiq al-ilāhiyya fī ʾl-radd ʿalā ʾl-Wahhābiyya*. Bombay: Maṭbaʿat Nukhbat al-Akhbār, 1306/1889.

Ibn Abī ʾl-ʿIzz, ʿAlī (d. 792/1390). *Sharḥ al-ʿAqīda al-Ṭaḥāwiyya*, 3rd ed., 2 vols. Ed. ʿAbdallāh ibn ʿAbd al-Muḥsin al-Turkī and Shuʿayb al-Arnaʾūṭ. Beirut: Muʾassasat al-Risāla, 1433/2012.

Ibn ʿAfāliq, Muḥammad ibn ʿAbd al-Raḥmān (d. 1163/1750). *Risāla ilā ʿUthmān ibn Muʿammar* [*Risāla* I]. Ms. Berlin, Staatsbibliothek zu Berlin, Pm. 25, ff. 36b–55b.

———. *Risāla ilā ʿUthmān ibn Muʿammar* [*Risāla* II]. Ms. Berlin, Staatsbibliothek zu Berlin, Pm. 25, ff. 56a–73b.

———. *Tahakkum al-muqallidīn fī muddaʿī tajdīd al-dīn*. Ms. Tübingen, Universität Tübingen, Ma VI 138, ff. 41a–52b.

Ibn ʿAmr, ʿAbdallāh ibn ʿAlī (d. 1326/1908f). *Jawāb qaṣīdat Ibn Siḥmān*. Ms. Mecca, Maktabat al-Ḥaram al-Makkī, *ʿĀmm* 4242, 171–76.

———. *Risāla ilā ʾl-amīr Muḥammad ibn Rashīd*. Ms. Mecca, Maktabat al-Ḥaram al-Makkī, *ʿĀmm* 4242, 168–71.

Ibn ʿAqīl al-Ẓāhirī, Muḥammad ibn ʿUmar. *Maʿārik ṣuḥufiyya wa-mashāʿir ikhwāniyya wa-fawāʾid ʿilmiyya*, 2 vols. Riyadh: Dār Ibn Ḥazm, 1427/2007.

———. *Masāʾil min tārīkh al-jazīra al-ʿarabiyya*, 4th ed. Riyadh: Dār al-Aṣāla, 1415/1994.

———. *Rujūʿ al-Amīr al-Ṣanʿānī ʿan madḥ al-shaykh al-muṣliḥ Muḥammad ibn ʿAbd al-Wahhāb raḥimahu ʾllāh fī mīzān al-tawthīq al-tārīkhī*. Unpublished manuscript, 1411/1991.

Ibn ʿAtīq, Ḥamad ibn ʿAlī (d. 1301/1884). *al-Difāʿ ʿan ahl al-sunna wa ʾl-ittibāʿ*. Ed. Ismāʿīl ibn Saʿd ibn ʿAtīq. Riyadh: Dār al-Hidāya, 1410/1990.

———. *Sabīl al-najāt wa ʾl-fikāk*. Ed. al-Walīd ibn ʿAbd al-Raḥmān Āl Furayyān. Riyadh: Dār Ṭayba, 1409/1989.

Ibn ʿAtīq, Saʿd ibn Ḥamad (d. 1349/1930). *Kitāb al-majmūʿ al-mufīd min rasāʾil wa-fatāwā ʾl-shaykh Saʿd ibn Ḥamad ibn ʿAtīq*, 4th ed. Ed. Ismāʿīl ibn Saʿd ibn ʿAtīq. Riyadh: Dār al-Hidāya, 1415/1995.

Ibn Baṭṭa al-ʿUkbarī, ʿUbayd Allāh (d. 387/997). *al-Sharḥ wa ʾl-ibāna ʿalā uṣūl al-sunna wa ʾl-diyāna*, 2nd ed. Ed. ʿĀdil ibn ʿAbdallāh Āl Ḥamdān. Riyadh: Dār al-Amr al-Awwal, 1433/2011f.

Ibn Bāz, ʿAbd al-ʿAzīz (d. 1420/1999). *Majmūʿ fatāwā wa-maqālāt mutanawwiʿa*, 2nd ed., multiple vols. Ed. Muḥammad ibn Saʿd al-Shuwayʿir. Riyadh: Dār Ulī ʾl-Nuhā, 1413/1993.

Ibn Bishr, ʿUthmān ibn ʿAbdallāh (d. 1290/1873). *ʿUnwān al-majd fī tārīkh Najd*. Riyadh: Maktabat al-Malik ʿAbd al-ʿAzīz al-ʿĀmma, 1423/2002.

———. *ʿUnwān al-majd fī tārīkh Najd*, 2 vols. Ed. Muḥammad ibn Nāṣir al-Shathrī. Riyadh: n.p., 1433/2012.

Ibn Dāwūd al-Zubayrī, ʿAbdallāh (d. 1212/1797f). *al-Ṣawāʿiq wa ʾl-ruʿūd raddan ʿalā ʾl-shaqī ʿAbd al-ʿAzīz Suʿūd*. Ms. Patna, India, Khuda Bakhsh Oriental Public Library, HL 1238.

Ibn Duʿayj, Aḥmad ibn ʿAlī (d. 1268/1851f). *Tārīkh Ibn Duʿayj*. Ed. Sulaymān ibn Ṣāliḥ al-Kharāshī. Beirut: Rawāfid, 1439/2008.

Ibn Fayrūz, Muḥammad ibn ʿAbdallāh (d. 1216/1801). *al-Radd ʿalā man kaffara ahl al-Riyāḍ wa-man ḥawlahum min al-Muslimīn*. Ed. al-Azharī. N.p.: n.p., 2010.

———. *Tarājim mā kāna fī jihat al-Aḥsāʾ min ʿulamāʾ al-Ḥanābila*. Ms. Princeton, Princeton University, Garrett 651Y, ff. 77a–79a.

Ibn Ghannām, Ḥusayn ibn Abī Bakr (d. 1225/1810f). *al-ʿIqd al-thamīn fī sharḥ aḥādīth uṣūl al-dīn*. Ed. Muḥammad ibn ʿAbdallāh al-Habdān. Riyadh: Dār al-Qāsim, 1424/2002.

———. *Rawḍat al-afkār wa ʾl-afhām*. Ms. Lucknow, Maktabat Dār al-ʿUlūm li-Nadwat al-ʿUlamāʾ, *Tārīkh* 2130.

———. *Tārīkh Ibn Ghannām al-musammā Rawḍat al-afkār wa ʾl-afhām li-murtād ḥāl al-imām wa-taʿdād ghazawāt dhawī ʾl-Islām*, 2 vols. Ed. Sulaymān ibn Ṣāliḥ al-Kharāshī. Riyadh: Dār al-Thulūthiyya, 1431/2010.

Ibn Gharīb, Muḥammad ibn ʿAlī (d. 1208/1793). *al-Radd ʿalā ʾl-Wahhābiyya*. Ms. Cambridge, University Library, Or. 738 (9) (not attributed).

———. *al-Tawḍīḥ ʿan tawḥīd al-khallāq fī jawāb ahl al-ʿIrāq*, 2 vols. Ed. Amīn ibn Aḥmad al-Saʿdī. Riyadh: Dār al-Tawḥīd lil-Nashr, 1435/2014.

Ibn Ḥajar al-ʿAsqalānī, Aḥmad ibn ʿAlī (d. 852/1449). *Fatḥ al-bārī bi-sharḥ Ṣaḥīḥ al-Imām Abī ʿAbdallāh Muḥammad ibn Ismāʿīl al-Bukhārī*, 13 vols. Ed. Muḥibb al-Dīn al-Khaṭīb. Cairo: al-Maktaba al-Salafiyya, 1380/1960f.

Ibn Ḥamdān, Sulaymān ibn ʿAbd al-Raḥmān (d. 1397/1976f). *Tarājim li-mutaʾakhkhirī ʾl-Ḥanābila*. Ed. Bakr ibn ʿAbdallāh Abū Zayd. al-Dammām, Saudi Arabia: Dār ibn al-Jawzī, 1420/1999f.

Ibn Ḥanbal, Aḥmad (d. 241/855). *Musnad al-imām Aḥmad ibn Ḥanbal*, 52 vols. Ed. Shuʿayb al-Arnaʾūṭ and ʿĀdil Murshid. Beirut: Muʾassasat al-Risāla, 1413–29/1993–2008.

Ibn Hishām, Abū Muḥammad ʿAbd al-Malik (d. 218/833). *al-Sīra al-nabawiyya li ʾbn Hishām*, 2nd ed., 2 vols. Ed. Muṣṭafā ʾl-Saqqā, Ibrāhīm al-Ibyārī, and ʿAbd al-Ḥafīz Shilbī. Cairo: Maṭbaʿat Muṣṭafā ʾl-Bābī al-Ḥalabī, 1375/1955.

Ibn Ḥumayd, Muḥammad ibn ʿAbdallāh (d. 1295/1878). *al-Suḥub al-wābila ʿalā ḍarāʾiḥ al-Ḥanābila*, 3 vols. Ed. Bakr ibn ʿAbdallāh Abū Zayd and ʿAbd al-Raḥmān ibn Sulaymān al-ʿUthaymīn. Beirut: Muʾassasat al-Risāla, 1416/1996.

Ibn Ibrāhīm al-Ṭabāṭabāʾī, Yāsīn (fl. 1190/1776f). *Radd ʿalā Ibn al-Amīr al-Ṣanʿānī*. Ms. Tübingen, Universität Tübingen, Ma VI 143, ff. 1a–5b.

Ibn al-ʿImād, ʿAbd al-Ḥayy ibn Aḥmad (d. 1089/1679). *Shadharāt al-dhahab fī akhbār man dhahab*, 10 vols. Ed. Maḥmūd al-Arnaʾūṭ. Damascus: Dār Ibn Kathīr, 1406/1986.

Ibn ʿĪsā, Aḥmad ibn Ibrāhīm (d. 1329/1911). *al-Radd ʿalā shubuhāt al-mustaghīthīn bi-ghayr Allāh*. Ed. ʿAbd al-Salām ibn Barjas Āl ʿAbd al-Karīm. Riyadh: Dār Ṭayba, 1409/1989.

Ibn ʿĪsā, Ibrāhīm ibn Ṣāliḥ (d. 1343/1925). *ʿIqd al-durar fīmā waqaʿa fī Najd min al-ḥawādith fī ākhir al-qarn al-thālith ʿashar wa-awwal al-rābiʿ ʿashar*. Ed. ʿAbd al-Raḥmān ibn ʿAbd al-Laṭīf Āl al-Shaykh. Riyadh: al-Amāna al-ʿĀmma lil-Iḥtifāl bi-Murūr Miʾat ʿĀm ʿalā Taʾsīs al-Mamlaka, 1419/1999.

———. *Tārīkh baʿḍ al-ḥawādith al-wāqiʿa fī Najd*. Ed. Ḥamad al-Jāsir. Riyadh: al-Amāna al-ʿĀmma lil-Iḥtifāl bi-Murūr Miʾat ʿĀm ʿalā Taʾsīs al-Mamlaka, 1419/1999.

Ibn Jāsir, Ibrāhīm ibn Ḥamad (d. 1338/1919). *Rujūʿ al-shaykh Ibrāhīm ibn Jāsir*. Ms. Mecca, Maktabat al-Ḥaram al-Makkī, *ʿĀmm* 4242, 177–80.

Ibn al-Jawzī, Abū ʾl-Faraj ʿAbd al-Raḥmān (d. 597/1200). *Kitāb talbīs Iblīs*. Ed. Aḥmad ibn ʿUthmān al-Mazīd. Riyadh: Dār al-Waṭan lil-Nashr, 1423/2002.

Ibn Jirjīs, Dāwūd ibn Sulaymān (d. 1299/1881). *Naḥt ḥadīd al-bāṭil wa-barduhu fī adillat al-ḥaqq al-dhābba ʿan ṣāḥib al-Burda*. Beirut: Dār al-Kutub al-ʿIlmiyya, 1425/2004.

———. *Risāla fī ʾl-radd ʿalā ʾl-marḥūm al-sayyid Maḥmūd afandī al-Ālūsī*. Bombay: Maṭbaʿat Nukhbat al-Akhbār, 1306/1888f.

———. *Ṣulḥ al-ikhwān min ahl al-īmān wa-bayān al-dīn al-qayyim fī tabriʾat Ibn Taymiyya waʾbn al-Qayyim*. Bombay: Maṭbaʿat Nukhbat al-Akhbār, 1306/1888f.

Ibn Kathīr, ʿImād al-Dīn Ismāʿīl ibn ʿUmar (d. 774/1373). *Tafsīr al-Qurʾān al-ʿaẓīm*, 2nd ed., 8 vols. Ed. Sāmī ibn Muḥammad al-Salāma. Riyadh: Dār Ṭayba, 1420/1999.

Ibn Laʿbūn, ʿAbd al-ʿAzīz ibn ʿAbdallāh. *Nuqūlāt ʿUnwān al-majd min tārīkh Ibn Laʿbūn: Ibn Bishr ʿalā khuṭāʾbn Laʿbūn*. Kuwait: Dār Ibn Laʿbūn, 2014.

Ibn Laʿbūn, Ḥamad ibn Muḥammad (d. 1260/1844f). *Tārīkh al-shaykh Ḥamad ibn Muḥammad ibn Laʿbūn al-Mudlajī al-Wāʾilī*. Ed. ʿAbd al-ʿAzīz ibn ʿAbdallāh ibn Laʿbūn. Kuwait: Dār Ibn Laʿbūn, 1429/2008.

Ibn Lādin, Usāma ibn Muḥammad (d. 1432/2012). *Majmūʿ rasāʾil wa-tawjīhāt al-shaykh al-mujāhid Usāma ibn Lādin*. N.p.: Nukhbat al-Iʿlām al-Jihādī, 1436/2015.

Ibn Mājah, Abū ʿAbdallāh Muḥammad (d. 273/887). *Sunan Ibn Mājah*, 2 vols. Ed. Muḥammad Fuʾād ʿAbd al-Bāqī. Cairo: Dār Iḥyāʾ al-Kutub al-ʿArabiyya, 1372–73/1952–54.

Ibn Māniʿ, Muḥammad ibn ʿAbd al-ʿAzīz (d. 1385/1965). *Risāla ilā Sulaymān ibn Siḥmān*. Ms. Riyadh, Dārat al-Malik ʿAbd al-ʿAzīz, *Wathāʾiq* 15/909.

Ibn Manṣūr, ʿUthmān ibn ʿAbd al-ʿAzīz (d. 1282/1865). *Fatḥ al-ḥamīd fī sharḥ al-tawḥīd*, 4 vols. Ed. Suʿūd ibn ʿAbd al-ʿAzīz al-ʿArīfī and Ḥusayn ibn Julayʿib al-Saʿīdī. Mecca: Dār ʿĀlam al-Fawāʾid, 1435/2004f.

———. *Manhaj al-maʿārij li-akhbār al-khawārij biʾl-ishrāf ʿalāʾl-isrāf min dīnihim al-mārij*. Ms. Cairo, Dār al-Kutub al-Miṣriyya, al-Taymūriyya 2144.

———. *al-Radd al-dāmigh ʿalāʾl-zāʿim anna shaykh al-Islām Ibn Taymiyya zāʾigh*. Ed. Sulaymān ibn Ṣāliḥ al-Kharāshī. Riyadh: Dār al-Tadmuriyya, 1425/2004.

Ibn Mufliḥ, Shams al-Dīn Muḥammad (d. 763/1362). *Kitāb al-furūʿ*, 12 vols. Ed. ʿAbdallāh ibn ʿAbd al-Muḥsin al-Turkī. Beirut: Muʾassasat al-Risāla, 1424/2003.

Ibn Qāḍī Shuhba, Abū Bakr ibn Aḥmad (d. 851/1448). *Tārīkh Ibn Qāḍī Shuhba*, 4 vols. Ed. ʿAdnān Darwīsh. Damascus: al-Maʿhad al-ʿIlmī al-Faransī lil-Dirāsāt al-ʿArabiyya, 1977.

Ibn Qāsim, ʿAbd al-Raḥmān ibn Muḥammad (d. 1392/1972), ed. *al-Durar al-saniyya fīʾl-ajwiba al-Najdiyya*, new ed., 16 vols. Riyadh: Warathat al-Shaykh ʿAbd al-Raḥmān ibn Qāsim, 1433/2012.

Ibn Qayyim al-Jawziyya, Shams al-Dīn Muḥammad ibn Abī Bakr (d. 751/1350). *Badāʾiʿ al-fawāʾid*, 5 vols. Ed. ʿAlī ibn Muḥammad al-ʿUmrān. Mecca: Dār ʿĀlam al-Fawāʾid, 1425/2004f.

———. *al-Dāʾ waʾl-dawāʾ*. Ed. Muḥammad Ajmal al-Iṣlāḥī. Mecca: Dār ʿĀlam al-Fawāʾid, 1429/2008f.

———. *al-Furūsiyya al-Muḥammadiyya*. Ed. Zāʾid ibn Aḥmad al-Nushayrī. Mecca: Dār ʿĀlam al-Fawāʾid, 1428/2007f.

———. *Ighāthat al-lahfān fī maṣāyid al-shayṭān*, 2 vols. Ed. Muḥammad ʿUzayr Shams. Mecca: Dār ʿĀlam al-Fawāʾid, 1432/2010f.

———. *Iʿlām al-muwaqqiʿīn ʿan rabb al-ʿālamīn*, 6 vols. Ed. Abū ʿUbayda Mashhūr Āl Salmān. al-Dammām, Saudi Arabia: Dār Ibn al-Jawzī, 1423/2002.

———. *Madārij al-sālikīn bayna manāzil iyyāka naʿbudu wa-iyyāka nastaʿīn*, 6 vols. Ed. Nāṣir ibn Sulaymān al-Saʿwī, ʿAlī ibn ʿAbd al-Raḥmān al-Qarʿāwī, Ṣāliḥ ibn ʿAbd al-ʿAzīz al-Tuwayjirī, Khālid ibn ʿAbd al-ʿAzīz al-Ghunaym, and Muḥammad ibn ʿAbdallāh al-Khuḍayrī. Riyadh: Dār al-Ṣumayʿī, 1432/2011.

———. *Ṭarīq al-hijratayn wa-bāb al-saʿādatayn*, 2 vols. Ed. Muḥammad Ajmal al-Iṣlāḥī. Mecca: Dār ʿĀlam al-Fawāʾid, 1429/2008.

———. *Zād al-maʿād fī hady khayr al-ʿibād*, rev. ed., 5 vols. Ed. Shuʿayb al-Arnaʾūṭ and ʿAbd al-Qādir al-Arnaʾūṭ. Beirut: Muʾassasat al-Risāla, 1435/2014.

Ibn Qudāma, Muwaffaq al-Dīn (d. 620/1223). *al-Mughnī sharḥ mukhtaṣar al-Khiraqī*, 3rd ed., 15 vols. Ed. ʿAbdallāh ibn ʿAbd al-Muḥsin al-Turkī and ʿAbd al-Fattāḥ Muḥammad al-Ḥilw. Riyadh: Dār ʿĀlam al-Kutub, 1417/1997.

———. *Taḥrīm al-naẓar fī kutub al-kalām*. Ed. ʿAbd al-Raḥmān ibn Muḥammad Dimashqiyya. Riyadh: Dār ʿĀlam al-Kutub, 1410/1990.

Ibn Rabīʿa, Muḥammad (d. 1158/1745f). *Tārīkh Ibn Rabīʿa*. Ed. ʿAbdallāh ibn Yūsuf al-Shibl. Riyadh: al-Amāna al-ʿĀmma lil-Iḥtifāl bi-Murūr Miʾat ʿĀm ʿalā Taʾsīs al-Mamlaka, 1419/1999.

Ibn Rajab, ʿAbd al-Raḥmān ibn Aḥmad (d. 795/1393). *al-Dhayl ʿalā Ṭabaqāt al-Ḥanābila*, 5 vols. Ed. Sulaymān ibn Muḥammad al-ʿUthaymīn. Riyadh: Maktabat al-ʿUbaykān, 1425/2005.

———. *Majmūʿ rasāʾil al-Ḥāfiẓ Ibn Rajab al-Ḥanbalī*, 2nd ed., 5 vols. Ed. Ṭalʿat ibn Fuʾād al-Ḥulwānī. Cairo: Dār al-Fārūq al-Ḥadītha, 1434/2012.

Ibn Riḍwān, ʿImrān ibn ʿAlī (d. 1280/1863f). *Mukhtārāt min qaṣāʾid al-shaykh ʿImrān ibn ʿAlī Āl Riḍwān*. Ed. ʿAbd al-Salām ibn ʿAbdallāh al-Sulaymān. Riyadh: n.p., 1426/2005.

Ibn Sanad, ʿUthmān (d. 1242/1827). *Maṭāliʿ al-suʿūd bi-ṭīb akhbār al-wālī Dāwūd*. Ed. ʿImād ʿAbd al-Salām Raʾūf. Beirut: al-Dār al-ʿArabiyya lil-Mawsūʿāt, 1431/2010.

———. *Sabāʾik al-ʿasjad fī akhbār Aḥmad najl Rizq al-Asʿad*. Ed. Ḥasan ibn Muḥammad Āl Thānī. Doha: Markaz Ḥasan ibn Muḥammad ibn ʿAlī Āl Thānī lil-Dirāsāt al-Tārīkhiyya, 2007.

Ibn Shabīb, Yūsuf. *Naṣīḥat al-muʾminīn fī ʾl-dhabb ʿan takfīr al-Muslimīn*. Amritsar: Maṭbaʿ al-Qurʾān waʾl-Sunna, 1325/1907f.

Ibn Siḥmān, Sulaymān (d. 1349/1930). *al-Asinna al-ḥidād fī radd shubuhāt ʿAlawī al-Ḥaddād*. Bombay: al-Maṭbaʿa al-Muṣṭafawiyya, n.d.

———. *al-Bayān al-mubdī li-shanāʿat al-Qawl al-mujdī*. Amritsar: Maṭbaʿ al-Qurʾān waʾl-Sunna, n.d.

———. *al-Dīwān al-musammā bi-ʿUqūd al-jawāhir al-munaḍḍada al-ḥisān*. Bombay: al-Maṭbaʿa al-Muṣṭafawiyya 1337/1919.

———. *al-Ḍiyāʾ al-shāriq fī radd shubuhāt al-mādhiq al-māriq*. Ed. ʿAbd al-Salām ibn Barjas Āl ʿAbd al-Karīm. Riyadh: Riʾāsat Idārat al-Buḥūth al-ʿIlmiyya waʾl-Iftāʾ, 1414/1992.

———. *Fatwā fī ʾl-dawla al-turkiyya waʾl-naṣārā*. Ms. Riyadh, Maktabat al-Malik Salmān, 3422, 134–45.

———, ed. *al-Hadiyya al-saniyya waʾl-tuḥfa al-Wahhābiyya al-Najdiyya*. Cairo: Maṭbaʿat al-Manār, 1342/1923f.

———. *Ibn Siḥmān: tārīkh ḥayātihi wa-ʿilmihi wa-taḥqīq shiʿrihi ʿUqūd al-jawāhir al-munaḍḍada al-ḥisān*, 2 vols. Ed. Muḥammad ibn ʿUmar ibn ʿAqīl al-Ẓāhirī. Riyadh: Maktabat al-Rushd, 1427/2006.

———. *Iqāmat al-ḥujja waʾl-dalīl wa-īḍāḥ al-maḥajja waʾl-sabīl ʿalā mā mawwaha bihi ahl al-kadhib waʾl-mayn min zanādiqat ahl al-Baḥrayn*. Delhi: al-Maṭbaʿ al-Mujtabāʾī, 1332/1913.

———. *Irshād al-ṭālib ilā ahamm al-maṭālib*. Ed. Badr ibn Jalwī al-ʿUtaybī and Sāyir ibn Saʿd al-Ḥarbī. Kuwait: Dār al-Khizāna, 1438/2016.

———. *Irshād al-ṭālib ilā ahamm al-maṭālib*. Ed. Rashīd Riḍā. Cairo: Maṭbaʿat al-Manār, 1340/1921f.

———. "al-Jawāb al-fāʾiḍ li-Arbāb al-qawl al-rāʾid." Ed. Fahd ibn ʿAbd al-Hādī al-ʿArjānī. Ph.D. dissertation, al-Jāmiʿa al-Islāmiyya biʾl-Madīna al-Munawwara, 1428/2007.

———. *al-Juyūsh al-rabbāniyya fī kashf al-shubah al-ʿAmriyya*. Ed. Sulaymān ibn Ṣāliḥ al-Kharāshī. Riyadh: Dār al-Ṣumayʿī, 1430/2009.

———. *Kashf al-awhām wa ʾl-iltibās ʿan tashbīh baʿḍ al-aghbiyāʾ min al-nās*. Bombay: al-Maṭbaʿa al-Muṣṭafawiyya, 1328/1910.

———. *Kashf ghayāhib al-ẓalām ʿan awhām Jalāʾ al-awhām wa-barāʾat al-shaykh Muḥammad ibn ʿAbd al-Wahhāb ʿan muftarayāt hādha ʾl-mulḥid al-kadhdhāb*. Bombay: al-Maṭbaʿa al-Muṣṭafawiyya, n.d.

———. *Kashf al-shubhatayn*. Ed. ʿAbd al-Salām ibn Barjas Āl ʿAbd al-Karīm. Riyadh: Dār al-ʿĀṣima, 1408/1987f.

———. *Kashf al-shubhatayn ʿan risālat Yūsuf ibn Shabīb wa ʾl-qaṣīdatayn*. Bombay: Maṭbaʿat Kulzār Ḥasanī, 1327/1909f.

———. *al-Mawāhib al-rabbāniyya fī ʾl-intiṣār lil-ṭāʾifa al-Muḥammadiyya al-Wahhābiyya*. Ms. Riyadh, Maktabat al-Malik Salmān, 3989.

———. *Minhāj ahl al-ḥaqq wa ʾl-ittibāʿ fī mukhālafat ahl al-jahl wa ʾl-ibtidāʿ*. Ed. ʿAbd al-Salām ibn Barjas Āl ʿAbd al-Karīm. ʿAjmān, UAE: Maktabat al-Furqān, 1417/1996f.

———. *Minhāj ahl al-ḥaqq wa ʾl-ittibāʿ fī mukhālafat ahl al-jahl wa ʾl-ibtidāʿ*. Ed. Rashīd Riḍā. Cairo: Maṭbaʿat al-Manār, 1340/1921f.

———. *al-Radd ʿalā ʿAbdallāh ibn ʿAmr*. Ms. Riyadh, Dārat al-Malik ʿAbd al-ʿAzīz, al-Murshid 8.

———. *Risāla ilā ʾl-ikhwān*. Ms. Ḥāʾil, Maktabat al-Shaykh Ṣāliḥ ibn Sālim Āl Bunayyān.

———. *al-Ṣawāʿiq al-mursala al-shihābiyya ʿalā ʾl-shubah al-dāḥiḍa al-Shāmiyya*. Bombay: al-Maṭbaʿa al-Muṣṭafawiyya, 1335/1916.

———. *Taʿaqqubāt al-shaykh al-ʿallāma Sulaymān ibn Siḥmān ʿalā baʿḍ taʿlīqāt al-shaykh Rashīd Riḍā ʿalā kutub aʾimmat al-daʿwa*. Ed. Sulaymān ibn Ṣāliḥ al-Kharāshī. Riyadh: Dār al-Ṣumayʿī, 1420/2009.

———. *Tahniʾa lil-imām ʿAbd al-ʿAzīz lammā aghāra ʿalā arkān Ḥāʾil*. Ms. Riyadh, Maktabat al-Malik Salmān, 3422, 93–95.

———. *Taʾyīd madhhab al-salaf wa-kashf shubuhāt man ḥādda wa ʾnḥarafa wa-duʿiya bi ʾl-Yamānī Sharaf*. Bombay: al-Maṭbaʿa al-Muṣṭafawiyya, 1323/1905.

———. *ʿUqūd al-jawāhir* (see *Ibn Siḥmān: tārīkh ḥayātihi*... for the al-Rushd ed.; *al-Dīwān al-musammā*... for the al-Muṣṭafawiyya ed.)

Ibn Taymiyya, Aḥmad ibn ʿAbd al-Ḥalīm (d. 728/1328). *al-Ikhnāʾiyya aw al-Radd ʿalā ʾl-Ikhnāʾī*. Ed. Aḥmad ibn Mūnis al-ʿAnazī. Jeddah: Dār al-Kharrāz, 1420/2000.

———. *Iqtiḍāʾ al-ṣirāṭ al-mustaqīm li-mukhālafat aṣḥāb al-jaḥīm*, 2nd ed., 2 vols. Ed. Nāṣir ibn ʿAbd al-Karīm al-ʿAql. Riyadh: Dār Ishbīliyā, 1419/1998.

———. *al-Istighātha fī ʾl-radd ʿalā ʾl-Bakrī*, 4th ed. Ed. ʿAbdallāh ibn Dujayn al-Sahlī. Riyadh: Maktabat Dār al-Minhāj, 1436/2014f.

———. *Jāmiʿ al-masāʾil*, 8 vols. Ed. Muḥammad ʿUzayr Shams. Mecca: Dār ʿĀlam al-Fawāʾid, 1422/2001f.

———. *al-Jawāb al-ṣaḥīḥ li-man baddala dīn al-masīḥ*, 7 vols. Ed. ʿAlī ibn Ḥasan ibn Nāṣir, ʿAbd al-ʿAzīz ibn Ibrāhīm al-ʿAskar, and Ḥamdān ibn Muḥammad al-Ḥamdān. Riyadh: Dār al-ʿĀṣima, 1419/1999.

———. *Majmūʿ fatāwā shaykh al-Islām Ibn Taymiyya*, 37 vols. Ed. ʿAbd al-Raḥmān ibn Muḥammad ibn Qāsim. Riyadh: Maṭābiʿ al-Riyāḍ, 1381–86/1961f–66f.

———. *Minhāj al-sunna al-nabawiyya fī naqḍ kalām al-shīʿa al-qadariyya*, 9 vols. Ed. Muḥammad Rashād Sālim. Riyadh: Jāmiʿat al-Imām Muḥammad ibn Suʿūd al-Islāmiyya, 1406/1986.

———. *Qāʿida fī ʾl-maḥabba*. Ed. Fawwāz Aḥmad Zamurlī. Beirut: al-Maktab al-Islāmī, 1420/1999.

———. *Qāʿida jalīla fī ʾl-tawassul wa ʾl-wasīla*. Ed. Rashīd Riḍā. Cairo: Maṭbaʿat al-Manār, 1327/1909f.

———. *Qāʿida mukhtaṣara fī qitāl al-kuffār wa-muhādanatihim wa-taḥrīm qatlihim li-mujarrad kufrihim*. Ed. ʿAbd al-ʿAzīz ibn ʿAbdallāh al-Zīr Āl Ḥamad. Riyadh: n.p., 1425/2004.

———. *al-Ṣārim al-maslūl ʿalā shātim al-rasūl*, 3 vols. Ed. Muḥammad ibn ʿAbdallāh al-Ḥalwānī and Muḥammad Kabīr Shawdrī. al-Dammām, Saudi Arabia: Ramādī lil-Nashr, 1417/1997.

———. *al-Siyāsa al-sharʿiyya fī iṣlāḥ al-rāʿī wa ʾl-raʿiyya*. Ed. ʿAlī ibn Muḥammad al-ʿUmrān. Mecca: Dār ʿĀlam al-Fawāʾid, 1429/2008.

Ibn Turkī, ʿAbd al-Wahhāb ibn Muḥammad (fl. 1257/1841f). *Tārīkh Najd*. In *Khizānat al-tawārīkh al-Najdiyya*, 10 vols., ed. ʿAbdallāh ibn ʿAbd al-Raḥmān Āl Bassām, 4:137–84. N.p.: n.p., 1999.

Ibn Yūsuf, Muḥammad ibn ʿAbdallāh (fl. 1207/1792f). *Tārīkh Ibn Yūsuf*. Ed. ʿUwayḍa ibn Mitayrīk al-Juhanī. Riyadh: al-Amāna al-ʿĀmma lil-Iḥtifāl bi-Murūr Miʾat ʿĀm ʿalā Taʾsīs al-Mamlaka, 1419/1999.

"The Islamic State." *Vice News*, August 2014.

Jabartī, ʿAbd al-Raḥmān ibn Ḥasan al- (d. 1240/1825). *ʿAjāʾib al-āthār fī ʾl-tarājim wa ʾl-akhbār*, 4 vols. Būlāq, Cairo: al-Maṭbaʿa al-Amīriyya, 1297/1897f.

Jābir, Jāsim ibn Muḥammad al-. *al-Luʾluʾ al-naqī fī turāth al-ʿallāma Muḥammad ibn Ḥasan al-Marzūqī al-Qaṭarī*. Medina: Maktabat al-ʿUlūm wa ʾl-Ḥikam, 2012.

Jackson, John. *Journey from India, towards England, in the Year 1797*. London: T. Cadell and W. Davies, 1799.

Jackson, Sherman A. "Ibn Taymiyyah on Trial in Damascus." *Journal of Semitic Studies* 39 (1994): 41–85.

Jaḥḥāf, Luṭf Allāh ibn Aḥmad (d. 1243/1827f). *Durar nuḥūr al-ḥūr al-ʿīn bi-sīrat al-Manṣūr ʿAlī wa-dawlatihi ʾl-mayāmīn*. Ed. ʿĀrif Muḥammad al-Raʿawī. Sanaa: Wizārat al-Thaqāfa wa ʾl-Siyāḥa, 1425/2004.

Jāsir, Ḥamad ibn Muḥammad al- (d. 1421/2000). "Muʾarrikhū Najd min ahlihā (1)." *al-ʿArab* 5 (1391/1971): 785–801.

———. "Muʾarrikhū Najd min ahlihā (2)." *al-ʿArab* 5 (1391/1971): 881–900.

Jones Brydges, Harford. *An Account of the Transactions of His Majesty's Mission to the Court of Persia in the Years 1807–11*, 2 vols. London: James Bohn, 1834.

Juhany, Uwaidah M. Al. *Najd Before the Salafi Reform Movement: Social, Political and Religious Conditions During the Three Centuries Preceding the Rise of the Saudi State*. Reading, UK: Ithaca Press, 2002.

Kamālī, ʿAbdallāh ibn ʿAbd al-Qādir al-, ed. *Raghbat al-muwaḥḥidīn fī taʿallum aṣl al-dīn*. N.p.: Maktabat al-Aṣāla waʾl-Turāth al-Islāmiyya, 1431/2010.

Karkūklī, Rasūl Ḥāwī al- (d. 1243/1827f). *Dawḥat al-wuzarāʾ fī tārīkh waqāʾiʿ Baghdād al-zawrāʾ*. Ed. and trans. Mūsā Kāẓim Nawras. Beirut: Dār al-Kātib al-ʿArabī, n.d.

Kearney, John. "The Real Wahhab." *The Boston Globe*, August 8, 2004.

Keating, Aileen. *Mirage: Power, Politics, and the Hidden History of Arabian Oil*. Amherst, NY: Prometheus Books, 2005.

Khān, Aḥmad. *Muʿjam al-maṭbūʿāt al-ʿarabiyya fī shibh al-qārra al-hindiyya al-bākistāniyya*. Riyadh: Maktabat al-Malik Fahd al-Waṭaniyya, 1421/2000.

Kharāshī, Sulaymān ibn Ṣāliḥ al-. *Aqwāl al-ʿulamāʾ fīʾl-risāla al-mansūba ilā shaykh al-Islām Ibn Taymiyya fīʾl-jihād*. N.p.: Ṣayd al-Fawāʾid, 1424/2003.

———. *Taʿaqqubāt al-ʿulamāʾ ʿalā Lawāmiʿ al-anwār al-bahiyya lil-imām al-Saffārīnī*. Kuwait: Dār Īlāf al-Dawliyya, 1438/2017.

"Khiṭāb jalālat al-malik." *Umm al-qurā*, 6 Dhūʾl-ḥijja 1347/May 16, 1929.

Khoury, Dina Rizk. "Who Is a True Muslim? Exclusion and Inclusion Among Polemicists of Reform in Nineteenth-Century Baghdad." In *The Early Modern Ottomans: Remapping the Empire*, ed. Virginia H. Aksan and Daniel Goffman, 256–74. Cambridge: Cambridge University Press, 2007.

Kohlberg, Etan. "*Barāʾa* in Shīʿī Doctrine." *Jerusalem Studies in Arabic and Islam* 7 (1986): 139–75.

Kostiner, Joseph. "On Instruments and Their Designers: The Ikhwan of Najd and the Emergence of the Saudi State." *Middle Eastern Studies* 21 (1985): 298–323.

Kramer, Martin. *Islam Assembled: The Advent of the Muslim Congresses*. New York: Columbia University Press, 1986.

Krawietz, Birgit. "Transgressive Creativity in the Making: Ibn Qayyim al-Ǧawziyyah's Reframing Within Ḥanbalī Legal Methodology." *Oriente Moderno*, Nuova Serie, Anno 90 (2010): 47–66.

Krawietz, Birgit, and Georges Tamer, eds. *Islamic Theology, Philosophy and Law: Debating Ibn Taymiyya and Ibn Qayyim al-Jawziyya*. Berlin: Walter de Gruyter, 2013.

Kurdī, Muḥammad ibn Sulaymān al- (d. 1194/1780). *Fatāwāʾl-imām al-ʿallāma waʾl-ḥibr al-fahhāma khātimat al-muḥaqqiqīn al-shaykh Muḥammad ibn Sulaymān al-Kurdī*. Cairo: al-Maktaba al-Tijāriyya al-Kubrā, 1357/1938.

Lacroix, Stéphane. *Awakening Islam: The Politics of Religious Dissent in Contemporary Saudi Arabia*. Trans. George Holoch. Cambridge, MA: Harvard University Press, 2011.

Laoust, Henri. *Essai sur les doctrines sociales et politiques de Takī-d-Dīn Aḥmad b. Taimīya*. Cairo: Imprimerie de l'Institut français d'archéologie orientale, 1939.

Lauzière, Henri. *The Making of Salafism: Islamic Reform in the Twentieth Century*. New York: Columbia University Press, 2016.

Lav, Daniel. "Ashʿarism, Causality, and the Cult of Saints." *Jerusalem Studies in Arabic and Islam* 50 (2021): 225–312.

———. *Radical Islam and the Revival of Medieval Theology*. Cambridge: Cambridge University Press, 2012.

———. "Radical Muslim Theonomy: A Study in the Evolution of Salafi Thought." Ph.D. dissertation, Hebrew University of Jerusalem, 2016.

Leaman, Oliver. "The Developed *Kalām* Tradition (Part I)." In *The Cambridge Companion to Islamic Theology*, ed. Tim Winter, 77–90. Cambridge: Cambridge University Press, 2008.

Longrigg, Stephen Hemsley. *Four Centuries of Modern Iraq*. Oxford: Oxford University Press, 1925.

Lorimer, John Gordon. *Gazetteer of the Persian Gulf, 'Omān, and Central Arabia*, 2 vols. Calcutta: Superintendent Government Printing, India, 1915.

Mach, Rudolph. *Catalogue of Arabic Manuscripts (Yahuda Section) in the Garrett Collection, Princeton University Library*. Princeton: Princeton University Press, 1977.

Mahdi, Wael. "There Is No Such Thing as Wahhabism, Saudi Prince Says." *The National*, March 18, 2010.

Majmūʿat al-rasāʾil wa ʾl-masāʾil al-Najdiyya (see Riḍā, Rashīd).

Majmūʿat rasāʾil wa-fatāwā fī masāʾil muhimma li-ʿulamāʾ Najd al-aʿlām. Cairo: Maṭbaʿat al-Manār, 1346/1927f.

Makdisi, George. "Hanbalite Islam." In *Studies on Islam*, ed. and trans. Merlin L. Swartz, 216–74. New York: Oxford University Press, 1981.

———. "Ibn Taimīya: A Ṣūfī of the Qādiriya Order." *American Journal of Arabic Studies* 1 (1973): 118–29.

Mānīʿ, Khālid ibn Zayd al-. *al-Āthār al-makhṭūṭa li-ʿulamāʾ Najd*. al-Dilam, Saudi Arabia: n.p., 1426/2006.

———. *Nāsikhū ʾl-makhṭūṭāt al-Najdiyyūn*. Riyadh: n.p., 1431/2010.

Maqdisī, Abū Muḥammad al-. *Kashf al-niqāb ʿan sharīʿat al-ghāb*. Minbar al-Tawḥīd wa ʾl-Jihād, n.d.

———. *al-Kawāshif al-jaliyya fī kufr al-dawla al-Suʿūdiyya*, 2nd ed. N.p.: Minbar al-Tawḥīd wa ʾl-Jihād, 1421/2000f.

———. *Millat Ibrāhīm*. Minbar al-Tawḥīd wa ʾl-Jihād, n.d.

———. *Wa-lākin kūnū rabbāniyyīn*. N.p.: Muʾassasat al-Taḥāyā, 1436/2015.

Maqdisī, Abū Yaʿqūb al- (d. 1440/2018). *al-Bāʿith ʿalā itmām al-nāqiḍ al-thālith*. N.p.: Maktab al-Buḥūth wa ʾl-Dirāsāt, 1439/2017.

March, Andrew F. *Islam and Liberal Citizenship: The Search for an Overlapping Consensus*. Oxford: Oxford University Press, 2009.

Mardam, Khalīl (d. 1379/1959), ed. "Majmūʿa makhṭūṭa." *Majallat al-Majmaʿ al-ʿIlmī al-ʿArabī* 5 (1343/1925): 61–69.

Massignon, Louis. *The Passion of al-Hallaj: Mystic and Martyr of Islam*, 4 vols. Trans. Herbert Mason. Princeton: Princeton University Press, 1982.

Matroudi, Abdul Hakim I. Al-. *The Ḥanbalī School of Law and Ibn Taymiyya*. New York: Routledge, 2006.

Melchert, Christopher. "The Relation of Ibn Taymiyya and Ibn Qayyim al-Jawziyya to the Ḥanbalī School of Law." In *Islamic Theology, Philosophy and Law: Debating Ibn Taymiyya and Ibn Qayyim al-Jawziyya*, ed. Birgit Krawietz and Georges Tamer, 146–61. Berlin: Walter de Gruyter, 2013.

Mengin, Felix. *Histoire de l'Égypte sous le gouvernement de Mohammed-Aly*, 2 vols. Paris: Chez Arthus Bertrand, 1823.

Meri, Josef W. *The Cult of Saints Among Muslims and Jews in Medieval Syria*. Oxford: Oxford University Press, 2002.

Michot, Yahya. "Un important témoin de l'histoire et de la société mameloukes à l'époque des Ilkhans et de la fin des croisades: Ibn Taymiyya." In *Egypt and Syria in the Fatimid, Ayyubid, and Mamluk Eras*, ed. Urbain Vermeulen and Daniel de Smet, 335–53. Louvain: Uitgeverij Peeters, 1995.

Mirza, Younus Y. "Ibn Taymiyya as Exegete: Moses' Father-in-Law and the Messengers in *Sūrat Yā Sīn*." *Journal of Qur'ānic Studies* 19 (2017): 39–71.

———. "Was Ibn Kathīr the 'Spokesperson' for Ibn Taymiyya? Jonah as a Prophet of Obedience." *Journal of Qur'ānic Studies* 16 (2014): 1–19.

Mouline, Nabil. *The Clerics of Islam: Religious Authority and Political Power in Saudi Arabia*. Trans. Ethan Rundell. New Haven: Yale University Press, 2014.

Mudayhish, Ibrāhīm ibn ʿAbdallāh al-. "Min ʿulamāʾ Najd alladhīna raḥalū ilā ʾl-Hind li-ṭalab al-ʿilm." *al-Jazīra*, April 18, 2013.

Muqarrar fī ʾl-tawḥīd. N.p.: Hayʾat al-Buḥūth waʾl-Iftāʾ, 1436/2014f.

Murad, Hasan Qasim. "Ibn Taymiyya on Trial: A Narrative Account of His Miḥan." *Islamic Studies* 18, no. 1 (1979): 1–32.

Murādī, Muḥammad Khalīl ibn ʿAlī al- (d. 1206/1791). *Silk al-durar fī aʿyān al-qarn al-thānī ʿashar*, 4 vols. Būlāq, Cairo: n.p., 1291–1301/1874f–83f.

Musil, Alois. *Northern Neǧd: A Topographical Itinerary*. New York: American Geographical Society, 1928.

Muslim ibn al-Ḥajjāj, Abū ʾl-Ḥusayn (d. 261/875). *Ṣaḥīḥ Muslim*, 5 vols. Ed. Muḥammad Fuʾād ʿAbd al-Bāqī. Cairo: Dār Iḥyāʾ al-Kutub al-ʿArabiyya, 1412/1991.

Mustafa, Abdul-Rahman. *On Taqlīd: Ibn al Qayyim's Critique of Authority in Islamic Law*. Oxford: Oxford University Press, 2013.

Mutawallī, Tāmir Muḥammad. *Manhaj al-shaykh Muḥammad Rashīd Riḍā fī ʾl-ʿaqīda*. Jeddah: Dār Mājid ʿAsīrī, 1425/2004.

Muṭīʿ al-Raḥmān, Muḥammad ibn Sayyid Aḥmad, and ʿĀdil ibn Jamīl ʿĪd. *al-Fihris al-mukhtaṣar li-makhṭūṭāt al-Ḥaram al-Makkī al-Sharīf*, 4 vols. Riyadh: Maktabat al-Malik Fahd al-Waṭaniyya, 1427/2006.

Nābiʿ, al-. *al-Shaykh al-Baghdādī ʿalā khuṭā ʾl-imām Muḥammad ibn ʿAbd al-Wahhāb*. Muʾassasat al-Minhāj, n.d.

Nafi, Basheer M. "A Teacher of Ibn ʿAbd al-Wahhāb: Muḥammad Ḥayāt al-Sindī and the Revival of *Aṣḥāb al-Ḥadīth*'s Methodology." *Islamic Law and Society* 13 (2006): 208–41.

Nuwayṣir, Muḥammad ibn ʿAbdallāh al-. *al-Muʿāraḍa li-daʿwat al-Shaykh Muḥammad ibn ʿAbd al-Wahhāb fī ʾl-Aḥsāʾ*. Ph.D. dissertation, Jāmiʿat al-Imām Muḥammad ibn Suʿūd al-Islāmiyya, 1410/1990.

O'Kinealy, James. "Translation of an Arabic Pamphlet on the History and Doctrines of the Wahhábís." *Journal of the Asiatic Society of Bengal* 43 (1874): 68–82.

Ovadia, Miriam. *Ibn Qayyim al-Jawziyya and the Divine Attributes: Rationalized Traditionalistic Theology*. Leiden: Brill, 2018.

Özervarlı, M. Sait. "Divine Wisdom, Human Agency and the *Fiṭra* in Ibn Taymiyya's Thought." In *Islamic Theology, Philosophy and Law: Debating Ibn Taymiyya and Ibn Qayyim al-Jawziyya*, ed. Birgit Krawietz and Georges Tamer, 37–60. Berlin: Walter de Gruyter, 2013.

———. "The Qur'ānic Rational Theology of Ibn Taymiyya and His Criticism of the *Mutakallimūn*." In *Ibn Taymiyya and His Times*, ed. Yossef Rapoport and Shahab Ahmed, 78–100. Karachi: Oxford University Press, 2010.

Palgrave, William Gifford. *Narrative of a Year's Journey Through Central and Eastern Arabia (1862–63)*, 2 vols. London: Macmillan and Co., 1865.

Pearson, Harlon O. *Islamic Reform and Revival in Nineteenth-Century India: The Ṭarīqah-i Muhammadīyah*. New Delhi: Yoda Press, 2008.

Peskes, Esther. "ʿAbdallāh b. Muḥammad b. ʿAbdalwahhāb und die wahhabitische Besetzung von Mekka 1803." In *Islamstudien ohne Ende: Festschrift für Werner Ende zum 65. Geburtstag*, ed. Rainer Brunner, Monika Gronke, Jens Peter Laut, and Ulrich Rebstock, 345–53. Würzburg: Ergon, 2002.

———. *Muḥammad b. ʿAbdalwahhāb (1703–92) im Widerstreit: Untersuchungen zur Rekonstruktion der Frühgeschichte der Wahhābīya*. Beirut: In Kommission bei Franz Steiner, 1993.

Philby, Harry St. John. *Arabia*. New York: Charles Scribner's Sons, 1930.

———. *Sa'udi Arabia*. London: Benn, 1955.

Picken, Gavin N. "The Quest for Orthodoxy and Tradition in Islam: Ḥanbalī Response to Sufism." In *Fundamentalism in the Modern World*, vol. 2, ed. Ulrika Mårtensson, Jennifer Bailey, Priscilla Ringrose, and Asbjørn Dyrendal, 237–63. London: I. B. Tauris, 2011.

Qabbānī, Aḥmad ibn ʿAlī al- (fl. 1159/1746). *Faṣl al-khiṭāb fī radd ḍalālāt Ibn ʿAbd al-Wahhāb*. Ms. Baghdad, Dār al-Makhṭūṭāt al-ʿIrāqiyya, 9284.

———. *Kashf al-ḥijāb ʿan wajh ḍalālāt Ibn ʿAbd al-Wahhāb*. Ms. Hyderabad, State Central Library, *Kalām* 1238.

———. *Naqḍ qawāʿid al-ḍalāl wa-rafḍ ʿaqāʾid al-ḍullāl*. Ms. Princeton, Princeton University, Garrett 3788Y, ff. 41a–63a.

Qadhi, Yasir. "Reconciling Reason and Revelation in the Writings of Ibn Taymiyya (d. 728/1328): An Analytical Study of Ibn Taymiyya's *Darʾ al-taʿāruḍ*." Ph.D. dissertation, Yale University, 2013.

Qāḍī, Muḥammad ibn ʿUthmān al-. *Rawḍat al-nāẓirīn ʿan maʾāthir ʿulamāʾ Najd wa-ḥawādith al-sinīn*, new ed., 3 vols. Riyadh: Dār al-Thulūthiyya, 1433/2012.

Qādirī, Muḥammad ibn Muḥammad al-Shāfiʿī al- (fl. 1211/1796f). *Radd ʿalā risālat ʿAbd al-ʿAzīz ibn Suʿūd*. Ms. Riyadh, Maktabat al-Malik Salmān, Jāmiʿat al-Malik Suʿūd, 6803.

Qāsim, ʿAbd al-Malik ibn Muḥammad al-. *al-Shaykh ʿAbd al-Raḥmān ibn Qāsim: Ḥayātuhu wa-sīratuhu wa-muʾallafātuhu*. Riyadh: Dār al-Qāsim, 1425/2005.

Qaṭṭān, Aḥmad al- (d. 13th/19th c.). *Tanzīl al-raḥamāt ʿalā man māt* (part 2). Ms. Mecca, Maktabat al-Ḥaram al-Makkī, *Tarājim* 2790.

Qūrshūn, Zakariyyā. *al-ʿUthmāniyyūn wa-Āl Suʿūd fī ʾl-arshīf al-ʿUthmānī*. Beirut: al-Dār al-ʿArabiyya lil-Mawsūʿāt, 1425/2005.

Radīsī, Ḥamādī al- (= Hamadi Redissi), ed. *al-Radd ʿalā ʾl-Wahhābiyya: Nuṣūs al-sharq al-Islāmī*. Beirut: Dār al-Ṭalīʿa, 1433/2012.

———. "The Refutation of Wahhabism in Arabic Sources, 1745–1932." In *Kingdom Without Borders: Saudi Political, Religious and Media Frontiers*, ed. Madawi Al-Rasheed, 157–81. New York: Columbia University Press, 2008.

Rapoport, Yossef. "Ibn Taymiyya on Divorce Oaths." In *The Mamluks in Egyptian and Syrian Politics and Society*, ed. Michael Winter and Amalia Levanoni, 191–217. Leiden: Brill, 2004.

———. "Ibn Taymiyya's Radical Legal Thought: Rationalism, Pluralism and the Primacy of Intention." In *Ibn Taymiyya and His Times*, ed. Yossef Rapoport and Shahab Ahmed, 191–226. Karachi: Oxford University Press, 2010.

Rapoport, Yossef, and Shahab Ahmed, eds. *Ibn Taymiyya and His Times*. Karachi: Oxford University Press, 2010.

Rasheed, Madawi Al-. *A History of Saudi Arabia*, 2nd ed. Cambridge: Cambridge University Press, 2010.

———. *Politics in an Arabian Oasis: The Rashidi Tribal Dynasty*. London: I. B. Tauris, 1991.

Rentz, George S. *The Birth of the Islamic Reform Movement in Saudi Arabia: Muḥammad Ibn 'Abd al-Wahhāb (1703/4–1792) and the Beginnings of the Unitarian Empire in Arabia*. London: Arabian Publishing, 2004.

Riḍā, Rashīd ibn ʿAlī (d. 1354/1935), ed. *Majmūʿat al-ḥadīth al-Najdiyya*, 2nd ed. Cairo: Maṭbaʿat al-Manār, 1342/1923f.

———, ed. *Majmūʿat rasāʾil wa-fatāwā fī masāʾil muhimma tamussu ilayhā ḥājat al-ʿaṣr*. Cairo: Maṭbaʿat al-Manār, 1346/1927f.

———, ed. *Majmūʿat al-rasāʾil waʾl-masāʾil al-Najdiyya*, 4 vols. Cairo: Maṭbaʿat al-Manār, 1344–49/1925f–30f.

———, ed. *Majmūʿat al-tawḥīd al-Najdiyya*. Cairo: Maṭbaʿat al-Manār, 1346/1927f.

———. *Tafsīr al-Qurʾān al-ḥakīm*, 13 vols. Cairo: Maṭbaʿat al-Manār, 1324–53/1906f–34f.

———. *al-Wahhābiyyūn waʾl-Ḥijāz*. Cairo: Maṭbaʿat al-Manār, 1344/1926.

Riexinger, Martin. "'Der Islam begann als Fremder, und als Fremder wird er wiederkehren': Muḥammad b. ʿAbd al-Wahhābs Prophetenbiographie *Muḫtaṣar sīrat ar-rasūl* als Programm und Propaganda." *Die Welt des Islams* 55 (2015): 1–61.

———. "Rendering Muḥammad Human Again: The Prophetology of Muḥammad b. ʿAbd al-Wahhāb (1703–1792)." *Numen* 60 (2013): 103–18.

Rihani, Ameen Faris. *Ibn Sa'oud of Arabia: His People and His Land*. London: Constable & Co. Ltd., 1928.

Risāla li-muʾallif majhūl. Ms. Mecca, Maktabat al-Ḥaram al-Makkī, *ʿĀmm* 4242, 164–66.

Ross, Edward Denison. *Catalogue of the Arabic and Persian Manuscripts in the Oriental Public Library at Bankipore*, 25 vols. Patna: Government Printing, 1908–42.

Rousseau, Jean Baptiste Louis (d. 1831). *Mémoire sur les trois plus fameuses sectes du Musulmanisme*. Paris: Chez Masvert, 1818.

———. "Notice sur la horde des Wahabis." *Gazette Nationale ou Le Moniteur Universel*, May 23, 1804, 1101–2.

Rudayʿān, Ḥassān ibn Ibrāhīm al-. *Manbaʿ al-karam waʾl-shamāʾil fī dhikr akhbār wa-āthār man ʿāsha min ahl al-ʿilm fī Ḥāʾil*. Ḥāʾil: Maktabat Fahd al-ʿArīfī, 1340/2009.

Rutter, Eldon. *The Holy Cities of Arabia*, 2 vols. London: G. P. Putnam's Sons, 1928.

Sacy, Antoine-Isaac Silvestre de. "Observations sur les Wahhabites." *Magasin Encyclopédique* 59 (1805): 35–41.

Sadleir, George Forster. *Diary of a Journey Across Arabia from El Khatif in the Persian Gulf, to Yambo in the Red Sea, During the Year 1819*. Bombay: Education Society's Press, Byculla, 1866.

Saffārīnī, Muḥammad ibn Aḥmad al- (d. 1188/1774). *al-Ajwiba al-najdiyya ʿan al-asʾila al-Najdiyya*. Ed. Mubārak ibn Rāshid al-Ḥathlān. Amman: Dār al-Fatḥ, 1436/2015.

———. *Jawāb al-ʿallāma al-Saffārīnī ʿalā man zaʿama anna ʾl-ʿamal ghayr jāʾiz bi-kutub al-fiqh*. Ed. Walīd ibn Muḥammad al-ʿAlī. *Liqāʾ al-ʿashr al-awākhir bi ʾl-Masjid al-Ḥarām*, vol. 10, sec. 119. Beirut: Dār al-Bashāʾir, 1439/2008.

Sahsawānī, Muḥammad Bashīr al- (d. 1326/1908). *Ṣiyānat al-insān ʿan waswasat al-shaykh Daḥlān*. Ed. Rashīd Riḍā. Cairo: Maṭbaʿat al-Manār, 1351/1933f.

Saleh, Walid A. "Ibn Taymiyya and the Rise of Radical Hermeneutics: An Analysis of *An Introduction to the Foundations of Qurʾānic Exegesis*." In *Ibn Taymiyya and His Times*, ed. Yossef Rapoport and Shahab Ahmed, 123–62. Karachi: Oxford University Press, 2010.

Ṣamʿānī, Nāṣir ibn Sulaymān al-. *al-Shaykh Sulaymān ibn Siḥmān: ḥayātuhu wa-shiʿruhu*. Master's thesis, Jāmiʿat al-Imām Muḥammad ibn Suʿūd al-Islāmiyya, 1412/1992.

Samin, Nadav. *Of Sand or Soil: Genealogy and Tribal Belonging in Saudi Arabia*. Princeton: Princeton University Press, 2015.

Sanad, ʿAbdallāh ibn Muḥammad al-. *Juhūd ʿulamāʾ Najd fī taqrīr al-walāʾ wa ʾl-barāʾ fī ʾl-qarn al-thālith ʿashar al-hijrī*. Master's thesis, Jāmiʿat al-Imām Muḥammad ibn Suʿūd al-Islāmiyya, 1417/1996f.

Saqqāf, ʿAbdallāh ibn Muḥammad al- (d. 1380/1960f). *Tārīkh al-shuʿarāʾ al-Ḥaḍramiyyīn*, 5 vols. [Various places]: [various publishers], 1353–63/1934f–44.

Sarḥān, Suʿūd Ṣāliḥ al-. "Ḥaqīqat al-khilāf bayna Muḥammad ibn ʿAbd al-Wahhāb wa-akhīhi Sulaymān." Unpublished paper, 2010.

Sarrió, Diego R. "Spiritual Anti-elitism: Ibn Taymiyya's Doctrine of Sainthood (*Walāya*)." *Islam and Christian-Muslim Relations* 22 (2011): 275–91.

Schöck, Cornelia. "Jahm b. Ṣafwān (d. 128/745–6) and the 'Jahmiyya' and Ḍirār b. ʿAmr (d. 200/815)." In *The Oxford Handbook of Islamic Theology*, ed. Sabine Schmidtke, 55–80. Oxford: Oxford University Press, 2016.

al-Shaghdalī, Ḥamūd ibn Ḥusayn (d. 1390/1971). *Tanbīh al-muṣliḥ al-ṣāḥī ʿalā tabriʾat al-ikhwān mimmā ʾftarahu ʾl-Malāḥī*. Ms. Ḥāʾil, Maktabat al-Shaykh Ṣāliḥ ibn Sālim Āl Bunayyān.

Shahīd, Ismāʿīl ibn ʿAbd al-Ghanī al- (d. 1246/1831). *Risālat al-tawḥīd*. Trans. Abū ʾl-Ḥasan ʿAlī al-Nadwī. Medina: Wizārat al-Shuʾūn al-Islāmiyya waʾl-Awqāf waʾl-Daʿwa waʾl-Irshād, 1417/1996f.

Shamsy, Ahmed El. *Rediscovering the Islamic Classics: How Editors and Print Culture Transformed an Intellectual Tradition*. Princeton: Princeton University Press, 2020.

Shathrī, Ṣāliḥ ibn Muḥammad al- (d. 1309/1891f). *Radd ʿalā ʾbn Duʿayj*. Ms. Ḥāʾil, Maktabat al-Shaykh Ṣāliḥ ibn Sālim Āl Bunayyān.

———. *Radd ʿalā ṣāḥib al-risāla al-maʿrūf bi ʾbn Duʿayj*. Ms. Riyadh, Maktabat al-Malik Fahd al-Waṭaniyya, 58/86.

———. *Taʾyīd al-malik al-mannān fī naqḍ ḍalālāt Daḥlān*. Ed. Muḥammad ibn Nāṣir al-Shathrī. Riyadh: Dār al-Ḥabīb, 1421/2000.

Shaṭṭī, Muḥammad Jamīl al- (d. 1379/1959). *Mukhtaṣar ṭabaqāt al-Ḥanābila*. Damascus: Dār al-Taraqqī, 1339/1920f.

Shawkānī, Muḥammad ibn ʿAlī al- (d. 1250/1839). *al-Badr al-ṭāliʿ bi-maḥāsin man baʿd al-qarn al-sābiʿ*, 2 vols. Cairo: Maṭbaʿat al-Saʿāda, 1348/1929f.

———. *al-Durr al-naḍīd fī ikhlāṣ kalimat al-tawḥīd*. Ed. Abū ʿAbdallāh al-Ḥalabī. Riyadh: Dār Ibn Khuzayma, 1414/1993f.

Shiliwala, Wasim. "Constructing a Textual Tradition: Salafī Commentaries on *al-ʿAqīda al-ṭaḥāwiyya*." *Die Welt des Islams* 58 (2018): 461–503.

Shuqayr, ʿAbd al-Raḥmān ibn ʿAbdallāh al-. "al-Madhhab al-Ḥanbalī fī Najd: dirāsa tārīkhiyya." *al-Dāra* 28 (1423/2002): 71–102.

———. *Ṭibāʿat al-kutub wa-waqfuhā ʿind al-malik ʿAbd al-ʿAzīz*. Riyadh: Dārat al-Malik ʿAbd al-ʿAzīz, 1424/2003.

Sibāʿī, Aḥmad ibn Muḥammad al- (d. 1404/1984). *Tārīkh Makka: dirāsāt fī ʾl-siyāsa wa ʾl-ʿilm wa ʾl-ijtimāʿ wa ʾl-ʿumrān*, 2 vols. Riyadh: al-Amāna al-ʿĀmma lil-Iḥtifāl bi-Murūr Miʾat ʿĀm ʿalā Taʾsīs al-Mamlaka, 1419/1999.

Sirriyeh, Elizabeth. "Wahhābīs, Unbelievers, and the Problems of Exclusivism." *Bulletin of the British Society for Middle Eastern Studies* 16 (1989): 123–32.

Steinberg, Guido. *Religion und Staat in Saudi-Arabien: Die wahhabitischen Gelehrten, 1902–1953*. Würzburg: Ergon Verlag, 2002.

———. "The Wahhabi Ulama and the Saudi State: 1745 to the Present." In *Saudi Arabia in the Balance: Political Economy, Society, Foreign Affairs*, ed. Paul Aarts and Gerd Nonneman, 11–34. New York: New York University Press, 2005.

Subkī, Tāj al-Dīn ʿAbd al-Wahhāb ibn ʿAlī al- (d. 771/1370). *Ṭabaqāt al-Shāfiʿiyya al-kubrā*, 10 vols. Ed. Maḥmūd Muḥammad al-Ṭanāḥī and ʿAbd al-Fattāḥ Muḥammad al-Ḥilw. Cairo: Maṭbaʿat ʿĪsā ʾl-Bābī al-Ḥalabī, 1964–76.

Subkī, Taqī al-Dīn ʿAlī ibn ʿAbd al-Kāfī al- (d. 756/1355). *al-Rasāʾil al-Subkiyya fī ʾl-radd ʿalā ʾbn Taymiyya wa-tilmīdhihi ʾbn Qayyim al-Jawziyya*. Ed. Kamāl Abū ʾl-Munā. Beirut: ʿĀlam al-Kutub, 1403/1983.

Surūriyya, Gharīb al-. "al-Dawla al-Islāmiyya imtidād lil-daʿwa al-Najdiyya." Telegram, May 30, 2017.

———. "Sīrat aʾimmat al-Islām fī hadm mawāḍiʿ al-shirk wa ʾl-ṭughyān." Blog post, July 23, 2015, http://ghareeb-assourouria.blogspot.com/2015/07/blog-post_23.html?m=1 (link defunct).

Swartz, Merlin L. "A Seventh-Century (A.H.) Sunnī Creed: The ʿAqīda Wāsiṭīya of Ibn Taymīya." *Humaniora Islamica* 1 (1973): 91–131.

Ṭabarānī, Sulaymān ibn Aḥmad al- (d. 360/971). *al-Muʿjam al-kabīr*, 2nd ed., 25 vols. Ed. Ḥamdī ʿAbd al-Majīd al-Salafī. Cairo: Maktabat Ibn Taymiyya, n.d.

Ṭabarī, Abū Jaʿfar Muḥammad ibn Jarīr al- (d. 310/923). *The History of al-Ṭabarī*, vol. 8. Trans. Michael Fishbein. Albany: State University of New York Press, 1997.

———. *Tafsīr al-Ṭabarī: Jāmiʿ al-bayān ʿan taʾwīl āy al-Qurʾān*, 26 vols. Ed. ʿAbdallāh ibn ʿAbd al-Muḥsin al-Turkī. Cairo: Dār Hijr, 1422/2001.

———. *Tārīkh al-Ṭabarī*, 10 vols. Ed. Muḥammad Abū ʾl-Faḍl Ibrāhīm. Cairo: Dār al-Maʿārif, 1960–69.

"Taḥwīl ism Mamlakat al-Ḥijāz wa-Najd wa-Mulḥaqātihā ilā ʾsm al-Mamlaka al-ʿArabiyya al-Suʿūdiyya." *Umm al-qurā*, 22 Jumādā I 1351/September 23, 1932.

Ṭanṭāwī, ʿAlī ibn Muṣṭafā al- (d. 1420/1999). *Muḥammad ibn ʿAbd al-Wahhāb*, 2 vols. Damascus: Dār al-Fikr, 1381/1961.

"Taqrīr mukhtaṣar ḥawl silsilat rasāʾil al-ṭawḥīd al-khāliṣ li-Maktabat al-Himma." N.d.

Taylor, Christopher S. *In the Vicinity of the Righteous: Ziyāra and the Veneration of Muslim Saints in Late Medieval Egypt*. Leiden: Brill, 1998.

Tirmidhī, Abū ʿĪsā Muḥammad ibn ʿĪsā al- (d. 279/892). *al-Jāmiʿ al-ṣaḥīḥ wa-huwa Sunan al-Tirmidhī*, 5 vols. Ed. Aḥmad Muḥammad Shākir, Muḥammad Fuʾād ʿAbd al-Bāqī, and Ibrāhīm ʿAṭwa ʿAwaḍ. Cairo: Maṭbaʿat Muṣṭafā ʾl-Bābī al-Ḥalabī, n.d.–1395/n.d.–1975.

Traboulsi, Samer. "An Early Refutation of Muḥammad ibn ʿAbd al-Wahhāb's Reformist Views." *Die Welt des Islams*, New Series, 42 (2002): 373–415.

Tuwayjirī, ʿAbd al-ʿAzīz ibn ʿAbd al-Muḥsin al- (d. 1428/2007). *Li-surāt al-layl hatafa ʾl-ṣabāḥ: al-Malik ʿAbd al-ʿAzīz dirāsa wathāʾiqiyya*. Riyadh: Riyāḍ al-Rayyis lil-Kutub waʾl-Nashr, 1418/1997.

ʿUbūdī, Muḥammad ibn Nāṣir al-. *Muʿjam usar Burayda*, 23 vols. Riyadh: Dār al-Thulūthiyya, 1431/2010.

ʿUmarī, Ṣāliḥ ibn Sulaymān al-. *ʿUlamāʾ Āl Salīm wa-talāmidhatuhum wa-ʿulamāʾ al-Qaṣīm*, 3rd ed. Burayda, Saudi Arabia: n.p., 1431/2010.

ʿUṣfūr, ʿAbd al-ʿAzīz ibn Aḥmad al-, ed. *Fatāwā ʿulamāʾ al-Aḥsāʾ wa-masāʾiluhum*, 2 vols. Beirut: Dār al-Bashāʾir al-Islāmiyya, 1422/2001.

ʿUtaybī, Juhaymān ibn Muḥammad al- (d. 1400/1980). *Rafʿ al-iltibās ʿan millat man jaʿalahu ʾllāh imāman lil-nās*. Minbar al-Tawḥīd waʾl-Jihād, n.d.

ʿUthaymīn, ʿAbdallāh ibn Ṣāliḥ al- (d. 1437/2016). *Buḥūth wa-taʿlīqāt fī tārīkh al-Mamlaka al-ʿArabiyya al-Suʿūdiyya*, 2nd ed. Riyadh: Maktabat al-Tawba, 1411/1990.

———. *Muḥammad ibn ʿAbd al-Wahhāb: The Man and His Works*. London: I. B. Tauris, 2009.

———. *al-Shaykh Muḥammad ibn ʿAbd al-Wahhāb: ḥayātuhu wa-afkāruhu*. Riyadh: Dār al-ʿUlūm, 1399/1979.

Vassiliev, Alexei. *The History of Saudi Arabia*. Trans. P. A. Seslavin. New York: New York University Press, 2000.

Vikør, Knut S. *Between God and the Sultan: A History of Islamic Law*. Oxford: Oxford University Press, 2005.

Voll, John. "Muḥammad Ḥayyā al-Sindī and Muḥammad ibn ʿAbd al-Wahhāb: An Analysis of an Intellectual Group in Eighteenth-Century Madīna." *Bulletin of the School of Oriental and African Studies* 38 (1975): 32–39.

Wagemakers, Joas. "The Enduring Legacy of the Second Saudi State: Quietist and Radical Wahhabi Contestations of *al-Walāʾ wa-l-Barāʾ*." *International Journal of Middle East Studies* 44 (2012): 93–110.

———. *A Quietist Jihadi: The Ideology and Influence of Abu Muhammad al-Maqdisi*. Cambridge: Cambridge University Press, 2012.

———. "The Transformation of a Radical Concept: *al-Wala' wa-l-bara'* in the Ideology of Abu Muhammad al-Maqdisi." In *Global Salafism: Islam's New Religious Movement*, ed. Roel Meijer, 81–106. New York: Columbia University Press, 2009.

Wahba, Ḥāfiẓ (d. 1387/1967). *Jazīrat al-ʿarab fī ʾl-qarn al-ʿashrīn*. Cairo: Lajnat al-Taʾlīf waʾl-Tarjama waʾl-Nashr, 1354/1935.

Wallin, George Augustus. "Narrative of a Journey from Cairo to Medina and Mecca, by Suez, Arabá, Tawilá, al-Jauf, Jubbé, Háil, and Nejd, in 1845." *The Journal of the Royal Geographical Society of London* 24 (1854): 115–207.

Wazzān, Khālid ibn ʿAlī al-, and ʿAbdallāh ibn Bassām al-Basīmī. "Manhaj al-shaykh ʿUthmān ibn Manṣūr fī tadwīn al-tārīkh waʾl-ansāb." *al-Dāra* 36 (1431/2010): 45–130.

Weismann, Itzchak. "Genealogies of Fundamentalism: Salafi Discourse in Nineteenth-Century Baghdad." *British Journal of Middle Eastern Studies* 36 (2009): 267–80.

———. "The Naqshabandiyya-Khâlidiyya and the Salafî Challenge in Iraq." *Journal of the History of Sufism* 4 (2003–4): 229–40.

Weisweiler, Max. *Verzeichnis der arabischen Handschriften*. Leipzig: Harrassowitz, 1930.

Winder, R. Bayly. *Saudi Arabia in the Nineteenth Century*. New York: St. Martin's Press, 1965.

Yāsīn, Yūsuf ibn Muḥammad (d. 1381/1962), ed. *al-Kitāb al-mufīd fī maʿrifat ḥaqq Allāh ʿalā ʾl-ʿabīd al-musammā Majmūʿat al-tawḥīd*. Mecca: Maṭbaʿat Umm al-Qurā, 1343/1925.

Zabīdī, Muḥammad Murtaḍā ibn Muḥammad al- (d. 1205/1790). *al-Muʿjam al-mukhtaṣṣ*. Ed. Niẓām Muḥammad Yaʿqūbī and Muḥammad ibn Nāṣir al-ʿAjamī. Beirut: Dār al-Bashāʾir al-Islāmiyya, 1427/2006.

Zaman, Muhammad Qasim. *Islam in Pakistan: A History*. Princeton: Princeton University Press, 2018.

———. *Modern Islamic Thought in a Radical Age: Religious Authority and Internal Criticism*. Cambridge: Cambridge University Press, 2012.

INDEX

Abā Buṭayn, ʿAbdallāh ibn ʿAbd al-Raḥmān, 251–53, 257, 275–76
ʿAbduh, Muḥammad, 317
ʿAbdallāh Bāshā (governor of Baghdad), 220–22
Abraham (Prophet): *al-walāʾ wa ʾl-barāʾ*, 3, 165–67, 182–83, 235, 278, 280, 282
Abū Bakr al-Ṣiddīq: *māniʿū ʾl-zakāt*, 174, 175–76, 178–80, 202
Abū Jahl, 168, 280
Aflāj, al-, 14, 265
ahl al-ḥadīth, 98. *See also* theology
Ahl-i Ḥadīth (India), 189, 266–69, 272, 274
Aḥsāʾ, -al, 12–13; first Saudi state and, 210–15, 340–41; Ibn ʿAbd al-Wahhab and, 35–39; Ottoman occupation of, 240, 247–50; refutation of Wahhābism in, 51–52, 69; third Saudi state and, 295, 314; Wahhābī views of, 248–49, 285–86, 314
Āl ʿAbd al-Muḥsin, Ibrāhīm ibn ʿUbayd, 24, 290
Āl Bassām, ʿAbdallāh ibn ʿAbd al-Raḥmān, 25
Āl Bunayyān, Ṣāliḥ ibn Sālim, 266, 273
Āl Ḥumayd, Sulaymān ibn Muḥammad, 66
ʿAlī ibn Abī Ṭālib, 158, 163; and Khārijites, 174, 176
ʿAlī Kahyā, 86n256, 214
Āl Musharraf, ʿAbd al-Wahhāb ibn Sulaymān, 34, 39–40
Āl Musharraf, Sulaymān ibn ʿAlī, 34
Āl Rashīd, 240, 260, 283–84, 288–89, 292–93. *See also* Rashīdī emirate
Āl al-Shaykh, 3, 8, 208–9
Āl al-Shaykh, ʿAbdallāh ibn ʿAbd al-Laṭīf, 264–67, 311; and dispute in Trucial ʿUmān, 303; and *fitna* in al-Qaṣīm, 274–91; and the Ikhwān, 296, 307, 309–11; and *iẓhār al-dīn*, 281; and *takfīr* of Ottoman Empire, 297n9; and *al-ʿudhr bi ʾl-jahl*, 160, 303; and *al-walāʾ wa ʾl-barāʾ*, 280–81
Āl al-Shaykh, ʿAbdallāh ibn Muḥammad, 144, 209; and *iẓhār al-dīn*, 171–72
Āl al-Shaykh, ʿAbd al-Laṭīf ibn ʿAbd al-Raḥmān, 4, 160n122, 241–43, 250, 264–65, 269, 276, 282, 291; and Ibn Jirjīs, 252–53, 258–59, 268–69; and Ibn Manṣūr, 256–59; and Ottoman occupation of al-Aḥsāʾ, 247–50; and Saudi civil war, 243–47; and *takfīr* of Ottoman Empire, 248
Āl al-Shaykh, ʿAbd al-Raḥmān ibn ʿAbd al-Laṭīf (d. 1406/1986), 25
Āl al-Shaykh, ʿAbd al-Raḥmān ibn Ḥasan, 4, 24, 29–30, 229–30, 241, 249, 265, 269, 276, 291, 312; and Ibn Jirjīs, 253; and Ibn Manṣūr, 255–59; and *iẓhār al-dīn*, 232; and portrayal of Ibn ʿAbd al-Wahhāb as divinely inspired, 41; and reading of *ʿadāwa* as *jihād*, 184; and reading of *fitna* as *shirk*, 184, 236; and second Egyptian occupation, 231–40
Āl al-Shaykh, Ḥasan ibn Ḥusayn, 298, 303, 310n59, 311n61
Āl al-Shaykh, Ḥusayn ibn Ḥasan, 298–99, 302–5, 327–28
Āl al-Shaykh, Ḥusayn ibn Muḥammad, 209; and *iẓhār al-dīn*, 171–72

Āl al-Shaykh, Ibrāhīm ibn ʿAbd al-Laṭīf, 265, 287n113; and dispute in Trucial ʿUmān, 303; and *al-ʿudhr bi ʾl-jahl*, 160, 303
Āl al-Shaykh, Isḥāq ibn ʿAbd al-Raḥmān, 4, 159–60, 266–69; and *fitna* in al-Qaṣīm, 282, 285–86; and *iẓhār al-dīn*, 282, 285
Āl al-Shaykh, Muḥammad ibn ʿAbd al-Laṭīf, 265, 276, 302, 311; and the *Ikhwān*, 310n59, 311n61, 314–15; and *takfīr* of Ottoman Empire, 276, 297n9; and Western businessmen in Arabia, 324–25
Āl al-Shaykh, Muḥammad ibn ʿAbd al-Wahhāb. *See* Ibn ʿAbd al-Wahhāb, Muḥammad
Āl al-Shaykh, Muḥammad ibn Ibrāhīm, 325n114, 332–34
Āl al-Shaykh, Sulaymān ibn ʿAbdallāh, 3–4, 225–26, 234, 236, 249, 339; and Ibn Taymiyya's anti-Mongol *fatwās*, 180n202; and reading of *ʿadāwa* as *jihād*, 183–84; and reading of *fitna* as *shirk*, 181
Āl Sulaymān, Zayd ibn Muḥammad, 271
Āl Suʿūd, 2, 8, 208–9
Āl Suʿūd, ʿAbdallāh ibn Fayṣal, 240–41, 243–47, 263, 266
Āl Suʿūd, ʿAbdallāh ibn Suʿūd, 224–25
Āl Suʿūd, ʿAbdallāh ibn Thunayyān, 233, 236
Āl Suʿūd, ʿAbd al-ʿAzīz ibn ʿAbd al-Raḥmān, 290, 294–98; and the British, 296–97, 313–14; and the Ikhwān, 305–307, 310–15, 310–11; political vision of, 325–27, 331; and Rashīd Riḍā, 316–17, 322–23; and Wahhābī scholars, 298, 313, 323–28, 331–32; and Western businessmen in Arabia, 324–25
Āl Suʿūd, ʿAbd al-ʿAzīz ibn Muḥammad, 8–9, 21, 87, 214–16; assassination of, 219; letters of, 87, 220; as military leader, 203, 206, 211; as ruler of first Saudi state, 207
Āl Suʿūd, ʿAbd al-Raḥmān ibn Fayṣal, 240, 246, 263–64, 294
Āl Suʿūd, Fayṣal ibn Turkī, 229–31, 233, 240, 260, 263
Āl Suʿūd, Khālid ibn Suʿūd, 231, 233
Āl Suʿūd, Muḥammad ibn Salmān, 341
Āl Suʿūd, Suʿūd ibn ʿAbd al-ʿAzīz, 88, 207–8, 214, 216; letters of, 220–24; as military leader, 211–14, 217–19
Āl Suʿūd, Suʿūd ibn Fayṣal, 240–41, 245–47, 249, 264
Āl Suʿūd, Turkī ibn ʿAbdallāh, 228–29, 260
Ālūsī family, al-, 268–69
Ālūsī, Maḥmūd Shukrī al-, 268, 273
Ālūsī, Nuʿmān ibn Maḥmūd al-, 268–69, 273
Amīr al-Ṣanʿānī, Muḥammad ibn Ismāʿīl al-, 80–84, 88, 91, 187–89, 268n19
ʿAmmāriyya, al-, 14, 68, 200
ʿĀriḍ, al-, 14, 33–34, 40, 62–63, 66, 142, 192, 200, 205, 253, 294
Arslān, Shakīb, 316
Arṭāwiyya, al-, 306, 311, 315
Ashʿarīs, 97–100; as Jahmiyya, 100, 104; and "Universal Principle," 101
ʿAtāqī, Asʿad ibn ʿAbdallāh al-, 57–58
ʿAtīqī, Ṣāliḥ ibn Sayf al-, 85, 210
ʿAwda, Salmān al-, 335
ʿAẓamī, Mukhtār ibn Aḥmad al-, 274

Bābṣayl, Muḥammad Saʿīd, 270, 272–73
Badawī, Aḥmad al-, 159
badw, 13, 230; Ibn ʿAbd al-Wahhāb's *takfīr* of, 206, 312; role in first Saudi state, 206
Baghdādī, Abū Bakr al-, 340
Bakrī, Nūr al-Dīn al-, 108
Banū Khālid, 66, 204–205, 212
Basra, 1–2, 219, 254–55, 262; Ibn ʿAbd al-Wahhāb and, 35–39, 40n55, 44, 51, 58, 64, 151, 196–97; refutation of Wahhābism in, 43–44, 61, 64, 81, 86, 213, 255
Bassām, ʿAbdallāh al-, 24
bin Ladin, Osama, 18, 335
Bray, Norman, 307
Burayda, 254, 289; struggle over Wahhābism in, 274–91
Būṣīrī, Saʿīd al-, 47, 252–53, 257
Burckhardt, Johann Ludwig, 15–16

Collingwood, R. G., 12
Commins, David, 9–10, 19, 41

Cook, Michael, 18, 56, 95, 192
Cox, Percy, 297
Crawford, Michael, 19, 157, 246
creed. *See* theology
cult of saints, 5–7, 104–7; Ahl-i Ḥadīth and, 267; decline of, 330; defense of, 48, 50–51, 57, 75–76, 83, 89, 91, 122–25, 251–52, 257, 259, 270; early modern Islamic revivalism and, 80–81, 188–89, 267–68; Ibn ʿAbd al-Wahhāb and, 1–2, 5–7, 16–17, 36, 38, 40, 44–48, 62, 64–65, 79, 81–82, 116, 122, 131–36, 139–45, 150–52, 155–57, 159, 166–67, 171–73, 185–86, 338; Ibn al-Qayyim and, 5, 111, 118, 146–47, 154, 165; Ibn Taymiyya and, 5, 50–51, 55, 104–10, 120–25, 130–31, 134–36, 146, 149, 153–54, 317; later Wahhābīs and, 3–4, 215, 223, 242, 252–53, 262, 275, 290, 299, 301, 320, 323; in Mamlūk Sultanate, 105; in Najd, 45–47, 62, 64–65, 116, 142, 155, 192, 230; in Ottoman Empire, 151, 290; Rashīd Riḍā and, 320. See also *istighātha, tawassul*

Dāghistānī, ʿAlī Afandī ibn Ṣādiq al-, 37
Daḥlān, Aḥmad ibn Zaynī, 25, 215, 270–74
Dallal, Ahmad, 187–88
Dawīsh, Fayṣal al-, 313–15
Dhahabī, Shams al-Dīn al-, 107–8, 112, 273; Ibn ʿAbd al-Wahhāb's admiration for, 113
Diffelen, Roelof Willem van, 17–18
Dilam, al-, 14
Dirʿiyya, al-, 8, 14, 33–34, 40; destruction of, 224–25; Ibn ʿAbd al-Wahhāb's relocation to, 66–68
Doughty, Charles, 253–54
Durar al-saniyya fī ʾl-ajwiba al-Najdiyya, al-, 19–20, 337

El-Rouayheb, Khaled, 100, 188
Ende, Werner, 10, 18n51

Fahad, Abdulaziz Al-, 10, 19
Fākhirī, Muḥammad al-, 23, 23n67
Faraj, ʿAbd al-Salām, 337
fiqh: Ibn ʿAbd al-Wahhāb and, 53–55, 115–16
first Saudi state, 8, 68; destruction of, 224–26; early expansion of, 199–206; expansion of beyond Najd, 210–20; as improbable occurrence, 191–92; and requirements of subjugated towns, 201–2, 206–7; role of nomadic tribes in, 206; and summons to Islam, 205; warfare of as defensive *jihād*, 199–200; warfare of as offensive *jihād*, 202–3
Fodio, ʿUsman dan, 187
Furaʿ, al-, 14, 231, 244

Goldziher, Ignaz, 17, 96

Ḥaddād, ʿAlawī al-, 32, 88–90, 270n33, 274
ḥaḍar, 13, 192
Hadiyya al-saniyya wa ʾl-tuḥfa al-Wahhābiyya al-Najdiyya, al-, 20, 318n86
Ḥāʾil, 14, 205, 261–64; *jihād* of third Saudi state against, 296. *See also* Āl Rashīd, Rashīdī emirate
Ḥajjāwī, Mūsā al-, 53, 55, 120, 122–24, 157–58
hajr, 279–80, 308–313
Ḥanafīs: and Māturīdism, 97–98; and refutation of Wahhābism, 91n276
Ḥanbalīs, 5; and approach to Ibn Taymiyya in eighteenth century, 124–25; Islamicists' neglect of, 15; and Najd, 13, 34, 53; and refutation of Ibn ʿAbd al-Wahhāb, 90–91; theology of, 97–99
Ḥashwiyya, 108
Ḥawālī, Safar al-, 335
Haykel, Bernard, 188
Haytamī, Ibn Ḥajar al-l, 270, 273
Heraclius, Prophet's letter to, 196, 221–24
Ḥijāz, 12; first Saudi state and, 210, 215–17; Ibn ʿAbd al-Wahhāb and, 35–38
hijra, 54, 170–72; as duty in Wahhābism, 171–72; and *fitna* in al-Qaṣīm, 274–91; and the Ikhwān, 305–306, 310; and Ottoman occupation of al-Aḥsāʾ, 249–50, 259–60; and second Egyptian occupation, 231–32, 235–40, 259. See also *iẓhār al-dīn*; *al-walāʾ wa ʾl-barāʾ*

Hodgson, Marshall, 187
Holtzman, Livnat, 111
Hoover, Jon, 97, 100n31
Ḥuraymilāʾ, 8, 14, 39–40, 42, 200; apostasy of, 76–77
Ḥusayn (Najdī saint), 45, 64
Ḥuṣayyin, ʿAbd al-ʿAzīz al-, 215–16

Ibāḍīs, 299–301
Ibn ʿAbdallāh, Thuwaynī, 86n256, 213–14
Ibn ʿAbd al-Laṭīf, ʿAbdallāh, 37, 51, 93
Ibn ʿAbd al-Muḥsin, Barrāk, 212–13
Ibn ʿAbd al-Wahhāb, Muḥammad, 1–3, 215; *Arbaʿ qawāʿid fī ʾl-dīn*, 64–66, 72, 90, 141–45, 399; *Arbaʿ qawāʿid tadūru ʾl-aḥkām ʿalayhā*, 52–55, 90; as author of catechisms, 141–42; career's resemblance to Prophet Muḥammad's, 196–97, 226; corpus of, 30; and cult of saints, 1–2, 5–7, 16–17, 36, 38, 40, 44–48, 62, 64–65, 79, 81–82, 116, 122, 131–36, 139–45, 150–52, 155–57, 159, 166–67, 171–73, 185–86, 338; death of, 208–10; and destruction of tombs and trees, 42–43, 58, 82; and divine inspiration, 41, 63–64; early life and career of, 33–42; epistle to Riyadh and Manfūḥa, 62–63, 86, 90, 119, 154–55, 158, 161; and *fiqh*, 53–55, 115–16; and *ghurbat al-Islām*, 119, 197; and *hijra*, 171; and Ibn Taymiyya's anti-Mongol *fatwā*s, 178–80; and *ijtihād*, 49–50, 60, 117, 119–120; and *iẓhār al-dīn*, 171; and *jihād*, 72–73, 79–80; 173–85, 199–200, 202–203; *Kalimāt* epistle, 1–2, 5, 44–48, 90, 132–36, 140, 167–68, 182, 257, 280n78; *Kashf al-shubuhāt*, 71–73, 90, 257, 317, 339; *Kitāb al-tawḥīd*, 30, 40–41, 269; *Mufīd al-mustafīd*, 78–80, 82, 90, 166, 178–79, 182, 202–3; *Mukhtaṣar sīrat al-rasūl*, 30, 170, 179n198; *Nawāqiḍ al-Islām*, 122, 157–58, 170, 302; and reading of *fitna* as *shirk*, 180–81; and relocation from Ḥuraymilāʾ to al-ʿUyayna, 42; and relocation from al-ʿUyayna to al-Dirʿiyya, 66–68; revolutionary ambitions of, 172–73, 183, 192–93; and role in first Saudi state, 200–2, 207–8; and role of *ʿulamāʾ* in politics, 198; and stages of Prophet's career, 196; *Sittat mawāḍiʿ min al-sīra*, 168–69, 257, 312; and stoning of adulteress, 66–67; and *takfīr*, 60–62, 65, 79, 122, 145–62; and *takfīr* of *badw*, 206, 312; and *tawḥīd*, 128–45; teachers of, 36–39, 41, 54, 59, 62–64; *al-Uṣūl al-thalātha*, 119; and *al-walāʾ wa ʾl-barāʾ*, 1–5, 7, 46–47, 65, 79, 137, 156–57, 166–70
Ibn ʿAbd al-Wahhāb, refutation of, 42–91; accusation of claiming prophecy, 62, 270; accusation of fighting and killing Muslims, 68–70, 74–75, 78, 82, 257; accusation of having no teachers, 37–39, 54, 62, 83; accusation of *ijtihād*, 49–50, 54–55, 60, 65, 78, 88, 93; accusation of imitating Ibn Taymiyya, 49–51, 55, 90–93, 270, 272; accusation of imposing *hijra*, 75, 78; accusation of insanity, 57–58; accusation of Khārijism, 70–71, 78, 81, 88, 255, 257; accusation of misusing Ibn Taymiyya, 75–78, 83, 87–91, 93–94, 251–52, 257–59; accusation of pronouncing *takfīr* on Muslims/*umma*, 48, 55, 57, 59, 65, 69, 71, 75, 78, 82–83, 93, 161, 255, 257, 270; accusation of prophetic mimicry/imitation, 63–64, 69–70, 75, 88; accusation of satanic influence, 44, 48, 62, 86; accusation of rejecting *fiqh* tradition, 54, 60, 88; portrayal as Musaylima, 48–49, 81, 210
Ibn ʿAbd al-Wahhāb, Sulaymān, 35, 39, 85, 94, 123–24, 150, 202; anti-Wahhābī refutation of, 76–77, 274
Ibn Abī ʾl-ʿIzz, 112, 138
Ibn ʿAfāliq, Muḥammad, 37, 52, 88, 93–94, 122–23; letters to ʿUthmān ibn Muʿammar, 73–75, 85; *Tahakkum al-muqallidīn*, 52–56, 270n33
Ibn ʿAjlān, Muḥammad, 243–46
Ibn al-Amīr al-Ṣanʿānī. *See* al-Amīr al-Ṣanʿānī
Ibn ʿAmr, ʿAbdallāh, 275–80, 282–91, 304, 313, 328; and *iẓhār al-dīn*, 285–86
Ibn ʿAqīl, Abū ʾl-Wafāʾ, 98n23, 106–7

Ibn ʿArabī, 59–60, 104, 130, 246
Ibn ʿAtīq, Ḥamad, 4, 227, 231, 241–43, 250, 257, 264–66, 267n14, 281, 291, 333, 339; and distinction between *bughḍ* and *ʿadāwa*, 11, 235, 239; and *iẓhār al-dīn*, 234–36, 239, 287; and Saudi civil war, 243–47; and second Egyptian occupation, 231–40; as source of Wahhābī extremism, 283, 291; and *takfīr* of Ottoman Empire, 227, 233–34
Ibn ʿAtīq, Saʿd ibn Ḥamad, 266–68, 282; and the Ikhwān, 310n59, 311n61, 314; and Western businessmen in Arabia, 325
Ibn Baṭṭa al-ʿUkbarī, 106–7, 128n5
Ibn Bāz, ʿAbd al-ʿAzīz, 81n236, 325n114, 333–34
Ibn Bijād, Sulṭān, 313–15
Ibn Bishr, ʿUthmān, 21–23, 29, 209, 258
Ibn Dāwūd al-Zubayrī, ʿAbdallāh, 32, 85, 128, 138n49; and *al-Ṣawāʿiq wa ʾl-ruʿūd*, 86–88, 89
Ibn Dawwās, Dahām, 68, 199–201, 204
Ibn Duʿayj, Aḥmad, 237–39
Ibn Dujayn, ʿUrayʿir, 204–205
Ibn al-Fāriḍ, 59–60, 246
Ibn Fayrūz, ʿAbdallāh, 37–38, 40, 42, 51, 88, 124
Ibn Fayrūz, Muḥammad, 69, 85–86, 89–90, 142, 209, 213
Ibn Fawzān, Sābiq, 277–82, 287, 288n117
Ibn Ghannām, Ḥusayn, 21–22, 29, 269, 340; and portrayal of Ibn ʿAbd al-Wahhāb in prophetic terms, 41; and portrayal of Islamic lands as dominated by *shirk*, 151, 319; *Rawḍat al-afkār wa ʾl-afhām*, 21, 269, 272–73
Ibn Gharīb, Muḥammad, 29, 84, 87n262
Ibn Ḥanbal, Aḥmad, 163, 300, 338
Ibn Ḥithlayn, Ḍaydān, 315
Ibn Ḥumayd, Muḥammad, 25, 95
Ibn ʿĪdān, Ḥasan, 77–78
Ibn ʿĪsā, Aḥmad ibn Ibrāhīm, 258–59
Ibn ʿĪsā, Ibrāhīm, 24
Ibn Isḥāq, Muḥammad, 193–94
Ibn Jāmiʿ, ʿUthmān, 209–10
Ibn Jāsir, Ibrāhīm, 275–77, 280, 290
Ibn al-Jawzī, Abū ʾl-Faraj, 98n23, 107
Ibn Jirjīs, Dāwūd, 250–53, 256–5, 268–69, 274, 280, 289, 291
Ibn Kathīr, ʿImād al-Dīn, 111–12, 180, 273; Ibn ʿAbd al-Wahhāb's admiration for, 113, 180.
Ibn Laʿbūn, Ḥamad, 23
Ibn Māniʿ, Muḥammad ibn ʿAbd al-ʿAzīz, 321
Ibn Manṣūr, ʿUthmān, 250–51, 254–59, 275, 280, 289, 291
Ibn Muʿammar, Ḥamad, 216
Ibn Muʿammar, ʿUthmān, 42, 66–67, 73
Ibn Mufliḥ, Shams al-Dīn, 112, 121
Ibn Muḥsin al-Anṣārī, Ḥusayn, 267
Ibn Musāʿid, Ghālib (Sharīf), 215–18, 223
Ibn Muṣliḥ, Siḥmān, 265–66
Ibn Muṭlaq, ʿĪsā, 52
Ibn Nabhān, 232–33
Ibn Qāsim, ʿAbd al-Raḥmān, 19
Ibn Qayyim al-Jawziyya, 5–6, 7, 111; and cult of saints, 5, 111, 118, 146–47, 154, 165; and *ghurbat al-Islām*, 118–19, 147; and *ijtihād*, 116–117; influence on Ibn ʿAbd al-Wahhāb, 42, 112–13, 116–19, 125–26, 150–51, 155–56, 166, 169–70, 185–86; *Iʿlām al-muwaqqiʿīn*, 116–19, 155–56; and *jihād*, 194–96; *al-Kāfiya al-shāfiya*, 111, 125–26; *Madārij al-sālikīn*, 165, 317; and *ṭāghūt*, 155–56; and stages of Prophet's career, 195–96; and *al-walāʾ wa ʾl-barāʾ*, 162–67; *Zād al-maʿād*, 30, 118, 147, 169–70, 194–96
Ibn Qudāma al-Maqdisī, 107, 124
Ibn Rajab, 112, 185n220; Ibn ʿAbd al-Wahhāb's admiration for, 113
Ibn Rashīd, ʿAbd al-ʿAzīz ibn Mutʿib, 287–88, 294–95
Ibn Rashīd, ʿAbdallāh ibn ʿAlī, 261–63
Ibn Rashīd, Muḥammad ibn ʿAbdallāh, 263–64, 266, 282–83, 286–88
Ibn Rashīd, Ṭalāl ibn ʿAbdallāh, 262–63
Ibn Sabhān, Sālim, 263–64
Ibn Sabʿīn, 246
Ibn Ṣafwān, Jahm, 94–95, 100, 299. *See also* Jahmiyya
Ibn Salīm, Muḥammad ibn ʿAbdallāh, 275–76, 287

Ibn Salīm, Muḥammad ibn ʿUmar, 275–76
Ibn Sallūm, Muḥammad ibn ʿAlī, 85, 254–55
Ibn Sanad, ʿUthmān, 25, 255
Ibn Sayf, ʿAbdallāh ibn Ibrāhīm, 36, 38–39
Ibn Shabīb, Yūsuf, 299–300, 302
Ibn Siḥmān, Sulaymān, xiii–xiv, 4, 264–66, 327, 333; and ʿAbd al-ʿAzīz Āl Suʿūd, 295–97; and Āl Rashīd, 283–84, 288–89, 292–93, 296; and character of refutations, 273; and dispute in Trucial ʿUmān, 300–305; and European powers, 297–98; and *fitna* in al-Qaṣīm, 274–92; and fondness for poetry, 271; and *ghurbat al-Islām* in Rashīdī interregnum, 292–93; and the Ikhwān, 296, 307–15; and ʿĪsā al-Malāḥī, 305n41; and *iẓhār al-dīn*, 4, 278, 284, 286–87; and *millat Ibrāhīm*, 278, 284, 292, 308, 312; and Rashīd Riḍā, 317–21; ridicule of, 287, 302; and *takfīr* of Ottoman Empire, 287, 289–90, 297n9; and *al-ʿudhr bi ʾl-jahl*, 160, 301, 303–304; and Wahhābī epithet, 270–71; and Wahhābī publishing in Egypt, 318; and Wahhābī publishing in India, 269–74; and *al-walāʾ wa ʾl-barāʾ*, 4, 278, 284, 286–87, 289–90, 292, 301–2, 308, 320; and Western businessmen in Arabia, 325
Ibn Suḥaym, Sulaymān, 58–62, 85, 170
Ibn Suʿūd, Muḥammad, 8, 33–34, 67–68, 192, 199, 207–8
Ibn Taymiyya, Taqī al-Dīn, 5–6, 7, 55, 96, 243–45; *al-ʿAqīda al-Wāsiṭiyya*, 109–110, 113; anti-Mongol *fatwās* of, 175–80; and congruence of reason and revelation, 101; and cult of saints, 5, 50–51, 55, 104–10, 120–25, 130–31, 134–36, 146, 149, 153–54, 317; *Darʾ taʿāruḍ al-ʿaql wa ʾl-naql*, 101; and divine attributes, 100–101, 109–110, 138; followers of, 110–112; and free will, 102–3; *al-Ḥamawiyya al-kubrā*, 109; and Ḥanbalī theology, 97–103, 106–107; and *ijtihād*, 109; influence on Ibn ʿAbd al-Wahhāb, 42, 112–13, 115–16, 120–22, 125–26, 128, 131–39, 144–45, 166, 178–80, 184–85, 185–86; *Iqtiḍāʾ al-ṣirāṭ al-mustaqīm*, 105–6; *al-Jawāb al-ṣaḥīḥ*, 104, 195; and *jihād*, 173–78, 181, 184–85, 194–95; and *Kalām* theology, 99–103, 130, 153; *Kitāb al-īmān*, 114, 115; and perpetual creativity, 102; and religious authority, 113–15; *al-Siyāsa al-sharʿiyya*, 174, 181; and stages of Prophet's career, 196; and Ṣūfism, 104–107, 130; and *takfīr*, 146–50, 153–54; and *taqlīd*, 109, 114; and *tawḥīd*, 128–36, and *al-walāʾ wa ʾl-barāʾ*, 162–67, 184–85
Ibn al-Ṭayyib al-Maghribī, Muḥammad, 58, 88
Ibn Turkī, ʿAbd al-Wahhāb, 23
Ibrāhīm Bāshā, 224–26, 237
Idrīs (Najdī saint), 45–46, 64
Ikhnāʾī, Taqī al-Dīn al-, 108–9
Ikhwān, 295–96, 298, 305–7, 324; doctrines of, 308–14; and *hijra*, 305–6, 310; and Wahhābī scholars, 307–16
ijtihād, 49, 80; Ibn ʿAbd al-Wahhāb and, 49–50, 60, 117, 119–120; Ibn al-Qayyim and, 116–117; Ibn Taymiyya and, 109. *See also* Ibn ʿAbd al-Wahhāb, refutation of
iqāmat al-ḥujja. See *al-ʿudhr bi ʾl-jahl*
Islamic State, 158n117, 339–41
istighātha, 47–48, 50–51, 79, 91–93, 104–105, 108, 133–34, 215; as distinct from *tawassul*, 105n46. *See also* cult of saints
iẓhār al-dīn, 171–72, 232, 234–36, 239, 249, 259, 278, 281–82, 284–87, 298, 333; as equivalent of *millat Ibrāhīm*, 284–85. See also *hijra*; *millat Ibrāhīm*; *al-walāʾ wa ʾl-barāʾ*

Jabal Shammar, 14
Jabartī, ʿAbd al-Raḥmān al-, 25
Jackson, John, 213
Jaḥḥāf, Luṭf Allāh ibn Aḥmad, 25, 144
Jahmiyya, 94–95, 100, 299; Ashʿarīs as, 100, 104; Mālikīs of Trucial ʿUmān as, 299–305
Jazīra al-Ḥamrāʾ, al-, 298–305
jihād, 173–85; as duty in Wahhābism, 3, 7–8, 231; and Ibn ʿAbd al-Wahhāb, 178–85; and Ibn Kathīr, 177–78; and Ibn Taymiyya, 173–78, 181; and Ottoman occupation of

al-Aḥsāʾ, 249–50; and second Egyptian occupation, 231–33, 236–37; and *al-walāʾ wa ʾl-barāʾ*, 182–85
jihādism, xv, 28, 336–41
Jihādī Salafism. See *jihādism*
Jīlānī, ʿAbd al-Qādir al-, 45, 57, 133, 159
Jones Brydges, Harford, 214
Jubayla, al-, 43, 57–58

kalām, 97–99, 102, 125, 130, 153
Karbalāʾ: Wahhābī sacking of, 218–19, 221
Karkūklī, Rasūl Ḥāwī al-, 25
Khārijites: the Ikhwān as, 307–8; Prophet's willingness to fight, 73; as *ṭāʾifa mumtaniʿa*, 174–76; Wahhābīs as, 70–71, 78, 81, 88, 189, 223, 255, 257; and *al-walāʾ wa ʾl-barāʾ*, 163. *See also* Ibāḍīs
Kharj, al-, 14, 45–46, 62, 140, 142, 205, 236–37
Khūrshīd Bāshā, 231, 239
Kramer, Martin, 323
Kūrānī, Ibrāhīm al-, 273
Kurdī, Muḥammad ibn Sulaymān al-, 49n94, 68, 270n33

Laoust, Henri, 18, 96
Lāt, al-, 168, 280n78
Lav, Daniel, 339

Majmūʿat al-rasāʾil wa ʾl-masāʾil al-Najdiyya, 20, 318
Majmūʿat al-tawḥīd, 20, 269
Majmūʿī, Muḥammad al-, 37–39
Makdisi, George, 15, 103
Mālikīs: and Ashʿarism, 98
Manfūḥa, 14, 40, 62, 68, 199–200
Maqdisī, Abū Muḥammad al-, 336–38
Margoliouth, David, 18
Marīsī, Bishr al-, 94–95
maṭāwiʿa, 56
Māturīdism, 98
Mecca: as *dār al-kufr*, 242, 284; and first Saudi state, 144, 216–17
Medina: Ibn ʿAbd al-Wahhāb and, 35–38
Miḥmal, al-, 14, 204
millat Ibrāhīm, 165, 278, 284–85, 292, 312–13, 337–38. See also *al-walāʾ wa ʾl-barāʾ*
Mīrghanī, Amīn ibn Ḥasan al-, 57
Mizzī, Jamāl al-Dīn al-, 112, 273
Mongol Īlkhānids, 175–80, 227, 244
Mouline, Nabil, 10, 19, 332
Muḍāyifī, ʿUthmān al-, 216
Muḥammad (Prophet): career progression of, 193–96; career's resemblance to Ibn ʿAbd al-Wahhāb's, 196–98; and letter to Heraclius, 196, 221–24; and preaching in Mecca, 3, 167–70, 173, 193–95
Muḥammad ʿAlī, 224, 231, 233
Mulaydāʾ, battle of al-, 264, 294
Muṭayr, 13, 264, 306, 313–14
Muʿtazila, 94, 97, 99
Muways, ʿAbdallāh al-, 70–71, 85, 256

Nadhīr Ḥusayn al-Dihlawī, 267
Najd: as accursed land, 75, 78; as favorable terrain for emergence of Wahhābism, 192; geography and demography of, 12–14; historiography in, 20–24
Niebuhr, Carsten, 15

Ottoman Empire, 13, 91n276, 192, 295, 316; and destruction of first Saudi state, 224; and occupation of al-Aḥsāʾ, 240, 247–50; and Rashīdī emirate, 263, 294–96; Wahhābī opposition to travel in, 274–91; Wahhābīs as rebels against, 223; Wahhābī *takfīr* of, xiii, 214–15, 227, 233–34, 248, 276, 287, 289–90, 296, 297n9

Palgrave, William, 16–17, 241–42, 261–63
Philby, Harry St. John, 17
positive law. See *qānūn*

Qāʿida, al-, 18, 336
Qabbānī, Aḥmad ibn ʿAlī al-, 43, 56, 91, 92–93; *Faṣl al-khiṭāb*, 43–51; *Kashf al-ḥijāb*, 61, 63–64; *Naqḍ qawāʿid al-ḍalāl*, 64–66
Qāḍī, Muḥammad ibn ʿUthmān al-, 25
Qaḥṭān, 13, 206

qānūn, 248–49, 282, 285, 297, 314, 334, 338
Qaṣīm, al-, 14, 60, 205, 231, 251–54; *fitna* in, 274–91
Quraysh, 3, 194, 244
Quṭb, Sayyid, 336, 338–39

Rapoport, Yossef, 109
Rashīdī emirate, 261–64, 294–96; and Ottoman Empire, 263, 294–96; Wahhābī *takfīr* of, 296
Rāwī al-Baghdādī, ʿAbdallāh Afandī al-, 84
Rāzī, Fakhr al-Dīn al-, 101
Razīnī, ʿAbd al-ʿAzīz al-, 94–95
Rentz, George, 6n17, 18n51, 23n66
Riḍā, Rashīd, 20, 298, 316–23, 328–29, 331; and ʿAbd al-ʿAzīz Āl Suʿūd, 316–17, 322–23; and publishing Wahhābī texts, 317–19; and the Wahhābī scholars, 318–22
Rihani, Ameen, 306–7, 323–24
Riyadh, 14, 40, 62; as capital of second Saudi state, 8, 228; capture of by ʿAbd al-ʿAzīz Āl Suʿūd, 294; and Rashīdī emirate, 263–64; and war with al-Dirʿiyya, 68–69, 75, 199–202, 204–6
Rousseau, Jean Baptiste Louis, 219–20
Rutter, Eldon, 331

Sabala, battle of al-, 315
Sacy, Antoine-Isaac Silvestre de, 15
Sadleir, George Forster, 16, 224–25
Saffārīnī, Muḥammad ibn Aḥmad al-, 49, 70–71
Sahsawānī, Muḥammad Bashīr al-, 267, 272
Ṣaḥwa, 335
Salafism, 7; Jihādī Salafism (see *jihadism*)
Sanūsī, Muḥammad ʿAlī al-, 187
Saudi civil war, 240, 246–47
Ṣayrāmī, ʿAbd al-ʿAzīz ibn Ṣāliḥ al-, 322
second Saudi state, 8, 228–30, 240
Shāfiʿīs: and Ashʿarism, 98–99; in Mamlūk Damascus, 99, 108, 111; and refutation of Ibn ʿAbd al-Wahhāb, 90–91
Shahīd, Shāh Ismāʿīl ibn ʿAbd al-Ghanī al-, 189
Shāh Walī Allāh, 187
Shaʿīb, al-, 14, 33, 204
Sharīf Ḥusayn, 297
Shathrī, Ṣāliḥ ibn Muḥammad al-, 238, 271
Shawkānī, Muḥammad ibn ʿAlī al-, 80, 187–88, 189n234
Shīʿa: in al-Aḥsāʾ, 13, 245, 248, 285, 324, 340–41; first Saudi state and, 210–13, 218–19, 340–41; Ibn ʿAbd al-Wahhāb's views on, 210; in Jabal Shammar, 261–62
shirk: contemporary *shirk* as worse than *shirk* of pagan Arabs, 64, 139–44; distinction between *akbar* and *aṣghar*, 76, 78–79, 83, 88, 91; eradication of as basis for Wahhābī *jihād*, 8, 180–81, 184, 203; *fitna* as meaning of, 180–81, 184, 236; *fiqh* as, 115; supplication as, 1, 36, 38, 40, 44–47, 55, 105, 120–23, 131–36, 140–41, 149, 215, 252; reverence of scholars as, 114–15; as widespread in Islamic world, 1, 5, 7, 11, 44–46, 146–47, 149–51, 156, 189, 197, 242, 290.
Ṣiddīq Ḥasan Khān al-Qannawjī, 267
Sindī, Muḥammad Ḥayāt al-, 37–39, 187–88
Shamsān (Najdī saint), 45–46, 64, 116, 133, 140, 155
Steinberg, Guido, 10, 19, 333–34
Subkī, Taqī al-Dīn al-, 108, 110, 270–71, 273
Sudayr, 14, 205, 254
Ṣūfism, 103–7, 116, 124, 130
Sulaymān Bāshā (governor of Baghdad), 84, 86n256, 213–15, 218
Sulaymān Bāshā (governor of al-Shām), 222–23
Surūriyya, Gharīb al-, 340–41
Surūr Zayn al-ʿĀbidīn, Muḥammad, 336
Suwaydī, ʿAlī al-, 273

Ṭabāṭabāʾī, Yāsīn ibn Ibrāhīm al-, 81
ṭāghūt, 45, 155–56, 171; apostate rulers as, 337, 340; Ibn ʿAbd al-Wahhāb as, 94; saints in al-Kharj as, 45–46, 62, 64, 142, 151, 155–57, 172
Ṭāʾif, al-, 216–17, 306
Tāj (Najdī saint), 45, 64, 114, 116, 119, 140, 155

takfīr, 57, 59, 145–62, 215; as duty in Wahhābism, 3, 7, 154–58; Ibn ʿAbd al-Wahhāb and, 60–62, 65, 150–62; Ibn Taymiyya and, 146–50, 153–54. See also *al-ʿudhr bi ʾl-jahl*; Ibn ʿAbd al-Wahhāb, refutation of
taqlīd, 49–50, 57, 60, 80, 83, 92–93, 109, 116–119. See also *ijtihād*
Tamīmī, Mirbad ibn Aḥmad al-, 82
Ṭandatāwī, ʿAbd al-Wahhāb al-, 56–58, 124, 189
Ṭanṭāwī, ʿAlī al-, 329–31
Ṭarīqa-yi Muḥammadiyya, 189
ṭawāghīt. See *ṭāghūt*
tawassul, 47–48, 50–51, 57, 92–93, 105, 215n104, 270; as distinct from *istighātha*, 105n46. *See also* cult of saints
tawḥīd, 55, 128–45; distinction between *tawḥīd al-rubūbiyya* and *tawḥīd al-ulūhiyya*, 128–32; and Ibn ʿAbd al-Wahhāb, 1–2, 7, 46, 50, 63, 72, 119–20, 128–45; Ibn Taymiyya and, 128–36; *tawḥīd al-asmāʾ wa ʾl-ṣifāt*, 138
Thādiq, 14, 201, 204
Tharmadāʾ, 14, 204n48
theology, 55, 97; Ḥanbalī, 97–99, 108; Taymiyyan, 97–112. See also *ahl al-ḥadīth*; Ḥanbalīs
third Saudi state, 8, 288–90, 294–98; and the British, 296–97, 313–14; and oil, 324–25; retitled Kingdom of Saudi Arabia, 326
Trucial ʿUmān: dispute over *takfīr* in, 298–305
Turaba, 306
Ṭūsūn Bāshā, 224

ʿudhr bi ʾl-jahl, al-, 78; Ibn Taymiyya and, 148–50; Ibn ʿAbd al-Wahhāb and, 151–54, 159, 186; later Wahhābīs and, 301–5. See also *takfīr*
ʿUmar ibn al-Khaṭṭāb: and *māniʿū ʾl-zakāt*, 175–76
ʿUnayza, 14, 205, 251–54, 276n57, 289
Ushayqir, 34
ʿUtayba, al-, 13, 306, 313
ʿUtaybī, Juhaymān al-, 335–36
ʿUyayna, al-, 8, 14, 33–35, 40, 42–43, 66, 68, 73, 173, 198–202, 206
ʿUzza, al-, 168, 280n78

Vassiliev, Alexei, 18n51, 295
Voll, John, 187

Wahhābism: early refutation of, 42–91; decline in zeal of, 330; and early modern Islamic revivalism, 186–90; European travelers on, 15–17; as revolutionary doctrine, 172–73, 192–93; as term, 5–7; Western scholarship on, 17–19. *See also* Ibn ʿAbd al-Wahhāb, Muḥammad
walāʾ wa ʾl-barāʾ, al-, 162–73, 225–26; distinction between *bughḍ* and *ʿadāwa*, 11, 235, 239; duty of showing hatred and enmity, 1–5, 7, 9, 11, 46–47, 65, 79, 137, 156–57, 163–70, 232, 234–40, 280–81, 285–86, 289, 301–302; and example of Prophet Abraham, 3, 165–67, 182–84, 234–35, 278, 280, 282; and example of Prophet Muḥammad, 167–70, 280, 301–2; Ibn ʿAbd al-Wahhāb and, 1–5, 7, 46–47, 65, 79, 137, 156–57, 166–70; Ibn al-Qayyim and, 162–67; Ibn Taymiyya and, 162–67, 184–85; and *jihād*, 182–85; Khārijism and, 163; and Ottoman occupation of al-Aḥsāʾ, 249–50; and second Egyptian occupation, 231–40; Shīʿism and, 163; and *tawḥīd al-ulūhiyya*, 162–66. See also *hijra*; *iẓhār al-dīn*; *millat Ibrāhīm*
Wallin, George, 262–63
Washm, al-, 14
Winder, R. Bayly, 260

yāsā, 177–78
Yūsuf (Najdī saint), 45–46, 116, 140, 155
Yūsuf Bāshā (governor of al-Shām), 222

Ẓafīr, 13, 206
ziyāra. *See* cult of saints

A NOTE ON THE TYPE

This book has been composed in Arno, an Old-style serif typeface in the classic Venetian tradition, designed by Robert Slimbach at Adobe.

GPSR Authorized Representative: Easy Access System Europe - Mustamäe tee 50, 10621 Tallinn, Estonia, gpsr.requests@easproject.com

www.ingramcontent.com/pod-product-compliance
Lightning Source LLC
Chambersburg PA
CBHW021847230426
43671CB00006B/300
9780691241616